IMMIGRATION OFFICE No. 112 R. O. OF KOREA

DEPARTMENT OF IMMIGRATION
PERMITTED TO ENTER
AUSTRALIA
24 APR 1986
on
For stay of 12 Month
SYDNEY AIRPORT 54

IMMIGRATION DIVISION BANGKOK THAILAND
A
72
DEPARTED
- 6 FEB 1988
SIGNED

IMMIGRATION & ETHNIC AFFAIRS
..........Person
30 OCT 1989
DEPARTED
AUSTRALIA
SYDNEY 32

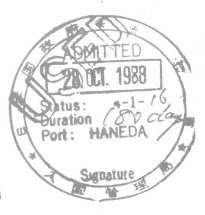

TRAVELER'S
INDIA
COMPANION

中华人民共和国
广东省公安厅

上陸許可
ADMITTED
15. FEB. 1986
Status: 4-1-4
Duration: 90 days
NARITA(N)
Immigration Inspector
日本国

ADMITTED
20 OCT. 1988
Status: 4-1-16
Duration 180 days
Port: HANEDA
Signature

№ 011278

THE UNITED STATES
OF AMERICA
NONIMMIGRANT VISA
ISSUED AT
Air Port

SED

U.S. IMMIGRATION
170 HHW 1710
JUL 2 0 1983

D1501675

The 1999–2000 Traveler's Companions

ARGENTINA • AUSTRALIA • BALI • CALIFORNIA • CANADA • CHILE • CHINA • COSTA RICA •
CUBA • EASTERN CANADA • ECUADOR • FLORIDA • HAWAII • HONG KONG • INDIA • INDONESIA •
JAPAN • KENYA • MALAYSIA & SINGAPORE • MEDITERRANEAN FRANCE • MEXICO • NEPAL •
NEW ENGLAND • NEW ZEALAND • PERU • PHILIPPINES • PORTUGAL • RUSSIA • SPAIN •
SOUTH AFRICA • SOUTHERN ENGLAND • THAILAND • TURKEY • VENEZUELA •
VIETNAM, LAOS AND CAMBODIA • WESTERN CANADA

Traveler's INDIA Companion
First Published 1999
The Globe Pequot Press
6 Business Park Road, P.O. Box 833
Old Saybrook, CT 06475-0833
www.globe.pequot.com

ISBN: 0-7627-0358-X

By arrangement with Kümmerly+Frey AG, Switzerland
© 1999 Kümmerly+Frey AG, Switzerland

Created, edited and produced by
Allan Amsel Publishing, 53, rue Beaudouin
27700 Les Andelys, France. E-mail: Allan.Amsel@wanadoo.fr
Editor in Chief: Allan Amsel
Editor: Anne Trager
Original design concept: Hon Bing-wah
Picture editor and designer: Roberto Rossi

Printed by Samhwa Printing Co. Ltd., Seoul, South Korea

TRAVELER'S INDIA COMPANION

by Kirsten Ellis and Chris Taylor

Photographed by Robert Holmes

Kümmerly+Frey

The Globe Pequot Press

OLD SAYBROOK

Contents

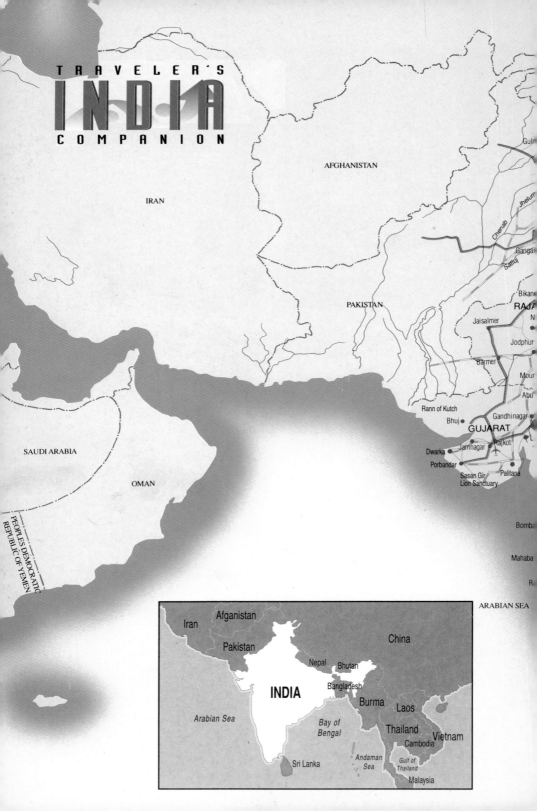

TRAVELER'S **INDIA** COMPANION

AFGHANISTAN

IRAN

PAKISTAN

Guln

Jhelum

Chenab

Ganga

Satluj

Bikane

RAJA

N

Jaisalmer

Jodphur

Barmer

Mour

Abu

Rann of Kutch

Bhuj

Gandhinagar

GUJARAT

Rajkot

Dwarka

Jamnagar

Porbandar

Palitana

Sasan Gir
Lion Sanctuary

SAUDI ARABIA

OMAN

PEOPLES DEMOCRATIC
REPUBLIC OF YEMEN

Bomba

Mahaba

R

ARABIAN SEA

Iran

Afganistan

Pakistan

China

Nepal

Bhutan

Bangladesh

INDIA

Burma

Laos

Arabian Sea

Thailand

Vietnam

Bay of
Bengal

Cambodia

Sri Lanka

Andaman
Sea

Gulf of
Thailand

Malaysia

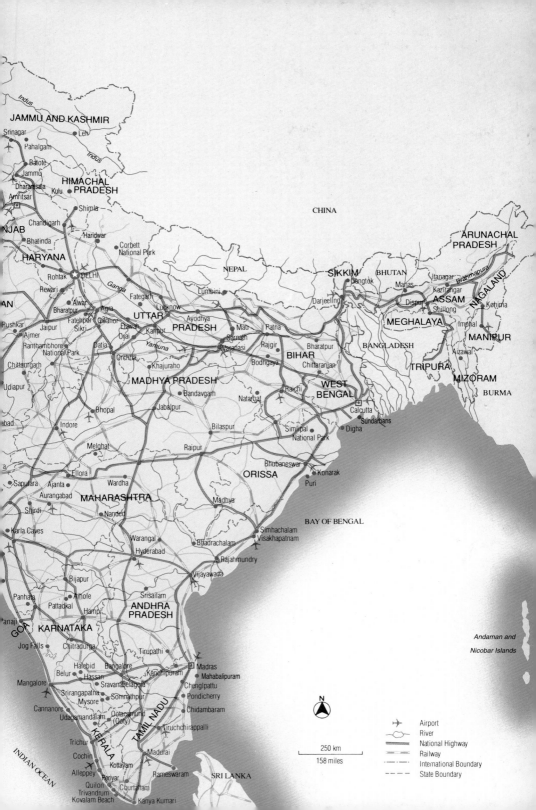

TOP SPOTS

Gaze on the Taj

OF THE TORRENTS OF INK THAT HAVE POURED FROM WRITERS' PENS ON THE SUBJECT OF THE TAJ MAHAL, Rabindranath Tagore's line about "a teardrop on the cheek of time" is easily the most memorable. It captures the fragility of this architectural triumph, while simultan-eously suggesting the lost love that inspired its construction.

After all, it is this meeting of architectural genius and a universal ideal that draws travelers from the world over. It's hard to imagine that any of them come away disappointed. You might travel the length and breadth of the subcontinent, seeking out its wonders, and still be taken aback by the splendor of the Taj when finally you cross its portals.

It's the oddest of sensations. So odd in fact that for a moment you may even forget the would-be guides and fellow travelers at your side. There it is, famously, just the way it looks on the postcards and in the coffee-table volumes: mounted on its marble plinth at the end of those

reflective ponds, its four tapering minarets nudging the heavens, its unparalleled pear-shaped dome summoning your gaze.

It is, of course, as ravishing a structure to look upon as its origin makes a compelling story to listen to. How does it go again? Well, in short, the Taj was built in 1631 by Emperor Shah Jahan in memory of his second wife Mumtaz Mahal, a Persian princess. You might imagine her as a willowy maid, but this is unlikely given she died giving birth to her fourteenth child. Nevertheless, the emperor was so crushed when she died that it is said his hair and beard turned utterly white within months. The mausoleum he constructed in her memory was like no other seen before. Somewhat inevitably, it has become India's "symbol of eternal love."

Whether you subscribe to the "eternal love" hype or not (and you are likely to get rather tired of hearing about it while you are in Agra), it does give you something to think about as you stroll around the grounds of the Taj. In a land teeming with shrines to obscure gods, this is a singularly secular "temple." There is something about it that we twentieth-century Westerners can understand: if its architecture is exotic, its symmetry is not; and if it is grand in a way that we no longer do things, it is at least the product of an ideal that makes sense to us.

Not that you should let such thoughts detract from your enjoyment. Find yourself a quiet corner away from the guides and their well-rehearsed patter in Taj apocrypha (designed by an Italian, once had a dark twin across the river, and such nonsense) and photographic advice, and sit in reflective peace as the sun swells with color and drops behind the Taj's captivating cupola-topped minarets.

Glowing like an opalescent pearl, the marble surface of the Taj Mahal, with its floral inlaid motifs and stylized caligraphy, is a masterpiece of exquisite ornamentation.

Ride the Palace on Wheels

TOURIST BROCHURES TRUMPET IT AS THE "JOURNEY WORTHY OF KINGS." And given that its carriages were built for royalty, perhaps for once they are not exaggerating. One of the world's most luxurious train journeys, the Palace on Wheels is a locomotive extravaganza through the best of royal Rajasthan.

And what a journey it is. Imagine reclining in the bar coach sipping a cocktail, perhaps browsing through a leather-bound atlas from the library, before retiring to a three-course meal; knowing that ahead of you lies a journey during which you will see sand dunes, hilltop fortresses, elephants, camel trains, and bazaars.

The eight-day odyssey sets out from Delhi and arrives in the walled, "Pink City " of Jaipur the next morning. As if the prospect of Jaipur, with its ornate Hawa Mahal or Palace of Winds, its City Palace, and its beguiling bazaars peopled by radiantly attired Rajasthanis were not enough, you are greeted on arrival by caparisoned elephants. Lunch is provided at Rambagh Palace — it's not every day you are escorted to lunch in a palace on elephant-back.

The next day you arrive at what was once the stunning fortress city of Chittaurgarh and what today is a collection of fascinating ruins whose history holds stories of heroism and sacrifice. The fortress ruins are, however, just a whistle stop on the road to the city of Udaipur, probably Rajasthan's most romantic destination. After all, few can resist Udaipur, with its palaces, temples, parks, its city-side lake and its famed Lake Palace, now transformed into one of the world's top hotels.

On the fourth day, hold your breath for the hauntingly beautiful, tenth-century fort of Ranthambhore. Surrounding the rocky ramparts is the Ranthambhore National Park, a Project Tiger reserve (see NATIONAL PARKS, page 28, in THE GREAT OUTDOORS for more on Project Tiger), though a tiger sighting on this occasion is only likely if one decides to board the train and have you for lunch. And this would be a pity because it means you would miss out on the next day's destination: Jaisalmer, one of the highlights of the entire journey.

Jaisalmer is the fortress among the dunes we all dream of when our thoughts drift into the never-never land of the Arabian nights. Behind its honey-colored walls is a tangled skein of alleyways lined with *havelis* — the mansions of rich merchants — and Jain temples. But the highlight of the Jaisalmer stopover is a jaunt on camelback out into the

dunes, where dinner is served under the stars to the strains of live Rajasthani folk music.

Few leave Jaisalmer without regret, but at least your next destination, Jodhpur, is unlikely to disappoint. The "Blue City" — every city in Rajasthan seems to have a color to itself — is home to one of Rajasthan's most awe-inspiring fortress: a place of cannon-protected ramparts that defend a labyrinth of palace apartments.

After such a week, it may be hard to imagine that there could still be something to look forward to. But then perhaps you have forgotten Agra, the last stop before you chuff back into Delhi.

Agra is reached, via Bharatpur — where Keoladeo Ghana National Park, a UNESCO World Heritage Site, is home to 300 species of birds — and Fatehpur Sikri, where you can gaze on the palaces and tombs of the Mughal emperor Akbar. It is all a prelude to your very last afternoon as a royal traveler. And what better way to spend it than gazing on the Taj Mahal as its colors shift in anticipation of the closing night?

OPPOSITE: Exotic scenes and sounds await the traveler in Jaisalmer, perhaps Rajasthan's most hauntingly beautiful fortress cities. ABOVE: Mosques, such as this one in Ajmer, are a common sight throughout Rajasthan.

Cruise the Backwaters

THERE'S A SPLASH OUTSIDE YOUR WINDOW, AND THE CHIRPING OF EXOTIC BIRDS. You roll out of bed, rub your eyes and find yourself gazing out across a startlingly blue skein of water at a swaying crowd of coconut palms.

Kerala's backwaters are one of India's most compelling destinations. Here, the morning paper is delivered by boat and children go to school by boat. Indeed, until the recent introduction of roads, the Kerala coastline, with its network of lakes, canals and rivers, was a watery world where all commerce was conducted by *kettuvallam*, the traditional straw-roofed vessel with arching prows introduced by the Chinese centuries ago.

Today the *kettuvallam*, which was mostly used for transporting rice, has been converted by some astute travel agents into a houseboat, in which you can cruise the beautiful backwaters by day and moor up close to a traditional village with an electricity source by night.

Unlike the houseboats of Kashmir, which unfortunately are off-limits to tourists anyway, the houseboats of Kerala *go* somewhere, giving you an ever-changing vista of village life and tranquil scenes. Watch fishermen flinging

filigree nets out into the water; see families paddling to church in dainty canoes; pass buffaloes lounging in the shallows; and let your gaze linger on women hanging out rainbow fabrics to dry on the outskirts of their villages.

Hours can pass like moments as you glide through remote areas of Kerala, poled along by your crew of two. And before you know it the sun is falling behind the palms and fireflies are beginning to wing through the air. The sweet smell of coconut and spices quickly sets your stomach rumbling as your houseboat chef prepares a curry with some freshly caught fish he bought just moments ago from a fisherman who pulled up alongside in a skiff. Just don't forget to save some room for that traditional Kerala desert — baked banana.

For more information about organizing your own private houseboat tour of Kerala's backwaters, contact Green Palm Travel and Tours at ℭ/FAX (484) 338172 E-MAIL greenpalm@kerala-interactive.com, 32/2512, PJ Anthony Road, Palarivattom, Kochi (Cochin) 682 025.

Pamper Yourself in a Palace

IN THE MODERN WORLD, PALACES — THOSE THAT REMAIN — are for the tourists to gawk at from a distance. Not in Rajasthan. In the Land of Maharajas, the legacies of a number of former kingdoms live on in royal homes that have now flung open their doors to anyone who can afford a night of the high life.

For starters you might travel to the "Pink City" of Jaipur, where set in manicured grounds the five-star Rambagh Palace combines the period charm of a maharaja's palace with first-rate modern facilities — the much remarked upon polo grounds are an added attraction. Also in Jaipur, though not quite in the same league, is the Jai Mahal Palace, which offers palatial pleasures at somewhat more affordable rates.

Continue on to walled fortress city of Jodhpur, and stay at the Umaid Bhawan Palace, which is considered by some to be the best of Rajasthan's converted palace hotels. Everything about this 347-room splendor, from the art-deco lobby to the basement swimming pool and the trophy-lined billiard room, is like a vision conjured from another age.

ABOVE: Fishermen cruise the tranquil backwaters of Cochin. OPPOSITE TOP: Skilfully flinging out a filigree net in Kerala. BOTTOM: No traveler should pass up the opportunity to enjoy the pleasures of one of India's palace hotels, like the Rambagh Palace Hotel.

Given the unique ambiance of the place — some wings are still home to Jodhpur's former royal family — many guests opt to stay in the suites. Each is a minor palace unto itself fitted out in authentic period furniture and features balconies and up to six rooms. Fondest memories are reserved for evenings on the terrace listening to the descant tinkling of exotic instruments played by turbaned musicians.

In the oasis town of Bikaner, meanwhile, who could resist the Lallgarh Palace, an exotic mirage in the desert, that appears at first glance to have been mysteriously deserted by its once royal masters? Inside, modern amenities combine gracefully with an *Arabian Nights* atmosphere.

But for many, the highlight of Rajasthan's palace hotels is the unforgettable Lake Palace, which rises out of Udaipur's Pichola Lake like a fairytale vision. The palace itself dates back to 1746, but it has been added to and renovated within by the Taj hotel group, making it one of the world's most memorable places to stay. Among its innumerable five-star treats and antique wonders, what could be more memorable than being poled across the lake at dusk by a gondolier to the marble steps of the palace in which you will be spending the night?

In the Embrace of the Gods

REMOTE KHAJURAHO IS LIKE NO OTHER PLACE ON EARTH. Built by the Chandella dynasty from 950 to 1050, three groups of temples dedicated to the three principal gods in the Hindu pantheon — Brahma, Vishnu, and Shiva — exhibit a showcase of human passion. Following their "discovery" in 1838 by Captain T.S. Burt of the British Army, the ensuing debate as to the meaning of the libidinous displays has shown no more sign of abating than have the numbers of intrigued and titillated tourists turning up daily for a firsthand peek.

Not that Khajuraho is just about sex. Far from it. In fact, only a tenth of the temple sculptures are erotic. In certain temples, the sculptures and friezes are almost austere, causing those with a serious interest in Khajuraho to throw up their hands in disgust at the prurient place it occupies in the traveler's imagination.

Be that as it may, for the casual visitor to Khajuraho it is the erotic carvings that leave the deepest impression. It is not simply the acrobatic improbability of some of them — the lover balanced on his head and assisted in his exertions by three curvaceous and beautiful women — but the sensual air that much of the sculpture bears, rather like that of Angkor with its dancing *apsaras*. These temples, you realize as you wander around them, depict life at its most passionate, rather like a Hollywood version of ancient times, complete with battling armies, full-bodied women, and steamy love affairs.

If there is anything to lament in Khajuraho, it is simply that all its passion is depicted in stone. All the more reason to try to be there for its annual weeklong Dance Festival, which is held in early March. At this time, the long-deserted ruins of Khajuraho come to life once again; as India's best classical dancers and musicians gather to stage magical evening performances against the backdrop of the ancient temples. At such a moment, it is almost possible to believe that the ancient passions depicted in stone have come to life and stolen into the present under the watchful gaze of Khajuraho's gods.

In the Holy City

VARANASI, ONCE KNOWN AS BENARES, IS INDIA'S HOLIEST CITY. It is a city of temples — more than 800 of them. It is a city of pilgrims —thousands stream in by road and rail daily. But mostly it is the city of the *ghats*, those flights of steps that descend to India's most sacred river, the Ganges.

The ghats that line the western bank of the Ganges in Varanasi number more than 100 and are the setting for what is perhaps India's most otherworldly scene — a daily pageant of pilgrims, penitents, and the pious, drawn to the banks of the river that is said to flow from the toe of Vishnu.

Mind you, following the lead of the pilgrims and bathing in the river is not recommended, and neither — heaven forbid — is drinking its water, which you will inevitably see some overzealous pilgrims doing. Far better you play the tourist and drink up the atmosphere of Varanasi rather than its waters.

The banks of the river are such a riot of color that it is easy to forget that Varanasi's sanctity is as much about death as it is about life. Anyone who dies on the banks of the Ganges in Varanasi achieves instant *moksha*, or enlightenment, which makes Varanasi a particularly holy place to dispose of the dead. The bodies are cremated, their ashes scattered in the waters of the Ganges; but it happens from time to time that the bodies of those whose families are too poor to afford a cremation will be seen floating in the river.

Chances are, however, as you push off from Dashaswamedh Ghat in the predawn darkness for an obligatory sunrise river journey, you will not see anything quite so gory. Garlands

of flowers tossed into the water by pilgrims are a far more likely sight.

As the sun pushes up over the horizon on the rural eastern bank of the Ganges, it begins to throw its light on one of the most bizarre waterfronts in world — a jumbled collection of spires and domed palaces, temples and opulent manors. It's a spectacularly antique scene in appearance, but surprisingly most of the buildings date back only as far as the eighteenth or nineteenth centuries, built by maharajas seeking a holy vacation home.

And with the first light of dawn, the crowds begin to arrive. You will find yourself sharing the river with boatloads of Indian tourists, with backpackers who look like they've been teleported from the 1960s, with trident-bearing *sadhus* (Hindu holy ascetics). It's all part of the grand spectacle that is Varanasi.

As you drift in towards the *ghats*, you will see jostling pilgrims splashing into the river, perhaps a lone man up to his neck in water, his hands raised heavenward in prayer. Young men limber up high on the *ghats* before diving in. Women dressed in saris descend modestly into

OPPOSITE: Early morning activity on the ghats, Varanasi. ABOVE: A meditative image in a Jain Temple, Jaisalmer.

the water. Brahman priests deliver sermons under palm umbrellas. Wild-eyed yogis with hair like brine-encrusted rope sit in contorted devotion.

It is, as you may imagine, not a scene — not a place — for the fainthearted. Some come away from Varanasi shaking their heads half in disbelief, half in horror. Others fall prey to the heady intoxication of its medieval magic. But no matter what their reaction to the city, all would agree that to visit India and not see its holiest city would be like visiting Italy and failing to see Rome — an omission of the gravest variety.

Chase the Raj in Calcutta

CALCUTTA IS A CITY THAT TURNS PRECONCEPTIONS ON THEIR HEAD. And you have to admit, on the preconception front, few places have it worse. Mother Theresa, the *City of Joy*, the infamous Black Hole prison — which has sadly become almost synonymous with the very word Calcutta — all crowd the popular imagination, distorting its views of the city.

For the locals Calcutta is the victim of "bad press." If you want to see poverty, they say, go to Bombay. Calcutta is about clubby tradition, not poverty.

And of course, they're right in their way. Not only is Calcutta the city of poets, most famously Nobel prizewinner Rabindranath Tagore, and filmmakers — Satyajit Ray among them; it was also once, as many observers point out, the second city of the British Empire.

The greatness lingers. Take the Writer's Building, whose burnt-sienna façade overlooks what was formerly Dalhousie Square. The name itself gives off a musty air, and the interior seems little changed since the East India Company built it in 1780 for its clerks, or "writers," as they were then known. "Inside," says a policeman lounging at the entrance, "are 15,000 locks opened by 15,000 keys. Ten thousand people work in there." Listlessly they preside over mounds of yellowing paperwork — the Raj is dead: long live the ledgers.

Of course, it's not just triplicate and red ink that lingers in Calcutta; it's Remington typewriters, rickshaws, and regal nostalgia. For as Geoffrey Moorehouse, Calcutta's most eloquent champion, has said, this is a city "pickled in its origins." He's right. And if you doubt it, ask yourself where else in Asia you can find a massively enthroned bronze statue of Queen Victoria.

The statue sits midway along the main drive that leads to the palatial Victoria Memorial. Built in 1921, the memorial was Viceroy Lord Curzon's vision, his Taj Mahal. As travel writer Jan Morris has noted, its founding being

coincident with the death of Victoria herself, it is a kind of "allegorical sepulcher." It is renaissance in inspiration, oriental in its flourishes — its minarets and centerpiece Taj-like dome. But mostly it impresses you with its pomp, with its sheer size. It fills you with wonder that, more than 50 years after independence, it could still be chock-a-block with oils and busts of the erstwhile empress.

Rolling away from the Victoria Memorial is the Maidan; the six-square-kilometer (two-square-mile) expanse of parkland that has been called Calcutta's Regent's Park, or more colloquially its "lungs." It was created in the late 1800s to allow a clear line of fire from Fort William, the biggest of Anglo-India's military complexes. As it turned out, no shot was ever fired in anger — and the Maidan became a popular escape for promenades, impromptu games of cricket, and poetry readings, as it still is today.

The fort still presides over the western edge of the park, while to the south is Saint Paul's Cathedral, its vaulting steeple (modeled on the Bell Harry Tower at Canterbury Cathedral) clearly visible across the lawns and trees. To the east is Chowringhee Road, once Calcutta's proudest thoroughfare.

Today you'll find Chowringhee in a state of sad neglect. Shoe-shiners and hucksters huddle in its colonnaded shop fronts, and its once-famous residences of the nabobs look like they have been invaded by listless squatters. Of course you still have the Oberoi Grand Hotel, now the jewel in the crown of the Oberoi chain, but once a guesthouse for the minions of the empire run by one Mrs. Annie Monk. But the Grand, though still a marvel — with its chandeliers, marble floors and massive ballroom — is an international-class exception to the spirit of Calcutta, which is mostly informed by nostalgia.

And if you have doubts that this is so, you need look no further than the city's lodgings. To be sure, the Grand has maneuvered its way into the international luxury stakes. But just around the corner from the Grand, in a street otherwise famous for its budget flop houses, is the Fairlawn Hotel. Here Mr. Edmund Smith and his Armenian wife Violet preside over a gracefully decaying shrine to English comforts, aided by a retinue of "retainers" and "bearers" dressed in full Raj regalia. Meals — three-course British fare — are announced by the single toll of a bronze gong. It's worth being there simply to watch the arrival of Mrs. Smith, whose tumbling entourage of lap dogs leap up into the seat beside her, only to be

Picnickers in the lush statuary-dotted gardens of the pompously grand Victoria Memorial.

scattered by the ever-tardy arrival of her portly husband.

There's more. Mrs. Joyce Purdy's Old Kennilworth Hotel looks like it hasn't seen a lick of paint in decades, but stands in endearingly cobwebbed neglect in a leafy garden. Or the Great Eastern Hotel, 1-3 Old Court Street, where Rudyard Kipling once languished filing dispatches for the *Civil and Military Gazette*, and which doesn't look as if it's been refurbished since.

After all, neglect, curiously enough, is another of the Calcutta's charms. You find it too at the Marble Palace, a colonnaded mansion housing a bizarre collection of *objets d'art* accumulated from around the world.

But that's Calcutta. It's a dreamy, forgetful place, a once-wealthy family that still displays its silverware — undusted. The talk is still of the glory days. And as for that infamous hole… try finding it. It's said to be memorialized by a plaque on the General

Post Office. If it is, it's long forgotten, near impossible to locate. And don't even think about asking for directions.

Head for the Hills

IN THE DAYS OF THE RAJ, WHEN THE HEAT ON THE PLAINS BECAME UNBEARABLE, IT WAS TIME TO HEAD TO THE HILLS. Today nothing has changed (except that the vast majority of refugees from the sun are Indian vacationers), and a hill-station vacation is an essential part of the Indian experience for those who are there in the hot season.

For the quintessential hill station experience, where could be better than Darjeeling, once known as the "Queen of the Hill Stations?" Apart from the fact it grows some of the world's best tea, is home to a lively Tibetan community, and sports sweeping views of Mounts Kanchen-junga and Everest from its perch at 2,134 m (7,000 ft) above sea level, Darjeeling is also a charming lost corner of Anglo-India.

Not that it is all Anglo-Indian charm. Darjeeling town is a fascinating coincidence of labyrinthine cobbled streets, cascading cobbled stairs, boisterous bazaars selling fragrant local tea and handicrafts from all over the Himalayas, and a melting-pot mix of colorful mountain peoples.

Indeed, it is not until you check into your hotel that the old days come to life. Splash out if you can and spend a night or two in one of Darjeeling's "steeped in tradition" hotels. The Windamere Hotel is the ideal choice — complete with floral fittings and log fires in the rooms — though for half the price you can forget the twentieth century in the similarly Anglophile New Elgin Hotel. If you're worried about missing those log fires, don't be, the New Elgin has them too.

Don't spend all your time in your hotel, though. You are in the mountains after all — get out and see them. A predawn journey to Tiger Hill, which offers a 2,590-m (8,482-ft)-high vantage of Mounts Kanchenjunga and Everest as the sun paints the sky with rosy brush strokes, is obligatory. Hike on further from Tiger Hill to the Buddhist Ghoom Monastery, which was established in 1850 by a Mongolian astrologer-monk and contains a giant seated image of Maitreya, the "Buddha to Come."

But, as everyone avers, the best part about Darjeeling is getting there. The last leg of the journey from Calcutta takes place on the "Toy Train"—the toast of railway buffs the world over. It huffs and puffs through jungles, tea plant-ations, and ranks of pines, before shuddering onto the "Agony Loop" just outside Darjeeling.

It must be said, however, that Darjeeling's miniature railway is not for those in a hurry. Speeds of around 10 kph (six mph) are the norm. But then arguably Darjeeling itself is not for those in a hurry. You go to the hills to get away from the hustle and bustle of India. And when you get there, you relax with tea beside the fire, take walks, and perhaps catch the sunrise on the Himalayas. Cucumber sandwiches will be waiting for you at the hotel.

Visit a Deserted City

FOR THE PORTUGUESE IT WAS THEIR "ROME OF THE EAST," A HONG KONG BEFORE ITS TIME, a trading town that got rich and bred majestic churches, monasteries, and mansions, and attracted a population that grew until, by the sixteenth century, it exceeded even that of London.

A series of three plagues — one every 100 years from the sixteenth to eighteenth centuries — ended Goa's glory days and decimated its population, driving those who remained to nearby Panaji and leaving only the buildings they once lived and worshipped in as a reminder of the city's former greatness.

Today, Old Goa, as the city is referred to, is still a quiet place. The tourists in this part of India are mostly here for the beaches or the parties, which means you can sometimes have the half a dozen or so churches that still stand here to yourself.

OPPOSITE TOP: A lone tiger in Rajasthan's Ranthambone National Park. BOTTOM: Spring blooms at the Shalimar Gardens just outside Srinagar. ABOVE: A sweeping view of the world's loftiest peak, Mount Everest.

Having contemplated the Inquisition and paused in reflection on the state of Xavier's remains more than four hundred years after his death, it may be time to simply enjoy Old Goa's Portuguese architecture.

Italian friars built the beautiful Church of Saint Cajetan to resemble Saint Peter's basilica in Rome. While the Convent and Church of Francis of Assisi has exquisite panel frescoes, and also houses the Archaeological Museum, where you can see a portrait gallery of former Portuguese worthies who governed the colony.

In such moments, you find yourself wondering about all the buildings that are now gone. Stroll up Monte Santo (holy hill), where the Saint Augustine Tower is the only reminder of what was once Goa's biggest church. It once bustled with worshippers. Now it's empty.

Bazaars, Mosques, and Minarets

HYDERABAD MAY NOT BE ONE OF INDIA'S MORE FAMOUS CITIES, BUT IT IS CERTAINLY ONE OF ITS MORE INTRIGUING — an outpost of Islam in the overwhelmingly Hindu south, a labyrinthine city in which palaces, mosques, and minarets rise from amongst some of the subcontinent's most colorful bazaars.

There are few better places to begin exploring the city than the sixteenth-century Charminar, the magnificent archway topped by four tapering minarets that is emblematic of Hyderabad. If you're lucky, someone will be on hand to let you take a spiraling climb up one of the minarets for an unparalleled view of the city.

Should more luck be on your side, once you have made the climb, at your feet will be the Old Bazaar, one of India's most intoxicatingly medieval markets. The snaking alleys are cheek by jowl with merchants, slow-moving buffalo, craftsmen working pearl ornaments (this is the center of India's pearl trade), *burqa*-clad women on shopping missions, silversmiths pounding out wafer-thin silver leaf, touts and rickshaw *wallahs*. If you can steel yourself to plunge headfirst into the mêlée, a cornucopia of treasures awaits you down there: pearls, handcrafted enamel jewelry, gilded Korans, silks, exotic spices, the locally produced *bidri* ware (made with black metal inlaid with silver), and much more. Look as you stroll around for the stone buildings with shops downstairs and living quarters upstairs — many date back from the sixteenth-century founding of the city.

Chief among them is the Cathedral of Saint Catherine da Sé, said to be the biggest cathedral in Asia. Perhaps it's something about the empty vastness of the place, but it somehow seems to speak for the whole of Old Goa: its desertion, its slide from riches to weeds and echoes.

Founded by the Dominicans and built in the Tuscan style, it's a miraculous thing to behold here by the shores of the Arabian Sea. Stroll inside and take a look at the decorated panels around the center altarpiece depicting Saint Catherine's life. If you are here at the right time of the day (5:30 AM, 12:30 PM, or 6:30 PM), you will hear the tolling of the "Golden Bell," one of the cathedral's five bells and one of the biggest in the world. As it peals out, cast your thoughts back, if you have the stomach for it, to the days when it was used to announce the burning of pagans and heretics during the Inquisition — for the ruins of the Palace of the Inquisition stand just across the road from the cathedral.

You can soak up more of the atmosphere of Old Goa at the Basilica of Bom Jesus where, in an airtight silver and glass casket, lie the sacred remains of Saint Francis Xavier, Goa's patron saint. A student of Ignatius Loyola, the founder of the Jesuit order, Xavier's remains go on public display once every ten years.

Note too — not that you can miss it — the vast Mecca Masjid, which dates from the

early seventeenth century. One of the world's largest mosques, with room inside — if you include the courtyard — for some 10,000 believers. It was built from massive granite slabs quarried, it is said, 12 km (about seven and a half miles) away and carted into the city by teams of more than 1000 bullocks. The red bricks in the entranceway are said to have been made with clay brought from Mecca.

There are any number of similarly impressive sights in Hyderabad: Faluknuma Palace, which audaciously brings together Mughal and classical architectural influences; Salar Jung Museum, an eclectic collection of 35,000 exhibits spanning 35 galleries; and some very fine European-influenced architecture — but in the end it is to the bazaars that most visitors return.

After all, what is more evocative of the whole India experience than the push and shove of the bazaar? Where else could you

turn your gaze from a stall crammed with bags of multicolored spices to find yourself confronting three blind men begging for alms, their faces creased with blissful smiles? Where else but the bazaar can you give yourself up momentarily to the sights, smells, and sounds of a world that has changed barely at all in hundreds of years? You might come away with some Hyderabadi pearls — about 20% cheaper than you would pay at home if you know how to haggle — or some of the city's celebrated enamelware. But, as at all Indian bazaars, the most treasured prize is the memory of having once explored an antique world of buying and selling that has long disappeared in the West.

OPPOSITE: The Qutub Shahi Mausoleum in Golconda, near Hyderabad. ABOVE: The Mecca Masjid Mosque, the largest mosque in predominantly Hindu southern India.

YOUR CHOICE

The Great Outdoors

For most visitors India's attractions are first and foremost cultural. But India is also home to stunning national parks — some offering the opportunity to catch a safari glimpse of tigers and other exotic animals, and some of the world's most breathtaking mountain scenery.

TREKKING

Most people associate Himalayan trekking with Nepal, but congestion on the trails of that Buddhist kingdom has led to a boom in walking opportunities in India over recent years.

One of the most popular regions for trekking is Himachal Pradesh, where the hot spots are currently **Shimla**, **Chamba**, the **Kulu Valley**, and the **Kangra Valley**. Most treks are possible from May to October, but the best time to be up in the hills of Himachal is from July to September, when the high-altitude rhododendrons come splendidly into bloom.

Northern Uttar Pradesh is a far less visited trekking region but is highly rated by those who make the effort to get there. The best region is **Garhwal** and **Kumaon**, where you will find the fabled Valley of Flowers and **Nanda Devi**, India's highest mountain. It's possible to walk in the region at any time of the year, but May to October are the best months.

Some travelers undertake short treks in the Tibetan state of **Ladakh**. The high altitude there is challenging for those who have not spent some time acclimatizing, and the climate offers just a small window of opportunity — June to September — for serious trekking. But such treks provide a rare opportunity to visit remote Tibetan villages and temples.

Also popular is **Darjeeling**, which among its many popular hikes is included the relatively untaxing climb to the summit of Tiger Hill. Nearby **Sikkim** also provides superlative trekking opportunities and is a magnet to those looking to get off the beaten track. October to November offers the best visibility in both these regions, though you should be prepared for some cold weather.

Trekking in the above destinations can be organized *in situ* with a minimum of fuss — guides and equipment are easy to come by and rarely expensive. But for those who are pressed for time, it may be wise to book ahead.

In the United States, High Adventure Travel ((415) 912 5600 US TOLL-FREE (800) 350 0612 E-MAIL airtreks@highadv.com WEB SITE www.highadv.com, 4th Floor, 442 Post Street, San Francisco, CA 94102, specialize in India trekking: they offer many interesting options,

OPPOSITE: Gorgeously-hued prayer flags fluttering from Leh Gompa. ABOVE: A porter labors under his load in the rocky hills above Darjeeling.

with highly experienced guides, and can also arrange customized treks. Mercury Himalayan Explorations US TOLL-FREE (800) 661 0380, Second Floor, 300 East 42 Street, New York, NY 10017, is another specialist.

In the United Kingdom, Exodus Expeditions ((0181) 675 5550, 9 Weir Road, London SW12 OLT offer a number of treks.

French travelers should contact Nouvelle Frontières ((08) 03 33 33 33 FAX (01) 45 68 75 41 WEB SITE www.nouvelles-frontieres.fr, 87, boulevard de Grenelle, 75015 Paris.

NATIONAL PARKS

India offers the chance to walk on the wild side, to see and photograph some of the world's most majestic creatures — tigers, lions, elephants, rhinos, leopards, and wild bears. After all, India has a rich variety of wildlife — over 350 species of mammals, 900 species of reptiles, 2,000 species of birds, and over 30,000 varieties of insects and butterflies, to be reasonably exact.

Although aristocratic maharajas joined the British colonialists in *shikar*, the sport of game hunting, wildlife conservation actually has a long history in India. It began over 2,000 years ago when Emperor Ashoka forbade his subjects to destroy forests or slaughter wildlife. Ancient Aryan nature-worship wove animals into Hindu myth, legend, and religious belief.

Today India has more than 400 wildlife sanctuaries, national parks, and bird reserves scattered from Ladakh in the Himalayan mountains to the southern tip of Tamil Nadu, and covering a combined total of more than 90,000 sq km (35,000 sq miles), some three percent of India's total land. They are vital to the conservation of endangered species, such as the Bengal tiger, the Asiatic elephant and lion, the snow leopard, and the Siberian crane. India's most successful conservation effort is **Project Tiger**, launched in 1973 by the government and the World Wildlife Fund to create strongholds for the tiger when the beast was on the edge of extinction. There are now 15 of these reserves throughout the country, and some 4,000 tigers.

Your chances of catching a glimpse of one of these tigers are probably best at the massive **Kanha National Park** in Madhya Pradesh, which was the setting for Rudyard Kipling's *Jungle Book*. Tigers are the main attraction here, but you should also be able to catch glimpses of gaur, India's rare wild ox. The disadvantage of Kanha National Park is its inaccessibility. From Varanasi trains take around 13 hours to reach the city of Jabalpur (south of Khajuraho), from where it's around eight hours of rough bus travel to the park via Kisli. The park is open from November

through June; the best months to visit are March and April.

Also particularly famous for its tigers is **Corbett National Park** in Uttar Pradesh. It's one of India's most touristed national parks, but this is no reason to pass up a visit. Besides tigers, lucky animal lovers will have opportunities to catch glimpses of leopards, elephants, and muntjacs.

What many visitors to India do not realize is that not only can you see tigers, but if you are very lucky, you might also get to see an Asiatic lion. The last refuge of these creatures exists at **Sasan Gir Lion Sanctuary** in Gujarat. Note, however, that the park is closed from May to October.

Bird lovers should go to **Keoladeo Ghana National Park** in Rajasthan, India's most popular bird sanctuary, and from September to February home to large numbers of migrating

waterfowl from as far away as Siberia. Another highlight for bird lovers, although very inaccessible, is **Vedanthangal Water Bird Sanctuary** in Tamil Nadu, home to enormous flocks of birds during the breeding season (November to January, approximately).

Most of India's national parks and wildlife sanctuaries have good lodges — some of them in former royal hunting reserves. They also usually come equipped with adequate restaurants, and almost always offer excellent tours for visitors, often with the option of hiring jeeps, tame elephants, or in some cases, boats for exploring. Local forest departments can provide guides and trackers. If arranged in advance, it's possible to stay in the department's rest houses and hideaways, usually tucked within dense forest — good for "spying" on the local wildlife. You will almost never be allowed to meander off into the jungle without an experienced guide.

Go well prepared with binoculars, a good camera (preferably with wide-angle and zoom lenses), rolls of camera film, plenty of mosquito repellent, and/or a mosquito net. Its best to wear olive green, khaki, and dull brown colors.

The national parks featured in this book are as follows:

DELHI AND THE NORTH
UTTAR PRADESH Corbett National Park (see page 119), MADHYA PRADESH Kanha National Park (see above).

RAJASTHAN
Ranthambhore National Park (see page 160), Keoladeo Ghana National Park in Bharatpur (see page 135), and the Sariska National Park (see page 160).

A Tawny Royal Bengal tiger.

BOMBAY AND THE WEST

GUJARAT Nal Sarova Bird Sanctuary (see BIRD WATCHING, page 52). Don't miss the Sasan Gir Lion Sanctuary (see page 248).

CALCUTTA AND THE EAST

ASSAM Kaziranga Wildlife Sanctuary (see WILDLIFE PARKS, page 274), Manas Wildlife Sanctuary (see WILDLIFE PARKS, page 274). WEST BENGAL Sunderbans (see MANGROVES AND TIGERS, page 264), Sajnakhali Bird Sanctuary (see MANGROVES AND TIGERS, page 264). ORISSA Chilka Lake Bird Sanctuary (see ALONG THE COAST, page 284).

ACROSS THE DECCAN

KARNATAKA Bandipur Wildlife Sanctuary and Nagarhole National Park (see KARNATAKA'S WILDLIFE SANCTUARIES, page 309). TAMIL NADU Mudumalai Wildlife Sanctuary (see OOTY EXCURSIONS, page 311).

MADRAS AND THE TEMPLE TOWNS

MADRAS Guindy National Park (see MADRAS, WHAT TO SEE AND DO, page 321). TAMIL NADU Vedanthangal Water Bird Sanctuary (see above); Point Calimere Bird Sanctuary (see BIRD WATCHING, page 52).

THE DEEP SOUTH

KERALA Periyar Wildlife Sanctuary, Thekkady (see PERIYAR, page 348).

Sporting Spree

Surprisingly, you *can* indulge some sporting interests in India, but as you might expect it is not most people's first choice when it comes to a sporting vacation.

Five-star travelers will have few problems — providing they stick to India's premier destinations — finding somewhere for a game of tennis, squash, golf, or to simply keep fit swimming laps or working out. But outside the top hotels, your opportunities for sporting exercise will be scarce.

For Indians themselves, the top sport nationwide is without a doubt that most quintessentially English of games, **cricket**. When international matches are in progress the country appears to come to a standstill. As you travel around the country, you will see amateur games being played wherever there is an open piece of greenery.

As for **golf**, Britain may have started it but India was second. The Royal Calcutta Golf Club, established in 1829, was not only India's first golf club, but also the first to be established outside Britain.

There are far too many golf courses in India nowadays to be able to list them all. Some, such as the 18-hole Bombay Presidency Golf Club, Dr. Choitram Gidwani Road, Chembur, and the Royal Calcutta Golf Club, 18 Golf Club Road, Calcutta, were established in the early nineteenth century and are venerable places to putt and drive a ball. Others, such as the nine-hole Agra Golf Club, which sports views of the Taj Mahal, are memorable for their locations.

But wherever you find yourself in India, rest assured you will alwasys be able to find somewhere to play golf. It is, however, recommended that you bring your own clubs *and* a good supply of balls.

Some of India's better 18-hole courses include Bangalore Golf Club, 2 Sankey Road, High Grounds, Bangalore; Cosmopolitan Club Golf Annex, Saidapet, Madras; Delhi Golf

Club, Dr. Zakir Hussain Marg, New Delhi; Madras Gymkhana Club Golf Course, Guindy, Madras; Ootacamund Gymkhana Club, Ooty; Shillong Golf Club, Polo Grounds, Shillong; and Tollygunge Club, 120 Deshpran Sasmal Road, near Calcutta.

One of the best places for whitewater rafting in India is in Uttar Pradesh, close to Rishikesh. Professionally run excursions lasting two or three days can be organized in Delhi through Himalayan River Runners ((011) 6852602 FAX (011) 6865604, F5 Hauz Khas Enclave, New Delhi.

Not many people realize it but you can go **skiing** in India. Should the mood take you, Uttar Pradesh is the place to go. The Garhwal and Kumaon Hills are one of India's premiere skiing destinations, offering powder snow and long-distance skiing "year-round," if some claims are to be believed.

The best skiing in India is widely considered to be Auli, 16 km (10 miles) from Joshimath, also in Uttar Pradesh. Facilities here compare favorably with other international skiing destinations.

The skiing season at Auli runs from December to May, and information can be obtained from the Tourist Office ((091) 26817 FAX (091) 24408, Garwhal Mandal, Vikas Nigaam, 74/1 Rajpur Road, Dehradun.

Among the few agents that offer tours to India's skiing destinations, Global Adventures ((604) 940 2220 TOLL-FREE (800) 781 2269 FAX 604 940 2233 E-MAIL global@portal.ca, PO Box 123, Delta, British Columbia, Canada V4K 3N6, is recommended.

India's premiere surf and sand getaway, Goa, offers all the water sports travelers expect of a beach holiday.

The Open Road

Driving yourself around India is a risky endeavor. Scant regard is paid to road rules, and erratic behavior from your fellow drivers is to be expected at all times. In addition, the flow of traffic is extremely sluggish, so that it can often be considerably slower to travel by road than by rail (not to mention air). Night driving is particularly hazardous and is not recommended: pedestrians, cattle, and hurtling darkened vehicles combine to make the risks of an accident very high.

Another problem to consider if you are thinking of driving yourself is the generally miserable condition of India's roads. These can be bad enough in the big cities, but get out into rural India and they more than often go completely to pot — literally.

Rental cars are available in India's major cities but, all things considered, it's far better to hire a car with a driver than to rent your own vehicle. It will cost you little more, and you can relax and let someone else worry about the traffic. Drivers can also be good sources of information, providing you don't travel so far that you are no longer in territory they are familiar with.

Bear in mind, however, that most drivers with cars tend to own a Hindustan Ambassador, an unreliable and remarkably uncomfortable vehicle — not something you want to be doing

long-distance travel in. Shop around for a driver with something more modern, though in out-of-the-way destinations this may not be possible.

Some travelers elect to take to the roads on a motorbike (the Enfield Bullet, which comes in 350 cc and 500 cc models, is the bike of choice for most foreigners). Again, while a bike gives you freedom to explore India at your own pace, you are guaranteed to have some hair-raising moments en-route. In India, as in the rest of Asia, size counts for everything on the roads, and a motorbike is very low on the vehicular pecking order.

If you're planning a long motorbike trip in India you will have to buy a bike. Indian-made bikes are relatively inexpensive and surprisingly reliable. Be sure, however, that all the paperwork is in order. You will need a certificate of ownership and third-party insurance, both of which it should be possible to obtain for a small fee through whoever sells you the motorbike.

Backpacking

India probably qualifies as the backpacking capital of the world. For many young New Zealanders, Australians, and Europeans (less

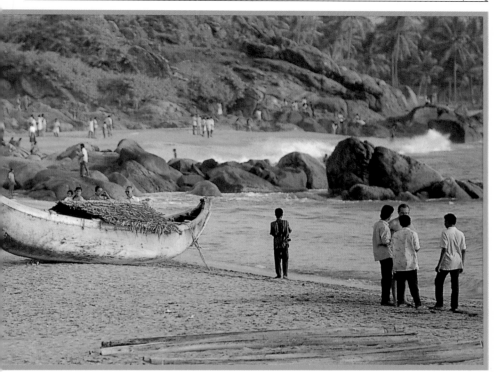

among Americans) an Indian journey has become a rite of passage.

It's not difficult to see why. Budget prices, exotic sights, sounds and smells, geographic diversity, and high adventure all combine to make India a compelling destination.

THE BACKPACKING TRAILS

Backpacking trails crisscross India, leaving few corners of the country untouched. But where the crowds are at any given time is largely a function of the climate. Varanasi and Agra, for example, tend to be dropped from most travelers' itineraries during the oven-like summer months, at which time the mountain retreats of Himachal Pradesh fill up with travelers.

Many travelers fly into New Delhi, and spend days there seeing the sights and adjusting to India. From Delhi, Agra — the home to the Taj Mahal — is just a couple of hours away. Tour groups often take in the Taj as a day trip, but backpackers usually spend a couple of days there in one of the budget guesthouses that sit just a stone's throw from the Taj itself.

From Agra some travelers go southwest to the camel-train deserts of Rajasthan, to the citadel cities of Jaipur and Jaisalmer, while others continue east to the Hindu holy city of

Varanasi. Those taking the latter route might consider a detour via Khajuraho, which is famed for its erotic carvings.

When the heat gets to be too much for you, remember the mountains are never far away in the north of India. Popular backpacker haunts include the old Raj-era hill station of Shimla, the mostly Tibetan Dharamsala, and the now legendary Manali. Another possible mountain destination in season is India's own foothold on the Tibetan plateau, Ladakh.

It's easy to forget that India is also a popular beach destination, though if it's sand and sun you're after you will need to go south. Most beach enthusiasts fly into Bombay (an expensive city that few backpackers linger in), and from there head to Goa, which is one of India's most popular backpacker destinations nowadays. Farther south is the beach center of Kovalam.

GETTING AROUND

India is a vast place, and if you want to get around on a budget your most valuable commodity is time — nothing in India, whether on the roads or by rail, moves

OPPOSITE: A beturbaned Rajput calls to mind the days when his people were feared warriors.
ABOVE: Goa's beaches are fabled.

particularly fast. Most backpackers do the long hauls by train and the shorter hops by bus. Flights are, as you would expect, expensive.

For the long train journeys, those looking to save money will have to face the question of just which class to travel. You can try the extremely inexpensive non-air-conditioned second class and (the increasingly rare) third class, but be prepared to upgrade: the crowded conditions, heat, and dust of the economy classes can try the patience of even the most hardened travelers.

A good middle road between budget discomfort and luxury is to take an air-conditioned second-class sleeper, which averages out at a very reasonable US$50 per 5,000 km of rail travel. Inexpensive meals are served on board, and although sleeping arrangements are somewhat cramped — six beds in two tiers per berth — the air conditioning at least ensures that you get some sleep.

Buses are nobody's favorite mode of locomotion, but there will be times when you have no choice — getting into the mountains of Himachal Pradesh from Delhi for example. Wherever possible, avoid local buses. Agreeably, you can save a little money traveling on them, but after an hour or so of countless stops and horrible overcrowding you will rue the choice. Better to seek out the state-run (every state has its bus company) luxury buses: few appreciate the high-decibel Hindi pop music, and the presence of the video machine is dreaded by all foreign travelers, but

at least you will have an assigned seat, legroom and air-conditioning that, more often than not, actually functions.

WHERE TO STAY

Finding budget accommodation in India is rarely a problem, and if you are traveling as a couple you can halve your costs by taking doubles.

In many parts of India, particularly in the more remote destinations, but even in popular destinations like Agra, it is possible to find a double room with a basic "splash yourself down" bathroom for as little as US$2 to US$3. Exceptions to this rule are the big cities of Delhi, Bombay, and Calcutta, where if you want to stick to a rock-bottom budget you will need to seek out dormitory accommodation.

Upcountry the government-run tourist bungalows are often a good deal. Rooms generally range from around US$3 to US$8, and there is usually a decent restaurant attached.

If you are going to have an early morning train journey or will be arriving in a town very late at night, ask for the Railway Retiring Rooms, which are nothing more than rooms in a railway hotel — they are inexpensive and as a rule well maintained, though standards vary from one station to the next.

Living It Up

Those looking to indulge themselves will find no shortage of opportunities to do so in India. In the major cities you will find fine dining and five-star hotels, and scattered around the country are numerous splendid hotels that have been converted from the palaces of maharajas. Another treat to look forward to is the occasional hotel that lingers on in renovated glory from the Raj era.

Contact information for the hotels and restaurants recommended here can be found in the relevant destinations chapters.

EXCEPTIONAL HOTELS

New Delhi, as you might expect, has India's highest concentration of top-notch hotels. Major chains, such as Hilton, Hyatt, and Sheraton, have branches here that meet the usual international standards, and there are also competitive local chains like the Oberoi and Taj groups.

ABOVE: Kumbh Mela is perhaps the world's most exotic religious festival. OPPOSITE TOP: India has no shortage of international standard luxury hotels. BOTTOM: A suite at the Rambagh Palace Hotel, Jaipur, Rajasthan.

In Agra, you can retire from your Taj Mahal sunset excursion to the award-winning **Mughal Sheraton**, a five-star hotel that for many locals rivals India's premier tourist attraction as a place of wonders.

Although in Delhi and Agra you will find top-class accommodation with all the obligatory subcontinent and Raj flourishes, it is in Rajasthan, where converted maharajas' palaces abound, that Indian travelers truly get to pamper themselves.

In Jaipur the **Rambagh Palace** and the **Jai Mahal Palace** are two palatial accommodations open to the public, the former sporting a polo ground. In Jodhpur the **Umaid Bhawan Palace** is considered by many to be India's best palace-style hotel. In Bikaner the hauntingly beautiful **Lallgarh Palace** is a must. And in Udaipur, the most famous of them all, is the **Lake Palace**, now a modern Taj-Group hotel constructed around a medieval kernel.

Bombay is the commercial heart of the subcontinent, and as you might expect home to the nation's most expensive real estate. Don't expect any bargains, but do expect the best in service and amenities. Such international-class standards are best summed up at the **Taj Mahal Hotel**, a 1903 blend of Rajput, Renaissance, and Gothic architecture. The Taj is at its best in its period-piece, sea-view rooms of the hotel's old wing. Nowadays, however, they are no secret — be sure to book well ahead.

Rivals to the Taj can be found at the **Oberoi Bombay Hotel** and the **Oberoi Towers**, both of which sport splendid views of the sea from fashionable Nariman Point. While there is no faulting either hotel when it comes to luxury standards, they do, however, lack the old world ambiance of the Taj.

Even Goa, which started out as a backpacker getaway, has some five-star luxury accommodation these days. In the northern beach area of Sinquerim the **Fort Aguada Beach Resort** is a tasteful Taj Group operation set in extensive gardens and featuring the ruins of a seventeenth-century fort.

In the southern beach area of Varca, meanwhile, the **Goa Renaissance Resort** is Goa's top place to dip into the good life. Take your pick of six restaurants and four bars, try your luck at the casino, or perhaps enjoy a round of golf at the resort's nine-hole course.

Calcutta's reputation in the West as a place of grinding poverty is belied by hotels such as the **Oberoi Grand**, a long-running establishment that has come through the days when it was the first hotel of the Empire's second city into a less blessed era with its

poise intact. Nothing, from the sweeping Georgian façade to the top-notch theme suites, fails to impress.

On a final note, it would be wrong to talk about India's luxury hotels without at least a nod in the direction of that Indian institution, the hill station. Most of the Raj-era institutions have seen better days, and the newer establishments tend to be about ersatz luxury for the mass honeymoon industry, but a few charming and luxurious places can be found here and there.

Chief among them would have to be the **Windamere Hotel** in Darjeeling. All right, perhaps this is not quite the luxury you might have become accustomed to elsewhere around India, but the time-warped library, Fawlty Towers bar, sweet garden, miniature golf course, and badminton court combine to create a whimsical charm that can be matched by few hotels in the world.

EXCEPTIONAL RESTAURANTS

You will find India's best restaurants in the capital, New Delhi, although Bombay also has some excellent dining too.

In Delhi, while some excellent cuisine can be found in extremely unexpected places, the very best is where you would expect it — in the top hotels.

For a journey into India's aristocratic culinary traditions, try the Maurya Sheraton's **Dum Pukht**. At the same hotel, treat yourself to a meal at **Bukhara**, which is renowned for its *raan*, or roasted spiced lamb, chicken *tikka* and charcoal-grilled kebabs, and, not least, its "dig-in" atmosphere.

Other similarly top-notch Indian restaurants in the capital include the Oberoi's **Kandahar**, where exquisite Mughalai cuisine rubs shoulders with classic European decor. **Dasaprakash**, in the Ambassador Hotel, is the place to sample a three-course, southern-style *thali* meal. And as for that Raj touch, the **Curzon Room** is a long-runner that indulges both the fantasies and the palates of those seeking nostalgia.

In Rajasthan, you will find yourself more often than not dining in your palace — why venture out anyway? All of Rajasthan's palace hotels offer superb dining opportunities, usually to the accompaniment of live musical entertainment, but the Rambagh Palace's huge Italian, marble-lined **Savaran Mahal**, with its retinue of regal waiters, is a particularly memorable place to dine on the finest in Mughalai cuisine.

When in Bombay, the Oberoi's **Kandahar** restaurant serves northern-style cuisine to die for. The Oberoi also offers a luxurious break from Indian cuisine at **La Rôtisserie**, renowned throughout town for its excellent French cuisine and seafood. Also recommended in Bombay is the Taj Mahal's **Tanjore** restaurant, which some say does the best Hyderabadi, Mughalai, and Punjabi cuisine in town, and also demands an evening on account of its evening program of classical Indian dance and music.

In Calcutta, the Oberoi Grand is not only the place to stay, it is also the place to eat. For Mughalai cuisine, **Gharana** is a memorable dining experience, while **Baan Thai** offers an opportunity to take a break from Indian cuisine and enjoy one of the best Thai restaurants in the country.

Family Fun

India is probably not the best place in the world to take your children, particularly if they are still very small. At the very least you will want to take a more upmarket approach to travel if you don't want your journey to be a misery.

OPPOSITE: A sage-like Muslim teacher.
BELOW: A scene from the ancient streets of Jaisalmer Fort, Rajasthan.

One thing to bear in mind if you're taking a family vacation in India is that the vast majority of India's attractions are of a cultural nature and will not hold the attention of small children for very long. Think instead about taking them on a "safari" to one of India's national parks, where the opportunity to see tigers and other exotic creatures is sure to pique their curiosity (see NATIONAL PARKS, page 28, in THE GREAT OUTDOORS).

Another consideration is the inevitably chaotic aspect of getting around in India. Just getting to the railway station and onto a train can at times be an undertaking requiring immense reserves of both patience and strength. For this reason, it's not a bad idea to consider a tour if you are traveling with children.

Cultural Kicks

For many travelers India is first and foremost a cultural destination. An ancient and dynamic society, you will find no shortage of cultural diversions while you are in the country.

MUSEUMS

With a history spanning millennia, India is a treasure house of art and history. New Delhi, the national capital, naturally has some of India's best museums, although the finest is agreed by most to be the Indian Museum in Calcutta.

New Delhi's most impressive museum is the **National Museum**, which features exhibits from prehistory to modern history. Spread over three floors, if your interests are wide you will need at least a full day to appreciate all that the museum has on offer. Watch Indian history unfold — first through displays of terracotta pottery dating back as far as 2700 BC, later through exquisite sculpture, and later still bronzes. Other displays feature paintings, India's maritime history, antiquities from Central Asia, and musical instruments.

Other interesting museums in Delhi include the **Crafts Museum**, which not only features superb tribal and regional crafts but also incorporates a village complex, in which you can examine some of India's rural architectural styles.

Purists will no doubt deplore the linking of trains and culture, but there's no denying that the collection of locomotives in the **National Rail Museum** — which is also in Delhi — present a fascinating picture of the evolution of India's most indispensable mode of transportation.

India's (and perhaps Asia's) biggest and best museum is the **Indian Museum** in Calcutta. The thirty six galleries might well keep you busy for days, although some of the multitude of exhibits are gathering dust and others are so obscure as to be of interest only to the specialist. The main attraction, however, is the museum's fabulous collection of sculpture gathered from all over the subcontinent — armies of art students can be seen squatting on the floor and reverently sketching the artwork. Another highlight of the museum is the massive collection of coins, which alone could take up hours of your time.

In Madras, don't neglect to visit the **Government Museum** and **National Art Gallery**, which apart from a rich collection of sculpture also houses India's largest and finest display of ancient bronzes.

Don't restrict your attention to just the bigger museums, however. You will find fascinating museums scattered all over India, in cities, towns, and attached to historical sights. Some of them may be small, some perhaps neglected, but they invariably contain something of interest, and rarely cost much to enter.

DANCE AND MUSIC

India has extraordinarily rich traditions of both classical and folk dance and music, woven inextricably together. It also offers a wealth of gifted artists, and performance festivals, sometimes against the original backdrops of ancient temples. In the large cities, five-star hotels often lay on performances in their restaurants as an extra draw for tourists, but more authentic happenings can be found by scanning details of events in the English-language newspapers.

There are several well-defined classical dance forms, each having evolved from a particular part of the country. All are rooted in the ancient religious tradition of dance as a form of worship, and their themes tend to concentrate on Hindu myths and the legendary exploits of the gods. In fact, dance is said to have originated with Lord Shiva, who in the form of Nataraja (Lord of the Dance) performed the energetic *tandava* or cosmic dance.

The most ancient classical form is *bharata natyam*, performed for centuries by *devadasis*, girls who were dedicated to Dravidian temples in Tamil Nadu. It is performed solo by a woman who begins with *alarippu*, a dance symbolizing that she is offering her body for the pleasure of the gods. The fluid, sensuous style combines *nritta* (pure dance) with expressive facial and hand movements and jingling ankle bells in order to depict maidenly love.

The dance-drama *kathakali* from neighboring Kerala is derived from a form of strenuous yoga. It is easily the most spectacular of all India's dances and is always performed by males in outrageously burlesque mikado-like costumes that require hours of preparation.

Odissi, from the eastern state of Orissa, is the most lyrical and erotic of all devotional temple dances, while *kuchipudi* from southern Andhra Pradesh consists of decorative dance dramas. The northern Indian *kathak* is a fast-paced, Muslim-influenced dance with complicated footwork, whirling pirouettes, and rhythmic sensuality. It was once performed by *nautch* — or dancing courtesans — in the Mughal court.

Apart from these main styles are many regional folk dances, tribal martial arts, and drama traditions, such as the graceful Manipuri style, and Bengal and Orissa's tradition of *chahau*, a masked dance. There are many others — ritualistic dances to welcome the birth of a child or chase away demons, and some involving balancing tricks with jugs of water or juggling knives.

Dance in India is unthinkable without music and song. According to legend, *nada* (sound) was the cosmic boom that accompanied earth's creation. Musical, rhythmical chanting of holy scriptures is as old as India's earliest civilization. Classical Indian music and its accompanying singing has a timeless, spiritual quality that must be experienced to be understood. Broadly speaking, it can be divided into two distinct styles: northern Hindustani and southern Carnatic, the former being more earthy and improvisational, steeped in Muslim and Persian influences, while the latter is more melodic and devotional. The music has two basic elements, the *tala* and the *raga*. *Tala* is the rhythm and is characterized by the number of beats, while the *raga* provides the melody.

The best known of the Indian instruments are the sitar and the tabla. The sitar is the large stringed instrument popularized by Ravi Shankar, while the tabla, a twin drum, is rather like the western bongo. Other less known instruments include the stringed *sarod* and *sarangi*, the latter played with a bow, and the reed trumpetlike *shehnai* and *tampura*.

OPPOSITE: A colorfully painted bull, sacred to India's Hindus. ABOVE: Do your best to see an Indian dance performance during your travels.

Shop Till You Drop

It's nearly impossible to leave India unburdened with purchases. Few places on earth can offer so much in the way of temptation and at such bargain prices. But before you even start shopping you will need to learn to bargain.

BARGAINING
Bargaining is an art form. It's not a simple matter of browbeating somebody into giving you the price you want. It's a game of sorts, and those who learn to play it well have usually been practicing for years. Not that you should let this intimidate you. It's still possible, even as a beginner, to knock a price that you already thought was very reasonable down to a level that makes you feel like you've got a bargain — it's unlikely you will have, but that's hardly the point.

First of all, before you do anything else, try to get a feel for the market. Most Indian handicrafts and souvenirs can be found in branches of the Central Cottage Industries Emporia in all the major cities. Prices in these shops are fixed and the quality of the products is usually high. You most definitely should not pay higher prices for such items elsewhere.

Secondly, be aware that even for the seasoned traveler Indian traders are amongst the canniest around, and will use almost any ruse to get you into their shop and to make you pay far more than you should for something you probably didn't even want to begin with. Acquire a firm but friendly air of aloofness. If someone pretends to be offended by your distance, don't be fooled, it's all part of the game — just watch the way Indians shop.

In bargaining, a few simple common-sense rules apply. First, don't get angry. Second, never make obvious how much you want something. Third, always remember you can walk away (a very effective bargaining tool, if used at the decisive moment). Finally, bear in mind that if you quote a price and a trader agrees to it, you are obligated to buy.

CARPETS
Without a doubt, one of India's most popular purchases among foreigners is a carpet.

Kashmiri carpets are among the world's finest. Travel to Kashmir is inadvisable at present and is unlikely to become so in the near future. Nevertheless, Kashmiri carpets can be still be found for sale in the bazaars and handicraft emporia of northern India.

If you are genuinely interested in buying a Kashmiri carpet you should either shop in one of the Central Cottage Industries Emporia or learn something about Kashmir carpets — if you have time, check prices at home before leaving for India. Recognizing quality in a carpet doesn't take that long, but it does require a little research.

A genuine Kashmiri carpet should have a tag underneath it that tells you what it is made of (silk or wool, or a combination of the two) and the density of knots per inch — naturally the more the better. In a government-accredited shop, the information on this tag will be reliable; elsewhere, you may not be so lucky (see also KASHMIRI HANDICRAFTS, page 204).

Tibetan carpets are widely available in the Tibetan communities of Himachal Pradesh, and can also be found in Delhi, Darjeeling and Gangtok. They are far less expensive than Kashmiri carpets, and some travelers are taken in by their earthy, "ethnic" colorings.

TEXTILES AND CLOTHING

Mahatma Gandhi was the great champion of homespun cloth, as anyone who saw the eponymous movie knows. Homespun, hand-printed cloth is known as *khadi*, and can be found in emporia and bazaars all over India. Every state has its unique printing styles. The simple variety that Gandhi espoused can still be purchased in what is known as a "Nehru jacket."

Silk is a very popular buy with foreign travelers, and it can be bought anywhere in India. The best places for silk shopping, however, are Varanasi and Kanchipuram (Tamil Nadu).

All over India you will see fascinating items of local clothing that can be purchased inexpensively. Just what you would do with it when you get home is another question. The *sari*, which can look elegant on an Indian woman, can look positively inelegant on

someone who does not know how to wear one. As for the southern-style *lungi*, which as some point out is more like a sheet than an item of apparel, it's hard to imagine where you might have an opportunity to wear one away from the beach. Nevertheless, they do at least make interesting souvenirs.

Lastly, remember that tailoring can often be remarkably inexpensive and that tailors are very capable in India. Buy your textiles and take them to a tailor with a design and — in the major cities at least — you should end up with something you would be proud to wear anywhere.

OPPOSITE TOP: A colorful market scene in Ajmer. BOTTOM: Indian pottery, such as this collection in a Rajasthan market, is inexpensive and attractive. ABOVE: Bangle-makers at work.

JEWELRY

Old hands will tell you to shop for silver jewelry and not gold, which is generally poor quality and expensive to boot. Few Westerners find Indian gold jewelry attractive anyway. Silver jewelry is widely available, but the more popular varieties are produced in Rajasthan and Bengal. Travelers to Tibetan areas such as Darjeeling and Dharamsala should consider buying some of the chunky silver jewelry Tibetans adorn themselves with.

Gems are a risky proposition for those who do not know what are they are doing, and are best avoided. Visitors to Jaipur — a major gem center — will invariably be dragged into gemstone shops and tempted by dazzling stones; they may be genuine, they may indeed be a bargain; but then again they may not be.

ANTIQUES

Bear in mind if you're shopping for antiques, that anything over 100 years old requires a clearance certificate — almost impossible to obtain — before it can be exported. If you're shopping at a *bona fide* antique agency, this should be no problem, but should there be any doubt check with the nearest branch of the Archeological Survey of India.

In actual fact, you are highly unlikely to end up taking a genuine antique out of India. Most of the "antiques" you see in shops will be cleverly aged items that were made weeks ago rather than centuries ago. This does not mean they are not attractive, and the wise shopper shops for good fakes rather than the genuine article.

Short Breaks

India is so vast and difficult to come to terms with that few people stop off for a short break or take a stopover vacation in one of its major cities. Nevertheless, there is at least one compelling reason to consider doing so if you have a stopover in New Delhi — Agra, home to the Taj Mahal.

With the daily 6:15 AM *Shatabdi Express* you can be in Agra within two hours, enjoying a breakfast of coffee, toast, and eggs en-route. Return is at 8:15 PM, which gives you a full day to explore Agra and its environs, perhaps taking in the nearby ruins of Fatehpur Sikri in the morning and Agra Fort in the afternoon, before ending the day with the Taj.

Travelers facing a Bombay stopover don't have anything quite so compelling to lure them out of town. Still, you might consider hightailing it to the former Portuguese colony of Goa, which is a short flight away or

around seven hours by a daily high-speed catamaran service.

Goa, some might argue, is not really India, but if it's a simple vacation you're after, it makes the perfect getaway. Attractions include white-sand beaches, accommodation to suit all tastes and budgets, exciting nightlife, delicious food, and beuatiful old Portuguese-style architecture in old Goa.

Travelers passing through Madras might consider a visit to the former French colony of Pondicherry, which is around four hours away by bus or train. Pondicherry has no major attractions to its name, but it does sport some attractive French colonial architecture and is home to a number of splendidly inexpensive French restaurants.

Festive Flings

The Indian calendar brims with thousands of festivals and many fairs all year round. For its most special days, India explodes with dazzling color, religious pageantry, trumpets, fireworks, tinsel, feasting, glorious costumes, brocade-showered idols, and magical outdoor processions of caparisoned elephants.

India has festivals to celebrate everything under the sun — from the latest military hardware to the arrival of the monsoons, not to mention sacred cows and cobras. There are Muslim, Sikh, Buddhist, Jain, Parsi, and Christian festivals. But the infinite pantheon of Hindu gods generate the most. Every temple has its own special festival, often occasions for its deities to receive a bath or a ritual anointment, or to be reunited with a spouse.

In a nutshell, Indian festivals are an excellent excuse for most Indians to put their work aside, forget their hardships, dress up, and have fun. The major festivals attract the country's best performers of classical and folk dance, music and theater. They also attract thousands of pilgrims, strolling players, and the merely curious from all over India. The party spirit extends to all aspects of Indian life — from cities to villages, from the annual Republic Day parade to individual wedding celebrations.

The dates of most festivals are calculated according to the Indian lunar calendar, and can be determined only by around October the previous year. At this time your nearest Government of India tourist office should have the full list of upcoming festival dates.

A smiling paint-splattered youth after a busy morning of Holi festivities.

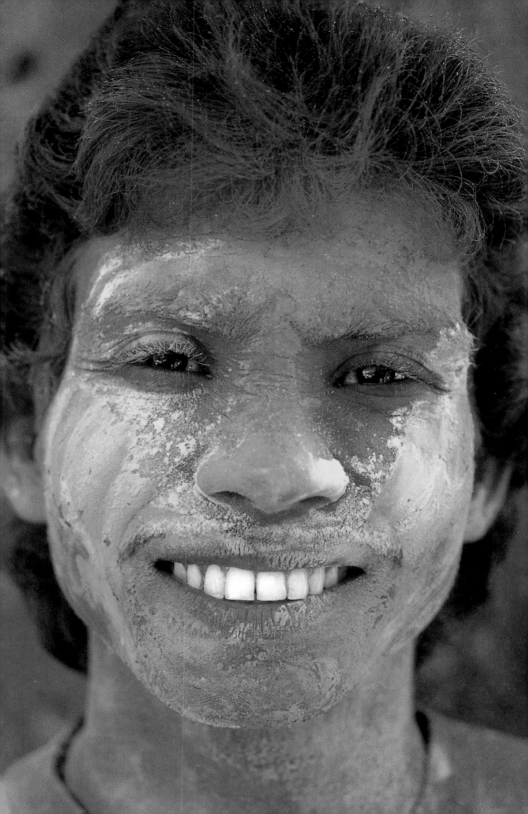

The most interesting and worthwhile festivals and fairs, together with their approximate dates and the best place to see them are listed below.

JANUARY

Pongal or **Sankranti** is south India's most exuberant harvest festival. It lasts three days and is best seen in Tamil Nadu and Karnataka. Villagers decorate cattle with fragrant blossoms, *ghee* (clarified butter), and mango leaves, feed them *pongal* (sweet rice) and parade them in lively processions accompanied by drums and music. Its highlight is a sort of Dravidian rodeo, where local lads try to wrest bundles of currency from the horns of ferocious bulls.

Republic Day on January 26 is an important national festival celebrated all over India. It's at its most spectacular in New Delhi, where it features a magnificent military parade with regiments in full dress, bands, richly caparisoned camels and elephants, floats and colorful folk dancers on Rajpath. It is followed by a two-day festival of music and dance and culminates with the famous dusk "Beating the Retreat" held on January 29 at Raj Bhavan.

JANUARY/FEBRUARY

Vasant Panchami honors Saraswati, the Hindu goddess of knowledge, and is celebrated with colorful processions and kite-flying. It is best seen in West Bengal. Paint brushes, ballpoint pens, and musical instruments are reverently placed at Saraswati's shrine, as if to encourage continued creativity.

The Float Festival is held in the famous temple town of Madurai in south India, marking the birth anniversary of Tirumali Nayak, the city's seventeenth-century ruler.

Jaisalmer's popular three-day **Desert Festival** coincides with the full moon and brims with a carnival, Rajput atmosphere. Highlights include camel polo, camel races, turban-tying competitions, desert music, and dance.

The **Nagaur Livestock Fair**, located half a day's drive from Jodhpur, rewards adventurous travelers with four days of camel races, livestock competitions, and colorful Rajasthani dancing and singing. Old India hands rate it just as highly as its better-known cousin, the Pushkar Fair.

Goa's Carnival is no longer as exuberantly spectacular as in former days, but it still attracts devotees for its free-flowing *feni* (a cashew or coconut based alcohol) and party atmosphere.

Sikhs don traditional attire to celebrate the birthday of Guru Gobind Singh.

FEBRUARY/MARCH

Shivarati marks the day when Hindus across India pay their respects to Shiva, the religion's father figure. The most colorful pageantry occurs at the largest Shiva temples at Khajuraho, Varanasi, Mandi, Chidambaram, and Kashmir. Devotees fast for a day, then fall upon dates, fruits, nuts, sweet potatoes, and rice — Shiva's favorite snack.

Holi is India's color-doused version of April Fools day. Spring is celebrated with explosive Bacchanalian, paint-squirting revelry that breaks down all traditional barriers of caste and religion in an atmosphere of playful flirtation. Picasso never visited India, but he was so impressed by the idea of Holi that he once staged it at his Spanish villa. It's best to soak up the carnival atmosphere of a "real" rural Holi in one of the smaller Rajasthan towns where you'll be drawn into exuberant folk dance, music, and gentle pelting with clouds of saffron, emerald, turquoise, pink, and red powder. Large cities are often not so much fun — and unwary foreigners may not enjoy the experience of being sloshed with buckets of paint from rooftop pranksters. Go prepared like everyone else by purchasing plenty of powder, paint, and water pistols, and wear clothes that can be thrown away the next day. Don't despair: you may resemble a walking artist's palette for days, or even weeks later, but the color will eventually come out!

Khajuraho Dance Festival is held early March in the famous temple, with a weeklong program of evening performances by the country's best artists to a backdrop of floodlit temples and glittering stars.

MARCH/APRIL

Gangaur is best seen in Rajasthan, especially Jaipur and Udaipur, and in West Bengal and Orissa. It pays tribute to Shiva's wife Parvati, in her incarnation of Gangaur, goddess of marital happiness, abundance, and fertility. In Jaipur, idols of Shiva and Gangaur are paraded on floats pulled by caparisoned horses and elephants amid trumpeting and singing. Everywhere else, marriage parties add to the atmosphere.

Mahavir Jayanti is a Jain festival dedicated to Mahavira, the twenty-fourth Jain *tirthankara* or saint, best seen at Jain shrines at Jain centers in Gujarat or at Mount Abu in Rajasthan.

APRIL/MAY

Urs Festival in Ajmer is held for six days in April to May and is a dramatic annual display of *qawwalis* (mythic poems set to classical raga modes), exuberant fairs, and feasts.

Baisakhi celebrates the beginning of the Hindu solar New Year. Hindus throng to the sacred Ganges River to bathe and worship, since the goddess Ganga is thought to have descended to earth on this day many millennia ago. Festive processions are best seen in the holy cities along the Ganges river in north India, as well as in Srinagar's Mughal Gardens and in Tamil Nadu. Sikhs also celebrate it to commemorate the day in 1689 that Guru Gobind Singh founded the Khalsa or militant brotherhood of the Sikhs. In Punjab farmers start harvesting and perform the *bhangra* dance, as wild and vigorous as that of the Cossacks.

Pooram in Trichur, Kerala, is one of India's temple festival highlights with its 30 decorated elephants, *dhoti*-clad priests, trumpets, and fireworks.

Meenakshi Kalaynam in Madurai, celebrates the annual mock-marriage of the "fish-eyed" goddess Meenakshi and Shiva with ten days of nonstop revelry in the courtyards of the famous Meenakshi Temple. Artists dance, priests chant, children dress as gods, and musicians play enchanting devotional music.

MAY/JUNE

Buddha Purnima celebrates Buddha's birth, death, and enlightenment, and is best at thefamous Buddhist centers of Sarnath andBodhgaya.

Hemis Festival is held at the largest monastery in Ladakh and celebrates the birth anniversary of the Guru Padmasambhava. Masked dances, fairs, and the ornately-dressed Ladakhis are the highlights.

JUNE/JULY

Id-ul-Fitr, also known as Ramazan-Id, is a major Muslim celebration which marks the end of Ramadan, the Islamic month of fasting. Thousands of devout Muslims stream into the major mosques to pray, then rejoice and feast. It's best seen in Delhi, Lucknow, Hyderabad, and Calcutta.

Rath Yatra, held in Puri, Orissa, is the most spectacular of all temple festivals, with a cast of devout thousands, like an Indian version of a Cecil de Mille epic. Held in honor of Lord Jagannath, three enormous temple chariots carrying the idols of Jagannath and his siblings, Balabhadra and Subhadra are dragged by sweating devotees.

JULY/AUGUST

Nag Panchami is held in honor of Naga, the great thousand-headed serpent on which Vishnu reclined in contemplation. It is most dramatic in Jodhpur, where giant colorful

effigies of Naga are erected, and women worship visiting snake charmers for fertility. Throughout India, cobras are fed with milk and sweets.

Teej celebrates both the onset of the monsoon and the reunion of Shiva and his wife Parvati (Gangaur). Nubile girls dress up in tinsel-fringed saris, jewelry, and bright green veils, playfully push each other on garland-bedecked swings, and pray for a faithful, loving husband. It's best seen in Jaipur, where gaily, vividly dressed villagers swarm to see the pageantry as caparisoned elephants, dancers, and musicians escort the Parvati idol from her parent's home into Shiva's waiting arms.

Independence Day is celebrated all over India on August 15, notably in New Delhi.

SEPTEMBER/OCTOBER

Ganapati (Ganesh Chaturthi) honors the elephant-headed god of good luck and inspires grand processions everywhere, but especially in Bombay.

Dussehra is a 10-day festival celebrated with performances across India, but the most colorful pageantry takes place in Kulu, Mysore, and West Bengal. In Delhi and Varanasi it is known as **Ram Lila**.

Diwali, or the "festival of lights," traditionally takes place on the first full moon following Dussehra. It's the gayest and most riotous of all Indian festivals, with a night-long display of fireworks, illuminations, and general pageantry.

Throughout India, houses are cleaned and repainted to honor Lakshmi, the goddess of wealth and the home, then bedecked with hundreds of oil-lamps. It is best seen in northern India and at Mysore in the south.

NOVEMBER/DECEMBER

Pushkar's Camel and Cattle Fair is a definite "must-see" tourist highlight (see page 162).

Exotic piety is at its most spectacular in Goa on **Christmas Day**, where glorious sixteenth-century cathedrals stage candlelit mass with hymns and pompous religious celebrations.

The **Madras Dance and Arts Festivals** last from mid-December to early January and offer a potpourri of excellent performances by the nation's best artists.

FESTIVAL FOOTNOTE

India's **Kumbh Mela** is undeniably the most ancient and spectacular religious carnival on the planet, revealing to astonished Western eyes all that is most mysterious, bizarre, and awesome about Hinduism, a faith that was born some three thousand years ago. It is held every three years, moving consecutively from one to another of the four venues: Allahabad (in Uttar Pradesh), Nasik (Maharashtra), Ujjian (in Madhya Pradesh), and Haridwar (again in Uttar Pradesh). The most recent one was held

A marching band announces and celebrates a wedding.

in Haridwar in April 1998. Ancient legend relates that demons once stole the sacred nectar of immortality from the gods, in a *kumbh*, or vessel, and during the ensuing battle between the gods and the demon thieves, the nectar spilled at twelve different places in the universe — eight of these spills were in the heavens and four were on earth — forming these four most sacred of Indian cities.

The Kumbh Mela begins when the astrological positions of the sun and moon are most auspicious, and millions of pilgrims and thousands of holy men (sadhus) of every order bathe in holy rivers, believing the holy rivers suddenly run with life-preserving nectar. Ash-smeared, leopard skin-clad "gurus" preside over captive audiences; "god" children bestow regal blessings; naked ascetics perform miraculous feats of endurance amid a temporary city erected from tents on huge sand belts near the river.

The holiest of all the Kumbh Melas occurs every 12 years at Allahabad, the confluence of the Ganges, Yamuna, and the mythical Saraswati rivers. It is scheduled to occur in Allahabad in 2001.

Galloping Gourmets

The cuisine of India is generally underrated in the West. This perhaps is partly due to the fact that in the popular imagination India and curry are inextricably linked.

In fact, and frequently to the surprise of visiting Westerners, what is generally referred to as "curry" in the West is not actually a particular dish but can be any of a huge number of *masalas*, or "mixes" of spices. These spices include turmeric, saffron, chili, cinnamon, coriander (— or cilentro — both leaf and seed), ginger, garlic, cardamom, mustard (seeds), and cumin — among others. Just which of these spices are mixed together and in what quantities will make a vast difference to the flavor of the meal you are presented with.

For many first-timers the most accessible of the myriad Indian cuisines is the Muslim-influenced Mughalai cooking of northern India, which has become so popular nowadays that it can be found in cities and even villages throughout India.

Mughalai cooking is rich — often creamy and impregnated with nuts and raisins — and meaty. It's not the kind of thing you order for a light meal. But if it's something substantial you want, Mughalai, with its kebabs, breads — oven-baked *naan* is a popular choice — and rich *pulau* accom-

paniments is a treat.

Rogon josh (curried lamb), *gushtaba* (spicy meat pounded to pâté-consistency, formed into balls and simmered in spiced yogurt), and *biryani* (chicken or lamb in orange-flavored rice, sprinkled with rosewater, almonds, and dried fruits) are well known northern-style dishes.

Tandoori — which refers to the clay oven (*tandoor*) in which the food is cooked, at extremely high temperatures — is revelatory when applied to either chicken or lamb. If it is done properly, the marinated meat (marinated in a pungent blend of yoghurt, saffron, and spices) will emerge from the oven moist and succulent. Boneless meat cooked in the same manner is known as *tikka*, and is also excellent, whether served alone or in one of a variety of *masala* sauces. *Naans, paratha* — plain or stuffed with vegetables, meat, oreven dried fruits — stuffed *kulcha*, and handkerchief-thin *romali roti* breads are served alongside (see also WHERE TO EAT, page 116, under DELHI for more information on north Indian cuisine).

In the south of India you are much more likely to be dining vegetarian, or at least on seafood. Plain rice, rather than breads, is the usual staple.

To make a foray into southern-style cuisine — which tends to be spicier than the food in the north — try a *thali*, which is more of a tempting platter of individual dishes. You will be presented with a pile of steaming rice, some crisp *poppadums* (usually), and a number of small bowls of deliciousvegetable curries —and perhaps some chutney too, often lime or mango. There is just one thing that is to be watched out for down south: you will often be required to eat with your fingers. As you look around at your fellow diners, you will realize quickly that it is really quite an art.

The great snack of the south, although it is not exactly in the high cuisine stakes, is the *masala dosa*, a potato-based curry wrapped in a crispy pancake. Throughout India you will find many other delicious snacks, perhaps most notably *samosas* — those more-ish deep-fried triangles of "vegetable curry pie" — and *pakoras* — a tantalizing combination of fresh vegetables cooked together in a blend of sweet spices and then dipped in chick-pea flour before being crispily deep-fried (see SOUTH INDIAN CUISINE, page 317, for further details on the particularities of this vast and varied cuisine).

Spice stalls are amongst the most colorful in any Indian market.

There are several staples without which no meal on the subcontinent would be complete. A day without bread for most Indians would be unthinkable — like a Frenchman without his baguette. Certain unleavened breads such as the common *chapati*, *roti*, and millet *paratha*, originated 4,000 years ago. Slapped to the side of a tandoor oven or fried over charcoal braziers, they still dominate most meals. Dairy products are liberally used in both the north and the south — so that it is not difficult to understand why the Indians regard the cow as sacred.

One aspect of Indian cuisine that is often neglected by less adventurous travelers is the desserts. You will find these served in special sweet shops accompanied by lightly sweetened milk tea.

If you want to leap in at the deep end, where Indian sweets are at their sweetest and sickliest, try a *gulab jamun*, a kind of thick sponge-ball that has been soaked in a rosewater-scented syrup.

More palatable for most Westerners is *barfi*, which is a curious fudge-like substance made from boiled-down milk. It's quite addictive once you develop a taste for it.

Also worthy of note is *kulfi*, a frozen sweet made from the winning combination of pistachios and cardamom.

You can find a spectacular variety of fresh fruit — mangoes, pomegranates, melons, pineapples, fig-like pitchouts, an endless variety of bananas, coconuts, Kashmiri apples, and tangerines — right across India, and most of it will be extremely cheap. Always buy complete fruits though, and peel them yourself. If grapes and tomatoes look particularly appetizing, take care to wash them in sterilized water before you eat them.

It's common to end your meal by chewing palate-cleansing handfuls of *sof*, or aniseed. The addictive *paan* (a mixture of betel nut and spices wrapped in a betel leaf) is also served and is the cause of all those red-stained lips and teeth.

India's national drink is *chai*, the army-style brew made from boiled up tea, milk, and spoonfuls of sugar, served at every railway station and *dhaba* or roadside café. If you ask for "tray tea," it is served the conventional way. If you don't like sugar, ask for *"ek chai neh chini"* (one tea, no sugar). Local south Indian coffee is excellent, and is available from the extensive network of Indian coffeehouses in most cities and towns.

For thirst-quenchers, *nimbu* — or lime soda served sweet, salted or plain — or freshly squeezed juices are the most refreshing "safe" beverages. Yogurt-based

lassi and milk straight from the king coconut are also very cooling and cleansing. Fizzy, bottled soft drinks — with improbable names such as Limca, Thrills, Campa Cola, and Thums Up — can be bought virtually anywhere and consumed with relative safety, but are very sickly. A bag of oranges is probably a healthier, more satisfying alternative. Bottled mineral water is widely available, but check first that its seal has not been tampered with.

Imported wine and spirits are available in top hotels, but at very high prices, which is why bottles of Scotch are so gratefully received as presents in India. Indian alcohol is cheaper, craftily confusing matters by its name: "Indian Made Foreign Liquor" or "Foreign Liquor" for short. Indian-made beer, wines, and whiskey are not terribly memorable (except the morning after) and

are served in most hotels except in "dry" Gujarat and Tamil Nadu states, where liquor permits must be collected from the nearest tourist office. Popular brands of beer, good for drinking with spicy curries, include Golden Eagle, Punjab, Kingfisher, Rosy Pelican, and London Pilsner. Bangalore has excellent draft beer served on tap in many English-style pubs. In the ex-Portuguese enclave of Goa, coconut and palm-leaf *toddy*, and cashew-nut *feni* make a piquant, interesting variation — and goes down very well with fresh, grilled seafood on a tropical star-filled night.

OPPOSITE: Women sorting nutmegs.
ABOVE: An early morning cyclist takes chickens to market in Hyderabad.

Science and Technology, Cochin University, Cochin, Kerala 682022; **Himachal Pradesh University**, Shimla, Himachal Pradesh 171005; **Indira Gandhi National Open University**, Maidan Garhi, New Delhi, 110068; **Jawaharlal Nehru University**, New Mehrauli Road, New Delhi, 110067; **Rabindra Bharati University**, 56A Barrackpore, Trunk Road, Calcutta, West Bengal 700050; **University of Bombay**, University Road, Fort, Bombay, Maharashtra 400032; **University of Calcutta**, Senate House, College Street, Calcutta, West Bengal 700073; **University of Delhi**, Delhi, 110007.

BIRD WATCHING

With more than 1,200 native species, India is a magnet to serious bird watchers. The main places to see the birds are the national parks that have been put aside with precisely this purpose: **Keoladeo** (Rajasthan), **Nal Sarova** (Gujarat), **Point Calimere** (Tamil Nadu) and **Vedanthangal** (Tamil Nadu) bird sanctuaries.

For more detailed information, a good place to visit is the Oriental Bird Club WEB SITE www.ee.princeton.edu/~vivek/indbird.html. Another good source of information is *A Pictorial Guide to the Birds of the Indian Subcontinent* by Salim Ali, S. Dillon Ripley (Oxford: Oxford University Press, 1995). It is illustrated and describes the habitats and ranges of almost all of India's native species. It is readily available in India.

Special Interests

SPIRITUAL

Ever since the Beatles decamped there, India has been a favored destination for those with an interest in spiritual matters. **Rishikesh**, the original Beatles' destination, is nowadays a yogic boomtown, with any number of inexpensive ashrams you can stay in and study matters such as Hindu philosophy, meditation, and yoga.

Other ashrams are scattered throughout India, such as the Krishnamurti Foundation in **Madras** and the Osho Commune in **Pune.**

Dharamsala, as home to the Tibetan Government in Exile, is the best place in India to learn about Tibetan Buddhism or to study the Tibetan language.

LANGUAGE STUDY

Hindi is the Indian language that most foreigners choose to study, and there is any number of universities around India that offer courses. The major ones are as follows (address your inquiries to the Director of International Programs): **Banaras Hindu University**, Varanasi, Uttar Pradesh 221005; **Bangalore University**, Jnana Bharathi, Bangalore, Karnataka 560056; **Cochin University of**

Taking a Tour

Given its vastness and the difficulties of doing it alone, a tour is often a sensible way to approach India for the first time.

In the United States, a reliable all-round operator for India tours is **Himalayan Travel** ((203) 359 3711 TOLL-FREE (800) 225 2380 FAX (203) 359 3669 E-MAIL worldadv@netaxis.com, 110 Prospect Street, Stamford, CT 06901.

If you're looking for a less conventional experience, **High Adventure Travel** ((415) 912 5600 US TOLL-FREE (800) 350 0612 E-MAIL airtreks@highadv.com WEB SITE WWW .highadv.com, 4th Floor, 442 Post Street, San Francisco, CA 94102, offer many exhilarating trips throughout India, including some spectacular journeys to the most varied and beautiful parts of the country. They specialize in trekking in the Himalayas, and their trips include hiking, rafting, climbing, and other physical activities. **Above the Clouds** ((508) 799 4499 TOLL-FREE (800) 233 4499 FAX (508) 797 4779 E-MAIL sconlon@world.std.com, PO Box 398, Worcester, Massachusetts 01602 0398, is another good choice for trips to the more remote India.

Another operator that focuses on "unusual" interests is **Geographic Expeditions** ((415) 922 0448, 2627 Lombard Street, San Francisco, CA 94123. The camel safari specialists are **Wilderness Travel** ((510) 558 2488 TOLL-FREE (800) 368 2794 E-MAIL webinfo@wildernesstravel.com, 1102 Ninth Street, Berkeley, CA 94710.

Mountain Travel/Sobek is a well-established agency offering a variety of exotic tours. It has offices in the United States ((510) 527 8100 FAX (510) 525 7710, 6420 Fairmount Avenue, El Cerrito, CA 94530; the United Kingdom ((1494) 448901 FAX (1494) 465526; and Australia ((029) 264 5710 FAX (029) 267 3047.

In the United Kingdom, **Abercrombie and Kent** ((0171) 7309600, Sloane Square House, Holbein Place, London SW1 8NS, are well regarded and offer suitably upmarket tours of the subcontinent. For similar levels of comfort but slightly more imaginative

programming, contact **Mysteries of India** ((0181) 515966, 92 The Green, Southall, Middlesex, UB2 4B6.

For other specialist interests (everything from trekking to golf), **Indian Encounters** ((1929) 480548, Creech Barrow, East Creech, Wareham, Dorset BH20 5AP.

In India itself, all the major travel agencies that operate tours have head offices in Delhi. A reliable agency is **Cox and Kings** ((011) 373 8811, H Block, Connaught Circus, New Delhi, which offers general tours. For trekking tours, contact **Mercury Travels** ((011) 373 2268, Jeevan Tara Building, Sansad Marg, New Delhi.

OPPOSITE: Sikhs gaze on the Qutb Minar Minaret in Delhi. ABOVE: The Friday mosque in the forsaken city of Fatehpur Sikri, near Agra.

Welcome
to India

A PERSON WHO TELLS YOU THEY FOUND WHAT THEY expected in India is probably not telling the truth. No traveler is ever fully prepared for the first experience of India, or leaves feeling untouched. Many approach their arrival with excited anticipation — for here, they have been told, exists all that is most extraordinary and most shocking, most marvelous and most bizarre.

The first glimpse of the vast subcontinent is very often misleading. This is the India that is revealed in the bright fluorescence of its international airports, where jet-lagged newcomers usually land during the early hours of the morning — the arrival time of most international

flights. As the doors of the air-conditioned airport close behind you, you are enveloped by waves of sticky heat and pungent, unfamiliar scents from the darkness, as you step unsteadily into what seems a flickering Hades of shouting Indians, bundle-like pavement sleepers, car horns bleeping in unison, and urgent scrums of taxi touts pulling at your shirtsleeves. Most travelers feel they are instantly caught off guard, catapulted into confrontation with a strange alien land.

Yet India has many guises. India offers its visitors majestic temples and tombs, erotic sculptures, forlorn royal palaces and fabled mountains, and great natural beauty.

ABOVE: A village market scene in Goa. OPPOSITE: A Trivandrum coconut shealer pauses to give a typically warm smile. BELOW: A three-wheeled taxi can make for a fun ride.

A tour through this ancient, vast, and crowded land is always an authentic adventure though — sometimes daunting, often moving, but always stimulating and memorable. This colossal pendant-shaped continent is a place where breathtaking extremes are accepted almost as commonplace, and where the traveler learns to expect the most unexpected.

India covers a land mass roughly the size of Europe and is home to a fifth of humanity — more than 960 million people — who form a diverse multitude of cultures, languages, religions, and dress. Its domain extends 3,300 km (2,000 miles) from the northern snowcapped peaks of the Himalayas to the steamy palm-dotted plains of the southern tip of Kanya Kumari, and sprawls for 2,700 km (1,700 miles) between the mountainous frontiers of China and Burma to the arid desert wasteland at the border of western Rajasthan. Its people speak 1,652 dialects, of which only 15 are officially recognized. It prides itself on being the world's largest democracy and a leader of the Third World, but it remains overwhelmingly a peasant nation rooted in often brutal traditions that have barely changed for centuries. It is the cradle of one of the greatest ancient civilizations — and during its heyday, one of the wealthiest — with a history that spans more than 4,000 years, offering today's visitors a glimpse of an infinitely diverse, rich cultural heritage.

Above all, India is a flesh-and-blood encounter with the Indian people, for no country can ever be judged by its spectacle alone, nor can a traveler be insulated from its ocean of faces. It is they who will reveal India to you in all its baffling, rich, and often exasperating complexity. There may be moments during your travels when you feel intoxicated by the diversity and splendor India has to offer, and others when you just want to fly home as quickly as possible. India demands a lot of patience and tolerance from its visitors. It can seem to be just too big and overwhelming to understand.

In a headlong rush to get visas and immunization jabs, many tourists overlook two very essential items of luggage for travel in India: an open mind and a well-developed sense of humor. If you manage to keep these intact throughout your stay, you will have mastered the knack of appreciating India.

While you'll probably never see the entire country, or ever feel you completely understand it, you will very likely come away with an enduring fascination for India — exerting a pull that may bring you back time and time again. Memories of India's pageant-like street-life, teeming with endlessly moving crowds and infused with dust-laden light, vivid flashes of color and spicy scents, and its bewildering landscape that is layered with the majestic relics

of lost empires, leave an indelible impression, touching what seems to be a human hunger for all that is most exotic, bizarre, and elusive.

The purpose of this guide is to present the most worthwhile and accessible Indian destinations and to help plan your itinerary within a broad framework of travel options. Whether you are backpacking, traveling in luxury, or taking a midway compromise between the two, this guide contains up-to-date information on hotels, restaurants, and transportation to help you fully appreciate each place.

Unless you plan to stay for several months — and there are some who end up staying in India for years — you'll need to be very selective about where you go. It is usually best to focus on one or two main regions, rather than attempting a crammed, all-encompassing tour of India, a nation best appreciated on a loose schedule. An itinerary that looks good on paper may not account for ever-lurking complications of traveling in India, such as an odd "off-key" day due to a bout of the notorious "Delhi-belly," or missing a crucial connection due to an unforeseen act of God.

To do justice to India, an Indian expedition should be at least three weeks long. Most people take at least three or four days to acclimatize after arrival, not just from the usual jet-lag, but to the overwhelming "strangeness" of India's climate, pace, and culture. Conversely, few newcomers to the subcontinent tend to stay longer than six weeks. Most people find it both exhilarating and exhausting, a place that rivets the senses and triggers such a complex array of reactions to its varied sights that before long they find themselves needing a break from their vacation. Responding to India's idiosyncrasies — as baffling or downright frustrating as these may seem at the time — is what makes the country such a special destination. If you maintain a fairly relaxed attitude, have plenty of enthusiasm, and are able to put it all down to experience, then you are likely to have some of the most fantastic and unforgettable experiences of your life.

Hardy but genial Rajasthani nomads of the arid Thar desert, swaddled against the sands in colorful camel-hair rugs.

India
and Its
People

TO VISIT INDIA IS TO BE GIVEN A TANTALIZING GLIMPSE of one of the world's most ancient and complex cultures. The 4,000 to 5,000 years of India's recorded past have seen its soil annexed countless times by history's shifting fortunes. Dynasty has usurped dynasty, empire has followed empire, and the lives of ordinary people have been plunged into suffering and turmoil from one century to the next. India's civilization has been of crucial importance to world history and culture, particularly within the regional context of central and southeast Asia. India's creative and intellectual tradition has produced more major works than the entire European tradition — even more impressive considering its extraordinarily destructive tropical climate, which has devoured vast quantities of sculpture, paintings, textiles, and manuscripts.

Vacationing travelers, whose interest in India's history is often sparked by a desire to learn more about the people they have begun to encounter, or about the awe-inspiring relics of fallen empires that stand before them, may find that trying to understand India can be a maddeningly elusive occupation. Even if you travel from the proverbial "Kashmir to Kanya Kumari," pride yourself on taking the rugged trail through the "real" India of mud-hut villages and earthy peasants, or arrive well-primed by novels and history books, you'll probably find India still skittishly defies comfortable definition. Perhaps, in the end, only a lifelong scholar of things Indian could come to grips with the question: What makes India, India? The best that can be done in a book such as this is to give India's past a comprehensible perspective. The history as recounted here deals not just with India's present boundaries with Pakistan and Bangladesh, but with the entire subcontinent.

ECOLOGY IS HISTORY

Just as some people hold that biology is destiny for individual human beings, so too it may be said that ecology has determined the history of India. The story begins with the Indus river, the very lifeblood of prehistoric India, from which the country's name is derived. Along its lushly forested banks, the early Indus Valley civilization flourished more than four thousand years ago. The early settlers — and many future conquerors — were lured by the region's fertile soil: the legacy of the physical forces that shaped the surfaces and climate of the subcontinent long before man existed.

Nature bequeathed India with the mighty 2,692-km (1,600-mile)-long chain of the Himalayas, the "resting place of the snows," without which the land would be little more than a desert. The Indus and northern India's other two great river systems, the Ganga–Yamuna and the Brahmaputra, all fed by Himalayan glaciers, still continue to sweep vast quantities of sedimentary topsoil downstream to form rich alluvial valleys and plains right across the north. Worshipped as goddesses by Hindus, these formidable rivers gave rise to India's greatest ancient cities. Their inhabitants tapped the river waters to irrigate a crop-growing hinterland and set off on them to distant destinations for trade. It was in the most bountiful region, watered by five upper tributaries of the Indus and hence called "land of five rivers" (Panch-ap, or Punjab) that the immigrant Aryans composed India's first ancient literary work, the *Rig Veda*, some 3,000 years ago.

India's destiny was shaped by the idiosyncrasies of its geographical isolation. It was cut off from its Asian neighbors by the sea around its coasts, by the protective natural barriers imposed

by the Himalayas on its northern frontier with Tibet and China, and by the vast stretches of virtually impenetrable jungle-clad hills blocking contact with Burma. In the south, the spinelike wall of the Vindhya and Satpura mountain ranges presented another barrier to easy communication between north and south India, encouraging the development of almost completely independent cultures and empires. Even today, few people in the Tamil-speaking south can speak Hindi, the national language. But most significantly, India's earliest migrants and invading armies swept in from its most accessible corner — and its historical Achilles' heel — the northwest frontier. They came along a series of well-known passes — the Khyber, the Bolan, and the Khurram passes — now shared by Afghanistan and Pakistan. For this reason, India's northwestern corner has always been its most turbulent battleground, with each invasion adding to India's ethnic patchwork, whether zealously spurred on by visions of conquered wealth and glory, or more recently, by the zeal of Islam or Christianity, or by profits of commercial enterprise and power.

OPPOSITE: Village woman stands in the courtyard of a temple in Khajuraho, Madhya Pradesh. ABOVE: Sunset over Dal Lake in Srinagar, Kashmir.

ANCIENT INDIA

Evidence suggests that protohuman life existed in India during the Paleolithic Age, when nomadic tribes of primitive men first began drifting across the subcontinent, leaving stone implements and crude hand axes as the only clue to their existence. A sketchy evolutionary trail, fueled by finds in the Sind province of Pakistan of terracotta pots, mother goddess figurines, phallic symbols, fragments of bronze as well as copper, suggests that some sort of village culture might have developed as early as 4000 BC. Exactly how long it took India's early villagers to make the extraordinary leap to urban settlement is not yet known.

Although a lot of India's early history lies in legend, it's not disputed that its earliest major civilization was established in fertile, forested pockets beside the Indus River, and that it thrived for at least a thousand years beginning around 2500 BC. Its people were thought to be Dravidians, whose descendants still inhabit the far south of India. The ruins of its major cities — located at Harappa (Hara is one of Shiva's names) and Mohenjo-Daro ("Mound of the Dead"), now in present-day Pakistan, and to a lesser extent at Lothal and Kalibangan in Gujarat and Ropar in Punjab — all indicate highly rigorous town planning. As many as 70 unearthed sites have also been found right across the northwestern region of Punjab and Sind. Informed speculation has it that some buried cities still await discovery beneath Indian soil.

Archaeologists compare the systematically laid-out sites to what has been unearthed at Pompeii. Excavations reveal that large-scale commercial operations flourished in these ancient cities. Their citizens, who enjoyed a hitherto unknown high standard of living, subscribed to religious beliefs and had some knowledge of script. Kiln-baked bricks, as opposed to simple mud bricks, were the standard building material. (In contemporary Mesopotamia in Egypt, kiln-baked bricks would have been regarded with fascinated awe.) Mining and working of several metals such as bronze, copper, lead, and tin were undertaken. Some cities, like Mohenjo-Daro, must have existed for centuries, as nine layers of construction were unearthed. Streets and lanes were laid out according to an axis grid running from north to south; houses were spacious units built around a central courtyard that ensured privacy; a bathroom and kitchen were de rigueur; evidence of stairs suggests double stories. Well-covered sewage drains existed, both inside private homes and on the streets, as did hot and cold public baths, deep wells, public buildings, trading posts, and harbor ports. Indeed, Lothal, in southwest Gujarat, was once a port whose inhabitants bartered with their northern neighbors at Harappa and Mohenjo-Daro, as well as in the Persian Gulf and Sumeria (Iran), using the Indian currency of the day — ornamental conch shells, bone-inlay goods, cotton, pearls, and possibly even peacock feathers and apes.

Discovery of these ancient ruins came relatively late in the mid-nineteenth century — when India's history was commonly believed to have begun only from the time of Alexander the Great's invasion in the fourth century BC. British engineers laying a railway between the Punjab and Karachi observed that local laborers seemed to have an unlimited supply of bricks with which to build the track's foundations. The timeworn bricks remained an enigma until the 1920s when archaeologists explored the region and changed history books by uncovering Mohenjo-Daro along the Indus and Harappa on the Ravi.

Surviving artifacts offer intriguing glimpses into the art and culture of the Indus people. Perhaps one of the most famous finds is that of a bronze naked dancing girl striking a provocative pose. Large numbers of excavated female figurines with their overemphasized hips, protuberant breasts, and pudenda seem to indicate fertility worship. Among the discoveries are hundreds of small, ornately inscribed steatite seals with pictographic portraits of Brahmanic bulls, "unicorns," tigers, and other animals, and also pictographic signs thought to have been used by merchants to brand their wares, like an early form of trademark.

Despite extensive ongoing research, comparatively little is known about the Indus Valley civilization's development and eventual decline, nor has their script ever been deciphered. The current theory has it that sometime after 1750 BC, the efficient, wealthy settlements at Harappa and Mohenjo-Daro suffered a series of earthquakes and floods, spelling complete disaster. Evidence at Mohenjo-Daro suggests that, as with Pompeii, homes were hastily abandoned: cooking pots scattered across kitchen floors and crushed skeletons of people attempting to flee have been found caught in the debris of walls and ceilings.

ARRIVAL OF THE ARYANS

Sometime after 2000 BC, semi-barbaric tribes of fair-skinned Aryans swept into India, probably from northeastern Iran and the region around the Caspian Sea. By 1500 BC they had snatched control from the Harappans, whose developed way of life had all but collapsed, and had become well ensconced in the Punjab. The Aryans were a pastoral race who had stormed the fortified cities of the Indus wielding bronze axes and riding in horse-drawn chariots. Unlike the Harappans, they lived in tribal villages with their migrant herds, and these dwellings, made from bamboo or light wood, did not survive the ravages of time. The Aryans became known as Hindus, from the word "Indus," and they worshipped a pantheon of gods, most of them nature's elements such as the sun, wind, water, and fire. These gods did not replace the mystical fertility or earth gods of the Dravidians — all found room within the same evolving religious faith that was eventually to become Hinduism.

It's thought that Aryans were the original architects of the caste system, invented to ensure that their racial distinctiveness was kept "pure." Early Aryan society was broadly divided into four hereditary social strata, called *varna* or "colors." The priestly Brahmans were the aristocrats of the social pyramid. Next came the Kshatriyas, the warriors, whose duties involved warfare and government, and the Vaishyas, who tended to be farmers, merchants, or skilled artisans. At the bottom were the Sudras, the menial laborers. Beneath them were the indigenous dark-skinned slaves, scoffed at by the sharp-featured, fair Aryans as the "noseless ones." Each *varna* was associated with a distinguishing color: white for Brahmans, red for Kshatriyas, brown for Vaishyas, and black for Sudras.

Along with their Caucasian genes, the Aryans brought with them a new, rich and precise language: Sanskrit. This was a branch of the Indo–European family of languages and it was later perfected to express in literary form the hymns and epics of the Vedas, the Upanishads and the *Bhagavad-Gita*. These huge compilations of myth and folklore were the seminal religious texts of virtually the whole of Indian thought to follow. Even the unorthodox religions, Buddhism and Jainism, were influenced by the Vedas to some extent. Before Sanskrit was written, however, the Aryans had to rely entirely on rote learning of hymns and rituals by the priestly caste, the Brahmans. From the epics written by these Vedic Aryans, it seems they were an earthy bunch who adored gambling, music, and large quantities of *soma* (an alcoholic drink heavily laced with hashish), as well as war and chariot racing. The epic poem *Mahabharata*, whose core is thought to reflect Indian life at about the time of 1000 BC, starts with King Santanu's obsessive love for the beautiful goddess Ganga, whom he "marries," symbolizing the Aryan advance east across the Ganges river.

At about this time, the Aryans had mastered the art of smelting iron ore for tools and weapons, and had ventured further inland — perhaps lured there by rumor of large iron ore deposits — to Uttar Pradesh, Bihar, and Orissa. New cities rose to prominence: Indraprastha (site of present-day Delhi), Kashi (Varanasi), and Pataliputra (Patna in Bihar). All this eastward colonizing meant that they failed to maintain their crucial hold on the northwest frontier. Inevitably, this led to invasion and yet further cross-fertilization of different cultural influences.

CHALLENGE FROM THE WEST

The first invaders were Persians, under Cyrus, followed by Darius (521–485 BC) who occupied the Indus Valley region of Punjab and Sind. They later recruited Punjabi soldiers who fought with Darius' son Xerxes in the Persian invasion of Greece (479 BC). Fantastic tales of India had been circulating ever since the return of their first official envoy, Scylax, a decade previously. Darius the Great, Emperor of Persia had deposited him near the headwaters of the Indus and instructed him to sail down the river to its mouth and make his way home by the Red Sea. In so doing, Scylax was to follow the same route used by the Phoenicians of the Levant who traded with western India as early as 975 BC and went on forays for ivory, apes, and peacocks.

Scylax's accounts of his adventures were taken up by Herodotus who had a great deal to tell about India at the time: for instance, that there were two races, the dark aboriginals and the fair Aryans, "white like the Egyptians." He told of "gold-digging ants who labored in gold-strewn plains," of the crocodiles of the Indus, of the extremes of temperature in the Punjab, and of the novel cotton clothes worn by the Indians. He also described a religious sect whose members lived on grain and ate nothing which had life — a reference perhaps to the Jains. Scribes also described the existence of marriage markets where impoverished parents sold their daughters and the practice of immolation of widows on the funeral pyres of their dead husbands — the economically motivated tradition known as sati (or suttee).

No wonder the world's greatest young general, Alexander the Great of Macedonia, was spurred to lead his armies, estimated at some 25,000 to 30,000 men, on his epic march in the spring of 326 BC from Greece across the Indus to this exotic, distant land. Alexander first occupied Taxila, then Pakistan, and then usurped the Persians and proceeded further inland, defeating the Aryan King Porus and his vast army of elephants. Following this crushing defeat no Indian ruler seriously contested Alexander's advance, but the further inland he moved, the more mutinous his travel-weary army became.

Drunk on conquest, Alexander was anxious to venture on to the "Eastern Sea," (which may have been the Ganges river) but was forced to accept the will of his men. Leaving behind a few officers as petty princes in the Upper Indus Valley, the Greek army turned back to the homeland that Alexander himself never lived to see again. He died in 323 BC, at the age of 36, in Babylon.

Despite the sowing of seeds into India's gene pool by his soldiers (still said to be the cause of blond hair and blue eyes among children in the upper Himalayas), Alexander's most lasting legacy to India was the development of Gandhara art, a mixture of Roman–Hellenic artistic ideals — including draped toga-like garments and bare torsos — and Buddhism, the emerging "radical" religion of the time.

THE GROWTH OF RELIGION

The Aryan epoch marked the emergence of the subcontinent's greatest religion, Hinduism, and the two born in revolt against it: Buddhism and Jainism. Few religions in the world can claim such an ancient tradition as Hinduism. Its essential beliefs can be traced to the Indus Valley civilization, where it is thought that Shiva was revered by *lingams*, or phallic stones, excavated at various Indus sites. It was left up to the nature-worshipping, priest-dominated Aryan society to lay the framework for the development of Hinduism. Some time between 1500 to 1200 BC they wrote their sacred religious texts, the Vedas, which are thought to refer to actual historical events. They tell of the victory of Brahma over Indra, god of thunder and warfare — a fable that is thought to refer to the revival of Brahmanism (the Indus Valley's embryonic form of Hinduism) in the wake of the Aryan invasions.

The majority of Indians today still believe in the idea that the Aryan priests formulated of karma — meaning "one's deeds" — with its notion of cause and effect on the reincarnation of the soul: what is done in one life has direct repercussions on the next, for better or for worse. This posed a Catch-22 situation to society's underdogs, since any protest about oppression or injustice in one's present life could be easily attributed to bad behavior in one's past life for which punishment was required to earn a better life in the next.

In the sixth century BC two contemporary figures emerged — first Buddha, then Mahavira — both challenging orthodox Vedic solutions to the question: Why is there so much suffering in life? Buddha, like Mahavira, was born into the Kshatriyas, the warrior class, which permitted religious learning but precluded priesthood.

Both of these two great religious reformers rejected Hinduism's central ethos and its rigid caste system, but from this point their paths diverged: Mahavira's led to Jainism, a relatively hermetic faith, while Buddhism emerged as a formidable religious force, supplanting Hinduism as the official religion under Emperor Ashoka and being gradually adopted throughout Asia.

Procession of high-ranking Hindu priests during the Kumbh Mela, India's holiest and most spectacular religious gathering, which is held every four years.

India and Its People

At this time Theraveda or Hinayana ("Lesser Vehicle") Buddhism was in vogue, in which the image of Buddha himself was never revealed in case it inspired physical desire — thus causing attachment to life on earth and distracting from the striving towards nirvana (release from the cycle of birth and rebirth). Instead, Buddha was alluded to through such symbols as stupas, footprints, trees, or animals. The more populist, less monk-centered schism — the Mahayana, or "Great Vehicle," form of Buddhism (which exists more or less in its original form among Buddhists today) — emerged several centuries later, with its more tactile images of Buddha's various incarnations, from animal to human, as well as with the Bodhisattva, or the potential Buddha.

ASHOKA AND THE MAURYAN AGE

The departure of Alexander the Great left a power vacuum that was to be rapidly filled by India's first imperial family, a mighty Aryan clan who used the peacock as their totem. These were the Mauryas (326–184 BC) who rose to prominence under the leadership of Chandragupta, himself perhaps inspired by Alexander's catalytic invasion of the Indus. From their capital at Magadha, built on the site of ancient Pataliputra and present-day Patnain Bihar, they were to unify the warring kingdoms and tribes along the Ganges under a single imperial umbrella for 140 years.

A fascinating insight into the Mauryan society and India's earliest foreign policy ploys was given by the contemporary ambassador from Greece, Megathenes, at the court of Chandragupta's son, Bindusara. He cites a rather amusing correspondence between Bindusara and the Greek ruler Antiochus I: the former had apparently requested Antiochus not only to send him samples of Greek wine and raisins, but also philosophers to teach him the art of arguing. Antiochus replied dryly that the wine and raisins had been dispatched, but that the Greeks drew the line at trading in philosophers.

THE BIRTH OF BUREAUCRACY

It's thought that the genius behind the Mauryan throne was Chandragupta's chief minister Kautilya, who wrote the *Arthashastra*, or *Science of Material Gain*, a treatise on the art of government and taxation. He was diabolical and shrewd enough to have given even Machiavelli a few pointers. Kautilya realized that the path to a powerful empire lay in a strong civil administration and punishment of those who trespassed its laws — Kautilya also introduced a state tax on everything from land and harvested crops to gambling and prostitution.

Mauryan society marked a unique transition from a rural monarchy to a strictly enforced civil administration — an indication that bureaucracy took indigenous root in India then and not after the arrival of the British, as it is commonly argued. Megathenes noted seven "classes" within Mauryan society, the highest class consisting of royal councilors, whom he ranked above the priests or Brahmans. The others were agriculturists, soldiers, artisans, police (including spies), and last but not least, the bureaucrats. At the peak of Mauryan power it is thought that more than a million men acted as imperial administrators, soldiers, and spies.

The Mauryan state controlled all the major industries — everything from winemaking to road-building — with strict pay scales and taxes imposed on artisans and professionals alike. The great Magadha capital was administered by the traditional *panchayat* (five-member) council of elders, a structure that was established throughout the Mauryan empire to govern India's villages, guilds, and castes, along with its towns and cities. Even today the *panchayat* remains a strong force in modern Indian villages.

THE ENLIGHTENED EMPEROR

The Mauryan empire reached its zenith under Chandragupta's grandson, the legendary Ashoka, "The Sorrowless One." During his reign — stretching from 269 to 232 BC — Ashoka emerged as India's most powerful and possibly most enlightened emperor. In its heyday, Ashoka's empire ruled over more of India than any other invader until the British some 2,000 years later, claiming revenue from Kashmir to Mysore and Bangladesh to Afghanistan. Only three of the Dravidian kingdoms in the far south — Kerala, Chola, and Pandya — remained independent from their reach.

Following the advice of the *Arthashastra*, which instructed that "any power superior in might should launch into war," Ashoka invaded the frontier tribal kingdom of Kalinga to the south, in modern-day Orissa, subduing it after the bloodiest war of his era. The sight of the battlefield's terrible carnage was to haunt him for the rest of his life, causing him to renounce violence as an instrument of policy. He became a Buddhist, and spread his faith by inscribing some 5,000 words of moral advice on 30 pillars (of which only 10 survive) and 18 rock-faces across his enormous domain, notably in Orissa, Gujarat, Delhi, Sarnath, and Sanchi. The most famous of his pillars, adorned with lions, has now been adopted as the symbol of modern India.

Honey-colored gateway within the medieval fortress of Jaisalmer in Rajasthan.

Ashoka's reign is best distinguished by his paternalistic toleration of every faith and tongue of his subjects. He abandoned the traditional annual royal hunt in favor of a *dharma yatra* or "pilgrimage of religious laws," which sent him off on regular and long journeys throughout his realm. An offshoot of this was that India gained an early network of tree-lined highways, leading from the capital. Ashoka is also said to have informed his subordinates that wherever he was, whether eating or in his harem, he was always "on duty" to carry out the business of the state. His Mauryan capital Pataliputra soon became Asia's foremost center of art and culture, while Mauryan administrators were posted to every far-flung region of the empire, and they were rotated regularly to avoid corruption—a system with numerous similarities to the way British "collectors" were later to operate.

Under Ashoka, Buddhism spread throughout the society—Ashoka's own son Mahendra became a monk and was to take the gospel of Buddha to Ceylon, now Sri Lanka. Another by-product of Ashoka's conversion to *ahimsa* (nonviolence) was that vegetarianism was adopted by the masses.

POST-EMPIRE OPPORTUNISM

Fifty years or so after Ashoka's death in 232 BC, the Mauryan empire had collapsed. Some historians would have it that his pro-Buddhist stance led to insidious resistance from power-hungry Brahman priests, while others believe that his pacifist ways allowed the military strength of the empire to wane leaving it highly vulnerable to fortune hunters from central Asia. It might just have been that Ashoka's successors were weak and ineffectual, lacking what it takes to hold a vast empire together.

Whatever the reason, the Mauryan empire had collapsed by 184 BC. Confusion and warfare reigned as various triumphant Central Asian and Persian tribes warred to take advantage of the political void. For more than five centuries, from 232 BC to AD 320, power shifted from one dynasty to another, ushering in half a millennium of unsettled often barbaric rule which largely undermined the great civilization and unity of the Ashokan era.

First had come Alexander the Great's successors, the Greek Bactrians. They captured Peshawar in 190 BC and, a decade later, with the collapse of Mauryan rule, established control throughout the Punjab. Many of these Greeks accepted Indian religions, the most famous conversion being that of their powerful king, Menander (circa 150 BC), who publicly embraced Buddhism. The most enduring legacy of this Bactrian bridge between east and west can be seen in the distinctive classical Buddhist art—

known as the Gandhara school — examples of which can be seen today in many of India's national museums.

Then, in around 50 BC, the Greek Bactrians fought in vain against a double-pronged attack by two foreign nomadic tribes: the Scythians or Shakas over the Kabul Valley in the north and the Parthians or Pallavas over the Bolan Pass further south; both managing to win solid power bases in the Indus Valley in the following century. Neither proved a match for the next spate of invasions by the more powerful Central Asian Kushan warriors. The Parthians fell in battle, while the Scythians simply melted away inland, adopting Kshatriyan names and becoming Indianized.

The Kushans (circa AD 50–240) sent their armies along the Ganges as far as Benares, now Varanasi. Their most famous king, Kanishka had a utopian fantasy that his dynasty would rule forever. He gave India a new calendar, intended as a historical tabula rasa that began with the year he commenced his reign — AD 78. Like Ashoka and Menander, Kanishka converted to Buddhism, and he hosted the Fourth Great Buddhist Council in Kashmir, which gave rise to the radical new schism of Mahayana Buddhism. During Kanishka's reign, the very first carved images of Buddha began to appear.

Meanwhile, against this backdrop in the north, Brahman rulers had established themselves further southeast in the Indo-Gangetic plains; the former Mauryan domain in Bihar had been directly inherited by the Sungas (184–70 BC), while the central Deccan region was ruled for more than four and a half centuries after 230 BC by the Telugu-speaking Andhras.

Although for some five centuries post-Mauryan era India was thrown into political fragmentation, many impressive artistic and scientific contributions emerged at this time. Foreign influence — from the Greek Bactrians — allowed Hellenistic ideas to percolate into Indian thinking, and vice versa. In particular, medicine and astrology flourished. In medicine, India was already rather advanced, with the ancient Hindu science of Ayurvedic medicine and its many herbal medications and potions being widely accepted in many parts of India. Interesting enough, during Ashoka's reign, yoga gained imperial patronage — an indication perhaps of how seriously longevity was taken in those days. In astronomy, the solar calendar's seven-day week and the hour seem to have been Hellenistic imports, along with the zodiac, which the Indians adopted zealously.

This was also an era of greatly expanded trade via the sea and the fabled Silk Road, the long and often perilous overland trading route traipsed by merchants, camels, oxen, and donkeys that crisscrossed the subcontinent. It began near what is now the port of Tyre in Lebanon and crisscrossed through what is now northern Iran, Afghanistan, Soviet Central Asia, and China — making India the economic center of Sino-Roman trade. Increased trade and wealth inspired both Indian thought and art in various ways. Indian merchants, who set aside some of their fortunes as donations to religious orders, usually Buddhist, in the belief that such piety would be well rewarded in the next life, or preferably in obtainment of the blissful "ultimate release" from life's cycle of rebirths (nirvana). Consequently, virtually all the great artistic and architectural remains from this period are Buddhist.

The Buddha image, which first emerged under Kanishka with the new Mahayana sect, sparked an artistic religious fervor to represent the Enlightened One in all his many guises and symbolic poses; with varying hand gestures (*mudras*) to depict his various messages, including his most famous gesture of reassurance, the "forget fear" gesture, which Gandhi later adopted as one of his favorite symbols. This prompted Buddhist monks to raise monasteries, temples, and beautifully decorative stupas, of which the most famous can be seen at Sanchi with its gateway of voluptuous *yakshi* (mother-goddess figures), dancing elephants, and other carved figures intended to depict stories of the Buddha's previous incarnations.

Perhaps the most extraordinary Buddhist legacy can be seen in a series of great monolithic, rock-hewn temples throughout the Deccan, the most magnificent of which are shaped from crescent-shaped ridges at Ellora and Ajanta, near Aurangabad in Maharashtra state, where the earliest temple caves date back to 200 BC. The tradition of creating these fabulous cave grottoes was to continue over the centuries until the thirteenth century. Yet it was during the imperial reign of the Guptas that artisans working here executed the most ambitiously monumental temples together with the most exquisite relief sculptures and large-scale fresco paintings, all constructed for the greater glory of Buddha.

THE CLASSICAL AGE

India's greatest Hindu dynasty, the Guptas (320–700) is noted for its grand cultural contribution to Indian history. Under its auspices, the arts blossomed as never before, while Sanskrit poetry and literature reached celebrated heights of sophistication. The Guptas, like the Mauryas, established their base of imperial power in Magadha where they controlled rich sources of iron ore. The dynasty was founded by Chandragupta I, and although their empire never matched that of the Mauryas, these powerful

rulers lost no time in usurping pettier princelings, and could soon claim a territorial triangle extending from the Punjab in the north to Bengal in the northeast and to the Deccan plateau in the south. Imperial cities rose throughout the domain, most importantly at Ayodhya. Soon, Kashmir too was claimed — a rare and highly coveted jewel in the Gupta crown.

With the Guptas on the throne, India entered its so-called "classical age," a golden epoch of peace, prosperity, and stability. This era produced India's "Shakespeare," the brilliant court poet-playwright Kalidasa, whose seven major Sanskrit classics marked the flowering of purely secular Indian literature. Many new theories in

algebraic mathematics and astronomy also surfaced. Ironically, the Guptan astronomer Aryabhata I, who calculated that earth moved around the sun and not the other way around, as was commonly believed at the time, was completely ignored. Royal patronage was tolerant, extending to Hindu, Buddhist, and Jain faiths, as can be seen in the cave art and sculpture perfected at Ajanta. However, the Guptas artistic effort culminated in the classical architecture of the Hindu temple.

Importantly, the Guptas brought about a wholesale revival of Hinduism. Its popularity had sagged in the post-Mauryan era, when Buddhism predominated amid a bevy of other fashionable "alternative" sects, ranging in practices from fatalistic determinism to ritualized human sacrifice — with everything in between.

The rise of Hinduism automatically reconditioned the caste system, tightening up the social hierarchy and regulating its conduct. Untouchables and slaves came to be little more than two-legged chattels. They were confined to the outskirts of towns and villages and designated the

Dravidian women walk bare-footed through the ancient temples of the Five Rathas in Mahabilpuram, Tamil Nadu.

"unclean" menial jobs of scavenging, cleaning, tending the dead, and making leather goods. Even accidental contact with an untouchable by a high-caste person was considered a contamination, and required ritual cleansing. The visiting Chinese Buddhist pilgrim Faxian (Fa-hsien), who traveled though India for six years at the beginning of the fifth century, was rather taken aback to find that untouchables carried gongs to warn passing upper castes to stand clear in order to avoid being "polluted" by their presence.

Another important social change under the Guptas concerned the status of women. The Guptas were the first to legalize the practice of arranged marriages, and codified a system that

had existed for centuries, making women legal wards under the power of fathers, husbands, sons, and brothers.

Perhaps one of the most fascinating windows on the world of the upper castes during this time is the *Kama Sutra* by Vatsyayana, referred to by the Guptas as a classic textbook on the art — and gymnastics — of love. It also describes the highly hedonistic lifestyle a wealthy young man of the time might well pursue for the benefit of his education. According to the *Kama Sutra*, days should also be spent appreciating poetry, music, sculpture, painting, and delectable food, all in a haze of delicate perfume, fresh flowers, and elegantly coiffed young women. However, it's important to stress that the *Kama Sutra* dealt with only one aspect of a courtier's life — the period of being a "good householder" — sandwiched in between "celibate studenthood" and "sagacious old age."

Ultimately, the Gupta empire was weakened by invading barbaric White Huns. By the sixth century the Huns had gained control of Punjab and Kashmir, and had splintered the former Gupta stronghold across northern India into a number of separate Hindu kingdoms, which would not become united again until the coming of the Muslims.

THE LEGACY OF THE SOUTH

Few of the political intrigues occurring in north India had much, if any, bearing on the contemporary political climate of the south. At this time the south was divided into three major ancient Tamil "kingdoms": the Chola on the east coast at Tanjore near present-day Madras, the Chera or Kerala in the west, and the Pandya in the center based at Madurai with a domain reaching down to Kanya Kumari in Tamil Nadu. Madurai, still one of south India's greatest temple cities, was the center of Tamil literary culture with its prestigious *sangams* or academies where some 500 poets are reputed to have congregated along with philosophers and artists.

In the face of attacks from the north, these three Tamil kingdoms formed political alliances, but during rare moments of peace they schemed and plotted against one another. Early in the fourth century, another Tamil dynasty appeared on the scene, the Pallavas ("robbers") who managed to oust the Chola monarch from Kanchipuram and set about leaving an incredible architectural legacy, as the vast *goporams,* or gateways, so distinctive of the south testify.

Unlike the Aryan caste system, the Tamils had their own pyramidal social structure, divided into "castes" that were really a kind of geographical identity: for instance, hills people, plains people, and forest, coastal, and desert dwellers. Within each of these five groups were divisions relating to employment; these included pearl divers, fishermen, boat-makers, and boatmen. At society's apex sat the supreme ruler, the monarch who was considered part deity. These Tamil Dravidians also had a tradition of matrilineal succession, which survived right up until early in the nineteenth century. They had the custom of cross-cousin marriage and were repelled by the northern practice of arranged marriage to "strangers."

This was a prosperous and cosmopolitan region, with well established seaborne trade with other civilizations, notably the Romans and the Egyptians, and later with Bali, Sumatra, and Java. Spices, teak, ivory, exotic birds, onyx, precious gems, cotton goods, silks, and even Ayurvedic medicine were bartered for gold coins, while India's art, philosophies, and religions were inadvertently included in the bargain.

A new and important foreign influence in the south was Christianity, brought by Saint Thomas the Apostle when he arrived in Kerala in AD 52. He was said to have been martyred at Mylapore, a suburb of Madras in AD 68, and ever since Christianity has retained a foothold in India's deep south. The tiny Jewish community of Cochin is also thought to have been founded during the first century.

THE IMPACT OF ISLAM

The Muslim conquest of India had the most profound impact on the political, social, and cultural life of the country. Islam spread like wildfire, and India was never the same again. With Hinduism and Islam being as incompatible as water and fire, the blend of religions was far from amicable. To somewhat puritanical Muslim eyes, the whole Hindu way of thinking was suspect. Hindus were seen as caricatures: caste-bound cow-worshippers with a slavish devotion to thousands of different gods whom they worshipped in the form of idols — anathema to followers of the monotheistic Islam. Hindus, on the other hand, saw Muslims as gross oversimplifiers with a doggedly single-minded perception of a complex elemental cosmos. Hindus saw no need to recruit fresh converts, since anyone not born a Hindu was automatically excluded from their faith. Conversely, Muslims were great proselytizers. Proselytizing was not always peaceful, as Muslims brandished not only the Koran but battle swords as well. Islam did not acknowledge that any person was better than another by reason of race, skin color, or social class; although women did not enjoy the same status as men. Evidence given by a woman, for example, was (and still is today in Islamic countries) only half as credible as that given by a man.

THE FIRST MUSLIM INVASIONS

The first Muslims to arrive were peaceable Arab traders who landed on India's west coast from what is today Saudi Arabia as early as the seventh century, not long after the death of Islam's founder, the Prophet Muhammad, in 632. Although Muslim merchants returned home laden with exotic imports and tales of India's wealth — creating the impression that the country was ripe for plundering — more than two centuries passed before Islamic armies launched a full-scale invasion. This was left to Mahmud of Ghazni, "the Sword of Islam," who mounted 17 separate attacks between 1000 and 1027, leaving a bloody trail as he and his Turkic hordes zealously smashed countless Hindu temples to dust and descended upon India's cities in a frenzy of murder and rapine.

His most successful campaign netted him so much booty from the holy Shiva temple at Somnath on the Arabian sea in Gujarat that not even a giant caravan of elephants, camels, and mules was able to carry it all away. Mahmud's court chronicler may have exaggerated, but he recorded that more than 50,000 Hindus were slaughtered that day. Certainly, Mahmud's credo

was convert or die, for in his opinion, Islam tolerated no rivals. Vanquished Hindu chieftains were lucky if Mahmud spared them their lives — and even if he did, he was known to sever their fingers as trophies to add to his ever-growing collection. As much as he enjoyed these periodic sprees of acquisitive mayhem, Mahmud was a bandit at heart, and had no great political designs on India.

It was not until 1192 that Muslim power took firm root in India, this time with another fierce Turko-Afghan Muslim warlord at the helm, Muhammad of Ghur. Within a decade, his armies had forced the Hindu kingdoms of the Gangetic valley to collapse, one by one, like dominoes. Only

the valiant Rajputs never completely surrendered, although they suffered horrific losses.

During this expansion, Buddhists were especially vilified, with monasteries destroyed and thousands of monks sent fleeing to Nepal and Tibet. Exiled from the land of its birth, Buddhism was not to be restored in any significant way in India until the twentieth century. Subjugated Indians were treated as second-class citizens, and were forced to pay their new rulers hefty tax. The Muslim title *zamindar*, or landlord, dates from this period of feudal rule.

After Muhammad of Ghur's death in 1206, his slave lieutenant, Qutb-ud-Din Aybak, promptly declared himself to be the Sultan of Delhi, commemorating the event by erecting a victory tower, the Qutb Minar, and what is supposed to have been India' first mosque — symbolically constructed from the remnants of 27 Hindu temples. His Sultanate is also known as the "Slave Dynasty," referring to martial slavery which allowed ambitious, lowborn young men an opportunity to rise above their status.

OPPOSITE: Lonely, boulder-strewn moonscape surrounding the Thikse monastery in Ladakh.
ABOVE: Detail of the Taj Mahal, considered the most sublime architectural achievement of the Mughal Emperors.

During the 320 years of its existence, the throne of the Delhi Sultanate changed hands among six successive Turko-Afghan dynasties. Next came the Khalji monarchs, notably Alauddin Khalji (1296-1316) whose reign spanned 20 years and who together with his general Malik Kafur not only conquered the Deccan but also the kingdoms of south India — although these did not stay subjugated long. Despite their iconoclastic and almost wholesale destruction of Hindu architecture, these Muslim sultans imported the imposing building styles of Central Asia, introducing two features without which Islamic architecture would later be unrecognizable: the minaret and the dome.

The Delhi Sultanate was beginning to weaken by the fourteenth century, during the reign of the next Turkic dynasty, the Tughluqs, who ruled from 1320 to 1397. The second Tughluq rulers was Muhammad ibn Tughluq, who was notorious for his insane zealousness, a sort of Indian "Grand old Duke of York" who first marched his subjects to his new capital in the Deccan, then marched them all back again.

Discontent and rebellion pockmarked the 26 years of his reign, and two southern regions of his Sultanate broke away and formed independent kingdoms in the north of present-day Karnataka, one Hindu, one Muslim. The Hindu Vijayanagar kings built a magnificent capital at Hampi, forming a united Hindu front against the flood-tide of Islam in the north. Meanwhile the Bahmani Muslim empire emerged, later splitting into the warring provincial kingdoms at Berar, Ahmednagar, Bijapur, Golconda, and Ahmedabad, all leaving behind impressive medieval fortresses.

The waning Delhi Sultanate proved an irresistible lure to one of the most dreaded names roaming the wilderness beyond the northwest frontiers, the ruthless warlord Tamerlane or "Timur the Lame." His devastating raid across the Punjab to Delhi in 1399 left "towers built high" of severed heads and mutilated bodies and Delhi itself laid waste with famine and pestilence. His invasion resulted in a catalytic shift of power — severing India once more into two parts. The north reverted to the Turkic Afghan princes, while the south once more regained its independent status as a conglomerate of Hindu kingdoms. Slightly more than a century later, Timur's great grandson Babur, an Uzbek prince, would return to found his Mughal dynasty on the same site.

MUGHAL POWER AND DECADENCE

No other age in India's history was as dazzling, as affluent, or ultimately as decadent as that of the Mughal Empire, a two-century-long era spanning six major emperors and reaching its zenith while Elizabeth I ruled in England. The period saw a remarkable blend of Indian, Persian,

and Central Asian influences manifested in an impressive legacy of magnificent palaces, forts, tombs, and landscaped gardens — including India's most famous building, the Taj Mahal.

Mughal is a corruption of *Mughul*, the Persian word for Mongol, since the Mughal rulers were partly descended from the great medieval Mongol leaders; Genghis Khan and Timur. But the Mughals were more Persian-influenced Turks than Mongols, and they spoke a language among themselves known as Turkic.

In 1526 the Mughal chieftain Babur swept down on the Hindu plains from current-day Afghanistan and at the Battle of Panipat his army killed Ibrahim Lodi and 20,000 soldiers, laying open the road to Delhi where the young warlord proclaimed himself emperor.

"Do not hurt or harm the flocks or herds of these people, not even their cotton ends or broken needles," Babur was recorded as telling his soldiers. "Beware not to bring ruin on its people by giving way to fear or anxiety. Our eye is on this land and on this people. Raid and rapine shall not be."

Babur dispatched his son Humayun to capture Agra, where the conquerors acquired the fabulous Koh-i-noor diamond from the disintegrated armies of the Lodi dynasty. Babur's legacy in Agra is the Ram Bagh garden, where the emperor liked to compose poems. Despite his success, Babur disliked India and the Indians, writing in his diary: "Three things oppressed us in India, heat, violent winds and dust." All he found to praise was India's countryside, its monsoon, and its gold. He died homesick for the cool fragrant air of Kabul, where his body was later taken for burial.

Humayun succeeded Babur at the age of 23, but was a natural recluse who lacked his father's military skills and the acumen required to hold together the new empire. He preferred to study languages, mathematics, philosophy, and astronomy, and was also fond of illuminated manuscripts and opium. Humayun was ousted in 1540 by a brilliant Afghan commoner, Sher Khan Sur (later known as Sher Shah), who captured Delhi and slaughtered 8,000 Mughal soldiers. While Humayun skulked in exile in Persia, Sher Shah earned popularity during his five-year reign for impressive civil policies, the construction of Delhi's sixth city Shergarh, numerous state highways, and for active promotion of Hindu employees and Rajput soldiery.

Humayun developed sufficient experience in diplomacy in his 15-year exile, and in 1556 he brought Delhi and Agra back under Mughal rule. His taste of victory was to be brief. Just weeks after reinstating himself in Delhi he died from a fall down some stairs, aptly enough in his library. His contribution to Mughal architecture is his impressive namesake tomb in suburban Delhi that strongly resembles the Taj Mahal.

Akbar, destined to be the mightiest emperor, was only 13 when he succeeded his father in 1556, although he took six years to shake off power-hungry guardians. Born of exiled parents, Akbar's unsettled childhood denied any chance of a formal education and he remained illiterate throughout his life, yet he was able to memorize vast tracts of Persian and Arabic poetry, displaying the brilliant intellect that later earned him the sobriquet "Akbar the Great." Historian Philip Mason wrote that Akbar "tried to give India the unity she had nearly attained under Ashoka and once again under the Gupta dynasty; his was the third attempt and the fourth was to the British."

Akbar, through a series of military campaigns, pushed the borders of the Mughal empire three-quarters of the way across the subcontinent, always creating an efficient bureaucracy in conquered areas. He encouraged harmony between Hindus and Muslims, setting an example by marrying a Rajput princess from Jaipur and appointing her Hindu kinsmen to powerful positions. He patronized the arts on a grand scale and had such a fascination for other religions that his courtiers privately expressed doubts that he was a Muslim at all. He devised his own faith, the Din-i-Ilahi, a mix of Islam and Hinduism and other dogmas, with himself as the supreme godhead. This enlightened experiment proved short-lived, but its memory is preserved in Akbar's greatest architectural achievement, his beautiful city of Fatehpur Sikri, abandoned just 14 years after it was built 37 km (23 miles) from Agra.

When Akbar died in 1605, his powerful empire passed to his son, the despotic and frequently drunk Jahangir, who expanded his domain with calculated brutality. He once coolly calculated that his hunting exploits had killed a total of some 17,000 animals and 14,000 birds. Yet at the same time, he was an aesthete whose patronage of painters produced gauche miniatures illustrating court life, love, and natural history of unsurpassed delicacy. He also built exquisite marble tombs, mosques, and Mughal gardens, but did not share his father's vision of a united, secular India.

The fifth Mughal, Shah Jahan, executed all possible rivals as soon as he sat on the throne in 1627 and further unraveled Akbar's achievements by destroying sacred Hindu temples and waging brutal wars against Hindu Rajputs and the Deccan Muslims. Yet now he is remembered for the elegant beauty of his architectural masterpieces: the infamous Taj Mahal, the Pearl Mosque in Agra, and the Jama Masjid and Red Fort in Old Delhi. His colossal expenditure on grandiose architecture became so profligate his son Aurangzeb finally locked him up to save the dynasty from financial ruin. Shah Jahan spent his last years imprisoned in Agra Fort, where from his quarters he could gaze across the Yamuna River to the Taj Mahal.

Aurangzeb took the throne in 1658 and his 51-year-long reign is remembered for fanatical imposition of Islamic orthodoxy. He aroused the hatred of his Hindu subjects by making them second-class citizens and building mosques with the rubble of their holy temples. Although he extended the Mughal Empire's boundaries to their furthermost, he also paved the way for its eventual collapse by alienating the rulers from the ruled. Aurangzeb lived frugally, never touching opium or visiting his harem or banning dancing girls and musicians from his court. His paranoia about losing power led him to systematically exile, imprison, and in some cases execute his male relatives. He even imprisoned his favorite wife and daughter and had them deliberately insulted by eunuchs. Aurangzeb died in 1707 and his grave is a Spartan affair covered only with earth and open to the sky at Khuldabad, near Aurangabad.

DECLINE AND TRANSITION

After Aurangzeb, the Mughal dynasty fell into slow decay. Eleven successive kings ruled over its dwindling fortunes, each as ineffectual and profligate as the last. Fresh contenders for power sensed that the Mughals were on their last legs, and the first serious blow came in 1739 when the Persian king Nadir Shah stormed Delhi. He slaughtered more than 30,000 people and returned home with 1,000 elephants, 7,000 horses, and 10,000 camels laden with booty, including the symbol of Mughal power, the fabulous Peacock Throne.

The seams of the Mughal empire were splitting and by the middle of the eighteenth century India had seen numerous shifts in power and influence, with many regions falling to strong Hindu rulers. Some subject Indians revolted, such as the Sikhs and the Jats, but the most formidable were the west-Indian Marathas, the militant anti-Muslim group that rose to prominence under the low-caste warrior Shivaji. Villagers in present-day Maharashtra state still relate anecdotes of Shivaji's daring military exploits. The Marathas gradually controlled most of north India except Punjab. They were soon to face a challenge by new and unexpected rivals from across the seas, and one that would eventually prove more formidable than the declining Mughals: the British East India Company.

ARRIVAL OF THE EUROPEANS

The European vanguard arrived even before the Mughals, when adventurous Portuguese explorers made forays into India in the late fifteenth century. Six years after Christopher Columbus discovered America, Lisbon's own Vasco da Gama landed at modern day Kerala in

1498, succeeding in his dream to rediscover the fabled Indies related by Marco Polo 200 years previously. His men set about zealously converting Indians to Christianity and sending home shiploads of exotic spices, which reaped colossal profits in European markets.

The Portuguese enjoyed a century-long monopoly on this lucrative trade before other European powers followed suit and began to sail east. Pepper became known as "black gold" and spices in Europe were highly valued as preservatives and flavoring. The Portuguese established bases at Daman and Diu in Gujarat and made their headquarters at Goa, an enclave captured in 1510 and kept under Lisbon's rule until 1961.

The Dutch inadvertently brought about the British Raj, as Elizabethan Englishmen grew envious of their coastal neighbor's success in the Indonesian spice trade and resolved to compete for the booming markets in the East Indies. A

series of bruising battles forced them to retreat to India, where they were enticed by tales of the decadent Mughals' treasures. Stories percolated back to England of kings who weighed themselves in gold, of stores of silver, silks, and jewels in ornate palaces filled with dancing girls, eunuchs, and exotic animals such as peacocks and elephants.

In 1600 Queen Elizabeth I granted the British East India Company a trade charter, and eight years later the corporation of wealthy English merchants landed a vessel at Surat in Gujarat during the reign of Emperor Jahangir. The Portuguese, Dutch, French, and Danes were all active in the East during this period but it was the English who were fated to found an Indian empire. By the end of the seventeenth century, the Company's various settlements were dominated by three Presidencies: Madras founded in 1640, Bombay in 1668, and Calcutta in 1690.

broke out on Indian soil in 1746 when a French army based at the trading post of Pondicherry captured British Madras, only to lose it back to the East India Company three years later. Tension between French and British posts remained long after peace returned in Europe, and both sides frequently provided local Indian rulers with arms, supplies, and expertise in attempts to hasten each other's end.

The Company's first full-scale military intervention in Indian politics was both accidental and decisive. Bengal was one of the several independent kingdoms that arose as the Mughal empire disintegrated, and in 1756, its nawab or prince, Siraj-ud-Daula, captured the British garrison at Calcutta and the infamous Black Hole incident took place (see CALCUTTA, page 253). One year later, Robert Clive's forces easily defeated the nawab and his French supporters on the field of Plassey, and finding himself in control of Bengal, Clive put his own candidate, Mir Jafar, on the throne.

In the south, the so-called "Tiger of Mysore" Tipu Sultan and his father Haider Ali inflicted a series of defeats on the British, but they were overcome in 1799, opening up the region for British exploitation. In the west, British forces defeated the Marathas in 1803, and two Sikh wars left Punjab in British hands in 1849. The East India Company had become the effective sovereign of most of India. English armies also defeated Nepalese troops and annexed Burma.

BIRTH OF THE RAJ

British domination of the subcontinent by the late eighteenth century stemmed both from their timely opportunism as the Mughal empire collapsed, and their pragmatic policy of toleration towards the conquered, indirectly employing the same rules that Akbar had employed so success fully. However the British initially made no attempt to interfere with Indian religions, customs, and culture, and made it clear that their interest in India was in making fortunes, not conversions.

With British muskets at their throats, so to speak, local rulers saw no choice but to accept British suzerainty. For the next 50 years, the British focused their attention on gaining complete political control. In 1803, the blind emperor Shah Alam was formally taken under British protection. Deference continued to be paid to him as the Great Mughal and it was officially he who ruled an empire but in reality he was a puppet of the British Resident in Delhi. Disgust with the Mughals was no secret among the British. Lord Thomas

The British East India Company expanded during the next 250 years, exporting cotton, cloths, silks, saltpeter, indigo, and opium from poppies, which was sent to China in exchange for that other valuable commodity, tea. From the outset, the Company had a structured hierarchy upon which the Indian Civil Service was gradually super-imposed. At the bottom were the "writers," or clerks. At the top were governors, who ruled like mini-emperors from palatial mansions. In order to bolster official salaries, private enterprise flourished and created the breed of social-climbing Company-men known as "nabobs" who accu-mulated vast fortunes and returned to England to build themselves country estates, to hobnob with aristocrats, and often to enter Parliament.

By the mid-eighteenth century, tensions between England and France were simmering in Europe when the War of Austrian Succession began, followed by the Seven Years War. Hostilities

The lakeside Shiv Niwas Palace and City Palace complex in Udaipur. Of all the ruling Rajput clans, only the Udaipur Mewars managed to remain virtually independent of the Mughal yoke.

Macaulay derided Aurangzeb's heirs as "a succession of nominal sovereigns, sunk in indolence and debauchery, sauntering away life in secluded palaces chewing bang, fondling concubines and listening to buffoons."

The British froze the borders of numerous Indian kingdoms, ranging from the largest and grandest, like Hyderabad and Kashmir, bigger in area than many European nations, to the smallest and most insignificant enclaves. On the upside of the coin, rulers of these so-called princely or native states enjoyed a security of tenure that their predecessors had never enjoyed. The aristocratic Rajput maharajas, the Muslim Nizams and nawabs, and the few remaining

Maratha generals were obliged to swell British coffers with generous annual revenues and acknowledge British paramountcy, but were otherwise autonomous in the administration of their territories.

Company agents were amassing enormously inflated personal fortunes, often by highly unscrupulous tactics. Tales of greedy excess filtered back to London, resulting in the India Act in 1784, which established the British government's control over the Company, although the Company was retained as a full partner in trade. London appointed a Board of Control to supervise all civil, military, and revenue matters, and the body was presided over by the Company's governor-general, the first being Warren Hastings who ruled from 1774 to 1785.

The British poured their mercantilist energies into large-scale iron and coal mining, developing tea, coffee and cotton production, and creating a vast network of railways, highways, postal and telegraph services, and irrigation and agricultural programs. English was the official language of the civil service and education, and still remains the lingua franca among India's administrative classes. By the mid-nineteenth century, some 1,000 Englishmen governed the affairs of some 221 million people. The British never allowed Indians

into the upper government echelons, but they established numerous schools and universities that led to the birth of an educated Indian elite.

Governor-general William Bentinck, influenced by philosophies of humanitarian liberalism fashionable in London in the 1830s, for the first time introduced laws against certain Indian cultural practices. He outlawed human sacrifice, the practice of suttee (the ritual suicide of widows upon the death of husbands), and acted against the Thugs, a secret society estimated to have strangled some 30,000 travelers a year in obeisance to the Hindu goddess of destruction, Kali. Not all British reforms were destined for success, and their tactics of delegating responsibility had dubious success in many rural areas. They bestowed administrative powers on *zamindars*, local landowners who generally abused their authority and forced many peasants into bonded labor in order to pay exorbitant taxes. The shortsighted policy gave birth to a class of impoverished peasantry, whose plight of living in near-slavery is still rife across India.

THE SEPOY REVOLT

British missionary zeal in reforming India led to considerable Hindu and Muslim antipathy, which in 1857 and 1858 took the conquerors completely by surprise. The revolt of the sepoys, British-employed foot soldiers, is called the "Indian Mutiny" in the West but titled the "War of Independence" in modern Indian school primers. Either way, both sides spilled much blood. The rebellion's unlikely symbolic figurehead was the last Mughal emperor, Bahadur Shah II, whose talents were more suited to perfecting poetry than revolutions.

The rebellion began in Meerut, near Delhi, where sepoys were incited by a rumor that new bullets being issued were greased with animal fat from pigs, which are deemed unclean to Muslims, and cows, which are sacred to Hindus. In the space of an afternoon, 47 battalions mutinied and began a spontaneous bloody trail of destruction across the north, killing every *feringhi*, or foreigner, they could find. A cheering mob proclaimed Bahadur Shah II the Emperor of Hindustan, and reinstated the octogenarian Mughal in Delhi's Red Fort.

The British contained the rebellion to the northern plains by disarming sepoys based in other areas and recruiting Sikhs and tribal irregulars to assist them in reasserting control. The campaign was marked by extreme brutality on both sides, and it took the expeditionary force six months to reach numerous besieged garrisons and eventually recapture Delhi in January 1858. Bahadur Shah was banished to Burma, signaling the final defeat of the Mughal Empire.

SEEDS OF REBELLION

The traumatic experience of the mutiny made London reassess its position in India. The Company was abolished in 1858 and its authority replaced by the British Crown. Queen Victoria was proclaimed Sovereign Empress of India, where a Viceroy would be her representative and chief executive. The industrial revolution was in full swing in England, and India — the "jewel in the crown" — became a key source of raw materials for the "workshop of the world."

The full-blown era of the Raj (from the Hindi for "rule") ran from 1858 until 1900. Ironically, British-founded educational institutions created an Indian intelligentsia who soon became incensed that principles of democracy fastidiously upheld in Britain were not applicable to Indian subjects.

National pride was also fueled by a growing awe for India following numerous revelations on its grandeur and complexity as the site of ancient civilizations. Archaeologists unearthed cities twice as old as Rome and discovered that Buddha was an Indian. Scholars deciphered ancient Sanskrit texts that revealed several millennia of formerly unknown kings and emperors. They pieced together the significance of coins, paintings, and sculptures, and uncovered long-lost philosophical, artistic, and literary achievements.

The Hindu renaissance and will for social reform was spearheaded by a handful of modern thinkers: Ram Mohan Roy, Ramakrishna, Swami Vivekananda, Dayanada, and even the English Annie Besant, president of the Theosophical Society and founder of the Central Hindu University, which later became Banaras Hindu University. They preached a common philosophical ground between modern Hinduism and Western thought, and called for the religion to break away from its domination by high-caste Brahmans.

The movement found its voice in the Indian National Congress, started in 1885 from the efforts of another reformist Englishman, Allan Hume. The Congress gradually came to articulate Indian desires for self-rule. Its creation led to the 1906 birth of the All-India Muslim League, whose founders derided plans of an India dominated by Hindu "Brahmans, moneylenders, and shopkeepers" and called for separate political representation.

Violence flared between the two communities and intensified under Lord Curzon's ill-conceived plan to divide Bengal into eastern and western administrative zones respectively dominated by Moslems and Hindus. The British also passed, in 1909, the Morley–Minto reforms, which called for separate electorates for Hindus and Moslems. Clashes between Moslem separatists and mostly Hindu unionists prompted Curzon in 1911 to reverse his Bengal partition plan, but the two British

schemes, intended to placate the demands of the two communities, had instead exacerbated the rift.

GANDHI AND INDEPENDENCE

Widespread demands for self-rule at the end of the 1800s were temporarily abandoned during World War I. Thousands of Indians served the British with honor, and wanted their loyalty to be recognized by an act of imperial generosity granting similar terms to India as Australia and Canada, which both enjoyed considerable self-rule as dominions within the empire. When London offered nothing in 1918, disillusionment among educated Indians turned to anger.

Congress began to expand its appeal, largely due to the inspiration of Mohandas Karamchand Gandhi, a young lawyer who returned to India in 1915 fresh from campaigning for human rights in South Africa. Gandhi called for the Congress to broaden its attitudes and membership and include the rural classes and the illiterate poor. He realized the near-impossibility of ousting the British through armed might, and instead insisted that all agitation should be based on *ahimsa* (nonviolence) and *satyagraha* (passive resistance). Gandhi's inspired views soon earned him the title of Mahatma ("Great Soul"), and he undertook a series of famous fasts to urge Hindus and Muslims to lay aside their differences and create a national unity that would cut across caste, community, and religious barriers. He insisted on the dissolution of untouchability, and called upon Brahmans to remove their sacred threads that symbolized their place in the elite caste.

OPPOSITE: Shah Jehan's Red Fort in Delhi, which saw the dethronement of the final Mughal emperor, Bahudur Shah in the aftermath of the 1857 Mutiny. ABOVE: Dapper regiments at the annual Republic Day in New Delhi when India proudly shows off its latest military hardware and martial might.

Gandhi dreamed that India would once more experience Rama Raj, a mythical golden age under the benign Hindu god Rama, when food was abundant and all people lived in peace and equality. He wanted the Indian flag to bear the spinning wheel, the symbol of his philosophy, and hoped that once the British left, India's economic future would be assured through small-scale cottage industries in which the rural masses could happily produce handicrafts, enjoying the utility derived from their labor.

With Gandhi's prompting, Indian women first began to involve themselves in politics and social movements. One of the most effective tactical weapons he used against the British was the ancient Hindu custom of *hartal*, or boycott, in which the daily functioning of the government ground to a halt due to nationwide strikes affecting all sectors of the economy.

A horrifying event in 1919 proved catalytic to the independence movement. General Reginald Dyer ordered his Gurkha troops to open fire on a peaceful but illegal protest meeting in Amritsar, killing 379 people and wounding 1,200 others in the sealed courtyard of Jallianwala Bagh. Sikhs, whose loyalty to the British had remained steadfast even throughout the Sepoy Mutiny, largely changed their alliance to the Congress. Gandhi shrewdly began campaigning against products and practices that made the British presence in India profitable. He agitated against taxes on Indian-produced salt as well as urging boycotts against British manufactured textiles, symbolizing his protest by learning to spin cotton thread, and by wearing only handwoven cloth, or *khadi*.

Although Gandhi spent several years in jail for his efforts, the British gradually accepted they must relinquish India, but their departure was complicated as officially they only controlled three-quarters of the subcontinent. One fifth of the population lived in some 600 princely states, whose rulers mostly did not relish the thought of sacrificing their typically lavish lifestyles.

Confrontations escalated between the Congress Party led by Jawaharlal Nehru and the Muslim League's leader, the sharp-witted Muhammad Ali Jinnah, who rallied the large Muslim minority behind his call for an independent Islamic homeland.

Viceroy Lord Wavell further infuriated Indians by announcing without consultation that they would fight for the empire in World War II, but many rallied to the cause and fought in Africa, Europe, and Asia against the Axis. The war stymied the independence movement, but peace was marked a new wave of Congress civil disobedience marked by mass arrests, riots, and bloodshed.

All parties now conceded that independence was inevitable, but Gandhi's call for the British to "Quit India" was now matched by Jinnah's slogan

"Divide and Quit." The results of central and provincial elections in India — as well as intensifying bloody clashes between Hindus and Muslims — made it clear that India's future lay either in partition or in a possible civil war.

A new British Viceroy, Lord Louis Mountbatten, was charged with the responsibility of handing over full control of India and the date was set for midnight on August 14, 1947. Both Nehru and Jinnah preferred partition to the alternative of a loose federation, which had been proposed by the British as early as 1945. Jinnah in particular refused to budge, proclaiming, "I will have India divided or India destroyed." Only Gandhi remained unmoved by the mood of jubilation, believing that India should be fully united.

Princely states were released from British sovereignty and obliged to decide which nation to join. The evacuation of some 200,000 British *sahibs* and *memsahibs* in India was surprisingly smooth, almost anticlimactic as India exploded with celebrations to mark its newborn freedom. However, the euphoria was soon overshadowed by the holocaust of partition.

The subcontinent was sliced into two new nations, its geographical boundaries imposed by religion. Pakistan was comprised of two completely separate regions: West Pakistan, which included half of the fertile, affluent Punjab, Sind province and several mountainous tribal states; and more than a thousand miles away, East Pakistan, made up of the eastern half of Bengal, which has became Bangladesh. At the time of partition, India was home to 35 million Muslims, while the newly created Pakistan housed millions of Hindus. In the months-long upheavals triggered by partition, more than ten million people migrated in each direction across the divided Punjab — the largest human exodus in history.

The price of the operation was to be paid in frenzied communal bloodshed and suffering. Estimates of how many people, mostly villagers, died in the terrible slaughter range between 200,000 and one million. Communal violence between Hindus, Sikhs, and Muslims spread so fast and so far that the Indian Army without the aid of British troops was quite unable to contain it. Trains were found in the middle of nowhere, their carriages spilling with mutilated corpses. Convoys of trucks were ambushed, and entire villages wiped out to the last man, woman, and child.

So extreme was the murderous madness that Jawaharlal Nehru, India's first prime minister, saw no option but to hand back responsibility to Mountbatten, who had by then become the first governor-general of the independent nation. Gandhi came to Delhi and went on a prolonged hunger strike for reconciliation and an end to communal violence. His assassination by a Hindu fanatic, on January 30, 1948, so shamed the nation that the bloodletting ceased. "The light has gone out of our lives," Nehru announced in a voice choked with grief. The impact of Gandhi's assassination was national psychological shock, sapping the will from communal violence and allowing Nehru time to turn his attention to the task of building a new India.

One of his most pressing concerns was resolving the status of the 362 major princely states. Kashmir, the last state to join India, had at its helm a vacillating Hindu maharaja governing a predominantly Muslim population and who refused to make his mind about which side he wanted to go. His decision was made for him when Pakistan-backed tribal members invaded the strategic state in October 1948, and he was forced to seek help from the Indian Army. New Delhi's forces halted the invaders, but lost about one third of Kashmir, which is now divided by a United Nations-mediated frontier.

AN INDIAN DYNASTY

The 1950s were the golden years of Indian independence, during which Prime Minister Jawaharlal Nehru formed what he hoped would be the guiding principles of his modern nation — secularism, democracy, social justice, and political nonalignment. His great personal charm and integrity, his intellectual stature, and his westernized sophistication singled him out as the leading international spokesman for newly independent Third-World nations. A Socialist, but not a Marxist, Nehru's goal was to create a modernized, self-sufficient India that would never again be beholden to another power. Nehru's socialist stance softened somewhat after consultations with the industrialists and Congress-backers, J.R. Tata and G.D. Birla, the Indian equivalents of Ford and Rockefeller. He established a protected and centralized economy through a series of five-tear plans aimed at encouraging massive industrialization and agricultural reforms.

Despite Nehru's policy of nonalignment, India increasingly found itself linked to the Soviet Union — partly in response to its month-long rout by China in 1962 and partly by America's increasing support for its arch foe, Pakistan. Gandhi's belief in peaceful neutrality was laid to rest when Beijing's forces poured across their mutual Himalayan frontier and relations between the world's two most populous nations remain bedeviled by disputes over two border areas.

Nehru died in 1964 and one year later his successor, Lal Bahadur Shastri, successfully repulsed Pakistan's twin attack on India — in the Rann of Kutch and in Kashmir. In January 1966, Shastri died, and Indira Gandhi, Nehru's daughter and no relation to the Mahatma, won a landslide victory at the polls to replace him. Skeptics darkly predicted that Indira would share the fate as India's only other woman ruler, the thirteenth-century Muslim Slave Queen, Razia, whose three-and-a-half-yearlong reign ended with a palace coup and her murder at the hands of her armed protectors.

With her election slogan "India is Indira and Indira is India," she was to prove them all wrong. During her 15 years in power she was both revered and severely criticized. Writer Salman Rushdie observed, "Her use of the cult of the mother — of Hindu mother-goddess symbols and allusions was calculated and shrewd." Mrs. Gandhi's most trying problem was sectarianism, in the form of

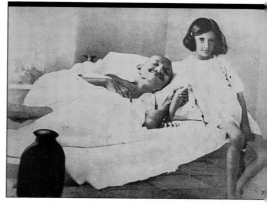

Congress Party splits or conflicts with neighboring powers. Agitation in East Pakistan against subjugation of the Bengali population by Islamabad erupted in 1971 into a civil war that culminated in Indian involvement. New Delhi's troops fought Islamabad's forces in both Kashmir and East Pakistan, from where nine million refugees flooded into India. After 12 days of fighting, Islamabad yielded its shaky hold over its eastern section and sued for peace, resulting in the creation of the independent nation of Bangladesh.

Mrs. Gandhi's travails were by no means over. National debt caused by the war and the refugee crisis and mounting inflation and unemployment led to popular opposition to her rule. Sensing that the tide was turning against her and prompted by a low-level indictment that she had used government money for electioneering, the prime minister imposed an 18-month-long state-of-emergency involving suspension of civil liberties and imprisonment of thousands of her political opponents. India ceased to be a democracy during

Two icons of twentieth century Indian history: A fast-weakened Mahatma Gandhi with Nehru's daughter Indira, who later succeeded her father as prime minister of India.

this period. Indira's zealous son, Sanjay, who she was grooming as her successor, incensed the populace with radical programs including the forced sterilization of more than 11 million villagers, and slum-clearing with bulldozers.

Mrs. Gandhi called an election in 1977 under the misguided belief that she remained popular and was ousted in a wave of support for the newly-formed Janata Party, largely comprised of disgruntled, Congressmen. Its elderly, pedantic leader Morarji Desai is remembered largely for his idiosyncratic habits of drinking urine, protecting cows, and banning alcohol and Coca-Cola, rather than for solving India's pressing economic problems. After their brief honeymoon, the Janata Party crumbled into squabbling factions and a 1980 election placed "Mrs. G" back on her pedestal in the nation's hearts and on its ruling seat.

Mrs. Gandhi valiantly tried but failed to conquer escalating economic and social ills, as well as bitter intercommunal unrest. Extremist Sikhs began agitating for the creation in northern Punjab of a theocratic nation named "Khalistan," or "Land of the Pure." The radicals began stockpiling arms in Amritsar's Golden Temple, Sikhdom's holiest shrine. Mrs. Gandhi retaliated in June 1984 with "Operation Bluestar," a massive weeklong army assault on the shrine that left some 600 people dead, mostly Sikhs.

The carnage and desecration of the shrine enraged Sikhs and led to the October 31, 1984 retaliatory assassination of Mrs. Gandhi by two of her Sikh security guards. Communal violence raged across northern India, where an estimated 3,000 Sikhs died at the hands of Hindu mobs. The mantle of the Nehru dynasty was passed onto Mrs. Gandhi's oldest son Rajiv, a former Indian Airlines pilot inducted into politics since the death of Sanjay in a 1980 plane accident.

Rajiv Gandhi was swept to power in 1984 on an unprecedented wave of popularity. Dubbed "Mr. Clean," he began with radical plans to liberalize the Indian economy, but soon ran into opposition. He was accused of accepting kickbacks in an arms contract and unceremoniously lost his mandate in 1989. Two years later, Rajiv Gandhi himself was assassinated, this time in a suicide-bomb attack allegedly masterminded by the Tamil Tigers, his death adding even greater dimensions to the Greek tragedy-style saga of the Gandhi family.

In mid-1996 the long rule of the Congress party came to an end when elections brought the Bharatiya Janata Party (BJP), or Indian People's Party, to power under Prime Minister Atal Bihari Vajpayee, who had formerly served as India's foreign minister during the socialist government from 1977 to 1979. BJP rule has seen rising Hindu nationalism, with more militant stances being taken with Pakistan over the Kashmir issue.

INDIA TODAY

Take a glance at the front page of any Indian newspaper for stories of mayhem and excess matched by few other nations. Political unrest could come from any region — perhaps from Sikh separatists in the Punjab, from the remote northeast where there are several tribal insurgencies, from near-feudal Bihar where peasant militia clash with private armies funded by landowning families, or anywhere where the centuries-old enmity between Hindus and Moslems may flare.

In the capital, headlines may cry of corruption in high places, prompting opposition members to walk out of Parliament, "amid uproarious scenes." Farmers, lawyers, or students may have called for hunger strikes, processions, or sit-ins that have brought the nation's businesses grinding to a halt. There may be another of God's terrible acts — drought or floods, ferries overturning, or buses plunging off ravines. There may be bizarre stories of a child being revered as a God, a movie star turning to politics, a widow throwing herself on her husband's funeral pyre, girls cutting off their tongues to honor Lord Shiva, or an elephant stampede destroying a remote village.

However startling to a Western eye, none of these yarns mean India is falling apart. The nation still lives in the shadow of the utopian dreams of Gandhi and Nehru, whose legacy lives in the yet unshaken ideals of unity, secularism, and social justice, maintained imperfectly perhaps, but nonetheless cherished as necessities. Beyond the story of sectarian violence is the telling fact that Hindus, Sikhs, Muslims, Buddhists, Parsis, Jains, and many other groups have lived together in India's nearly 600,000 villages for many centuries. Hinduism, the nation's most pervasive religion with some 700 million adherents, exerts a strong binding moral and spiritual force. Its central worldview is one of flexibility and absorption.

India can point to an impressive record of modernization, but it cannot shake the growing burdens of the rural poor or its mountain of untrained and unemployable people flooding the cities. In a nation of 960 million people, there are only around 50 million wage-paying jobs. Seventy percent of Indians live in the villages, yet their water supply is barely adequate, and they have no electricity, nor can many of them read or write. One statistic simply speaks for itself: one in every ten people who walk on this earth is an illiterate Indian.

But the foremost problem facing the nation today is its ever-growing population. India's population is estimated to be about 960,000 million, and with one baby born every two seconds, it adds an Australia to its ranks each year. Nothing can halt the population reaching one billion by the year 2000.

India is very proud of its scientific community, the world's fourth largest, be they producing locally made space rockets, battleships, atomic power stations, or computer software. Indeed India startled the world and nearly made itself into an international pariah by conducting nuclear tests in mid-1998 that were inevitably imitated shortly later by its archrival Pakistan.

India's nuclear tests were carried out in a spirit of immense public support, in what some thought to be a frightening form of Hindu nationalism. Mere months later, the tests seemed forgotten, and India was again going about the daunting task of turning itself into a modern nation. At the time of writing, both India and Pakistan were under intense international pressure to sign the Comprehensive Test Ban Treaty (C.T.B.T.) before September 1999.

INDIA'S ARTISTIC LEGACY

India's spectacular artistic heritage began 6,000 years ago when ancient tribesmen began fashioning buxom mother goddesses from clay: the earliest surviving artifacts to have been dug up at the Indus Valley sites in present-day Pakistan. It was not until the Mauryan age in the third century BC that India experienced a burst of artistic brilliance, notably in Buddhist art during the reign of Ashoka. The remarkable stone carving of this period can be seen at its most impressive at Sarnath and Sanchi, in Madhya Pradesh. Succeeding dynasties — the Sungas and Satavahanas — adapted Mauryan motifs and techniques and were very keen on using symbols to indicate Buddha's all-seeing eye, such as a footprint, the sacred wheel, and the stupa.

The next artistic wave was Alexander the Great's legacy from his subcontinental foray near present-day Peshawar: Gandhara art was classic East meets West, a mixture of Greco-Roman knowhow and Buddhist inspiration. Gandhara art is recognizable by its classical Grecian-style torsos, draped toga-like folds that are thought to be the inspiration behind saris and *dhotis*, and its "avant-garde" depiction of Buddha in human form. At the same time, a major school developed in Mathura, midway between Delhi and Agra, that reflected the revival of Hinduism and also featured busty *iyakshinis*, or nymphs, who were the dumpy forerunners to the sophisticated ladies of Khajuraho.

During the "golden age" of the Guptas, an artistic renaissance led to the development of classical style of Indian art. The painting and sculpture of this time have a fluid and sensuous look, with a consummate fascination for detail yet contriving an effect of utter simplicity. During this period, images of Buddha's stylized attitudes, clothing, and hand positions evolved to perfection

and are today mimicked by modern mass-produced images in Buddhist countries. Just as the Guptas were taking Buddhist art to its zenith, Dravidian artisans in the south were developing a strongly Hindu tradition, with new sculptural forms crafted in stone and bronze.

The next millennium saw a steady evolution from stylized, rather static Buddhist art towards almost decadent freneticism as the medieval Hindu revival entered full swing, perhaps best illustrated at the rock-cut caves of Ajanta and Ellora in Maharashtra. By then, sculpture had become an inseparable part of architecture, whose every surface displayed carved activity. Examples are best seen at the Hoysala temples at Karnataka, the

Sun Temple at Konarak, and the celestially carnal temples at Khajuraho.

The arrival of the temple-bulldozing Muslims undoubtedly wiped out great chunks of the Hindu artistic tradition. In their zeal to build empires these early invaders had little time for art, and only under the Mughal Emperor Akbar did a truly creative style of art emerge. This was miniature painting, concocted from a blend of Islamic and Persian styles, at first primarily portraiture and depictions of battles and courtly life. Under Jahangir, exquisite wildlife and nature studies were produced. An artist's palette included malachite, lapis lazuli, gold, silver, and an ingenious substance called *peori*, a yellow dye extracted from the urine of cows fed on mango leaves.

Throughout the Hindu states of northern India, artists were quick to take their cue from the Mughals, combining their own religious and artistic traditions with those that had been established by the Mughal school. Provincial styles differ greatly and are divided into different schools, notably Rajasthani or Mewar, Jammu or Pahari, Basolhi and Kangra, all former hill states of the Punjab.

A master musician instructs his pupils in a Madras school.

Although they are best remembered for their remarkable architecture, the Mughals represent the last great period of exclusively Indian artistic activity. During the British Raj, the British East India Company commissioned Indian artists to paint picturesque landscapes in oils and watercolors, and this became known as the Company school. Modern Indian painting gained impetus in the 1930s with the so-called Bengali school, a distinct style of painting developed by a group of artists who took inspiration from traditional watercolor techniques and folk-art motifs. India's most famous twentieth-century artists, whose work is rooted in the Indian tradition yet reflect western influences, include Amrita Shergill, M.F. Husain, and Krishen Khanna.

THE SACRED FLAME: RELIGIONS OF INDIA

The nation's founding prime minister, Jawaharlal Nehru, once described India as "a madhouse of religions." He spoke only half in jest. Religion is the heartbeat of the nation, and its influence, symbolism, and superstitions pervade every facet of life.

Four of the world's most influential religions — Hinduism, Buddhism, Islam, and Christianity — have flourished on Indian soil. The first two were born in India. In addition, India also saw the rise of Jainism, Sikhism, countless minor sects and tribal cults, as well as playing host to Judaism and Zoroastrianism.

India has long been perceived as a land of mystic wisdom and spirituality, standing in contrast to Western society with its emphasis on material gain. Yet outsiders often find it near bewildering to grasp how important religion is to the average Indian — as sustaining and inseparable to their existence as air, water, and food. As casual spectators to this fairground of faiths, tourists will catch glimpses of its influences almost every day they spend in India.

Glittering ornate temples are found even in the most remote villages. Some are ancient and exquisite, others modern and gaudy, but all are busy with devotees making offerings (*puja*) to brightly painted deities, chiming temple bells, and filling the air with wafts of incense and marigold blossoms. In the courtyards, sacred poems are read, hymns are chanted, and dances are performed.

Just as noticeably, on Fridays, the Muslim day of rest, the nation's mosques throng with white-capped Muslims who chant verses from the Koran, bow, and cup their hands to Allah.

Drivers adorn their dashboards with incense sticks, flowers, and the images of their faith. Sikhs enshrine the image of Guru Nanak, their religion's founding father; Hindus paint the ancient Aryan

swastika symbol around gaudy pictures of favorite gods or goddesses. Many homes have shrines — or even a whole room — set aside for worship.

The Indian calendar is peppered with religious festivals, some of them drawing pilgrims by the million. The Hindu religion has the most — 360 for an average of almost a festival a day. Just as important are the innumerable commonplace rites and observances performed almost unconsciously each day: a Hindu's predawn *puja*, a Muslim's Mecca-facing five prayers, a Sikh's uncut hair wound up in a turban.

Indian society is dominated by Hindus, who make up some 83% of the population; Muslims comprise some 10%; and Sikhs and Christians

combined make up a further five percent, while a handful of other minorities, namely Jains, Parsis, and Buddhists, make up the remainder.

HINDUISM

The world's most ancient living faith, Hinduism is not so much a religion as a philosophy. It has more adherents than any other religion in Asia: more than 670 million Indians are Hindus.

Although its origins can be traced back to the fertility cult of the Indus Valley civilization,

OPPOSITE: A towering *goporum,* or gateway, typically adorns the giant temple complexes of South India. ABOVE: Stylized stone carving dating from the Hoysala dynasty (1006–1310) which marked a peak in Dravidian temple architecture that can be seen at Somnathpur, Belur, and Halebid.

Hinduism formally emerged some 3,500 years ago as a distinct religious tradition with the Sanskrit-speaking Aryan invaders. Unlike most major religions, it neither claims a specific founder nor can point to a single "holy book" as its ultimate spiritual reference. Instead it has many, the earliest being the four sacred Vedas, notably the Rig Veda, composed between 1600 and 1000 BC, formally marking the birth of Hindu mythology. Other scriptures include: the *Upanishads*; the *Bhagavad-Gita* (described by Mahatma Gandhi as his "spiritual dictionary"); the *Puranas*; and two remarkable epic poems — the *Mahabharata* and the *Ramayana* — which are written in a tradition that was later to be echoed in Homer's Iliad and the Odyssey.

Hinduism has survived numerous periods of both prosperity and decline, demonstrating a resilient capacity to absorb and assimilate opposing faiths, rather than forcefully seeking converts. Its central view of religious tolerance was encapsulated in the Upanishads (800–400 BC) which state: "The Great God is One, and the learned call him by different names." Far from diluting itself out of existence, Hinduism seemed to gain strength from its flexibility and religious synthesis. It allows an astonishing freedom of worship. Under its umbrella can be found monotheists, polytheists, pantheists, totemists, animists, agnostics, and even the odd atheist!

Despite its inherent pluralism, Hinduism has several essential beliefs that tie its various creeds together. The ultimate objective of life is essentially the renunciation of life by achieving *moksha*, or perfection, thus breaking the soul's cycle of birth and rebirth. The passage leading to this desirable state is determined by an individual's *karma*,

which roughly translates as "actions" but means a law of cause and effect whereby a person's deeds in this and previous lives tally up to influence their status in the next life. *Dharma*, an individual's moral duties to perform in life, also comes into play. Both are inextricably bound to the concept of reincarnation, which offers both solace and hope in the belief that present troubles are the wages of a former life's sins and that pious and unselfish actions hold the key to a better life in the future.

The rules for reincarnation can be extraordinarily complex. The 2,000-year-old *Manu Smriti* (Laws of Manu) codified ancient precepts of law and sacred duty, punctuating them with digressions on what kind of rebirth punishes which sin. For example, if a man steals silk he becomes a partridge; if he steals cotton cloth he becomes a crane; if linen, a frog, and so on.

Although the larger esoteric concept of attaining an unblemished soul is important, Hinduism has its feet firmly on the ground and encourages its adherents in *kama* (earthly and notably sensual pleasures) and *artha* (prosperity and material wealth). According to Hindu beliefs, life passes through four stages — the stage of the learner, demanding self-control and abstinence; the stage of the householder, when *kama* and *artha* are healthy pursuits; the stage of detachment or gradual turning away from worldly things; and the stage of ascetic renunciation, when a person becomes devoted only to spiritual meditation and yoga, preparing for *moksha*.

An interesting feature of Hinduism is its cult of peripatetic sadhus, or holy men. They are rarely seen outside their mountain retreats, where they endure great hardships to show renunciation of the material world, only occasionally congregating at large religious festivals. Foreign visitors to India have for centuries been mystified by sadhus' bizarre acts, such as lying on beds of nails and being buried for weeks on end. Many deliberately cultivate their bedraggled appearance by smearing their half-naked bodies with ash and growing their hair and beard in matted dreadlocks. Sadhus often brandish tridents in obeisance to Lord Shiva, to whom they ritually smoke hashish.

A Pantheon of Gods

Hinduism recognizes an ultimate omnipotent force known as the Supreme Universal Soul, or *Parabrahma*, which has three physical manifestations: *Brahma*, the Creator; *Vishnu*, the Preserver; and *Shiva*, the Destroyer. All three are represented with four arms, while Brahma also has four heads to depict his all-seeing wisdom. He is said to have delivered the four sacred Vedas from each of his mouths.

Orthodox Hinduism is divided into two main sects: *Shaivism*, comprised of those who worship Shiva, and *Vaishnavism*, comprised of those who

The spectrum of faith in India is as infinitely varied, startling and mysterious as the country itself. ABOVE: Totemic image of Kali, the fearful Hindu goddess of destruction. OPPOSITE TOP: Sikh clerics within the exquisitely ornate sacred citadel of the Golden Temple at Amritsar. BOTTOM: Naked Naga sadhus, clad only in marigold garlands and Rastafarian dreadlocks converge at Hardwar for the Kumb Mela.

India and Its People

worship Vishnu. Unlike these two, the other member of the holy trinity, Brahma, has almost no temples. However, at Pushkar there is a shrine where you can see his "steed," the sea turtle.

This trinity symbolizes the three essential stages of life — birth, life, and death — and presides over a vast pantheon of some 330 million Hindu gods. Despite such a profuse array of gods, most people concentrate their devotional energies on a select few.

Vishnu, the most revered of the gods, possesses cosmic powers more formidable than Einstein's Theory of Relativity: when Vishnu sleeps, the universe goes into spasms of agitated flux that only normalize when he wakes up again. Vishnu is

usually depicted sitting on his vehicle; a human-faced eagle called Garuda. Vishnu has had nine incarnations (*avatars*), including a fish, a tortoise, a boar, a half-man, a beggar-dwarf, and the axe-wielding Parashurama, and is scheduled to return once more as the horse-headed Kalki. On his seventh call, he came as Rama with a Herculean mission to destroy the demon king Ravana of Lanka (Sri Lanka). The remarkable story of his success, aided by the faithful monkey-god Hanuman, became one of India's greatest epics, the *Ramayana*.

Vishnu made his eighth visit as Krishna, the handsome blue-skinned cow-herder god, who like Christ is said to have lived on earth in human form. Unlike Christ however, Krishna was something of a Casanova who decked himself out in yellow silk, peacock feathers, and jasmine-bud garlands. He was the heart-flutter of all the Mathura *gopi* (milkmaids), whom he married en masse after delivering them from the clutches of the demon king Naraka. Krishna is said to have had some 16,000 girlfriends, but Radha was his favorite and their romantic love was woven into Hindu myth to symbolize the relationship between the human soul and the Divine Spirit.

Vishnu's ninth and most daring incarnation was Buddha himself, apparently the result of an

inventive ploy to lure breakaway Buddhists back to the Hindu fold.

Each of the Hindu trinity has a consort, representing the feminine side of their powers. Brahma is married to his own daughter Saraswati, Goddess of Knowledge, who travels about on a swan. Vishnu's consort is the gorgeous Lakshmi, the Lotus Goddess of wealth and prosperity. Shiva's first wife was Sati, but after her tragic demise as India's first sati (or suttee) victim, he married the beautiful Parvati, the Goddess of Cosmic Energy, whose soul splintered into innumerable incarnations: Kali, the terrifying Goddess of Destruction, capable of inflicting disease and misery but also of healing, and depicted with a necklace of writhing snakes and skulls; Durga, the Slayer of the Buffalo Demon, a female warrior usually depicted riding around on a tiger and waving weapons held in each of her ten hands; and Shakti, the Goddess of Creative Energy. In addition to Ganesha, Parvati had another son by Shiva: the six-headed god of war, Kartikeya.

Modern-day Hinduism is steeped in elaborate legends about heroes and demons and the courageous exploits and playful idiosyncrasies of these flamboyant, larger-than-life gods and goddesses. Mythology is inseparable to all Indian art — sculpture, paintings, classical music, and dance — and fairs, festivals, and folk songs keep the tradition alive today.

Caste

One of the most pervasive aspects of Hinduism is caste, the schematized division of society into four *varnas*, or "colors": Brahmans (priests and teachers), Kshatriyas (leaders and warriors), Vaishyas (merchants), and Sudras (farmers, artisans, and laborers). The fair-skinned Aryans invented caste as a form of social apartheid (see THE ARRIVAL OF THE ARYANS, page 64). A more romantic explanation describes the four castes springing from the mouth (Brahmans), arms (Kshatriyas), thighs (Vaishyas), and feet (Sudras) of the creator, Brahma. Over the centuries, these four castes splintered into thousands of sub-castes or *jati*, so that their original job-definitions have lost their meaning. Only the Brahmans, by virtue of their high-caste status, have preserved their exclusivity, and regardless of their profession, they tend still to occupy privileged positions within society.

Inextricably bound to the notion of caste are the concepts of purity and pollution. Higher castes, especially Brahmans, have their lives regulated by a bewilderingly complex laundry list of prohibitions. Cardinal "don't do's" include the eating of beef and any contact with lower castes or items of food, water, or objects touched by them. Highborn castes often refuse to perform tasks deemed polluting. This is why many Indian households employ a bevy of servants — a Brahma cook, a Sudra sweeper, and a sub-Sudra toilet cleaner, and so on. To transgress these rules requires rigorous ritual, such as bathing in holy waters, and extra time spent at the temple.

The most infamous aspect of the caste system, however, lies outside its boundaries: untouchability. Traditionally, untouchables have always been considered social pariahs who are given the tasks considered lowly and contaminating to all other castes, such as sweeping houses and streets, cleaning sewers, and removing corpses. With independence, the new constitution abolished untouchability; renaming members of the out-caste harijans, or "children of god," and giving them full democratic and human rights.

JAINISM

Jainism was the first major sect to rise in rebellion against Hinduism and was founded around 500 BC by Vardhamana Mahavira, an older contemporary of Buddha and the most recent of the 24 Jain saints or *tirthankaras*. He rejected the Hindu gospel that a Supreme Creator had engineered the universe, believing instead that it was infinite and eternal. Mahavira preached the complete renunciation of desire and the material world as the most direct path to spiritual salvation, encouraging his adherents to follow the path of asceticism, austerity, and nonviolence.

Nevertheless, breaking customs that have existed for thousands of years is difficult. Caste still determines the kind of work a man accepts, the woman he will marry, the people he will and won't mix with, and the type of religious observances he will perform.

Religion in Revolt
From Hinduism emerged two breakaway ideologies, one propounded by Vardhamana Mahavira and the other by Gautama Buddha, both opposed to extravagance, hierarchical rule, and violence. Both philosophers were Kshatriyas, who stood against the complications and prejudices of caste. Both advocated a return to a simpler, more direct lifestyle and boundless compassion for all beings. Both encouraged an ascetic approach focused on belief in "One Soul" — everything that exists within the material world lives on an equal plateau.

Jain monks became noted for their extreme asceticism. Many of them adopted the habits of the Hindu sadhus or holy men, taking to the road dressed in nothing but a loincloth with only a begging bowl and a stave as possessions. The Jain cardinal doctrine of *ahimsa*, non-injury to any living creature, stems from the belief that all matter is eternal and that every object has a soul, even pebbles or grains of sand. Plants and trees have at least two souls, while animals are thought to have three. As a result, some Jains

OPPOSITE: Restoring the frescoes of a Rajput temple requires both skill and a certain religious fervor. ABOVE: This pilgrim takes elaborate measures to preserve her precious cargo of water from the Ganges River in Varanasi, which Hindus believe has the power to cleanse the soul. OVERLEAF: Communal breadbaking at a Sikh festival in the Punjab.

wear thin muslin masks over their mouths to prevent them from breathing in small insects. These devotees do not eat after dark in case insects should accidentally fall into their food and die. Many sweep the ground before them as they advance, to avoid inadvertently treading on small creatures.

The Jains are just as preoccupied as Hindus with the theory of rebirth, and becoming a monk is thought to provide a fast track to release. Lay Jains traveling the slower route try to refrain from telling lies, from being devious, and from indulging in sensual pleasures.

In the first century AD the Jains split into two sects: the white-clad Svetambaras and the

misogynist, space-clad or naked Digambaras. The latter were so zealously disdainful of possessions that they refused to don clothes at all. They also regarded women as the scourge of humanity, whose charms were an evil temptation to those trying to tread the path of straight and narrow.

Jain temples are frequently exquisite, with ornately carved marble pillars and sculptures. The most impressive of these can be seen in the three main Jain centers: Rajasthan (Mount Abu), Gujarat (Palitana and Junagadh), and Bombay. The Jains have four and a half million adherents in India today. Despite their ascetic beliefs, the Jain community maintains a strong presence in the business world as traders, bankers, and philanthropists, running rest houses for pilgrims, homes for widows and orphans, and even hospitals for sick birds.

BUDDHISM

The Buddhist religion was the second religious schism to emerge from Hinduism, and it proved to be far more influential. Buddha was born Siddhartha Gautama, the son of a local prince, between 563 and 556 BC in what is now Nepal. He lived at first in luxury, marrying and fathering

a son. Then, at the age of 29, he left the comforts of the palace to embark on a long quest for truth and for an understanding of human mortality and suffering. After several years of rigorous asceticism, he sat down under a bodhi tree at Uruvela, near Gaya in Bihar state, and achieved "enlightenment" or nirvana. He spent the next 45 years of his life preaching that everyone, not just priests or ascetics, was capable of aspiring to enlightenment in their own lifetime, without having to passively await a better incarnation in the next life.

Gautama's answer to the problem of suffering was contained in his "Four Noble Truths." He explained that human suffering is rooted in terminal dissatisfaction and insatiable desire. In order to become free of suffering you must escape desire, and the way to escape desire is to follow the Eight-fold Path. This path details how to become disentangled from all desire for worldly gratification.

At Sarnath's Deer Park near Benares (Varanasi), Gautama met five Brahmans who became his disciples. Called the the Enlightened One or "Buddha," Gautama reputedly died at the age of eighty, having eaten poisoned food.

Buddhism was clearly a radical departure from Hinduism or Jainism. Buddhism renounced the need for extreme asceticism and instead emphasized living in the present.

Buddhism at first flourished in India, adopted by the great Emperor Ashoka who ruled from 269 to 232 BC. It was carried to every part of his extensive empire, and spread in time to Burma, Thailand, Sri Lanka, Korea, China, Vietnam, Nepal, Tibet, Central Asia, and notably to present-day Japan.

Buddhism was soon divided by a schism, leading to two main schools of Buddhist thought. The Hinayana or "lesser vehicle" held that enlightenment was an individual pursuit, whereas the Mahayana or "greater vehicle" held that enlightenment was a collective pursuit, with the ultimate aim of bringing humanity to salvation. The Hinayana referred to Buddha in external symbols (the lotus for his birth, the bodhi tree for his enlightenment, the wheel of law for his first sermon, and the stupa for his enshrinement). The Mahayana took Buddha's last words as gospel, "Be a lamp unto yourselves, be a refuge unto yourselves, seek no refuge outside of yourselves."

However, Buddhism later waned in popularity in India — the land of its birth — largely because of the challenges it faced first from Hinduism and then later from Islam. Although Hinduism and Buddhism were almost diametrically opposed theories, these religions and Jainism still coexisted relatively peacefully for many centuries until the advent of Islam.

ISLAM

Muslims form the largest religious minority group in India, with more than 105 million adherents, almost as many as in Pakistan. They are mainly scattered throughout northern India. Only in Kashmir are they a regional majority. The Muslims first came to India as powerful, iconoclastic conquerors, generally making the bulk of their converts from low-caste Hindus. Today, however, the most visible legacies of India's Islamic heritage can be seen in the nation's Mughal forts, mosques, and domes, and in the Mughalai cuisine and art.

Arab traders sowed the first seeds of Islam in India when they beached their sailing vessels along the southern coast during the seventh century, bringing news of the recently founded faith of the Prophet Muhammad. They also brought the Koran, a collection of messages that Allah (God) had spoken to Muhammad. The overwhelming feature of Islam was its forceful zeal to spread the word — and by the sword if this was deemed to be required. Beginning in Arabia, Islam spread east over the centuries and eventually took firm root in three continents. Unlike the Hindu religion, which requires its adherents to be born Hindus, conversion to Islam is easy — to become a Muslim merely requires saying the words "There is no god but Allah and Muhammad is his prophet."

Very early on in its history, Islam experienced a schism that still remains with them to this day.

The majority of Muslims are Sunnites, whose allegiance is to the direct descendants of Mohammed's immediate successor, the Caliph. Other Muslims are Shiites who follow the descendants of the prophet's son-in-law, Ali. Both aspire to make a pilgrimage to Mecca — the prophet Mohammed's birthplace.

SIKHISM

The Sikh religion is relatively new, having broken away from Hinduism in the sixteenth century, in response to frictions between Hindus and Muslims in the Punjab. Founded by Guru Nanak (1469–1538), Sikhism was inspired by the Hindu doctrine

of *bhakti*, or passionate devotion: it originated as a pacifist, caste-rejecting movement, seeking to fuse the best from both Hinduism and Islam. Its essential message can be found in the Sikh Bible, the *Adi Granth*, which includes the collected writings of the faith's 10 gurus or teachers, along with various Hindu and Muslim devotional poetry.

Sikhs became increasingly martial towards the end of the seventeenth century, as a result of Hindu and Muslim persecution. The Mughal Emperor Aurangzeb in fact so detested the Sikhs that he offered a reward of gold coins for any citizen who brought to him the severed head of a Sikh.

Provoked by Aurangzeb 's prize-offering, the sixth Guru of the line, Guru Gobind Singh

OPPOSITE: An elephant fresco in Shekhavati district, Rajasthan. ABOVE: A diptych of elderly bibliophiles.

(1675–1708) turned the Sikh religion into a military brotherhood whose members all took the surname Singh or "Lion." He enjoined male Sikhs to observe "the five K's": they must wear the four symbols of Sikh faith — a *kara*, a steel bangle; *kaccha*, soldiers' shorts; a *kangha*, a wooden or ivory comb; and a *kirpan*, a dagger; and they must never cut either their hair or their beard (*kes*).

The Sikhs have only one god and their temples are known as *gurdwaras*. The holiest Sikh shrine is the Golden Temple in Amritsar, in northern Punjab state. Sikhs are generally notable for their pragmatism, their earthy good humor, their capacity for hard work, and their skill in mechanical matters.

Although Sikhs make up only two percent of the population of modern-day India, with some 18 million adherents, they are a very proud and visible community throughout the country.

ZOROASTRIANISM

The tiny community of Zoroastrians, more popularly known as Parsis, are mostly concentrated in Bombay and are thought to number around 10,000. Their religion is one of the world's oldest, founded in Ancient Persia by the prophet Zoroaster during the sixth century BC. After the Islamic conquest of Iran many intrepid Zoroastrians left their homes and sought refuge in India. The first group is said to have reached Diu in Gujarat around AD 766. They caused no tension or religious conflict, probably because they made no attempts to convert others. They were considered

desirably fair-skinned, and they were astute — as they are still considered to be — in business and intellectual matters.

Their scripture, the Zend-Avesta, contains psalms describing the ongoing battle between Truth and Lie. They worship Ahura Mazda (the "Lord Wisdom"), who is symbolized by fire. Parsis worship nature's elements and particularly fire, keeping the symbol of their belief burning in their temples. They are probably best known for their rather macabre habit of leaving their dead in "Towers of Silence" to be devoured by vultures, thus avoiding polluting the sacred purity of the elements — fire, earth, water, and air — by burying or cremation.

The numbers of Parsis are on the wane today due to increasing intermarriage. Indira Gandhi was married to a Parsi but her son Rajiv could not be a Parsi even if he wanted to — it takes two Parsi parents to make a Parsi child.

CHRISTIANITY AND JUDAISM

Many people are surprised to learn that Christianity first took root in India within half a century of Christ's own lifetime. The apostle Saint Thomas arrived in Kerala in AD 52 and spread the Syrian Christian faith. Christianity was by no means unknown when Catholic and Protestant missionaries made converts in various Portuguese, Dutch, and English settlements during the sixteenth century, mainly among low-caste Hindus. Today India has some 22 million Christians, many of them living in the ex-Portuguese enclave of Goa, as well as a quarter of the population of Kerala. The populations of two small northeastern states — Mizoram and Nagaland — were also sufficiently impressed by intrepid Christian missionaries to soon convert in large numbers.

In Kerala again, Cochin's Jewish community should get a special mention — their ancestry dates back to 973 BC, when King Solomon's merchant fleet began trading for spices and other fabled treasures. Scholars say that Jewish immigrants first settled along Kerala's Malabar Coast soon after the Babylonian conquest of Judea in 586 BC. The immigrants were well received and the Dravidian king of Cochin granted a title and small principality to one Joseph Rabban, a Jewish leader. Although only a handful of so-called White Jews remain in Cochin, their synagogue is worth visiting, older than any in the Commonwealth.

ABOVE: An infamous Indian "sacred" cow, elaborately clad for the harvest festival of Pongol in South India. OPPOSITE TOP: Worshippers at the Sufi shrine of Dagah. BOTTOM: Unorthodox Hindu temple with Belgian chandeliers and slumbering devotees in Goa.

India and Its People

Delhi
and
the North

THE CAPITAL: A TALE OF TWO CITIES

Completed at the tail end of the British Raj in 1931, New Delhi was a ready-made capital inherited by India's new leaders 16 years later. It still manifests a perceptible hangover from the Raj-era, not only in much of its old-world architecture but in the British systems of parliament, law, and bureaucracy which survive more or less intact, albeit idiosyncratically. An early illustration of this, just after India became independent in 1947, was when many of the original 6,000 servants who kept the Viceroy's Palace pristine during the Raj, and lived behind the palace in a township of their own, were first dismissed in a show of egalitarianism, but soon asked to resume their old jobs in the newly-named Rastrapati Bhavan.

The social life of Delhi's rich and powerful is played out against a backdrop of genteel clubs, five-star hotels, and Raj-era bungalows, where gossip is spiced with the latest wafts of scandal and sycophancy. On the flip-side, Delhi also houses thousands of homeless on its streets, many of them Rajasthani villagers fleeing the ravages of drought to find work as laborers on the city's numerous construction sites. After a day or so in Delhi, you'll see these hordes of gaunt workers, who look like sun-blackened skeletons draped in bright rags, balancing impossible loads on their heads as they labor on medieval-looking work sites. At night, you'll see their makeshift cardboard hovels go up on pavements and traffic islands next to slumbering cows, barely a stone's throw from the capital's luxury hotels and embassy colonies.

Delhi can be a rather deceptive introduction to India — with its built-up urban sprawl, large influx of foreign tourists, and Sten-gun-toting security patrols — but its historic sights merit a stay of at least four or five days. Of all the large Indian cities, it offers the gentlest transition to life on the subcontinent, with some of the country's best hotels and restaurants. It's also the most efficient center from which to make bookings and gather information, and is a convenient base for exploring northern India, with easy access by air and train to the ever-popular "Golden Triangle" route of Agra and Jaipur, and to the rest of Rajasthan, to Varanasi and Khajuraho, and to the Himalayan resorts of Himachal Pradesh and Ladakh.

BACKGROUND

Historically, Delhi represented a crucial foothold on the subcontinent that none of India's prospective invaders could afford to ignore. It commanded the strategic northeastern routes from Central Asia and the high valleys from Afghanistan, where Delhi's early conquerors came from — many of them in the footsteps of Alexander the Great — and provided a bastion for plundering the rich lowlands of the Ganges delta.

Competition for the control of Delhi began in the eleventh century, much of it marked by gruesome Oriental despotism and valiant victories. The city was raised, fought over, destroyed, deserted, and rebuilt no fewer than seven times, although archaeologists argue that as many as eight other cities existed, and also suggest that idol-smashing Muslims may have wiped out remnants of ancient Hindu settlements.

The antiquity of Delhi may be traced to the legendary city of Indraprastha, the capital of the Pandavas, the mythical heroes of the *Mahabharata*

epic. Legend has it that their city was founded on the banks of the river Yamuna over 3,000 years ago, although archaeologists trace the earliest settlements in Delhi to 1200 BC. Indraprastha was said to be located where the sixteenth-century Purana Qila now stands — where shards of fine gray earthenware have been found that seem to give substance to this myth.

Invading Rajput dynasties were responsible for the first citadels, whose decaying ruins can be seen 10 km (about six miles) south of Connaught Place near the Qutb Minar. Of these, the first was Lal Kot, built by the Tomar Rajputs in 1060, who brought with them the mysterious Iron Pillar with its fourth- or fifth-century Sanskrit script. It is said to be more than 2,000 years old and made of such

Mahatma Gandhi depicts the "Father of the Nation" in a characteristically stalwart pose.

pure iron that it has never rusted. Even more enigmatic than the origin of the Iron Pillar is the only great ancient Hindu shrine left intact in Delhi's environs, 17 km (10.5 miles) south of Delhi, known as Suraj Kund. Thought to have been constructed by the Tomar Rajputs, it is a pool surrounded by wide amphitheater-like steps, with the remains of a large temple nearby, dedicated to the sun god, Surya.

Feudal battles ensured that Lal Kot soon fell to another Hindu Rajput clan, the Chauhans, in the twelfth century. They considerably expanded this original domain, renaming it Qila Rai Pithora.

Then in 1206, Delhi trembled to the rumblings of India's Spartacus, the former Turkic slave Qutb-ud-Din Aybak who became Delhi's first Muslim Sultan. He pounded his predecessor's cities to rubble before laying the base for Delhi's second city with his two significant edifices: the Quwwat-ul-Islam Masjid, one of India's first mosques, built from the remains of 27 Hindu temples — with the looted Iron Pillar given pride of place in its courtyard — and his famous tower of victory, the Qutb Minar, situated south of New Delhi and celebrating the Muslim defeat of a Hindu king.

The line of the so-called Slave Kings ended in 1296, when Sultan Alauddin of the Afghan Khaljis stormed through India, capturing the Rajput fortress of Chittaurgarh and founding Siri, Delhi's second city. The Khaljis left a magnificent sprawling fort that visitors will find surrounded by encroaching modern tenements in the present-day Hauz Khas suburb.

By 1321 the Afghans had been ousted by the Muslim Tughluqs, a formidable Islamic warrior dynasty who constructed no fewer than three cities here during the fourteenth century. The first, Tughluqabad, built by Ghiyas-ud-Din, is now a ruined ghost of a fort city, dotted with tombs and fortified by massive sloping walls, 10 km (about six miles) southeast of the Qutb Minar. Whether or not the city is haunted — as the story goes — by the ghost of a vengeful saint is a matter for speculation, but it was abandoned only five years after its construction due to a shortage of water. Today it is inhabited only by the Gujars, a gypsy tribe.

The next Tughluq city, Jahanapanah, was also rapidly deserted. Its founder was the mad quixotic Sultan Muhammad ibn Tughluq, an Indian Nero renowned for fiendish ways — among his many exploits, the most vicious was crushing his elderly father to death beneath a specially-constructed "ceremonial welcome" archway. Acting on imperial whim he decided to quit his father's domain and force-marched his subjects 1,100 km (563 miles) to his new capital at Daulatabad, near present-day Aurangabad. According to an eyewitness account, two subjects attempted to evade the Sultan's Long March and suffered the ruler's wrath. The first, a cripple, was butchered,

and the other, who was blind, was prodded all the way to Daulatabad by soldier's lances. It was later observed that only the poor man's severed leg, a macabre trophy, eventually arrived. Seventeen years later, the Sultan grew tired of debauched amusements at his Deccan fortress, and marched his subjects all the way home to Delhi again.

Delhi's fifth city was the final and most impressive achievement of the Tughluq rulers, founded in 1351 by the Sultan Muhammad's considerably more tolerant cousin, Feroz Shah. His 37-year reign was relatively peaceful and he was able to indulge in building and repairing the existing buildings of the Qutb Minar complex. Today visitors explore the crumbling ruins of his historic capital's core in the site known as Feroz Shah Kotla, just to the south of the Red Fort, where you can see on one of two third-century pillars the edicts of Emperor Ashoka in the Brahmanic script deciphered by James Prinsep in 1837.

After Feroz's death, confusion about the succession of the Tughluq line weakened the kingdom, and when in 1398 Timur the Lane — the dreaded Tamerlane, Emir of Samarkand and conqueror of Persia, Afghanistan, and Mesopotamia — invaded India he met with only slight resistance. But after two weeks sacking the city, Timur led his armies back to Samarkand, taking 120 elephants as useful booty but not bothering to set himself on Delhi's throne. The last of the Tughluqs died in 1414, and power passed to the Sayyids, descendants of the Prophet who barely made a dent in Delhi's history, and to three generations of Pathan Lodi kings who built a necropolis of tombs and mosques, but little else before moving to Sikandra, just outside Agra, in 1504.

The first of the Great Mughals to arrive in Delhi was Babur, a feudal overlord from Samarkand who claimed the blood of both Genghis Khan and Timur ran in his veins. He swept through Delhi before marching his armies onto Agra, where he acquired the Koh-i-noor diamond and founded the Mughal dynasty. Babur died in 1530, and his son Humayun moved north to Delhi, building a fort-capital known as Purana Qila on the banks of the Yamuna river, where his magnificent tomb stands today. Humayun called his capital Danpanah, or Asylum of the Faith, but he had to flee to Persia (using the Koh-i-noor to bribe his way out in safety) when an Afghan adventurer, Sher Shah Suri, arrived on the scene in 1540. The usurper was able to add several impressive monuments to what became Delhi's sixth city, Shergarh, before Humayun reclaimed his throne with a vengeance in 1555.

From then on into the seventh century, Delhi and Agra became twin jewels in the Mughal crown, and not until 1638 did Humayun's great-grandson, Shah Jahan, transfer the seat of his empire to Delhi. Completed over a decade, the seventh Delhi, Shahjahanabad, became India's regal center. It was dominated by a magnificent sandstone walled fortress now called the Red Fort, the giant Jama Masjid mosque, and the broad processional avenue Chandni Chowk, or "moonlight bazaar," named for a wide canal which once ran down its center. The contemporary American traveler Robert Minturn described Chandni Chowk as the "gayest scene in India;" filled with "scarlet ladies" and gloriously clad "natives" gadding about on howdahed elephants and Arab steeds. With this in mind, it's easy to picture the pride of Mughal Delhi's architect Shah Jahan, who inscribed his famous claim: "If there is paradise on the face of this earth, it is here, Oh! It is here!" in gold above his marble audience hall in the Red Fort.

Delhi after a day's gallop to bayonet every European in sight. The sepoys secured the reluctant support of their symbolic emperor, Bahadur Shah, in their bid to oust the *feringhi* or foreigners.

The insurgents were later strung up by avenging British troops, so incensed at the sight of their mutilated womenfolk and children that they not only blew up mutineers by placing them over the mouths of their cannons, but seriously debated blowing up the Jama Masjid too, with the notion of raising a Christian cathedral in its place. At Kashmir Gate, slightly north of the Red Fort, you can still see the pockmarks of shot and shell, where the dwindling number of British were forced to retreat to defend themselves. Bahadur Shah was

However, the Mughal empire was fated to fall into decay, and a century later, in 1739, Delhi's prized gem-studded Red Fort fell to the plundering Nadir Shah, the emperor of Persia.

By this time the weakened Mughals were no match for the British, who had long ago established footholds in Madras and Bengal. In 1803 the British placed under their yoke the last Mughal, the blind old poet Bahadur Shah, who was in reality only a puppet king. All that remained to him was his title, his palace, and a pension bestowed by the new rulers. But the British suffered a severe setback with the yearlong Sepoy Mutiny in 1857, sparked in Meerut by protesting sepoys, or native soldiers, whose principal objection seems relatively straightforward in retrospect: pig and cow fat, used to grease Muslim and Hindu cartridges. The British reaction was one of classic hubris, and the enraged sepoys went on a murderous spree, arriving in

packed off in disgraced exile to Rangoon, but during a spate of crossfire at Humayun's Tomb, a vigilante British officer "bagged" the last Mughal's sons for the greater glory of the Empire.

Delhi remained a provincial town set amid hyena-infested wilds and magnificent relics until 1911 when, for the first and only time, a ruling English monarch came to India to be crowned Emperor in Delhi at the Coronation Durbar. This was where the new King George V broke the news of the shift of India's imperial capital from Calcutta to "this beautiful and historic city." His words so traumatized the British in Calcutta that they omitted to print the numbing news in the next day's papers, fearing perhaps their new Emperor was suffering from a bad bout of sunstroke.

Dawn breaks over the medieval Jama Masjid, casting its distinctive silhouette across old Delhi's skyline.

GENERAL INFORMATION

Consult the monthly *Delhi Diary* for its extremely useful directory that covers all the information centers, travel reservation offices, restaurants, theaters, embassies, hospitals, and so forth that you could possibly need. Delhi is the place to stock up on information for your next destinations, as well as doing as much advance planning and booking as possible to save hassle later. The main **Government of India Tourist Office (** (011) 3320005, at 88 Janpath, is open from 9 AM to 6 PM from Monday to Friday, 9 AM to 2 PM Saturday, and is closed Sunday. It answers queries about all Indian destinations and usually stocks a good map of Delhi. This is where you book conducted tours for New Delhi (morning) and Old Delhi (afternoon), run by both the India Tourist Development Corporation (ITDC) and the Delhi Tourist Development Corporation (DTDC). See also TRAVELERS' TIPS, on page 361, for addresses of appropriate Government and State tourist offices.

WHEN TO GO

The best time to visit Delhi is between mid-September and March, when the days are crisp, fine, and sunny and the evenings cool. Winters can be surprisingly chilly — so if you plan to arrive between December and January, you'll need warm socks and sweaters. Winter is also India's marriage season and so a good time for seeing spontaneous processions of brocade-clad, turbaned grooms resplendent on white horses, their glittering brides, and their entourage of drunken guests, lamp-*wallahs*, and trumpet-tooting bandsmen in old epauletted uniforms. Delhi has a fleeting but beautiful blossoming splendor during the spring months of February and March.

One of Delhi's most spectacular annual festivals is Republic Day, held on January 26, when India displays its martial might along the Rajpath with parades of dapper regiments (including the famous Camel Corps), brass bands, folk dancers, and India's latest military hardware. Don't take along anything valuable, as all baggage has to be left with security. At dusk, crowds watch silently as camel-mounted soldiers perform their ritual for the Beating Retreat.

Delhi is also particularly lively during the 10-day Ram Lila (Dussehra) festival in September or October. Continuous plays, marathon readings, and music and dance are performed by weird and wonderfully dressed actors on chariots in Old Delhi. They recount episodes from India's epic poem, the *Ramayana*, which tells the story of the

god Rama's victory over the demon king Ravana and the rescue of Rama's abducted wife Sita. The festival culminates in a procession of immense, firework-padded, brightly painted effigies of the evil ten-headed Ravana and his henchmen to the Ram Lila fairground (located where Old Delhi ends and New Delhi begins), where they are set ablaze to the roar of thousands of onlookers.

The Muslim festival Bakr Id, in April, is also very dramatic, with hundreds of thousands of devotees kneeling in prayer outside the Jama Masjid. The only festival you might want to avoid in Delhi is Holi, in March — which is possibly India's most delightful festival in small villages or amongst friends, but can turn nasty in big, impersonal cities when gangs of young men use it as a excuse to pelt unwitting passersby, particularly young women and tourists, with paint, colored water, stones, or even kerosene and battery acid.

GETTING AROUND

New Delhi's grid-like boulevards are relatively easy to find your way around — roads are well signed and all the street names uniformly belong to the post-Independence era. But the city is very spread out, leaving many travelers with the impression that they've spent much of their time in Delhi just getting from one place to another. To a large extent, whether you stay in Old Delhi or New Delhi has a significant effect on which aspect of the city you end up experiencing.

Travelers tend to concentrate their sightseeing efforts in three major areas: in and around the central hub of Connaught Place and Janpath, where you'll find all the banks, shops, emporia, tourist and airline offices, and many tourist-orientated restaurants and budget hostels; near the Red Fort, to explore the old walled city's bazaars and sights, close to Old Delhi Railway Station and, a little further north, the Interstate Bus Terminal near Kashmiri Gate; and around the Paharganj area, situated two kilometers (a mile and a quarter) north of Connaught Place, next to the New Delhi Railway Station, and with a reputation as a backpacker's haunt for its cheap accommodation and cafés. Unless you are staying at one of the five-star hotels within Lutyens' residential New Delhi to the south of the city, it's often easy to neglect this exceptionally pleasant area, but it's well worth making time to explore the tranquil Lodi Gardens, the tombs of Safdarjang and Humayun, and the imperial Rastrapati Bhavan complex.

Of all the Indian cities, Delhi's varied and spread-out attractions require you to be selective and organized about sightseeing. It helps to have a good city map so that you have at least some idea where your driver is supposed to be taking you, otherwise you may find yourself being

---

Humayan's Tomb, the majestic prototype of the Taj Mahal, is one of Delhi's best preserved monuments.

taken for a ride! You can begin on a city-wise note as soon as you arrive in Delhi's airport terminal by heading for the "Pre-Paid Taxi" booth and utilizing the no-hassle system of paying your fare in advance, with the rate calculated against your desired destination. The fare from the airport to Connaught Place is around US$10, but may be cheaper depending on which taxi service you use.

It might take a while to adjust to the anarchic haphazardness on the capital's roads, where a combination of relatively well-paved roads and fatalistic disdain of road rules often proves fatal. According to statistics, Delhi's roads are the second most dangerous in the world after Nairobi, and there seems every indication that they will stay that way. You'll need to adopt a little Hindu fatalism to stay cool, but you'll soon get used to seeing lurching over-crammed sardine-can buses or snail's-pace motor-scooters atop which an entire family have arranged themselves. After a few days of observation on Delhi's roads, you'll come away with some new discoveries about the Average Indian versus the Laws of Physics and some new ideas about different ways of utilizing vehicles. You should have learned how to detect subtle suicidal urges in potential auto-rickshaw or taxi-drivers. For instance, glazed bloodshot eyes are telltale signs that they have recently been sipping *bhang*, which is a marijuana-based concoction to which many drivers are addicted. It's also worth noting that it's not always wise to follow up your driver's invitation to change money on the black market, as a good number of them are paid as police informers. Just put it all down as good character assessment practice for being out in the "field"!

You may wish to ride a Delhi bus just for the experience. But they are very crammed and often downright unpleasant, particularly for women. It's far more fun to watch the macho sport that young Indian men seem to regard as a sort of rite of passage — they'll go to astonishing lengths to self-consciously loiter until the bus has begun to accelerate, then sprint after it for a highly competitive (highly amusing) last-ditch effort to hurl themselves aboard, often left desperately half-dangling — to the cheers of onlookers!

Auto-rickshaws provide the cheapest, most convenient way of negotiating short distances in Delhi. They tend to be slow and kidney-rattling, and so are obviously less practical for longer distances, like going out to the airport or to the Qutb Minar.

With any motorized transport, always agree on the price first (this deflects the driver's inclination to waste his gasoline on driving you around in circles) or make sure that the meter is being used. Drivers will wait quite happily if you want to retain them while you hive off for an hour

of so of sightseeing or shopping — but you must agree on the waiting charge, usually about Rs 20 an hour for taxis. Taxi-drivers are legally entitled to charge you 25% "night charge" after 11 PM, but their "10% extra charge" story is bosh at all other times. You're free to tip drivers liberally if they have been particularly helpful. In Old Delhi, you can get about the bazaars by cycle-rickshaw or horse-drawn *tonga* — both are good for laid-back, open-air sightseeing.

WHAT TO SEE AND DO

Most travelers are still working off jet-lag when they arrive in Delhi and spend their first couple of days simply getting acquainted with the Indian sights, sounds, and smells of their immediate neighborhood. If you're not in the mood for a foray into the Old City or over the ramparts of Tughluqabad, try the tourist office's four-hour morning tour. It will whisk you around many of Delhi's far-flung places of interest, allowing you to see a sizeable chunk of the city's most famous sights with minimal effort and expenditure. (See GENERAL INFORMATION, page 102, on where to book conducted tours). If you want to tackle Delhi's sights at your own pace, then the suggested routes below should serve as a useful framework, best spread over three or four days.

Old Delhi: Mosques and Moneylenders
Make Shah Jahan's medieval walled city your first sightseeing stop in Delhi for a taste of the "real" India. It's a total contrast to Lutyens' spacious green city, a place of vibrant color, tangled alleys, pungent scents, and frenetic crowds. Here you can stroll in Chandni Chowk's bazaars and visit Jama Masjid and old Delhi's majestic centerpiece, the Red Fort. This combined destination will probably fill an entire day.

Old Delhi is dominated by the gigantic rust-colored **Red Fort**, or Lal Qila, which looms 18.5 m (60 ft) at its highest watchtowers and is enclosed by nearly two and a half kilometers (one and a half miles) of snaking battlements. The fortress-palace became the courtly hub of the Mughal empire when Shah Jahan decided to shift the seat of power from Agra to Delhi, sparking a construction boom between 1638 and 1648 to create his new capital, Shahjahanabad. The emperor-architect prided himself on the unequaled grandeur of the Red Fort — no small thing for the man who designed the Taj Mahal — and tantalizing reports of his precious gem-studded palace, its marbled fountains, the ceremonial pomp, and above all, his solid gold jewel-encrusted Peacock Throne spread the Red Fort's fame. Shah Jahan was soon deposed by his fanatical son, Aurangzeb, who was the last of the Great Mughals to rule from Delhi. Shah Jahan's palace, once considered a symbol of monumental wealth, now has a desolate, plundered look — all its precious gems, gilt, and silver were plucked bare in the aftermath of the 1857 mutiny.

Entry is through the massive **Lahore Gate**, so-named because it faces Lahore in what is now Pakistan. It leads you into the vaulted shopping arcade known as **Chatta Chowk**, formerly where royal *memsahibs* would inspect the latest creations of court goldsmiths, jewelers and weavers, but today full of "antiques" (usually "aged" by pros down in the old city), tourist junk, and frantically gesticulating touts.

At the end of Chatta Chowk is the two-storied **Naubat Khana**, where court musicians used to serenade passing nobles on their way across the garden to the colonnaded **Diwan-i-Am**, or public audience hall. This was a sort of impromptu law court where any commoner had the right to plea their case before the emperor, who gazed down from an ornate palanquined platform. Beyond lies a large formal garden and six palace *mahals*, through which ran the network of lotus-shaped marble fountains Shah Jahan named Naher-i-Bahisht or "Stream of Paradise," which has sadly been allowed to fall into disrepair. To the far right is **Mumtaz Mahal**, now a museum open from 9 AM to 5 PM, and close to it is **Rang Mahal**, once an elaborate painted boudoir. As you move left, you'll pass through the emperor's former trio of apartments known collectively as the **Khas Mahal**.

The palace's citadel was the adjoining **Diwan-i-Khas**, the majestic private audience hall where the emperor received his most important visitors, seated on his priceless Peacock Throne. The name came from two peacock forms outlined in jewels and forming the main part of the design. After the plundering Nadir Shah took it back with him to Persia, it was broken up and so no longer survives. Shah Jahan's famous inscription can still be seen above the entrance to the hall. Close by are the **hamams**, or baths, where royal parties took hot saunas and perfumed baths and could cool off by parading down the fort wall, which overlooks the Yamuna River. Next to the baths is Aurangzeb's **Moti Masjid**, or Pearl Mosque, built in 1622 for his own private worship.

Note that the Red Fort has a highly recommended **sound-and-light show** nightly that dramatizes the Red Fort's history. English performances are held at 7:30 PM from November to January, at 8:30 PM from February to April, and at 9 PM from May to August.

Directly opposite the Red Fort sprawls **Chandni Chowk's** arterial row of bustling bazaars. It was laid out in 1648 by Shah Jahan's daughter Jahanara Begum with a central canal flanked by merchants and nobles' mansions. Despite the invasion of buzzing traffic, the essential nature of the place has changed little over the centuries. Be warned, however, it takes a long-term resident to navigate its maze of narrow alleys — the visitor must be prepared to be happily lost. There will be plenty to feast your eyes on: scrawny coolies laboring under impossible burdens; pavement barbers lathering and snipping up a storm; street photographers immortalizing clients with turn-of-the-century cameras; matronly hagglers scouring the jewelry stalls for bargains; wobbling rickshaws carting mountains of satiated shoppers home; and perhaps the odd ash-smeared ascetic waving a trident and a begging bowl.

Chandni Chowk's historic lanes offer the most in thrills and spills — **Pul-ki-Mandi** for flowers; **Dariba Kalan** for moneylenders, weight-priced gold and silver; **Kinari Galli** for wedding garb, tinsel and turbans; and **Nai Sarak** for perfume. And don't forget **Paratha Wallah Gully**, the Alley of the Bread Sellers (see WHERE TO EAT, page 116), if all this walking has given you an appetite.

The push and shove of the bazaar can be exhausting. If your nerves begin to go, climb aboard a cycle-rickshaw and let your driver worry about navigational hazards while you take in the view.

At the eastern end of the Chowk is the seventeenth-century **Digambar Jain Mandir**, better known by tourists for the **Bird Hospital** within its grounds, where hundreds of sick birds are administered splints and medicine and even given ceremonial cremations on the banks of the Yamuna if they die. Non-vegetarian birds, like vultures, are considered spiritually unclean, and are only allowed in as "outpatients"! Visitors are welcome and donations help keep the birds in grain.

From here, just let your feet wander. Landmarks include the seventeenth-century Sikh **Gurudwara Sisgani**, dedicated to Tegh Bahadur, a Sikh guru beheaded by Aurangzeb, and the *kotawali* (police station) where the British hanged mutineers after the 1857 Mutiny. Make sure you pay a visit to the lively **Spice Market** at the end of the Chowk near Fatehpuri Masjid.

It's impossible to miss the tapering minarets and onion domes of the **Jama Masjid**, India's largest mosque, opposite the Red Fort. Built predominantly from red sandstone and white marble and adorned with exquisite Mughal inlay, it was commissioned by Shah Jahan in 1644 and completed by Aurangzeb 14 years later. There are three main gateways, each approached by steep flights of stairs (the magnificent eastern gate was reserved for the Emperor riding in magnificent procession to attend Friday prayers). It's the epicenter of India's Muslim community — you'll notice black flags, which mourn the death of Muslims in communal violence — and on Fridays and during Islamic festivals thousands of white-capped devotees prostrate themselves in its central courtyard, which accommodates up to 20,000. A small booth at the entrance sells tickets to the 46-m (150-ft)-high **South Minaret**, where a 122-step climb earns you one of the best views across the old city. Women must be accompanied by "responsible family members," a rule imposed after several incidents of molestation up in the tower. Within the courtyard is a small marble crypt containing various treasures—an alleged whisker from the Prophet's beard, the imprint of his foot at Mecca, and ancient Urdu parchments.

Civil Lines: The Cusp of Old and New

Civil Lines was the British cantonment in Delhi before New Delhi was dreamt up. North of the old city near Kashmiri Gate, the area is dotted with crumbling historic homes — the scene of brutal murders of Europeans during the 1857 Mutiny — worth a stroll if you are especially fascinated by the Raj era in India.

Places of interest include the Greco-colonial **St. James Church** (consecrated in 1836), built by the larger than life Sir James Skinner, the son of a Scotsman and his Rajput mistress, who founded the Indian Army's yellow-clad Skinner's Horse Cavalry Regiment. Inside are beautiful stained-glass windows, oak pews, and fascinating plaques to deceased "Who's Who" of nineteenth century Anglo-India, swarms of whom perished at the sepoys' hands. Skinner's own tomb is by the altar and his many family members were buried outside. When he died 64 men contested his estate claiming they were his sons. Sunday services are held in English, but at all other times, between 8 AM and 5 PM, a church attendant should be on call to let you in with a key.

Nearby you can also see the nineteenth century **Lothian Road** and **Nicholson Cemeteries** and the once select, now seedy **Raj-era Mall** near Kashmiri Gate.

On Rani Jhansi Road, which winds uphill onto North Ridge, you'll see the **Mutiny Memorial**, known as "Jeetgarh" or victory fort, which looks like a lopped-off Gothic cathedral spire. It marks the spot where the party of cholera-stricken, beleaguered British, Gurkha, and Sikh soldiers camped out for several weeks before mounting their assault and commemorates those who died in the attempt. Farther up the road on your right is a motley-looking **Ashoka Pillar**, (third century BC) patched up after being broken into many pieces and with most of its Brahma script worn away. It was brought to Delhi by Feroz Shah Tughluq, a Sultan of the fourteenth century. **Flagstaff Tower** stands on the crest, slightly off the road, with a gate entrance. Terrified British *memsahibs* and children fled here on May 11, 1857 as sepoys began rampaging in Civil Lines. The nearby **Oberoi Maidens Hotel** is a good place for a tea break.

Several other Raj-era treasures lurk nearby, difficult to hunt down unless you are especially zealous. Closest are the **Old Secretariat** just north of here and the once-magnificent **Metcalfe House**, located not far from Delhi University at the northern end of Mahatma Gandhi Road. Built in 1835 it was the museum-piece home of Sir Thomas Metcalfe, British Resident of the Mughal Court, who transferred all his family art treasures from England to India. Metcalfe died in this house in 1853. It was later occupied by his nephew, Sir Theophilus, Joint Magistrate and a key figure in rousing Delhi's Europeans to arms against the mutineers.

New Delhi: Imperial Inheritance

In New Delhi, start with **Connaught Place**, built to commemorate the Duke of Connaught's visit in 1920. This paint-splintered ring of ever-widening colonial arcades is lined with dusty shop fronts, airline offices, restaurants, and squatting merchants selling everything from piles of books to shoeshines. Other eccentric Raj-era oddities can still be ferreted out, like solar topees, military attire, and old regimental silver — or you can pick through Janpath's overflowing Tibetan market — and there's plenty to occupy an entire morning.

Leaving Connaught Place, turn down Sansad Marg to arrive at the **Jantar Mantar**, the astronomical observatory of Maharaja Jai Singh II of Jaipur. Built of sandstone and marble in 1724, this was the experimental prototype of five similar structures scattered across India, the most famous of which can be seen in Jaipur. It comprises four "instruments," including the huge "Prince of Dials" sundial, each designed to measure with exactitude the position of the sun, planets, and stars, as well as to predict eclipses. Set in pretty gardens, it's open from sunrise to 10 PM daily.

Hail an auto-rickshaw to visit the garishly elaborate **Lakshmi Narayan Temple**, on Mandir Marg, west of Connaught Place, built by the industrialist Birla family in 1938, and usually referred to as the **Birla Temple**. A "modern" Hindu, Birla wanted his temple to symbolize unity of faith so he broke all the traditional rules and caste barriers and came up with something novel. Constructed from a medley of different stones instead of the usual sandstone or marble, it is a mixture of many different types of Hindu architecture, but more radically, it's open to all Hindus, including harijans, or untouchables. And instead of being dedicated to just one god, it not only worships a whole gamut, but incorporates icons of other religions too, including Buddhist and Sikh wall frescoes and a giant Chinese Buddhist bronze bell. The main attraction is Krishna's mirrored shrine, designed to reflect the deity's face whichever way you look at it.

OPPOSITE: TOP: Old traditions live on at Delhi's Polo Club. BOTTOM: The Lodhi Tombs, in the gardens of the same name — one of Delhi's most restful retreats.

It's a short rickshaw hop to **Sansad Bhavan**, the circular colonnaded house of parliament designed by Lutyens' colleague, Sir Herbert Baker. Originally created for the Chamber of Princes, the Council of State, and the Legislative Assembly, it now houses the Rajya Sabha (Upper House) and Lok Sabha (House of the People). It's quite easy to arrange a visit to watch India's political turbines churning — sessions are often, in *Times of India* parlance, "uproarious" and when tempers run high, certain members of parliament have been known to hurl their shoes in rage. Contact your embassy for a letter of introduction and then go to the reception office on Raisina Road for a pass for front row seats.

Beyond is Lutyens' magisterial Indo-Baroque **Rastrapati Bhavan**, the former Viceroy's Palace now used as the official residence of India's president and flanked by imposing secretariat blocks, both inaugurated in 1931. As pompous and awe-inspiring as this sprawling apparatus of empire was, the British proved only temporary tenants, and its keys were handed to India's politicians only 16 years after its inauguration. Somewhere beneath the palace lies a foundation stone originally laid by King George and Queen Mary. It was originally laid at a site later deemed impractical because too far north of the old city, so to save face the stones were secretly exhumed at night and carted off to the new site. Lutyens never really forgave his collaborator, Sir Herbert Baker, for miscalculating the steep gradient of the slope upon which this complex stands — the result of which obscured the view from India Gate up to Lutyens' Rastrapati Bhavan. You can wander through the main entrances of Baker's secretariat buildings, now North and South blocks, where crucial executive decisions are made in an ambience rendered eccentric by nesting pigeons, aged shuffling tea "boys," and huge stacks of yellowing files.

Curious tourists aren't allowed inside Rastrapati Bhavan (where servants still use bicycles to get from one wing to another) but you can visit the adjacent four-hectare (10-acre) **Mughal Gardens** between February and March when they are gloriously in bloom.

At the end of stately Rajpath is **India Gate**, the 42-m (138-ft)-tall memorial arch with its "eternal flame." The arch was built by the British in memory of the 90,000 Indian soldiers killed during the World War I, and in the ill-fated 1919 Afghan expedition. After the 1971 war with Pakistan, Indira Gandhi added a smaller arch to honor even more war casualties. Enveloping it is the **Maidan**, the imperial village green, which is mowed by oxen and is a magnet on hot summer nights for ice cream *wallahs*, lolling families, and courting couples.

The Historic Trail

Delhi's most famous landmark, the **Qutb Minar**, is best visited in the sunlit peace of early morning (avoiding scrums of tourists and irritating "hullooing" touts). Located about nine and a half kilometers (four miles) south of New Delhi this "tower of victory" was the Empire State Building of ancient India — and at 72.5 m (239 ft) high it's still the country's tallest man-made tower. It was built by the Turkic "Slave king" Qutb-ud-Din Aybak in 1199 to celebrate his victory over Delhi's last Hindu ruler. Modeled on the tower at Ghazni and adorned with Islamic arches, motifs, and bold script, the red sandstone and marble five-storied structure has survived lightning and earthquakes (which destroyed the topmost cupola in 1803, at that time enjoyed by Europeans as a surreptitious picnic spot). After a gruesome accident in which many people were killed in 1981, visitors are not allowed up its tower stairway for spectacular views.

Within the Qutb Minar complex lies Delhi's first mosque, the **Quwwat-ul-Islam,** or the Might of Islam. Begun in 1193 it was modeled on the Prophet's house in Medina and built with many decorative remnants from 27 demolished Hindu temples — images of gods and goddesses that the Muslims found offensive were defaced and turned inward. Within the mosque's courtyard is the Iron Pillar, erected here in the fifth century. According to lore, if you stand with your back against the pillar and clasp your hands around it, your wish will be granted. See also the richly carved tomb of Aybak's son-in-law Iltutish, built in 1235, and the structures erected by the Khalji ruler Alauddin, the architect of Delhi's second city at Siri: the Alai-Darwaza (south gateway); the vast base and unfinished 27-m (88-ft)-high Alai Minar tower; and his own tomb amid the rubble of his college for Islamic studies.

From here you can either drive eastwards to the rampart ruins of **Tughluqabad** (from which the huge amphitheater at Suraj Kund is a convenient detour south) or head back into residential New Delhi to explore some of the city's remaining monuments and tombs.

Should you take the latter course, bear in mind there is no need to tackle them all at once — in fact it's best to leave them until you feel in the mood for a quiet garden stroll away from the hectic bedlam of Delhi proper. Like all Delhi's historic places, they are open from sunrise to sunset.

Start perhaps with **Safdarjang Tomb** at the end of Lodi Road. It was built from 1753 to 1754 for the second Nawab of Oudh, Safdar Jang, making it one of the last of the great garden tombs to be constructed by the waning Mughals.

It's barely two minutes stroll to the **Lodi Gardens**, a picturesque necropolis of over 50 large octagonal-shaped, blue-domed tombs that date from the Sayyid (1414–1451) and Lodi dynasties (1451–1526), set amid a leafy park. Schoolboys play cricket on the green, retired civil servants read Hindu epics to rapt cross-legged illiterates, *ayah's* wander about with toddlers in tow, and politicians and diplomats jog breathlessly here. Tombs litter the gardens, although sadly a large number have been defaced by graffiti. Look especially for the Bara Gumbad with its large dome and the Sheesh Gumbad, which still has much of its blue-tiled roof intact and which sports splendid inlay floral designs on its exterior. The tomb of Muhammad Shah here, which was erected in 1450, is one of the earliest prototypes of Mughal design.

A far more sophisticated version of this basic design can be seen at **Humayun's Tomb**, at the intersection of Lodi Road and Mathura Road (half-an-hour's stroll further on). Flanked by four impressive archways and four garden squares, this black and white marble and red sandstone tomb is considered to be the architectural precursor to the Taj Mahal, with its octagonal base plan, grand arches, a lofty double dome, and fountains in its central canal.

The tomb was built between 1555 and 1569 by Humayun's senior widow, known as Haji Begum, nine years after the emperor's death. Her tomb lies here, along with those of other Mughal royals, including that of Dara Sikoh, Shah Jahan's favorite son. It was at Humayun's Tomb that the last of the Mughals, Bahadur Shah Zafar, hid before giving himself up to the British—his two sons were killed here by a trigger-happy officer.

The Lodi-style tomb outside belongs to the nobleman Isa Khan and was built in 1547; the Mughal-style tomb of Khan-i-Khanan, a military general under Akbar, was built in 1627. Across the road is the fourteenth century Sufi village of **Nizamuddin**, which is still an exclusively Muslim precinct, having sprung up around the *dargah* (shrine) of Sufi saint Sheikh Nizamuddin Christi. He died in 1325 at the age of 92, and his tomb is the most famous in the village's Muslim cemetery. Life here follows a medieval pattern: women live in strict purdah; goats are tethered in mud-bricked courtyards; shop stalls are a jumble of perfumed rose water, embroidered caps and hookah pipes. To reach the shrine, take the narrow path near the police station on Mathura Road. Along with Ajmer in Rajasthan, Niza-muddin attracts flocks of pilgrims for the Urs festival (dates vary from year to year) with poetry readings, fairs and performances of *qawwalis*, or mystical verses.

From here, it's only a ten-minute rickshaw ride north along Mathura Road to **Purana Qila**, which is said to straddle the legendary city of Indraprastha. The walled fort's original structure was initiated by Humayun, but the Afghan

Sher Shah expanded it from 1538 to 1545 in the interim decade before the ousted emperor returned from his exile to wrest Delhi back. Two main gateways still stand — the northern Talaqi Darwaza or "Forbidden Gate" and the southern Lal Darwaza, which overlooks Delhi's Zoo. Inside look for the Sher Mandal, a two-storied octagonal tower which Humayun had converted into his library. A year later he stumbled on the stairs in his haste to attend the muezzin's call to prayer, dying from his injuries three days later. Just beyond is Sher Shah's **Qila-i-Kuhna** mosque (1541) as well as an interesting museum housing the site's archaeological finds, which date back to 1000 BC.

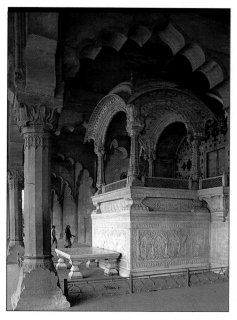

Purana Qila is flanked by **Delhi Zoo**, India's largest. It is open-plan with water canals rather than cages and is notable for its rare white tigers. Opening hours are 9 AM to 5 PM daily, except Fridays.

The nearby **Pragati Maiden** exhibition grounds, built for the Asian Games in 1982, are worth visiting for their excellent **Crafts Museum**. It displays traditional icons, rare religious wooden figurines, tribal *bhutas* (folk deities) from Karnataka, terracotta figures from Tamil Nadu, textiles, and brass crafts and utensils. Outside is a "village" collection of rustic huts peculiar to each Indian state, and a courtyard where village artisans are invited to demonstrate how traditional Indian

ABOVE: The emperor's marble canopied throne, within the Red Fort's Diwan-i-Am public audience hall. OVERLEAF: Impregnable and forbidding, the Lahore Gate looms at the entrance to the Red Fort, flanked by crenelated battlements.

crafts are made. You can buy Rajasthani fabrics, terracotta pottery, bronze miniatures, Hyderabadi *bidri* ware, and many other crafts at reasonable prices. It's open 9:30 AM to 6 PM and the crafts demonstration program lasts from October 1 to June 30.

Slightly northeast of this area on Mathura Road is Delhi's fifth city, **Feroz Shah Kotla** (or Ferozabad), built during the fourteenth century by Emperor Feroz Shah Tughluq. Much of it was wrecked to build Shahjahanabad, but its ruins are still impressive and contain one of Ashoka's inscribed pillars dating back to the third century BC. From here it's a 10 minute walk northeast down Mahatma Gandhi Road to **Raj Ghat** on the banks

of the Yamuna River. A simple black marble slab marks the place where Mahatma Gandhi was cremated following his assassination on Friday, 31 January 1948. Members of India's ruling Nehru dynasty have had their funeral pyres here: Jawaharlal Nehru, India's first prime minister in 1964; then his grandson, the heir-apparent Sanjay Gandhi in 1980; Indira Gandhi in 1984; and Rajiv Gandhi in 1991. Various dignitaries have planted trees including Mikhail Gorbachev, Queen Elizabeth II, Gough Whitlam, Dwight Eisenhower, and Ho Chi Minh. Opposite Raj Ghat is the **Gandhi Memorial Museum**, open 9:30 AM to 5:30 PM except Mondays.

Museum Round-Up

If you have time, Delhi's lesser-visited sights are very worthwhile. The **National Museum**, on Janpath just below the Rajpath intersection,

contains one of the largest and most precious collections of Indian art and artifacts. It houses many key finds from the prehistoric and Indus Valley civilizations, terracotta figures dating from the seventh and eighth centuries, miniature paintings, and sculpture from the Maurya, Gandhara and Gupta periods. Central Asian antiquities are well represented (with some Tibetan objects secretly smuggled out of Lhasa during the Younghusband mission in 1904), and there's a wing devoted to folk, classical, and tribal musical instruments. The museum shop offers inexpensive replicas of famous sculptures and shows good films at 2:30 PM on Saturdays and Wednesdays. The museum is open daily except Mondays from 10 AM to 5 PM.

Since her December 1984 assassination, Indira Gandhi's residence has been preserved as the **Indira Gandhi Memorial**, at 1 Safdarjang Road. It is now a museum featuring a photographic display along with many of the former prime minister's personal effects. Her recorded voice accompanies visitors through the garden, and the site where she fell is covered by glass, her blood stains preserved.

For another chapter in India's modern history, go to the **Nehru Memorial Museum** on Teen Murti Road near Chanakyapuri, where the residence of India's first prime minister has been converted into a fascinating repository of documents and photographs about his life. There's a sound-and-light show every night about Nehru and the independence movement. To see where Mahatma Gandhi was killed, visit the **Gandhi Smriti Museum** in Tees January Road. All three museums are open from 10 AM to 5 PM and are closed Mondays.

Rail buffs won't need encouragement to visit Delhi's interesting **Rail Transport Museum** in Chanakyapuri (behind the Bhutanese Embassy), where highlights include an 1855 steam engine, a 1908 Viceregal dining coach, and a museum stuffed with fascinating rail lore: the most eccentric exhibit is the fractured skull of a wild elephant that charged a Calcutta-bound train in 1894. Original sepia plates of trains are also on sale for around US$25 to US$50. Opening hours are 8:30 AM to 11:30 PM and 4 PM to 7:30 PM (April to June), 10:30 AM to 5 PM (July to March).

Other notable museums include: the **International Dolls Museum** on Bahadur Shah Zafar Road, with over 6,000 dolls from 85 different countries; the **National Gallery of Modern Art** on Dr. Zakir Hussain Road near India Gate; and **Tibet House**, 1 Institutional Area, Lodi Road, which displays ceremonial items brought out of Tibet when the Dalai Lama fled the Chinese invasion. Tibetan handicrafts are sold, and there are often lectures and discussion sessions, which visitors are welcome to join.

Shopping

If you plan to return from India laden with exotic purchases, then Delhi is the best place for serious shopping. As India's competitive marketplace, its shops are overflowing with goods from all over the country. Hard bargaining pays off in Delhi as prices are often hugely inflated for the tourist market — but often dropped just as quickly for the city-wise. The biggest center is **Connaught Place** and this is the best place to start browsing are at the fixed-price **Government Emporia**. Even if you don't buy anything here, you'll gain an insight into the range, quality, and price of goods to expect in bazaars and shops elsewhere.

The two-storied, merchandise-crammed **Central Cottage Industries Emporium ℂ** (011) 332 1909, on Janpath, has a fine range of fabrics, crafts, furniture, pottery, carpets, *dhurries* (flat-weave floor coverings), and jewelry. On the other side of Connaught Place on Bhagat Kharak Singh Marg you'll find the long row of state emporia, each specializing in the crafts of a single state — they make a fascinating morning's excursion. Especially good are **Poompuhar** (Tamil Nadu), for colorful appliqued lanterns and umbrellas; **Zoon** (Kashmir), for carpets and shawls, giant terracotta animals, bronzes, and papier-mâché masks; **Bihar,** for fine raw silk; **Nagaland,** for woven tribal rugs and bamboo baskets; **Orissa,** for unusual *ikat* fabrics and toys; and **Gujarat,** for fine weavings, embroidered fabrics, and lacquered furniture. The only drawback with the state emporia (open 10 AM to 6 PM) is the archaic system of sale (bills in triplicate done at one counter, collection at another).

Also in Connaught Place, in the Regal Building, is **Khadi Gramadyog Bhavan**, which has a fascinating assortment of goodies ranging from handmade paper to khadi cotton. The underground bazaar of **Palika** in Connaught Place has over 400 stalls with a wide range of products. It's a good place to hone your bargaining skills.

Despite the good shopping, it's a good idea to get out of the Connaught Place area and explore some of the shopping centers that are popular with locals. **Hauz Khas Village**, in particular, is worth a visit. It is located southwest of town, about 10 km (six miles) from Connaught Place. Restaurants, galleries, and stylish boutiques abound, and it's possible to shop for everything from antiques to high fashion. The **Ambawatta Complex** at Mehrauli Village, about 15 km (nine miles) southwest of Connaught Place, is another high-fashion stop, and also features tasteful furnishings at the Good Earth shop.

All the main hotels have shopping arcades, but the best are found at the Taj Group's **Khazana** shops, at the Maurya and the Imperial.

Aside from Chandni Chowk's curio shops (clustered around the Jama Masjid), it's fun to witness the lively Sunday market along Mahatma Gandhi Road, known as **Chow Bazaar**. Originally started during the Mughal period, this Indian version of London's Portabello Road has an extraordinary assortment of old and new. Crowds also come to see itinerant circus performers doing death-defying stunts.

For essential oils, rose water, henna, and ornate sandstone-carved bottles — all perfect for gifts — visit the unique **Chhabra Perfumery** at R-Expo, 1115 Main Bazaar, Paharganj.

For antiques and curios you need go no further than **Sunder Nagar Market**, located midway between the Oberoi Hotel and Purana Qila on Dr. Zakir Hussain Road, with some 40 antique and art shops. If you're unsure about the authenticity of an antique or item of jewelry, you and the shop-owner can always pay a visit to the National Museum or to the Government Gem Laboratory on Barakhamba Road.

Delhi is an excellent place to stock up on reading material before heading farther afield. At Khan Market (near Lodi Gardens) **The Bookshop** has up-to-date book releases. On Connaught Place, head to the **Oxford Book House** in Scindia House. The **Bookworm**, 29 B Connaught Place, is also worth a visit.

For the finest Indian tea, also prettily gift-wrapped, go to the **Tea Room Aap Ki Pasand**, Netaji Subhas Road, opposite Golcha Cinema in Old Delhi. Stop here after exploring the old city and for delicious iced lemon tea. Shops in general are open from 10 AM to 6 PM daily except Sundays.

WHERE TO STAY

Delhi is one of India's busiest entry points for foreign visitors, expatriates, and business people. On the accommodation front it has everything from five-star deluxe hotels sporting international standards and international rates to budget dives that cost no more than a few dollars a night.

Luxury

Don't expect bargains at Delhi's luxury hotels. Rates of US$250 and upward are the norm at the best establishments. But you can at least expect top-notch facilities: excellent restaurants, 24-hour coffee shops, recreational facilities and swimming pools (a definite plus during summer), business desks, travel agents, shopping arcades, bakeries, bars, astrologers, and discotheques.

Most of the luxury hotels are miles away from the center of town (close to the city's Fort Knox grid of diplomatic embassies at Chanakyapuri), a downside when it comes to sightseeing but a

A paan-wallah awaits customers in Chandni Chowk.

plus for those in need of respite from the maddening congestion of central Delhi. Advance bookings are recommended for five-star accommodation, particularly during the peak season months between October and March.

Making recommendations in the top league — for which you can expect to pay around US$300 a night — is no easy matter as competition is stiff. The Oberoi Intercontinental, New Delhi Hilton, Le Meridien, Maurya Sheraton, Taj Palace, and Taj Mahal hotels all rank amongst the best in the Sub-Continent and offer very similar standards at very similar rates.

Location is critical for some travelers and, if this is the case for you, **Le Meridien Hotel** ((011) 3710101 FAX (011) 3714545, Windsor Place, Janpath, is a good choice. The futuristic atrium is not to everyone's taste, but the facilities and restaurants are topnotch.

Similarly well situated is the **New Delhi Hilton** ((011) 3320101 FAX (011) 3325335, Barakhamba Avenue. One of its most popular features is its third-floor terrace swimming pool — the perfect place to be on a sweltering Delhi afternoon.

Most of Delhi's other five-star luxury hotels are south of the city center. **The Oberoi Intercontinental** ((011) 4363030 FAX (011) 4360484, Dr. Zakir Hussain Road, is recommended. It overlooks a golf course and is easily one of Delhi's most opulent places to stay.

Similarly exclusive is the **Maurya Sheraton** (Welcomgroup) ((011) 6112233 FAX (011) 6113333, Sadar Patel Marg, which has some very highly rated restaurants and a solar-heated swimming pool (if you happen to find yourself in Delhi during its brief winter).

Those who enjoy the grand style of the Taj chain should stay at the **Taj Mahal Hotel** ((011) 3016162 FAX (011) 3017299, 1 Mansingh Road, which is one of the Taj group's best: impeccable service, lavishly fitted, with some of the city's best views.

Several impeccably-kept colonial hotels offer less expensive elegance with plenty of period flair as well as efficiency for those arriving in Delhi to embark on their Indian adventure. The fairly central **Claridges** ((011) 3010211 FAX (011) 3010625, 12 Aurangzeb Road, offers room rates at about half the price of the five-star deluxe chains and is housed in a delightful, pukka Georgian-style building. Facilities include a swimming pool, lawn tennis, restaurant dining, and a health club.

Less expensive again and less conveniently located is the **Oberoi Maidens,** ((011) 2525464 FAX (011) 2915134, 7 Sham Nath Marg, built in 1900 just north of Old Delhi, in the former Raj

cantonment of Civil Lines. It has spacious, comfortable rooms and, if such things are important to you, this is where Lutyens stayed as he planned his new city. The gardens are a particularly welcome feature in frenetic Delhi.

The **Hotel Imperial** ((011) 3341234 FAX (011) 3342255 has a lot to recommend it: reasonable room rates, a peaceful garden and a great location on central Janpath. Inside you will find a refurbished 1930s decor, a good shopping arcade, a swimming pool, a period bar, and a pretty terrace and lawn for al fresco meals and afternoon teas. The Imperial Hotel, like the Ashok, Claridges, Maurya, and the Kanishka hotels, allow non-guests to use their pool for a small fee.

Mid-range

Mid-range travelers have a good range of centrally located hotels to choose from. It is, however, essential to book ahead, as the more popular hotels rarely have vacancies at short notice.

The **Ambassador Hotel** ((011) 4632600 FAX (011) 4632252, Sujan Singh Park, is at the upper end of the middle category but comes complete with a swathe of facilities. The South Indian restaurant downstairs is very highly regarded by Delhiites.

The **Lodhi Hotel** ((011) 4362422 FAX (011) 4360883, also in south Delhi, on Lala Rajput Rai Path, is less expensive. It has comfortable rooms and an excellent restaurant.

Nirula's ((011) 3322419 FAX (011) 3324669, L Block, Connaught Place, is as central as it is possible to be, located right next to one of New Delhi's most popular restaurant complexes. Room rates are very reasonable given the well-appointed rooms and excellent location.

Also on Connaught Place and a super value is the **Hotel Fifty-Five** ((011) 3321244 FAX (011) 3320769, H Block, Connaught Place. This small, award-winning hotel has just 15 rooms so advance bookings are essential.

The ITDC-run **Ashok Yatri Niwas** ((011) 3344511 FAX 3368153, 19 Ashoka Road, is a less personal but similarly priced choice. It's a giant 545-roomed complex with basic but adequate rooms and a good South Indian restaurant.

Lastly, the most popular of Delhi's four "Y's" is the **YMCA Tourist Hostel** ((011) 3746668 FAX (011) 3746032, near the Regal Cinema on Jai Singh Road. It offers excellent value, with comfortable single rooms, a good restaurant, and gardens.

Budget

The budget center of Delhi is the Main Bazaar of the Paharganj area, opposite New Delhi station. It's a shock to the system if you are a new arrival in India, but for those with the stomach for it, Paharganj combines a convenient location (you can walk from the station) with a wide range of

---

The twelfth century Qutb Minar, with its intricately fretted and embellished tower, seen through the archways of India's oldest mosque, the Quwwat-ul-Islam.

inexpensive accommodation options. You are advised to ignore the touts who work this area and choose your own room.

A recommended choice on Main Bazaar itself is the **Vivek Hotel (** (011) 7777062 FAX (011) 7537103, at 1534 50 Main Bazaar. The rooftop restaurant is popular by night and the "air-cooled" and air-conditioned rooms, complete with hot showers, are good value.

Delhi's most famous — read notorious — budget hotel is the **Ringo Guesthouse (** (011) 3310605, 17 Scindia House, not far from Connaught Place, an institution that has been providing dormitory beds and stuffy private rooms to overlanding backpackers for as long as

and exotic spices which the Mughals brought with them when they left Persia in the sixteenth century. It's served with a variety of breads to mop up its sauces, the most popular being the delicious fluffy, yogurt-leavened *naan*, which is baked clinging to the side of a tandoor clay oven. Other flat breads include wholewheat *rotis*; *romali* (handkerchief) *rotis*, or *parathas*, layered and stuffed with minced meat or *paneer* cheese — almost a meal in themselves.

Tandoori mutton, poultry, and fish are a famous Mughalai specialty. These dishes attain their distinctive succulence from being marinated in a mixture of yogurt, crushed garlic, turmeric, salt, and sometimes papaya pulp. Then, skewered, they

anyone can remember. A recommendation is perhaps not in order, but there is no denying the continuing popularity of this place.

WHERE TO EAT

As the nation's cosmopolitan capital, Delhi offers some great eating experiences. You can either dine at its luxury hotels which employ top chefs and usually have a varied range of Indian, Western, and Chinese restaurants and coffee shops, or there's a wide choice of well-established eating houses scattered across town.

Indian Cuisine

Delhi is probably the best place in the world to sample delicious, authentic north Indian Mughalai food. This strongly meat-based cuisine is very rich, redolent of the thick yogurt, onions,

are cooked over the tandoor's glowing coals. Don't be alarmed by the fiery red of your tandoori chicken — the color comes from the marinade, not from being smothered with chilies!

There is also the classic *biryani* of basmati rice and spiced meat cooked with saffron in a sealed pot to sticky, fragrant perfection. Another favorite is chicken Mughalai, which comes in a thick, creamy sauce with onions, cashews, and raisins. Mughalai vegetable dishes tend to be equally sumptuous. Try *dal makhni* (rich spiced lentils with coriander), *shahi paneer* (cheese in cream and tomatoes), *khatte alloo* (spiced potatoes), or *baingan mumtaz* (stuffed eggplant).

Desserts are generally prepared from milk or Indian cottage cheese that is flavored with cardamom or saffron. *Firni* is the most popular, a kind of exotic rice pudding served in earthenware bowl. There's also *kheer*, a rich thickened milk with raisins and nuts, and a summer favorite is *khulfi*: Indian ice cream accompanied by transparent sweet vermicelli called *falooda*.

Foreigners and diplomats who live and work in Delhi swear that the major hotels offer the best cuisine, and they rate the Maurya Sheraton and the Oberoi Intercontinental as two of the very best (see WHERE TO STAY, above). Arguably, these two hotels offer the most memorable Mughalai cuisine in town. Naturally, you can expect to pay much more — perhaps US$10 more per head — eating in these restaurants than you would if you ate elsewhere in Delhi. But it remains absurdly good value if you consider what a comparable meal would cost at home. Imported wines and spirits will rapidly escalate costs. Reservations are strongly recommended: popular restaurants are lionized by socializing Delhiites.

The Maurya Sheraton's very elegant restaurant, the **Dum Pukht** ((011) 6112233, recreates the aristocratic traditions and atmosphere of the nabobs. Also at the Sheraton is the popular **Bukhara** ((011)6112233,renowned for its delicious northwest frontier dishes, notably its succulent *raan*, or roasted spiced lamb, chicken *tikka*, and charcoal-grilled kebabs, all served in mock-rustic surroundings where guests are invited to put on aprons, eat with their fingers like baronial Mughals, sip frothy Indian beer from pewter goblets, and watch chefs deftly gouging rows of skewers behind huge glass windows. This place is so popular, they don't take reservations after 8:30 PM.

The Oberoi's **Kandahar** ((011) 4363030 has similarly excellent fare served in classic European surroundings, where the tone is set by bow-tied waiters, subdued lighting, and elegant silver platters; although true to Mughal form you'll find no knives or forks on the table.

For those interested in taking a look at how the less affluent enjoy their Mughalai cuisine, **Karim's** ((011) 3269880, near Jama Masjid, has been running for 70 years and is celebrated locally as probably the most authentic restaurant of its kind in Delhi.

Colonel's Kababz ((011) 4624384, Defence Colony Market, is a restaurant that enjoys immense popularity in the Defence Colony area south of Jawaharlal Nehru Stadium. From small-time beginnings there are now those who say the *tikkas* and kebabs created by the retired army colonel who runs the place rival those of the five-star hotels — and at nearly a tenth of the price! Also in the same area you will find **Sagar** ((011) 4698374, one of Delhi's best south Indian restaurants. A vegetable *thali* here costs just a few dollars.

For more exceptional south Indian food (which tends to be much lighter on the palate if you're still adjusting to the Indian diet) in more sumptuous surroundings, head for **Dasaprakash** ((011) 4632600, which is located in a cavernous, lamp-lit dome in the lobby of the Ambassador Hotel and is always crammed with avidly eating locals. Try their three-course *thali* meal; waiters are always hovering to refill your platter with varieties of *subze* (spiced vegetable dishes) and puffed *puri* bread — as much as you can put away. Fresh grape juice, *lassis*, and creamy mango milkshakes are the house specialties. Also recommended is **Sona Rupa** ((011) 3326807, 46 Janpath, where you might sample a typical Madras-style breakfast of steamed *idlis* (rice cakes) in spicy *sambar* gravy.

If you're in Connaught Place on the prowl for a solid meal, try one of Delhi's oldest, most eccentric haunts, **Gaylord** ((011) 3360717, 16 Regal Building (it opened in the early 1950s, and still retains the original waiting staff, damask tablecloths, and chandeliers), or **Kwality** ((011) 3732352, just around the corner on Sansad Marg (Parliament Street) — both are air-conditioned havens where you can feast on good Indian food for about US$8 for two.

The truly adventurous will enjoy a visit to the **Paratha Wallah Gully**, the Alley of Bread Sellers, which is wedged in Chandni Chowk's lanes. Originally established in 1875, this row of historic "cafés" is run by high-caste Brahmans employing Oliver Twist-like urchins as adept street "chefs," and over the decades has catered to everyone from colonial British administrators to jailed opposition party leaders. Its fame rests on its fresh unleavened *paratha* sprinkled with cumin, sesame, caraway, or stuffed with peas, onions, or potato. While the restaurants barely conform to Western standards of cleanliness, you'll dine extremely well here on insatiable amounts of sizzling, fragrant *paratha*, all served with rounds of delicious, freshly cooked *subze* (spiced vegetables), banana chutney, and curd. It's Chandni Chowk's most popular lunchtime spot and has an enthusiastic clientele of travelers disillusioned with the expensive, less authentic fare of New Delhi's five-star hotels. You should have no problem finding a rickshaw-*wallah* or taxi driver who knows where it is if you are in the Chandni Chowk area.

International Cuisine

On the international front, Chinese cuisine deserves a first billing simply because there is so much of it about in Delhi. Perhaps Delhi's most celebrated Chinese restaurant is the **Tea House of the August Moon** ((011) 6110202 at the Taj Palace, which comes complete with a pagoda and

Tea House of the August Moon at the Taj Palace is typical of elaborate restaurants in Delhi's five-star hotels.

goldfish pond. The *dim sum* are good. Less expensive and centrally located on B Block inner circle of Connaught Place is **Zen** ((011) 3724455, a stylish Chinese restaurant that serves up tasty and vaguely recognizable dishes in a relaxing environment.

For Continental cuisine in a Raj era setting, a visit to the Oberoi Maidens is recommended. The **Curzon Room** ((011) 2914841 is a delightful period piece, though don't be surprised to see Indian offerings on the menu nowadays.

Delhi's best formal French restaurant is the Oberoi's pricey **La Rochelle** ((011) 4363030, where you can dine on quails, oysters, and steaks and sip imported wines.

La Piazza ((011) 6181234, at the Hyatt Regency, Bhikaji Cama Place, probably has the best pizzas in town, all prepared in a wood-fired oven, but if you wander over to the E Block of Connaught Place you can find branches of both **Domino's** and **Pizza Express**.

The **Orient Express** ((011) 611 0202, at the Taj Palace, allows diners to feast in a mock-up Orient Express railway carriage. It's not a cheap night out, but the Continental four-course dinners and the nineteenth-century ambiance make for an unforgettable evening.

Connaught Place is the best area in town to seek out inexpensive international cuisine and fast food. The long-running **Nirula's**, located in L Block, Connaught Place, is an Indianized fast-food parlor that comes complete with a popular vegetarian lunch buffet. In the same complex you will also find the **Chinese Room** — Delhi's oldest

Chinese restaurant — and a cake and pastry shop, an ice cream parlor, and two popular stand-up fast-food annexes selling everything from *dal* and *chapatis* to pizzas and India's very own Campa-Cola and Thums Up.

Travel-weary Brits may be tempted to make a beeline for **Wimpy** in Connaught Place, just along from the Tourist Office at 5 Janpath, which serves burgers made from almost everything except beef, but they still taste okay.

NIGHTLIFE

While Delhi is not as lively as cosmopolitan Bombay, top classical dancers and musicians perform here far more regularly. If you're determined to experience at least something of India's dazzling cultural heritage — be it dance, drama, or music — scan the morning's *Times of India* or *Indian Express* for their daily listing of what's on, check out the *Delhi Diary* sold at most newsstands, or consult the tourist office's fortnightly *Program of Events*.

Performances tend to start around 6:30 PM and there's a central ticket office at Cottage Industries Emporium, Janpath. One regular event to catch is the Dances of India program at the **Parsi Anjuman Hall** ((011) 3318615, Bahadur Shah Zafar Road, Delhi Gate, a popular showcase of *bhavai*, *kathak* and *bharata natyam* styles. Performances begin at 7 PM every night; tickets cost US$2.50.

If you want to experience the technicolor thrills, wet saris, and outrageous fortunes of Hindi movies, join the scrums at the **Regel Cinema** complex in Connaught Place or the modern **Sheila** opposite New Delhi Railway Station. More modern cinema complexes (where you will find English movies) include the **Basant Lok** complex in Vsant Vihar and the **Satyam Cinema** in Ranjeet Nagar. The **British Council** ((011) 3711401, 17 Kasturba Gandhi Marg, has occasional screenings of more highbrow offerings.

Delhi is not particularly well endowed with bars, but for an inexpensive beer the cafés on the inner circle of Connaught Place, such as **El Rodeo**, **Zen**, and **Café 100**, are reliable options. The **Jazz Bar** ((011) 6112233, at the Maurya Sheraton is deservedly popular and as its name suggests features live jazz nightly. **Someplace Else** ((011) 3733737, at the Park Hotel on Sansad Marg, is another busy Delhi watering hole. It becomes a dance club later in the evenings.

Most discos enforce strict dress codes, have a cover charge, and will turn away unaccompanied male revelers. **Ghungroo**, at the Maurya, is popular but entry is not guaranteed if you are not staying at the hotel. **CJ's**, at Le Meridien, is also selective about who it lets through the door. If your tastes in dance music run to the conservative, **My Kind of Place**, at the Taj Palace, features "oldies but goodies."

HOW TO GET THERE

As the capital, New Delhi is second only to Bombay as a transport hub. Flights fan out from Indira Gandhi International Airport to destinations around the world, while the domestic airport (of the same name) has flights to all major — and many minor — national destinations, making Delhi an excellent place to fly into and to arrange onward travel.

Delhi has two major train stations: New Delhi station and Old Delhi station. Most trains depart from New Delhi, which is conveniently close to Connaught Place. If you have a departure from Old Delhi, always leave more time than you think you will need to get there, as traffic in the old city can be terribly congested.

The best place to make your rail bookings — and Delhi is one of the best places in India to do this — is the upstairs foreign tourist booking office at New Delhi station. Service can be a little slow at times, but it is still infinitely better than lining up local-style for a ticket downstairs.

If you're feeling adventurous you might like to head over to the Interstate Bus Terminal at Kashmir Gate to organize your own bus tickets; it's far easier of course to let an agent do this for you — any travel agent will deal in bus tickets.

For the most part, travelers opt to leave and arrive in Delhi by rail or air, but for certain destinations — Katmandu, Shimla, and Dharamsala, for example — the bus is the only option for those who are watching their money, or who don't have time to wait for a seat on limited flights. In some rare cases, such as the bus services to Jaipur, it is actually quicker to travel by bus than it is by train.

CORBETT NATIONAL PARK

India's most famous, gloriously scenic, and well-organized tiger sanctuary is 267 km (140 miles) northeast of Delhi in Uttar Pradesh, and is easily reached in six hours by car, or by rail to Ramnagar, the nearest station, 50 km (31 miles) away. It's named after Jim Corbett who spent a lifetime hunting down man-eaters and leopards in these parts from 1907 to 1939 and whose ripping yarns and instinctive understanding of these mesmerizing beasts spawned a series of books, notably *The Man-Eaters of Kumaon*.

It is the lure of seeing a tiger that draws visitors here. But in reality your chances of getting a glimpse of one are slim. Nevertheless, Corbett Park has crocodiles, elephants, leopards, Himalayan black beer, hog deer, chital (spotted dear) and spectacular birdlife (585 species), so there will be many other wildlife sightings to compensate for missing the park's elusive big cats.

Accommodation is provided in "forest lodges," all of which are comfortable and inexpensive, and offer modest menus, but with confusingly identical names. In **Dhikala**, at the main entrance to the park, one has a choice among the "luxury" New Forest Rest House and Annex, the New Forest Rest House, the Old Forest Rest House, and individual cabins.

Luxury accommodation can be found on the fringes of Corbett, notably at the **Tiger Tops Corbett Lodge** ((05945) 85279 FAX (05945) 85278, which counts luxurious rooms, a bar, swimming pool, and elephants among its amenities. Room rates are over US$170, but if you want to do your tiger-spotting in style, this the place to be.

Slightly cheaper but still no slouch in the luxury stakes is the **Claridges Corbett Hideaway** ((05945) 85959 FAX (05945) 85959, where guests are put up in rustic cottages. There's a swimming pool here too.

You can explore by elephant and jeep, or hide out in *machans* (watchtowers). The park's Ramganga river brims with trout and mahseer, and you're free to go fishing as long as you have a permit from the Dhikala Game Warden. The best season to visit is between November and May, with the park most beautiful between January and March.

Note that steep "permit" fees of over US$100 per day are levied on any travelers with video or movie cameras.

AMRITSAR

Amritsar, the Sikh holy city, is Punjab state's premier tourist destination and the only reason most foreigners, apart from overlanders heading for Pakistan, enter this once vast state. The Golden Temple, the Sikh's holiest shrine, makes an excursion to Amritsar worthwhile in itself.

OPPOSITE: India is still home to such medieval sights as performing bears. ABOVE: Decaying colonial colonnades in Connaught Place.

The Golden Temple was the scene of an intense standoff and fierce fighting when the Indian army laid siege to the temple in mid-1984. Sikh extremists led by Jarnail Singh Bhindranwale holed up in the complex for months before being blasted into submission by armored vehicles and tanks. The Indian army was under strict instructions not to damage the Hari Mandir central temple, but the Akal Takht — traditional headquarters of the Sikh religious authority, and where Bhindranwale was finally killed (in the basement) — was badly damaged. You would never know it today. Repairs have been carried out to faithfully restore the complex to its former grandeur, and tourists are once again flocking to gaze on the temple.

GENERAL INFORMATION

The Golden Temple has an information office (along with a branch of the Punjab Bank and a post office). The local tourist office is not really worth bothering with but can be contacted at ((0183) 231482.

WHAT TO SEE AND DO

The Golden Temple

The Golden Temple is to Sikh's what Mecca is to Muslims, a place of pilgrimage and great sanctity. The centerpiece is the **Hari Mandir**, the Golden Temple proper. It was consecrated by the fifth Sikh Guru, Arjun; but Sikh ruler Maharajah Ranjit Singh created its grandiose marble structure and smothered its domes with anywhere from 100 to 400 kg (200 to nearly 900 lb) of gold (depending on who is counting).

Surrounding the Hari Mandir is the sacred bathing ghat from which the city gets its name: *amrit* (nectar) *sar* (pool). Crossing the ghat from the **Akal Takht**, or "Throne of the Timeless God," is the Guru Bridge. Pilgrims bring offerings of sweet *prasad* (a sweetened mixture of butter and flour), which is then distributed to all visitors who enter the Hari Mandir — it's good form to at least attempt a nibble.

Behind the Hari Mandir is a communal dining hall, open to all nationalities and creeds, which serves vegetarian meals free of charge at lunch and dinner times. The dispensation of food and communal dining is in keeping with the central Sikh tenet of equality.

Lastly, although anyone may enter the Golden Temple, you should follow the local rules. Shoes and socks are out, and you should keep your head covered. Tobacco and alcohol are forbidden in the precincts of the temple, and if you have an umbrella with you this should be left with your shoes too.

Other Sights

After you have visited the Golden Temple, take a stroll through the old city. You will see a scattering of mosques as well as one Hindu temple of particular note: **Durgiana Temple**, dedicated to the goddess Durga.

Just 90 m (100 yards) northeast of the Golden Temple, the park of **Jallianwala Bagh** marks the spot where, on April 13, 1919, General Dyer ordered his Gurkha troops to fire on peaceful protestors. Over 300 people died and the massacre ignited anti-British hatred in the struggle for independence. The bloodshed is depicted in a memorable scene in the movie *Gandhi*.

Amritsar's best hotel is the **Mohan International** ((0183) 227801 FAX (0183) 226520, in Albert Road, where rooms come in a choice of standard "European plan" or the slightly more luxurious "American plan." Despite the shopping arcade, swimming pool, health club, and other amenities, the Mohan's comforts are a far cry from the luxury standards of Delhi. "European plan" room rates start from around US$30.

The **Ritz Hotel** ((0183) 226606 FAX (0183) 226657, 45 The Mall, is a close runner up but not quite as good value as the Mohan. Nevertheless, if the Mohan is full, it's a reliable mid-range hotel for a night in Amritsar.

Lower mid-range and budget travelers have a number of hotels to choose from. **The Grand** ((0183) 62977 FAX (0183) 229677, Queen's Road, has reasonably priced air-conditioned rooms and the hotel comes with a bar and a decent Chinese restaurant. The **Hotel Airline's** ((0183) 227738 FAX (0183) 229812, Cooper Road, is another popular mid-range choice, with air-conditioned rooms starting at around US$15.

WHERE TO EAT

Popular with tourists passing through is the **Kwality Restaurant** ((0183) 224829 on Mall Road. It does a mix of Chinese, continental, and Mughalai cuisines and also serves beer. The **Crystal Restaurant** ((0183) 225555, at Crystal Chowk, is another reliable diner, with similar offerings on its menu.

HOW TO GET THERE

The ideal way to reach Amritsar from Delhi is by train. Flights are limited, and buses — which are at least frequent — are uncomfortable. Most train services take 10 hours from the capital, but if you take the *Shatabdi Express* you can cover the distance in relative comfort and in just seven hours. It is possible to take onward connections by rail to Varanasi and Calcutta on the *Amritsar-Howrah Mail.*

Sikhs in ceremonial costume guard the sacred pool lake precincts of the Golden Temple complex at shrines. Amritsar, the holiest of all Sikh shrines.

Agra and India's Heartland

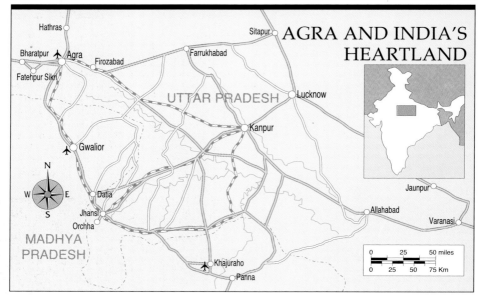

AGRA AND INDIA'S HEARTLAND

AGRA AND THE TAJ MAHAL

Agra is the medieval Mughal city of the famous Taj Mahal, the creation of a dynasty that dedicated its spoils to building architectural masterpieces. It was a strategic Aryan stronghold some 3,000 years ago, and its origins are recounted in the epic *Mahabharata*, in which it is referred to as "Agrabana" or "Paradise."

The city first rose to prominence as the capital of Sikander Lodi during the early sixteenth century. But it was soon usurped by the Mughals, and both Babur and Humayun made some early efforts to establish it as their power base. In 1566 the 24 year-old Akbar ordered the construction of his red sandstone fort beside the Yamuna River, and the city of Agra grew up around its lofty crenellated battlements, massive watchtowers, and giant gateways. It was the dynasty's first major architectural venture, and it remained the center of imperial activity during the early years of Mughal rule.

At its peak, tales of Agra's splendor and the lavish patronage of its powerful rulers lured emissaries, traders, missionaries, musicians, scholars, artists, physicians, philosophers, and craftsmen from practically every civilization, ushering in a period of creativity comparable to the Italian Renaissance. The mightiest of the Mughals, Akbar not only established control across almost three-quarters of the subcontinent, but also created an efficient bureaucracy and fostered the arts on a grand scale.

Akbar's rule was marked by religious tolerance, and he set an example by taking a Hindu

wife, Jodhai Bai from Amber, and raising her Rajput kinsmen to positions of eminence. His vision of creating a secular state prompted him to devise an eclectic faith, the Din-i-Ilahi or "Ultimate Religion of God," combining what he considered the best elements of Islam, Zoroastrianism, Hinduism, Jainism, and Christianity into a single, unifying religion — with himself as the divine godhead.

Akbar's legacy also includes the nearby city of Fatehpur Sikri, described by author Geoffrey Moorehouse as "the most enduring, elegant ghost-town that man ever abandoned," and from which Akbar ruled between 1570 and 1585 before leaving, apparently due to its poor water supply.

Nevertheless, despite his grand achievements, it is not Akbar but his grandson, Shah Jahan (ruled 1627–1658), whose name is most romantically linked to Agra. He was a compulsive builder, addicted to monumental architecture inlaid with jewels and semiprecious stones (and to his harem as well, apparently, whose population numbered some 5,000). He created the Jami Masjid, an array of lavish marble palaces, pavilion gardens, and an exquisite mosque within Agra Fort — all executed with such finesse it was said of the Mughals that they "designed like giants and finished like jewelers."

But the greatest of Shah Jahan's achievements, of course, was the Taj Mahal, the breathtakingly elegant mausoleum for his beloved Empress Mumtaz Mahal, whom he called "The Light of the Palace." She had died at 39 after delivering him his fourteenth child (only half of his children survived to adulthood). "Empire has no sweetness, life itself has no relish left for me now," Shah Jahan was said to have mourned when he heard the news.

Although he was to outlive his wife by 35 years, Shah Jahan became progressively reclusive and devoted himself to what, apart from Mumtaz, had always been his passion — architecture.

As the "seventh wonder of the world", and perhaps its most enduring symbol of human love, the Taj Mahal is still India's most popular tourist attraction. For many, it is one of the main reasons for visiting India, usually inspiring even the most seasoned traveler. Yet Shah Jahan grew restless at Agra, and by 1648 he had prepared his magnificent new capital of Shahjahanabad, now Old Delhi, as the new seat of Mughal power. He never ruled there. Within a decade he was deposed by his own son, the fanatical Aurangzeb, and he spent the rest of his days confined to royal quarters in Agra Fort; from which the imprisoned monarch could gaze across the river to his finest creation, the Taj Mahal.

Under Aurangzeb, the Mughal empire fell into slow decline, suffering random sieges by local Marathas and Jat forces, who wreaked havoc, even pillaging the Taj Mahal. By 1803 the British had marched their troops in, establishing their capital of the North Western Province (now Uttar Pradesh). Their stately cantonment town, to the south of Agra fort, now known as **Sardar Bazaar**, is an oasis of peaceful bungalows and gardens, but was the scene of violent battles during the Sepoy Mutiny in 1857.

Few visitors linger long in Agra. Fabulous sights it may have, but the tourist hordes have turned the city into a haven for assertive touts, beggars, and tourist shop hucksters. Sadly, many a visitor to Agra has come to the fast conclusion that it is best to trust nobody. It's worst at the Taj Mahal itself, where droves of prospecting con artists swarm over sightseers, waving soiled testimonials, smudged postcards, and bad advice. Studious refusal to stop and converse and sharp "no thank-yous" are the best responses.

Still, it's worth at least overnighting in Agra rather than day-tripping from Delhi. To see the Taj at its best, it's essential to see the monument in the changing light of both dawn and dusk. Stay two nights and you can extend your Agra sightseeing to a selection of surrounding sights such as Sikandra, Fatehpur Sikri, and Keoladeo Ghana National Park in Bharatpur, one of the finest bird sanctuaries in the world. Other easily accessible destinations from Agra include Jaipur in Rajasthan and Gwalior, Datia, and Orchha in Madhya Pradesh.

Like Delhi and most of central India, Agra is at its best during October to March, when days are warm, the nights just cool enough for a sweater, and the landscape filled with exuberant bursts of bright bougainvillea and mustard flowers. Attempting sightseeing during high summer entails distinct discomfort — temperatures can soar as high as 50°C (122°F) and choking dust storms, or *simoons*, sweep across the plains.

Agra and India's Heartland

WHAT TO SEE AND DO

Taj Mahal

Described by Rudyard Kipling as "the embodiment of all things pure, all things holy and all things unhappy," the Taj Mahal is India's ultimate symbol. The so-called "Crown of Palaces" has been eulogized by poets and artists so often that even as early as when he visited in 1897, Mark Twain felt himself "drunk on someone else's cork." All the same, like him, few can come away without feeling that simply laying eyes on the Taj is more than ample compensation for traveling halfway around the globe.

The Taj was Shah Jahan's greatest architectural project, completed in 1659 after 22 years of construction by some 20,000 artisans — including representatives from Iran, France, Italy, and Turkey. Beneath its tons of seamless white marble lies plain red sandstone, wrought to jewel-like brilliance by exquisite pietra dura inlay of precious stones and Urdu verses from the Koran, fretted marble kiosks, and bulbous domes. The marble came from Makrana in Rajasthan, and over a thousand elephants were required to transport it and work the construction pulleys. Its cost in those days was well over five million rupees; by today's standards this marble alone is priceless.

Pollution smudges have done little to diminish the majesty of the building (though sulfur dioxide pollution and dubious restoration efforts remain a serious threat to the monument), perhaps the most photographed in the world. The Taj is ever elusive, its Makrana marble taking on different hues with changing light, emanating a ghostly phosphorescent glow in moonlight, an oleander-pink glow at dawn and dusk, and a blinding white glare in the heat of the day.

The contours of the Taj Mahal are never less than breathtaking.

Like lifting the veil from a beautiful woman, it was designed to captivate visitors with a series of tantalizing glimpses as they pass through the courtyard leading to the huge red sandstone entrance gate, where all its splendor is revealed. Raised on a central marble plinth, flanked at each corner by minarets and silhouetted against the sky, the huge domed mausoleum gives the illusion of "hovering" above its reflected image in the central watercourse. Classical Mughal symmetry is achieved by precisely laid-out formal gardens and water pavilions, and by balancing the great tomb with two subsidiary buildings; one a mosque, the other an assembly hall. Remarkably, during the early years of the Agra cantonment, the British held moonlit balls here — although after the Mutiny in 1857 this was deemed a tad too inflammatory for local sensibilities!

As with any temple or mosque, you're required to take off your shoes before entering the cenotaph chamber. Alternatively you may rent a pair of peculiar regulation canvas "slippers" to fit over your shoes, a practical concession to tourists who are sometimes (quite naturally) wary of entrusting their footwear to the official "shoe minding" service.

The entrance level contains false tombs of Mumtaz and Shah Jahan, who actually were laid

to rest in precise duplicates in a lower-burial vault, surrounded by a superbly fret-worked marble screen decorated with thousands of inlaid semiprecious stones. Once there was a golden screen around them, but in the eighteenth century this was looted by the Jats of Bharatpur, who also took away the original silver entrance doors. The tombs are engraved with floral patterns of jaspers, emeralds, sapphires, and other precious stones.

Mumtaz's sarcophagus is the more elaborate, in line with an order from Shah Jahan, who wanted his wife's grave continually covered in flowers. The screen and the dangling Cairine lamp were donated by former British Viceroy, Lord Curzon, in 1909.

Rumors and myths galore have coalesced around the Taj. According to Indian guides, Shah Jahan planned to build an identical tomb in black marble on the other side of the Yamuna, joining the two with a bridge. The story is probably apocryphal, but intriguing all the same. Large quantities of old brickwork have indeed been unearthed on the other side of the river opposite

The Taj Mahal, the most enduring symbol of India, seen from the monsoon-swelled Yamuna River.

the Taj, giving substance to the story, but they were later identified as the remains of walls and pavilions of one of Babur's gardens. Another lesser-known rumor concerns the late Shah of Iran's tour of India during the 1970s, and whether or not Indira Gandhi granted his private request to be able to spend a night in the Taj Mahal with his wife, in the hope that she might conceive a heir.

Purists say the Taj Mahal is best seen in the moonlight, but despite continuing talk of opening the monument on full-moon evenings, it remains open to the public only from dawn to dusk. The only way to see the Taj at night is to book a hotel room with a view directly overlooking it.

Agra Fort

Built by Akbar between 1566 and 1573, Agra Fort was created as his much-needed military stronghold from which to govern the burgeoning Mughal empire. Determined at any cost to have an impregnable citadel, Akbar ordered it encircled by nearly two and a half kilometers (one and a half miles) of monumental

15-m (50-ft)-high turreted walls and wide moats, constructed from sandstone slabs so skillfully joined that Akbar's court historian wrote that even "a hair could not fit between them."

Aside from Akbar's sturdy earthbound battlements, few of his original buildings remain, for his son Jahangir and grandson Shah Jahan replaced them with their more opulent structures. Most of the fort's interior belongs to Shah Jahan's reign, whose residential jewel-encrusted palaces are linked by pavilions and terraces from which to gaze across at the Taj Mahal and the plains beyond.

Entrance is through the main southern Amar Singh Gate, named for the Maharaja of Jodhpur who was killed nearby after coming to blows with Shah

Jahan's soldiers in the Diwan-i-Am in 1644. It is emblazoned with the words Allah-o-Akbar, the traditional Islamic call to prayer, which means "God is Great."

Within, the first buildings visitors see were built by Akbar: **Akbari Mahal**, Akbar's former quarters; and his son's Jahangiri Mahal, unusual for its Hindu decorative motifs. Look for the stone pool nearby in which Jahangir's wife Nur Jahan ("Light of the World") used for her rosewater baths.

Within the center of the fort is Shah Jahan's **Diwan-i-Am**, the hall of public audience, a pavilion supported by 40 carved pillars, where the emperor once sat in state, consulting with officials and receiving petitioners. No ordinary citizen was permitted to venture further.

Beyond lies the **Moti Masjid**, the pearl mosque, where the emperor, his family, and attendants gathered for private prayer. From its domed ceiling once hung a huge priceless pearl. Near the mosque are a group of arcaded sandstone structures, the site of the annual New Year Meena Bazaar, when the aristocratic ladies took on the role of flirtatious purveyors, selling exotic wares to the princes, nobles, and even the emperor himself. As a local guide pamphlet curiously puts it, "Emperor Akbar used to attend in feminine disguise so that he could mix up with the female sex!" It was here that Shah Jahan, then a prince, met and fell in love with Mumtaz Mahal.

The fort's true citadel of power was Shah Jahan's **Diwan-i-Khas**, or private audience hall, which glittered with solid gold, silver, and precious stones. Here the emperor would receive important dignitaries or foreign ambassadors. Close by are the **Khas Mahal**, Shah Jahan's private pavilions, linked by colonnaded terraces set amid a formal garden. An adjacent sunken courtyard once served as a pool stocked with exotic species of fish, for the emperor was fond of angling. Look especially for the **Sheesh Mahal**, the royal bathing quarters, where the light of a single lamp is reflected in thousands of tiny mirrors embedded in the walls and ceiling. Water here once cascaded down marble chutes into vast intricately carved Turkish-style tubs.

Within the courtyard stairs lead up to the octagonal **Mussamamman Burj**, or **Jasmine Tower**, named for its adornment of mosaics, flower-wreathed columns, and beautiful marble filigree screens. It was here that Shah Jahan spent the last eight years of his life as a prisoner, before dying in 1666. Like most of Agra's monuments, the fort is open from sunrise to sunset.

Mughal Tombs

Agra Fort's **Delhi Gate** faces the squat domed Jami Masjid, built by Shah Jahan in 1648 and dedicated to his daughter Jahanara Begum, who loyally stayed with her father during his imprisonment.

From here, hire a taxi or auto-rickshaw for the 15-minute ride across to the opposite bank of the Yamuna River, about a kilometer (two-thirds of a mile) northeast of Agra Fort, to the **Itmad-ud-Daulah**, known as the "Baby Taj"—less frequented, smaller, and yet somehow more delicately beautiful than its grander, more famous cousin. Completed in 1628, it is the resting place of Nur Jahan's father Mirza Ghiyas Beg (alias Itmad-ud-Daulah, the "Pillar of the State").

Ghiyas Beg, a Persian noble, is less interesting than his daughter. Having fallen out with the Safavid king Abbas of Persia, Beg fled to India with his wife and small daughter, but the journey was so difficult, and money and morale so low, that they decided to abandon the little girl to speed the journey. Allah intervened, or so it seemed, when a caravan traveling behind the penniless couple found the child and returned her to her parents. Ghiyas Beg soon rose to prominence in the Mughal

court, and his rescued daughter, Mehrunissa, became the beautiful young wife of a Persian general. On her husband's sudden death in 1607, the 30 year-old Mehrunissa returned to Agra and became a lady-in-waiting to one of Akbar's widows. Here she was spied by the young Emperor Jahangir, who made her his Empress Nur Jahan in 1611. Despite being in purdah, Nur Jahan wielded formidable power, and as her frequently drunken husband became increasingly ruled by his three main passions — art, hunting and his harem — she proved herself an exceptional administrator. Many of her family members rose in the Mughal ranks, including her niece, Mumtaz, the woman who inspired the Taj Mahal.

Itmad-ud-Daulah was the first Mughal tomb to incorporate the Persian technique of pietra dura, the inlay of semiprecious stones in marble that was later popularized by Shah Jahan in the Taj. A feminine touch prevails in its intricate geometric and floral mosaics and lace-like pierced screens, similar in style to the tomb Nur Jahan built for Jahangir, near Lahore in Pakistan.

Farther north, you'll see the **China-ka-Rauza**, the "China Tomb," notable for its giant enameled dome, constructed for posterity by Afzal Khan, a noble in Shah Jahan's court. Continuing two kilometers (one and a quarter miles) north along the riverside lies **Emperor Babur's Ram Bagh Garden**, laid out in 1528. Unfortunately, restoration efforts seem to have foundered on apathy and there's little to see here today. It's said that Babur was temporarily buried here before being permanently interred as was his wish at Kabul in Afghanistan.

Finally, visit **Sikandra**, 10 km (six miles) north of Agra, to see Akbar's vast, beautifully carved, but ravaged red-ocher sandstone tomb set in a lush

Cane Sheathers near Agra.

garden and completed by his son, Jahangir in 1613. Guarded by four monumental gateways, its architecture blends Muslim, Hindu, Sikh, and Christian designs, reflecting Akbar's secular faith, with the lavish, more typically Mughal pietra dura inlay work added out of filial duty by Jahangir.

SHOPPING

Agra brims with handicraft shops and emporia and is famous for its pietra dura marble inlay work, embroidery, leatherwork, carpets, and jewelry. It's also notoriously touristy, with plenty of shabbily produced goods pumped out for impulse-buyers. Every taxi or auto-rickshaw driver will spin a story

In nongovernment run shops, you are advised to take care with credit card payments. Don't allow staff to disappear to a "back room" with your credit card. Cases of credit card fraud are not unheard of in Agra.

WHERE TO STAY

Agra's constant flood of tourists has ensured that there is a good range of accommodation choices around town. Note, however, that many hotels touting "Taj views" are in fact miles from the Taj. The only "hotels" in town with good Taj views (and even then from the roof only) are the basic cheapies in the Taj Ganj area.

about their "brother's" shop, but if you take up an offer of visiting a certain shop, they're liable to rake as much as 40% profit on anything you buy, meaning the overall price is inflated.

As with most large Indian cities, make the government emporia your first stop so that you'll be able to compare quality and prices when picking through curio shops later. The **Cottage Industries Exposition**, Fatebahd Road, is one such place, though bear in mind that prices are inflated. Good shopping areas include **Sardar Market**, near the Mall, and farther up Balu Ganj, where hundreds of "factories" churn out marble inlay goods, painstakingly fitting in mosaic patterns in a process little changed since the days when the Taj Mahal was built. The easiest way to tell bona-fide marble from inferior soapstone or alabaster is to scratch it surreptitiously: alabaster marks, marble remains clear.

Expensive
Agra's top hotel is the five-star **Mughal Sheraton** ((0562) 331701 FAX (0562) 331730, Taj Ganj, a design award-winning marble edifice with cascading fountains, terrace swimming pool, and landscaped gardens. As far as the locals are concerned, this is Agra's true "Taj Mahal," a mecca of chic restaurants and international amenities. It certainly offers some of the city's best Mughalai food, accompanied by Indian musicians, as well as several other good restaurants. Unusual features such as croquet and a yoga center complement the usual luxury facilities such as swimming pool, health center, and tennis here. Rooms are in the expensive range.

The nearby **Taj-View Hotel** ((0562) 331841 FAX (0562) 331860 is less expensive but also quite luxurious, featuring a fitness center, a swimming pool, a shopping arcade, restaurants, a bar, and even poolside barbecues in season (October to March).

In a similar league to the Taj-View, though looking slightly down-at-heel in comparison, is the **Clarks Shiraz** ((0562) 361421 FAX (0562) 361428, 54 Taj Road, situated within the leafy cantonment area, just next to the Indian Airlines office. It has a popular rooftop restaurant.

Mid-range

A good mid-range choice is the **Hotel Amar** ((0562) 331885 FAX (0562) 330299, Fatehabad Road, which has a slew of luxury facilities — swimming pool, health club with Jacuzzi, restaurant, and bar — and rates of less than US$30 for a double.

Similarly good value is the **Trident Hotel** ((0562) 331818 FAX (0562) 331827, Fatehabad Road, which sports Mughal-theme decor and all modern conveniences in its rooms. As is the case elsewhere in this price-range, the Trident has a swimming pool and restaurant dining.

The **Grand Hotel** ((0562) 364014 FAX (0562) 364271, 137 Station Road, Agra Cantonment, is looking a little shabby these days, but it's not without a certain faded Raj-era charm. Rates are slightly cheaper than at the Trident and the Amar, but you will have to forego a dip in the pool: there is none.

Budget

The Taj Ganj district, just spitting distance from the famous mausoleum itself, is the place to seek out budget rooms. Some of the budget guesthouses in this area — many of which offer Taj views from their rooftops — are often not as bad as you might expect. Always take a look at the rooms before checking in, though.

Probably the best choice in this category is the relatively new **Hotel Raj** ((0562) 331314, a mere stone's throw from the southern gate of the Taj Mahal. It has an average restaurant, but the air-conditioned rooms with attached bathroom are a bargain at less than US$10.

WHERE TO EAT

As well as its legacy of Mughal architecture, Agra also offers a chance to sample fine Mughalai cuisine, refined by court chefs to tantalize the taste buds of emperors. For stylish authentic fare, try the Mughal Sheraton's **Nauratna** ((0562) 331701 restaurant, excellent for succulent spiced tandoori *burra* kebabs, *rogan josh* (curried lamb), mutton *biryani*, and rich *rasgulla* (cream cheese balls soaked in sugared rose water). Or opt for a *thali* platter, either for lunch or dinner, which has a delicious selection of meat and vegetable dishes. Musicians and *ghazal* singers entertain while you eat. Also within the hotel complex, you'll find Agra's best Chinese Sichuan restaurant, and an outdoor garden café for barbecue dishes.

The Clarks Shiraz has good-value dinner buffets at its **Rooftop Restaurant**, with a choice of Indian, Chinese, and continental dishes.

Outside the hotels, try **Kwality Restaurant** at 2 Taj Road, near the tourist office, for reasonably priced, promptly served Indian food in air-conditioned surroundings. Nearby in Sadar Bazaar, **Lakshmi Vilas** is a cheap and excellent south Indian restaurant that is particularly popular with locals for breakfasts of fluffy *idlis, vadas*, and banana *lassi*, but it is open all day.

Tour groups often end up at the **Only Restaurant**, 45 Taj Road, for lunch. The atmosphere is pleasant and generally, if you stick to the Indian standards, the food is very good.

At night, the hotel-lined Fatehabad Road transforms into a long strip of alfresco food *dhabas* or sidewalk stalls, all lit by hissing gas lamps and doing a roaring trade in meat and vegetable curries, griddle-hot chapatis, and stewed, sugary *chai*. It's very basic — with knee-high tables, rickety stools, and tarpaulins overhead — but always full of appreciative locals and street-wise tourists. The best to try is the **Amar Dhawa**, near the Raj Hotel.

In the budget Taj Ganj area most of the guesthouses have restaurants, some with rooftop views. As a rule the food is poor, but **Joney's Place**, despite its gruesome decor and unhygienic appearance, is generally packed with budget travelers and even the occasional refugee from the five-star cantonment — the northern style Indian cuisine is surprisingly good.

HOW TO GET THERE

Located 204 km (126 miles) southeast of Delhi, Agra is conveniently reached by direct daily flights from Delhi, Khajuraho, Varanasi, Jaipur, and Bombay.

OPPOSITE: Mughal columns within the Diwan-i-Am at the Red Fort. ABOVE: Detail of surface exterior at Itmad-ud-Daulah's tomb.

Few travelers, however, take the half-hour flight from Delhi, preferring to take the *Shatabdi Express*, which departs daily from the New Delhi railway station at 6:15 AM, and returns from Agra at 8:18 PM. The trip takes just two hours, and its air-conditioned first-class cabins are luxurious by Indian standards, with packed snacks and coffee provided free of charge.

The *Taj Express* is cheaper and slightly slower. Its chief advantage is that departures are at the more civilized hour of 7:15 AM. It returns to Delhi at 6:45 PM.

Bus travel between Agra and Delhi is not advisable: it's a five-hour journey. There are, nonetheless, hourly departures from the main Delhi interstate bus stand. Deluxe buses leave from the India Tourism Development Corporation (ITDC) Transport Counter, L Block Connaught Place, daily at 7 AM .

At Agra railway station, day-trippers may want to join the excellent daily government-run tour of Agra's key sights — including Fatehpur Sikri, Agra Fort, and the Taj Mahal — in air-conditioned comfort. The tours have informative guides and connect with the rail services to and from Delhi. Tickets can either be purchased on the *Taj Express* or from near the Platform 1 inquiry window. The state tourism bus leaves the railway station at 10:30 AM for Fatehpur Sikri, returning to Agra at 6:30 PM.

EXCURSIONS FROM AGRA

For an adventurous, unforgettable day's excursion, combine Agra's two most compelling surrounding sights — **Fatehpur Sikri** and **Keoladeo Ghana National Park**, often referred to as the Bharatpur Bird Sanctuary.

Agra and India's Heartland

FATEHPUR SIKRI

This gigantic, forsaken sixteenth-century city looms high above the dusty tableland 37 km (23 miles) southwest of Agra. Still almost perfectly preserved, it was the Mughal empire's most fleeting capital, and perhaps its most magnificent. Emperor Akbar conceived it as a "modern" utopian city — a meeting place of enlightened scholars, philosophers, and statesmen — and its distinctive architecture reveals far more of this ruler's brilliant and enigmatic personality than his enormous palace complex at Agra Fort.

For all his pragmatic hardheadedness, Akbar was inspired to build Fatehpur Sikri in a fit of romantic superstition. As the story goes, in his late twenties the emperor possessed as much territory and wealth as a monarch could ever hope for. Yet despite his many wives (and his extensive 800-strong harem), he lacked a legitimate male heir. Apparently the problem lay not in his fertility, but in the fact that his male children failed to survive. Akbar sought the advice of a Sufi Muslim saint, Sheikh Salim Chisthi, who successfully prophesied that the emperor's wives would soon produce three healthy male children. Sure enough the next year Jodhai Bai, one of Akbar's Rajput wives and the daughter of the Maharaja of Amber, gave birth to a son. He was named Salim in honor of the holy man and became the future emperor Jahangir. (The other two sons followed soon after.)

Overjoyed that his line was secure, Akbar announced his intention to move his royal capital from Agra to a brand new city built at Sikri, the home of the holy man. Work began in 1565, and for a decade the site teemed with the empire's best architects, masons, stonecutters, and sculptors, as well as some 10,000 coolies to help build what came to be known as Fatehpur or "City of Victory," named for Akbar's victory over Gujarat in 1573. Even by the heroic and decadent standards of the Mughals, Akbar's magnificent sandstone metropolis must have seemed a sumptuous court, filled with palaces, pleasure domes, mosques, gardens, courtyards, bathhouses, and stables, enclosed within a circumference of some 14 km (nine miles). A contemporary English traveler, Ralph Finch, wrote: "The king hath in Agra and Fatehpur Sikri 1000 elephants, 30,000 horses, 1,400 tame deer, 800 concubines and such other store of leopard, buffaloes, cocks and hawks that it is very strange to see. Agra and Fatehpur Sikri are very great cities, either of them much greater than

By far the most pleasant way to do this is to hire a taxi the day before — agreeing on the rate for a round-trip beforehand, usually in the range of US$25. Arrange to leave about 4:30 AM (you'll soon nod off in the taxi!) in order to arrive at Bharatpur by sunrise to see its exotic birdlife swooping and diving, fluttering brilliant plumage against the soft dawn sky. The return journey is then broken with an afternoon ramble through Fatehpur Sikri, arriving back in Agra around 5 PM in time to catch ongoing connecting flights or trains.

If you've more time to spare, it's much cheaper to make the hour-long bus trip to Fatehpur Sikri from Agra's Idgah bus station and continue onto Bharatpur that afternoon for an overnight stay. From Bharatpur, which is located in Rajasthan's southeastern corner, direct twice-daily trains run to Agra, Jaipur, and Delhi.

The magnificent citadel of Fatehpur Sikri with its stately arrangement of palaces, pavilions, gardens, shrines and administrative buildings, all in cinnabar-red sandstone. The world may not contain a larger, more beautiful and more perfectly preserved ghost city than this.

London." Yet by 1586, Akbar was forced to abandon Fatehpur Sikri, apparently when the water supply dried up, prompting a mass migration back to Agra.

Akbar's elegant inner citadel remains strongly evocative of his cultured Mughal court. His graceful buildings seem barely touched by the ravages of time, although only ruins remain of the original town on the periphery.

There are two entrances to the city: The official one through the **Shahi Darwaza**, where licensed guides can be hired; the other at the monumental 54-m (177-ft)-high **Buland Darwaza** or "Gate of Victory." The latter is visible for miles, and bears a Koranic inscription that today reads like an epitaph to Akbar's grand architectural ambitions: "The world is a bridge: pass over it but build no house upon it. He who hopes for an hour, hopes for Eternity, for the world is but an hour."

Buland Darwaza leads into an enormous congregational courtyard containing the Friday Mosque or **Jami Masjid**, said to be a copy of the main mosque at Mecca, and the white marble, jewellike tomb of Sheikh Salim Chisthi, ornamented with latticed screens and serpentine brackets. The holy man died in 1571, but the tomb was only completed some 10 years later on the orders of Akbar, and adorned with exquisite *pietra dura* later by Shah Jahan as an act of piety. It was built on the site of the Sheikh's favorite meditation place. Childless women of all religions come to pray at the Sheikh's tomb for his blessings. The mosque and shrine are cloistered outside the city's main secular enclosure and must be visited separately.

To the left of the Buland Darwaza is a very deep well filled with murky water into which local lads dare to dive if you give them a few rupees. From here, it's a five-minute stroll to the Shahi Darwaza. Within this royal citadel, past the royal stables, stretch seemingly endless palaces, each more majestic than the last. First looms the casket-like palace that belonged to Raja Birbal, Akbar's brilliant Brahman prime minister, one of the "Nine Jewels of Akbar's Court."

To your right lies the principal harem wing for the Hindu wives, over which Akbar's Wife No. 1, the Rajput princess Jodhai Bai, presided imperiously from her spacious purdah-screened salon. Within the *zenana* (harem) were spacious gardens, fountains and a mosque, and privacy was ensured by solid gates guarded by eunuchs. Two favorite wives had separate abodes: Akbar's Christian wife from Goa, Maryam, lived in the so-called Golden Palace, named for its gilded interiors; and his Turkish wife, Sultana Begum (who was, it is said, his favorite, despite her inability to provide him with a son), was the envy of all the harem for her elegant marble pavilion studded with precious jewels.

Look especially for the **Panch Mahal**, a five-storied architectural marvel and Akbar's personal citadel of pleasure, where he would wile away his evenings in the company of his harem. Close by, you'll see two of Akbar's quasi-bureaucratic chambers, the **Astrologer's Seat**, an ornamented pavilion where the resident astrologer played an important role in day-to-day court life, and the **Treasury**, or the **Ankh Michauli** (Hide and Seek) building, nicknamed for Akbar's favorite game in the harem but functioning as the imperial repository of gold and silver.

This section leads onto the **Pachesi Courtyard** where Akbar and his courtiers used slave girls attired in brilliant dresses of different colors as pieces to play the game *pachesi*, moving when ordered on a giant marble board, a notion that inspired India's famed filmmaker Satyajit Ray to create his classic *The Chess Players*.

Akbar's private quarters flanked those of the *zenana*, screened away from the courtyard, and his richly embellished "House of Dreams" or bedchamber is on the first floor.

Across the royal courtyard is Fatehpur Sikri's architectural gem, the **Diwan-i-Khas** (Hall of Private Audience). This single vaulted chamber is dominated by its massive central Lotus Throne Pillar, which supported Akbar's throne and is linked to the upper-level gallery by four suspended gangways. The central pillar is tiered with eclectic carved motifs from a potpourri of religions, reflecting the universal outlook of Akbar's faith. It is simultaneously the Hindu tree of life (of which the *bodhi* tree of the Buddhists is a version), the lotus flower stretching to the heavens, and the royal umbrella that protects the king and his subjects. Akbar's throne itself was designed to represent the nail of the river-god Indra, in an unmistakable allusion to the Hindu concept of the cosmos: the emperor in the middle and the universe radiating around him. Within this resplendent honeycomb chamber, Akbar would conduct philosophical debates with adherents of diverse faiths, some Hindu, some Muslim, others mystics of no particular persuasion, and even missionaries from the Portuguese trading posts on the southwestern coast of India.

Climbing to the roof of Diwan-i-Khas, you'll get a good view of the octagonal **Elephant Tower** to the north. Spiked with masonry "tusks," this tower is the tomb of Akbar's favorite elephant, Hiran "The Golden One." Even in Akbar's relatively tolerant court, Hiran was often called upon to perform one of the more gruesome punishments meted out by the Mughals. Convicted criminals sentenced to be "Crushed by Elephant" were placed strategically beneath his feet, whereupon he was usually ruthless. If the elephant seemed indifferent and refused to squash the victim three times in a row, this was considered divine intervention and the happy criminal would be set scot-free.

Farther north lie the remains of the caravansary, where visiting traders would stay, the Elephant Gate (one of nine gates that dot the massive city walls), and the imperial workshops and market.

Leaving the south door of the Diwan-i-Khas, you'll follow Akbar's route along a raised pavilion to the colonnaded **Diwan-i-Am**, designed for large public gatherings. Akbar sat at the center (flanked by unseen wives behind a carved *jami* screen), dispensing justice and hearing litigation. According to his biographer Abul Fazl, Akbar was "without harshness or ill-will," but if you examine the center of the lawn, you'll see the sickle-shaped stone where Hiran the elephant trampled convicted criminals to death.

You'll need a map and may wish to hire a licensed guide — both available at the Shahi Darwaza entrance. If you're keen to stay overnight in Fatehpur, the best place to stay is the **Gulistan Tourist Complex** ((05619) 2490, which has air-conditioned rooms, a restaurant, and even a bar. The **Archaeological Survey Rest House** provides absurdly inexpensive but quite comfortable accommodation if you book through the Survey's main (informative) office at 22 The Mall, Agra.

KEOLADEO GHANA NATIONAL PARK, BHARATPUR

Located in Rajasthan's eastern corner, 17 km (10.5 miles) from Fatehpur Sikri, Bharatpur is an ornithologist's paradise: one of the world's finest bird sanctuaries, with over 29 sq km (11 sq miles) of fresh water marshland, originally developed by the Maharaja of Bharatpur for his legendary duck shoots. The sanctuary was established in 1956, before which it had been a royal hunting domain for more than 200 years.

During British colonial times, English aristocrats and their supporting casts of young subalterns never refused an invitation to a shooting spree. Sepia photographs in the old hunting lodge, now a tourist guesthouse, record arch-imperialists Lords Kitchener and Curzon at shoots in 1902. But it was Lord Linlithgow, a former viceroy, who holds the Bharatpur record, shooting down 4,273 birds on November 12, 1938.

Thankfully, today the park's 370 species of birds live in lushly beautiful, protected peace. The sanctuary is open from September to February but is best visited from November to January, when about 150 different types of migratory birds wing in for a temperate winter, usually from China, the Arctic Circle, Afghanistan, and Siberia. Bharatpur's most famous residents are rare Siberian cranes, often as many as 40 out of some 2,000 believed to exist in the world. They take just under a week to reach India from Siberia. You will see the Indian sarus crane, dazzling white egrets, hunchback herons, water-dancing Chinese coots, gliding eagles,

extravagantly-colored storks poised on treetops, lapis-blue kingfishers, and many others, dipping, diving, and spiraling. If you want to bone up on birdlife, take along *A Pictorial Guide to the Birds of the Indian Subcontinent* by Salim Ali and S. Dillon Ripley (Oxford: Oxford University Press, 1995).

Arriving at dawn (armed with binoculars, camera, a sweater, and mosquito repellent) is an absolute must. As the mists rise, the sanctuary's feathered occupants stir into life, sending stereophonic bird-song echoing across the water. At the main entrance Forest Office, where tickets must be purchased, you can arrange bicycle (the best way to get around) and rowboat rental (for punting across the marshes), as well as hire one of their excellent guides, who are usually trainee ornithologists with a genuine enthusiasm for their subject.

Off the well-designated roads and marshland embankments, you may catch a glimpse of Indian antelopes and the odd wild boar. Cobras inhabit a small breeding patch within the park, and their mid-morning wriggle in the sun has become a small tourist attraction in itself — visit in the company of a guide. Jeeps and taxis can pick up passengers at a halt zone about eight kilometers (five miles) into the sanctuary.

After a morning's scout, you can proceed for a hot brunch at the **Forest Lodge** ((05644) 22760, the Maharaja's former hunting lodge and the sanctuary's nicest accommodation option, in the cheap range. Air-conditioning is available but usually not required in winter.

In Bharatpur town, opt for newly refurbished old-world palatial charm at the **Hotel Park Palace** ((05644) 23783, Agra Road. This former palace guesthouse brims with trophies, collector's item photographs, and faded frescoes. Meals are excellent, with vegetables picked straight from the garden. Rates are inexpensive. Other good options can be found in Bharatpur town, otherwise try the Rajasthan Tourism Development Corporation (RTDC)-run **Saras Tourist Bungalow** ((05644) 23700, on Agra Road, with practical, clean rooms, hot showers, and a basic menu, (very cheap).

Aside from the sanctuary, there's plenty to see in Bharatpur, a former British cantonment town. Its most impressive sight is the eighteenth-century **Lohagarh (Iron) Fort**, built by the Jat ruler Maharaja Suraj Mal, the founder of Bharatpur, and named for withstanding numerous attacks by the British. There's an interesting museum displaying artifacts from the region, open from 10 AM to 5 PM, closed on Fridays. It's also worth cycling to see the Jat dynasty's imposing palace and museum, where family heirlooms are displayed. Locals describe with relish how the present Maharaja's grandfather was renowned for his eccentric manner and how he used to don his flying goggles and take off in his World War I biplane, laughing maniacally as he strafed "moving objects" in the fields below!

KHAJURAHO

The famous erotic sculptures of Khajuraho are included by many travelers as a side trip from the "Golden Triangle" of Delhi, Agra, and Jaipur. Built between 950 and 1050 by the rich and powerful Rajput Chandella rulers, these temple sculptures, with their countless scenes in praise of earthly passion, are the very antithesis of India's modern, more censorious sexual mores.

Situated in the middle of the dry rural plains of Madhya Pradesh, Khajuraho was once a magnificent temple city, clustered with some 85 spire-peaked temples. Of these today only 22 remain,

seeming all the more extraordinary in their state of desolation.

A thousand years ago, Khajuraho was encircled by a fortress-like wall with eight gates, each flanked by two gilt date palms — inspiring the Chandellas to call their capital "Khajurvahika" or "city of the golden dates." The surviving temples have weathered the years remarkably well, revealing this ancient civilization's zest for life in all its forms: spirituality, sexuality, music, hunting, and martial conquest. They probably owe their continued existence to their remote location, escaping the destructive fury of icon-smashing Muslim armies as they swept across northern India during the eleventh century.

Why the Chandella kings — who claimed descent from the moon god Chandra and worshipped Lord Vishnu, God of Preservation — decided to build their capital in such a remote, barren spot remains a mystery. The pure technological feat of constructing these architectural marvels is impressive. The sandstone was dug from the Ken River 20 km (12 miles) away, and chiseled to crisp perfection by a laborious method involving cutting and carving every stone individually, then assembling it like a giant three-dimensional sandstone jigsaw. Believing that temple building ensured a place in heaven, this

dynasty erected the bulk of their temples in an intense burst of creative energy between the tenth and eleventh centuries.

Five hundred years later, the Rajput Chandella empire was on the wane, and their fabulous capital became obscured by undergrowth; the region became notorious for its ruthless *thugs*, or Kali-Worshiping bandits.

The temples were noted dismissively as "ruins" by a British military official surveying the region in 1819, leaving the discovery of Khajuraho's wonders to the more adventurous Captain T.S. Burt in 1838. However his excitement at uncovering such ancient masterpieces was tempered with the realization that "the sculptor had at times allowed his subjects to grow a little warmer… than there was any absolute necessity for doing so," perhaps the most classic under-statement of the Victorian era.

Today visitors are awed by the craftsmanship of the temple carvings. From a distance they resemble a kind of tiered, variegated beehive, but at close range, they depict a universal hierarchy of mythological gods and goddesses, warriors, seductive celestial nymphs or *apsaras*, animals, and changelings. The chief attraction is the scenes of carnivalesque orgy — countless loving couples locked in sexual union, *mithuna*, and even indulging in the odd bout of bestiality. But such scenes are presented as a natural and integral part of human nature. Above all, they celebrate man's union with the divine and the pleasures of the material world.

During the British Raj, unwitting young *memsahibs* reportedly fainted away when faced with the more lurid scenes. And after India's independence, when politicians were doing much soul-searching about their national heritage, they actually contemplated screening off "offensive" portions of Khajuraho's temples from public view and classifying their famous ancient treatise on the art of sex, the *Kama Sutra*, as obscene literature. For India is the heir to a religious tradition that took unashamed delight in sexuality, adopting the phallic *lingam* and the female genital-shaped *yoni* as its most widespread objects of worship.

Various theories have been put forward about the purpose of the sculptures. One story has it that the copulating couples were a test of the monk's celibacy, another that the figures were a graphic reminder to the worshipers to leave all earthly thoughts behind before entering the temple's hallowed inner sanctum. The most outlandish explanation was that the temples were built for purposes of sex education when the population was in serious decline!

Khajuraho's highlight is its annual weeklong Dance Festival, held in early March, when India's top classical dancers and musicians perform every evening against the floodlit backdrop of ancient temples, rekindling the traditional practice of the *devadasis* (girls dedicated to Indian temples), an unforgettable experience for performers and audience alike. Tickets range from about US$1 to US$5 per "seat" (a cushion space). Advance bookings for hotels and flights are essential.

While Khajuraho is small enough to see within an afternoon, it's best to plan to spend at least two days to appreciate its temple architecture by leisurely bicycling, returning for the charmed light of dawn and dusk.

Lastly, avoid Khajuraho's blistering summer and arrive between November and February for cool comfort.

entrance at 9:30 AM and 2:30 PM. Otherwise make your way across the road to Raja's Café, where talented graduate guides are available for about US$5 for half a day, or US$7 for a full day, as well as lunch allowance and "language allowance" if you happen to be French, German, or Japanese. It's well worth getting a copy of Krishna Devi's informative pamphlet sold at the museum.

As a general introduction, the temples follow a distinct pattern, externally resembling a sort of giant textured beehive, tiered with rising spires or *shikhara*. Each comprises five parts: an *ardhamanadapa* or entrance porch leading onto a pillared *mandapa* hall, then an *antarala* or

WHAT TO SEE AND DO

The Temple Tour

Khajuraho's medieval temples are found in three areas. The most famous is the Western group, located at the center of town, and fringed by tourist cafés, lodges, and shops. The Eastern group lies one and a half kilometers (just under a mile) away near the old village. The Southern temples are some four kilometers (two and a half miles) away.

Opening hours are from sunrise to sunset, but you can explore all three groups in about five to six hours if you rent a bicycle or take an autorickshaw or taxi. It's a good idea to hire a guide if you want to get the most out of your sightseeing — you can always return to appreciate them alone later. The Archaeological Survey conducts free lecture tours of the Western group twice daily except on Fridays and holidays, leaving the main

Agra and India's Heartland

vestibule, and finally an enclosed corridor or *pradakshina* that encircles the central inner sanctum or *garbhagriha*. The temples can be divided into two groups: those dedicated to Vishnu, Lord of preservation; and those dedicated to Shiva, Lord of destruction. Traces are also found of Buddhism, Jainism, sun worship, animism, and various other cults that indicate the eclectic tastes of their architects. They also stand on high platforms, some two and a half meters (eight feet) above the ground, causing speculation that the Chandellas may have flooded these enclosures to create the illusion of a lake of floating temples.

OPPOSITE: An amorous couple entwined in one of Khajuraho's less explicit, perfectly chiseled embraces. ABOVE: The beehive-shaped temples of Khajuraho teem with countless *mithunas* or love-making scenes.

Start with the famous Western group, first visiting its fascinating **Archaeological Museum**, located just outside the enclosure. It contains a rich collection of relics found within the area and is open from 9 AM to 5 PM daily except Friday. Remember to keep your ticket (with its strategic rip!), which also allows you to enter the Western group of temples. Just next door you'll see a shrine dedicated to the region's former ruling Maharaja Sri Pratap Singh Dev, touchingly laid out to recreate his personal bedroom, complete with a blown-up photograph of the deceased ruler and many personal effects.

Set within beautifully maintained gardens, the Western group represents the zenith of

with over 900 sculptured figures, its spectacular main spire soaring to a height of 31 m (108 ft). Friezes depict deities on their cosmic plateau, observing the activities of mere mortals beneath swarming into epic battles with phalanxes of elephants and dragons (the symbol adopted by the Chandellas) or reclining with curvaceous young women on their return home. Every detail of contemporary life is captured here, portrayed with exuberant realism and humor. Above all, the friezes celebrate the ideal woman with her hourglass waist and high, provocative breasts, smoldering with saucy sensuality in countless poses and moods. As if they have been caught unseen, these seductive creatures go about their

Chandella art. Just to the left, stands a quartet of early temples, all dedicated to Lord Vishnu. The base of **Lakshmana** (circa 930–950) features a frieze of hunting and battle scenes that celebrates the martial might of the Chandellas. Also featured are numerous fine figures of *apsaras* and erotic art.

Two small temples stand nearby, **Lakshmi** and **Varah**, the latter bearing a huge statue of Vishnu in his incarnation as a boar. Slightly south of the enclosure is the **Matangeswara Temple**, the fourth of the group, with its giant lingam. This is Khajuraho's most popular "living" temple and on festival days comes alive with clanging bells and vividly dressed villagers laying flowers and sweetmeats around its central shrine.

Walking westwards, you'll find the **Kandariya Mahadev** (circa 1025–1050), the most artistically magnificent of all Khajuraho's temples, teeming

toilette, combing their hair, applying eye shadow, preening themselves in their mirrors, or perhaps joyfully coupling with their lovers. Here are found Khajuraho's most energetic and explicit *mithuna* (lovemaking scenes), graphic illustrations of the *Kama Sutra*.

Just north is the small **Dev Jagdamba** temple, thought to have been dedicated to Goddess Parvati and on close inspection, filled with formidably athletic orgiastic sequences.

In the northeastern corner is the **Chitragupta Temple**, dedicated to Surya, the sun god, who is portrayed driving his chariot drawn by seven horses. There are interesting exterior reliefs that show hunting scenes, dancing nymphs, rural processions, and even fights between incensed elephants. Inside look for the 11-headed Vishnu in the central niche, each head representing one of his various incarnations.

Completing the temple circuit is the **Parvati Temple**, notable for its inner frieze of the Goddess Ganga using a crocodile as a carpet, and the **Vishvanatha Temple**, dedicated to Shiva and flanked by a large Nandi bull.

It takes about 15 minutes to cycle to the eastern group of temples, following the dirt road to Khajuraho's medieval village. This walled enclosure is more evocative of the sedate influence of Jainism, lacking the frenetic erotic fervor of the Western group.

The largest and finest of these Jain temples is the central **Parsvanatha Temple**, with its elegantly chiseled *apsaras* engaged in prosaic day-to-day activities: fondling a child, writing a letter, applying makeup, removing a thorn from a foot. Within the inner shrine stands an ornamental throne and ornate carved bull, the emblem of the first Jain *tirthankara*, the saint Adinath. Just outside is a circular museum that houses a fine collection of relics, columns, and broken-off friezes from the site.

The Eastern group's Hindu temples are scattered in the surrounding fields nearby: the **Javeri**, dedicated to Vishnu, located near the village; the **Vamana**, 200 m (217 yards) north, dedicated to Vishnu's incarnation as a dwarf and notable for its bands of dazzling maidens in a variety of come-hither poses; and the **Brahma Temple**, one of the oldest at Khajuraho. Nearby, you can't miss the giant luridly orange statue of Hanuman, the monkey god, guarding a modern temple on the road out to the Jain enclosure.

For more, temple addicts can venture out to the Southern group, four kilometers (two and a half miles) away to admire the two interesting temples, the **Duladeo** and the **Chaturbhuj**.

A highly rewarding day excursion is out to the fantasy tree-house built by Khajuraho's lovable eccentric, Gilles Bohnenblust, a Swiss who considers India his adopted home, and who runs the Raja Café with his English wife Betty. His designer tree-abode has to be seen to be believed, perched high above the gushing torrents of the Ken River in Panna District, 23 km (14 miles) away. Among those eager to stay and experience life among the leaves have been actors Julie Christie and Vivien Leigh. It's certainly a pleasant place to linger — they have possibly the world's most unique bar — and Gilles and Betty may offer guests the opportunity to experience luxurious tree life. If you're curious to see and possibly stay, contact the staff at the Raja Café on Main Square.

WHERE TO STAY

Khajuraho has several good-value luxury hotels, set in large gardens and convenient to the airport, located four kilometers (two and a half miles) from the temples.

The Taj-run **Chandella** ((07686) 42355 FAX (07686) 42366, has moderately priced rooms, an idyllic swimming pool, a health club, and serves an array of Indian, Chinese, and continental food. The **Jass Oberoi** ((07686) 42344 FAX (07686) 42345 offers comparable accommodation and also has a good swimming pool and shopping arcade.

The **Hotel Clark's Bundela** ((07686) 2363 FAX (07686) 2359 is the new kid on the block and offers similar standards and amenities.

The **Khajuraho Ashok** ((07686) 2024 FAX (07686) 42239 is a long running mid-range hotel, but room rates here are only a little less than the preferable Chandella and Jass hotels. It's a reliable choice, however, if the latter are closed.

A good mid-range choice is the **Hotel Jankhar** ((07686) 2063 FAX (07686) 42330, not far from the Jass Oberoi on Airport Road. Comfortable, well appointed doubles with air-conditioning cost less than US$15, and Chinese, Indian and continental cuisine is available in the restaurant.

Khajuraho is popular with budget travelers and there is no shortage of lodges and guesthouses catering to their needs. The **Rahil Hotel** ((07686) 2062 has a good central location and clean rooms, though it is not going to win anyone over for its decor. The **Tourist Bungalow** ((07686) 2064 has rooms in the very cheap to cheap range for air-

Despite its popularity with tourists, Khajuraho remains very rustic and unspoilt, with an unhurried pace of life. OPPOSITE: Bullocks being used to draw water in Khajuraho village. ABOVE: An old man soaks up the morning sun.

cooled doubles. Other options include the **Sunset View**, on Airport Road, the **New Bharat Lodge** or the **Jain Lodge** (very cheap and both on Jain Temple Road), which are all popular with backpackers, clean and within a minute's walk from the Western group of temples.

WHERE TO EAT

Both the Chandella and the Jass Oberoi hotels have excellent Indian restaurants and Western-style coffee shops. Beyond that, locals have cottoned on to foreign tastes and set up a row of open-air cafés near the entrance to the Western Temples, prettily lit up at night with fairy lamps. The best of these is the long-running Swiss-managed **Raja's Café**, on the Main Square, good for full breakfasts of eggs, toast, and coffee and popular for its cheap, delicious Indian meals as well as its apple pancakes and banana fritters.

Other highly patronized spots include the **Safari Restaurant** with good-value *mewari thalis*, the **Madras Coffee House** (Jain Temple Road), and the all-vegetarian **Gupta Restaurant**. **Mediterraneo** is an Italian restaurant that is run by an Indian-Italian couple. It's on Jain Temple Road.

HOW TO GET THERE

Khajuraho is small enough to cover in a day and many visitors fly in on the shuttle flight from Delhi in the morning and return the same evening. Daily flights also link Khajuraho with Agra and Varanasi.

Arriving overland can be problematic. From Delhi, Mumbai and Chennai the most convenient railhead is Jhansi, 175 km (108 miles) away. From Calcutta and Varanasi the nearest railhead is Satna, 120 km (74 miles) away. Regular bus services link Khajuraho with Agra, Jhansi (six hours), and Satna (four hours).

GWALIOR

Gwalior attracts few tourists, yet it offers one of India's most spectacular Rajput forts and is a good base for exploring two fabulous, deserted medieval cities nearby — Datia and Orchha.

Gwalior Fort, a colossal honey-colored sandstone citadel set some 91 m (300 ft) along a crest-like rock face, is the city's principal attraction. Akbar was said to have been influenced by it when building his own Fatehpur Sikri.

BACKGROUND

According to legend, the fort's history began in the fourth century when a sun-worshipping, leprous Rajput chieftain named Suraj Sen encountered a faith-healing ascetic called Gwalipa on the fort's site. Granted a miracle cure,

he built the first fortress in gratitude. The ascetic gave him the new name of Suhan Pal and further prophesied that for as long as he and his descendents kept the surname Pal his line would reign successfully in Gwalior. Suhan Pal and 83 of his successors did indeed rule after him, until the eighty-fourth took the name Tej Karan and lost the kingdom.

By the late fourteenth century the Tomars were in power and it was the Tomar king Man Singh (1486–1516) who built the six-towered Man Singh Palace, considered to be the finest example of Hindu architecture extant in India. It has been fought for and conquered three times: first by Sikander Lodi, later by the Mughal Emperor Babur, and lastly by the Marathas, whose descendants are now Gwalior's ex-First Family.

WHAT TO SEE AND DO

Gwalior Fort

You'll need at least a full morning or afternoon to do justice to this magnificent Boy's Own fortress, whose rambling battlements wind in a circle for five long kilometers (three miles). Approach it by the southwest Hindola Gate, passing the giant Jain statues carved from the rock faces (defaced by Babur in a fit of pique). Inside is Man Singh's palace, a quintessential Oriental "wonder" with its six onion-dome cupolas and myriad rooms adorned with dazzling lapis lazuli tiles, encrusted with broken jasper and emerald mosaics, filled with a menagerie of carved gargoyles and peacocks; it even has a natural air-conditioning system. The subterranean quarters beneath were used by the Mughals as dungeons, notable as the place where Aurangzeb hanged his brother, a possible successor to his throne.

Don't forget to visit the cluster of marble palaces built by the Mughals. These comprise the two eleventh-century **Sasbahu Temples** (literally "Mother-in-law" and "sister-in-law") along the eastern wall and the ninth-century **Teli-ka-Mandir**, a curious temple built for newlyweds with erotic sculptures to instruct young brides in the art of pleasing their husbands.

There's an excellent museum housed in the fifteenth-century **Gujari Palace**, just inside the Hindola Gate, with a fascinating collection of inscriptions, carvings, Gupta sculptures, and miniature paintings.

As at Amber (near Jaipur), caparisoned elephants carry passengers up to the fort's gate. The entire complex is open daily except Mondays 8 AM to 11 AM and 2 PM to 5 PM. From April 1 to September 30, 7 AM to 10 AM, 3 PM to 6 PM.

Other Attractions

Other sights in Gwalior include the ornate Italianate **Jai Vilas Palace**, built between 1872 and 1874 by the madly decadent Maharaja Jayaji, whose tastes ran to glass furniture, gilt brocade, kitsch erotica (see Leda in a loving embrace with a swan), and tiger-head trophies. Built when the British still occupied Gwalior Fort, it was designed by one Lieutenant Colonel Sir Michael Filose of the Indian Army as a princely showpiece for the Prince of Wales (the future King Edward VII) to sojourn in during his tour of India. Its gem-like **Durbar Hall** contains two immense chandeliers, reputed to be the largest in the world. Each is nearly 13 m (42 ft) high, carries 248 candles, and weighs three tons. Before they could be hung, three elephants were hoisted to the roof to make sure that it was going to stand the strain.

Not to be outdone the next resident, Madhav Rao Scindia, built a silver train set that chugged its way around the dining table delivering mutton vindaloo, port, and cigars. This gleeful Maharaja charmed the pants off the British — as legendary for his schoolboy pranks and unerringly accurate water pistol attacks as for enthusiastically modernizing his state. He also staged perhaps the most elaborate tiger shoots in India for the benefit of the British aristocracy. One observer estimated that if all the Maharaja's combined kills were laid out, they would stretch for more than four kilometers (two and a half miles). Even more eccentrically, he managed to be the only Indian to fight with the British expeditionary force against the Chinese in Peking at the time of the Boxer uprising.

Also in town, you'll find the tomb of Tansen, the brilliant bard whom Akbar made Master of Music at his court in 1562. According to local lore, chewing the leaves of the tamarind tree nearby gives you a mellifluous singing voice.

WHERE TO STAY

Stay overnight in Gwalior at the Welcomgroup's **Usha Kiran Palace** ((0751) 323993 FAX (0751) 321103, Jayendragunj, a stylish palace guesthouse crammed with 1930s furniture, set within well-maintained grounds. Rooms are air-conditioned and cost from around US$80 for doubles.

For standard middle-range accommodation, the **Hotel Gwalior Regency** ((0751) 340670 FAX (0751) 343520 is a comfortable, air-conditioned option.

Slightly cheaper rates apply at the **Tansen Hotel** ((0751) 340370 FAX (0751) 340371, 6 Gandhi Road, where you have a choice of air-conditioned or fan-cooled rooms.

Lastly, the **Hotel Vivek** ((0751) 329016 FAX (0751) 429878, Topi Bazaar, is one of the better budget hotels in town. There is no air-conditioning here, but the air-cooled rooms come with attached bathrooms and are a good value.

WHERE TO EAT

Gwalior is no gourmet paradise, but the restaurants at both the Usha Kiran Palace and the Hotel Gwalior Regency both serve the familiarly eclectic mixture of Indian, Chinese, and continental cuisine.

The **Kwality Restaurant**, outside the southeast corner of the fort is an excellent place to escape the heat and enjoy some Indian cuisine.

HOW TO GET THERE

Gwalior is just 118 km (73 miles) from Agra and is also conveniently on the Delhi-Mumbai rail line. Flights connect Gwalior with Delhi and Mumbai. Buses from nearby Agra should take a little over three hours.

EXCURSIONS FROM GWALIOR

It's worth visiting Gwalior just to make the memorable day-trip to the hauntingly forlorn palace-cities of Datia (69 km or 43 miles away) and Orchha (129 km or 80 miles away), both of which see very few visitors.

Regular buses run from Gwalior to the city of Jhansi, 11 km (nearly seven miles) from Orchha, but hiring a taxi makes for speedier, more relaxed sightseeing. Leave at dawn for a journey past tiny hamlets and fields of swaying wheat to arrive at Datia in the morning cool.

At **Datia**, the seven-story hilltop **Gobinda Palace** (dating from 1614) is a fabulous maze of latticed corridors, verandahs, pillared cupolas, and fresco-covered rooms, once studded with semi-precious gems. It's to the west of the surrounding town, which is encircled by a seventeenth-century stone wall.

Both the Datia and the Orchha palace-complexes were financed by Raja Bir Singh Deo, a Bundela Rajput ruler based in Jhansi in the seventeenth century. This rather Machiavellian character won sway and great wealth in Jahangir's court and was rewarded for his services to the emperor-to-be when Jahangir was still Prince Salim and plotting to depose his father, Akbar. As one of Jahangir's sidekicks, the Raja was entrusted with the task of murdering one of the heir-apparent's key rivals — Akbar's personal friend and chief advisor, the influential Abul Fazal, an outstanding writer whose voluminous works provide an intimate account of India under the Mughals.

Up until the 1930s Datia was a standard item in viceregal itineraries, hosting the British Governor-General Lord Hastings in 1818 and the Viceroy Lord Curzon in 1902. Today it is a forgotten treasure, and gypsies camp in its decaying ruins with herds of goats.

Nevertheless, **Orchha** is the more magnificent and better preserved of the two fort cities. With its palaces and temples rising from overgrown foliage, inhabited by deer and nesting birds, it's perfect for a quiet picnic and some solitary exploring.

Tucked away on the fringes of Orchha is a tiny village with small shops and tea-stalls. It is connected to the medieval palace by an impressive seventeenth-century stone bridge.

Orchha's monuments are a rich amalgam of different architectural styles, incorporating Mughal, Jain, Persian, and even European features. Its most impressive structure is the perfectly symmetrical **Jahangir Mahal**, which combines lofty walls with numerous, delicate *jali* screens and ornate carvings. Close by is **Raj Mahal** the royal chambers, which are connected by a maze of colonnaded corridors lined with silver doors and exquisite wall paintings, found even along the curving ceilings. Other palaces are reached by crossing Mughal-style gardens studded with pavilions and fountains serviced by underground pipes.

Orchha also has some beautiful and unusual temples. The **Lakshmi Narain Temple**, dedicated to the goddess of wealth, Lakshmi, is covered in paintings depicting the pomp of Orchha court life, now sadly defaced by graffiti. The large **Chaturbhuj** temple, dedicated to the four-armed Vishnu, has a layout that visually reproduces each of his four limbs.

Another minor attraction is the rows of domed **cenotaphs** lining the Bewa River and housing the ashes of Orchha's former rulers.

For those considering spending a night in Orchha, it is actually possible to stay within the palace quarters, which have been partly converted into the delightful **Hotel Sheesh Mahal** by the Madhya Pradesh tourism authorities. Its most beautiful deluxe suite has its own sun-filled courtyard and a large marble bathroom with a wall-size mirror. Suites and double rooms are in the inexpensive range, all with running hot and cold water and attached bathrooms—food is extra and perfectly adequate for a day or so. Book through the Madhya Pradesh Tourist Office ((011) 336 6528, B8, State Emporia Building, Bhagat Kharak Singh Marg, New Delhi.

CITY OF LIGHT: VARANASI (BENARES)

Varanasi, as Mark Twain put it in 1896, is "older than history, older than tradition, older even than legend, and looks twice as old as all of them put together." Once known as Benares — a British corruption — the spiritual heart of Uttar Pradesh state is one of the world's oldest continuously inhabited cities. It was a bustling metropolis when its main counterparts were the ancient centers of Thebes, Nineveh, and Babylon.

Hindus flock to Varanasi for purification and death, to bask in the *Kasha* (divine light) that they believe emanates from the ancient holy city's thousand or more temples clustered along the Ganges river. Washing in the sacred waterway is said to cleanse away all sin. To die next to the river and have one's ashes scattered into the water is the goal of every devout Hindu, who hold that this guarantees release from the eternal cycle of birth and rebirth.

Every dawn in Varanasi involves spiritual devotion on an epic scale. As temple bells peal across the city, thousands of pilgrims throng the *ghats* (stone waterside steps) leading down to the khaki-colored sacred waterway. Bearing ritual brass vessels, marigold garlands, and earthen oil lamps they immerse themselves in the Ganges and reverently cup water to their lips as the sun rises. In soft, almost evangelical light, Varanasi's teeming riverfront canyon of spire-topped temples, decaying eighteenth-century palaces and ashrams, presents a haunting, unforgettable sight. Behind the ghats lies a medieval maze of tangled alleys crammed with glittering bazaars, ascetic priests, dusky-skinned urchins, turmeric-smeared fakirs with rope-like hair, white-clad widows, chanting mendicants, and plump, painted cows.

Hinduism's umbilical attachment to the Ganges river is thought to have begun with the Aryans, who understood that the waterway saved much of north India from being a barren desert. The 2,525-km (1,565-mile)-long river begins as a spring at Gangotri in the Himalayas and snakes through the northern plains into a mammoth delta of fertility before flowing into the Bay of Bengal. With its current it carries the hopes, the prayers, and in death the ashes of millions of Indians. Other holy towns in Uttar Pradesh also line its banks: Allahabad, Rishikesh, and Haridwar.

Holy though Ganges water may be—countless people drink it—the river is severely polluted by the millions of liters of raw sewage and industrial waste pumped into it each day. The problem is compounded by the Hindu practice of forbidding cremation of children, holy men, and disease victims, who comprise the estimated 60,000 corpses annually thrown straight into the Ganges.

Archaeologists believe the city's mythological name, Kashi, probably derived from its earliest inhabitants, the aboriginal Kashia tribe, who settled by the river some 3,000 years ago and eked out a living by bartering woven matting made from local grass and known as *kushasans*. The mats are still made and used as umbrellas to shield meditating holy men from the often fierce sun.

Pilgrims throng Varanasi's ghats or steps to bathe and pray beside the Ganges River, which devout Hindus believe has the power of cleansing away cumulative sins.

Agra and India's Heartland

The Hindu Aryans occupied the site from around 800 to 900 BC, and the city soon became a magnet for philosophers, poets, mathematicians, and pilgrims. The origins of Buddhism can be traced to nearby Sarnath, where, in the sixth century BC, Prince Siddhartha preached his first sermon after gaining enlightenment.

Varanasi emerged as a prestigious and wealthy metropolis of gilded temples and shrines dedicated to the city's special deity, Lord Shiva. Local rulers constantly contested the right to claim its considerable revenue, and plundering northern invaders periodically laid siege. No wonder: Its rich silks, brocades, cotton textiles, and woolen cloth were coveted from China to Rome. Muslims frequently held the city to ransom from the eleventh century onwards, but the most ruthless destroyer of Hindu temples was the Mughal Emperor Aurangzeb, who converted the Lord Vishwanath Temple, said to be the original home of Lord Shiva, into a mosque. Hindu Rajas came to power in 1738, giving Varanasi a spell of local rule until it was ceded to the British in 1775.

The city has long been renowned as a center of creativity and culture and is still the best place to hear the graceful *thrumri* and *dadra* melodies of Indian classical music. Spectacular enactments of Hindu epics have been performed since the seventeenth century, and the Banaras Hindu University, founded in 1916 by the nationalist Madan Mohan Malviya, is now India's premier school for Sanskrit and Hindu studies. Internationally renowned musician Ravi Shankar hails from Varanasi, as do many of the country's most talented sitar and tabla players. And tucked away in the city's medieval old center are thousands of families, many of them Muslims, engaged in making Varanasi's famous silks and brocade fabrics, intricately carved wooden toys, and hand-loomed carpets.

GENERAL INFORMATION

There are two main tourist offices: the **Government of India Tourist Office** ((0542) 343744, at 15B The Mall, Cantonment; and the **Uttar Pradesh State Tourist Office** ((0542) 343486, Parade Kothi, opposite the railway station. The Government of India office is the better of the two, providing advice on city sights, shopping, music, dance, and festivals. Bookings can be made at both offices for inexpensive tours led by experienced guides.

The Indian Airlines Office ((0542) 345959, in Mint House, Cantonment, runs a bus shuttle to the airport, but the service can be erratic if you are in a hurry.

The *Northern India Patrika* newspaper has good entertainment sections. The best local guidebooks are *Glimpses of Varanasi* by K. Jaycees or *Benares* by S.N. Mishra. *Benares: City of Light*

by Diana Eck (Princeton University Press) has detailed information on each ghat and temple in particular, as well as Hinduism in general.

WHEN TO GO

Every day in Varanasi is dedicated to one of the gods in the Hindu pantheon, and pilgrims ensure that the city is lively all year around, but the weather is best between October and March. By late May and all the way through until late September temperatures soar in Varanasi, making sightseeing near impossible.

From September to October Varanasi is host to India's most flamboyant festival, the Ram Lila, or Dussehra, a 10-day extravaganza of pageants, dance, and musical performances.

Music festivals are the best showcase for Varanasi's extraordinary talents, the best being

Agra and India's Heartland

held at the Sankat Mochan Temple in early April, when top musicians perform for four to six nights as a tribute to the Monkey-God, Hanuman. Others to watch out for include the Lalit Sangit Parishad in December, the Rimpa in January, and the Dhrupad Mela in late February. Admission is free, but bring a blanket to wrap yourself in as evening concerts often end at dawn.

WHAT TO SEE AND DO

The Ghats
The city's life revolves around its seven-kilometer (4.3-mile)-long sweep of about 100 bathing ghats that skirt the west bank of the Ganges. Most were built in the eighteenth century, along with palaces and temples constructed by Hindu maharajas of Varanasi, Jaipur, Udaipur, Gwalior, and Mysore.

No visitor should miss taking a boat ride along the ghats at dawn for a grandstand view of the magical light filtering across one of the most spectacular scenes of devotional pageantry on earth. Rise at 4 AM — you can always have a siesta — and take an auto-rickshaw to the central **Dashaswamedh Ghat** (note that auto-rickshaws can't take you directly to the ghat itself, but will drop you around five minute's walk away) where you'll find plenty of boatmen willing to ferry you around at reasonable rates. A good introductory hour-long tour is to go upriver to Assi Ghat and then to return and proceed downstream to Panchganga Ghat.

Varanasi's riverside ghats stretch along the river's edge for nearly seven kilometers like a medieval canyon of plaster-peeling residences, eighteenth century palaces and ornate temples.

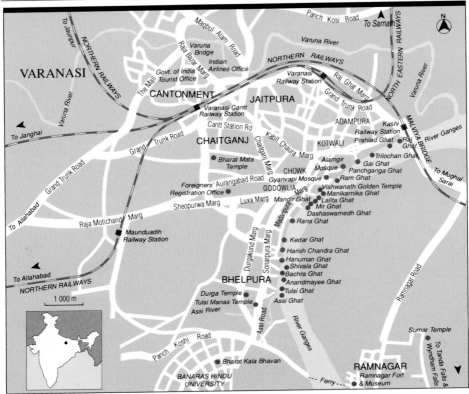

You will see the faithful throng the water's edge, perform Hindu rites, and energetically lather themselves with suds from head to toe. Young men strut about and limber up with exercises before making daredevil dives from temple spires. Women surreptitiously bathe in their saris. Brahman priests hold court on plinths beneath palm umbrellas and give sermons about the Hindu epics. Pavement barbers shave heads of their penitent customers, *dhobi-wallahs* process mountains of soapy cloth, and half-naked yogis sit frozen in contorted positions. Wrestling is a favorite pastime, and crowds cheer as they watch combatants tussle in a special pit in contests to clamber up a *malkham* or smooth wooden pole.

Most travelers return from Varanasi with graphic tales of the city's death industry. Your boatman will no doubt take particular pleasure in pointing out "Ganga people," the whitened rubbery corpses that float downstream accompanied by marigolds and plastic bags. Locals shrug these sights off with Asiatic calm and humor, regarding them as all part of the flotsam and jetsam of Varanasi's great spiritual recycling of life and death. Some startled tourists have an overwhelming urge to hurry straight back to their hotels. But most find that curiosity wins over squeamishness.

The busiest cremation or "burning" ghats are Manikarnika and Harishchandra. Corpses are wrapped in white muslin cloth and covered with orange marigold flowers, before being borne on bamboo stretchers to the pyres on the water's edge, traditionally set ablaze by the deceased's eldest son. Varanasi's caste of undertakers are the untouchable "doams," recognizable by their shaved heads and loincloths. The Doam Raja is their hereditary leader who is held in great awe since his blessing is said to ensure a superior reincarnation. He surveys his domain from a house above Manikarnika Ghat that is decorated with two life-size plaster tigers, symbolizing death's imminence.

The doams dispatch the dead with alacrity, building pyres, sloshing wood with flammable cooking oil, and enthusiastically swinging ceremonial staffs to burst open flaming skulls and ensure the soul escapes from the body. At Manikarnika Ghat, wealthy families vie to have their relatives cremated on the Chandrapaduka slab, which is believed to be marked with the footprints of the god Vishnu. Grief is rarely evident, as Hindus believe that once the soul is released, the body is just a discarded shell. But do not try and photograph the proceedings, as this greatly offends the participants and has caused numerous brawls between mourners and unwitting tourists, sometimes resulting in cameras being hurled into the Ganges.

During your boat trip, make sure you see the five most sacred ghats, the Asi, Dashaswamedh, Manikarnika, Panchganga, and Raj. Pilgrims who bathe in each one consecutively believe their prayers will be fulfilled.

The furthermost upstream ghat is **Assi Ghat**, which marks the confluence of the Ganges and the Assi rivers. Next is **Tulsi Ghat**, which honors the poet Gosain Tulsi Das, who translated the *Ramayana* and died here in 1623. The city's sewage pumps out under **Janki Ghat**, and nearby is the government's first electric crematorium: an experiment that hopes to bring modern efficiency and hygiene to a messy but time-honored sacred ritual.

Bachra Ghat is used by Jains and has three Jain temples. Beside it is the ornate **Shivala** or **Kali Ghat**, the most impressive of the royal ghats, and one that is still used daily by the former Maharaja of Benares — it can be distinguished by its huge Shiva *lingam*.

Hanuman Ghat attracts hordes of devotees paying their respects to the monkey-god. Nearby, the **Dandi Ghat** is used by ascetics, fakirs, and yogis. Past Harishchandra's smoking pyres is **Kedar Ghat** with its fine temples. **Mansarowar Ghat** is named after a Tibetan lake at the foot of Mount Kailas, Shiva's Himalayan home. **Someswar** or "Lord of the Moon" **Ghat**, is said to have magical healing powers and attracts droves of hopeful lepers, cronies, and terminally ill. Next is the ghat of **Ahalya Bai**, an eighteenth-century queen of Indore.

Dashaswamedh Ghat is Varanasi's liveliest bathing place, named to honor the site where Brahma sacrificed (*medh*) ten (*das*) horses (*aswa*). One of its many temples is dedicated to Sitala, the goddess of smallpox. Nearby is the grand **Man Mandir Ghat** and an observatory built by Jai Singh in 1710. **Mir Ghat** leads to a Nepalese temple that is decorated with erotic paintings, and further inland is the **Golden Temple** (see below), Varanasi's most sacred shrine. Nearby are the two holiest burning ghats, the **Manikarnika** and the **Jasain**, a favorite cremation spot for India's elite.

At the northern end is **Dattatreya Ghat**, named after a Brahman saint; **Panchganga Ghat**, where India's five holy rivers are said to merge; **Trilochan Ghat**, marked by its two turrets; and **Raj Ghat**, the final goal of pilgrims.

The City

Back on land, set off and explore the city's atmospheric medieval gullies, or lanes, to seek out bazaars, temples, peering and decaying palaces. No accurate map exists of this remarkable web of

stone-paved corridors, barely more than an arm's span wide, often dark and slippery, both enchanting and claustrophobia-inducing at the same time. Getting lost is all part of the fun. If all else fails, locals claim that following a sacred cow will lead you to the river.

Start from the old city's main forum, the Dashaswamedh Ghat/Chowk are, and take a stroll down Vishwanath gully, which leads to the famous **Golden Temple**. Hindus believe Shiva lives here, so it's far too holy a place for non-Hindus to view, although tourists can peer inside from the old house next door. The original temple (built in 1600) was later to be destroyed by the Mughal Emperor Aurangzeb who, in a display of

dominance over his Hindu subjects, had his Gyanvapi Mosque built on top of the site. A Maratha queen, Ahalya Bai, in 1776 reconstructed the present shrine next door and dedicated it to the god held by Hindus to be the lord of the universe. The solid gold plating that you see on the towers was given by the Maharaja Ranjit Singh of Lahore in 1835. Stalls along the lane sell flowers by the kilo, along with horsehair fly-whisks, religious paraphernalia, ornate toys, glass bangles, and filigreed jewelry.

To the south is the red-ochre **Durga Temple**, built in the north Indian Nagara style by an eighteenth century Bengali Maharani. It is dedicated to Durga, a fearsome incarnation of Shiva's wife, Parvati. She is placated by periodic goat sacrifices — watch out though, as the temple is renowned for its resident tribe of clever monkeys that often whisk away visitors' glasses and handbags.

Nearby is the modern shikhara-style **Tulsi Manas Temple** engraved with verses and scenes from the *Rama Charit Manas*, the Hindi version of the Ramayana written by the medieval poet Tulsi Das.

Faded clothes being hung out to dry at the Washing Ghat, Varanasi.

Farther south, 11 km (6.8 miles) from the city center, is the **Banaras Hindu University**. It is open daily except Sundays from 11 AM to 4 PM and has an excellent miniature painting and sculpture collection inside its Bharat Kala Bhavan.

From here you can either take a ferry or a taxi to reach the eighteenth-century **Ramnagar Fort** across the river, 16 km (10 miles) from the city center. The ex-Maharaja still lives here in a splendid suite overlooking the Ganges, although part of his ancestral home is now a well-organized museum with liveried guards and eccentric treasures giving a whiff of former glories: gem-encrusted weapons, moth-balled howdahs, palanquins, astrological clocks, decadent Kashmir vestments, ostrich eggs, and vintage cars. It is open from 10 AM to noon and from 1 PM to 5 PM.

Sarnath

Sarnath is a serene Buddhist pilgrimage center about 10 km (six miles) from Varanasi. It was the deer park where Buddha preached his first sermon around 528 BC to his five close disciples after receiving enlightenment at Bodhgaya in Bihar. The sermon was "Setting in Motion the Wheel of Righteousness," and it laid down the Buddhist doctrine of the "Middle Way," which pointed to the path of righteous moderation as the means to spiritual salvation, or nirvana.

Sarnath probably derived its name from one of Buddha's titles, Saranganath, Lord of the Deer. It became a monastic center, gaining official patronage as the capital of the Buddhist religion under Emperor Ashoka (circa 269–232 BC), the warlord-turned-pacifist who erected several memorial towers or stupas as well as one of his famous pillars here. The Chinese Buddhist pilgrims, Faxian (Fa-hsien) and Xuanzang (Hsuan Tsang), who visited in the fifth and seventh centuries respectively, both recorded impressions of their stay. The latter wrote of Sarnath's vast monastery with lakes, extensive gardens, magnificent giant stupas, 1,500 monks, and the Emperor Ashoka pillar.

Over the centuries, however, Buddhism lost its initial momentum, and successive Muslim invasions in the twelfth and seventeenth centuries destroyed much of Sarnath's fabled grandeur, although the sprawling remains of this religious capital are still impressive. The huge swastika-covered **Dhamekh Stupa** dates from around AD 500 and is thought to mark the place where Buddha gave his sermon.

The excellent **Archaeological Museum** is open 10 AM to 5 PM except on Fridays. Its prize exhibit is the four-faced lion capital, which originally crowned the Ashoka pillar and is now the official symbol of modern India. It is a treasure house of sculptures from the major periods of artistic activity at Sarnath — Mauryan, Kushan, and

Gupta — as well as later Hindu images from the ninth to twelfth centuries.

Sarnath's annual festival is Buddha Purnima, which commemorates Buddha's birth with a colorful fair and procession of his relics held on the full moon of May/June.

SHOPPING

Varanasi's famous silk and brocade fabrics are used by leading American and European designers and have always been valued by wealthy Indians as wedding attire, to be passed down as heirlooms. Quality handwoven silk brocades are called *kinkhab* and are highly decorative tapestries threaded with pure gold and silver and patterned with delicate motifs. Saris, stoles, and cloth woven by craftsmen can cost up to US$1,200 a piece, but there are plenty of perfectly exquisite, much cheaper ones.

For browsing or buying, you can view the finest selections at **Brij Raman Das** and **Ushnak Malmulchan** in the central Chowk area. The **Silk Corner**, next to the Indian Airlines office in the Mall, has a large range of reasonably priced good quality silks sold by the meter, as well as silk boxer shorts, cushion covers and ties.

The bazaars offer a plethora of goods, and it is easy to compare prices and bargain. The main **Chowk** and **Godowlia** areas are good for silks, brocade, perfume, paan, and carved walking sticks; **Vishwanath Gully** for painted toys and images of gods and goddesses; **Thatheri Bazaar** for ornamental brass work and lacquered glass bangles; **Satti Bazaar** for saris.

Varanasi is also the best place in the world for sitar shopping. Serious students are welcomed by the senior sitar-maker, **Radhey Shyam Sharma**, who is a disciple of Ravi Shankar and has a workshop at 52/34E Luxmi Kund behind the New Imperial Hotel. A fine quality instrument costs around US$70 to US$200. Cheaper varieties priced around US$20 to US$50 can be found in **Nichi Bagh** off Chowk.

WHERE TO STAY

Expensive

Varanasi's few luxury hotels are frequently over-booked, so try to reserve well in advance.

Two hotels vie for number one billing in Varanasi's luxury accommodation stakes. Quite honestly, there is little to choose between them. Both do an admirable job of bringing modern comforts to a city that elsewhere looks like it has been time-warped from the Middle Ages. The leafy Cantonment area, which houses the luxury hotels and some good value middle-range hotels too, is a welcome retreat from the push and shove of the old city.

One is the **Hotel Taj Ganges** ((0542) 345100 FAX (0542) 348067, Nadesar Palace Grounds. If possible, request a room on one of the upper floors, particularly one with a view across the leafy garden, swimming pool, and the adjacent Nadesar Palace of the former Maharaja, where Englands Queen and Prince Phillip stayed in 1955. Facilities include several excellent restaurants, a shopping arcade and a travel desk.

The **Hotel Clarks Varanasi** ((0542) 348501 FAX (0542) 348186, The Mall, Varanasi Cantonment, is similarly luxurious and offers almost identical amenities. Rates at both the Taj and the Clarks start at around US$100 for a single. Non-guests are welcome to use the swimming pools and garden for a nominal fee.

Mid-range

A good mid-range choice is the all air-conditioned **Hotel Varanasi Ashok** ((0542) 346020 FAX (0542) 348089, The Mall, Varanasi Cantonment, a somewhat bland experience, but nevertheless good value considering its facilities, which include a swimming pool.

The **Hotel de Paris** ((0542) 346601 FAX (0542) 348520, The Mall, Varanasi Cantonment, on the other hand is dripping with atmosphere. A former guesthouse of the Maharaja of Benares, it has eccentric, natty charm, with a huge garden filled with hammocks and deck chairs, and a dining room crammed with sepia photographs and deer heads. Facilities are somewhat basic, but with room rates of little more than US$20 for a spacious air-conditioned double it's difficult to complain.

If you are looking for a mid-range hotel closer to the old city, the **Hotel Hindustan International** ((0542) 351484 FAX (0542) 350931, C-21/3 Maldahiya, is a reliable, fully air-conditioned hotel with rates only slightly higher than those at the Hotel de Paris. It includes a swimming pool among its facilities.

Budget

The rock bottom accommodation is mostly in the heart of the old city, overlooking the ghats. The great advantage to this, of course, is that within minutes of getting up you can be beside the Ganges with the local population, enjoying the coolness of early dawn.

Not all the budget hotels in this area are as grim as you might imagine. The **Vishnu Resthouse**, Pandey Ghat, has simple but clean air-cooled rooms with attached bathrooms, and has a delightful patio café that overlooks the ghats and the river. It's frequently full.

Also recommended — if you're the adventurous type — is the **Shanti Guesthouse** ((0542) 322568, Manikarnika Ghat, a towering building (by local standards) with a profusion of rooms — some of them air-cooled and with attached

bathrooms — and a splendid rooftop restaurant that provides views across the old city, the ghats and the river.

WHERE TO EAT

The **Hotel Clarks Varanasi** ((0542) 348501 probably has the best restaurant in town. Treat yourself to a pre-dinner cocktail in the garden before tucking into their superb Mughalai, Lucknow, or Chinese food that costs around US$5 per head. Lunchtime poolside barbecues are also popular. The **Taj Ganges** ((0542) 345100 offers similar fare, as well as atmospheric garden buffet dinners.

Locals swear by the generous portions and reasonable prices of the less than glamorous **Diamond Hotel** ((0542) 310696 at Belapur, especially good for splurging on rich Mughalai cuisine, fluffy *naans*, and *kulfi* ice cream. For light, nourishing south Indian food, seek out the **Kerala Café**, also at Belapur, open all day and excellent for lightly spiced *dosas*, lunchtime *thalis*, and aromatic Mysore coffee. Other popular eateries can be found in the central Lohurabir area, including the **Tulasi Restaurant** for simple Indian cuisine. Nearby, **Kwality** has an extensive menu of Mughalai, Chinese, and continental food.

Varanasi is famous for its sumptuous sweetmeats — *rasgulla* (cream cheese balls soaked in sugared rosewater), *chum-chum* (oval-shaped, sprinkled with desiccated coconut, and stuffed with *malai* cream), *kheer* (a rich thickened milk with raisins and nuts), *pista burfi* (*halwa* sweets), and others — best sampled from stalls in **Thatheri Bazaar** in the Chowk area.

Residents often start their day with *thundai*, an aromatic concoction of milk, saffron, almonds, black pepper, and ground-up marijuana or bhang. Many people are addicted to the brew and also consume bhang in their *paan* mixtures.

HOW TO GET THERE

Indian Airlines connects Varanasi with flights from Delhi, Mumbai, Agr, Khajuraho, Hyderabad, Calcutta, Lucknow, Allahabad, and Patna, and there are also connections to Katmandu. Vayudoot flies from Delhi and Agra. A regular bus links the airport to the city, and the 22-km (13.6-mile)-long route costs about US$7 in a taxi.

Northern and North-Eastern railways link Varanasi to major cities, and overnight sleepers from Calcutta (12 hours) and New Delhi (17 hours) are the most comfortable rail option.

Jaipur
and
Rajasthan

VIBRANTLY COLORFUL AND EXOTIC, RAJASTHAN — the "land of the rajas" — is in many ways India's ultimate destination. It is a barren and inhospitable land: shifting desert sands under a blazing sun, a fantastic timeworn realm of medieval fortresses. And yet somehow it still pulsates with a rich diversity of life and color. Rajputs are proud, handsome people. Lithe and graceful, clad in many-hued cloth and adorned with sparkling silver, they seem to the visitor's eye almost otherworldly. But Rajasthan is not so much another world as another time: In Rajasthan one feels at times the twentieth century has been little more than a rumor or a half-remembered dream.

JAIPUR

Known as the "Pink City" because of the color of the stones used in its architecture, Jaipur is the bustling capital of Rajasthan. Nestled amid the craggy Aravalli Hills, it was founded in 1727 by the brilliant astronomer-king Jai Singh II to replace his ancestral hill fortress of Amber, 11 km (seven miles) away.

By the time Jai Singh II came to power at the age of 13, his family had earned the dubious distinction of being the first Rajput power to align with the Mughals through a strategic royal marriage. Jai Singh proved a formidable statesman, and the Mughal alliance brought peace and privilege to his domain.

A man of his times, Jai Singh was an enthusiastic student of contemporary sciences. He laid out Jaipur on a grid system consisting of seven rectangular blocks of buildings fronted by seven magnificent gates and precisely crisscrossed by broad 33.8-m (111-ft)-wide arterial avenues that intersected at the city's core — the City Palace — in keeping with the principles of the ancient Hindu architectural treatise, the *Shilpa Shastra*. In the new city, traders and artisans under court patronage were given their own lanes, a tradition that persists today. Until town planners went on a demolition binge after Independence, the city's encircling walls were completely intact. Sadly, today only portions remain.

But the city retains a fairytale exuberance, with its courtly palaces, colorful bazaars, and nearby fort. Its streets are a spice-scented mêlée of bobbing turbans, women in tinsel-fringed scarlet robes clutching kohl-eyed babies, gamboling monkeys, camel-drawn carts, and jingling cycle-rickshaws. It's still the "highly ornamented curiosity… all in the soft, rich tint of strawberry ice cream" described by Mark Twain when he visited the city in 1897.

Actually, Jaipur's overall "pinkness" was then only a recent phenomenon, dating from 1876 when the city was painted up for the visit of the Prince of Wales, later King Edward VII. Today, every shop-owner within the historic Pink City Boundary is required by law to maintain his shop's façade.

As the final destination in the tourist's popular "Golden Triangle" of Delhi-Agra-Jaipur, the city is well endowed with hotels, restaurants, and shops — but also, unfortunately, with pushy touts and con-artists. Watch out for overpricing and overbooking.

Jaipur — indeed, all of Rajasthan — is best visited from October to February, when the days are sunny and crisp and the evenings cool. Jaipur celebrates all the major festivals, but it's especially worth visiting during Diwali in October or November, and the elephant processions and exuberant paint-throwing mayhem of March and

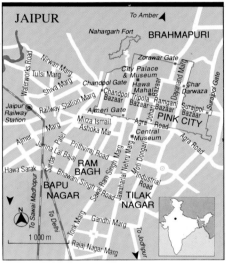

April, when both Holi and the Rajasthani Gangaur festivals take place. Also during March, polo fever hits Jaipur, with tournaments of elephant, horse, camel, and even bicycle polo being staged.

GENERAL INFORMATION

Of the six Rajasthan Tourist Offices around town the one at the Railway Station ((0141) 315714 is particularly useful and offers good local information, maps, guide services, and reasonably priced car rental for out-of-town excursions. The head office ((0141) 370180 is at the Tourist Hotel on Mirza Ismail Road (known as M.I. Marg).

WHAT TO SEE AND DO

Jaipur's sights are concentrated within the old city in and around the City Palace complex. You can spend the best part of a day seeing them at your own pace, enjoying the colorful bazaars and

A typical scene from the jostling streets of Jaipur.

street life in between. When this gets tiring, climb aboard a cycle-rickshaw and be whisked down Jaipur's wide boulevards — the best way to get around and still feel part of the color, scent, and activity all around you.

Watch out for glint-eyed auto-rickshaw and taxi-*wallahs*, particularly those who besiege befuddled tourists emerging from the railway station. They have a pathological dislike of using their meters, so always agree on the fare in advance.

Jaipur has plenty of bike-rental places, including a rank outside the rail station. If you are in tip-top shape, you might consider tackling the steep Aravalli ridge on the Jaipur-Delhi Road to Amber, 11 km (seven miles) away, stopping halfway to admire the eighteenth-century **Jal Mahal** or Water Palace, originally used by the maharajas as a summer residence.

You'll need at least two full days to see Jaipur's highlights and to poke through its bazaars for shopping bargains. The RTDC morning guided tour is a good time-saver, with comfortable buses and English-speaking guides. The full-day tours can be exhausting, and some visitors complain that they attempt to cram too much in. Tours leave from the railway station as a rule but can be organized through the RTDC ((0141) 370180.

The Old Royal City
Start just outside the City Palace complex at Jaipur's famous **Hawa Mahal** or Palace of the Winds. Named for the cool westerly winds that blow through it, its five-tiered pink façade is ornamented with delicate overhanging balconies and gilded arches, and yet it is only one room deep. It was built in 1799 so that veiled royal women could peer down unseen by the world through its 593 stone screens. You can climb to the top for a purdah-view of Jaipur between 10 AM and 4:30 PM daily. There is also a good "Jaipur Past and Present" display.

houses part of the City Palace museum, displaying a fine collection of antique textiles and royal costumes. Among the extensive displays of Rajput weaponry are such curiosities as crystal-handled gold daggers, guns tailored for a camelback rider, and gruesome instruments designed to spring open in the unfortunate victim's abdomen. To your right is the ornate **Singh Pol**, the Lion Gate, with its guardian marble elephants, which leads into a magnificent courtyard flanked by tiered buildings of oleander stucco. In the center of the courtyard is the marble **Diwan-i-Khas**, or Private Audience Hall. The two silver urns here, said to be the world's largest, were made to store six months' supply of Ganga water for a Jaipur maharaja while he attended King Edward VII's coronation in London.

On your left, a gateway leads to the Peacock Courtyard; its four gateways are studded with glass mosaics and polished brass, each depicting one of the four seasons. Nearby is the seven-tiered **Chandra Mahal** or Moon Palace, the maharaja's personal abode. Its mirror-decorated topmost chamber affords fine views across the Jai Niwas Gardens, the eighteenth-century Sri Gobind Dev Temple, and the towering Clock Tower.

Back in the main courtyard, the facing gateway leads to the **Sawai Man Singh II Museum**. On display here are some magnificent medieval carpets, most of them from Afghanistan and Pakistan, and a collection of Jaipur and Mughal school miniatures and rare Sanskrit and Koranic manuscripts. Royal palanquins, gilt-studded ivory howdahs, and one of India's largest chandeliers complete the collection.

The City Palace is open daily from 9:30 AM to 4:45 PM, except on public holidays and festivals.

Directly opposite the City Palace is Jai Singh's fascinating astronomical observatory, the **Jantar Mantar**. Jai Singh's obsession for astronomy inspired him to pore over ancient texts, to ponder the calculations of Euclid and Ptolemy, and to pick holes in contemporary European theories of astronomy. He was the first Indian astronomer to emphasize scientific observation rather than theory, and he went on to revise the Indian lunar calendar and astrological tables. The observatory is open from 9 AM to 5 PM daily.

One final place to visit in town is the grand nineteenth-century Indo-Saracenic-style **Central Museum** (Albert Hall), south of the walled city in the sprawling Rang Niwas Gardens, which also contains a small zoo. This vast, eccentric collection includes a fascinating display on Rajasthan's tribal groups, lore, costumes, and arts. Among its more bizarre exhibits are 100 wax models of gruesomely contorted G-string-clad yogic sadhus or holy men, an Egyptian mummy, many bald stuffed birds,

Behind the Hawa Mahal, a large square filled with *chai* stalls and fluttering pigeons leads to the oleander-pink **City Palace**, the symbolic heart of the capital. It is still used as a royal residence and as a backdrop for special state festivals. Jai Singh's eighteenth-century palace is an enchanted miniature metropolis in itself, occupying one-seventh of the entire old city area. The complex — with its confection-like pink façades edged with delicate lacy white borders, arched pavilions, and marble courtyards — has been described by architecture buffs as India's "most daring and successful synthesis of Mughal and Rajput styles." The palace courtyards are full of indolent, picturesquely dressed guards with bulky red turbans, many of them old retainers of the former maharaja.

Just within the entrance courtyard of the City Palace stands the dazzling white **Mubarak Mahal** or Palace of Welcome. Built in 1900, it was first a guesthouse, then the Royal Secretariat; now it

Horses graze in the lake beneath the majestic Amber Palace, the former capital of the royal Jaipurs.

snakes rotting in bottles, hundreds of Austrian rock samples, some very decrepit stuffed crocodiles, and one inexplicable display: an ancient fish dangling in a case, with a tag marked "Fish" tied around its belly — definitely worth a giggle or two!

Amber

Few visitors fail to be moved by the dramatic Rajput grandeur of Amber, the hilltop fortress-palace 11 km (seven miles) north of Jaipur. Surrounded by fortified battlements, it straddles two sepia-hued tundra ranges in the Aravalli Hills overlooking Maota Lake. Higher still, a craggy fortress crowns the summit, and sprawling, crenellated walls lattice the surrounding hills.

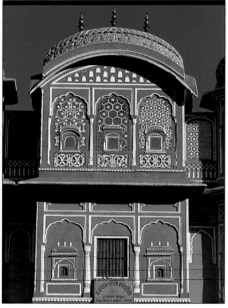

This was the citadel of the powerful Rajput Kachchwaha kings, whose illustrious descendant, Jai Singh II, founded Jaipur. Although they had ruled the region since the eleventh century, Amber palace was not built until the late sixteenth century, by which time the Kachchwahas had risen to power and wealth. You can either walk up the steep cobbled ramparts to the fort-palace complex or take the popular (but overpriced) ride on a caparisoned, painted elephant. Passing through the main entrance gate, you'll step into a small courtyard containing the marble-pillared **Kali Temple**, which has solid silver doors.

The multi-pillared **Diwan-i-Am** (Public Meeting Hall) nearby leads to Jai Singh's magnificent ceremonial **Ganesh Pol** or Elephant Gate — an ornamental masterpiece of intricate inlaid mirror mosaic, fresco, and scalloped stuccowork. It leads into a charming garden courtyard flanked by royal

apartments, many with elaborate frescoes, stained-glass windows, mosaics, plaster reliefs, and mirror-studded alcoves. The main attractions are the fountain-cooled **Sukh Niwas** (Hall of Pleasure), the glittering **Sheesh Mahal** (Mirror Palace), and the **Jai Mandir**, Jai Singh's royal abode, with glass and precious stones studded into a shining surface of powdered marble, eggshells, and crushed pearls. Behind the garden court lies the elaborately latticed *zenana*, where each of Jai Singh's wives had a separate suite.

Amber is best visited in the crisp cool of early morning, allowing plenty of time to wander through the labyrinthine passages leading to the servants' quarters, watchtowers, and dungeons. Bring bottled water and a packed lunch and do what few tourists do — clamber up the steep, boulder-strewn slopes to the fortress ramparts, where you'll find an interesting museum, cool drinks, and sublime views in all directions. Amber's fort-palace is open from 9 AM to 4:30 PM daily.

On the way back to town, stop at **Gaitor**, the cremation grounds of the Kachchwaha clan, to see the white marble *chhatris* or cenotaphs of Jaipur's rulers. Jai Singh II's is the most magnificent, supported by marble pillars and covered in ornamental friezes. Follow the steep road up the ridge to **Nahargarh (Tiger) Fort**, built by Jai Singh II in 1734 to defend his new city. Alternatively, it's one-and-a-half-kilometers (just under a mile) up a paved pathway northwest of the City Palace. Either way, it's Jaipur's loveliest sunset spot.

SHOPPING

Jaipur has the most colorful variety of things to buy in all of India, ranging from enameled blue pottery, exquisite gem-studded, enameled jewelry, and traditional block-printed fabrics to brightly patterned dhurrie rugs. It is tempting to forsake Jaipur's other attractions and spend hours poking about in the spice-scented lanes, drinking sickly-sweet tea, and chatting with artisans working at traditional crafts. The bazaars are concentrated to the south of the old city, while many of the modern shops and all the state emporia are on Mirza Ismail Road and Agra Road.

The bazaars are the best place to shop, but there are also some emporia worth taking a look at. On Mirza Ismail Road you will find the **Rajasthan Handloom House** and next door the **Rajasthali Emporium**. They provide an excellent opportunity to survey the handicrafts of Rajasthan and get an idea of prices. **Anokhi**, on Tilak Marg, opposite the Udyog Bhavan, is easily India's best shop for a large range of traditional hand-block printed cottons and stylish European-style dresses (it has a cult following with Delhi's diplomatic wives). There's another outlet in the Rambagh Palace Hotel, and opposite Delhi's Ashoka Hotel.

You can find the most famous of Jaipur's wares — polished gems, semiprecious stones, and exquisite enameled jewelry — in wide-open **Johari Bazaar**, near the Hawa Mahal. In the lane opposite **Gopalji Ka Rasta**, **Bapu Bazaar** and **Nehru Bazaar** are the places to find traditional tie-and-dye *bhandhani*-work and hand-printed textiles, as well as embroidered camel-skin *mojadis* or slippers, and local perfumes.

Along the **Tripolia Bazaar's** long arterial boulevard are endless rows of brassware, terracotta pots, and the famous Jaipur "blue" pottery, and **Chaura Rasta** is crammed with costume jewelry and bangles.

For quality gems and jewelry, there are two particularly good shops to visit — bearing in mind that bazaar jewelry is not always "pukka": **Gem Palace** and the **Jewels Emporium**, both on Mirza Ismail Road.

To see craftsmen making block-printed fabrics, marbled paper, and Jaipur blue pottery, make an excursion out to the charming village of **Sanganer**, 16 km (10 miles) south. The village is noteworthy for its palace ruins, imposing antique *toranas* or gateways, and several ornate Jain temples.

WHERE TO STAY

Expensive

Travelers to Jaipur have a reasonably good selection of luxury hotels to choose from, but the winning feature of Jaipur's top-end accommodation is that it offers the opportunity to pamper yourself with a stay in a royal palace.

The most magnificent of the royal palaces is the five-star **Rambagh Palace** ((0141) 381919 FAX (0141) 381908, Bhawani Singh Road. In the late-nineteenth-century, it was the official palace of the polo-playing maharaja Man Singh II, and the world's only private residence with its own polo ground. Set amid manicured gardens, this marble palace offers royal suites with period furniture, four-poster beds, and art deco marble bathrooms. The Polo Bar — judged one of the world's most famous watering holes — and cane chair-strewn veranda are Jaipur's most relaxing oases at sunset. Facilities include an excellent health club with squash courts, a beauty salon, an excellent shopping arcade, a delightful 1930s pavilion-enclosed marble-lined swimming pool, and a Jacuzzi. Modern rooms have standard five-star decor and are in the expensive range, but suites offer the proverbial lap of luxury for upwards of US$475.

Almost as lush and slightly cheaper is the **Jai Mahal Palace** ((0141) 371616 FAX (0141) 365237, Jacob Road, Civil Lines. There is less of the palace atmosphere here and more emphasis on modern amenities. Along with the usual shopping arcade, swimming pool, restaurants, bar, and 24-hour room service, an in-house astrologer is also available.

The best of the non-palace hotels (despite the name) is the **Rajputana Palace Sheraton** ((0141) 360011 FAX (0141) 367848, Palace Road. Room rates at this tastefully appointed, modern hotel, which is built around a swimming pool, start at around US$155 for a double.

Mid-range

The period-flavor **Raj Mahal Palace** ((0141) 381757 FAX (0141) 381887 is set in rambling gardens off Sardar Patel Road. A former British Residency, it was taken up by Jaipur's First Couple after they left the Rambagh. Prince Philip came here in 1965 and was introduced to the joys of Holi when showered with colored water by Jaipur's maharaja.

Downscaling your budget still further into the US$30 range does not mean you have to miss out on the palatial experience. Jaipur has a number of quaint mansions belonging to ex-nobles that have been converted into guesthouses, all set amid peaceful gardens.

The most charming of these is **Narain Niwas** ((0141) 563448 FAX (0141) 561045, Narain Singh Road, built in 1881. Its decadent suites are a repository of faded finery — four-poster beds, Afghan carpets, old lithographs, and flayed tiger skins. There are two little garden cottages, and

OPPOSITE: Detail of a typically ornate façade in the so-called "Pink City" of Jai Singh's time. ABOVE: The five-story pyramidal Hawa Mahal, (Palace of the Winds) in Jaipur is a classic example of traditional Rajput architecture with its *chhatris* domes, curved arches, and latticed windows giving the effect of architectural embroidery in cinnabar and white.

simpler comfortable rooms for US$15. Breakfast on the terrace with preening peacocks strutting past is Jaipur at its most seductive. Meals are prepared to order.

Also highly recommended is **Bissau Palace** ((0141) 304371 FAX (0141) 304628, Chandpol Bazaar, a charming and peaceful refuge in the heart of the old city. Guests can browse through a beautifully kept library, peer at heirlooms, cool off in a backyard pool, and sip tea on the veranda. Excellent Western breakfasts are served. Single rooms to well-furnished suites are within the inexpensive range, all with air-conditioning.

Budget

One of Jaipur's most charming budget hotels is **Khetri House** ((0141) 69183, a 1930s-style bungalow with pleasant and cheap rooms. There is no air-conditioning here.

The **Khasa Khoti** ((0141) 375151, Mirza Ismail Road, is slightly more expensive, but has a selection of comfortable air-cooled and air-conditioned rooms. A swimming pool, restaurant, and tourist office feature among the facilities.

Other hotels include the RTDC-run **Gangaur Tourist Bungalow** ((0141) 371641, on Mirza Ismail Road and **Teej Tourist Bungalow** ((0141) 374373, Collectorate Road, Bani Park, neither exceptional but both clean and well-priced.

WHERE TO EAT

Of the luxury hotels, the Rambagh Palace offers the most sumptuous dining experience. A candle-lit evening meal at its huge Italian marble-lined **Savaran Mahal** is an unforgettable treat. Regally attired waiters serve excellent Mughalai dishes — although it's possible to opt for less exotic Chinese and Western dishes — and there's an evening accompaniment of musicians and folk ballads. Dinner for two costs about US$20.

On Sansar Chandra Road, Mansingh Hotel's rooftop **Shiver** attracts scores of Jaipur businessmen for its super lunches, and has good views and evening music.

Of the dozens of restaurants clustered along Jaipur's main Mirza Ismail Road, the best are **Niros**, **Chanakaya** (for vegetarian Rajasthani dishes), and **Kwality**, all reasonably priced with prompt service. Niros, in particular, has become so popular nowadays that you may find yourself waiting for a table. It serves a familiar mixture of tandoori, Mughalai, continental, and Chinese cuisines.

For Sino-Indian fare, "masala-style" — no chopsticks — try the **Golden Dragon**, just off Mirza Ismail Road, around the corner from Niros.

One place where you can be assured of good food, fast service, and a friendly atmosphere without overstretching your budget is the **LMB Hotel** (Laxmi Misthan Bhandar) in the old city

near Johari Bazaar. It is always packed with discerning backpackers for its delicious vegetarian dishes, *kachori*, savory puffs served with hot chutney, and milk-based desserts of *rasmalai* and *halwa*. To round off a splash-out meal, Jaipur's best ice cream counter is just outside.

The **Copper Chimney Restaurant** on Mirza Ismail Road, is recommended for its Indian cuisine and friendly service.

HOW TO GET THERE

Indian Airlines has daily flights from Delhi to Jaipur, along with direct flights to Jodhpur, Udaipur, Ahmedabad, Bombay, and Aurangabad. Other airlines with Jaipur connections are UP Airlines, Modiluft, and Sahara airlines.

The best way to get to Jaipur by train is with the *Shatabdi Express*, which leaves Delhi at an ungodly hour, but does the journey in less than five hours and in relative luxury. The *Intercity Express* is another early morning service, taking about 40 minutes longer to do the trip. Rail connections from Agra are not so convenient — they tend to be slow and arrive at inconvenient hours. The *Howrah Express* has a late night departure and should arrive in Jaipur at around 6 AM, making it the best choice.

In some ways, buses are a better way of getting to either Agra or Delhi, though the real risks involved in hurtling down India's highways is worth considering before buying a ticket. Deluxe air-conditioned buses take less than six hours from either Delhi or Agra.

Jaipur is a perfect staging post for exploring the rest of Rajasthan by train or bus and has direct rail links to Alwar (Sariska National Park), Sawai Madhopur (for Ranthambhore National Park), Ajmer (Pushkar), Jodhpur, Udaipur, Abu Road, and Ahmedabad, and Bikaner (via a stop at Sikar to link with the fresco-filled region of Shekhavati).

SAMOD

If you can spare a night away from Jaipur, make a detour 42 km (26 miles) north to Samod, where there is an enchanting eighteenth-century palace built by Jai Singh II's finance minister, and now run by his descendants as a hotel.

Surrounded by barren scrubland and crowned by the battlements of an old fort up on the ridge, **Hotel Samod Palace** ((0141) 608942 FAX (0141) 602370 has exquisite jewel-box interiors, fine murals, gilt and painted surfaces, and *meenakari* (inlay of mirrors and stones) as fine as that of the Sheesh Mahal at Amber. It's splendidly romantic, with a grand central courtyard, antique carved

TOP: Chulgiri Temple and BOTTOM Ranaji Ki Nasia in Jaipur.

furniture, faded courtly photographs, old retainers, and posing peacocks. Evenings are spent in the fine Durbar Hall, being served Rajasthani cuisine and entertained by musicians. The rooms are furnished simply and well. The bathroom shutters open to reveal spectacular views. Doubles range from around US$100.

To get to Samod it's a good idea to hire a taxi or a RTDC car at Jaipur's railway station tourist office. Traveling by local bus involves a change at Chaumu, which is about an hour out of Jaipur.

RANTHAMBHORE NATIONAL PARK

Set between the Aravalli and Vindhya hills, Ranthambhore's 411 sq km (156 sq miles) of dry deciduous forest is tiger territory, full of picturesque pavilions and ruined temples with a thousand-year-old fort silhouetted against the hilltop skyline. Since the eighteenth century, the area served as a hunting ground for the maharajahs of Jaipur, who built a series of artificial lakes as vital watering holes for wildlife. The Project Tiger park also has leopards, hyenas, jungle cats, sloths, sambar (large deer), chital (spotted deer), and *chinkara* antelopes and *nilgai* Indian antelopes). Marsh crocodiles and monitor lizards can be seen slumbering on lake-banks, and the park attracts many migrant water birds.

Ranthambhore lies 162 km (100 miles) from Jaipur, and can be easily reached by car or train. The nearest station, Sawai Madhopur, is only 13 km (eight miles) away from the park entrance. From Delhi Ranthambhore is directly accessible on the Delhi-Bombay line.

Now the ex-royal **Jogi Mahal Lodge** is closed (it may reopen), the best place to stay is the **Sawai Madhopur Lodge (** (07462) 20541 FAX (07462) 20718, former residence of the maharaja of Jaipur and an oasis of luxury. Doubles start at around US$130, but there are only 22 rooms so it is wise to book ahead. It's around three kilometers (one and a half miles) from Sawai Madhopur station.

You can find considerably cheaper accommodation without compromising too much on atmosphere and comfort at the **Castle Jhoomer Baori Forest Lodge (** (07462) 20495, which was formerly a hunting lodge of the maharaja and which now provides spacious air-cooled rooms at budget rates to all paying customers. It's around seven kilometers (just over four miles) out of town, beautifully situated on a hill.

ALWAR AND SARISKA NATIONAL PARK

A train halt lying 143 km (90 miles) northwest of Jaipur and halfway from Delhi, Alwar has a gruesome martial past, yet today is a languid town dotted with palaces and lakes, dominated by a 300-m (1,000-ft)-high battle-scarred hilltop fortress hewn from the jagged Aravalli Hills. It was founded as an independent princely state late in Rajasthan's history in 1776, but it quickly made up for lost time with constant bouts of often brutal warfare against Delhi's Mughals. Following an alliance with the British, Alwar's rulers concentrated their efforts on building elaborate pleasure palaces and staging extravagant tiger shoots.

Alwar makes a picturesque staging post for a visit to Sariska National Park, 34 km (21 miles) away, staying overnight at either the **Sariska Palace (** (0146) 41322 (Sariska), one of the largest hunting lodges in India, or the RTDC-run **Lake Palace (** (0144) 22991, which overlooks the beautiful Siliserh Lake and wooded hills.

There's plenty to see in town, starting with the opulent 105-room **Vinay Vilas Palace**, built in 1925. In its prime, its stables accommodated 3,000 thoroughbred horses and a herd of royal elephants. To the right of the palace is the magnificent two-story gilt carriage designed to straddle the backs of four elephants and carry 50 people off on a tiger shoot. Among the highlights in its fascinating museum are a cup that is carved out of a single emerald, enemy-scuttling weaponry, and a rich display of eighteenth- and nineteenth-century Mughal and Rajput paintings. The palace is open from 10 AM to 5 PM, and is closed on Fridays and public holidays.

Clamber up to the fort for an eagle's view of the **Pujan Vihar** garden and summer house and the royal *chhatris*, temples, and pavilions near the tanks.

A former royal hunting ground, the **Sariska National Park** spans 800 sq km (300 sq miles) and is one of India's most beautiful tiger sanctuaries. You'll get as close as you would ever want to get to tigers by driving in jeeps or hiding in little *machan*-huts above the reserve's well-patronized waterholes (especially at dusk), and see plenty of leopards, sloth bears, hyenas, *nilgai* (Indian antelope), *chinkara* and four-horned antelope, and various birds.

Stay either at the Sariska Palace (see above) or at the budget **Tiger Den Tourist Bungalow (** (0146) 41322. The best time to visit is from February to June.

SHEKHAVATI

The dusty, fresco-filled region of Shekhavati lies in northwestern Rajasthan within easy reach by road or train of Jaipur, Bikaner, and Delhi. Once a semi-independent collection of *thikanas* (fief-doms), from the mid-eighteenth century wealthy Marwari merchants from near Jodhpur, created townships of fortress-like *havelis* decorated with life-size frescoes.

The frescoes were created using a technique similar to that developed during the Italian Renaissance, which consists of working rapidly on wet plaster — a method that has preserved many of the frescoes very well. The earliest examples depict popular gods, martial lore, and elephants, but later works feature such startlingly quirky subjects as a mourning Queen Victoria, King George V and Queen Mary on a visit to India, podgy pinstriped Indians waving farewell from a train, and even the Wright brothers in their odd-looking airplane.

You'll find the largest concentration of these beguiling creations in the districts of Jhunjhunu and Sikar at three major fresco centers: **Mandawa**, **Dundlodh**, and **Nawalgarh**, each within an afternoon's driving distance of moderately priced and charming palace-hotels.

WHERE TO STAY

One of the best places to stay is the **Castle Mandawa ((01592) 23124, 168 km (100 miles)** from Jaipur, 35 km (22 miles) from Sikar. Built in 1775, it is a breathtakingly atmospheric place to stay, particularly during the festivals of Holi in February/March, Gangaur in March/April, and Teej in July/August. From the moustached Rajput guards at the entrance to the brilliant peacocks fluttering across the rooftops, it offers a splendid base from which to explore the surrounding villages. At the end of the day, return for a hot shower, a good meal, and a delightful room with original furnishings, either in the castle or in the converted stables.

The same family run a **Desert Camp**, perfect for large groups with its deluxe Rajput huts (with attached modern bathrooms!) and village atmosphere, just two kilometers (a mile or so) from Castle Mandawa. Both can be booked through Old Mandawa ((0141) 381906 FAX (0141) 382214, Sansar Chandra Road, Jaipur 302001.

Also recommended in the region is the **Dera Dundlodh Kila ((01594) 52519 FAX (01594) 52519,** located 150 km (94 miles) from Jaipur, 25 km (15 miles) from Jhunjhunu, 14 km (nine miles) from Mukundagh. It was built in 1756 and can be booked through Dundlod House ((0141) 211276, Hawa Sarak, Civil Lines, Jaipur.

HOW TO GET THERE

The best way of exploring these fresco towns is by jeep or car. If you arrive at either Sikar or Fatehpur by train, there are plenty of drivers willing to bargain on rates for driving you around.

You can get there by taking the *Shekhavati Express*, which runs between Delhi and Jaipur daily and stops at Jhunjhunu, Mukundagh, and Sikar, or opt for the erratic bus services linking Shekhavati's towns with Sikar and Jaipur.

AJMER AND PUSHKAR

Located within central Rajasthan, at 130 km (80 miles) west of Jaipur and 198 km (123 miles) east of Jodhpur, the walled lakeside city of Ajmer is a curious Muslim toehold in a region dominated by Rajput Hindus. It is, in fact, India's most famous Muslim pilgrimage center, with its shrine of the Sufi saint Khwaja Muinudin Chisthi (1142-1256) who was a direct descendant of the Mohammed's son-in-law, Ali.

Ajmer's early history was scarred with bloody rampaging assaults by the Mahmud of Ghazni in 1024 and Muhammad Ghori in 1193, but it later

became an important religious and strategic oasis town for the Mughal emperors. It was annexed by Akbar in 1556, who built a fort-palace that has now been turned into a museum. After 1818, it was ruled by the British, who founded the Mayo College, the first-ever Indian public school for young princes.

The city is strewn with historic Islamic architecture. The **Adai-din-ka-Jhopra** is a remarkable mosque built by Muhammad Ghori's armies in just two days on the ruins caused by an orgy of destruction that razed an ancient Sanskrit college and 30 Hindu temples. The **Dargah**, a grand shrine built by Humayun, contains the relics of the Sufi saint.

The Dargah is the scene of Ajmer's spectacular annual festival of *Urs*, commemorating the saint's death. Held for six days in April or May, the festival draws thousands of pilgrims. Curious tourists go to witness the dramatic spectacle of continuous *qawwali* singing, exuberant fairs, and feasts cooked in iron tureens so vast that people dance in them (not during the cooking of course).

Ajmer is not exactly brimming with good accommodation. Even the best hotel in town, the **Hotel Mansingh Palace ((0145) 425855,** Vaishali Nagar, has a down-at-heel, neglected air about it, despite providing an impressive array of amenities.

Close-up of a fresco painting in Shekhavati district.

The only other recommendable hotel in Ajmer is the budget to mid-range **Hotel Regency** ((0145) 30296, Delhi Gate, which has reasonable air-conditioned doubles from around US$15.

Budget travelers tend to give Ajmer a miss entirely and head directly to **Pushkar**, just 11 km (seven miles) away, where there is an abundance of family-run inexpensive accommodation.

Hindus believe Pushkar's beautiful lake to be sacred, second only to the Ganges River in purifying those who immerse themselves in it. According to legend, the lake formed when Lord Brahma dropped a lotus flower while searching for a suitable place to do his *yagna*, or sacrifice. Pushkar also boasts one of the only Brahma temples in India.

But for most visitors, Pushkar means only one thing — the exuberantly colorful 10-day **Camel and Cattle Fair**, staged in November, when this tiny oasis town is suddenly crammed with up to 200,000 Rajput traders and 50,000 cattle for an endless round of livestock-dealing, camel racing, and fairs selling silver jewelry, embroidered shoes, camel-skin items, and woolen rugs, folk-dancing, music, and itinerant entertainers. You'll never have seen anything like it — the horizon massed with splay-legged camels and blazing with the most riotous bursts of color imaginable. It is a

ABOVE: A bridal procession makes its way through the streets of Ajmer. OPPOSITE TOP: Children dressed in Rajput finery for the Pushkar fair. BOTTOM: Jodhpur's citadel towers over the city. OVERLEAF: Beasts of burden and labor, camels are prized for their endurance in the harsh, sun-baked Rajasthan desert.

pageant of turbaned men and Rajput women in their swinging, multicolored *ghaghara* skirts, tie-dyed blouses embellished with silver tinsel, and bedecked with silver jewelry.

Be warned: during the fair, Pushkar's modest accommodation facilities are swamped. The **RTDC Tourist Village** ((0141) 310586 is open year round, but during the fair rates soar as much as tenfold, and bookings are essential. Accommodation is provided in double tents with shower and lavatory; food is included in the tent price.

Another nice place is the Maharaja of Jaipur's former palace, the chaotically RTDC-run **Hotel Pushkar Palace** ((0145) 72001. Ask for a good air-conditioned room: some of them have lake views.

JODHPUR

Lying on the edge of the Thar Desert and dominated by its medieval fortress citadel, the flat, sandy, leisurely paced city of Jodhpur was the former capital of the arid, drought-prone principality of Marwar (Land of Death).

The city was founded in 1459 by Rao Jodha, attracted by the natural defenses provided by its massive 125-m (400-ft)-high steep scarp. As a trading post on the main camel caravan routes, Jodhpur rapidly amassed vast wealth, and its merchant class, known as the Marwaris, are still renowned in India for their mercantile prowess.

Jodhpur's main attraction is its extraordinary fifteenth-century fort encircled by a snaking 10-km (six mile)-long stone wall punctuated by eight monumental gates. This fortress proved invulnerable even to the Mughals, who finally compromised by signing treaties with Jodhpur's rulers, exchanging wealth for military assistance to win Gujarat for the Mughal empire.

The patronage of the Mughals reached its height in the mid-sixteenth century, when Jodhpur's Rao Udai Singh married his sister to Emperor Akbar and his daughter to the emperor's son, Jahangir. Akbar may have secretly regretted the alliance — his Rajput wife, Jodhai Bai, managed to increase considerably the powers of the Jodhpurs, but more importantly for Akbar she made him give up "beef, garlic, onions and the wearing of a beard," according to a court chronicle.

Mughal patronage turned sour though when Jodhpur's Jaswant Singh backed the losing side in the Mughal struggle for power between the waning Shah Jahan and his formidable son, Aurangzeb. One of the first commands given by the new emperor Aurangzeb was for the murder of Jaswant Singh's posthumously born boy heir to the Jodhpur throne, who was then conveniently at the royal court in Delhi. The attempt failed (the boy was hidden in a basket of sweetmeats and whisked away to safety), but Aurangzeb wreaked his revenge in 1678 by sacking Jodhpur and

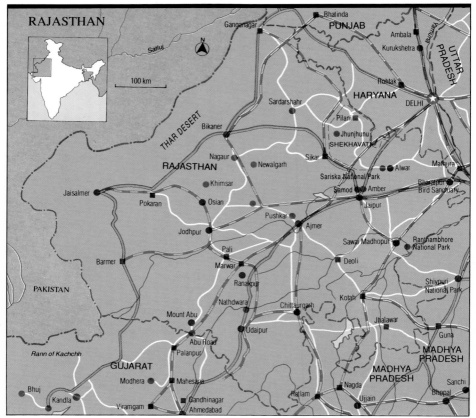

plundering the prosperous towns of Marwar. Ajit Singh, the boy-prince, recaptured his kingdom after an interval of 30 years, becoming in the process one of Jodhpur's greatest heroes.

Jodhpur was then thrown into a century of dynastic disarray and bloody battles with neighboring states. At the end of the eighteenth century, it was seized first by the Marathas and then by the British. During the early twentieth century, Jodhpur was ruled by the quixotic and powerful Maharaja Umaid Singh, who left the remarkable Umaid Bhawan Palace, one of the world's largest private residences, as his legacy. The palace was built to keep 3,000 of his starving population employed following a devastating famine in 1923. It was completed in 1945, just before the maharaja had to cede his princely state to a newly independent India.

Jodhpur remains curiously unappreciated by many travelers, who glimpse it only in passing, usually en route either to Jaisalmer further west or Udaipur in the south. But old-India hands rate its charms highly, for as well as its wealth of historic attractions and colorful bazaars, Jodhpur is a place where you can stray off the beaten track for a glimpse of village India.

WHAT TO SEE AND DO

A novel, but slow, way to get around Jodhpur is by nag-drawn *tonga* or the ubiquitous cycle-rickshaw. But for Jodhpur's main attraction, **Mehrangarh Fort**, five kilometers (three miles) from the town center, take a taxi or auto-rickshaw.

From Jai Pol (Victory) Gate, continue the steep climb on foot past cannon-shot-scarred battlements, souvenir shops, and busking musicians. Commissioned by Rao Jodha in 1459, this fortress aerie is a masterpiece of medieval defense. It is said that its unsuspecting architect was ordered buried alive so that he could not reveal its secrets.

Another grisly relic of the feudal past is the forlorn plaster row of delicate sati palm prints beside Lohapol (Iron) Gate, marking the spot of self-immolation by women whose husbands died in battle. Sati was idealized as an act of romance, sacrifice, and devotion, so that a king's prestige was quite literally measured by the number of women who elected to throw themselves on his funeral pyre. Of all Jodhpur's rulers, Ajit Singh claimed the greatest "honor" by having his six queens and 58 concubines share his flames in 1731.

Rudyard Kipling was suitably impressed by the fortress-palace, describing it as a creation of "angels, fairies and giants," though it is a description that could hardly have found favor with the full-blooded, larger-than-life Rajputs who built it.

The complex is maintained as a museum, and houses 18 different sections, each full of carefully displayed antiquities. Open 9 AM to 5 PM daily, the entrance fee includes the very useful services of knowledgeable, English-speaking guides.

Elderly royal retainers usher visitors through cordoned passages with a proprietorial air. Within lies a maze of interlocking palace interiors, inner marble courtyards, audience halls, and exquisite latticed *zenana* chambers. The *pièce de résistance* is the royal boudoir, an Arabian Nights fantasy of exotic paneling, dangling colored balls, and mirrored and mosaic walls. There are even swings, perfect for royal romps with the concubines, and an enormous bed upon which generations of Jodhpur's maharajas indulged in their peccadilloes. Another highlight is the eighteenth-century Dancing Hall, the ceiling of which is plastered with 80 kg (176 lb) of pure gold.

The museum rooms house a richly diverse collection of weaponry, including the swords of Akbar and Timur, gem-encrusted gilt elephant howdahs, royal cradles, rare miniatures, and many traditional Rajasthani musical instruments, many of which have now disappeared from common use. But pride of place is taken by a huge portable tent-palace, used by Emperor Shah Jahan on his tours.

Beyond the palace lie the fort's craggy ramparts, strewn with antique cannons. The view from the edge is unforgettable, like being atop Mount Olympus and spying on the activities of the world below. From the city rises the hum of massed humanity, with stray shouts, dog's barks, and snatches of song lifted suddenly with almost unnatural clarity.

As you drive down the fort road, you'll see the dazzling white marble **Jaswant Thada**, the cenotaph to Maharaja Jaswant Singh built in 1899. He was the first of the Rathore rulers not to have his cenotaph erected at Mandore, the historic capital. It's worth finding the *chowkidar* to let you inside to see the portraits of all the Rathore rulers.

In town, wander through Jodhpur's colorful marketplace, which spans out around the **Clock Tower Square** until late in the evening. It's too narrow for cars, but big enough for swarms of jingling bicycles, cows, carts, and camels. This is the fabled Old Market, now **Sardar Bazaar**.

In the general market, cows doze lethargically under giant tarpaulins, *dhoti*-clad merchants sprawl like odalisques amid pyramids of millet, women squat like monkeys sifting wheat from chaff, and swarms of flies and giggling children dog you step by step. Depending on which direc-

tion you take, you'll be plunged into anything from a locksmith's cul-de-sac to one stacked with oozing raw jaggery, silverware, sweetmeats, flower garlands, or medical textbooks. Good finds in Jodhpur include wooden puppets, painted horses, ivory-work, tie-dyed *bandhana* fabric, and embroidered slippers.

Tranquil strolls can be enjoyed in the leafy, well-kept **Umaid Public Gardens and Zoo**, full of bougainvillea, mango, and rosebushes.

To the northwest of the gardens is **Government Museum**, a taxidermist's nightmare with its balding, silverfish-infested menagerie, reminiscent of the famous Monty Python "dead parrot" skit. Other exhibits include antique Indian sculpture, scrolls, royal treatises, and a decorated Durbar Hall. It's open from 10 AM to 4 PM daily except Fridays.

It's worth reserving a morning or afternoon to see **Mandore**, the ancient capital of the Rathore Marwars, eight kilometers (five miles) north of town. It's a picturesque necropolis set in a lush, leafy garden, strewn with the *chhatris* of the Jodhpur rulers. The maharanis' *chhatris* are more desolately elegant, standing amid boulders along the hilltop ridge and reached by a steep winding path to the right of the garden.

Make sure you see the 18th-century Hall of Heroes, a gallery of 16 life-sized gods, goddesses, and Rajput warriors carved from a single rock.

Village Safaris

Between tours of princely palaces and marble mausoleums, many visitors to India lament that they missed a glimpse of the real India — the rural villages where people still live by their ancient customs. Maharaja Singh of Ajit Bhawan started the village safari tradition — which has now become a full blown tourist attraction, with many agencies around town offering them — as a one-day safari aboard a 1942 U.S. Army jeep through the villages in the near-desert terrain surrounding Jodhpur. His fascinating firsthand insights into Rajasthani rural life won glowing praise from Geoffrey Moorehouse, author of *India Britannica* and *Calcutta*.

"Everything in towns is evil," explains Singh. "It is on the farms, the uncorrupted areas away from electricity and telephones that the real beauties of life can be found."

The vestige of his previous role still exists, for at each stop the villagers offer an enthusiastic greeting, and still turn to him for guidance, to mediate disputes, and even to conduct wedding ceremonies. The maharaja and his small group of visitors are met by a beaming white-haired patriarch dressed in white and clusters of curious, brightly clad tribeswomen laden with chunky silver jewelry and ivory bracelets up the length of their arms.

Visitors are asked to take off their shoes before walking across the surprisingly pleasantly textured "protective" ring of mixed dried cow dung and urine around the hut: an ancient practice to ward off snakes and harness the "generative energy" of the cow, a sacred creature to the Hindus. Over spicy ginger tea (and sometimes a draft of *afion* (opium), taken infused in water from the cupped hand of the host) Singh holds court on subjects as varied as the plight of the Untouchables, the desert's deepwater wells, the significance of turban colors, and local courtship rituals. Visitors are shown how villagers make dhurries, and are encouraged to try their hand at making pots, grinding grain, and firing slingshots.

You will find village safaris on offer all around Jodhpur these days; the going rate is US$10 a head. The Umaid Bhawan Palace is a reliable choice. Although their tours lack the vigorous personality of Maharaja Singh, they are cheaper and the pageantry of village life remains as fascinating.

Consider combining a village safari with a night or two at the delightful sixteenth-century **Rohet Castle** ((02932) 66231, 42 km (26 miles) from Jodhpur, a mini-fortress stronghold of the region's ruling Rathore clan overlooking an oasis lake. Here you'll be well looked after by the present *thakur* (ruler), Siddarth Singh, and his charming family, fed mouthwatering Rajput cuisine, and if you are part of a small group, you'll be given a truly memorable welcome, ending with an uproarious dance on the lawns with infectiously gleeful Rajput villagers. Rooms

look out onto the garden and are inexpensive. Or you can opt to spend a comfortable night on the roof under a brilliant canopy of stars. For bookings, contact Rohet Castle, P.O. Rohet, District Pali, Rajasthan, or Rohet House, PWD Road, Jodhpur.

If you're getting about Rajasthan by rented car, Castle Rohet can be a good place to break the trip to see **Ranakpur's** wondrous fifteenth-century Jain temples, 116 km (72 miles) away. Intricately sculpted from rose marble, these 29 halls form India's most complex and extensive group of Jain temples, covering over 3,600 sq m (40,000 sq ft) and containing 1,444 ornate pillars, each unique and covered with carvings. From Ranakpur, Udaipur is only 60 km (37 miles) away.

WHERE TO STAY

Luxury
The magnificent oleander-colored sandstone **Umaid Bhawan Palace** ((0291) 33316 FAX (0291) 35373, residence of the former maharaja, is now India's most extraordinary luxury hotel, superbly maintained and run by Welcomgroup.

Replete with marble, gilt, and rich brocades, this vast 347-roomed palace is eccentric opulence on a grand scale. Massive crested brass doors usher visitors into an art deco lobby leading to soaring double-domed inner courtyards, the first with stuffed leopards poised on its sweeping twin marble staircases, the second with European gilt furniture and tiered spiraling stairwells leading up to a whispering gallery. Directly below is the basement swimming pool, and from the central courtyard branch trophy-crammed billiard rooms and libraries.

Much of the palace is given over to the hotel, while Jodhpur's former royal family inhabits the uppermost wings. The main reception halls hold the palace museum, with its rare antique clock and watch collection, Rajput Mughal miniatures, armor, *objets d'art*, and ambitious painted murals (open 9 AM to 5 PM).

Each room is different, but all are spacious and decorated with original period furnishings. The suites are positively splendid, with up to six rooms apiece and balconies overlooking the peacock-inhabited garden pavilions, and range from US$350 to US$990. There's even a novelty suite created to resemble the interior of a ship, but by far the grandest are the two Regal Suites, formerly occupied by the maharaja and his maharani, with mammoth beds, interior fountains, chandeliers, and glorious art deco marble bathrooms.

Evenings are best spent on the moonlit terrace, where turbaned musicians play every evening against a magical backdrop of pavilioned gardens and the illuminated fort. The excellent five-star facilities include an indoor pool with sun terrace, a health club, squash, tennis, and badminton courts, with croquet and golf on request.

If ostentation and maharaja palaces are not your style, you might decide to stay in the no-nonsense **Ratanada Polo Palace** ((0291) 31910 FAX (0291) 33118, where you'll find comfortable lower-end luxury standards and all the usual amenities.

Mid-range

Ajit Bhawan ((0291) 37410 FAX (0291) 63774, opposite Circuit House, is Umaid Bhawan's closest rival. Built for Umaid Singh's younger brother, this bougainvillea-covered ancestral

courtyard. Golf, squash, camel rides, and excellent village tours can be arranged. The maharaja is definitely the man to talk to about acquiring a pair of Jodhpur's classic sartorial amesake.

Another mid-range accommodation option is the **Hotel Karni Bhawan** ((0291) 32220 FAX (0291) 33495, Defence Lab Road. This modern hotel with good amenities — swimming pool, shopping arcade, and so forth — offers inexpensive and comfortable rooms, and has a very pretty breakfast courtyard too.

Budget

Budget travelers can take their pick of a number of cheap, reliable lodges. At the top of the range is

mansion has been transformed into a charming hotel brimming with family heirlooms, Raj-era bric-a-brac, hunting trophies, and a friendly atmosphere. It is run with great aplomb in the guesthouse tradition by a raconteurish descendant of Ajit, Maharaj Swaroop Singh — the uncle of Jodhpur's present maharaja — who cuts a very dashing figure in riding breeches, cravat, and turban.

There's a choice of air-conditioned or air-cooled double rooms within the mansion, or you can opt for one of the stylish cottages scattered around the pretty gardens, each designed like a traditional village hut but with very pukka tiled bathrooms. The room prices are inexpensive. Additional quirky glamour is provided by Ajit Bhawan's staff, all startlingly authentic in their Rajput costumes. Excellent breakfasts and home-cooked dinners are served in the garden or the

the uninspiring but clean and well managed **Adarsh Niwas Hotel** ((0291) 627338 FAX (0291) 627314. It's just near the rail station and has a popular courtyard cafeteria. Rooms are either air-cooled or air-conditioned, and they all come with attached bathrooms.

The RTDC-run **Ghoomar Tourist Bungalow** ((0291) 44010, on High Court Road near the Ajit Bhawan Gardens, is a popular travelers' halt. It also houses the Tourist Office, an Indian Airlines desk ((0291) 28600 or (0291) 20909, and a cafeteria. Rooms are shabbily worn, but clean, and quite acceptable for a night or so. Dorm beds are also available for a song.

OPPOSITE: A Rajput patriarch and his grandson. ABOVE: Within the monumental Umaid Bhawan Hotel, originally an Anglophile maharaja's fantasy palace built entirely of red sandstone in the 1920s.

WHERE TO EAT

Try to dine at least once at both Umaid Bhawan Palace and Ajit Bhawan, for each offers a unique style, spectacular settings, and good food.

Highlights at **Umaid Bhawan** include afternoon teas on the terrace and the excellent blowout buffet lunches in the grand Marwal Hall, with its dangling chandeliers, polished mirrors and stuffed tigers. **Ajit Bhawan** is perfect for sampling authentic West Rajasthani dishes in a prettily illuminated garden or courtyard — or, during Jodhpur's bitterly cold winter nights, around a blazing fire.

is the **Fort View**, a rooftop restaurant at the Mayur Hotel on Station Road. As its name suggests, views of the fort are a major attraction, but the *thali* platters are recommended too.

HOW TO GET THERE

Some 336 km (208 miles) from Jaipur, Jodhpur has direct flights to and from Delhi, Jaipur, Udaipur, and Mumbai.

Unless you're on a fly-by-night tour, Rajasthan is the perfect size to get around in by train. Overnight sleepers link Jodhpur with Delhi and the main Rajasthan centers of Jaipur, Jaisalmer, Udaipur, Abu Road, Bikaner, and Ahmedabad.

In town are two popular eating houses: the vegetarian **Pankaj**, at Jalori Gate, and the **Kalinga**, next to the Adarsh Niwas Hotel near the rail station, which is good for reasonably priced Mughalai dishes and as a place to linger before catching an overnight train.

Don't miss out on the famous Jodhpur treat, Makhania *lassi*, a divine concoction made from whipped cow's milk, butterballs, and cardamom —one taste, and you're hooked. It's served all over town, usually in suspiciously grimy glasses with a lump of ice added for good measure.

The **Sri Mishra Lal Hotel** at the Sardar bazaar gateway serves what are reputed to be Jodhpur's best *lassi*, claiming to sell 1,000 glasses a day. Another decadent Jodhpuri dessert is *mawaki-kachori*, a baklava-like pastry stuffed with caramelized nuts and coconut, smothered in syrup.

A popular haunt for locals and foreigners alike

NAGAUR

On the desert route between Jodhpur and Bikaner, 240 km (150 miles) away, are three sightseeing "musts." The journey is best made in a rented jeep, though local buses can be taken.

Some 100 km (62 miles) north of Jodhpur, nestled near the dunes of the Thar Desert, lies the fifteenth-century oasis stronghold of **Khimsar**.

Its moated, fortified **Royal Castle** is a delightful hotel — a mix of medieval architecture and 1920s decor, taken over by the Welcomgroup and run by its ancestral owner and Rajasthan M.P. Onkar Singh, and his family. Mr. Singh is not always in residence, however.

The rooms are fitted with modern amenities. Evening barbecues and delicious authentic Rajput dishes are served in the ramparts of the old fort. The surrounding plains and sandy dunes are filled with romping *nilgai* (Indian antelope), *chinkara* antelope, desert fox, and the Great Indian bustard, with partridges and imperial sand grouse often ending up as Royal Castle fare. For bookings, write to Onkar Singh, Royal Castle, P.O. Khimsar, District Nagaur, or contact the Umaid Bhawan Hotel in Jodhpur.

It's 65 km (40 miles) to the ancient town of **Osian**, worth seeing for its cluster of 16 ornate Hindu and Jain temples dating from the eighth to the eleventh century.

Also see **Nagaur**, 110 km (68 miles) from Bikaner, a medieval town with a particularly fine partridge-infested, twelfth-century Mughal fort. It's perfect for picnics and for clambering through. The *zenana* quarters have frescoes painted with crushed emeralds, pearls, and egg yolk; there are also mossed-over swimming pools and a mosque built by Akbar. So few visitors explore this remarkable fort that the guard beams with joy when they do appear, proudly producing a musty Visitors' Book for them to sign.

On the full-moon falling closest to the cusp of January and February, Nagaur attracts thousands of Rajput villagers for its livestock fair — bigger and less of a tourist trap than Pushkar — with camel races, folk dancing, strolling players, and mongoose fights.

JAISALMER: FORTRESS OF GOLD

Nothing quite prepares the traveler for the first breathtaking glimpse of Jaisalmer, the remote fortress city on the edge of Rajasthan's Thar Desert. (*Thar* means "abode of death.")

Jaisalmer, which lies 287 km (178 miles) from Jodhpur, at the edge of India's western border with Pakistan, is the most magically medieval of Rajasthan's desert cities, and certainly the most extraordinary, since all the buildings — from the humblest shop to the palace and temples — are carved from a burnished golden-yellow sandstone. Even today, houses are built in the medieval manner to merge in with the old.

The Bhatti Rajput chieftain Rawal Jaisal deserted his former capital Lodurva, 17 km (10.5 miles) away, to found Jaisalmer in 1156 — attracted by the site's large oasis and the natural defense provided by Trikuta (three-peak) hill. It was a tryst with destiny: Centuries before, Lord Krishna was said to have predicted that a distant descendant of his Lunar clan would one day rule from here. Jaisalmer's ruling family, who claimed both Lord Krishna and the moon as ancestors, kept only silver furniture in their palace quarters, believing that the moon-like color would give them talismanic strength.

Protected against the shifting sands and feudal marauders by a steep, double-tiered ring of giant stone ramparts, Jaisalmer became a prosperous, and coveted, stronghold on the great Spice Route which stretched across India from Persia and Afghanistan. It became a city of *caravansaries*, large buildings surrounding a central courtyard, in which the merchants took shelter.

The early Muslim king of Delhi, Alauddin Khalji, laid : iege to the city at the end of the thirteenth century when one of his particularly well-laden caravans was pillaged by the Jaisalmer ruler. The siege lasted eight years, and in a bizarre twist of fate the young Jaisalmer prince Rattan Singh befriended the enemy general, Nawab Mahboob Khan. The two were inseparable

companions and would meet to play chess until the war-horn sounded them into battle. Finally, in 1295 the Rajput clan knew that defeat was imminent. While Rattan Singh's sons were secretly delivered into the safe care of the nawab, Jaisalmer's entire community of women and children committed *johar*, or mass suicide, as their menfolk, clad in ceremonial saffron and delirious with opium, fought to the last.

The warlike Bhattis were soon back in their citadel, waging vendettas once again against neighboring tribes, and spinning webs of intrigue and treachery. Jaisalmer entered a more peaceful era, however, as part of the Mughal empire in the late seventeenth century, prospering as a trading

OPPOSITE: The exterior of the Umaid Bhawan Palace Hotel is a hint of the wonders within. ABOVE: A Jaisalmer village woman in her finery.

post famous for silks, spices, indigo dies, and opium. It was in this period that Hindu and Jain merchants, bankers, and artisans settled here and built magnificent *haveli* mansions with elaborate honeycomb-like balconies.

Jaisalmer's fortunes dwindled with the opening of the Bombay port in the eighteenth century, but it suffered an even worse crisis in the aftermath of Partition in 1947, when the time-honored trade routes to Pakistan were suddenly deemed illegal. Only when it became an important military base during the 1965 and 1971 Indo-Pakistan wars did Jaisalmer emerge from its almost medieval seclusion to be connected by road and rail to the rest of Rajasthan.

WHEN TO GO

Ideally, visit Jaisalmer from November to February when the days are warm, the skies clear, and the nights cold enough for a driftwood fire and a warm sleeping bag. Avoid the summer months, when the temperature shoots up as high as 53°C (127°F) and the raging *simoon* (dust-storm) turns Jaisalmer into a virtual ghost-town.

Jaisalmer is most popular during its annual three-day **Desert Festival**, which coincides with the full moon in February. It's a lively jamboree of camel polo, acrobatics, races, sword-swallowers, traditional Rajput *ghazals* (songs), and dance

Today, Jaisalmer's main source of revenue is tourism. Since the city's "discovery" in the early seventies, Jaisalmer's camel safaris have become one of India's most popular tourist activities, and the beautifully-woven local embroidery has itself become a major industry. There is also a burgeoning illicit trade of black market goods that are smuggled by camel drivers across the sanddunes which separate India and Pakistan.

GENERAL INFORMATION

Jaisalmer's Tourist Office is located in the RTDC Hotel Goomar, but it is not terribly helpful. You'll find more enthusiastic English-speaking guides, who claim to be part of the town's "Guide Association," at the entrance gate to the fort; they will show you every place of historical interest for about US$2 a day.

performances, turban-tying, and "Best Dressed Rajput" contests. Villagers from all around throng to Jaisalmer's bazaar to sell silver jewelry and handwoven wares. Prices for necessities such as mineral water, toilet paper, and beer suddenly soar, and accommodation and train seats are hard to come by. Many hotels solve the problem by erecting impromptu canopied rooms on their roofs, and a "tourist village" of basic tents and bathroom facilities is set up on the plateau beneath the fort in a style similar to that at Pushkar's Camel and Cattle Fair.

Jaisalmer is still one of the best places to witness the spectacle of **Holi** (February/March), a day of mock paint-splashing battles and giggling powder-bespattered chaos. On this day, villagers cram into Mandir Palace, where they playfully pelt the ex-maharaja's family, and the courtyard fills with the sound of the reedy pipe *sheenai* (folk songs) and the clapping rhythm of swirling Rajput dances. All of the important Rajasthan festivals — Dussehra, Diwali, and Gangaur — are celebrated here in the traditional exuberant way.

WHAT TO SEE AND DO

Fort and City Tour

A good walking tour begins at the fortress gate, from where a steep slope branches into a tangled maze of roughly cobbled, dim, and winding passageways. Here the bustle of life seems centuries old. Camels are herded into the shade of overhanging balconies while their owners crouch nearby over pots of syrupy tea; goods ranging

from ornate curled slippers to cartloads of fresh figs are hawked on the cobbles; and villagers, dressed in vivid Rajput costume, haggle over spice trays.

Walking is the only practical means of getting around, although Jaisalmer is so small and contained it can be enjoyed at a leisurely pace in a single morning.

It's a 10-minute walk to the **Gadisar Tank**, the large natural oasis just below the city walls to the southwest. The lake that led Jaisal to found his city is full only in the monsoon months, but there are many temples and shrines around it to explore. The beautiful carved archway leading to the tank is supposed to have been built by Telia, a well-known *nautch* courtesan, for her Bhatti prince lover. She slyly added a Krishna temple so that the monarch's disapproving royal matrons, who refused to use the gate, could not pull it down. For

glorious early morning views of the turreted fort, clamber up onto the temple roofs.

A short distance north is the **Fort**, entered by the Gadisar Gate. This majestic sandstone fortress buttressed by 99 cone-shaped bastions is perched high on Trikuta, or "three-peak" hill. The fort is the second-oldest to be found in Rajasthan, after Chittaurgarh fort, and its cannonball-scarred battlements are testimony to centuries-past sieges, most notably by the Tughluqs and the Mughals.

Just inside the thick gateway of the fort is the ornate seven-story city palace, which rises up from the traditional "blind" *zenana* ground floor to a riot of carved porticoes; and the four other *mahals* (palaces) which housed the royal queens and concubines. After a short stroll up the steep cobbled path, you'll enter a spacious square, dominated by a magnificent marble throne, the **Diwan-i-Am**, where the maharaja used to preside over public meetings, entertain visiting royalty, and celebrate weddings. It was also within this courtyard that *johar* took place.

Just beyond, past a low arched gateway, are the **Jain Temples**, an elegant group of seven interconnecting temples that were built by wealthy Marwari traders between the twelfth and fifteenth centuries and dedicated to the Jain saints Sambhavanathi and Rikhabdevji. Each temple is a marvel of elaborate design and intricate carvings; exteriors festooned with mythological deities and coy, curvaceous *apsaras* (celestial nymphs). Inside you will find incense-laden chambers lined with rows of meditating white marble *tirthankaras*, or Jain saints, whose eyes — all 6,666 pairs of them — flicker eerily with precious gems. Look especially for the priceless emerald icon of the Jain deity in the temple devoted to Mahavira.

Within the temple complex is an ancient library, the **Gyan Bhandir**, with a rare collection of manuscripts, miniature paintings, and books.

The temples are only open in the morning from 9 AM to noon, and only between 10 AM and 11 AM on Sundays.

Follow the path left of the temples and you'll come to the nearby **Dop Khana** (Place of the Cannon) which offers the best views across the maze-like walled city to the desert plains below. It's an enchanting place to return to at dusk, when you see what looks like a row of bobbing glow-worms in the darkness of the surrounding desert — the lantern trail of long chains of nomads astride their camels, arriving laden with goods destined for Jaisalmer's markets.

The magically medieval fortress city of Jaisalmer sits on a rocky promontory on the edge of the Thar Desert, with its amber turrets turning golden in the dusk light.

Havelis **and Palaces**

Descendants of the wealthy traders still live in beautiful *havelis*, some of which are centuries old. Jaisalmer is full of these magical eighteenth- and nineteenth-century mansions, their surfaces covered with intricate filigree carvings skillfully created by Muslim *silavats* (stone-carvers) for Hindu traders. The sandstone surface of the buildings crumbles slightly to the touch, creating an odd sensation of having breathed, for a moment, the dust of Jaisalmer's vanished opulence, the scent of silks, rich brocades, and thick incense.

Salim Singh Haveli is slightly north of the central market. Salim Singh was a despotic prime minister in the late seventeenth century, who built himself this Arabian Nights-style *haveli* with its impressive peacock-motif arched roof and unique sky-blue cupolas to outshine the mansions of other nobles. Renowned for his cruelty, he once had 3,000 people from a nearby village massacred in order to win sway with the ruling maharaja. According to local lore, he tried to build his *haveli* as high as the monarch's palace and even planned to build a connecting bridge to the royal chambers, but Rajput courtiers persuaded the king to destroy this skyscraping rival, and its upper stories were blown to bits. Although its façade is stunning, the interior has been left ransacked and Spartan.

Close by is the vast late-nineteenth-century **Mandir Palace**, built outside the city walls by the Maharawal Salivahan of Jaisalmer in the belief that a curse on the old city palace was killing off his family members in droves. It's unlike any other building to be found in Jaisalmer — an Indo-Saracenic extravaganza complete with fluted pillars, domed turrets, a tiered filigree-work façades, and interiors of silver furniture.

In a cul-de-sac just north of the palace is the most spectacular of all Jaisalmer's beautiful *havelis*, the **Patwon-ki-Haveli**, the collective name for five houses built between 1800 and 1860 by the wealthy Patwa brothers (who dabbled in opium dealing and gold smuggling, as well as trading precious gems). Two of the houses are museum showcases (open daily 10:30 AM to 5 PM), one is rented by a shopkeeper who seems quite happy to show people through, and the remaining two are private residences.

Lastly, don't miss the **Nathamal-ki-Haveli**, a late-nineteenth-century prime minister's house, with a marvelous fretted frontispiece that is flanked by sandstone elephants. You can ask to see the first floor, with its intricate painted walls and murals.

Camel Safaris

Not least of Jaisalmer's attractions is the romantic lure of the camel safari. This has to be one of India's unforgettable, once-in-a-lifetime adventures: a camel trek across the desolate wastes of the Thar,

the monotony broken by sudden magnificent glimpses of an age-old Indian desert culture — encounters with nomadic tribes dressed like theatrical troubadours, ancient palace ruins etched against an azure sky, and swift packs of *chinkara* antelope racing across the horizon.

Whether you make it an afternoon's camel jaunt or a full-fledged three-week Lawrence of Arabia epic journey is up to you. For most people, a single night spent by a thorn-tree fire under a dazzling umbrella of stars, with a glorious desert sunrise, and two days of a camel's odd, lolloping gait, with earthy meals of *dahl*, millet *chapatis*,

OPPOSITE TOP: Street-side vendors ply their trade in Amber Fort. BOTTOM: The beautiful filigree architecture of a traditional Jaisalmer haveli. ABOVE: Jaisalmer's maze of sheltered lanes are surprisingly cool, lined with merchants *havelis* with façades of honey-colored sandstone carved to weblike delicacy.

(great thirst-quenchers), coverall light cotton garments, strong comfortable shoes, and Lomotil tablets for emergency cases of diarrhea. A good book and a flashlight to read it with, plus plenty of camera film complete the ideal list.

Jaisalmer's camel safari season runs from October until March, but if you're planning a long camel safari, of around two weeks, it is only really practical between November and January when the desert is at its coolest and most enjoyable.

and *aloo choli* (spicy vegetables), is usually long enough to absorb the spirit of desert travel.

Virtually all Jaisalmer's hotels and guest houses can arrange camel and jeep safaris for the most popular two-day trail that does a circuit of local places of interest.

With so many different safaris on offer, recommendations are not a good idea. Shop around, but remember that cheapest is not best. Competition is fierce, and touts and hotel proprietors will pressure you to take their safaris from the moment you arrive in Jaisalmer.

The Hotel Narayan Niwas offers a deluxe version more suited to those seeking the comforts of the Raj. The party consists of camels (one each, plus one for luggage), a cook, bedding, World War II-style tents, hampers packed to one's predilections, filtered water tanks, onions to keep the snakes away, night watchmen, and wireless contact with the police. You can even request folk dancers to entertain the party in the evenings around the campfire. Prices for teh deluxe safaris are considerably higher.

Essentials for a camel safari include a pair of sunglasses (for the intense desert glare), a water bottle, a wide-brimmed hat, high-factor sun lotion, chapstick, mosquito-repellent, a bag of oranges

Short two- or three-day tours from Jaisalmer usually visit a handful of several ancient monuments in the desert. A short distance north is **Bada Bagh** (Big Garden), the cremation ground of Jaisalmer's rulers, dating back to the twelfth century. Here stand tiered, canopied rows of marble *chhattris*, or memorial cenotaphs, each carved with bas-reliefs. It's the perfect spot to take sunset photographs of Jaisalmer, blazing saffron-pink against the horizon.

Lodurva, 16 km (10 miles) northwest, is the archaic eighth-century Rajput capital, with fine ruins and an ornate Jain temple complex. One traveler reported stepping into this temple without taking his shoes off and being astonished to hear a voice exclaim in plummy Oxford vowels: "I say, old chap, you simply mustn't wear shoes here, you know!" The owner of this astonishing voice turned out to be a scantily clad, turmeric-smeared fakir squatting in a darkened niche!

Other stops on the trail include **Amar Sagar**, six kilometers (nearly four miles) northwest,

Few sights are as arresting in Rajasthan as the spectacle of its vivid and picturesquely dressed inhabitants. Four faces of Rajasthan: ABOVE: A young musician and a Rajput beauty, her arms covered in ivory bracelets, signifying her married status. OPPOSITE: A nomadic camel driver and a gypsy tribeswoman.

where a beautiful Jain temple stands near a dried-up oasis, and **Mool Sagar**, nine kilometers (almost six miles) directly west of Jaisalmer, a garden and large tank. In between you will pass through many small villages of beehive-shaped mud and cow-dung huts and grinning desert dwellers who find the sight of sunburned foreigners atop cantering camels as funny as a Marx Brothers comedy.

Longer treks include the **Sam Sand Dunes**, 40 km (25 miles) away — where you'll see the true Sahara-like desert landscape of Rajasthan — and the exotic fortress city of Bikaner, 280 km (174 miles) away, which takes about 11 days.

Another popular excursion from Jaisalmer is to **Khuri**, which is 40 km (25 miles) southwest of Jaisalmer and very close to the Pakistan border. Like the Sam, its chief attraction is its "real" desert landscape of smooth tidal waves of golden sand, which feels much more like authentic desert than does the empty scrubland surrounding Jaisalmer.

If you want to see the *real* Rajasthan, where people still live by their ancient customs, visit Khuri. The charming Rajput Sodha family — the rulers of this region for over 400 years until Independence in 1947 — run excellent camel safaris between October and March and also accommodate tourists in small, spotless mud guest huts in the village for about US$5 a day, which includes three delicious traditional meals of homemade cheese, a wide range of breads, vegetarian dishes, and nonstop cups of sweet cardamom tea. The Sodhas are dignified, warm-hearted hosts, and the two sons, Bhagwan and Tane Singh Sodha, make articulate, humorous escorts whether on a camel safari or a tour of the village.

To get to Khuri, either rent a jeep or take the early morning bus from Jaisalmer. Bhagwan Singh is always there to meet visitors when the bus arrives.

SHOPPING

One of the most enjoyable things to do in Jaisalmer is to wander the alleys seeking out the bazaars, where rummaging can uncover some wonderful treasures, often more unusual and of better quality than those geared for the mass market in Jaipur.

In tiny niche-like shops tucked up crooked stairwells, or in *haveli* basements, you'll find colorfully embroidered and mirror-inlaid cloths, decorative banners, and blankets.

Jaisalmer is also an excellent place to buy woolen dhurrie rugs, produced locally in many traditional designs and sizes. To get an idea of the selection, quality, and price, it's worth first taking a look at **Marudhar Handicrafts** in Patwon Haveli, or at the **Kamal Handicrafts Emporium**, just near the Jain temples in the fort. Also worth visiting when shopping for general Rajasthani crafts is the **Rajasthali Emporium**, Gandhi Chowk.

Along **Manik Chowk**, the main market square at the entrance to the fort, dozens of small

stalls provide the perfect accessories for a swash-buckling Rajput-style desert adventure: brightly embroidered, curving camel-skin *mojadis*, or slippers; camel saddles and whips; 14-m (45-ft) long turbans; and huge gathered *ghagras*, or skirts (taking up to seven meters— over seven yards — of cloth).

Small items like embroidered camel-leather belts and bags make wonderful gifts, but if you're looking for exotic trophies to take home from Rajasthan, this is the place to browse for unusual antique silk, heavy silver Rajput jewelry, and the unique wall-hangings patched together pain-stakingly by village women with fragments of embroidery.

WHERE TO STAY

Despite its popularity, Jaisalmer has little in the way of true luxury accommodation. Most of the best hotels are mid-range in price and standard. Even for the best suites in town you can expect to pay less than US$100.

The **Hotel Narayan Niwas** ((02992) 52408 FAX (02992) 52101 is Jaisalmer's most stylish hotel. A converted caravansary with 24 rooms, the hotel is quaintly romantic, but simple, with a deep open hall where the camels used to sleep but where guests can now recline on striped cushions and listen to the traditional Rajasthani musicians in canopied culs-de-sac each evening. There's an attached restaurant with a good evening buffet and highly exotic performances by dancers, sword-throwers, and musicians. Rooms are well furnished, air-conditioned, and are moderately priced. During the Desert Festival, colorful canopied tents, complete with beds, fresh linen, and toilets, are available.

The **Gorbandh Palace Hotel** ((02992) 51511 FAX (02992) 52749 is a dependable mid-range hotel a mile or so west of the fort. The modern amenities have been unobtrusively blended with a traditional design to make it a pleasing place to stay. It's centrally air-conditioned and has a

swimming pool. Well-appointed doubles are around US$25.

Outside the town walls, the **Jawahar Niwas** ((02992) 52208 FAX (02992) 52259 is less of a class act but is housed in a beautiful building. The ex-maharaja's former guesthouse, it is now a hotel of faded charm. It has a pleasant veranda and a large billiard room. Rates are inexpensive.

If you want stay inside the fort itself, the **Jaisal Castle** ((02992) 52362 FAX (02992) 52101 is an old 11-room courtyard house tucked into the fort's topmost ramparts. You'll find it — after asking directions many times by weaving up a sloping bottleneck of cobbled alleys. The views at sunset compensate only somewhat for the abysmal service and food — tea is served in chipped, stained cups and the promised fresh sheets, soap, and clean towels just never seem to materialize.

Close by too is the **Shreenath Palace Hotel** ((02992) 52907, a very basic hotel (despite the name) in which the authentic atmosphere of an old merchant's *haveli* is the only winning feature. It's cramped but quaintly furnished rooms are very cheap.

The **Hotel Neeraj** ((02992) 52442, set slightly outside the city walls, is a good inexpensive option, as is the RTDC **Moomal Tourist Bungalow** ((02992) 52392, though both hotels are an incon-venient distance (two kilometers, or just over a mile) from town. Both offer a choice of rooms ranging from air-conditioned "deluxe" doubles to basic singles and dormitories for budget travelers.

Jaisalmer has become a rabbit warren of small family-run lodges that offer very cheap accom-modation (including rooftop mattresses), basic local fare, and all the local information you need. Most of these budget hostels can reserve train tickets and organize camel treks, all with smiling desert hospitality.

One of the most popular is the **Fort View Hotel** ((02992) 52214, which has Spartan doubles (no bathroom), a clambering waiter who serves guests their meals on the rooftop, and an endearing manager whose "no-frills" camel safaris are extremely popular.

Other backpacker havens within the fort town that are worth investigating are the **Hotel Pleasure**, on Gandhi Chauk; and the **Hotel Shree Giriraj Palace**, all of which have very basic rooms and rock-bottom prices.

WHERE TO EAT

Stick to Jaisalmer's traditional desert fare, with its simple round of spiced vegetables, robust millet *rotis*, and curd. **Hotel Narayan Niwas** has an excellent evening buffet with local specialties such as nut-textured *kar-sangria* — made from dehydrated desert shrub beans — and *bajra ka sohita*, an unusual combination of ground millet and spiced mutton. Local sweets include *halwa*, made of lentils, and *ghewar*, a sugarcoated ball with a rich milky filling.

Clustered quite close together in the middle of the Fort area near the Maharaja's palace and museum, other reliably good restaurants in Jaisalmer include **Kalpana's**, the **8th of July Restaurant**, and **Gaylord Restaurant**, which all serve good Indian, Chinese, and continental food. Otherwise you can take your pick of the dozens of small family-run budget eating places which have mushroomed around the market square. Some are very unhygienic-looking, but they are usually safe for simple vegetarian dishes and spicy-sweet *chai*.

arduous ten-hour day journey, which passes through flat and monotonous desert, with gnarled fist-shaped trees, nomadic camels, and graceful lines of *paniharis* (women water-carriers). The hard-seated second-class carriages are the most entertaining, as they fill up suddenly at desert halts with spectacularly attired Rajput villagers who seem preserved from another age: tall, sinewy men jaunty in scarlet onion-dome turbans, glinting earrings, and ingeniously tied white *dhotis*; and women covered in silver jewelry and *chaori*, bracelets of ivory or bone which are worn from the shoulder to the wrist as a symbol of marriage.

Jaisalmer has become an extremely popular destination, and competition for the cov-

One restaurant in Jaisalmer that is worth recommending in particular is **Trio**, at Gandhi Chowk. The Mughalai cuisine here is superb at the price, and diners are entertained in the evenings by talented musicians. It is one of the very few restaurants in Jaisalmer that has any real ambiance.

HOW TO GET THERE

Indian Airlines flies to Jodhpur, the nearest airport, 287 km (178 miles) away. It's customary to make the journey from Jodhpur to Jaisalmer by train, Jaisalmer's main link to the outside world. There is at present just one rail service to Jaisalmer, but as Rajasthan's rail network is being upgraded, more services can be expected.

Make sure to bring along plenty of water, oranges, as well as an engrossing book for the

eted overnight sleepers can be fierce, so it's essential to reserve tickets as soon as you reach Jodhpur.

Jaisalmer is also connected by bus to Jodhpur, a 10-hour trip, and Bikaner, 280 km (174 miles) away, about eight hours. These are not exactly pleasure rides; train travel is vastly preferable.

BIKANER

Situated in the northern Thar desert, Bikaner is an ochre-colored sandstone fortress city surrounded by high medieval ramparts. It is famous for its distinctive Rajput architecture, martial camels,

OPPOSITE: Pastel-hued walls in a quiet alley, Bikaner. ABOVE: Dawn silhouette of *chhatris* spires, in Bikaner.

and exotic inhabitants. It was founded in 1488 by Rao Bikaji and his band of 300 loyal followers. Lying at the crossroads of the great medieval caravan routes, this prosperous stronghold became renowned for its military prowess over the course of a centuries-long vendetta that included many spectacular battles with the ruling Jodhpur clan.

Like many Rajputs, the Bikaners adored indolent pleasures — and court archives note their excessive consumption of opium and the aphrodisiac *asha*, a dubious concoction of powdered gold, silver, ground pearls, and goat brains. During the nineteenth century, Bikaner began to curry favor with the British, donating 200 camels to the Afghan Campaign in 1842 and offering shelter to many European refugees during the 1857 mutiny.

Present-day Bikaner owes many of its finest buildings to one remarkable man — the late Maharaja Ganga Singh (1880–1943) — who single-handedly transformed his backward feudal domain into Rajasthan's chief granary by building the Ganga Canal to transform the surrounding desert into green fields, and by then constructing a railway. This flamboyant monarch founded India's most prestigious military unit, the Camel Corps, and staged spectacular annual shoots for imperial sand grouse, complete with fleets of Rolls Royces and vast banquets. England's Prince of Wales (the future King Edward VII) attended a shoot in Bikaner in 1905. Ganga Singh's nineteenth-century Lallgarh Palace, built entirely in rose-colored sandstone, is now a luxury hotel— and looms on the edge of the desert like a vast mirage from Evelyn Waugh's 1945 classic novel *Brideshead Revisited.*

WHAT TO SEE AND DO

As with most of Rajasthan's smaller centers, transport around town is mainly by foot or pony-drawn *tonga*, although a few un-metered auto-rickshaws and taxis operate from the railway station.

The city is dominated by its imposing medieval **Junagarh Fort**, built entirely with red-ochre sandstone and marble between 1588 and 1593 by Raja Raj Singh, one of Akbar's generals. Successive rulers enlarged and embellished the fort over the next 400 years.

With its massive battlements and moat, it is one of the few forts in India never to have been conquered, although it was often attacked. Beyond the main **Suraj Pol** (Sun Gate) you can see the silver-fringed sati handmarks left by queens

The keeper of the Rat Temple seems unaware of a new addition to his turban.

and concubines over the centuries. Inside is a magnificent Mughal Durbar Hall and a maze of no less than 37 ornate palaces, with marble pillared halls, delicately painted chambers, mirror-encrusted ceilings, and ivory and woodcarvings.

The most sumptuous of all these palaces are the **Chandra Mahal** (Moon Palace), a jewel-box of delicate paintings, mirrors, and carved marble panels, and the **Phool Mahal** (Flower Palace), that is filtered with stained glass and studded with mirror mosaics. Other notable places to see within the fort include the Karan Mahal, Rang Mahal, Bijai Mahal, and the Anup Mahal palaces, the latter opposite the Har Mandir temple where royal marriages, births, and the annual Gangaur festival are still celebrated.

The fort museum brims with fascinating heirlooms, including rare manuscripts, jeweled weaponry, gold howdahs, antique hookahs, and a number of oddities, including two decaying World War I biplanes purchased by the patriotic Ganga Singh. The fort is open daily except Fridays from 10 AM to 4:30 PM and houses the Tourist Office.

Bikaner's old walled city has an equally medieval flavor. It is fun to spend an afternoon combing the filthy and chaotic bazaars that are clustered around **Kote Gate**; full of turbaned desert nomads, colorfully clad women, and pigeonhole stalls hawking everything from various lacquer-work to camel-skin lampshades, beautiful antique doors, and ivory bangles. The **Ganga Singh Golden Jubilee Museum**, in Gandhi Park close to the Tourist Bungalow, is well worth visiting for its rich collection of pre-Aryan archaeological finds, antique Indian sculpture, and fine Bikaner school miniatures. It's open from 10 AM to 5 PM, although it is closed on Fridays and public holidays.

If **Bikaner Jail's** Superintendent J.K. Sharma is in an affable mood, he will allow you to tour through this massive nineteenth-century stone prison, where inmates — a mixture of petty thieves and *dacoitish*-looking murderers — create carpets in a system begun by Maharaja Ganga Singh in the 1920s. The prison yard presents an unforgettable scene: hundreds of surly calico-clad men sit in dugout troughs amid a 40-m (130-ft)-long mesh of foot-peddled pulley contraptions and waterwheels that process raw wool into clean threads for the weaving looms — all beneath the burning sun and under the watchful eye of a pockmarked Tamerlane-like jailer. Hand-knotted carpets can be bought from the prison storeroom.

Out of town, don't miss a visit to the state-run **Camel Breeding Farm**, 10 km (six miles) west of Bikaner, home to about 300 gamboling baby camels and their parents. India's regimental Camel Corps plucks out the best and brightest

among them. Here you can go for a ride, chat with the traditional clannish keepers, the *Rebaris*, about camel lore, and sample still-warm camel milk. The farm welcomes visitors daily between 3 PM and 5 PM.

At **Deshnok**, which is 33 km (20 miles) south of Bikaner, stands the **Karni Mata Temple**, dedicated to the fifteenth-century mystic who prophesied Rao Bika's successes, but more famous as the "rat temple," where swarms of "sacred" rodents are protected in the belief they are shortly to be reincarnated as gifted humans. Lured with grain and sweetmeats, hundreds of rats squeak and scurry across the marble shrine — and over the bare feet of devotees. It's not for the squeamish, and visitors are given stern warnings not to stand on one accidentally. Curiously, even the temple priest and his assistant have rather rodent-like features.

The beautiful royal *chhatris*, or cenotaphs, at **Devi Kund**, eight kilometers (five miles) from Bikaner, are interesting memorials to the dead of the princely Rathores of Bikaner.

WHERE TO STAY AND EAT

Bikaner's grandest hotel is the **Lallgarh Palace** ((0151) 523963 FAX (0151) 522253, run by members of Bikaner's former royal family. Much of it remains uninhabited, as if magically deserted. Peacocks and squirrels make themselves at home in the echoing, marble-balustraded courtyards; the state rooms are swathed in dustcloths; and in the corridors are mounted trophies and exquisite *jali*-screened alcoves.

The hotel rooms are tastefully done, some of them featuring canopied twin beds, gloomy drapes, and mahogany furniture. Modern amenities include a swimming pool and tennis courts. Rates start at US$135 for a double.

The hotel's Palace Museum is brimming with royal memorabilia, including stuffed trophies, *objets d'art*, various military outfits worn by the portly maharaja, and a massive carpet woven by Bikaner's prisoners. There is a particularly fine photographic gallery for a fascinating close-up inspection of virtually all of India's princes, stiff-collared viceroys, and their formidable vicereines. The museum is open daily except Wednesdays, from 9 AM to 6 PM.

The management of the Lallgarh can arrange for you to stay at **Gajner Palace** ((01534) 5001, 32 km (20 miles) away, an elegant royal hunting lodge set on the lake of a wildlife sanctuary full of gazelles, wild boar, black buck, sambar, and imperial sand grouse.

A less expensive alternative to the palace is to stay at the **Hotel Bhanwar Niwas**, ((0151) 61880, a converted *haveli* with an intimate atmosphere and attractively appointed rooms.

Cheaper again, and a good budget hotel, is the **Thar Hotel** ((0151) 543050, which has 30 air-cooled and air-conditioned rooms — all with attached bathrooms. The hotel includes an excellent vegetarian restaurant, and they can organize camel safaris.

Amber Restaurant, on Station Road, is recommended for delicious, cheap vegetarian *thalis*, creamy *lassi*, and curd. Try their unusual "Amber Special Dosa," stuffed with cashew nuts and fruit and served with fresh coconut chutney.

For those with a sweet-tooth, Bikaner's famous *ghaver* (caramelized fudge) and the town's distinctive combination of hot milk, curd, and sugar, frothed up by sidewalk vendors with theatrical sloshes into brass beakers, can quickly become addictive.

The best restaurant in town is the one at the Lallgarh Palace Hotel. It's open for opulent lunch and dinner meals.

HOW TO GET THERE

Bikaner is easily reached by express trains, and is 8 to12 hours from Jodhpur (240 km or 150 miles), 10 to 11 hours from Jaipur (354 km or 220 miles), and 12 hours from Delhi (510 km, or 317 miles). Take a sleeper for minimum discomfort.

"Express" bus trips from these cities, as well as to Jaisalmer (320 km or 205 miles), take longer (mainly due to long halts at shanty tea stalls while the driver has a rollicking time with his mates) and are more grueling. Luxury air-conditioned coaches offer more comfort, but run only from Delhi and Jaipur. Bus is, however, the quickest way to get to and from Jaisalmer (around eight hours).

UDAIPUR

Udaipur , a languid lake city strewn with marble palaces, hibiscus-massed gardens, fountain pavilions, and cobbled medieval bazaars, is one of India's most romantic destinations. It offers a dramatic contrast to the desert-bound fortress towns more commonly associated with Rajasthan.

Udaipur, the "city of sunrise," was founded in 1567 by Maharana Udai Singh, after a sage told him if he built his new Mewar capital here it would never be captured. It was timely advice, for his ancestral fortress kingdom at Chittaurgarh had just been dealt a fatal blow by Akbar's army.

As Rajasthan's most ancient ruling family, the Mewars bore the title maharana, or "light of the Hindus," and felt themselves more distinguished than mere maharajas, claiming descent from the sun god Rama. (The royal escutcheon is a defiant-looking sun face.) The proud Mewars suffered the yoke of no foreign power for long and nursed a

Silhouette of *chhatris* spires, in Bikaner. The cupolas of the Shiv Niwas Palace provide quiet outlooks over the ancient town of Udaipur.

bitter grudge against those Rajput clans — most particularly Jaipur's Mansingh — whose kingdoms fell into the hands of the Mughals.

Udaipur had no sooner been founded than Akbar's armies laid siege to it. But despite formidable odds, Udai Singh's heir, the legendary Pratap Singh, kept them at bay for 25 years before finally being overpowered. Successive maharanas were involved in an almost constant round of feudal battles and intrigues, and Udaipur achieved a lasting peace only in 1818 when it came under British control and was rescued, along with the rest of Rajasthan, from the clutches of the Marathas.

Udaipur's most prolific builder was Maharana Jagat Singh, who during the seventeenth century

built much of the majestic City Palace. It straddles a sheer natural rock palisade almost one and a half kilometers (a mile) in length overlooking Lake Pichola. It is a vision of Rajput grandeur with its riot of kiosks, projecting balconies and turrets and is topped by a gold *kalash* (spire), the symbol of gods or independent kingdoms. Successive rulers kept adding wings until it became the largest and most imposing palace complex in Rajasthan.

At the same time, Jagat Singh created an exotic lake citadel — now the famed Lake Palace Hotel — on the island of Jagniwas. He also built the forlornly beautiful palace on the opposite island of Jagmandir later used as an abode-in-exile by Jahangir's rebellious son Shah Jahan; it was from here he proclaimed himself emperor when his father died. It was on Jagmandir, too, that several British families were given shelter following the Indian Mutiny of 1857.

With its tranquil atmosphere, glittering array of palaces, garden pavilions, and cool lake-fanned breezes, Udaipur is one of Rajasthan's most beguiling cities. You should plan at least four days visiting its many sights and attractions, including several historic temple complexes nearby. It is at its most beautiful between September and March, and just after the July monsoons.

GENERAL INFORMATION

The main Tourist Information Bureau ((0294) 23605, is located at the Kajri Tourist Bungalow. Their daily city tours leave from here at 8:30 AM and 1:30 PM. There is also an afternoon excursion to **Haldighati** (40 km or 25 miles away), the site of an historic battle between Maharana Pratap Singh and Akbar; the sacred eighteenth-century shrine to Lord Krishna at **Nathdwara Temple** (48 km or 30 miles away); and the large eighteenth-century temple complex of **Eklingi**, 22 km (about 14 miles) from town. This five-hour tour leaves at 2 PM and costs US$2. There are also tourist offices at the airport and railway station.

WHAT TO SEE AND DO

Udaipur's palaces and gardens clustered around the long lakeside boulevards make for a perfect day's cycling or walking. Bike-rental places are found along Lake Palace Road, and usually charge about US$1 per day. Otherwise you're at the mercy of Udaipur's taxi and auto-rickshaw drivers — agree on a price before setting off.

The **City Palace** houses a museum, open 9:30 AM to 4:30 PM. Visitors pass through an enchanting multitiered labyrinth of royal apartments, *zenana* quarters, courtyards, terraces, and pavilions. Every inch of wall and ceiling has been decorated (much of it by Hindu artisans who came to Udaipur after the sectarian Aurangzeb expelled them from Delhi's Red Fort) with jewel-colored mosaics, inlaid Chinese tiles, mirror-work niches, and fine paintings. In one room, beautiful Mewar princess Krishna Kumari drank poison and saved the kingdom from the wrath of her two rival suitors from neighboring states. Clamber up to the roof gardens and overhanging terraces for views of the lake.

There is another interesting museum near the main palace entrance, with fine Rajput miniatures, toys, and royal *objets d'art*. It is worth buying the museum guide for the detailed information it gives on each room.

Nearby is the eighteenth-century **Tripolia Gate** with its eight carved marble arches under which the ruler was weighed on his birthday and his weight in gold distributed to his people.

Directly behind are the steep stone elephant-steps leading to **Jagdish Temple**, a fine Indo-Aryan temple built by Maharana Jagat Singh in

1651 and notable for its black stone image of Vishnu as Jagannath, Lord of the Universe. You'll emerge into the cobbled Bara Bazaar, which winds its way down to the larger Bapu Bazaar, east of the City Palace, both of them overflowing with wooden toys, perfumes, silver trinkets, *pichwai* (cloth paintings), decorative earthenware pots, and giant troughs of bubbling sweetmeats.

To round up, visit the glorious **Gulab Bagh**, or Rose Gardens, laid out in 1881; cycle to the north of the city to see the ornamental **Saheliyonki Bari** gardens created for the royal concubines, then glide along the **Lake Fateh Sagar** esplanade, stopping to have tea at **Nehru Park**, a garden island with a restaurant, reached by boat; and visit

the fascinating folk museum, **Bhartiya Lok Kala Mandal**, near Chetak Circle, which displays tribal art objects, puppets, masks, dolls, folk deities, and musical instruments, and stages an excellent "puppet circus" from 6 PM to 7 PM.

It is also a pleasant excursion by bicycle to the beautiful royal Mewar *chhatris* at **Ahar**, three kilometers (almost two miles) east of town, where an interesting museum houses archaeological finds. For evening entertainment, traditional Rajasthani dances are performed from 7:30 PM every Tuesday, Thursday, and Saturday at the **Meera Kala Mandir (** (0294) 583176.

WHERE TO STAY

Luxury
The glorious **Lake Palace Hotel (** (0294) 527961 FAX (0294) 527924 rises from Pichola Lake like a

marble confection. Built by Maharana Jagat Singh in 1746, it is now run by the Taj Group as a luxury hotel, complete with shopping arcades, coffee shops, and standard modern rooms, and only the husk of its original medieval structure remains.

Five royal suites, complete with stained-glass windows and antique furniture, have been painstakingly restored and cost upward of US$300. Pretty interior courtyards and terraces and a spectacular little marble swimming pool are illuminated at night. A restaurant serving standard five-star fare draws those who aren't guests for sunset drinks and good buffet dinners. Gondoliers dressed in fraying navy-blue tunics ferry guests and visitors back and forth from the marble steps of the Lake Palace to the shore. The locals have never quite gotten over the excitement of having the James Bond movie *Octopussy* filmed here. The Lake Palace operates one-hour boat tours across to Jagmandir Palace at 5 PM to coincide with dusk's charmed light. These are well worth the cost.

The **Shiv Niwas Palace Hotel (** (0294) 528016 FAX (0294) 528006 is an extravagantly elegant five-star hotel — part of a grand eighteenth-century addition to the vast, rambling City Palace. It has served as a royal guesthouse, accommodating the likes of Queen Elizabeth, Jacqueline Onassis, and the Shah of Iran. Massive doors open onto a dazzling courtyard with a clear blue marble Grecian pool. The royal suites, furnished with Belgian chandeliers, four-poster beds, and surplus treasures from the City Palace, range from US$250 to US$600, while the "ordinary" rooms cost around US$125. Bookings can be made through any of the Taj Group hotels.

For less-expensive period elegance, one good place is the IDTC-run **Laxmi Vilas Palace Hotel (** (0294) 529711 FAX (0294) 525536, on Fateh Sagar Road. Another former palace guesthouse, it includes a swimming pool overlooking Fateh Sagar Lake, a shopping arcade, and other luxury amenities, at rates that start at around US$115.

Mid-range
Perhaps the pick of the numerous middle range hotels in Udaipur is the **Lake Pichola Hotel (**(0294) 421197 FAX (0294) 410575, an elegant 25-room hotel that is acclaimed by all who stay there above all for its incomparable views. The rooms too are well appointed, and with rates of US$30 upwards are superb value. Among its services, the hotel offers "boating" and "folk dances on request."

Udaipur also offers two excellent mansion "retreats," both set amid leafy forest at a slight

OPPOSITE: At the Karni Mata Temple at Deshnok, near Bikaner, a Rajput girl observes a "sacred" rat nibbling her proprietary offering of *prasad* or sweet-meats. ABOVE: A Jaisalmer village girl.

distance from town. The **Hotel Shikarbadi** ((0294) 583201, five kilometers (three miles) away, is a delightful nineteenth-century trophy-stuffed royal hunting lodge, with a swimming pool, old retainers, and leafy gardens. It's good for horse riding at dawn. Rooms are moderately priced and can be booked through the Lake Palace Hotel.

Cheaper, and rather more eccentric, is the **Pratap County Inn** ((0294) 236389, at Titadhra Village, six kilometers (just under four miles) from town. It's set amid lovely surroundings and there are free horseback and camel rides.

Budget

One of Udaipur's best budget choices is the **Rang Niwas Hotel** ((0294) 523891, Lake Palace Road. Located in the shadow of the City Palace, it is another former mansion guesthouse, run with boundless enthusiasm by the extremely affable Mr. Singh and his two sons. You can arrive at any time of the day or night and be assured of (at least) a stretcher bed in the ping-pong room; or choose from modest but clean US$8 rooms (supplied with buckets of hot water) or charming US$25 to US$30 "suites" with charming old furniture, hot water, and mosquito nets. Other attractions are a useful information board in the lobby, a sweet little courtyard, and Udaipur's best rooftop café. Mr. Singh is a great organizer — he'll warn against "fiendish" commission-seeking auto-rickshaw *wallahs*, rental bicycles, and help coordinate out-of-town tours with other guests to save on taxi fares.

Most of the rock-bottom budget accommodation is clustered close to the Pichola Lake, near the Jagdish Temple. **Jag Niwas Guesthouse** is one of the better ones, with some better quality doubles available.

WHERE TO EAT

Udaipur's two fantasy palaces both have pleasant bars and coffee shops and stage excellent candlelit dinners with a choice of Rajasthani, Indian, and continental dishes, often preceded by puppet shows or musical performances. The Lake Palace offers excellent US$11 buffet lunches.

The sunny rooftop café at the Rang Niwas Hotel is open all day, with modest but well-prepared food and prompt service. Newspapers can be rustled up along with excellent Western-style breakfasts (with perfect two-minute eggs, warm toast, and creamy fruit *lassi*). Main meal dishes offer a choice of Indian, Chinese, or Western food, and are reliably generous and cheap.

Another traveler's favorite is the **Mayur Café**, opposite the Jagdish Temple. Highlights include "Rajasthani Pizza" made with delicious local cheese, "France Frice," "Think-Shakes," and home-baked chocolate cakes.

Another popular place, particularly for its evening dinner buffets, is the **Rooftop Palace View**, Lake Palace Road. Don't go expecting superb views, but the food is worth a trip. The **Roof Garden Café** is another rooftop restaurant, near the Rang Niwas Palace Hotel. Its local food is excellent and is often accompanied by Rajasthani folk music performances.

Also try the modern A-framed, aptly-named **Feast Restaurant**, opposite the Saheliyonki Bari Gardens, for pleasant decor, well-dressed waiters, and classic Mughalai fare cooked up by the former chief chef at the Lake Palace Hotel. Downstairs is Udaipur's highly popular fast-food parlor, **Eat-Me-Up**, which serves nonstop *dosas*, hamburgers, french fries, and milkshakes.

HOW TO GET THERE

Indian Airlines links Udaipur with Delhi, Jaipur, Jodhpur, and Mumbai. The Indian Airlines office ((0294) 410999, is at LTC Building, Delhi Gate, and the airport is 24 km (15 miles) from town.

By rail, the daily *Chetak Express* takes 17 hours to reach Udaipur from Delhi, via Jaipur and Ajmer, but for the fastest service take the *Garib Nawaz Express*, which takes a little over 15 hours. The *Udaipur/Ahmedabad Express* makes the 14-hour journey to and from Gujarat's capital and halts at Abu Road Station, about five hours from Udaipur, for those traveling on to Rajasthan's hill station.

Daily luxury or RTDC express buses go to Ahmedabad and all major Rajasthan centers from the main bus stand near the railway line opposite Udai Pole. There are also frequent bus services to surrounding historic attractions such as Eklingi, Ranakpur and, only slightly further afield, Chittaurgarh.

CHITTAURGARH

Some 115 km (72 miles) east of Udaipur, the ancient Mewar capital of Chittaurgarh is the most famous and hallowed of all Rajasthan's fortress citadels. Situated on a 180-m (590-ft)-high precipice, this sprawling, battle-scarred, ghost-ridden fortress was sacked thrice, and thrice won back by the courageous Mewars. With its cannon-shattered battlements, carved marble memorials, and myriad sati palm prints, it is the very symbol of stoic Rajput heroism and sacrifice.

According to legend, the fortress was built by Bhim, one of the five Pandava heroes in the Hindu epic *Mahabharata*. From the seventh century it was the capital of the Mewars, effectively becom-

The towering Jai Stambha, or "Tower of Victory" in Chittaugurh.

Jaipur and Rajasthan

ing the ruling seat of Rajasthan and thus coveted by prospective invaders. Its long and traumatic history was a litany of brutal assault during which capitulation to the invading enemy was marked by grisly sacrifice. Preferring death to subjugation, its men drank drafts of opium, donned the saffron robes of martyrdom, and rode off for a final orgy of killing known as *saka*, while their women and children committed *johar* — mass immolation on giant pyres. Yet great care was always taken to preserve the royal lineage so that the ruler's son and heir could return to lead a guerilla war against the usurpers of the Mewar domain.

The Muslim Sultan of Delhi, Alauddin, was the first to sack Chittaurgarh, in 1303, in his frenzied desire to abduct the beautiful Chittaur queen Padmini, after having seen her unveiled face in a pool reflection. But his was a bitter victory, since the heroic queen threw herself into the flames beside her Rajput sisters. Chittaurgarh was plundered again in 1535 by the Gujarati sultan Bahadur Shah; 32,000 Rajput soldiers died in battle, and 13,000 women immolated themselves. Just 30 years later, Chittaurgarh was crushed once more, this time irrevocably, by Akbar's armies, compelling Maharana Udai Singh to found his new capital of Udaipur.

You'll need at least three hours to explore the rambling ruins, which need an experienced guide to bring them alive. Guides can be organized at the Tourist Office ((01472) 41089, on Station Road, not far from the train station.

See the ruined fifteenth-century **Rana Kumbha Palace**, which houses a Shiva temple, elephant and horse stables, and vaulted underground cellars, in one of which it is thought Maharani Padmini committed *johar*. Also see the Jain and Hindu temples, the beautiful seven-meter (23-ft)-high **Jai Stambha** (Tower of Victory) to the south, built to mark Kumbha's victory over the Sultan of Malwa in 1440, and the smaller, squat **Kirti Stambha** (Pillar of Fame). Husks of ruined palaces are found everywhere, including **Padmini's Palace** at the eastern end of the fort.

If you want more time to explore the fort, you can overnight in Chittaurgarh, though most options are uninspiring. The RTDC **Panna Hotel** ((01472) 41238 is near the railway station and has clean but basic rooms for under US$10. The **Hotel Pratap Palace** ((01472) 40099, near the post office, is a better class of establishment, offering some air-conditioned rooms, a good restaurant and even a bar. Room rates are budget.

Many visitors use Udaipur as a base to visit Chittaurgarh by bus (three hours), leaving before dawn and returning the same day. Chittaurgarh is also a convenient stopping-off place on the rail journey to Jaipur (320 km or 200 miles) via Ajmer (187 km or 116 miles) and on the bus trip to Bundi (156 km or 97 miles).

MOUNT ABU

Mount Abu is an anomaly. It is Rajasthan's answer to Shimla or Ooty, a lush nineteenth-century hill station dotted with date palms and royal summer palaces, nestled 1,200 m (4,000 ft) up in the craggy landscape of the Aravallis, the home of the colorfully-clad tribal Bhils. It is also an important center for Jain pilgrimage, with an exquisite temple complex dating back to the eleventh and thirteenth centuries.

During the mid-nineteenth century, Mount Abu came into vogue as a princely retreat, sprouting stately mansions. Later, during World War I, the British transformed it into a military cantonment, primarily for recuperating shell-shocked soldiers and tuberculosis patients. All these influences — as well as its burgeoning popularity as a honeymoon destination for Gujarati Indians, with its rash of kitsch "love hotels" — make it an eccentric, beguiling place to visit.

The origins of Mount Abu are steeped in Hindu lore. It gets its name from Arbuda, the serpent son of the Himalayas who supposedly rescued Shiva's bull, stranded in a chasm here; it is also where the gods scooped out the oasis-like Nakki Lake with their *nakks*, or nails. Mount Abu is as important to Rajput Hindus as Mount Olympus is to the Greeks for according to myth this was where the sage Vashisht lit a sacrificial fire from which the original Rajput warrior clans first emerged.

Like any Indian hill station, Mount Abu is at its most pleasant during the high summer months of March to June. Be warned, however, that high summer also brings with it masses of Indian honeymooners and tourists, putting a squeeze on accommodation. In winter, when the rest of Rajasthan is at its best, Mount Abu can be downright freezing: be sure to bring sweaters and socks.

WHAT TO SEE AND DO

North of town, the **Dilwara Jain Temples** are the main attraction. Set on a hill in a mango tree grove and built between the eleventh and thirteenth centuries, the temples are famous for their complex and intricate marble carvings. It's no exaggeration to say that these carvings alone are worth the journey to Mount Abu. They are so perfect, it is almost impossible to believe they were crafted from a sculptor's chisel. The temples, which deserve several visits, are most beautiful just before dusk. The temple complex is open to non-Jains only between noon and 8 PM; leather items — shoes, belts, bags, watch-straps, etc. — as well as menstruating females (as a bold sign declaims) are not permitted inside.

Otherwise, Mount Abu is a picturesque place for walking and relaxing. There are wonderful views from **Guri Shikar**, 15 km (nine miles) away, at 1,725 m (5,660 ft), making it the highest point in Rajasthan. At **Achalgarh**, 11 km (seven miles) away, there is an intriguing Shiva temple, with three stone buffaloes; and the rock-chiseled **Adhar Devi Temple** is reached by a flight of 200 steps.

Closer are Sunset and Honeymoon Points for stunning views, and Nakki Lake for boating. The town itself is interesting to stroll around.

The Tourist Office ((02974) 3151 is opposite the bus station. Its opening hours are rather strange — from 7 AM to 10 AM, noon to 2 PM, and 5 PM to 8 PM — perhaps because there is a Retail Beer shop nearby selling every type of Indian beer to thirsty refugees from "dry" Gujarat.

WHERE TO STAY AND EAT

There are no luxury hotels as such at Mount Abu, though some of the better middle-range hotels try hard and others compensate with some Raj-era atmosphere. Like other hill stations, Mount Abu's hotels offer off-season discounts of up to 50% before Indian tourists start arriving in mid-April.

The **Palace Hotel** ((02974) 38673 FAX (02974) 38674 (also known as Bikaner House), Dilwara Road, is a charmingly atmospheric place to stay. Set amid leafy grounds, with tennis courts and a private lake, its quaintly furnished rooms have nine-meter (30-ft)-ceilings, hot showers, and are inexpensive. Very large Anglo-Indian meals are available in the former dance hall (look for the purdah slats above), and there is a billiards room in the lounge.

Similarly atmospheric is **Connaught House** ((02974) 3360, Dilwara Road. It's the delightful former summer house of the British Resident attached to the ex-princely state of Marwar (Jodhpur). Owned by the Maharaja of Jodhpur, it has bougainvillea-sprayed bedroom cottages, each with complete privacy, good basic amenities, and simple Indian food. The "American plan" rooms in the new wing are more modern and range from around US$30.

Hotel Savera Palace ((02974) 38817 fax (02974) 38817, Sunset Road, is a reliable, if uninspiring, middle-range hotel with a swimming pool and "steam bath." **Hotel Hillock** ((02974) 3277 FAX (02974) 3467 is marginally better, offering well-appointed air-conditioned rooms with the full complement of amenities at US$40 and upwards.

A homely guesthouse option is the **Mount Hotel** ((02974) 3150, Dilwara Road. Run by a friendly family, it serves good authentic Parsi and Indian dishes.

If you're determined (and brave enough) to experience the interior of an Indian "love hotel," ask for a honeymoon suite at **Hotel Samrat** ((02974) 3173, near the taxi stand, and revel in nylon leopard-skin sheets on a bed shaped like a

chariot, "his" and "hers" heart-shaped pillows, Khajuraho-motif tiles, curtains, and bath-towels, and nonstop Hindi movies on television!

Outside the hotels, it's worth sampling the best of Mount Abu's gold mine of excellent Gujarati fare. The town center is full of *thali*-cafés, whose generous platters cost little more than US$1. One of the best of these is **Kanak Dining Hall**.

For a decent cup of coffee and good Indian snacks, hunt down the **Madras Café**, Nakki Lake Road. Proper Indian meals are served in the upstairs section.

The best hotel restaurant in town is at the Hotel Palace (see above). Prices are very reasonable given the generous portions.

Otherwise, stick to the string of friendly open-air eating places near the bus-stand, where barefoot boys in oversized jackets wait on tables. These places are good for spicy sweet ginger tea, *thalis*, *dosas*, and the addictive *pau bhaji* — a steaming hot mixture of pulverized potatoes, vegetables, garlic, ginger, and chilies served with a fried bun.

HOW TO GET THERE

Mount Abu can be a convenient place to stop before continuing on to Ahmedabad and Gujarat state. From Udaipur, 185 km (115 miles) away, it can be reached by train or by morning express bus (seven hours). Buses can be booked at most hotels or at the bus station in Udaipur.

If you arrive at Abu Road by train, you can either hop on a local bus or rent a jeep for the 27-km (17-mile) winding journey up to Mount Abu. On arrival, you'll find yourself surrounded by pram-pushing "porters," all vying for the task of shunting your luggage to your hotel for a few rupees.

Get around locally on foot, by the local "jeep" service, taxi, or by pony, or RTDC-conducted morning and afternoon sightseeing tours.

Entrance hall of the exquisitely carved Dilwara Jain Temples at Mount Abu.

The Mountain Trail

SHIMLA

The former summer capital of the British Indian empire, Shimla has colonial ghosts, nineteenth-century cottages with potted geraniums, beautiful alpine scenery, crisp pine-scented air, and monkeys. It sprawls along a 12-km (seven-and-a-half-mile)-long ridge, 2,200 m (7,218 ft) high in the northwest Himalayan foothills.

The setting for Rudyard Kipling's *Plain Tales From the Hills*, Shimla is thought to have derived its name from "Shamla," a title of the goddess Kali who is revered by local hill people. British officers stumbled on its exceptional scenic charms when driving invading Gurkhas from the region in 1819. Then in 1822 one Major Kennedy started a trend by constructing his permanent residence in Shimla.

The British developed an attachment to this remote Himalayan town that amounted almost to an obsession. During the summer months on the northern plains, government officers would develop a condition known as "Punjab head." The heat was so intense that efficient work and accurate decision-making became well-nigh impossible. Shimla soon became a glamorous summer bolt-hole for the Anglo-Indian elite, the heat-weary, and the invalid, complete with a busy social round of dinners, whist parties, picnics, amateur theatricals, and furtive assignations between young officers and so-called "grass widows," whose husbands labored on the burning plains below.

Shimla gained respectability in 1864 when the viceroy Lord Lawrence visited and pronounced it the official summer capital, observing rather soberly, "I believe we shall do more work in one day here than five down in Calcutta." Thus began the great annual exodus of the viceroy with his guards, private staff, and public attendants, along with his secretariat, army headquarters, Foreign Office, the representative of the Indian princes, and a vast entourage of cumbersome file-cases hauled up by pony-drawn tongas, and *memsahibs*, children, and traders. By 1904, the construction of the Kalka-Shimla railway finally provided easy access to the hill station.

Shimla's tiered ridge soon resembled a semi-suburban jumble of fanciful Anglo-Indian architectural styles — red-roofed Swiss chalets with names like Fairy Cottage and Windermere, Tudor and Georgian-style mansions, the Gothic tower of Christ Church with a bell made from a mortar captured in the second Sikh War, and palatial government buildings such as Barnes Court, Kennedy House, and Gordon Castle.

The Viceregal Lodge was so luxurious — with a staff of 300 domestics and 100 cooks — that it was said Indian income tax had been invented to pay for it. No carriages (excepting those of the viceroy and his retinue) were allowed in the center

of town, known as the Mall, so residents were carried about in *jhampans* (curtained sedan chairs) or four-man rickshaws by hardy coolies. When Sir Edwin Lutyens, the architect of imperial New Delhi, went to Shimla in 1913 he was apparently appalled and said, "If one was told the monkeys had built it all one could only say: What wonderful monkeys — they must be shot in case they do it again...."

Shimla, now the state capital of Himachal Pradesh, has changed surprisingly little in appearance since the days when *memsahibs* gathered to gossip at Scandal Point. The town itself is busy, lively and nostalgically "English," with quaint Raj-era hotels and buildings and beautiful walks through Himalayan mountains thick with oak, deodar cedar, and pine trees. It's a perfect place to indulge in fantasies of the Raj.

The best time to visit is from mid-April to October, the fragrant summer season when hyacinths, rhododendrons, violets, and lilies fill the meadows. Winters are bitterly cold and Shimla is carpeted in snow between December and March. Whatever the time of year, the nights are chilly.

GENERAL INFORMATION

The Tourist Office ((0177) 212591 is located on the Mall and runs useful tours out to surrounding vantage points. The National Book Depot, just up from the Tourist Lift, sells the excellent *Tourist Guide to Shimla*, full of useful information.

WHAT TO SEE AND DO

Shimla is a charming place with plenty of atmosphere and invigorating country walks. Its main forum is the crescent-shaped **Mall** lined with stylish English buildings, ice cream stalls, and souvenir shops. You can peer at sepia photographs in musty shop-fronts of 1930s Shimla debutantes and bristle-mustached officers, buy ornately carved walking sticks, Kulu shawls, discarded solar topees, or boxes of faded "at home" cards as souvenirs, and stop for refreshments in one of the many cafés and restaurants. The **South Indian Coffee House** serves excellent snacks and aromatic Mysore coffee.

At the top of the Mall near the Ridge is the Gothic **Christ Church**. Built in 1857, it is the second oldest church in northern India. Inside are beautiful stained-glass windows, murals, old oak pews, and fascinating plaques commemorating deceased army regiments. Sunday services are worth attending just to see the resident organist furiously pounding out "We Plough the Fields and Scatter."

See the mock-Tudor **Gaiety Theater** — where Gilbert and Sullivan tunes were de rigueur — and

The Onion-dome of a rustic mosque in Srinagar's old district on the banks of the Jhelum River.

the grand Scottish Baronial-style **Municipal Buildings**. Next to Christ Church is **Scandal Point**, the large open square that got its name 50 years ago when a dashing young Indian prince on horseback eloped from this spot with a young British *memsahib*. Steep terraces lead down to the crooked, zigzagging levels of **Middle** and **Lower Bazaars**, which brim with local handicraft stalls, cafés, and swarthy-featured men from the Pahari hill tribes.

Visit the **State Museum** to see good Pahari-school miniature paintings, costumes, textiles, jewelry, woodcarvings, bronzes, and stone-sculptures. It's open 10 AM to 5 PM daily, except Monday and every second Saturday. Also see the

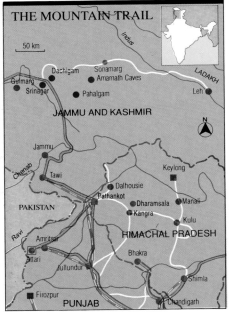

huge six-storied **Viceregal Lodge** on Summer Hill, which once hosted ceremonial balls and festivities and now houses India's Institute of Advanced Studies, which has a fine reception hall and library.

For the best view of Shimla, make the exceedingly steep climb up to **Jakhu Hill**, which, at 2,438 m (8,000 ft), takes anything from 40 minutes for strapping mountaineers to two hours for mere mortals. At the top is a little temple dedicated to the monkey god Hanuman and presided over by its resident ash-smeared sadhu and his tribe of monkeys. In 1874, Shimla's Victorian society was appalled when a young aristocrat, Charles de Russeth, became a disciple of the Jakhu sadhu and spent his time chanting to monkeys. Known as the "leopard fakir" for his fur headdress and loincloth, he was India's very first hippie.

Other pleasant walks include **Glen Forest**, four kilometers (two and a half miles) away near the

Annandale racecourse and cricket ground, which offers a pretty picnic spot with a waterfall; the 67-m (220-ft)-high **Chadwick Falls**, located west of town; **Summer Hill**, five kilometers (three miles) away), where you can see the elegant Georgian house of **Rajkumari Amrit Kaur** in which Mahatma Gandhi stayed during his visit to Shimla; and **Prospect Hill**, also five kilometers (three miles) away.

Good excursions by car or bus include **Wildflower Hall**, 13 km (eight miles) to the east, which was built by Lord Kitchener in 1903 to rival the Viceregal Lodge and was used as a peaceful hotel; **Kufri**, 16 km (10 miles) from town, a modest winter ski resort with equipment for rent; and **Chail**, 90 km (56 miles) away, with its summer palace of the Maharaja of Patiala, now a hotel, bird-sanctuary, and the world's highest cricket pitch.

WHERE TO STAY

Shimla attracts droves of vacationing Indians and has a good range of hotels, lodges, and facilities. Accommodation rates drop by 30% to 50% in the cold off-season months from November to mid-April.

Ideally, to soak up the flavor of Shimla you should stay in one of the old Raj-era hotels, which offer a delightful blend of colonial grandeur, eccentric service, and fussy decor combined with stunning views.

The Tudor-style **Woodville Palace Hotel**, ((0177) 223919 FAX (0177) 223098, is the most charming of these. Surrounded by pine trees and situated on the edge of town, it was used as a set in *The Jewel in the Crown* series, adapted from Paul Scott's *Raj Quartet* by Granada Television. It has moderate rates, spacious period suites crammed with curios and mahogany furniture, plenty of hot water, and a pretty garden for afternoon teas served by waiters in cummerbunds. Breakfasts are good, but if you value prompt service at other mealtimes take a stroll down to the Mall to avoid tiresome waits in the dining room for tepid, nursery-style Raj food.

The best hotel in town is the **Oberoi Clarkes** ((0177) 251010 FAX (0177) 211321, The Mall. One of Shimla's earliest hotels and build in the Tudor style, it has been tastefully transformed into a standard five-star hotel. It has only 39 rooms, so it is wise to book ahead, particularly during the busy summer season.

Good value budget rooms are available at the **Hotel Sangeet** ((0177) 202506 FAX (0177) 202506, The Mall. It's a modern place and, with rooms from around US$15, is one of the best deals in town.

Cheaper again is the **Hotel Dalziel** ((0177) 252691. The rock-bottom budget rooms in this older hotel are not particularly recommended, but the rooms at the back, each with a veranda and an attached bathroom, have good views and are pretty good value.

HOW TO GET THERE

Shimla's nearest airport is at an altitude of 1,372 m (4,500 ft), and above a sheer drop, at Juberhatti, 22 km (14 miles) away. Daily flights are operated by Jagson and Archana airways to and from Delhi.

A good alternative to flying direct is to take the daily Indian Airlines flight, a train, or a bus to Chandigarh, then proceed the 110 km (68 miles) to Shimla by the charming narrow gauge *Kalka Mail* "toy train," which departs from Kalka, 24 km (15 miles) north of the Haryana state capital. The scenic five-hour journey winds up the original steep track that was built from 1903 to 1904, a collector's item for rail buffs. Shimla's station looks like it is straight out of a series of children's books with its pretty flower-boxes, gleaming brass, and spick-and-span coolies in bright red jackets. Several state and luxury coaches run from Delhi (10 hours) and Chandigarh (four hours) daily.

THE KULU VALLEY AND MANALI

Kulu Valley, 205 km (127 miles) from Shimla, is famous for its beautiful scenery, apple orchards, and lively tribal music and dances. In recent years, with continuing strife in Kashmir, Manali has become the most popular of India's Himalayan hill resorts.

Enclosed by the last snow range of the Himalayas, with the Dhauladhar and Pir Panjal ranges running parallel to the south, the narrow terraced valley runs from Mandi north through Kulu and Manali all the way up to the Rohtang Pass. The Beas River flows through its fertile, flower-strewn meadows. It's an excellent base for walks, trout fishing, and gentle treks up through pine and cedar forests.

Gregarious local hill people dress in traditional homespun shawls, Kulu caps, wool jackets, and moccasins — all of which make wonderful purchases in the bazaar. They like to work hard, pray hard, and play hard. The region boasts more than 6,000 carved wooden temples, and religious festivities involve much merry consumption of *chang* (the local rice beer) as temple deities are dressed up and borne on elaborate palanquins in torchlight processions.

It's worth making a special trip to the Kulu Valley to see the most exuberant of all Kulu's festivals, Dussehra (September/October), 10 days of exuberant revelry, folk dances, and music played on traditional instruments. All over India, Dussehra is celebrated to commemorate Rama's victory over the demon king of Ravana. But in Kulu, festivities focus on the victorious god Raghunath. Some 200 gods from neighboring villages are carried here on palanquins and chariots to pay him tribute. Nightly folk-dancing competitions are held.

WHAT TO SEE AND DO

In Kulu you have a choice of a number of pleasant walks to either or both of the seventeenth-century Raghunathji **Vaishno Devi Temple** and the **Bijli Mahadev Temple**. There is a very good Himachal Pradesh State Museum. You can also visit two former Kulu capitals, one at **Nagar** that includes a castle (now a resthouse) and the other at **Jagatsukh**, the earlier Kulu capital, which has many interesting temples.

In Manali, see the nearby **Old Manali Village** and the fourteenth-century wooden **Hadimba Devi Temple**.

Treks up into the mountains have become extremely popular in Manali, and innumerable agencies around town have packages on offer. Himalayan Journeys, The Mall, is one such operator. The Himalayan Mountaineering Institute ((01902) 52342, near the Manali Ashok Hotel, can offer advice for treks, rents equipment, and has Sherpa guides.

Good two-day trekking excursions include **Hanuman Tibba** at 5,929 m (19,452 ft) and to the **Rohtang Pass** at 4,000 m (13,123 ft). Other worthwhile treks are to **Malana**, **Parbati**, **Solang**, and **Seraj** valleys and up the **Deo Tibba** (6,000 m or 19,685 ft). Beyond the Kulu Valley is the Kangra Valley, with its impressive Kangra fort.

Trout-fishing licenses are issued through the Tourist Office.

WHERE TO STAY

You can find accommodation — often in inexpensive lodges — scattered around the valley, notably in Mandi, Kulu, and Nagar. But if it's middle-range or luxury accommodation you want, the best choices are in Manali.

These Kashmiri schoolgirls seem to require little distraction to be lured away from their studies.

Very few travelers elect to spend the night in Kulu itself. It's not an unpleasant town, but it lacks the vacation atmosphere of Manali and the rustic charm of Nagar farther up the valley. Kulu's best hotel is the **Hotel Shobla** ((01902) 22800. It has a garden and spacious rooms, some of which overlook the river. The most popular budget hotel in town — and for good reason — is the **Hotel Bijleshwar View** ((01902) 22677. Some of the pricier rooms (everything is under US$10) have cozy fireplaces, if you're here in the colder months.

Manali is the place to be if you want to experience Indian hill station madness. There is a vast range of hotels to choose from. In New Manali you will find middle range and luxury hotels, many of them catering to honeymooners and domestic tourists; and in old Manali you will find inexpensive lodges inhabited by a host of budget European and American backpackers.

Manali's best hotel is the **Holiday Inn** ((01902) 52262 FAX (01902) 52562, Prini, just over two kilometers (one and a half miles) out of town. There are 55 rooms in three levels here, all of them tastefully appointed and featuring the usual luxury features — satellite television, direct-dial phones, minibar, and 24 hour room service. Each of the reasonably priced "junior suites" features a sitting area that opens onto a patio. The hotel has a coffee shop, a "multi-cuisine" restaurant, and a bar with mountain views.

Similarly luxurious is the **Manali Resorts**, ((01902) 52274 FAX (01902) 52174. It's around four kilometers (two and a half miles) out of town and has a glorious position overlooking the Beas River.

Ambassador Resorts ((01902) 52110 FAX (01902) 52173 features great views over old Manali. With restaurants, a bar, health center, spa, Jacuzzi, billiards, pony riding, and even trout fishing you hardly need to venture off the grounds. Rates start at around US$60.

For cheaper mid-range accommodation, the **Manali Ashok** ((01902) 52331 FAX (02902) 53108 is a pleasant retreat from the bustle of central Manali. It's a good family choice, with a children's playground, a games room, and even a doll's house. Other features include a gymnasium and a bar. Rates start at around US$40.

John Banon's Guesthouse ((01902) 32335 FAX (01902) 52392, has some well-furnished suites and a secluded position on the road to old Manali. Rates are inexpensive.

In the budget area of old Manali, the **Veer Guesthouse**, with its simple doubles and lounge-around veranda area, is one of the most popular places to stay amongst backpackers. The nearby **Dragon Guesthouse** is also highly recommended, with rates of under US$10 for clean doubles with an attached bathroom.

Moored *shikaras* on the glassy surface of Dal Lake, Srinagar.

How to Get There

Manali is the Kulu Valley's main tourist area and is easily reached from Delhi by air or bus.

There are daily flights with Jagson Airways from Delhi to the Kulu Valley's Bhuntar airport, which is 10 km (six miles) away from Kulu town and 50 km (31 miles) from Manali. Otherwise, fly to Chandigarh, then make the long 270-km (167-mile) — but exceptionally pretty — journey by road.

From Shimla, buses run daily to Manali on a hair-raising 205-km (127-mile), eight- to nine-hour journey that includes exhilarating views, perilous drops, and alarming road signs: "Arrive Late In This Life, Not Early In The Next," "Over-takers Will Meet Undertakers," and "Married Couples, Divorce Speed."

Adventurous travelers might consider taking a bus from Manali to Leh in Ladakh. This route is only open from June through December and has become popular due to the conflict in Kashmir. It's a rugged two-day journey with an overnight stop at a high-altitude tent site.

Buses also run daily from Manali to Rishikesh and Dharamsala.

DHARAMSALA

In 1959, the people of Lhasa rose up against their Chinese-installed government. The Chinese People's Liberation Army responded brutally, firing mortar shells into the Dalai Lama's summer residence, the Norbulingka. On the March 17, the Dalai Lama fled Lhasa, disguised as a soldier. Fourteen days later he crossed the Tibetan border into India. He has been there ever since, establishing a Tibetan Government in Exile in Dharamsala.

The Dalai Lama's government and the large Tibetan community that has coalesced around it are in McLeod Ganj, which is around 10 km (six miles) above Dharamsala proper. Foreigners come mostly to study Buddhism, meditation, and the Tibetan language, but Dharamsala and McLeod Ganj also offer the opportunity to take some bracing day walks and, like the Kulu Valley, do some more strenuous treks.

In the center of McLeod Ganj is a small Tibetan *chorten* (memorial shrine). It's not of enormous significance, but it attracts a steady stream of worshippers who circumambulate it and spin its prayer wheels.

Take the Temple Road south of town for a pleasant walk down to the **Dalai Lama Temple**. It enshrines images of Sakyamuni, the historical Buddha, Avalokiteshvara, the bodhisattva of compassion, and Guru Rinpoche, the Indian guru who is said to have brought Buddhism to the high plateau of Tibet centuries ago.

Those with an interest in Tibet can stroll down Jogibara Road to the **Library of Tibetan Works and Archives**. Tibetan language classes are held here, as are informal classes on Tibetan philosophy.

A pleasant and not particularly demanding walk involves taking Bhagsu Road east out of McLeod Ganj to the village of **Bhagsu**. From here there's a trail out to a nearby waterfall.

Ask around about performances of *lhamo*, Tibet's traditional folk opera. The **Tibetan Institute of Performing Arts** maintains a performance troupe, but shows are generally reserved for public holidays.

The Dalai Lama gives public audiences on an occasional basis. You will need to apply in advance, in person, with your passport for a free pass if one is being held during your stay. The place to apply is announced several days before the audience. Excitement runs high in the Tibetan community at such times.

McLeod Ganj has a wide selection of low-cost, mostly Tibetan-run lodges and guesthouses. One of the more popular is the **Green Hotel**, which has pleasant views of the town and the mountains rising out of the clouds in the distance. Take a look at the deluxe rooms, each with an attached bathroom, which are extremely good value at around US$6. The restaurant here is invariably packed.

For something slightly more upmarket, try the **Hotel Tibet (** (01892) 21587, which is a short stroll from the bus stand. Like the Green Hotel, it overlooks the valley, and its semi-deluxe rooms, all with satellite television and 24-hour hot water, are again very good value. The Tibet has a popular restaurant.

Also recommended is the **Hotel Natraj (** (01892) 22529, which is in the south of town (take the left fork in Temple road and walk past the Bookworm Book Shop). Rooms are similar in price and standard to those at the Tibet, but if you value your comforts opt for the deluxe rooms, which are probably the best in town. Rates are inexpensive.

Most of the hotels have restaurants, those at the Green and Tibet hotels being among the best. In the evenings, the **McClo Restaurant**, above the bus stand, is one of the most popular places to knock back a few beers — the food is only average. Numerous family-run Tibetan restaurants around town turn out *momos* (stuffed dumplings), *thukpa* (noodle soup), and other traditional Tibetan fare.

Buses run to Dharamsala and McLeod Ganj every other day from the Paharganj tourist enclave of New Delhi, and the journey takes around 13 hours. There are also direct buses to Manali and Rishikesh. The nearest railway station is Nagrota, about 30 km (17 miles) below McLeod Ganj, but it only has limited services — most people travel in and out of Dharamsala by bus.

RISHIKESH

Known as the "yoga capital of the world" and famous as the place where the Beatles met the Maharishi, Rishikesh attracts a steady flow of sadhus, yogis, and spiritually inclined Westerners. Many foreign travelers visit Rishikesh from Dharamsala, from where there are daily bus connections.

Rishikesh came into being as a pilgrimage town at the point where the Ganges river plunges out of the mountains onto the plains. The busy town center evinces little of these beginnings, but the ashram centers to the northeast, on either side of the Ganges, are interesting places to visit.

Although there are some pleasant forest walks around Rishikesh, the main attraction for most visitors is the town's yoga ashrams. Yoga fever reaches a high pitch during the **International Yoga Festival**, which is held annually from February 2 to 7. Unless you book ahead, you can expect accommodation to be hard to find at this time of year.

A good place to do an introductory course on yoga is the **Yoga Study Center** ((0135) 431196.

Accommodation in Rishikesh can be found in the town center, near the railway station, to the south of town, and to the northeast in the charming, but mostly budget, Swarg Ashram area.

The best place to stay is the **Hotel Ganga Kinare** ((0135) 431658 FAX (0135) 431658. It's a pleasantly situated middle-range hotel with views of the Ganges. Rooms are air-conditioned, and guests can make use of the hotel's free yoga library.

The **Interlok Hotel** ((0135) 430555 FAX (0135) 432855, on Railway Road, is in the town center and is another recommended middle-range hotel. The air-conditioned suites, in particular, are good value at less than US$30.

The Swarg Ashram area is popular with budget travelers. The **Green Hotel** has some spacious air-cooled doubles and is a good place to meet other travelers.

The easiest way to get to Rishikesh from Delhi is by train a journey of around 11 hours.

KASHMIR

Ever since the Mughal emperors made the Vale of Kashmir their summer haven, successive conquerors have fallen captive to the legendary beauty of this land. Nestled high in the Himalayas in India's far north, this lake-studded valley was the "Pearl of Hind" to the Mughals and a playground for the British Raj — a land of lofty snowcapped peaks, alpine forests, lily-strewn waterscapes, orchards of springtime blossoms, and patchwork meadows of riotous wildflowers.

Until 1989 Kashmir's spectacular natural scenery and bracing alpine climate attracted travelers all year round to indulge in nostalgic memories of the Raj on Srinagar's houseboats, or for trekking, trout fishing, and skiing in the Himalayan mountains. Jawaharlal Nehru, himself a Kashmiri, wrote of the land's "strange enchantment" and "fairy magic," and certainly Kashmir feels less like a part of India than a strange Oriental fable.

Today, Kashmir's tourism industry is moribund. A line of control between India and Pakistan divides the state, and Pakistan, it is believed by most observers, is actively supporting separatists who are struggling for a Pakistan-controlled government. For its part, India remains defiant that Kashmir will remain a part of India and maintains a military presence in the region that may number as many as 600,000.

Western governments discourage foreign tourism in Jammu and Kashmir. Tourist agencies in New Delhi, on the other hand, have a habit of hard-selling Kashmir to foreign tourists. Check with your embassy or consulate before taking the advice of agencies who have more interest in commissions than in your safety. In 1995, Kashmiri separatists kidnapped six foreign tourists. One escaped, one was executed, the others remain unaccounted for.

By all accounts the once charming city of Srinagar is virtually a city under siege. Since 1990, official figures put Kashmiri casualties at more than 20,000, though some human rights groups put the figure as high as 52,000.

At present, there are no signs of an impending solution to Kashmir's problems. Both India and Pakistan claim the entirety of the state as their own; both countries conducted nuclear tests in mid-1998, which has simply served to up the ante and, what's more, pose the threat of a nuclear war in south Asia.

The following information, then, should be regarded as background to a place of superlative beauty that will hopefully one day see peace again. Until that day, it would be irresponsible to recommend hotels and restaurants in the region, and even more irresponsible to recommend you visit.

BACKGROUND

Jammu and Kashmir state is made up of three distinct areas, each very different not only in landscape but also in the heritage, language, and religion of the people.

In the very south, at the periphery of Punjab's hot plains before the foothills of the Himalayas, lies Jammu city, once the stronghold of feudalistic Hindu and Sikh Dogra rajas, and then a winter capital. To the north, across dense, forested ravines and steep mountain passes, lies Kashmir Valley, an oval plateau 1,500 m (5,000 ft) above sea level, framed by three massive Himalayan ranges — the Karakoram, Zanskar, and Pir Panjal.

Srinagar, the state's summer capital, is nestled amid the valley's lakes, meadows, and floating gardens. The third main part of the state, the remote and arid region of Ladakh, is at the northeastern border with China where the 7,000-m (23,000-ft)-high peaks of the Zanskar Range are found. Sometimes referred to as "Little Tibet," Ladakh still looks and feels like a medieval, hermetic Buddhist kingdom, with ancient monasteries hewn into the mountain crags, legions of red-robed monks, and prayer flags fluttering everywhere.

Jammu and Kashmir is 94% Muslim, and the residents hold that their cultural links to Central Asia, Afghanistan, Persia, and the Middle East are stronger than those to mostly Hindu India. The

Tibetan prince. When the prince died in 1338, Shah Mir usurped the kingdom and founded the Sultan dynasty.

The eighth and most celebrated sultan was Zainul-Abidin — known as Badshah, or Great King — who encouraged studies in Hindu and Buddhist philosophy and patronized literature, dance, and music. Every Kashmiri artisan regards Badshah as a kind of patron saint, for he introduced new arts such as shawl embroidery, carpet making, papier-mâché, silver work, and carving, and invited entire guilds of craftsmen in Persia and Samarkand to settle in the valley.

The Mughal emperor Akbar conquered the region in 1586. Declaring Kashmir "my private

area's rich history as a major trading center along the ancient Silk Road is reflected in the potpourri of appearances: sharp — almost Grecian — profiles, fair skin, tawny hair, and hazel eyes.

The region's recorded history stretches back to the early second century BC, when it was renowned as an ancient land of scholars and mystics. Emperor Ashoka (269–232 BC) converted its inhabitants to Buddhism, and Kashmiri missionaries were largely responsible for spreading the doctrine across the mountain passes of the Silk Road to Central Asia, China, and Tibet.

A Hindu heyday followed in the seventh and eighth centuries with a line of Karkota kings who gave Kashmir its first impressive monuments and cities. But from the tenth to the fourteenth century, Kashmir entered a dark epoch of feudalistic disarray, in which power passed from a line of ruthless commanders to a Muslim

garden," he amused himself by boating, water-fowling, and indulging in eccentricities such as seeing how many of his valets could fit inside a hollow *chenar* plane tree — 34 was the impressive total! Four generations of Mughal emperors made Kashmir their summer idyll, creating elaborate pleasure gardens, delicate marble pavilions, and intricate irrigation systems still in use today, and eulogizing the vale in poems, songs, and paintings. In the meantime, they brought the Muslim faith to nearly all of the population.

As Mughal power waned in the eighteenth century, Afghan warlords occupied the area from 1756 to 1819, when they were ousted by Ranjit Singh, who conquered the valley and annexed it to his Punjab kingdom. After losing the first Anglo-Sikh war in 1846, the Sikhs could not afford the indemnity imposed by the British, and instead offered them Kashmir. The Dogra Maharaja of

Jammu offered London twice the amount, and became the ruler of the combined states of Jammu and Kashmir. His descendants ruled under the British until Independence in 1947.

The strategically situated state has been a battleground between India and Pakistan: notably in 1948, 1965, and 1971. Both countries still contest Kashmir's sovereignty. Troops from both sides frequently exchange gunfire at the restricted frontier areas, and a tense standoff is in force at Siachen Glacier, the world's highest battleground at 5,800 m (19,000 ft). At the same time, a section of Kashmir near Ladakh is under dispute between India and China and is another source of regional tension.

city like backdoor entrances to the sprawling Dal Lake and the smaller, more secluded, Nagin Lake.

Srinagar's old quarters on the banks of the Jhelum River, with their labyrinthine alleys and crooked, Tyrolean-looking houses, appear little changed since the reign of the Mughals.

Houseboats

By the late nineteenth century, the British had come to regard Kashmir as their cool Himalayan retreat during the furnace-like heat of the Indian summer. But the ruling maharaja balked at this seasonal invasion of his earthly paradise and prohibited the British from owning or building houses on his land, hoping that this would stem the flow of

SRINAGAR

After India's hot and dusty plains, Srinagar's cool alpine air, *chenar*-shaded meadows, and soaring snow-clad mountains are a revelation. With its lake-moored houseboats, Mughal gardens, mosques, and the lure of the nearby Himalayan mountains, Srinagar was, until the late 1980s, easily the most popular destination in northern India and the perfect base from which to explore the rest of Kashmir.

Srinagar, or "city of beautiful scenery," is thought to have originated some 2,000 years ago as a hamlet founded by Emperor Ashoka when his daughter Charumati took a fancy to Dal Lake during a pilgrimage to the area. The present city was established in the sixth century by the feudal king Raja Pravarasen II, who created many of the serpentine waterways that still wriggle through the

officers, crinolined *memsahibs*, and entourages of swaddled infants, nannies, and servants. With inventive literal-mindedness, the British created a floating colony of luxurious, carved mock-bungalows on Srinagar's Dal and Nagin lakes, thus launching the fashion for houseboating.

From these drifting cedar-scented Victorian parlors, they issued "at home" cards, drilled their Kashmiri cooks in Mrs. Beeton's gastronomic legacy, and went for pleasure cruises in *shikaras*, the hand-paddled, canopied taxi-gondolas with curtains and mattress-sized cushions on which to recline.

OPPOSITE: Elaborate gingerbread façades characterize Srinagar's houseboats. ABOVE: Experiencing domestic bliss aboard a luxury houseboat is one of Kashmir's most profound pleasures.

How many houseboats are still operating as floating hotels today is uncertain. In the late 1980s there were more than 1,000.

Shikara Rides and Floating Gardens

Srinagar's pleasures are concentrated on its placid, spring-fed Dal and Nagin lakes, where *shikara* rides prove an addictively indolent form of transport. Meandering canals are crossed by small Mughal bridges that wobble with the overhead traffic and are flanked by medieval-looking, half-timbered houses buried in bulrush thickets.

Off these liquid corridors are the backwater bayous, where the local river families live in clusters of derelict *doongas* (plain wooden house-

barges) with toddlers, mongrels, and chickens scrambling beneath the lines of washing hung on the decks. Gypsy-featured locals dart about in narrow skiffs like dragonflies, collecting water weed, fishing for carp, and stopping to gossip awhile at tiny shops raised on stilts.

Boat expeditions include crossing Dal Lake to the **Shalimar Bagh Gardens**. On the southern shore of the lake is the **Floating Gardens**, where the thick, buoyant mats of bulrushes are covered with earth and anchored by poles in the deep water. Locals lean out of their dinghies to harvest cucumbers and melons from these floating beds.

There is a secluded bird sanctuary on the northwest side of Nagin Lake, where Himalayan dippers, golden forktails, and golden orioles circle above the endless banks of flesh-colored water lilies amid dramatic views of the mountain-flanked valley.

Mughal Gardens

The pleasure gardens left by the Mughal emperors are as evocative of these legendary rulers as the more famous Red Fort in Delhi or the Taj Mahal in Agra. Kashmir was their summer playground, where they could breathe rose-scented air, gaze across the lake to the snowcapped mountains, frolic with an entourage of honey-skinned maidens, and banish thoughts of the hot and dusty plains below.

Scattered alongside upper Dal Lake, the two most beautiful gardens are the Shalimar and the Nishat Bagh, both pavilion-pieces with fountains, water-channels, cascades, and formal quadrangles of terraced wildflowers.

The **Shalimar Bagh Gardens**, 15 km (just over nine miles) away, were built in 1616 by the emperor Jahangir as a "garden of love" for his beloved wife, Nur Jahan.

Five kilometers (three miles) back toward the city is **Nishat Bagh**, or "garden of bliss." This larger and more ambitious version of the Shalimar was laid out in 1633 by Nur Jahan's brother, Asaf Khan, two years after Nur's death. Set on the lakeside slopes of the Zabarwan mountains, it has steep flights of terraces, leafy walkways, waterfalls, and pavilions. In the distance you'll see Hazratbal Mosque's shimmering marble-white dome against the mist-wrapped Pir Panjal mountains.

The **Cheshma Shahi**, or "royal spring," is the smallest of the gardens. It was begun by Jahangir and completed in 1632 by Shah Jahan, who added vineyards, fountains, and tanks. Its spring is believed to produce waters with magically tonic properties. Set in the slopes above are the ruins and gardens of **Pari Mahal**, once a Buddhist monastery and later converted into a school of astrology by Shah Jahan's son, Dara Sikoh.

Mosques and Monuments

The **Shah Hamdan Mosque** has an extraordinary exterior of ornate carvings and painted papier-mâché. Built between 1373 and 1398, it is named after a prominent Sufi from Persia, whose influence led to the peaceful conversion of millions of Hindus to Islamic mysticism during the fourteenth century.

Like a fanciful illustration for an exotic fairy tale, the mosque's interior glitters with still-bright seventeenth-century papier-mâché lacquered colonnades, latticed stairs, whimsical stained glass, and European glass chandeliers. The building signifies the five daily prayers offered to Allah, having five walls, five arches, and a repetition of the number five throughout. *Burqa*-covered Muslim women file into the screened purdah quarter adjacent to the mosque to whisper their prayers, but neither they nor any non-Muslim are allowed inside.

By rickshaw, the **Jamia Masjid** is less than five minutes away and is the largest and most popular mosque in Kashmir. Giant speakers strapped to its square-shaped minarets send the muezzin's cry booming to the faithful across Dal Lake. Originally built by Sultan Sikander in 1400 and expanded by his son Zainul-Abidin, it was razed to the ground by fire three times and rebuilt each time, although it still retains the original immense deodar pillars, 15 m (50 ft) high and carved from whole trees.

Today's Indo-Saracenic structure can accommodate up to 10,000 worshipers in its peaceful inner courtyard during the main Muslim festival, Id-ul-Fitr, which celebrates the end of Ramadan fasting.

Along the towering ridge of nearby **Sharika Hill** are the crumbling ruins of the eighteenth-century **Hari Parbat Fort**, built by Atta Mohammed Khan, an Afghan governor. Legend has it that the hill was formed after the goddess Parvati threw a pebble from the heavens, which grew as it fell to crush the wicked water demon, Jalobhava, who dwelt in the depths of a huge lake. Villagers claim that the stones strewn across Hari Parbat are all incarnations of gods from the almost-limitless Hindu pantheon. The emperor Akbar built the surrounding ramparts from local gray limestone in the late sixteenth century, beautifying them with fragrant groves of almond trees.

The elegant white marble **Hazratbal Mosque** has an Ottoman-style dome flanked by a single minaret like a finger pointed heavenward. Built on the site of the original 600-year-old shrine, it contains the valley's most sacred possession — a strand of the Prophet Mohammed's hair, or the *Moe-e-Muqaddas*, brought to India in 1635 from Medina. The Holy Hair disappeared in December 1963, and black flags flew from houses across the valley. The ensuing riots held the state government to ransom, and calm was only restored five weeks later when the relic was mysteriously restored. On certain Muslim festivals, it is displayed to massed crowds of pilgrims in the outside courtyard.

Just opposite Nehru Park is a hill path leading to the oldest Hindu shrine in the valley, the **Shankaracharya Temple**, which stands 300 m (1,000 ft) above the city on a hill known as **Takht-I-Sulaiman** (Throne of Solomon). It is thought that the temple was originally built by the emperor Ashoka's son Jaluka around 200 BC, and later enlarged by an unknown Hindu sage in the reign of Emperor Jahangir.

MOUNTAIN RETREATS

Unfortunately, Kashmir's continuing troubles have put two of India's most fabled mountain retreats out of reach to travelers: **Gulmarg** and **Pahalgam**.

Amid the towering pine-forested Pir Panjal mountains, two hours' drive (52 km or 32 miles) from Srinagar, Gulmarg is renowned for its spectacular alpine scenery and spring wildflowers which carpet the valley in a solid mass of color.

Gulmarg is both a summer and winter resort. Apart from its exhilarating mountain walks, treks, and pony-rides, it has the world's highest golf course at 2,650 m (8,612 ft) and during winter offers the best skiing on the subcontinent.

Originally called Gaurimarg (after Lord Shiva's wife), Sultan Yusaf Shah renamed it Gul (flower) Marg (meadow) in 1581. But for the muezzin's cry echoing across the valley and its swarthy Muslim hookah-smoking inhabitants, Gulmarg looks like a pastoral Swiss landscape.

Gulmarg's warm season lasts from mid-May to mid-October (May to June for spring flowers) and the peak skiing season is in January to February, when the valley is covered in thick, crunchy snow.

Pahalgam is a charming sleepy valley 96 km (60 miles) from Srinagar, set 2,130 m (7,000 ft) high among snowy peaks and forests of pine, conifer, and sycamore and crisscrossed by the Lidder and Shashnag rivers. Until recently it was a popular hill resort.

There are fragrant fields of purple saffron flowers at **Pampore**, 13 km (eight miles) away. **Avantipur**, 29 km (18 miles) away, was the ancient capital of Kashmir, built by King Avantivarman (855–883) and has two ninth-century temples dedicated to Vishnu and Shiva. Also nearby is **Achabal**, a Mughal garden laid out by Shah Jahan's daughter, Jahanara. **Kokernag** is famous for its curative springs. **Martand** has a huge Sun Temple built by the sixth-century king Lalitaditya.

JAMMU

Few of Kashmir's fabled charms are found in Jammu, the state's bustling commercial winter capital, with its ungainly urban sprawl across the banks of the Tawi River against a backdrop of sandstone foothills, small lakes, temples, and a ruined fort.

OPPOSITE and ABOVE: Cruising by *shikara* provides the most romantic form of transport across Dal and Nagin lakes.

Little is known of the city's early history. According to legend, it was founded by the ninth-century king Jambulochan, who built his monumental Bahu Fort overlooking the Tawi. In 1730, the region fell under the control of the warlike Dogra Rajputs, whose descendants retained power over the merged Jammu and Kashmir state until Independence. During the eighteenth and nineteenth centuries, Jammu was the center of a minor artistic renaissance, and its artists created the exquisite court miniatures known as the Pahari school.

With tourism to Kashmir no more than a trickle, Jammu — which was only ever regarded as a pit-stop on the road to Srinagar — sees very few foreign travelers nowadays.

The town itself has art galleries. The best is the **Dogra Art Gallery**, Gandhi Bhavan, facing the New Secretariat. Set up in 1954, it houses nearly 600 paintings, as well as terracottas, medieval weapons, sculpture, and ancient tar-leaf manuscripts. The other is the **Amar Mahal Museum**, built for Raja Amar Singh in 1907. It features a collection of rare Pahari miniatures and manuscripts.

Bahu Fort is five kilometers (three miles) above the town. Its ramparts swarm with devotees of the evil-eyed, black-faced goddess in the small Kali temple. Beneath the fort are the sloping terraces of the **Bagh-I-Bagu Gardens**.

The interior of the **Ragunnath Temple**, dedicated to Lord Rama, is coated with gold. Built in 1835 by Maharaja Gulab Singh, it is the most impressive of a cluster of nineteenth-century temples located within the lively and colorful bazaar area in the city center.

KASHMIRI HANDICRAFTS

Shopping in the region is no longer possible (or at least not recommended), but it is still possible to buy Kashmir's beautiful handicrafts in New Delhi.

Among the region's more tempting purchases are hand-knotted silk or wool carpets, unique feathery *pashmina* and *shahtush* shawls, exquisite embroideries, ornate papier-mâché, and walnut-wood carvings, as well as tailor-made fur coats, leather ware, and saffron.

The most coveted of all Kashmiri handicrafts are the exceptionally fine handmade **carpets**, usually woven in old Persian designs in varying combinations of silk and wool to create a special weave which looks dark from one side and light from the other. They are usually produced on large wooden looms by teams of young boys, and depending on the size and quality can take between six months and four years to complete. Because they are so popular, shops are flooded with inferior mass-produced carpets — particularly those made with cotton-derivative "staple" yarn, which imitates the appearance of silk but is far less durable.

You need to be very careful when choosing a carpet. Check the content and knot of the carpet — regardless of what the salesman tells you. A silk carpet will weigh at least two kilograms (four and a half pounds) less than yarn staple or wool. But the true test is to pluck a knot out and burn it — staple yarn ignites instantly, but pure silk smolders. Another test is to check the number of knots per square inch on the reverse of the carpet. A good silk or wool carpet should have around 360 knots per square inch (six and a half square centimeters), but the finest carpets have as many as 700 knots. Make sure that you scrutinize the carpet for any design or color faults, and that you are given a certificate of origin to save possible customs duty or import tax payments on your return home. If you want to ship your carpet back, you might feel happier if you make the arrangements yourself. If you don't have time, photograph or mark the carpet under the unfazed salesman's eye. That way he's less likely to send you an inferior or different "replica" of the one you purchased!

Far less expensive are the *namadas*, brightly chain-stitched rugs made from pounded fleece, or the unusual and decorative **crewelwork floor coverings** with an underside of white cotton fabric.

Then there are the legendary **Kashmiri shawls**, prized for centuries by Mughals and maharajas, who employed hundreds of skilled craftsmen to produce the *pashmina*, *shahtush*, and exquisitely embroidered *jamawar pashmina* shawls, the latter taking as many as 20 years to complete. Akbar launched the practice of giving shawls to foreign dignitaries, and as trade increased with Europe by the late eighteenth century, they became an item of aristocratic fashion in France. The French empress Josephine possessed between 300 and 400 of these shawls. According to one story, Napoleon — who liked to see her shoulders bared, while she preferred them decoratively draped — would dramatically whisk off her shawl and fling it into the fire, whereupon the empress would calmly send for another one.

By the mid-nineteenth century, the inexpensive mass-produced English imitation Paisley wool and silk shawls almost destroyed the market for exotic, handwoven Kashmiri shawls. Today, there are efforts to keep the craft alive, and shawls of all qualities are made.

Shahtush shawls are the most legendary of all. Spun from fleece gathered from the throats of ibex goats in Ladakh and Tibet, they are so airy and feathery they can be drawn through a ring, and so warm they can cook a wrapped egg after five hours. Unlike woolen and *pashmina* shawls, *shahtush* shawls are seldom dyed or embroidered. The rare 100% pure shawls are mousy brown in color and highly sought after, costing around US$360.

Kashmir's papier-mâché goods can be found all over India, but only in Srinagar can you find the most delicate work etched with real gold, not bronze dust or gold poster paint. The making of papier-mâché is a laborious process: pulped paper is first soaked in adhesive fluid, dried in a mold for at least a month, then painted with bright designs before being coated with varnish. Traditionally, men and boys do this work, and still use natural extracts for color: coral is ground for red, lapis for blue, charcoal for black, and cardamom for yellow.

LADAKH

Ladakh, or "Land of the Passes," is a region of stark beauty north of Kashmir that remains an unspoiled citadel of Buddhist religion and Tibetan culture locked within a snowy fortress of Himalayan gorges. Travelers have named the area "Little Tibet," the "Moonland," and the "Last Shangri-La" — all with some degree of truth. Leh, the area's ancient capital, sits on a 3,555-m (11,663-ft)-high plateau in the Indus Valley, and is dominated by a royal palace reminiscent of the Potala in Lhasa. The city is dwarfed by the ocher-hued crags of the mighty Karakoram mountains and is largely populated by Tibetan refugees who fled their homeland after China invaded it in 1950.

India, China, and Pakistan all have contesting claims over parts of Ladakh, which for centuries served as a strategic junction on the medieval Silk Road between Xinjiang in China and routes to the Indian plains and Persia. Ladakh was virtually closed to the outside world for most of the post-Independence period, until in 1974 New Delhi decided to open up the region to tourism. But the area still remains virtually untouched, retaining much of its character as a hermit kingdom where a "divine" monarchy and powerful priests rule over nomadic tribes who eke out a living from yaks, goats, juniper berries, and barley crops.

Sparsely vegetated and as ruggedly inhospitable as the Sahara, Ladakh is home to the legendary snow leopard. Tibetan eagles soar across the sky, while herds of wild Zaskari horses run in herds across the plains.

Its tough, Tartar-featured inhabitants are followers of Tibetan Buddhism. The religion is thought to have been first brought to Ladakh in the third century by missionaries sent by Ashoka, and the doctrine became mingled with the indigenous animistic Bon faith and ancient Hindu tantric cults.

Prayer flags flutter from every household rafter, *chortens* or shrines of holy relics dot the wayside, and villagers carry prayer wheels about with them like fetishes. The region is famous for its perilous cliff-top *gompas*, or Tibetan Buddhist

monasteries, which are brightly painted with murals of tantric gods and laden with gilded gem-studded statues of Buddha, religious icons, carvings, and scroll paintings or *thankas*. Many have in recent years been restored and refurbished from donations by tourists, some of whom serve among the red-robed monks.

GENERAL INFORMATION

Ladakh's high altitude and very thin air mean that you'll need to take it very easy for the first few days after arrival. This is when you are most vulnerable to dizziness, headaches, insomnia, or nausea, particularly if you fly direct to Leh from

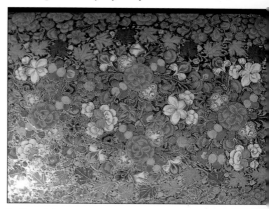

Delhi. If the problem persists, consult a doctor immediately. People with heart or lung conditions should take special care. Severe altitude sickness can be fatal, but it is more likely to affect overly active trekkers. The only cure is to descend to a lower level as soon as possible.

You should also go prepared for freak temperature changes, bringing light cotton clothes for warm summer days, woolen clothes for nippy nights. Lip salve, sunscreen, sunglasses, hats, and strong walking shoes are essential for all travelers. Binoculars and extra film also come in handy. Local agencies provide tents, mattresses, sleeping bags, and basic utensils for trekkers.

A powerful flashlight comes in handy when studying the interiors of dimly lit monasteries. Smoking in the *gompas* is considered very rude, as is touching art objects. While you are free to photograph in the *gompas*, Indian soldiers tend to get very excited when tourists take innocent vacation snapshots near bridges, airfields, and military installations, and the ensuing drama and confiscation of film and even cameras is not worth the trouble.

ABOVE: Detail of ornately hand-painted Kashmiri papier mâché box. OVERLEAF: Street scene in Leh town.

Make sure you have cashed your travelers' checks and foreign currency and have plenty of small denomination rupee notes before arriving in Leh, where both banks and small change are rare.

Finally, you can win big grins from the Ladakhis by peppering your speech with a few local words. *Jullay* is an all-purpose greeting that means "hello," "goodbye," and "how are you" all in one. *Katin chey* means "please," while *thukjechey* means "thank you."

When to Go

Religious festivals add special gaiety, color, and excitement during visits to the *gompas*. While most festivals occur during the winter months, summer

visitors have the opportunity to see the spectacular Hemis festival of masked dances and drama performed by monks held during June and July at **Hemis Gompa**, 40 km (25 miles) from Leh.

All *gompas* have large courtyards in which these religious festivities take place, but Hemis Gompa stages the most impressive of the genre. Dances are heralded by the discordant crescendo of three-meter (10-ft)-long brass trumpets, drums, and clashing cymbals played by red-robed acolytes in tall hats. Other monks are transformed into demons and gods by ornate padded costumes and garish masks, and they twirl, lunge, and shimmy while holding icons of Bon, Buddhism, and Tantra to enact tales from the scriptures. The victory of good over evil tends to be the basic theme of these dances, signifying the destruction of baser characteristics such as greed, lust, and anger, but sometimes monks enter trancelike states and act as oracles, making predictions and answering questions.

But the greatest spectacle is seeing thousands of Ladakhi villagers arrive in traditional dress bearing brass samovars containing yak-butter tea. The women wear elaborate robes with long felt headdresses studded with turquoise and heavy silver jewelry, and the men are swaddled in quilted *goncha* coats tied with colorful cummerbunds.

Archery contests coincide with every religious festival, and visitors are welcome to try their hand and to join in the music, dancing, and drinking. Check whether your trip coincides with a game of local polo — played at a fast and furious pace on local wild Zaskari ponies on the highest and most spectacular polo ground on the planet.

River rafting in the Indus River can be arranged during the summer (see below).

WHAT TO SEE AND DO

Leh Town

Start your sightseeing with a visit to the abandoned **Leh Khar Palace** (open 6 AM to 9 AM and from 5 PM to 7 PM) which sprawls across Tsemo Hill. It was built by King Singe Namagyl in the sixteenth century, taking its cue from Lhasa's Potala Palace. It still belongs to Leh's royal family, who now live in another palace at Stok. Despite its many wall paintings and royal *gompa*, it has a desecrated, pillaged look that dates from the Kashmiri invasion of Ladakh in the 1800s. The main attraction is the superb views from its top windows across Leh's fluttering prayer flags.

In town, visit the lively **marketplace** to see elderly Ladakhi women in traditional attire selling vegetables and household goods, spinning, and knitting.

Going to the *Gompas*

Sightseeing in and around Leh largely involves scrambling up steep lanes to see cliff-top *gompas*. The drab, baked-mud exteriors of these monasteries hide colorful tantric frescoes, silk or brocade *thankas*, and exquisitely carved statues. *Gompas* are places of worship, isolated meditation, and religious instruction for young monks, as well as the repository of Ladakh's wealth. The approach to a *gompa* is heralded by votive shrines, known as *mane* walls, and by stupas, known as *chorten*. Outer walls and entrances are lined with cylinders of wood or metal mounted vertically on spindles and placed in alcoves which are rotated during prayer.

In Leh, visit the fifteenth-century **Leh Gompa**, with its large Buddha (open from 7 AM to 9 AM and from 5 PM to 7 PM), and **Shanka Gompa**, with its gold statues, located two kilometers (one and a quarter miles) away.

It takes several days using a jeep or taxi to see the important *gompas* outside town. Buses run out to most places, and it is sometimes possible to stay overnight in the monastery. The closest are **Spituk** (eight kilometers or five miles), with fine Buddha icons, masks, and *thankas*; and **Shey** (15 km or just over nine miles), the ancient seat of the pre-Tibetan kings with a seven-and-a-half-meter (25-ft)-high copper statue of Buddha.

Also worth seeing is **Phyang** (19 km or almost 12 miles), a sixteenth-century *gompa* that belongs to the Red Hat sect of Tibetan Buddhists, and **Thikse** (19 km or almost 12 miles), a twelfth-century, 12-story clifftop *gompa* with 10 temples full of statues, images, stupas, and wall-paintings. It offers views across the green Indus Valley.

Stok Palace (16 km or about 10 miles) is the home of Leh's royal family. **Hemis Gompa** (40 km or about 25 miles), built in 1630, is the wealthiest, best-known, and biggest *gompa* in Ladakh. Its popularity stems from its annual festival that honors the anniversary of Guru Padmasambhava's birth. It has Ladakh's most extensive collection of wall-paintings, statues, and *thankas*, including the world's largest, which is unfurled every 12 years (the next time in 2004).

WHERE TO STAY AND EAT

With more tourists attracted to Ladakh each year, accommodation facilities are improving. Meanwhile, Leh has a range of hotels, lodges, and guesthouses, many of the latter private homes that rent rooms out to foreign visitors. Prices vary a great deal, dropping to half the peak-season rate in the off-season, with many places closed during the winter.

Upmarket hotels are all moderately priced, but then standards are fairly low too. The **Galden Continental** ((01982) 52373 has a good, central location and a pleasant inner courtyard for sitting out in the sun. Room rates are around US$30.

The **Kang-Lha-Chhen** ((01982) 52344 is also recommended. Again it has a courtyard, and it also exudes some atmosphere. The **Bijou Hotel** ((01982) 52331 is housed in a Ladhaki-style building with a garden.

For something slightly cheaper, the **Dragon Hotel** ((01982) 52339 is another traditional style building arranged around a garden. It only has a small number of rooms and is a popular place, so it is wise to book ahead.

There are a bewildering number of budget guesthouses in Leh. Almost all of them are at the mercy of the city's erratic electricity and water supplies. Take promises of hot water with a pinch of salt and shop around before committing yourself to a stay of more than one night at any particular place.

The **Old Ladakh Guesthouse**, in the center of town, is a long-runner and remains a popular place with budget travelers. In Changspa, which is just north of the town center, the family-run **Oriental Guesthouse** is another popular place to stay.

Tiger Tops Mountain Travel's **Ladakh Sarai** ((011) 752 3057 (Delhi) FAX (011) 777 7483 (Delhi), 11 km (seven miles) from Leh, offers comfortable Mongolian-style yurts pitched amid willow trees near the old Ladakhi village of Stok, famous for its royal summer palace and its archery contests. The circular, furnished tents are very cozy, with efficient solar-powered showers and modern toilet facilities. Lighting is provided by lanterns and candles so that the meadow's tranquillity is not spoiled by the sound of generators. Good Western and traditional Ladakhi cuisine is served in a separate dining tent. The Sarai is a good base for trips to the monasteries, short treks, and river rafting on the Indus. Most travel agents can book through the London or Delhi offices. The same company organizes trekking and rafting in Ladakh.

Ladakhi food does not constitute one of the world's most exciting cuisines. Ladakhis consume lots of roasted barley meal (*tsampa*), as well as quantities of salted yak-butter tea and *chang*, a potent barley brew. The better hotels and restaurants serve a choice of Indian, Chinese, and Tibetan dishes. Local chefs excel at delicious *momo* steamed dumplings, chow mein, and various other rice and noodle dishes, particularly good at **Dreamland Restaurant**, close to the center of town. Others to try are **Chopstick**, **Potala**, and **Hill Top**.

HOW TO GET THERE

Reaching Leh is an experience in itself. Although Ladakh is open to visitors throughout the year nowadays, winter flights from Delhi can often be delayed or even cancelled due to adverse weather conditions.

Indian Airlines runs regular flights from Delhi and Srinagar, with less frequent flights from Chandigarh. It's a flight that features spectacular aerial views across the snowy Himalayas. In season, however, from June to September, there is high demand for seats — book your return flights well in advance. Better still, make sure your schedule is flexible enough to accommodate an extra day or two to return, just in case you are left stranded waiting for the next available flight.

For variety, it's possible to fly one way and drive the other. The only problem with this is that most road travel nowadays is via the 480-km (297-mile) road that links Leh with Manali. It's a rough journey. The old route from Leh to Srinagar is still open, but not recommended.

Only about half of the road between Leh and Manali is paved. The journey involves crossing the Taglang Pass—which, at 5328 m (17,476 ft), is one of the highest passes in the world, and is guaranteed to make you short of breath and feel as if you have been struck down by a dose of the flu. There is an overnight stay in a tent village at Sarchu.

A remote hamlet is tucked amid dramatic mountain scenery in Ladakh.

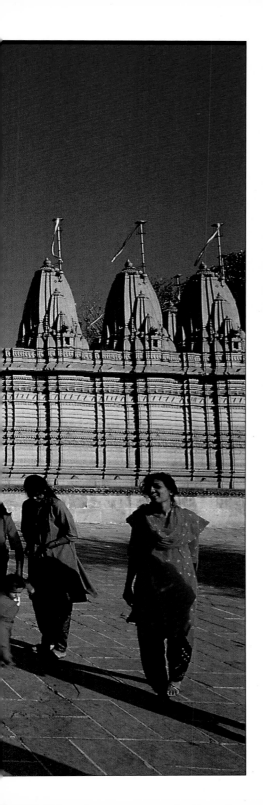

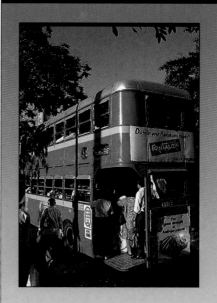

Bombay
and the
West

BOMBAY
(MUMBAI)

ARABIAN SEA

Buddhist Temple

To Airport

Maulana Abulkalam Azad Road

P Budhkar Marg

B Madhukar Marg

To Airport

Nalgum Rd

Jerbai Wadia Road

G Kadam Marg

Dr Annie Besant Road

Senpati Bapat Marg

N M Josh Road

N M Josh Road

Babasaheb Ambedkar Road

Acharya Donde Marg

Hospital Avenue

A P Ora Marg

Currey Road

Govt House Cafe Road

G D

Ambekar Road

Tokarsi Jivraj Rd

Sewri Road

Dr E Mosses Road

MAHALAXMI
Race Course

Haji Ali's Tomb

Lala Lajpatrai Marg

Keshavrad Khade Road

JACOB CIRCL

S G MAHARAJ CHOWK

Sane Guruji Road

E S Patanwala Marg

Victoria and
Albert Museum

Victoria
Gardens

Lakaria Bunder Road

Raay Road

G D

Bhulabhai Desai Road

J Dadajee Marg

Gopalrao Deshmukh Marg

S K Barodewala Marg

Fly Over N S Patkar Marg

Arthur Road

Com Bapurao Jagtap

Maulana Azad Road

Victoria Road

Motishah Road

Dr Mascarenhas Road

Souter St

Dr Anandrao Nair Road

Morland Rd

Clare Road

Bar Avant Singh

Mangaon Road

Wadi Bunder

Kemps Corner

August Kranti

J Boman Behram Marg

P Bapurao

Tardeo Road

NANA CHOWK

A Premji

Girgaum Road

Dr Dadasaheb Bhadkamkar Marg

Sukhlaji Street

Pupila Rd

Dimtimkar Rd

Road

Babula Tank Rd.

Kolabhat Ibarhyukati JLS

Jail Road

Tower of
Silence

Hanging
Gardens

Mani Bhavan
(Mahatma Gandhi
Memorial)

Maulana Shaukatali Road

Nanubhai Desai

Patel Road

NAL BAZAAR

Sardar

Patel Road

Nandalani Road

Kamala
Nehru
Park

Khar Marg

Padamji

Vithalbhai Patel Road

C P Tank

Mohammedali Rd

Lavinbai Jagmohan Das Marg

MALABAR
HILL

Bel Gangadhar

Walkeshwar Road

Netaji Subhas Road

Chowpatty Beach

Sardar

Jagannath

Dr B Jaykar Marg

R M R Marg

M P Marg

Bhuleshwar

Abdul Raman

Sheikh Menon Street

Sardar

Tilak Marg

D Mello Road

CROSS ISLAN

Walkeshwan
Temple

Aquarium

Sports
Clubs

Marine

BACK BAY

Mahamahi

Shankar Shet Road

Dr. C Hormusjy

Lokmaniya

Dadabhai Naoroji

Bombay Victoria Terminus

Raj Bhavan

MALABAR POINT

Netaji Subhas Road

Drive

1st Marine St

Karve

Sir V Thackersey Marg

Cross Maidan

Mahatma Gandhi Road

Mahapalika Marg

To Elephanta
Islands

HARI

Azad Maidan

Somani Marg

Fort St

W Hirachand Marg

Govt. of
India
Tourist
Office

Veer Nariman Road

D Wacha Road

Oval
Maidan

P Mehta Road

Dadabhai Naoroji Road

St. Thomas
Cathedral

Flora Fountain

Shoorji V

Mint

NARIMAN POINT

Madame Cama

Jam Bhaji

Maharshi Karve Road

Maharshi Karve Marg

Jehangir Art Gallery

K B Bhonsle Marg

Prince
of
Wales
Museum

Pju S S Sawali Marg

Electric
House

N Parekh Marg

Gateway of India

P J R Marg

Capt P Petrie Marg

Shahid Bhagat Singh Road

1 000 m

N

BOMBAY (MUMBAI)

Bombay, now officially renamed Mumbai, is India's most flamboyant and cosmopolitan city, with its fortune barons, chic socialites, movie magnates, street-smart hustlers, and above all, its diverse mixture of races and traditions.

The capital of Maharashtra state on the west coast, Bombay is India's financial, industrial, and trading center, with a prosperous skyline of gleaming skyscrapers, office towers, and five-star hotels. Bombay strikes a balance between a sort of worldly sang-froid and swaggering vulgarity. There's a fleshy, overripe veneer to the place — echoed in the lurid cinema billboards of paunchy villains and voluptuously sequined heroines that mushroom across town to advertise the latest Hindi *masala* extravaganza. This is where India manufactures her dreams, and cinema-hungry audiences worship stars like demigods: Bombay is the single-largest producer of films in the world, with about 200 movies produced in its studios each year.

Every aspect of Bombay is influenced by its mix of migrant communities. Like New York and Sydney, Bombay's dynamism lies in its mixture of imported cultures — and the adroit pragmatism of its communities of Hindus, Muslims, Parsis, Sikhs, Arabs, Jains, and Jews, many of whom originally settled here several centuries ago. Today the lure of work and wealth is just as strong, drawing thousands of refugees who drift in from the impoverished countryside to construct makeshift *bustee* hovels on the outskirts of town.

Despite the extreme poverty, Bombay is a progressive place and has surpassed Calcutta as the nation's leading city. Its port handles around 40% of the country's maritime trade, it sports a host of secondary and heavy industries, and its inhabitants provide nearly one third of India's entire income tax revenue.

First-time travelers to India often find Bombay the best choice as a starting point — its relaxed social mores, numerous international-class hotels, thriving nightlife, and its shops and restaurants make it easier to adjust to life on the subcontinent. It is also the gateway to western India, and the ideal starting point for journeys to Goa, Maharashtra, and Gujarat. Virtually all of India can be reached by air or rail connections from Bombay.

BACKGROUND

Bombay has been an important trading city with strong links to the West for more than three centuries. Portuguese adventurers in the sixteenth century coined and adapted a native name for the original seven swampy, malarial islands of "*Buan Bahia*," or "good bay." The name has stuck, but

the islands were long ago reclaimed and transformed into the isthmus upon which now sits one of the world's largest cities.

The small archipelago was the base for a succession of Hindu dynasties that ruled until 1348, when Muslim invaders based in Gujarat overran the area. It changed hands again in 1534, ceded by the Islamic conquerors to the Portuguese in exchange for protection from Lisbon's forces against the mighty Mughals of northern India. The Portuguese built several churches and large fortifications, but little remains of these earliest European occupiers, except the walled city at Bassein, still largely intact, some 50 km (31 miles) from Bombay.

Britain entered the scene in 1662, when Catherine of Braganza married Charles II and gave as her dowry the largest island, Mumbadevi. The six other islands were ceded three years later when the Portuguese retired to the coastal reaches of Goa. Samuel Pepys recorded that the marshy site was "but a poor place, and not really so as it was described to our King." The archipelago was leased out to the East India Company in 1668, which soon capitalized on its worth.

Scores of Gujarati, Parsi, Arab, Jewish, and Armenian traders and artisans were soon lured to the town, and salt flats around the islands were quickly transformed into a thriving center for trade in spices, silk, precious metals, cotton yarn, and

Movie stars achieve the status of demi-gods with Indian audiences. Bombay alone produces some 800 movies a year — a world record.

opium. The upsurge in cotton prices during the world shortage caused by the American Civil War and the opening of the Suez Canal were catalytic events for Bombay. The surplus funds prompted Governor Sir Bartle Frere to undertake a series of ambitious projects. He reclaimed land to link the islands into a single land mass, upon which were built dockyards, railways, spacious boulevards, and grand edifices in the Victorian-Gothic style. Bombay became a true city of Empire.

A hundred years ago, Bombay became the center for the "Quit India" movement led by the leaders of the nationalist movement, Mahatma Gandhi and Jawaharlal Nehru. Nehru became the first Indian Prime Minister after India was made independent in 1948.

Early Settlers

Most notable of Bombay's many immigrant communities are the Parsis, whose ancestors fled Persia and the religious persecution by the Muslims and migrated to India in the seventeenth century. A formidably successful community that includes many of Bombay's most influential families, the Parsis are Zoroastrians, who venerate fire, water, and earth. Believing the elements too sacred to pollute, the Parsis have a somewhat eerie practice for the disposal of their dead: at the "Towers of Silence" on Malabar Hill (just next to the Hanging Gardens), the dead are left in open wells to be consumed by vultures. Parsis tend to be tolerant in outlook, but generally remain a hermetic community, seldom marrying outsiders. However, Parsi traditions seem to be slowly dying out.

GENERAL INFORMATION

The **Maharashtra Tourism Development Corporation** (MTDC) ((022) 2026713 or 2027762, CDO Hutments, Madame Cama Road, runs well-organized conducted city bus tours that bulldoze through the main places of inte rest (daily, except Mondays, 9 AM to 1 PM, and 2 PM to 7 PM). Other guided tours include daily boat trips to the Elephanta Caves, 10 AM to 2 PM and 2:30 PM to 6:30 PM, and a full day's excursion that includes the Kanheri Caves, the Lion Safari Park, and Juhu Beach, 10 AM to 7 PM.

Government of India Tourist Office ((022) 2036854, at 123 Maharishi Karve Road, opposite Churchgate station, is open weekdays from 9 AM to 5 PM, alternate Saturdays from 9 AM to 12:30 PM, and is closed Sundays.

Consulates in Bombay include those of Australia ((022) 2181071, Canada ((022) 2876027, Germany

((022) 2832422, Italy ((022) 3804071, Japan ((022) 4933843, France ((022) 4950918, Switzerland ((022) 2884563, United Kingdom ((022) 2830517, and the United States ((022) 3637407.

Useful Reading

The monthly *Bombay Experience* has an extensive directory for all hotels, restaurants, information centers, travel reservation offices, museums, and so forth, and is available from hotels and newsstands. The Government of India Tourist Office also publishes a fortnightly diary of cultural events in Bombay.

WHEN TO GO

Bombay's climate, along with that of most of the western region, is at its best from October to February when the air is fresh, the days balmy, and the nights cool. In March, it becomes appreciably hotter and humid until summer reaches its sizzling zenith in June. Heavy monsoon rains often follow, frequently causing floods. During the cool peak season, and particularly just prior to and during the annual Derby (February to March), Bombay's hotels are thronged with travelers. It can prove extremely difficult to make short-notice connections to other cities, especially Goa, at this time, so it's wise to have all your hotel and travel connections reserved in advance.

GETTING AROUND

Bombay faces the Arabian Sea, and the original seven islands retain their names as the suburbs of Colaba, Mahim, Mazagoan, Parel, Worli, Girgaum, and Dongri. Metropolitan Bombay comprises five square kilometers (nearly two square miles) at the tip of the peninsula, into which are squeezed many of the city's 15 million people, along with its main administrative and commercial offices, docks, and factories. Behind it lies the residential area, covering 22 sq km (eight and a half square miles).

Getting around metropolitan Bombay is surprisingly straightforward, with most of the essential facilities — ticketing offices, post offices, hotels, restaurants, and shops — located in the thin three-kilometer (two-mile) strip between the Taj Mahal Hotel and Nariman Point. Bombay's meandering inner-city boulevards, narrow alleyways, bazaars, and its invigorating seafront are best explored on foot, but take a taxi to each area of interest and walk about from there.

Compared to Delhi, Bombay's taxi-*wallahs* are models of propriety: they usually take you directly to your destination and use their meters, which are outdated and show a fraction of the real cost — at the time of writing it was necessary to multiply the metered fare by a factor of 11. You are wise to look over the driver's shoulder when

---

A red double-decker bus passes in front of a magnificent Victorian-Gothic municipal building in downtown Bombay — reminders of the city's lasting British legacy.

he is scrutinizing his official "correction rates" card to check the additional amount you need to pay.

Bombay has a rapid electric train system servicing its outer suburbs. Hundreds of thousands of people cram into its open-air cabins each day, burrowing through the human mass when it is time to disembark (a mere 30-second halt at each stop). It is also a pickpocket's paradise, and so crowded during rush hours that commuters scale the sides and cling to the roof — predictably resulting in several fatalities each day.

Bearing this in mind, it is quite an adventure to rattle through Bombay's urban landscape, loitering first to admire the clustered gargoyles and Gothic magnificence of the Victoria Terminus,

1911, en route to make the startling announcement at the Delhi Durbar that New Delhi was to replace Calcutta as the capital of India. In Bombay, they were welcomed by a hastily constructed white plaster arch on the Bunder pier that was replaced in 1927 by the present Gateway of India, designed by George Wittet, with its cosmopolitan mix of traditional Hindu, Muslim, and Gujarati styles, notably the minarets and trellis-work *jalis*. The Gateway of India was also the site where on February 28, 1948, the Somerset Light Infantry, to the tune of *Auld Lang Syne*, wrapped up the Union Jack and boarded vessels for England, ending more than two centuries of British rule.

but one recommended for Sundays only when the carriages are virtually empty. Trains leave for the western suburbs from Churchgate and for the eastern suburbs from Victoria Terminus.

Auto-rickshaws cluster around the suburban train stations, but are banned from the streets of central Bombay. Local buses (London double-deckers) cost virtually nothing but are near impossible to use as the destinations and numbers are marked in Hindi script.

WHAT TO SEE AND DO

City Strolls
You could start your day with a swirled cappuccino and the Bombay edition of the *Times of India* at the Taj Mahal before crossing the road to the **Gateway of India**. This was where King George V and Queen Mary stepped ashore in

The **Sassoon Docks**, a pleasant one-and-a-half-kilometer (nearly one-mile) walk south of the Bunder, named after Bombay's famous Sephardic Jew, David Sassoon, are recommended for the dawn spectacle of fishermen unloading their catch. It's a 10-minute walk from here to the tranquil **Afghan Memorial Church of St. John the Evangelist**, built in 1847 to commemorate British soldiers killed in the Sind and Afghan campaigns of 1838 and 1843.

Adjacent to the Apollo Bunder is the bustling **Colaba** area — the main tourist center — crowded with antique shops, cheap lodgings (such as the infamous Stiffles Hotel, which bears a quaint resemblance to a New Orleans brothel and lists its room rates in Arabic), cafés, and street-stalls selling a medley of bright shirts, plastic flowers, good leather shoes, and electronic watches. Tucked behind the Taj is the **Royal Bombay Yacht Club**, an oasis of musty, nautical charm.

Nearby is the Wittet-designed **Prince of Wales Museum**, set in a circular garden on Mahatma Gandhi Road, which commemorates the Princes first visit to India. This leafy marble oasis in the midst of Bombay's bustle contains one of India's best collections of art and artifacts. The natural history section contains numerous strange creatures snared and stored in formaldehyde by proud Victorian men of science. There's an array of Harappan artifacts, Assyrian tablets, Tibetan-Buddhist sculptures and scrolls (and gruesome carvings from human bone), antique cloisonné-ware, and oil paintings. It is open daily except Monday from 10 AM to 6:30 PM and charges a small entry fee (but is free on Tuesdays).

Next door is the **Jehangir Art Gallery** (closed on public holidays) and its pleasant Samovar Café. Hawkers in this area sell factory seconds — acid-washed denim, cotton dresses, and bright shirts, giant balloons, and garish stuffed animals.

Nariman Point is the place to see small armies of sinewy, white Gandhi-capped *dabba-wallahs* delivering cartloads of lunch boxes to waiting office workers at lunchtime.

The Fort on Foot

The "Fort area" is a rather elastic term for the area that encompassed the original **Fort St. George** cantonment and is now the heart of civic Bombay. This is a fascinating place to stroll around, with its musty antique shops, architectural monuments, and colorful street-hawkers, notably the sandwich-*wallahs* who serve multilayered offerings from boxes strapped around their necks. In this area are some of the most daunting official buildings ever constructed on the outposts of the British Empire. These architectural examples of the High Victorian age were built when Bombay was flushed with commercial success and governed by an ardent imperialist, Sir Bartle Frere (1862 1867), who imported British architects to execute a massive palisade of public offices in the fashionable Gothic Revival style.

An excursion into the city's history can begin at the **Bandstand** south of the Oval Maidan, where cricket games are held on Sundays. Fronting the sea is a remarkable collection of buildings, beginning with the Venetian-Gothic **Secretariat**, flanked by Sir Gilbert Scott's 1874 French-Gothic **University Campus**, **University Library**, and the **Rajabai Clock Tower** (excellent for a view over the city). Farther along is the **High Court**, completed in 1878. In the noonday sun, bewigged lawyers flit about in its large courtyard like black crows, and affidavits are painstakingly drafted under flapping palm-mat awnings. The smaller building next to it is the **Public Works Building**, and adjacent is James Trubshawe's **Central Telegraph Office**.

An alternative tour starts from **Hautatama Chowk**, formerly Flora Fountain, where a short walk east brings you to Horniman's Circle and **St. Thomas' Cathedral**, whose foundation stone was laid in 1675. The ornate façade was a gift from the East India Company, and the cathedral still exhibits the chairs King George and Queen Mary occupied during their visit in 1911, and a profusion of brass plaques and marble figures.

Beyond the cathedral is a stately sweep of buildings, including the Doric-style **Town Hall**, designed by Colonel Thomas Cowper. Opened in 1833, it also functions as the Asiatic Society Library, the oldest and largest library in the city. The basement contains many cloth-covered statues of former colonial rulers, removed after Independence. Beyond this you can glimpse the **Mint**, built in 1829 (permission to visit requires an application to the Mint Master).

But the greatest building of all is the magnificently preposterous **Victoria Terminus** at the north end of the Fort, designed by Frederick William Stevens in 1888. Its façade teems with contorted gargoyles, turreted spires, and a petrified menagerie of rats, peacocks, and snakes. A life-size statue of Queen Victoria once stood in front of the façade, but it has been relocated (with regal hauteur intact) to a corner of the Bombay Zoo.

At dusk, the throngs of suburb-bound workers beneath the giant arches give Victoria Terminus the appearance of a metropolitan Hades, watched over sternly by busts of the founding company chairman and his managing director. Lady Dufferin, vicereine when the terminus was completed, thought it "much too magnificent for a bustling crowd of railway passengers."

The Markets

Crawford Market, built by Arthur Crawford in 1867, is the most grandiose market building in India. Tattered sunlight turns the dust into incense-scented screens as you wander through the chaotic maze of cool passages, each a division of wares. The best time to visit is around 7 AM, when armies of slender coolies balance silvery basins of fresh fish on their heads, chickens run riot, and immense troughs of fruits and vegetables are unloaded amidst a cacophony of squeals, shouts, and thuds. It has immense character: here you find sly Marwari traders hawking false mustaches and crocheted caps, the frail leaflike dried bummelo fish, giant sacks of grain, brightly colored spices, caged Assam parrots, labrador puppies, and fighting cocks. If you crane your neck, it's possible to make out Rudyard's father, Lockwood Kipling's bas-reliefs on the market's façade.

OPPOSITE LEFT: Boats docked in front of Bombay's famous Taj Mahal Hotel. RIGHT: The Raj lives on at the Prince of Wales Museum.

Within a two-kilometer (just over a mile) radius of Crawford Market and concentrated between Victoria Terminus and Maulana Shaukatali (Grant) Road are literally dozens of specialist bazaars set amidst a labyrinth of temples, mosques, and narrow, spindly seventeenth-century Gujarati houses. It's easy to spend hours strolling from one bazaar to another. Even Bombayites throw up their hands in mock despair when asked to name them all, but listed here are some of the most interesting.

North of Crawford Market, off Abdul Rahman Street, are the **Zaveri** and adjacent silver bazaars, where plump merchants recline on white cushions while prospective wives barter for gold and diamond jewelry — the more ostentatious the better. Around the corner is the sneeze-inducing dry fruits and spices bazaar, called **Mirchi Gully**, where every conceivable kind of chili is sold, along with piles of Afghani almonds and pistachio nuts.

For rows of glittering brass and copper, go to the **Bhuleshwar** area at the top of Kalbadevi Road, where you can also visit the Mumbadevi temple and tank, reconstructed from the original built in 1737 and a shrine of the Koli or fisherfolk, whose sacred goddess gave Bombay its name.

To the north, on Mutton Street, is the best of them all: **Chor** or **Thieves Bazaar**. Stroll past retired car engines to the antique section of the market where grandfather clocks, intricately carved rosewood furniture, chinaware, nautical instruments, and His Master's Voice gramophones are sold by shrewd dealers. The rest of Chor bazaar gets more peculiar — secondhand army surplus, rows of shoelaces, and even a section for stolen airline headphones. The **leather market** in Dhaboo Street is just parallel and worth exploring for wallets, bags, and shoes.

The Marine Promenade

Locals never call Marine Drive by its new name, Netaji Subhas Road; they prefer to call it "Queen's Necklace" for its sparkle of lamps at night. Reclaimed as recently as 1920, it stretches along the seafront from Nariman Point to Malabar Hill and is well patronized by early morning joggers, king-coconut sellers, and courting couples. Towards the Chowpatty end is the **Taraporewala Aquarium**, which is worth a visit. Opened in 1951, it houses a wide variety of marine and freshwater fish, and even sells fish and chips at its small café! Open 11 AM to 8 PM weekdays (except Monday) and 10 AM to 8 PM on Sundays, it charges Rs 5 entrance fee.

At the north end of Marine Drive is **Chowpatty Beach**, a stretch of sand offering fairground rides on man-powered Ferris wheels and merry-go-rounds, candyfloss, and piping-hot midnight snacks. This is also the focus for political rallies and where the **Ganesh Chaturthi** festival is staged every year during September's full moon.

Bombayites are devoted to the latter plump, elephant-headed fellow, the deity of material advancement, and honor him with a massive parade along Marine Drive, with as many as 6,000 Ganesha images, some towering to nine meters (30 ft) and strung with flashing lights and blaring loudspeakers. The grand finale is the immersion of these effigies in the sea at Chowpatty Beach amid cheers from the crowd as they either buckle and sink or float gaily toward the horizon. In the late nineteenth century, when political meetings were banned by the British, the early Independence Movement used the Ganesha festival as a way of communicating political messages through dance and drama.

From dawn to dusk, Chowpatty Beach is a drifting circus of scrawny beggars, hawkers, aimless sadhus with long tousled hair, and scrums of young men in flared trousers. Families flock here on Sundays, wandering from the donkey stand to impromptu wrestling competitions and the triple

row of Bombay's best fast food vendors. Here is the place to sample snacks with names like *channa bhatura*, *bhel-puri*, *ragada*, and the queen of Bombay's snacks, *pau bhaji*, a spicy vegetable gravy served with a fried bun.

It's about a 15-minute stroll to August Kranti Gardens, and **Mani Bhavan** — a little brown house at 19 Laburnum Road — is just parallel. This was Mahatma Gandhi's residence during his visits to Bombay between 1917 and 1934. From here, Gandhi launched many of his famous *satyagraha* (nonviolence) campaigns. Today, Mani Bhavan is a museum housing replicas of Gandhi's daily utensils, ascetic bed, spinning wheel, and well-worn sandals. There's a section depicting the Mahatma's life through a collection of dolls, a picture gallery, and an excellent library. Also on exhibit are copies of historic documents signed by Gandhi. It is open from 9:30 AM to 6 PM, except Sunday and charges and entrance fee of Rs 5.

Malabar Hill
At the top of nearby Malabar Hill are the **Hanging Gardens**, which were landscaped in 1881 and immediately became popular with *memsahib* watercolorists as a locale for botanical sketches. Despite the Gothic-sounding name, the gardens are very sedate but do have one intriguing attraction — a gardener who transforms his hedges into astonishing abstract art compositions.

Adjacent to the gardens in a private enclave and hidden by dense foliage is the **Tower of Silence**, the round stone construction in which the Parsis place their dead to be devoured by vultures. These structures are designed in much the same way as a lobster-net — to prevent vultures from flying out with body parts in their talons. A series of towers have been built since

Bombay's swish Marine Drive is known as the "Queen's Necklace" for its sparkle of lights at night.

the Parsi community acquired the one-square kilometer (just under a half-square mile) site in 1673, and today the area is potentially some of the most valuable real estate in Bombay, but is ardently protected by the Parsis. Visitors are strictly forbidden.

Just across the road is the **Kamala Nehru Children's Park**, with its colorful playground, floral clock, and spectacular views across Back Bay, Chowpatty Beach, and Marine Drive. Just near the park's entrance is the **Naaz Café**, where the top terrace is the best place for a chilled beer at sunset.

At the **Adishwarji Jain Temple**, on Bel Gangadhar Kher Marg, just down the road from the gardens, you can admire the intricate marble

addresses, where much of the city's famed socializing takes place. Majestic eighteenth-century mansions with ornately carved façades and marble fountains writhing with naked nymphs can be found here alongside the skyscrapers. On the southern tip, Malabar Point, is **Raj Bhavan**, the Chief Minister's residence, which is closed to the public but can be seen from Marine Drive. Nearby is the **Walkeshwar Temple**, dating back to the eleventh century, where legend has it Rama stopped to make a devotional *lingam* on his way to rescue his kidnapped wife, Sita, from the clutches of the evil Ceylonese god-king.

Opposite is the **Banganga Tank**, where Rama is supposed to have shot an arrow into the scorched

carvings, many of great antiquity, which were placed here after the temple's construction in 1903. Its upper story contains exquisite silver doors, and the ground floor has rows of recesses with statues of Jain *tirthankaras*.

One of the most colorful Jain ceremonies to witness here is the Siddh-Chakra, a purification ritual before marriage. (The best time to see it is just before the marriage season begins in December to January). Wearing *dhotis*, the young men undergoing the ritual cover their faces with the distinctive Jain gauze mask (to discourage the swallowing of insects) and sit amidst elaborate patterns of blossoms and symbolic *thali*-dishes, humming scriptures with the temple priests as musicians play stirring tunes — all recorded by proud parents on their video cameras.

Malabar Hill and the neighboring suburb of **Breach Candy** are Bombay's most exclusive

earth when he was thirsty. Today the ancient stone stairs are used to dry clothes and the tank's mythically pure water has turned to a chocolate-colored swill.

Haji Ali's Tomb and the *Dhobi* Ghats

Little is known about Haji Ali, the turreted mausoleum built in the late eighteenth century at the end of a rocky causeway near Mahalaxmi and reached only at low tide. According to popular belief, the tomb was built in memory of a merchant who renounced his wealth and lived on the barren rocks after a pilgrimage (hajj) to Mecca. His sister, Ma Hajiani, became his companion in ascetic suffering and a mausoleum was built for her a little distance away on Worli Bay. This is not the place to leave your shoes unguarded — the tomb is full of quick-eyed beggar urchins eager to whisk away your sneakers. Muslim pilgrims have developed a ritual to deal with the row of pitiful, wailing beggars who perform *khel* (beggar's tricks) along the narrow walkway — they exchange rupees for a handful of praise and distribute the equivalent of a few grains of rice to each one. At the entrance are dozens of stalls selling sticky white (and sickly sweet) *prasad*, reflective-glass scripture pictures, *burqa* (the encompassing garment worn by Muslim women), and plug-in Taj Mahal baubles that shine in the dark. There's also the **Hajiali Juice Center**, which makes the best fresh juice in town. Try their specialty, *sitafel* (custard apple) and pomegranate juice.

Two of Bombay's elite social institutions, the ultra-proper Willingdon Club and the **Mahalaxmi Race Course**, are close by. The racecourse is named for the goddess of the nearby Hindu temple, who is the deity of wealth. The annual Derby here in February and March creates a frenzy of social activity.

Stroll to the **Mahalaxmi Junction** station overbridge to see Bombay's *dhobi* ghats, where hundreds of *dhobi-wallahs* (washermen) live and work. It's a giant maze of troughs, bubbling with suds and echoing with the noise of stains being tirelessly whacked out of the city's laundry. Like the *dabba-wallahs*, the *dhobi-wallahs* operate almost infallibly on a system of hieroglyphic squiggles on each piece of fabric to identify the owner.

The Museum Roundup and Other Sights

The **Victoria and Albert Museum** is situated in spacious gardens close to the entrance of the Jijamata Udyan in Byculla, which was once the premier European suburb in Bombay. The museum has many Indian paintings, antique coins, and weaponry, but its highlight is "Bombay: a Photorama," which portrays the story of Bombay from 1661 to 1931 through a series of old prints, maps, and 250 old and rare photographs. It is open every day except Wednesday.

The **Victoria Gardens** are Bombay's best and largest, laid out in 1861 with broad paths, ornamental ferneries, and many rare species of tropical plants. A blackboard near the entrance lists "flowering" attractions of the day. The **Bombay Zoo** is here, and children can take elephant, camel, and pony rides. It is open from Thursday to Tuesday from 8 AM to 6 PM.

The **National Maritime Museum** is the only one of its kind in India, with a rich collection of naval and maritime memorabilia dating back to the time of Alexander the Great. It's located on Middle Island, a coastal battery owned by the Western Naval Command, and reached by tourist boats that leave from the nearby Gateway of India. It is open between 2 PM and 5:30 PM on Saturdays and 10 AM and 5 PM on Sundays and public holidays.

The **F.D. Alpaiwalla Museum**, located at Khareghat Memorial Hall in Khareghat Colony, houses an extensive collection of antique memorabilia, Gandhara sculptures, 80 albums of picture postcards, fragments of Sir John Marshall's Taxila excavations, Chinese porcelain, and a mummified hand from Egypt.

The **Nehru Planetarium** in Worli has daily stargazing shows in English at 3 PM and 6 PM (except Mondays).

EXCURSIONS FROM BOMBAY

On a small green island just 10 km (six miles) northeast of the Apollo Bunder are the four magnificent rock-cut cave temples of Elephanta, dating from 450 to 750 and dedicated to Lord Shiva.

It's an hour's journey to **Elephanta Island** and ferries leave every hour between 9 AM and 2 PM from the Gateway of India. The deluxe boats are preferable because they have archaeology graduates as guides.

Long before Bombay came into existence, Elephanta Island was the capital city of the Silahara Dynasty (first century AD) and was called Gharapuri, "place of idols." Much later, the Portuguese claimed part of the island and renamed it after discovering a massive elephant sculpture, which now stands in the Victoria Gardens. Portuguese soldiers used the carved temple deities for target practice, and natural decay has added to the damage.

From the primitive wooden jetty, the caves are reached by an easy climb (or by palanquins for those who don't mind being hoisted up the hill by four semi-naked men). The cave temples contain a combination of Hindu, Jain, and Buddhist iconography, and straitlaced Christian visitors considered the sinuous, enraptured figures shockingly Dionysian. On Sundays and public holidays, Elephanta Island is unbearable, with

OPPOSITE: Haji Ali's Muslim tomb of mysterious origin. ABOVE: Boats used for tours of the Elephanta Caves.

creaking ferry-loads of fellow tourists and a motley crowd of persistent hawkers. Avoid the rabble by taking the earliest boat during the week.

The **Kanheri Caves**, 42 km (26 miles) from Bombay, are far more impressive. This is one of the largest of a series of Buddhist rock-cut monasteries in western India, cut into the hills and valleys of the mountain chain known as the Western Ghats, of which the most famous are at Ajanta and Ellora. The pillars are hewn from the rock in such a way that they appear to support the weight of the mountain above. There are 109 caves in all, dating from about the first to the ninth century, and all are excavated from a gigantic circular rock.

The earlier caves belong to the Hinayana phase of Buddhist architecture. Many served as simple monks' quarters and are of little interest, but caves 1, 2, and 3 are notable for their massive pillars, sculptures, and stupas. Most impressive is cave 3, a *chaitya* (or chapel), with monumental pillars and elaborate images of Buddha.

The ruins at **Bassein**, 77 km (48 miles) from Bombay on the mainland, make a perfect picnic spot. This is where the Portuguese built a walled city overlooking the sea after taking possession of the territory from its Muslim rulers in 1534. It grew into a grand settlement, with cathedrals and elegant homes where the fiercely Jesuit Portuguese aristocrats lived in dissolute splendor, using Bassein as a naval base for converting the natives, often under threat of death, and amassing considerable wealth. They were forced to flee suddenly in 1739 during an invasion by the local

Mahratta army, and the ruins now serve as a poignant reminder of Portuguese rule. Trains run to Bassein Road station from Victoria Terminus, and the settlement ruins are only four kilometers (two and a half miles) away. It's best to make this a full day's excursion.

WHERE TO STAY

Luxury

Good accommodation in Bombay can be fiendishly hard to find in the peak January/February season if you arrive without advance bookings. The best hotels are often overbooked, so it's wise to have your reservations confirmed well in advance.

The world-famous **Taj Mahal Hotel**, ((022) 2023366 FAX (022) 2872711, opposite the Gateway of India, is the haunt of Bombay's glitterati and probably the best icon of the city's affluence, blending Rajput, Renaissance, and Gothic architecture.

There's a good range of restaurants and bars, notably the Apollo Bar for "designer" cocktails and a view across the Arabian Sea, and the stately Sea Lounge, where the well-heeled discreetly arrange marriages over tiered trays of cucumber sandwiches. It has a superb bookshop, health club, and swimming pool, a resident astrologer, and its shopping arcades make interesting browsing. Rates are very expensive, although the modern annex prices are a little cheaper.

The **Oberoi Bombay Hotel** ((022) 2025757 FAX (022) 2041505, is the Taj's nearest rival, a monolith of black marble and glass at Nariman

Point that outshines the neighboring Oberoi Towers hotel. The Oberoi offers the most modern suites and the best sea views in Bombay, stylish service, and reputedly the finest dining experiences in town. Rooms are also the city's most expensive, with singles at US$325, and doubles US$355 a night. Next door, at the **Oberoi Towers (** (022) 2024343 FAX (22) 2041505, rooms start at US$260. Both hotels have a varied range of restaurants, bars, coffee lounges, health clubs, and shops, but the new Oberoi is undeniably more elegant and more suited to business travelers.

Both Bombay's airport terminals — the Sahar (international) and Santa Cruz (domestic) — are situated at least an hour's drive from the city. Travelers who prefer a quick getaway can stay directly opposite at the five-star **Leela Kempinski (** (022) 8363636 FAX (022) 6360606. Among its many amenities and services, it proudly advertises: "recycling of garbage into manure." But don't let this put you off.

Mid-range

Bombay is well endowed with mid-range hotels, but if you have arrived from other parts of India you may well be surprised by the prices. Bombay is India's most expensive city, and this is reflected in the local room rates.

The **Hotel Marine Plaza (** (022) 2851212 FAX (022) 2828585, 29 Marine Drive, is definitely at the top end of the middle range, with rooms ranging from around US$150. It has a great location on Marine Drive and tastefully appointed rooms, complete with mini-bars. There's a swimming pool, a restaurant, and a terrace garden. The ground floor bar is one of Bombay's most popular expat watering holes, the perfect place to get together with business associates.

The **Fariyas (** (022) 2042911 FAX (022) 2834992, off Arthur Bunder Road, Colaba, combines a good central location with surprisingly good value (by Bombay standards) four-star rooms. It has a popular bar, a restaurant, a coffee shop, a health club, a gym, and a swimming pool.

The art deco-style **Ritz (** (022) 2850500 FAX (022) 2850494 has rooms for around US$100 and has some atmosphere too. Unfortunately, there's no swimming pool.

Budget

Bombay is an expensive city in comparison to other Indian destinations, but there are still some good deals to be had for US$50 or less. The best area to look is Colaba, where you will find a range of hotels with rooms from between US$20 and US$50.

The **Regent Hotel (** (022) 2871854 FAX (022) 2020363, Best Marg, Colaba, is a smart, functional business hotel. It's all air-conditioned, and rates run from US$25.

Close by is **Hotel Whalley's (** (022) 2834206, 41 Mereweather Road, a slightly frayed, endearing establishment with huge rooms and balconies. Similar is **Bentley's Hotel (** (022) 2841474, 17 Oliver Road. Bentley's also has some reasonably priced air-conditioned rooms. The doubles here are enormous and cost under US$20.

The quite modern **YWCA International Guesthouse (** (022) 2020445, 18 Madame Cama Road, is open to both men and women. Its US$20 doubles are such good value they are frequently booked in advance. Non-YWCA members can pay a "transient membership" fee of US$1.

WHERE TO EAT

No other Indian city can rival the quality and diversity of Bombay's restaurants. Here you can find excellent Portuguese-Goan, Iranian, Chinese, Italian, even Polynesian food, as well as every regional cuisine in India. No less exotic are Bombay's own specialties, such as Bombay Duck — feather-light, dried *bummelo* fish served crisp from a hot griddle. The famous Parsi *dhanshak* dish, made with fried rice and a chicken or mutton *dhal*, the local pomfret, and concoctions such as *ragada*, *bhel-puri*, and *pau bhaji* on Chowpatty Beach have also found their way into Bombay's culinary mythology.

There is an almost unlimited variety of restaurants in Bombay — from the most exclusive haunts of the top hotels and glitzy society havens to the proletarian Irani cafés and the city's renowned nocturnal street chef, the **Bade-Miyan** (meaning "big old Moslem"), who produces delicious brazier-hot kebabs and egg-rotis from his cart behind the Taj Mahal Hotel until one or two in the morning.

For truly exquisite dining, the Oberoi Bombay is a sure winner. The very sumptuous **Kandahar (** (022) 2025757 restaurant serves faultless Northwest Frontier food; the pool-level **La Rôtisserie (** (022) 2025757 is excellent for French cuisine and seafood, specializing in prime and imported meats; and La Brasserie, open from dawn to midnight, has breakfasts (fresh croissants, perfect freshly squeezed juices) to inspire deep sighs of content from homesick Europeans.

The Taj Mahal's **Tanjore (** (022) 2023366 restaurant is the best in town for regional Indian cuisine, particularly Hyderabadi, Mughalai, and Punjabi specialties, as well as for its evening program of classical Indian dance and music. (Second choice goes to the Oberoi Towers' **Mughal Room**.) Also excellent is the **Golden Dragon**, for authentic Sichuan food.

One of the world's legendary hotels, the Taj Mahal, boasts spacious suites and rooms overlooking the ocean and its large pool, as well as first-class restaurants and modern amenities.

Outside the hotels, there are literally hundreds of restaurants from which to choose. Currently in vogue with Bombay's glitterati is **Trishna** ((022) 2672176, 7 Rope Walk Lane, a deceptively shabby looking place that serves what some regard as the finest seafood (prepared Indian style) in Bombay. Prices are extremely reasonable.

Also in vogue is **Kailash Parbat** ((022) 2874823, near Colaba Market, which is renowned for its vegetarian snacks. The famous items on the menu are *puri* — puff-fried flat bread — dishes.

Copper Chimney ((022) 4924488 is one of the city's most celebrated tandoori restaurants. It has three locations: Dr. Annie Besant Road, K. Dubash Marg, and 524 Juhu Supreme Shopping Center.

In a city that is littered with Chinese restaurants, **China Garden** ((022) 8280842, Om Chambers, 123 August Kranti Marg, Om's Corner, is perhaps the most popular. This exceptional restaurant serves a variety of regional Chinese cuisine.

Other popular Chinese restaurants, include **Chopsticks** ((022) 2049284, 90 A Veer Nariman Road, with an atmospheric outdoor café extension, and the **Nanking Chinese Restaurant** ((022) 2020594, Phiroze Building, Shivaji Maharaj Marg, which is especially good for succulent steamed crab, prawns, and lobster at reasonable prices despite its popularity.

For authentic Thai cuisine, the **Thai Pavilion** ((022) 2150808, in the President Hotel, 90 Cuffe Parade, is one of the best in town. The President also has one of Bombay's most popular Italian restaurants, **Trattoria** ((022) 2150808. It's particularly popular with the late-night crowd.

Good Punjabi fare can be found at the **Sher-e-Punjab** on Bhagat Singh Road, a Sikh enclave where drying turban strips hang from the upper stories, with delicious northern specialties and a distinctive spinach dish made with rye and mustard seeds.

For pure idiosyncratic charm, nothing can match Bombay's Irani cafés, the dwindling legacy of the many hundreds founded by staunch Zoroastrian immigrants a hundred years ago, with their marble-topped tables, spindly-legged wooden chairs, salon-style swing doors, illustrated mirrors (often with spidery portraits of the Shah of Iran, George VI, and his Queen Elizabeth), and elderly, white-capped waiters who scuttle around like lizards with a dish in one hand and a tea-towel in the other. Irani cafés are all-day affairs, starting with *brun-maska*, hard crusts of buttered Irani bread eaten dipped in *phudhina*, mint tea made with milk and sugar. If Brain Fry In Eggs, or Chicken Dress Gravy seem best left to the imagination, ask for a *dibbe wala* meal of chicken or mutton instead. The oldest and most famous of the cafés are **Kyani** and **Bastani**, at Dhobi Talao toward the north end of Mahatma Gandhi Road); otherwise try the **Regal Restaurant** and the **Byculla Restaurant**, both of which are near the Byculla railway station, near Victoria Gardens.

In Colaba, don't miss the **Leopold Café**, down the road from the Regal Cinema. Everybody seems to end up in here at some point. The tandoori items are inexpensive and surprisingly good, and the chilled beer — try the London Pilsener — seems to make an appearance on every table in the house.

Just up the road from the Leopold is the **Café Mondegar**, which has a similar menu, also offers cold draft beer, and has a good jukebox.

Lastly, those who can't do without a decent a pizza, should call over to **Smok'in' Joe's** ((022) 2882254, Wodehouse Road, Colaba, or to **Domino's** ((022) 4375957, 3-4 Kohinoor Corner.

NIGHTLIFE

Bombay is without a doubt India's most vibrant city by night, with a thriving array of bars, restaurants, nightclubs, and theaters.

Of all Bombay's nighttime entertainment, to miss seeing a Hindi film would be like going to Stratford-on-Avon without seeing a production of a Shakespeare play. There are literally hundreds of cinemas here, showing a variety of films in Hindi, Marathi, and English. They usually screen at 3 PM, 6 PM, and 9 PM, with a few extra matinees at odd hours.

To get acquainted with Bombay's insatiable fascination for celluloid, buy one of the "screen gossip" rags sold at every newsstand and then find out from the local newspaper listings what's showing where. It's most fun to go to one of the old "talkies" cinemas with ornate façades dating from the 1930s: the **Eros** on JN Tata Road, Churchgate, and the **Metro** on Marine Drive. If your taxi/auto-driver doesn't know them, he's not worth his salt. Otherwise, opt for modern air-conditioned comfort at one of the three cinemas directly opposite Victoria Terminus — the **Excelsior**, the **Empire**, and the **Sterling**.

Currently Bombay's most favored bar for expatriates and moneyed locals alike is **Geoffrey's**, at the Hotel Marine Plaza. It's a popular spot for after-work drinks, and the food — fish and chips and so on — is good too. **Leopold Café** and **Café Mondegar** in Colaba also see busy crowds, though they have less of the pub atmosphere. **Tavern**, at the Fariyas Hotel, off Arthur Bunder Road in Colaba, is a long-running pub that still does good business.

For a look at where the in-crowd is, head over to the **Fashion Café**, formerly the Studio, Marzban Road. The chains on the mat black walls give this place a fetishistic air, but by 11 PM it is packed with a young, lively crowd. **The Ghetto**, Bhulabhai Desai Road, is another "in" place, though it has a "couples only" door policy.

For the city's best cocktails, jazz, and stunning views, the Oberoi's elegant **Bayview Bar** is a winner. **Not Just Jazz by the Bay**, 143 Soona Mahal, Marine Drive, is another jazz bar, though it is equally popular for its lunch and evening meals.

Bombay's nightclubs start opening their doors at around 10 PM, but don't really get going until past midnight, especially on Friday and Saturday nights. Virtually all are housed within five-star hotels, meaning that unless you are a guest or can sweet-talk your way past the bouncer, you'll need to pay an entry fee. Once inside, drinks — local liquor, unless specified — tend to be expensive.

The best is **1900s**, at the Taj Mahal Hotel, a belle époque-style haunt for Bombay's young, fashionable in-crowd, enlivened by the appearance of models and rising film stars. With teased hair and dangling earrings, girls from the wealthy upper class dance like pouting marionettes in the latest Western fashions. At the bar, a few heavy-jowled men wearing gold medallions drink neat whisky in silence, tapping snakeskin shoes in time with the beat until closing time. Open from 9:30 PM to 3 AM, the cover charge is US$10.

HQ, 166 Mahatma Gandhi Road, is popular with a younger set and is interesting for a glimpse of what Bombay's affluent youth are up to late at night.

Night owls head over to the **Copa Cabana**, Marine Drive, when everything else closes at around 3 AM. Be warned, however: this place gets packed and it can be difficult to get past the vigilant doormen without an introduction from a regular.

A half-hour drive north of Bombay is **Juhu Beach**, a mini-Malibu dotted with the kitsch mansions of film stars. Palms fringe an unswimmable beach, but at night it looks suitably romantic

— a glittering stretch of cafés, neon lights, and carnival-like stalls along the sands. One of the area's coolest hangouts these days is the **Razzberry Rhinoceros**, in the Juhu Hotel. It's a Hard Rock Café knock-off with a dance floor and pool tables too.

Nearby, the Holiday Inn and the Airport Plaza Hotel have standard discotheques, patronized mostly by airline crews on their stopovers.

For a glimpse the seamier underworld (depressing) of Bombay, its so-called "Cages," the lively brothel area is located in Colaba's Maulana Shaukatali (Grant) and Falkland Roads. It is named for the grilled windows through which the painted ladies peer. It's better to drive rather than walk late at night.

You could make one last stop at Chowpatty Beach, at the end of Marine Drive, which is still lively at 1 AM or 2 AM. It's a drifting circus of hawkers selling king coconuts, giant balloons, piping-hot midnight snacks, parents trailing small toddlers, and eccentric sideshows on the moonlit sands.

HOW TO GET THERE

Bombay, not Delhi, is India's hub for international flights, which means you can fly there from almost anywhere in the world. Santa Cruz domestic airport is also India's busiest domestic airport, and you can fly to almost any major Indian destination.

OPPOSITE: Tourist boats moor in front of the Gateway of India, scene of departure ceremonies when Britain left India in 1948, ending more than two centuries of rule. ABOVE: The pomp and squeals of an Indian brass band.

Travelers who do not arrive by air mostly travel by train or, in the case of Goa, perhaps by boat. Buses fan out from Bombay to destinations around the nation, and tickets can be bought at travel agents around town, but bear in mind that the trains are faster, more comfortable and safer.

Long-distance trains operate from Victoria Terminus and Churchgate Stations. Trains from Victoria Terminus service destinations to the south and to the east (notably Cochin and Madras), while trains from Churchgate travel north. Travelers to or from Delhi should take the *Rajdhani Express*, which covers the distance in around 17 hours and in relative comfort.

From Bombay, travelers usually explore western India by one or a combination of three routes through Goa, Maharashtra, and Gujarat. Many make Goa's sandy, palm-lined beaches and colonial Portuguese sights their first priority. But both Maharashtra and Gujarat are equally rewarding destinations, though they are often neglected by tourists.

GOA

Goa is justifiably famous for its dazzling 100-km (62-mile) sweep of palm-lined coast fringed by the turquoise Arabian Sea. Unspoiled and rustic, Goa's fertile green plains are covered with cashew nut, mango, and jackfruit groves, and they are crisscrossed by the Mandovi and Zuari rivers, from which rise forested hills up to the Western Ghats mountain range.

Goa has a seductive Latin atmosphere that feels peculiarly non-Indian, and is perfect for relaxing, swimming, sunbathing, and eating seafood.

BACKGROUND

The Mauryan Empire established settlements along this coastal sweep in the third century BC, and the area passed through a succession of rulers in seesaw wars and conflicts between the Muslims from the north and the Hindu-dominated dynasties of the south.

But Goa owes its exotic personality to the Portuguese, who seized it from the Bijapur kings of the Deccan in 1510 — under the command of Afonso Albuquerque — after failing to secure a base on the Malabar coast further south. Traders from Lisbon used Goa as well as the smaller possessions of Diman and Diu to the north in Gujarat as staging posts for plying the eastern spice routes to Indonesia and Sri Lanka in order to amass fortunes from spices including ginger, pepper, nutmegs, and saffron.

Zealous missionaries followed, and their terrifying threats of a fiery hell prompted mass conversions of local Hindus, aided by the arrival of an Inquisition party in 1560. At the height of its prosperity, Goa was a magnificent city, full of majestic cathedrals and mansions, some of which can still be seen in Old Goa today. But Portuguese power declined rapidly after the seventeenth century, falling prey to occupation by the Dutch in 1603, and later by the British during the Napoleonic wars in Europe.

During the full-blown days of the Raj, Goa was regarded as a quaint and harmless vestige, appreciated for its cheap wine. A British guidebook of 1898, *Picturesque India*, referred to Goa as "a pathetic wilderness of ruined churches and palaces." The Portuguese held control until 1961, when the remaining colonials were thrown out in a largely bloodless invasion by India.

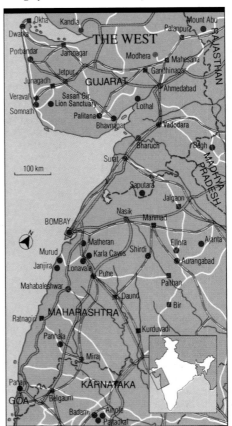

The colonial heritage is apparent everywhere, in the street tavernas, dilapidated Iberian-style villas, women's preference for frocks over saris, and numerous smatterings of Portuguese in the local Konkan vernacular.

Although India has some 6,000 km (3,700 miles) of coastline, most of it is completely undeveloped and Goa is India's most superior beach resort. This is as much due to its variety of beautiful beaches and hotels as it is to the gregarious Goanese who have a Mediterranean enthusiasm for their hybrid cuisine and locally brewed *feni*, a coconut or cashew whiskey.

GENERAL INFORMATION

Government of India Tourist Office ((0832) 223412 is in the Communidade Building, Church Square, Panaji, but the best place to go for information and maps is the **Tourist Information and Tour Counter (** (0832) 225583 or 225535 or 224757, Tourist Home, Patto Bridge, Panaji.

WHEN TO GO

India has few destinations where it is possible to feel comfortable all year round, but Goa is one of them. It's best to visit between October and February, but the monsoon period of June to September is often dramatically beautiful.

Goa's famous Carnival (generally held in February) is an exuberant, bacchanalian ritual of floats and costumes. If you are in Goa for any major Christian festival or for the *Novidades* harvest celebration on August 24, it's likely that bullfights will be staged, advertised by word of mouth only. During Easter and Christmas, Goa dons full sixteenth century regalia for remarkable processions in Old Goa's ghost city of cathedrals and basilicas.

GETTING AROUND

Goa looks deceptively tiny on the map, but in reality it is very spread out, and transportation is needed to appreciate its varied landscape. Taxis are freely available for day hire. Renting a motorbike is far more exhilarating, and rates are best negotiated on a weekly basis. Your hotel should be able to arrange a newish vehicle, but make sure you wear a crash helmet as the local constabulary often extract "simple police fines" from bareheaded tourists.

Goa's four main towns are connected by a regular bus service. **Panaji**, the center, is close to Dona Paula and Miramar beaches; **Mapusa** (13 km or eight miles away) has bus connections along the northern coast; **Margao** (34 km or 21 miles away) is very Portuguese, with fine parks and old mansions, and connects to the southern beaches of Majorda, Colva, Benaulim, Betelbatim, and Betel; and **Vasco da Gama** (30 km or 18.6 miles away) is close to the Oberoi Resort at Bogmalo Beach.

The nicest way to explore Old Goa from Panaji is by taking a mid-morning ferry for a languid chug down the Mandovi River. The tourist office runs enjoyable evening river cruises from Panaji's jetty at 6 PM. Full moon nights are spectacular, with dinner and lively Portuguese music and dancing on deck.

WHAT TO SEE AND DO

Panaji

Panaji still looks and feels like a sleepy Portuguese town. It is set along the southern bank of the salty Mandovi River, with broad avenues spilling into cobbled squares, grand public buildings, red-tiled houses, narrow lanes, and tavernas.

Start with the **Secretariat** building, originally built by the Sultan of Bijapur who quartered his Arabian horses and elephants in the Moorish courtyard. The Portuguese rebuilt it in 1615 as the official residence for viceroys and generals. Beyond Largo Da Palacio (Palace Square) is Panaji's lively quay where the steamer from Bombay arrives each morning.

Nearby is the baroque **Church of the Immaculate Conception**, with its distinctive twin towers. Just beyond the church is the residential Fontainhas area, a languid maze of shuttered, balustraded villas, painted ochre, blue, or mint green, behind which plump matrons slice spinach for the lunchtime Goan favorite, *caldo verde*. This area is full of musty, antiquated shops selling sacks of raw cashews and lumps of Goa's mango-flavored cheese. Shadowed lanes reveal cafés where old men in straw hats gather to sip *feni* during the siesta hours.

For a spectacular view across the town, take a 15-minute walk up to **Altino Hill** and the **Patriarch Palace**, where Pope John Paul II stayed during his 1986 visit.

Old Goa: Conquistadors and Cathedrals

The Portuguese called their prized Indian possession "Goa Dorada," or Golden Goa, but it was not the beautiful beaches they were referring to. Portuguese wealth and power was concentrated in Old Goa, its "Rome of the Orient," where the vast hybrid oriental-baroque cathedrals are layered with African gold.

In the sixteenth century, Goa was famed for its eight square kilometers (three square miles) of majestic churches, monasteries, convents, and stately mansions, boasting a larger population than Lisbon, Paris, or London. Old Goa was abandoned after a series of virulent plagues in 1534, 1635, and 1735 that wiped out nearly 80% of the population. The survivors created Panaji, nine kilometers (five and a half miles) away, as the new capital in 1835. Today, Old Goa is still fairly deserted, and its lime-white churches hover above the jungle like a Christian Angkor Wat.

The **Basilica of Bom Jesus**, completed in 1604, contains a remarkable Baroque gilded altar. In an airtight silver and glass casket lie the sacred remains of St. Francis Xavier, Goa's patron saint, who spent his life spreading Christianity through the Portuguese colonies. A naked bulb eerily lights his mottled skull. Beneath the basilica is a beautifully sculpted mausoleum donated by the Grand Duke of Tuscany. Xavier died in China in 1552, and his mummified corpse crisscrossed the globe before it was brought to Goa in 1613. For a "small donation" you can view his silver-encased feet.

Every 10 years, the basilica becomes a mad throng of pilgrims for the "public veneration" of the skeleton. A small gallery displays portraits and various relics attributed to the famous saint. The basilica is open 9 AM to 6 PM daily (open 10 AM Sundays for service).

Across the road is the majestic **Cathedral of Saint Catherine da Sé**, completed in 1619 and

beautifully carved woodwork, exquisite panel frescoes, and fascinating gravestones bearing coats of arms. It houses the Archaeological Museum, which has a gallery of portraits of Portuguese governors and viceroys and a notable collection of ancient Indian sculpture recovered from Goan Hindu shrines sacked by both Muslims and Christians in fits of religious monomania.

The **Church of Saint Cajetan**, near old Goa's ferry wharf, was built by Italian friars to resemble Saint Peter's Basilica in Rome. Look for the **Viceroy's Arch**, the ceremonial entranceway for disembarking Portuguese governors. On Monte Santo (holy hill) is the **Saint Augustine Tower**, all that remains of what was once Goa's biggest

dedicated to Saint Catherine of Alexandria, a pagan girl who became an ardent Christian and was later beheaded on the very same day, November 25, that Afonso Albuquerque gunned his way down the Mandovi to wrest Goa from the Muslims. Many regard the cathedral as Asia's most magnificent Christian church, a grand renaissance structure with an ornate gilded interior. Beautifully detailed panels around the center altarpiece depict Saint Catherine's life. The font is believed to have been used by Saint Francis Xavier. The cathedral has five bells, one of which is the "Golden Bell," one of the biggest in the world, which was used to announce the burning of pagans and heretics during the Inquisition.

The nearby **Convent and Church of Francis of Assisi**, built in the rare Manueline style, was originally a small Franciscan chapel. It was completely remodeled in 1661 with gilded,

church. Opposite is the buttressed, fortress-style **Convent of Saint Monica**, India's largest nunnery. A gate leads to the secluded **Church of Our Lady of the Rosary**, one of the earliest built in Goa, which contains the tomb of Dona Caterina, wife of the tenth governor and the first Portuguese woman to venture to Goa.

Stately Mansions

The tourist department in Panaji can provide a list of 20 private villas and mansions that can be visited by appointment. Some are more than 400 years old and still lived in by the original families, with very beautiful collections of Portuguese colonial and Indian furniture and fittings. The Alvarez mansion in Margao and that of cartoonist Mario Miranda at Lotulim are well worth a visit. Don't turn up on their doorsteps without ringing first, as these are private residences.

Museums and Art Galleries

The small **Archaeological Museum and Portrait Gallery** ((0832) 46006, Old Goa, has a mildly interesting collection that comprises European-style portraits and Hindu statuary. It is open from 10 AM to noon and from 1 PM to 5 PM every day, apart from Fridays.

The **Archives Museum of Goa** ((0832) 46006, Arhirwad Building, First Floor, Santa Inez, Panaji, is by no means a major attraction — sporting a neglected and eclectic collection of items of local interest — but it's worth an hour of your time. It's open from 9:30 AM to 1 PM and from 2 PM to 5:30 PM; it is closed Saturdays, Sundays, and public holidays.

unload their catch. During the mid-1960s, when hippies began colonizing Goa's beaches — to the slightly outraged astonishment of local villagers — Calangute became the center of Flower Power adherents. Stalls in Calangute still do a roaring trade in leather G-strings, hessian trousers, and ethnic sandals.

Two kilometers (just over a mile) farther north is **Baga Beach**, backed by a steep hill and probably one of the best of the northern beaches. Its uncluttered sands have an authentic feel, with traditional fishing boats hauled past the high-tide mark, and chaperoning nuns and schoolchildren spending the siesta under the coconut palms. Baga also has a good windsurfing school.

Sea and Sand

If you're not heading straight for the main luxury resorts at Aguada and Bogmalo beaches, then you face a daunting array of beaches and hotels from which to choose. Generally, the northern coastline is popular for a good range of hotels, beaches, and restaurants, while the southern coast is more primitive and secluded, though it contains two of Goa's resort hotels.

THE NORTHERN BEACHES

North of Fort Aguada are the twin beaches of **Calangute** and **Candolim**, a seven-kilometer (slightly over four-mile) sandy stretch scattered with dozens of hotels and lodging houses and, on the beachfront, makeshift bars and restaurants made from wood and palm leaves. Children cross the sands to tempt reclining tourists with their fruit baskets, and at dawn each morning fishermen

From Baga's northern headland, it is a 10-minute walk to **Anjuna Beach**, a faded paradise for the "love generation," who lived in crude matting shacks along the cliff face. Nowadays Anjuna is the center of Goa's rave culture, with massive parties held in season. Daily life here centers on exhibitionist yoga, Frisbee games, and the smoking of vast amounts of hashish from elaborate pipes. Worthwhile Anjuna institutions are the Wednesday flea market and the Friday evening Haystack, the brainchild of Goa's most noted musician, August Braganza, whose backyard turns into a canopied showcase for local talent, with folk dances, singing, and music performed and good Goan food served.

OPPOSITE: Church of Immaculate Conception, Panaji, Goa. ABOVE: The postcard-perfect waves and sands of Goa's Aguada Beach.

The small rocky inlets of **Chapora** and **Vagator** are three kilometers (just under two miles) farther north. Chapora is overlooked by the ruins of a Portuguese fort, built in 1717, with fine views from the ramparts. Vagator is more idyllic and secluded, with a couple of resorts. A number of local residents here rent out rooms in the village, and it's possible to rent an entire house inexpensively.

THE SOUTHERN BEACHES

Bogmalo is small by Goan standards and largely patronized by guests of the Oberoi's luxury resort, which dominates the crescent-shaped bay.

Colva's stretch of powdery sand and pristine, warm water is Goa's most paradisiacal. At least

the 1960s, the north has been more developed, but the south is catching up fast, particularly with the advent of direct charter flights to Goa from Europe.

The best idea is to head to one of the more developed beaches in the north or south initially, and then use it as a base to explore the area and perhaps find somewhere more to your liking. In the north, Sinquerim, Calangute and Baga are the most developed beaches — Anjuna, farther north again is a popular backpacker destination, and scene of the now famous "full moon parties." In the south, Colva, Benaulim, and Cavelossim are the most developed beaches.

It is also possible, of course, to stay at either of the nearby towns of Panaji and Vasco da Gama,

it was until recently. While tourist development has been more low-key here than at Calangute, Colva is, however, developing at breakneck speed. **Benaulim**, two kilometers farther south, is a more secluded place to stay and has equally beautiful beaches.

Farther south again, at **Varca** and **Cavelossim**, there are yet more pristine beaches. Development here has been mostly upmarket, of the sort exemplified by the Goa Renaissance, Holiday Inn and Leela Beach resorts.

WHERE TO STAY

Goa is a sprawling place, and deciding which area to be based in is no easy matter. The vast majority of arrivals opt for beachside accommodation, but this in itself presents the north or south dilemma. Traditionally, since travelers "discovered" Goa in

though this is an option taken by relatively few foreign visitors.

Panaji

Hotel Mandovi ((0832) 226270 FAX (0832) 225451, D.B. Bandodkar Road, Goa's oldest, still has a certain charm despite suffering from a 1960s decor overhaul. Nothing has changed much since Evelyn Waugh stayed here and observed that the hotel bookshop contained only cheap detective novels, sex psychology manuals, and rationalist education books. Rates start at around US$30.

The **Hotel Nova Goa (** (0832) 226231 FAX (0832) 224958, Dr. Atmaran Borkar Road, is of a similar standard, but it's a more modern venture and comes complete with a swimming pool.

The **Hotel Fidalgo (** (0832) 226291, 18th June Road, is another modern hotel, also with a swimming pool.

The Northern Beaches

The **Fort Aguada Beach Resort** ((0832) 276201 FAX (0832) 276044 is one of Goa's premier resorts, at Sinquerim, Bardez. Built by the Taj Group within extensive gardens and the ruins of a seventeenth-century fort, the hotel building has tasteful sea-facing rooms, some with terraces. It has a swimming pool, water sports, tennis courts, a Jacuzzi, and a gymnasium. On the hillside are tiers of self-contained cottages, perfect for a couple.

On an even higher level is **Aguada Hermitage Villas** ((0832) 276201 FAX (0832) 276044, a series of elite dwellings used for the 1983 Commonwealth heads of government conference, with one cottage named after Britain's former Prime Minister Margaret Thatcher. Rates average at around US$225, but double or halve in price depending on the season, for a one-bedroom cottage.

Right on the beach, is the **Taj Holiday Village** ((0832) 276201 FAX (0832) 276045, another grand hotel complex with the full complement of amenities and services.

Not far away, at Candolim Beach, a less expensive accommodation option is the **Whispering Palms Beach Resort** ((0832) 276140 FAX (0832) 276142, a mid-range resort that sees a steady traffic of package tourists in season.

For budget accommodation, you need only walk five to ten minutes north of the Whispering Palms to find an enclave of mostly family run "resorts" that charge rages of around US$15 in season. The **Alexandra Tourist Center** is a good choice, but take a look at some of the other nearby places before committing yourself to anything.

Calangute Beach is teeming with accommodation, though much of it is of the budget variety, with rooms for US$10 or less. The best choice is the **Varma Beach Resort** ((0832) 276077 FAX (0832) 276022, with large, moderately priced and well-kept, air-conditioned rooms. They serve excellent breakfasts of piping-hot Goanese bread, eggs, fruit, and delicious coffee. The Varma is closed off-season, between June and September.

Close by is the **Concha Beach Resort** ((0832) 276056 FAX (0832) 277555, a simple, but stylishly presented place with good value rooms.

Way down at the south of Calangute Beach, the **Paradise Village Beach Resort** ((0832) 276475 FAX (0832) 276155 is a sprawling development that is popular with the package tour groups. It has a swimming pool, a miniature golf course, and a beach frontage. High season rates are around US$50, but are discounted off-season.

For budget chalet accommodation, **Coco Banana** is one of the most popular choices on the beach.

If you are arriving in Goa without reservations, Baga beach, which is a northern extension of Calangute beach, is probably not such a good place to start. In high season, most of the hotels here are pre-reserved by package tours.

One of the best in this area is the **Hotel Baia Do Sol** ((0832) 276084 5 FAX (0834) 731415. Literally set on the sands, it has casual, well-kept rooms, a great outdoor seafood restaurant, and excellent value riverside cottages. The helpful staff can arrange motorbikes, river cruises, waterskiing, fishing, and traditional folk dances.

The **Ronil Beach Resort** ((0832) 276099 FAX (0832) 276068, a modern Spanish-style resort around a freshwater swimming pool with an outdoor restaurant is highly recommended and moderately priced. A last Baga Beach option is **Cavala** ((0832) 276090, which offers simple rooms without air-conditioning, and has a quaint bar and good Goanese restaurant.

At Anjuna, the **Bougainvillea** ((0832) 273271 FAX (0832) 262031 is a cut above most of its local competitors, featuring a swimming pool and smart, air-conditioned rooms, but it is also a bit of a hike from the beach.

The **Poonam Guesthouse** ((0832) 273247 is a better choice if you want to be in the thick of things, though the rooms are somewhat basic, no air-conditioning, but all come with attached bathrooms.

The beaches of Chapora and Vagator, to the north of Anjuna, are quieter and less developed. Accommodation is mostly in budget guesthouses, though some foreigners also stay long-term in rented houses. The best accommodation on Vagator beach is the **Sterling Resort** ((0832) 273276

OPPOSITE: One of Goa's upmarket beach resorts. ABOVE: A proud bridegroom garlanded with flowers parades in the streets Goa.

FAX (0832) 273314. It has both air-conditioned and fan-cooled cottages set in a spacious garden with a swimming pool. It's a quiet and friendly place that is ideal for a lengthy stay.

The Southern Beaches

Bogmalo beach is just a short drive from the airport. The beach is dominated by the **Park Plaza Resort** ((0834) 513291 FAX (0834) 512510. It has pleasant rooms; small balconies face either the sea or a beautiful rear garden. The resort boasts excellent water sports, a freshwater swimming pool, health club, and a variety of restaurants serving good traditional Goan and seafood dishes. And Colva, Goa's most spectacular beach, is close by. Rooms

one of the sea-view rooms—all come with attached bathrooms and some have air-conditioning.

Farther south, you will find some of Goa's best hotels. For five-star comforts, the **Goa Renaissance Resort** ((0834) 745208 FAX (0834) 745225, at Varca beach, is probably the pick of the pack. It boasts six restaurants, four bars (including one by the beach), a casino, a disco, a swimming pool, a nine-hole golf course, and innumerable other amenities. Rates, in season, start at US$300.

Farther south again at Cavelossim beach is the **Leela Beach Four Seasons Resort** ((0834) 746363 FAX (0834) 746352, with water sports, tennis courts, restaurants and bars. Also on the same beach is the friendly **Holiday Inn Resort Goa** ((0834)

start at around US$170 in high season, but drop to as low as US$55 from June through September.

Colva beach is Goa's most touristed and developed. If it's nightlife and watersports you want, this is probably the best place to be based. One of the better hotels here is the Colva's **Hotel Silver Sands** ((0834) 721645. It has good, air-conditioned rooms, but it wins no points for atmosphere. The nearby **Penthouse Beach Resort** ((0834) 731030 has a more winning ambience, featuring air-conditioned rooms in Goan-style cottages; it also has a swimming pool.

A more budget alternative to these two middle-range hotels is the **Sukhsagar Beach Resort** ((0834) 721888, which has mixture of air-conditioned and fan-cooled rooms. North of here, and with a position near the beach, the **Longuinhos Beach Resort** ((0834) 222918 is more expensive but a arguably better deal, particularly if you take

746303 FAX (0834) 746333. It's not quite in the same league as the Goa Renaissance or the Four Seasons, but is a reliable luxury choice all the same.

WHERE TO EAT

All over Goa, from city restaurants to the simplest village taverna, it's possible to eat magnificently. Here the unique hybrid cuisine finds a perfect companion in the famous *feni* — a potent local brew made from cashew, coconut, or apple. Goans are particularly proud of their robust cuisine, and never turn down an invitation to dine at a family home, where the most authentic food is found.

Indianized Portuguese dishes are usually spicy, but delicious, such as *xacuti*, a high-powered dish of either mutton or chicken with a coconut masala sauce, or *caldinhe*, a delicately seasoned fish dish. These are usually accompanied by *pau*, a small soft bread roll leavened with palm toddy. Pork is a staple meat and is used in *chourisso*, a sausage, and *sorpotal*, pig's liver pickled in a savory sauce.

But the real splendor of Goan cuisine is in the numerous preparations of fresh seafood — king prawns, lobster, kingfish, oysters, mussels, shrimps, and crabs — roasted, grilled, or curried in mouthwatering ways. Goan wines are unexceptional, though much cheaper than other Indian varieties, and all come in screw-top bottles. It is easy to develop a taste for *feni*, which is best taken diluted with soda. The smoother, double-distilled variant flavored with cumin, ginger, or sarsaparilla makes an unusual drink.

Every Goan has a list of favorite eating places, and the only bias tends to be proximity, as Goa is very spread out. Most of the main hotels have good indoor and outdoor restaurants, but the following places (in the same order as the hotels listed above) are highly recommended.

In Panaji a longtime favorite for Goan cuisine is **Venite (** (0832) 225537, on Janeiro Road. The atmosphere of this old colonial building, with its balconies overlooking the street, is every bit as good as its meals.

At Sinquerim beach, try the **Afonso de Albuquerque** at the Fort Aguada Beach Resort for seafood and Goan fare. Also recommended for its seafood, and close to the Taj Holiday Village, is **Nezvila**.

One of the most popular restaurants on Calangute beach is the beachfront **Souza Lobo**. It's best to stick to the seafood here, but if you're feeling adventurous you might try one of the dangerously inexpensive steaks.

Farther north, at Baga beach, the best place to head for after sunset is **Casa Portuguesa**, an exquisitely restored Portuguese villa owned by Francisco Sousa, a wealthy Goan lawyer. This may well be India's most elegant restaurant, with candlelit tables spread through the Iberian-style vaulted rooms, small veranda, and tropical garden. It serves classic Portuguese dishes and standard Goan fare, including such delicacies as whole shark *rachieada*, mussels in wine, and grilled oysters. Goa's cognoscente flock here as much for the wonderful food as to hear Francisco perform *fado*, the lugubrious Portuguese love songs. Try either to book or to come early — the Casa Portuguesa serves only dinner and fills up at about 9 PM.

On the Baga beachfront is **St. Anthony's Bar**, which has been part of Goan mythology since it opened in 1968. This weathered beach shack, with its peeling Formica-top tables, slumbering dogs, and rock-bottom prices, serves everything with a Midas touch, from fruit whips and waffles to grilled mackerel and clams cooked in coconut sauce.

Tito's Bar and Restaurant, a short way south of St. Anthony's and also on the beachfront, is another popular spot. The seafood is good, and the bar pulls in the crowds from around 10 PM onwards.

In Anjuna there are numerous inexpensive cafés and bars, most of them not far from the famous Wednesday flea market area. The **German Bakery** is one of the best. On the beach, not far north of the flea market, you will find several bars, including the **Shore Bar**, that are popular places at sunset.

At Vagator beach, the **Sterling Resort** has an excellent seafood restaurant. Close by is **Lobo's**, which serves similar fare at more budget prices.

Overlooking the southern end of Vagator beach, is the **Mahalakshmi Restaurant**, another good seafood place.

Moving south, at Colva beach you will find several strings of cafés and bars directly on the beachfront. Most do seafood meals and provide chilled beer in occasionally quite swish surroundings. Competition among them is fierce, which guarantees surprisingly high standards at relatively inexpensive rates.

The **Silver Sands**, at the hotel of the same name, right in the center of Colva beach, is one of the best of the restaurants, and along with the usual Indian and Continental offerings also does some superb Goan cuisine. For similarly upmarket Goan cuisine, also try the **A-Tartaruga Bar and Restaurant** at the Longuinhos Beach Resort.

Splash is the most popular of Colva's late night haunts, but while it's recommended for a drink, its food is disappointing.

At Benaulim beach you will find more beachside cafés — mostly in-season — though as a rule they are not as good as those at Colva. One recommended restaurant is the **Solitary Garden**

OPPOSITE: The ruins of the Portuguese Fort Aguada. ABOVE: Maharashtra girl hawking handicrafts on the beach.

at the Palm Grove Hotel. It has a relaxing alfresco ambience and a good selection of Goan specialties to choose from.

Farther south, at Varca Beach, the Goa Renaissance Resort, dominates the culinary agenda. **Castaways** is the place for Goan treats and barbecued seafood. The **Polynesian Hut** does "Polynesian-style" dinners in-season. The **Café Cascade** serves Indian, continental and Goan cuisine.

HOW TO GET THERE

One of the most popular ways to travel between Goa and Bombay is by high-speed Catamaran.

From Bombay, boats leave at either 10 AM or 10:30 AM daily (except Monday and Wednesday) and arrive in Goa at around 5 PM. The service is operated by Frank Shipping ((0832) 228711 (Goa) or ((022) 610 2525 (Bombay). There is a return service that operate daily (except Tuesday) at 10 AM. Tickets cost approximately US$40.

Goa's Dabolim airport is connected by Indian Airlines, Jet Airways, Modiluft, Spanair, Damania Airways, East West Airways, and NEPC to a host of Indian destinations. Panaji, the capital, is 27 kilometers(nearly 17 miles) away and the resort beaches are even further, so it's worth utilizing the free reception coaches provided by the major hotels for prospective guests. Otherwise, there's an inexpensive airport bus into town.

Train journeys to Goa's Vasco da Gama station, some 30 km (just under 19 miles) from Panaji, take as little as 10 hours from Bombay nowadays due to the recent conversion of tracks on this route to broad gauge.

Luxury buses take sixteen hours from Bombay, but most of these are notorious video-coaches. The best choice however is MTDC's air-conditioned "luxury" bus, one of the rare ones that doesn't inflict the ubiquitous onboard video, which departs at 3 PM daily (US$8).

AURANGABAD AND MAHARASHTRA

Set high on the dry, weathered Deccan Plateau, Maharashtra's craggy heartland stands in stark contrast to the tropical bustle of Bombay, the state capital. A rural patchwork of thatch huts, fields of giant sunflowers, cotton, and mustard plants, and deep, dried-out ravines, Maharashtra has an eerie, primitive beauty.

Although primarily used as a base for visiting India's finest ancient cave sculptures and frescos at Ajanta and Ellora, Aurangabad, has several historical attractions and some very interesting Buddhist caves of its own. Originally called Khadke, it was later renamed during the Mughal emperor Aurangzeb's reign from 1650 to 1670. Aurangabad is surrounded by crumbling fortifications and contains several fine Mughal monuments, including Aurangzeb's duplicate Taj Mahal, the Bibi-ka-Maqbara, built as a mausoleum for his wife.

BACKGROUND

The state of Maharashtra was once the center of the mighty Maratha empire, which ruled much of central India during the seventeenth century, waging fierce battles with Muslim invaders. Much earlier, however, between the second century BC and the thirteenth century AD, the area witnessed the creation of the finest of all cave temples and monasteries in India, a technical *tour de force* carved from solid rock with brilliant technical and artistic skill. These are the famous caves at Ajanta and Ellora, some 60 in total, near the city of Aurangabad. The work of itinerant communities of Buddhist — and later Hindu and Jain monks, who had among their ranks exceptionally skilled sculptors and artists, the caves at Ajanta and Ellora are so exquisite in their execution that they rank with the Taj Mahal, the temples of Khajuraho and Kanchipuram, and the ruined city of Fatehpur Sikri as the country's greatest wonders.

Today's tourists pass through the musty cave recesses to marvel at the skill and beauty of these caves, but for earlier generations of largely illiterate devotees they were an overwhelming visual sermon, enshrining the history of myth, religion, and architecture of ancient India.

After Buddhism declined in India, these cave masterpieces were neglected and fell into obscurity under layers of earth and vegetation until 1819, when a group of British soldiers stumbled upon a cave while tiger hunting on the Deccan Plateau.

GENERAL INFORMATION

Your first stop for information should be the **Government of India Tourist Office** ((0240)331217,

Krishna Vilas, Station Road. The **Government of Maharashtra Tourist Office** ((0240) 331513 Holiday Camp, Aurangabad, is another place to go for local information.

WHEN TO GO

The best season to visit is October to November, after the monsoon, when the fields brim with sunflower plantations, or December to March, when it is comfortably warm and sunny. As early as April to May, Maharashtra becomes unpleasantly hot, and a supply of mineral water is an absolute necessity.

GETTING AROUND

Aurangabad is a small, rather sleepy, town, with all the useful tourist facilities — railway station, central bus stand, hotels, restaurants, and tourist office — fairly close together. Auto-rickshaws seem to outnumber taxis, and are the best way to negotiate Aurangabad's narrow back-alleys, where the Muslim influence is strongly evident in street-side mosques and *burqa*-clad women.

With its better facilities, Aurangabad is perfect as a base for daily excursions to Ajanta and Ellora, and you should plan to spend at least two days here to see everything properly.

There are frequent buses to both Ellora (29 km or 18 miles) and Ajanta (106 km or 66 miles), but you may prefer to take either or both of MTDC's daily, well-conducted full-day Ellora and City Tour and the Ajanta Excursion. The former covers Daulatabad Fort, Grishnewshwar Temple, Ellora Caves, the Aurangabad Caves, the tomb at Khuldabad, Bibi-ka-Maqbara, and Panchakki, while the latter covers the Ajanta viewpoint and the Ajanta Caves.

These tours are a very economical way of covering all the main areas of interest in and around the city, and their accompanying guides are all knowledgeable archaeology graduates.

For those who prefer to study India's finest cave temples at leisure, an organized tour can be frustrating. If you are pressed for time, it is possible (but tiring) to see everything in one day. A hired Ambassador taxi (seats four) will cost around US$35 for the day, and there are many pleasant picnic spots along the way if you bring a packed lunch.

WHAT TO SEE AND DO

Aurangabad Caves
Few visitors to Aurangabad venture up the stony hillside rock-cleft three kilometers (just under two miles) out of town to see these unfinished, but still magnificent, cave temples. There are 10 of them in all, excavated by Buddhist monks between the third and the seventh century AD.

It's convenient to start with the western group of caves, by walking "backwards" from cave 10 to cave 6. Amongst this group, cave 7 is by far the most spectacular, with its central frieze depicting an enormous Siddhartha on the verge of his transformation into Buddha, praying for protection from eight fears — sword, fire, chains, shipwreck, lions, snakes, crazed elephants, and the writhing demons of death. Cave 6 has a curious mixture of Hindu and Buddhist iconography that indicates the gradual absorption of Buddhist thought into Hinduism.

From these caves, it's a rambling 20-minute stroll across to caves 1 to 5 on the eastern side of the hill. Cave 4 is the only *chaitya*, or temple, all the others being *viharas*, or monastery prayer halls.

It is best to travel to the caves in a solid Ambassador taxi — the alternative, an auto-rickshaw, is much bumpier. The caves are open from sunrise to 6 PM. A stroll back to Aurangabad is a pleasant finale, and it's easy to find your bearings: just stride across the empty plains towards the white minarets of the Taj-clone, **Bibika-Maqbara**, and from here you can hire a rickshaw for a ride back into town.

The orthodox Mughal emperor Aurangzeb built the Bibi-ka-Mqbara in 1679 for his wife, known as Rabia Durrani, ordering his architects to construct a masterpiece that would outshine his father Shah Jahan's then recently completed Taj Mahal in Agra. Thrifty even in his grief, Aurangzeb's mausoleum is far less ornamental, costing 300 times less than its immortal rival. It's open from sunrise to 10 PM.

Overlooking Aurangabad's Kaum River in the heart of the city is the **Panchakki**, an impressive pre-Mughal watermill harnessed to operate large grain-grinding stones. It was built in 1624 to commemorate the memory of the Sufi saint Baba Shah Musafir, whose tomb lies nearby. Open from sunrise to 10 PM.

Aurangabad is famous for its *himroo* shawls, cotton brocade, *bidri* ware, and Aurangabad silk, but the antiquated traditional handloom methods are rapidly disappearing. It's worth paying a visit to one of the few family businesses existing in the city. The most characterful is the Aurangabad Himroo Factory in Shahganj, opposite Gandhi Square, where the owner and arch-weaver, A.H. Qureshi, will explain the technique and mourn the death of the trade, while his spindly fingers blur in the motion of knotting and threading.

Daulatabad Fort
A remarkable medieval fortress towering high on a pyramidal hill above the dusty plains some 13 km (eight miles) from Aurangabad, Daulatabad's eerie beauty is haunted by its former despotic rulers

Dusk at Bogmalo Beach, Goa.

and bloody history. Originally it was the capital of the Yadava dynasty in the thirteenth century, who called it Devagiri, or "hill of the gods." It caught the quixotic imagination of the mad Delhi sultan, Muhammad Tughluq, who captured the fortress for his new capital, renaming it Daulatabad, or "fortunate city." His unfortunate subjects were forced to walk 1,100 km (680 miles) here from Delhi in 1327; then, only 17 years later, he realized the impracticality of the location and marched the remaining survivors back again.

The medieval equivalent of Fort Knox, Daulatabad is surrounded by six kilometers (nearly four miles) of thick walls, rows of terrifying spikes at its entrance to deter charging elephants, a huge moat that once seethed with hungry crocodiles, and dead-end passages where trapped intruders ended their lives under vat-loads of boiling oil.

With its labyrinth of musty passages, Daulatabad is fascinating to wander through, but bring a flashlight to avoid stumbling in its dark stairwells. Just inside the entrance gate is the 60-m (197-ft)-high **Chand Minar pillar**, built in 1435 as a monument of victory. From the dried-out moat, it's a half-hour climb to the top, passing the blue-tiled **Chini Mahal Palace** where prestigious nobles were kept prisoner. On the hill's crest stands a formidable cannon engraved with Aurangzeb's name, and there's a black, spiraling pit once used to hurl burning coals down onto invaders. It's open from sunrise to sunset.

Aurangzeb's Grave

When Aurangzeb died in 1707, he was buried according to his instructions in a bare earth grave open to the sky at Khuldabad ("heavenly abode"), 26 km (16 miles) from Aurangabad on the route to Ellora. Once a fortified village (Aurangzeb built the battlements around it), its most interesting monument is the **Karbala**, or holy shrine of Deccan Muslims, which contains the remains of many historical figures.

In his will, Aurangzeb stated that his funeral costs were to be covered only by the four and a half rupees earned from the sale of caps sewn by the emperor himself. As a final request, the money earned from the sale of his hand-copied Korans was to be divided amongst holy men on the day of his death. It would have displeased Aurangzeb to see the decorative marble screen that surrounds his grave — a donation from the wealthy Nizam of Hyderabad. As contrived as this austerity must have seemed, it came to symbolize Aurangzeb's troubled legacy, for although his descendants were to rule fitfully for another century and a half,

Carved out of solid rock over a period of some 400 years, the Ellora caves are the most elaborate cave temples in India.

Aurangzeb was the last of the Great Mughals. Standing in this tranquil sunlit spot, you may find your musings on this theme interrupted by a meaningful cough by the elderly mosque keeper with a carrot-colored beard, a well-thumbed Koran, and a monetary gleam in his eyes.

Ellora

Some 29 km (18 miles) from Aurangabad are the most elaborate cave temples in India. Although Buddhist monks began excavating in the seventh century, the site soon grew to include Hindu and Jain temples as the Buddhist faith waned in popularity. There are 34 caves — 12 Buddhist (AD 600–800), 17 Hindu (around AD 900), and five

Jain (AD 800–1000) — and they are numbered in that order as you progress from south to north.

It's convenient to start with the Buddhist caves, though these are the least interesting. Ten can be traced to the Mahayana schism by their contemplative images of Buddha vilified by the more orthodox relic-worshiping Hinayana sect which was responsible for building caves 1 and 7. The wealthy merchants who financed the construction of these caves did so in the belief that their pious contributions helped them to accumulate religious merit. Cave 10 is the only *chaitya* of the group, with its immense Buddha on a lion throne, surrounded by attendants and fronted by a nine-meter (almost 30-ft)-high stupa.

If you're on the MTDC tour you'll be whisked speedily past most of the Hindu temples, stopping to admire in detail only the most spectacular. This is cave 16, the Kailas Temple, named after Shiva's mountain home in the Himalayas. Begun in the eighth century, 7,000 stonecutters worked on it in squadrons constantly over a period of 150 years during the Rashtrakuta dynasty, an expenditure in manpower and rupees equal to that of conducting a major protracted war.

Carved from a single rock as large as the Parthenon in Athens, the Kailas Temple is an awesome feat of engineering: begun from the

top (much of which is now open to the sky) and chiseled down to the floor, creating arches, passageways, towers, and ornate friezes along the way. A bridge at the entrance leads to an enclosed courtyard, where immense flagstaffs and stone elephants surround the main two-storied shrine and Nandi pavilion. The cool, sandalwood-scented interior chambers are filled with ornate Dravidian sculptures depicting stories from the *Ramayana*.

The Jain temples are a short stroll to the north. Although noteworthy for their delicacy and detail, these appear rather anemic after the energetic brilliance of the Kailas Temple. The "Assembly Hall of Indra," cave 32, is the most interesting of this group, with its simple ground floor enlivened by curving lotus reliefs on the ceiling. The upper story is notable for its decorative friezes and lotus-design columns. The shrine is dedicated to Mahavira, the last of the 24 *tirthankaras* and founder of the Jain religion.

There are several hotels near Ellora if you want to spend more time looking at the caves, but none are particularly good. The best (and nearest to the caves) is the **Kailash Hotel** ((02437) 41043.

Ajanta

It's a long, winding drive from Aurangabad to the Ajanta caves (106 km or 66 miles), but at journey's end is one of the world's most fascinating collections of wall paintings and frescoes. Unfortunately, the wall paintings are becoming progressively bleached by exposure to the atmosphere and, despite efforts by experts to preserve them with sealing fluids, are slowly fading away. The light wreaks havoc with the delicate colors, so the caves are kept in murky darkness. Come prepared with a strong flashlight, or pay the "lighting charge" at the entrance. For a small sum, a wizened attendant in a Nehru cap will try to reflect rays of sunlight into the cave using a sheet of corrugated iron. If you're not with a tour, it's advisable to hire a "deluxe" guide from the entrance (the bone fide ones wear accredited badges).

The 30 caves chiseled into Ajanta's crescent-shaped granite gorge represent the highest artistic achievement of the Buddhist monks who arrived here in the second century BC to establish a monastic retreat. Most of the caves were completed by the second century AD; the others date from the fifth to the seventh century, before the site was mysteriously abandoned for nearby Ellora. For hundreds of years, the caves were obscured under thick foliage, and this accounts for the near-perfect state of preservation in which they were found.

The caves are a perfect showcase for understanding the progression of Buddhist art and thought. The early Hinayana school disapproved of earthly pleasures, believing that the best way to attain salvation was through pain. Caves 8, 9, 10, 12, and 13 date from the older Hinayana period, and images of Buddha are notably absent. In the second century BC, the more worldly Mahayana school's liberal ideas shocked Hinayana Buddhists to the core, but created a renaissance in Indian art. Here the frescoes are full of Brueghel-like scenes, far more diverting than the central theme of the Ajanta caves; the life and times of Buddha. This more realistic and sensual art reached its zenith in the Gupta dynasty, AD 320-647.

All the caves at Ajanta are monolithic: scooped out to create a complex granite husk complete with pillars, façades, dormitories, and galleries of sculpted Buddhas, all carved from the same piece

WHERE TO STAY

Aurangabad's best hotel is the **Taj Residency** ((0240) 381106 FAX (0240) 381053. It has a secluded position out of town and is set amidst manicured lawns. Amenities include a coffee shop, restaurant, bar, fitness center, 24-hour business center and swimming pool. Doubles start at US$90.

The **Welcomgroup Rama International** ((0240) 485441 FAX (0240) 484768, close to the airport, has rates and standards similar to those at the Taj.

The **Ajanta Ambassador Hotel** ((0240) 485211 FAX (0240) 484367 on Airport Road is moderately priced, with pleasant decor, from around US$65.

of rock. Beneath the frescoes are layers of clay, cow dung, powdered rice husk, and lime plaster. Crushed pebbles, ochre, and ground lapis lazuli were used as colors, and applied with squirrel-hair brushes.

Cave 1 is the largest and most impressive of the Ajanta caves, with the best frescoes and relief carvings. Caves 2, 16, 17, and 19 also contain beautiful frescoes. Cave 4 is the largest *vihara* (residence) cave, supported by 28 pillars. Along with caves 17, 19, and 26, it has the best sculptures in the group. The oldest cave is cave 10. The caves are open from 9:30 AM to 5:30 PM.

The only local accommodation is five kilometers (three miles) away in **Holiday Resort** ((02438) 4230. It has cheap, clean rooms and meals. The tourist hostel directly opposite the caves is a basic affair, but can be relied on to provide a room at a pinch.

Slightly cheaper, the **Vedant** ((0240) 333844 FAX (0240) 331923, Station Road, is somewhat characterless but has good, spic-and-span air-conditioned rooms, restaurants, a bar, and a swimming pool.

Of a similar standard and also in the heart of Aurangabad is the moderately priced **Hotel Aurangabad Ashok** ((0240) 332492 FAX (0240) 331328, in Dr. Rajendra Prasad Marg.

In the budget category **Hotel Rajdoot** ((0240) 352050 FAX (0240) 331328, which has both air-conditioned and air-cooled rooms from around US$6.

The **MTDC Holiday Resort** ((0240) 334259 is another excellent budget choice. Set in pleasant gardens, it features spacious rooms with attached bathrooms, a bar, and a restaurant.

OPPOSITE: Daulatabad Fort has an eerie beauty and a bloody history. ABOVE: Entrance to the Ellora caves.

WHERE TO EAT

The **Taj Residency**, the **Rama International** and the **Ajanta Ambassador** all have good Indian/continental restaurants.

The **Mingling Restaurant**, attached to the Hotel Rajdoot, is regarded by locals as the best Chinese restaurant in town. The **Kailash** restaurant at the MTDC Holiday Resort has the usual mixture of Indian, Chinese, and continental offerings.

The **Foodwallah's Tandoori**, on Station Road, is very popular and well worth visiting for its tandoori and *tikka* dishes, which are lauded as

among the best in town. Otherwise try the **Food Walla's Bhoj Restaurant**, also on Station Road, for good vegetarian fare.

HOW TO GET THERE

There are daily flights from Bombay to Aurangabad with Indian Airlines and NEPC. You can also fly to Aurangabad direct from Udaipur, Jaipur, and Delhi with Indian Airlines.

Trains run to Aurangabad from Bombay, but this is a long, awkward journey (eight to nine hours) involving a change at Manmad junction. It's still a popular route, however, and you are required to book four days in advance from Bombay. Jalgaon is the nearest railhead for the Ajanta Caves (56 km or 35 miles, from Aurangabad), and both Manmad and Jalgaon are linked to Bombay, Delhi, and Calcutta.

Of the overnight buses that ply the winding, mountainous route to Aurangabad, the best choice is the MTDC air-conditioned coach, which leaves Bombay at 8:30 PM.

GUJARAT

Few travelers venture to Gujarat, yet the state is saturated with historical attractions and, as a relatively untrodden tourist trail, has retained much of its traditional lifestyle. Gujarat is a colorful mixture of modern and age-old cultures. In the capital, Ahmedabad — one of India's most highly developed commercial cities — camels still traipse its main streets as they have done for centuries, and the whole city grinds to a halt during the siesta hours from noon to 4 PM. Rural Gujarat appears barely touched by the twentieth century; villagers still wear traditional dress and practice skilled crafts, particularly weaving and woodcarving.

Ahmedabad contains many relics of its grand Mughal past and fine art and textile museums. Nearby, the former princely capital, Vadodara (Baroda), is a stately city of Gothic palaces, parks, and museums. But the real pleasures lie in rural Gujarat, from its northern tip at the Rann of Kutch, the home of brightly attired tribal nomads, through to the Sasan Gir Lion Sanctuary and elaborate Jain temples in the south.

The Ajanta caves boast one of the world's most fascinating collections of wall paintings and frescoes.

BACKGROUND

Gujarat contains many of the ancient sites of Hindu mythology. The story goes that the Somnath shore temple in the south was built by Soma, the Moon God, to mark the creation of the universe. Legend also places Lord Krishna's kingdom at Dwarka, on Gujarat's west coast. Its first communities appeared with the Indus Valley civilization in about 2500 BC, and the world's earliest Asian and Western literature refers to the value of Gujarat's trade goods. Anti-caste Buddhists and Jains ruled until the end of the eighth century, and the latter are still a dominant

noticeably, Gujaratis are renowned for their shrewd business acumen, and many have emigrated and now thrive in communities around the world.

GENERAL INFORMATION

A good mini-tour of Gujarat begins with Ahmedabad and covers the main destinations of the Jain pilgrimage centers of Palitana and Junagadh, the Sasan Gir Lion Sanctuary and Somnath Temple in the south, and palace-filled Vadodara in the southeast. Adventurous travelers can explore the northern Rann of Kutch, a salt desert inhabited by the colorful nomadic Malderi tribe. Most of Gujarat's hotels are inexpensive and

force in Gujarat today, being responsible for the state's almost total vegetarianism.

During India's Middle Ages, these peaceful cultures were invaded by the feudal Hindu Rajputs, and for several centuries much of the present state fell under first Muslim, then Mughal, rule. Opportunistic Portuguese traders established key ports in Daman and Diu on the southern coast, retaining possession until 1961. With the expansion of the British Empire, mainland Gujarat was governed by the British, while the southern Kathiawar peninsula, now known as Saurashtra, had 282 princely states in an area roughly the size of Ireland.

Mahatma Gandhi, who was born in Gujarat's Porbandar state, believed that his penchant for pacifism and social reform was an inherent Gujarati trait, and took the motto "nonviolence is the supreme religion" from the Jains. More

simple but are subject to a sliding state-imposed luxury tax that can add 30% to the bill.

To see Gujarat (and parts of Rajasthan) in luxury, the *Royal Orient* does a seven-day journey from Delhi to Chittaurgarh, Udaipur, Junagadh, Veraval, Sasan Gir, Delvada, Palitana, Sarkhej, Ahmedabad, and Jaipur, before returning to Delhi. The costs are reasonable and all-inclusive of meals, accommodation (on board the train), and entry fees for sights. Bookings can be made via the **Tourism Corporation of Gujarat in Delhi** ((011) 373 4015 FAX (011) 373 2482.

WHEN TO GO

Gujarat has an abundance of fairs and festivals throughout the year, but it's well worth timing your trip to coincide with the **Makara Sankranti Kite Festival** on January 14, or the **Navrati Festival**, which celebrates the goddess Amba, held on the cusp of September to October, with nine days of impromptu street dances and *bhavai* folk theater.

The mild winter months from November to March are the best times for Gujarat, although the monsoon season has its own charm. Bring light clothes, and a sweater for winter evenings.

AHMEDABAD: GATEWAY TO GUJARAT

Ahmedabad's congested urban sprawl contains the husk of an original city built by the Muslim ruler Ahmed Shah during the fifteenth century, and much of this grand Islamic architecture still stands. Towards the end of the sixteenth century,

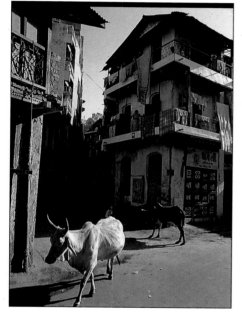

Ahmedabad had a thousand mosques, cenotaphs, and tombs, all surrounded by carefully kept gardens. In 1615, Sir Thomas Roe, the British emissary to Emperor Jahangir in Delhi, described Ahmedabad as being "as large as London, the handsomest city in Hindustan and perhaps the world." It was here that Mahatma Gandhi founded his *ashram* and later launched his famous Salt March to protest British hegemony.

Now an industrial center plagued by pollution and noise, Ahmedabad is no longer a beautiful city, but visitors will find it has many pockets of unexpected charm. It has fine museums and boasts a cultivated patronage of the arts that is quite unique in India. Beyond the remains of the medieval wall and its stone gateways, in the Byzantine confusion of Ahmedabad's old city, are many sixteenth-century *havelis*, so delicately carved they resemble wooden cobwebs, and the

pols, or living quarters, of the artisan and merchant communities. At almost any hour, weavers, hand-block printers, and woodworkers can be seen in these musty lanes toiling over their work.

Despite Gandhi's legacy, communal enmities run deep in Ahmedabad, which has seen grisly clashes between its Muslim and Hindu communities in the old city.

General Information

Government conducted tours covering the city's sights leave each day from the Lal Darwaja bus-stand at 8 AM and 2 PM, costing Rs 30. These are useful if you have very little time, and for getting your bearings. Contact the **Tourist Corporation of Gujarat** ((079) 449172, H.K. House, Ashram Road (open 10:30 AM to 1:30 PM and 2 PM to 5:30 PM) for details on their longer (four- or five-day) tours around north and south Gujarat and Saurashtra, costing about US$30 to US$40. There are also tourist counters at the airport and railway station.

What to See and Do

The domes and minarets of the Muslim mosques, pavilions, and monuments built during the fifteenth century are dotted throughout central Ahmedabad. Built of local honey-colored stone, these structures are a fusion of austere Islamic design and ornately decorative Hindu art, and mark the birth of the Indo-Saracenic style. The most beautiful are within the heart of the city. **Rani Sipri's Mosque and Tomb** (1514) is believed to have been built by a wife of Sultan Mehmood Begada after he executed her son in a fit of anger. Nearby is the **Rani Rupmati's Mosque** (1440), with its exquisite traceries and *jali* screens.

The gracious *Friday* mosque, **Jumma Masjid** (1424), was built by Ahmed Shah, the city's founder. According to local myth, the large black stone slab near the main door once formed the base of a Jain idol, which was buried upside down and trampled on to express distaste for other religions.

Just outside the mosque's east gate is **Ahmed Shah's Tomb.** Women are refused entry to the central chamber. The tombs of his queens are across the street, but almost impossible to find in the dense bazaars.

Sidi Saiyad's Mosque (1430), close to the river end of Relief Road, was built by one of Ahmed Shah's slaves. Its pierced marble latticework arches are alone worth coming to Ahmedabad to see. Their design and workmanship outshine even the windows of the Taj Mahal in Agra. Unfortunately, the mosque now forms part of a traffic island.

OPPOSITE and ABOVE: Pockets of unexpected charm are found in the bustling city of Ahmedabad, such as the Manek Chowk market area where sacred cows wander at will.

Also a Muslim creation, and unique to Gujarat, are the ornately carved *baolis* (step wells), resembling watery amphitheaters. The most beautiful is the **Adalaj Vav**, built in 1499 by Queen Rudabai of the Waghela dynasty, with its richly carved ornamental friezes and five-story structure, 19 km (12 miles) from the city.

Closer at hand is the **Dada Hari** *baoli* in town (closed from 1 PM to 4 PM), with spiral staircases and decorative friezes.

Just outside the Delhi Gate, to the north of the old city, lies the white marble **Hatheesingh Temple**, a well-patronized Jain citadel erected in 1848 by a wealthy merchant.

For restful strolls, the **Kankaria** artificial lake, almost one and a half km (a mile) long, is four kilometers (two and a half miles) southeast of the city. Built by the Sultan Qutb-ud-Din in 1451, it has an island palace where Emperor Jahangir and his beautiful empress Nur Jahan came to escape from the dust of Ahmedabad. Today, it's refreshingly peaceful, with lakeside cafés, boating, and a well-stocked zoo.

The **Sarkhej** monuments, 10 km (six miles) southwest of the city, make a pleasant excursion. This was once an isolated oasis around a stone-stepped *baoli*. The remnants of the palace, pavilions, mosque, and tombs, built by Sultan Mehmood Shah Begada and his queen Raj Bai in around 1460, are of an elegant, unembellished design.

The **Sabarmati Ashram** (six kilometers or just under four miles from Ahmedabad) was founded in 1915 by India's most famous Gujarati, Mahatma Gandhi (1869–1948). He moved here two years later with his wife, Kasturba, and remained until 1930. This was where he launched his great civil disobedience movement, which led to the freeing of India after two and a half centuries of British rule. It was from here that Gandhi began his famous Dandi march in 1930 to protest the British Salt Law, which effectively barred Indians from the salt business.

Of all the memorials throughout India associated with Gandhi, this small collection of whitewashed thatched cottages and personal possessions is the most moving. Open from dawn until the close of the nightly sound-and-light show (conducted in Hindi, Gujarati, and English on different nights), the Ashram contains a pictorial history of Gandhi's life, a handicrafts center, and a spinning wheel factory. The English sound-and-light show is held on Tuesdays, Thursdays, Fridays, and Sundays at 8:30 PM.

Old Ahmedabad is thick with bazaars and tiny shops selling a wonderful array of treasures. **Manek Chowk** is the old city's main marketplace, a bustling mêlée where merchants sell an array of embroidered beadwork, silver jewelry, antique carved wooden doorways, trays of spices, quaint stuffed toys, regimental silver, and brass teapots.

For serious shoppers, here you can find Gujarat's distinctive fabrics. Look especially for hand-painted or wood-blocked prints in the traditional black, maroon, red, and ochre patterns, *bandhana* (tie-dyed) silks and cottons, *zari* (gold) work, and the unusual patola silk sari — a traditional design woven with tie-dyed threads much coveted by Gujarati girls and costing anything from US$120 to US$1,800 depending on the quality.

If you're uncertain as to whether you are getting a bargain or being thoroughly hoodwinked, try either **Gurjari Handicrafts Emporium** or **Bangshree**, opposite Vidhyapith, both back in the commercial part of the city on Ashram Road. Both offer a good range of traditional products at government prices.

This is Ahmedabad's oldest residential area, divided into confusingly dense *pols*, or culs-de-sac, which house extended families or clans. Ask directions for the **Doshiwada-ni-pol**, where the most beautiful of the old *havelis* are found. Often only one room wide, they can be as high as five stories and are covered with beautiful carvings. Sadly, these are rapidly being dismantled and sold as antiques or placed in museums. In this area you'll see bird-feeding squares, called *parabdis*, where the nature-respecting Jains throw grain to the pigeons. In this most dense part of the old city, it's common to see men wearing the distinctive Gujarati dress — the white, pin-tucked and embroidered tunic worn to almost girlish effect — and *burqa*-clad women.

Ahmedabad's museums are wonderful, though they tend to be closed during the siesta hours and on state holidays. The best is the

Sarabhais' **Calico Museum**, a rare collection of textiles dating from the seventeenth century housed in the gardens of the family mansion in Shahibag, the old elite Civil Lines. There's also an extensive textiles reference library which can be seen on request. Open from April to June, 8:30 AM to 10:30 AM, July to March, 11 AM to noon and 3 PM to 5 PM; open daily, except Wednesdays and public holidays.

The Sarabhais are the barons of India's textile industry, a talented Jain family who made their fortune during the cotton boom of the 1800s and who live in great style in the leafy compound surrounding the museum. The stately old Sarabhai mansion can be visited and is now a center for Hindu studies.

The **Shreyas Folk Art Museum**, off Circular Road, which displays a unique array of tribal costumes, decorations, and crafts (open 9 AM to 11 AM and 4 PM to 7 PM, closed Wednesdays), and the **Tribal Museum** in Gujarat Vidhyapith, Ashram Road (open weekdays from 9 AM to noon and from 3 PM to 5 PM; closed Wednesday), provide a good introduction to Gujarati culture and mythology.

The **N.C. Mehta Museum**, housed in Le Corbusier's Sanskar Kendra Municipal Museum, Paldi, has a fine collection of Indian miniature paintings. It is open Tuesday to Sunday from 11 AM to noon and 3 PM to 5 PM. The **Vechaar Utensils Museum** in the Vishalla village (see WHERE TO EAT, below) is open Monday to Saturday, 5 PM to 11 PM and Sunday 5 PM to 10 PM.

Where to Stay

The accommodation situation in Ahmedabad has improved over recent years and there are now some reasonably good luxury hotels in town.

One of the best is the swish **Holiday Inn** ((079) 5505505 FAX (079) 5505501, next to the Sabarmati River near the Nehru Bridge. It has two restaurants, a coffee shop, and a bar, plus a health center and swimming pool. Rates start at around US$100 and include a complimentary breakfast.

Out at the airport, around 10 km (six miles) from downtown Ahmedabad, is the **Trident Hotel** ((079) 7864444 FAX (079) 7864454, which is fractionally cheaper than the Holiday Inn and offers similar standards and facilities.

The **Hotel Cama** ((079) 5505281 FAX (079) 5505285, on Khanpur Road, is pleasant and modern, with efficient staff, car rental, a poolside garden, a liquor shop, a good chemist, and a restaurant that serves delicious lunchtime *thalis*. It's a good mid-range choice, with doubles ranging from around US$60.

In a similar price range is the **Inder Residency** ((079) 6565222 FAX (079) 6560407, opposite Gujarat College. It's a modern place, with a shopping center and a swimming pool.

The **Ambassador Hotel** ((079) 5502490 FAX (079) 5502327, on Khanpur Road, is an inexpensive alternative, with well appointed air-conditioned doubles from around US$15.

The **Hotel City Palace** ((079) 2168145 FAX (079) 2113274, Relief Road, has a good central location and simple air-conditioned rooms with attached bathrooms from less than US$10.

Where to Eat

Ahmedabad's best evening entertainment and authentic Gujarati cuisine is a 15-minute drive south of the city center, at the mock-Gujarati **Vishalla** village, on Sarkhej Road. It's best to arrive no later than 8:30 PM and then to wander about

the decorated mud huts where artisans pot, weave, and make *paan*. The excellent Vechaar Utensils Museum situated here houses a remarkable collection of 2,500 metal utensils collected from all over Gujarat — including betel nut cutters, hookahs, guns, unique vessels for milking camels, and dowry items — and stays open until 10 PM.

To the accompaniment of folk music or a traditional puppet show, dinner is taken in true cross-legged Gujarati style, served on a brass *thali*. A superb feast of subtly spiced vegetable dishes, fragrant rice, lightly fried *puris*, and chutneys, followed by mugs of sweet buttermilk, and outrageously sweet *jalebis* for dessert. Lunch is equally pleasant, served from 11 AM to 1 PM.

Ahmedabad is a city of monuments, mosques, and temples. OPPOSITE: Jami Masjid, known as the Friday mosque. ABOVE: Hutheesingh Temple.

' Both the **Holiday Inn** and the **Cama** have good restaurants, but Ahmedabad's modest, proletarian-style eating houses are more authentic. The best of these are the popular **Chetna Dining Hall**, next to the Krishna Talkies on Relief Road, with all-you-can-eat *thalis* for US$1.50, and the **Gopi Dining Hall**, near the Town Hall on Pritamrai Road.

Gujaratis are usually strict vegetarians. Popular dishes include *undhyoo* — a winter dish of eggplant, potato, broad beans, and sweet potato which is traditionally cooked by being buried under a hot fire — *srikand*, hot *puris* eaten with rich candied yogurt, and *khaman dhokla*, a chickpea flour cake.

If you have the stamina, it can be fun to experience a lengthy train ride at least once, and the Delhi to Ahmedabad journey (626 km, or 390 miles, taking sixteen hours) has a drawn-out charm. Stops along the way include Ajmer and Jaipur, as well as Mount Abu, and the train passes through dry desert tundra that is enlivened by clusters of nomadic camels, brilliant splashes of dandified tribal dress, vendors who wander through the swaying train, and various itinerant musicians who jump aboard and sing evocative Rajasthani *ragas*.

There are bus services from Bombay, Mount Abu, and Udaipur, and from Ahmedabad to destinations throughout the state.

Gujarat makes India's best ice cream, crammed with fruit and nuts, and with unusual seasonal favorites such as custard apple and cashew. Gujaratis have a fetish for it, and there's a parlor on every block. The **Ghandi Cold Drinks House**, Khas Bazaar, is a good place for Gujarati ice creams at their best.

How to Get There

There are daily flights to Ahmedabad's airport (eight kilometers, or five miles, away) from Bombay, Delhi, Calcutta, Jaipur, and Jodhpur, and you can also fly to Ahmedabad from Vadodara, Bangalore, Madras, Hyderabad, Aurangabad, and Srinagar.

Trains run to Ahmedabad from Bombay (the 492-km, or 306-mile, trip takes around nine hours by the fast mail train and fifteen hours by the normal service).

LOTHAL

The famous archaeological ruins at Lothal, 87 km (54 miles) from Ahmedabad, are well worth a day's excursion. It was once an important Harappan port that traded with Egypt and Mesopotamia in around 2400 to 1500 BC, and is thus the earliest known civilization in the subcontinent. Other major Harappan sites are in Pakistan at Mohenjo-Daro and Harappa.

Discovered in 1954, excavations reveal a systematically planned port city, with a scientific knowledge of the tides applied to its underground drains, planned streets and houses with baths and fireplaces, burial grounds, and dockyards. Terracotta figurines, ivory and shell objects, beads, bangles and semiprecious stones, painted bowls, bronze and copper implements, and seals with Indus Valley script are on display at an excellent on-site museum.

PALITANA

The most revered of the Jains' five temple-covered sacred hills, Palitana's nearby **Shatrunjaya Hill** is a marble jungle of some 863 magnificent Jain temples, some of which date back to the eleventh century. The other sacred hills are at Girnar, near Junagadh, Mount Abu in Rajasthan, Parasnath in Bihar, and Gwalior in Madhya Pradesh.

Jainism became a powerful force in the sixth century BC, largely in reaction to strict, caste-bound Hinduism. It was founded by Prince Mahavira (559–527 BC), the twenty-fourth and last Jain *tirthankara* (saint), who became a *jina* (conqueror of spiritual knowledge), and his disciples.

The temple complex, known as the "abode of the gods," is a marvel of complex architecture, each temple within a *tuk*, or enclosure, and richly ornamented with carved spires and towers.

The temple chambers are frequently thronged with Jain pilgrims who prostrate themselves before the rows of impassive-looking idols, whose eyes gleam out fiercely in the gloom. Wiry, shaven-headed priests administer to the temple duties and keep a watchful eye out for tourists who neglect to leave their shoes at the door. A stern sign at the entrance to the complex forbids menstruating women to enter, lest they defile the temple's purity. The largest and most ornate temple is the Chaumukh temple, built by a wealthy banker in 1618 in the hope of saving his soul. But most pilgrims make a beeline for the most sacred temple, dedicated to Sri Adishwara, the first *tirthankara*, whose image is studded with gold and enormous diamonds. An unusual addition is the Angar Pir, a Moslem shrine, where childless women make offerings of miniature cradles and pray for children.

The magnificence of these temples is due largely to the Jain belief that reincarnation and salvation can be influenced by, amongst other things, temple building and *ahimsa*, reverence for all life. The truly devout are not only complete vegetarians, excluding even eggs and milk from their diet, but also wear white gauze masks to prevent the accidental swallowing of small insects.

It's best to make Palitana an early morning expedition, before the heat makes climbing the four kilometers (two and a half miles) of steps unbearable. At dawn, the route throngs with white-clad pilgrims, the aged and disabled carried in *dolis*, string sedan chairs, which are also utilized by exhausted tourists. Priests hand a ticket to each leaving visitor who, after an hour's tiring descent, can exchange it for a restorative breakfast of sweetmeats and sugary tea. It's open from 7 AM to 7 PM, when even the priests withdraw to leave the gods to themselves.

Where to Stay

Palitana has many resthouses but these are exclusively for Jain pilgrims. There's a choice of either the state-run **Hotel Sumeru Toran (** (02848) 2327, on Station Road, which has some air-conditioned rooms, or the more basic **Hotel Shravak (** (02848) 2428, opposite the bus station, offering rooms or dormitories and cheap *thalis* at mealtimes. If hunger strikes at odd hours, try the popular snack alley next to the Shravak.

It's far preferable to stay in the larger port city of **Bhavnagar**, 56 km (35 miles) away, at the **Nilambag Palace Hotel (** (0278) 424241. This local maharaja's former palace has charming, period suites from around US$50.

How to Get There

Bhavnagar, 244 km (152 miles) from Ahmedabad, has the nearest airport, which has regular flights to Bombay.

To get there from Ahmedabad, you will need to take a train or a bus, both or which take around five hours. From Bhavnagar, there are regular train and bus services for visiting Palitana.

JUNAGADH

A picturesque city of much archaeological importance, Junagadh is rather off the beaten track, but of great significance to Jains for the sacred, temple-covered **Girnar Hill** nearby, which is no less impressive than Palitana, and a much gentler climb at only 2,000 steps! Betrothed couples come to worship at the topmost Amba Mata temple to ensure a harmonious marriage. It's a good place to spend a day before continuing on to Sasan Gir Lion Sanctuary, 58 km (36 miles) away.

Junagadh is thought to date back to around 250 BC, when the Mauryan emperor Ashoka ordered his edicts inscribed on a boulder, which can still be seen on the way to Girnar Hill. On Junagadh's outskirts lies **Uparkot**, a walled city with its own palace, Jami Masjid, and Buddhist caves with spiral staircases, built by the militaristic Chudasamal Rajputs during the ninth century. It was the scene of an epic 12-year siege over the heart of a beautiful potter's daughter who rejected the advances of a neighboring king and married the Rajput ruler of Junagadh instead. In 1094, the Junagadh raja was slain — in a Pyrrhic victory, since the coveted woman committed sati shortly afterwards.

In town, see the **Rang Mahal**, the nineteenth-century palace now used as government offices, in which the dog-loving Nawab of Junagadh staged canine weddings and gave each of his 800 dogs its own room with a telephone and servant.

OPPOSITE LEFT: Textile factory at Aurangabad.
RIGHT: Darwaza Market, Ahmedabad.

At the time of Partition, the nawab wished to have his tiny state merged with Pakistan, and having failed to do so, lived in disgraced exile. Within the palace is the **Durbar Hall** museum, with palace relics, weaponry, and a portrait gallery. It is open from 9:30 AM to 11:45 AM and from 3 PM to 5:30 PM. The tourist office is right next door.

Also see the ornate **Maqbara**, the royal mausoleum, with minarets and spiral staircases; the **Sakkar Bagh** museum and zoo; and the **Rupayatan Institute for Handicrafts**, where craftsmen work on traditional embroidery and patchwork.

Where to Stay

There are a number of small, cheap hotels in Junagadh, but none is very good. One of the better choices is the **Hotel Girnar ℂ** (0285) 21201, which has a small selection of clean, air-conditioned rooms and some cheaper air-cooled rooms. There's an attached vegetarian restaurant.

How to Get There

The nearest airport is Keshod, 47 km (29 miles) away, with flights from both Bombay and Ahmedabad. The *Somnath Mail* runs between Ahmedabad and Veraval/Somnath via Juna- gadh, a 13-hour journey. Buses connect Junagadh with Ahmedabad, Veraval/Somnath, Palitana, and the Sasan Gir.

SOMNATH

According to Hindu myth Somnath Temple, which overlooks the Arabian Sea, was built by Soma, the Moon God, at the dawn of creation. Archae- ologists date the shore temple to around the first century AD.

Although destroyed and rebuilt more than seven times, the present temple retains much of its legendary beauty. By the sixth century, Somnath was renowned as the richest temple in India, and consequently was sacked by the Mahmud of Ghazni, who required a vast caravansary of elephants, camels, and mules to carry all the gold and precious ornaments. Over the next 700 years, the temple was repeatedly smashed, then rebuilt by devout priests. The Mughal Aurangzeb, vowing to crush the "heretical" temple, powdered it to dust in 1706. Only in 1950 was it restored to its present state.

Somnath contains one of the 12 *jyotirlingas*, or Shiva shrines, in India and has two major festivals: the vibrant **Kartika Poornima**, a village fair with traditional dance, theater, and chanting of Vedic hymns, held in November/December, and the **Mahashivratri**, held in February/ March, which attracts hundreds of thousands of Indian pilgrims.

It's best to visit at sunrise or sunset, when the priests perform an elaborate ritual to worship Shiva.

The nearby government-run **Prabhas Patan Museum** is very disorganized, but contains ancient relics of the various versions of Somnath Temple. It is open from 9 AM to noon, 3 PM to 6 PM daily, except Wednesday.

Somnath has only one decent hotel — the **Hotel Mayuram ℂ** (02876) 20286, Triveni Road.

How to Get There

Trains run from Ahmedabad to Veraval (12 hours), which is just five kilometers from Somnath.

SASAN GIR LION SANCTUARY

One of India's finest wildlife sanctuaries, set in 1,295 sq km (500 sq miles) of lush deciduous forest, the Sasan Gir Sanactuary is the final refuge of the rare Asiatic lion, once found throughout the Middle East and both north and east India, but hunted as a coveted trophy item during the British Raj era.

The famine of 1899 so decimated the Asiatic lion population that Lord Curzon cancelled his shoot at Gir, where he was staying as the guest of the Nawab of Junagadh. Curzon persuaded the nawab to protect the remaining lions, who now number around 200. The sanctuary is open from mid-October to mid-June, but the cool season between November and February is the best time for sighting the lions, who generally retire to the forest's interior during the summer.

General Information

The Gujarat State Tourism Corporation offers a special two-day package tour to the Sasan Gir Santuary. The trip includes reception at Keshod, the nearest airport (an 80-minute flight from Bombay, and 90 km (56 miles) from the sanctuary), accommodation at the Forest Lodge, a sanctuary tour, and a visit to Somnath. The **Government Gujarat Tourist Office ℂ** (011) 334 0305, A 6 Bhagat Kharak Singh Marg, New Delhi, will supply further details.

What to See and Do

The forest also has wild boar, bears, panthers, antelopes, hyenas, leopards, and the unusual Indian *chowsingha* (antelope) whose buck has four horns. The monsoon months of July to September are good for seeing almost 200 varieties of birds.

The Gir Forestry Department provides jeeps and guides on a daily basis, though it's best to turn up early at 7 AM when the office opens if you want a good chance of actually sighting a lion. Be prepared to come away from your mini safari disappointed, as although lion numbers are on the increase they still remain elusive.

Within the Gir Forest are the scenic **Tulishyam Hot Springs**, 90 km (56 miles) from the sanctuary's entrance, where you can bathe in the natural sulfur springs and, if desired, find cheap accommodation at the Holiday Camp Lodge.

Where to Stay
The best place to stay is at the **Gir Lodge** ((028) 85521 FAX (028) 85528, a surprisingly luxurious 29-room operation (all air-conditioned) close to the Forest Lodge. It has a library stocked with information about the local wildlife. Doubles range from US$105.

The **Forest Lodge** ((028) 85540, is a budget alternative, with a small collection of air-conditioned rooms at the US$12 mark.

How to Get There
The nearest transport hub is Veraval, which is connected to Ahmedabad by rail. Buses and trains from Veraval to Sasan Gir take around two hours.

VADODARA (BARODA)

Located 120 km (75 miles) southeast of Ahmedabad, the former capital of the vastly wealthy Gaekwads of Baroda (whose name means "protector of cows"), is a city of sprawling parks and lakes, palaces and museums, with a campus atmosphere. Predictably, perhaps, its charms are muted by ugly industrial expansion. It's a good base for excursions to the beautiful ruined fort of Champaner, 47 km (29 miles) away.

What to See and Do
On the city's periphery is the **Lakshmi Vilas Palace**, a Gothic-domed, Indo-Saracenic extravaganza with a 150-m (500-ft) façade. It was completed in 1890 for the Maharaja of Sayajirao, who campaigned against purdah and tried to introduce a form of separation for unhappily married women. His legendary wealth included the Baroda collection of jewels, a pearl carpet studded with diamonds, rubies, emeralds, and woven with gold, and thick gold anklets worn by the palace elephants. Unfortunately, the palace and its fabulous collection of armor and sculpture are rarely open to the public.

Back in the city, the **Baroda Museum and Art Gallery** in the **Sayaji Park** (complete with a zoo, miniature train, and large lake) has an excellent collection of Mughal miniatures and European paintings. It is open Fridays and Sundays from 9:30 AM to 4:45 PM, and Saturdays, 10 AM to 5:45 PM.

Nearby is the **Maharaja Fateh Singh Museum**, the Gaekwads' lavish art collection, which includes works by Titian, Raphael, Murillo, and displays of Greco-Roman, Chinese, Japanese, and Indian paintings. Situated within the palace

grounds, the museum is open Tuesdays to Sundays from 9 AM to noon, 3 PM to 6 PM from July to March, 4 PM to 7 PM from April to June.

Old Baroda's faded splendor is best appreciated by visiting several of the Gaekwads' smaller palaces scattered around the city, the most impressive being the **Pratap Vilas Palace**, now used as the Railway Staff College. The **Maharaja Sayajirao University of Vadodara** is a grand palisade of Gothic-inspired architecture leading to Sayaji Park, with a renowned Arts faculty that organizes regular evening performances by India's top artists. Its Art College is considered one of India's best.

Other places to see are the **Kirti Mandir**, the Gaekwads' family vault, and the exquisite **Tambekarwada**, a four-story *haveli* covered with murals. Managed by the Archaeological Survey of India, it is open daily and hard to find, so obtain directions from the Tourist Office opposite the railway station.

The **Naulakhi** well, just near the Lakshmi Vilas Palace, is a good example of Gujarati *baoli*, or step-well. The Islamic **Maqbara** has beautiful filigree carvings, and the **Sarsagar Lake** is good for boating.

Some 47 km (29 miles) northeast of Vadodara, the ruins of **Champaner**, Sultan Mahmud Shah Begada's fortified fifteenth-century palace-town, and its grand Jami Masjid mosque lie on the flame-red Pavagadh Hill. It's a sight worth seeing, and it's possible to stay at Champaner's Holiday Home.

Where to Stay
The only five-star accommodation is the **Welcomgroup Vadodara Hotel** ((0265) 330033 FAX (0265) 330050, R.C. Dutt Road, with a swimming pool, an excellent Mughalai restaurant, and a good travel counter.

Also on R.C. Dutt Road, a reasonable mid-range to stay is the characterless **Express Hotel** ((0265) 337001 FAX (0265) 330980. It's an air-conditioned monster of a place but the US$30 to US$50 doubles are good value.

Hotel Surya Palace ((0265) 361361 FAX (0265) 361555, is moderately priced, and comfortable with an excellent restaurant for great value Gujarati *thalis*. It has some inexpensive air-cooled rooms for budget travelers.

How to Get There
Vadodara connects by air with both Delhi and Bombay, and by rail with Ahmedabad as well as Bombay and Delhi.

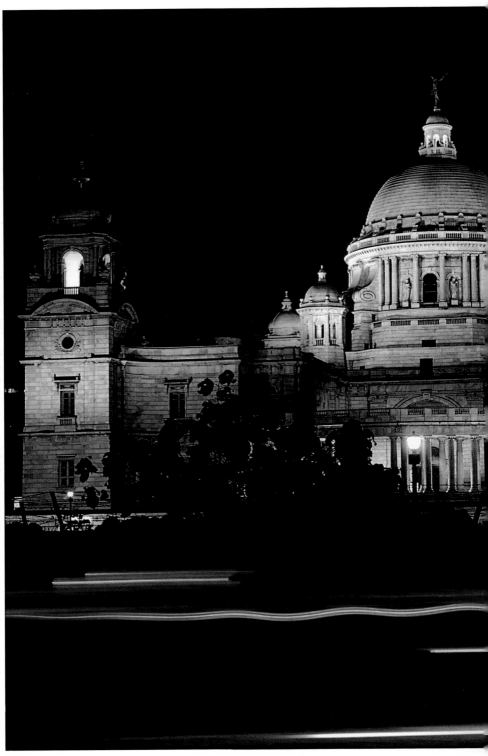

Calcutta and the East

CALCUTTA

Calcutta offers unexpected charms, perhaps even more striking when contrasted with the image of impoverishment it is more widely associated with. It is easily the country's most fascinating city, a unique and compelling mixture of Raj-era relics, Bengali culture, and communist politics. The state capital of West Bengal, it is one of the world's largest cities, with a population of more than 12 million.

Once Calcutta was the second city of the British empire, after London, and it remains above all a monument to imperial decline, for it is the most British of all Indian cities. It has a legacy of patrician English Classical buildings, fine museums, the university, the prestigious Royal Asiatic society, the Botanical Gardens and its Pall Mall stretch of exclusive social clubs, not to mention the Edwardian turns of phrase so beloved by the local English langauge press.

Calcutta is the action-packed center of the exuberant Bengali culture, and here literature, politics, and visual and performing arts thrive as the city's ruling passions. The Bengalis are a civilized, gregarious people, given to volatile outbursts but quick to smile and offer their help and hospitality. Calcutta is India's "Left Bank" with its "café society, Bohemian airs, political argument and love of gossip" wrote Trevor Fishlock in *India File*.

The city both mocks and fulfills a prophecy, apparently attributed to Lenin, that the "road to world revolution lies through Peking, Shanghai and Calcutta." For decades, flags emblazoned with the hammer and sickle have fluttered from the state Secretariat, the former British Writers Building. Its central Maidan has statues of Lenin and the local hero Netaji Subhas Chandra Bose who courted both Hitler and the Japanese during World War II in the hope they would rid India of the British, dying in a wartime plane crash before his plans came to fruition. With deliberate tongue in cheek, Calcutta authorities renamed historic Clive Street after Bose, just as they renamed the street in which the American consulate is located after Ho Chi Minh during the Vietnam war.

BACKGROUND

By Indian standards, Calcutta is comparatively young. It was founded for trade and profit in 1690 by Job Charnock, the local British East India Company agent. Desiring a permanent trading post in wealthy Bengal, Charnock selected the site of three villages amid swamp and jungle. One of these was called Kalikata, named by locals after the most fearsome goddess in the Hindu pantheon, Kali, the destroyer. These early settlers lost no time in Anglicizing it to Calcutta and erecting the first Fort William near the present Dalhousie Square six years later.

They faced heavy losses, not only from random bloodshed when defending their patch from regional Muslim officials, but because their immune systems balked at a whole host of hitherto unknown diseases. Calcutta became known as Golgotha, or "Place of Skulls," long before it was to earn the sobriquet "City of Palaces" for the Palladian mansions and grand English classical buildings that rose with the city's fortunes. Malaria and other tropical diseases, and Calcutta's unrelenting heat and stifling humidity, saw mortality rates of the European population climb to above 50% during the eighteenth century.

Calcutta grew steadily as trade prospered. Opportunistic merchants soon began reaping vast profits in jute, tea, indigo, cotton, silk, and minerals, luring scores of young men to make the 18-week journey from England to work as Company hacks or "writers," counting on making their fortunes by dabbling in free trade. The British Residency of Calcutta received a temporary setback when Fort William was attacked by the Nawab of Murshidabad in 1757. It was recaptured by Robert Clive, though he arrived too late to rescue 123 Europeans who perished in an underground cellar. The same cellar later came to be called the "Black Hole of Calcutta."

Soon Calcutta boasted a second, well-fortified fortress town, and in 1772 it was proclaimed the capital of British India by its first Governor, Warren Hastings. The grand imperial architecture represents Calcutta at its zenith, when the British lived and worked behind the iron gates of their splendid homes, offices, and social clubs, attended by ever-increasing tiers of servants. James Morris sets the scene in *Pax Britannica*: "In the evenings, the richer British box-*wallahs* emerged in top hats and frock coats to promenade the Maidan, driving steadily here and there in broughams, hansoms and victorias, exchanging bows and transient assessments."

During the nineteenth century, Calcutta was the focus for the early independence movement, motivating the British to shift the viceregal seat to Delhi in 1911. After Independence it lost its commercial clout with the waning of colonial-based trade, when new industries sprang up in Bombay — and its grand imperial infrastructure fell into neglect and decay.

Calcutta's modern reality is one of impossible overcrowding, pavement slums, congested traffic, inoperable phones, daily electricity blackouts, with water shortages alternating with floods — living conditions that by any standards are intolerable. It was Kipling's "city of dreadful night… the packed and pestilential town." It is true that Calcutta is a virtual synonym for dreadful squalor. It remains off the beaten track for many travelers, and tales of the city's suffering and filth do not add to its attractions. Yet Calcuttans defend their city with a kind of fierce pride, and few would choose to live anywhere else. Travelers who sample its peculiar, yet stimulating, attractions often find that, above all, this city radiates an unforgettable triumph of the human spirit, and few fail to be moved by its unique energy.

GENERAL INFORMATION

The best **Government of India Tourist Office** ((033) 2421402 is at 4 Shakespeare Sarani. It's both friendly and well stocked with information. The **West Bengal Tourist Bureau** ((033) 2488271 is at 3/2 BBD Bagh.

Both the state and national tourist offices have counters at the airport. Both run daily morning and afternoon conducted city tours, good for orientation, if you don't have time to sightsee at leisure, and for getting out to far-flung sights.

In the Dalhousie Square (BBD Bagh) area, you can make overseas calls at the Central Telegraph Office, 8 Red Cross Place, and collect *poste restante* letters at the large General Post Office. It is also possible to make international calls from almost all hotels and from innumerable private operators nowadays.

Lastly, you'll save yourself much time and energy by entrusting your travel plans to a reliable travel agent. Good ones to try include American Express ((033) 2486181, 21 Old Court House Street; Mercury Travels ((033) 2423535, 46C Jawaharlal Nehru Road; and Thomas Cook ((033) 2475354, 230A, AJC Bose Street. Indian Airlines can be reached at ((033) 2472356, 39 Chittaranhan Avenue.

For rail bookings, there are two main offices situated quite close together, both within BBD Bagh (Dalhousie Square), including Eastern Railways ((033) 2206811, at 6 Fairlee Place, BBD Bagh. You can waste hours negotiating endless reservations lines, so if possible, let a travel agent handle your bookings. The main bus terminus for city and state transport is off Jawaharlal Nehru Road.

WHEN TO GO

"Enough to make a doorknob mushy." So said Mark Twain of Calcutta's intensely humid climate, which is exacerbated by its proximity to the sea and its low altitude. For comfort, avoid the torrential monsoon from June to September and visit instead between November and February.

Calcutta explodes with revelry during its spectacular three-week **Durga Puja** festival in September/October, when tinseled glitter, colorful pageantry, music, dance, and infectious gaiety spill out on the streets. This is the Bengal version of Dussehra, celebrating the goddess Durga, destroyer of evil, portrayed riding a tiger. On the final day, floats of ornate idols are paraded through the main boulevards and later dunked in the

Hooghly at sunset, accompanied by cheering crowds, flashing strobes, and Hindi "disco" music.

Calcuttans adore festivals and are as enthusiastic about the Diwali and the Muslim Id as they are about Christmas, the latter culminating in a grand candlelight mass at St. Paul's Cathedral. Since there are about 20 official holidays in the Bengali year, it's rare to arrive when there is not at least some kind of festivity in progress. Bengali New Year in April/May is riotous but hot.

GETTING AROUND

Calcutta is immense. Its greater area sprawls for some 102 sq km (39 sq miles), and just crossing the relatively compact, but very congested city center can easily take an hour by taxi.

The central core of Calcutta sprawls along the west bank of the Hooghly River from the Zoological Gardens in the south to the Howrah Bridge some five kilometers (three miles) to the north. Over the bridge is the industrial ship-building and jute industry heartland, and the beautiful Botanical Gardens.

At the heart of the city is the huge green expanse of the Maidan. It's hugged by the bustling strip popularly known as Chowringhee, now renamed Jawaharlal Nehru Road, where most of the hotels, restaurants, travel agencies, and airline offices are found. At the southern end of Chowringhee you'll find the Government of India Tourist Office, the Birla Planetarium, St. Paul's Cathedral, and the Victoria Memorial. Slightly north lies BBD Bagh (Dalhousie Square), where the General Post Office, the international telephone office, the West Bengal Tourist Office, various railway reservation offices, the Writers Building and the American Express office are located.

Calcutta can be a dastardly city for getting around. Visitors are often perplexed by its duplication of street names, since nobody seems to know whether to use the old Raj-era or new post-Independence version. Even maps aren't consistent.

The best way to deal with Calcutta's anarchic traffic is treat it as one of the city's most amazing "sights" — an endless heaving tide of garishly painted lorries, double-decker buses, clanging trams, bullock carts and Ambassador taxis, with man-powered rickshaws pulling decorously perched passengers, weaving to and fro. Astonishing things happen on the streets. During one 10-minute ride, for example, I saw a naked sadhu, a flock of goats milling at the university gates, rows of cycle-rickshaws pulling school-children in cages, and an Ambassador taxi masquerading as an ambulance, with a man leaning out the window waving a red flag and making siren noises.

Rush hour literally lasts all day, easing up only in the early hours of the morning and after 7 PM.

The subway — India's first — has helped to solve some of Calcutta's transportation problems. After years of tunneling, delayed by waterlogging brought on by the annual monsoon, it now cuts a convenient north-south swathe through town, from Dum Dum, near the airport, to Tollygunge, taking in the important Chowringhee district en-route. It's an astonishingly clean and efficient alternative to the bedlam above. Many tourists make use of it to get out to Kalighat, which takes 10 minutes by the underground contrasted with up to an hour's drive.

Taxis and auto-rickshaws provide the most comfortable transportation and can be found at any time of the day in the Sudder Street area. Taxi drivers will usually use their meters, but posted fares are subject to a complex conversion procedure that will multiply the fare tenfold or more. It's often best to agree on a fixed fare beforehand. Buses are a test of Darwinian fitness: watch Calcutta's office-workers hurling themselves wildly into the mêlée before deciding whether this mode of transportation is for you.

Calcutta is the world's last stronghold of the human-powered cart rickshaw — originally introduced by the Chinese immigrants during the eighteenth century and now an enduring symbol of the city. Over 30,000 ply the inner city trade, and they have their own union for protection against Calcutta's authorities who have often tried to eradicate them as an embarrassing reminder of human degradation. Tourists often feel guiltily imperialistic perched above a struggling rickshaw *wallah* — but it's worth remembering that they depend on miserly wages (and generous tips) to fill their stomachs. At night they hook themselves into their contraptions to slumber. For short hops, they can be invaluable for weaving in and out of clogged traffic.

WHAT TO SEE AND DO

For those unfamiliar with the city, "sightseeing" in Calcutta might sound like a contradiction in terms. But many travelers stay far longer than they first intended, becoming increasingly intrigued by this tumultuous city with its fascinating repository of Raj-era architecture and its rich cultural life.

A successful itinerary is planned on the basis of geographical proximity rather than attempting to see things in a particular order. Walking around town without an accurate Calcutta map is not only confusing, but the distances involved make it exhausting work too. So hail some form of transportation — be it mechanical, animal, or in the case of Calcutta, even human — and move on to wherever else seems the most interesting. The tours devised below are tailor-made for this approach and are best spread over several days of sightseeing.

City Tour
If you're staying in the central Chowringhee / Sudder Street area, the most decadent start to any sightseeing is to have breakfast in the Oberoi Grand Hotel, followed by a short stroll down Chowringhee — which is now officially called Jawaharlal Nehru Road. It's lined with decaying Palladian palaces and mansions, formerly inhabited by the wealthy and powerful British and Bengali *bhandralok*, the enterprising Westernized Indian middle class.

Today most of these buildings are used as commercial offices, amid Chowringhee's frenetic mêlée of garish movie billboards, bazaars, cafés, and hotels.

Across the road is the **Maidan**, Calcutta's three-kilometer (two-mile)-long Hyde Park, where everything from massive political rallies to early morning yoga lessons takes place. Itinerant performers, ash-smeared sadhus, and tired tourists alike enjoy the shade of its leafy trees, and it's also famous as the venue for the "Mukta Mela," a sort of informal cultural fair held from time to time, in which poets recite their verses to one another, artists discuss their canvases and freethinkers bring along their soapboxes.

The Maidan was created in the wake of the massacres of the Indian Mutiny of 1857, when the British decided to replace their original Fort William near Dalhousie Square with a new more massive and impregnable version, whose whitewashed fortifications and trenches overlook the Hooghly River farther west. The Maidan was originally designed to give the fort's cannons a clear line of fire — today it echoes with the sound of cricket shots. Indian cricket was actually born on the Maidan in 1802, when a two-day white-flannel match between the "Old Etonians" and a "Calcutta" brigade of East India Company nabobs was held.

A nag-drawn *tonga*, or traditional horse-drawn taxi, outside Howrah Station.

To the south lies the Royal Calcutta Turf Club, which has an active season from November to mid-March, but draws India's horse-mad elite for its climactic annual Queen Elizabeth II Derby in January.

At the southern end of the Maidan rises the dazzling white marble **Victoria Memorial**, one of the most pompous, grandiloquent edifices ever built by the British in India. When the poet W.H. Auden visited during the 1950s, he recorded being vastly amused when a freelance guide told him that it had been designed by the same man who created the Taj Mahal! It has been called an imperial "blancmange" of Classical and Mughal architecture, and it was in fact inspired by the Taj

Mahal, with its four rudimentary minarets, gleaming white dome, and exterior of solid Macarana marble.

It was commissioned by Lord Curzon, Viceroy of India, and raised entirely with money from voluntary contributions as the ultimate compliment to Queen Victoria after her death in 1901. Built between 1906 and 1921 at an estimated cost of Rs 7.5 million, it's set amid 26 hectares (64 acres) of lawns, fountains, and herbaceous borders and is dotted with statues of former British rulers that used to adorn street corners all the way along Chowringhee and the Maidan. Looking dourly imperious, the Empress of India sits enthroned in bronze at the entrance marble staircase, wearing the regal Order of the Star of India. Above her, a 4.9-m (16-ft)-high bronze winged Angel of Victory is poised to fly from atop the central dome.

Inside houses the most remarkable collection of memorabilia of British India ever amassed under one roof — 3,500 exhibits on 25 galleries. The entrance dome is etched with the text of Queen Victoria's imperial proclamation speech. The surrounding galleries are crammed with paintings depicting the monarch's life, along with personal possessions such as the baby-grand piano on which she played as a child, her personal writing desk, and an embroidered armchair. There are even scrapbooks of her letters in Hindustani, for she was tutored in the language by her favorite Indian attendant Abdul Karim.

Entire wings are lined with portraits and busts of famous British figures who each in their own way made their contribution to British India, including Robert Clive, General Stringer Lawrence (father of the Indian army), Lord Bentinck, who outlawed suttee, William Makepeace Thackeray, who was born here, and Florence Nightingale, who only ever took a distant interest in India. Among the many excellent paintings, look especially for Burne-Jones's portrait of Rudyard Kipling, Verestchagin's monumental depiction of the Prince of Wales (the future King Edward VII) making his grand tour of Jaipur in 1876, the works of the Victorian artists Thomas and William Daniells, and Johann Zoffany's portrait of William Hastings and his family. Rare extant documents and treaties, an armory, and a Historic Calcutta exhibition complete the fascinating collection. The Publications Office sells excellent catalogues, books, and posters. It's open Tuesdays to Sundays, from 10 AM to 4:30 PM from March to October, and until 3:30 PM from November to February, closed on public holidays.

St. Paul's Cathedral, barely five minutes walk across the gardens is the first Church of England cathedral of British India, built in 1847 with East India Company funds as their Gothic imitation Canterbury Cathedral. Inside see the ornate communion plate presented by Queen Victoria, Burne-Jones's stained glass west window, Francis Chantrey's statue of Bishop Heber and Sir Arthur Blomfield's mosaics around the altar.

Further southeast lie the **Zoological Gardens**, off Belvedere Road, open sunrise to sunset, its main attraction being a captive rare white tiger from Rewa.

Opposite is **Raj Bhawan**, the Government House from which viceroys ruled India until 1911. It was built in 1803 upon the orders of the governor-general of Bengal, Lord Wellesley, who was determined to have a palace equal to his station. He tactfully omitted to mention how palatial his palace was, only sending the bill to his superiors in London when it was safely completed, and the East India Company was forced to foot the cost — then two million rupees. However, future viceroys found this replica of Kedleston Hall in Derbyshire very much to their tastes. Inside is a grand marble hall dominated by 12 busts of Caesar, staircase sphinxes — and the various contributions left behind by previous occupants: Warren Hasting's gravel from Bayswater, Lord Ellenborough's Chinese cannon on a brass dragon, Lord Curzon's fretted-iron lift. It's now part-residence of the Chief Minister and part-Secretariat of West Bengal, and is not open to the public.

Close by, along Council House Street, you'll find the Greco-colonial **Saint John's Church**, Calcutta's oldest British cemetery. It was built in 1787, modeled on London's Saint Martin-in-the-Fields and used as a temporary cathedral by the East India Company's burgeoning populace until St. Paul's Cathedral was completed. Its quaint interior is dominated by Zoffany's Raj-version of the "Last Supper," whose saintly disciples actually resemble their less-than-angelic sitters, a corps of young clerks who, Zoffany later dryly noted, passed the time taking swigs at brandy bottles. Within the overgrown churchyard, crammed with moss-encrusted masonry, one of the oldest tombstones belongs to Job Charnock, who died in 1692, two years after founding Calcutta. Admiral Watson, who supported Clive in retaking Calcutta from Siraj-ud-Daula, is also buried here. Other tombstones illustrate the perils faced by the early British settlers — premature deaths caused by heat, exotic diseases, too much port, or ill-fated adventures.

From here, it's a twenty minute stroll down to **Dalhousie Square**, now renamed **BBD Bagh**, in memory of Benoy, Badal and Dinesh, three freedom-fighting Bengali martyrs. For more than 150 years, Dalhousie Square was British India's headquarters, and it is still Calcutta's commercial hub. Bengali bureaucrats, lawyers, stockbrokers, and businessmen deftly pick their way past beggars, coolies, shattered pavements, and rattling trams. To Western eyes, this imperial muddle of dilapidated Victorian buildings, swept-up Doric colonnades, grand mahogany doors and Romanesque-lettered brass nameplates looks eerily familiar, yet with its overlapping chaotic squalor it is almost like a sort of post-Holocaust London.

Half-naked men and boys briskly lather themselves in muddy gushes sloshed from burst pipes and clean their teeth with *neem* twigs; thin pavement clerks hunch over battered Remingtons typing out applications for lines of Indians; tiny urchins chatter over shared chapatis. Once this was Job Charnock's Tank Square, where *bheesties*, or water carriers, serviced the houses of the early European settlers. The tank still brims today and its high fence does nothing to discourage early morning swimmers and tribes of *dhobi-wallahs*, who tirelessly thwack spirals of cloth against the concrete slopes.

The square is dominated by the huge 14-story **Writer's Building**, built in 1880, with its Early English porticos and burnt–sienna façade crowned by rooftop statues who strike allegorical poses representing imperial ethos: Justice, Virtue, Faith, Charity, and so on. Originally it was just a squat barrack-house where the runtish clerks or "writers," who came out with the East India Company, lived and worked. As Bengalis are apt to explain, India's notoriously complex bureaucracy dates back to when these early British "writers" scribbled records of business transactions in this very building, now used as the Secretariat of Communist West Bengal.

Their modern counterparts, the Bengali *bapus*, maintain a long tradition of painstakingly typing letters and insisting on receipts and memoranda in triplicate. The few outsiders who venture within find labyrinthine passages, branching off into dusty cavernous rooms where peons shuffle papers, sip tea, and wile away time in a trance against pyramids of yellowing files.

West of Dalhousie Square is the imposing Corinthian-pillared **General Post Office**, on the site of the original Fort William, demolished by Nawab Siraj-ud-Daula in 1756. Calcutta's infamous "black hole" was actually a guardroom at the northeast corner of the General Post Office, but since independence all indications of its presence have been removed, save a tiny brass plaque.

It's fascinating to walk along Netaji Subhas Road, Calcutta's main business strip adjoining the square, lined with the old British commercial houses that continue to flourish in Indian hands. Whiffs of tea grow stronger nearer **R.N. Mukherjee Street**, where the city's tea auctions are held. Frenzied dealing goes on at the Lyon's Range Stock Exchange, just beyond Clive Street.

OPPOSITE: A cheerful smile from a Muslim teacher. ABOVE: A curious young woman gazes out from a doorway.

A Patchwork of Legacies

The colossal cantilevered **Howrah Bridge** is the city's most famous landmark. The 27,000-ton plank joining Calcutta with the jute-mill and shipbuilding settlement of Howrah across the khaki waters of the Hooghly opened in 1943 and is now one of the busiest bridges in the world, with some two million people crossing it daily. No other sight captures Calcutta's hectic energy quite so dramatically — from dawn until late into the night it's a permanently choked tide of sardine-can buses, taxis, hideously polluting trucks, buffalo-drawn carts, and clanging hordes of bicycles and rickshaws. Astonishingly, during high summer, this steel mesh bridge

ornate *objets d'art* and paintings collected from auctions and dispossessed households across the globe — all slowly consumed by Dickensian decay, mildew, and dust.

Lurking somewhere in this charmed gloom hang oils by Titian, Sir Joshua Reynolds, Murillo and Rubens — amid a jumble of Venetian glass, statues of Greek gods, enormous chandeliers, Parisian furniture, gilt goblets from Bohemia, and Teutonic stag heads. An unusually nubile-looking Queen Victoria dominates a red marble room, facing many po-faced plaster busts. Guests are free to wander through between the hours of 10 AM and 4 PM, although it's not a museum, but is the private home of the Mullick family.

expands some four feet each day in the heat, shrinking back to normal during the night. Beneath it along the river banks is a constant jamboree of itinerant masseuses, barbers, and flower sellers.

Some three kilometers (nearly two miles) north of the city center, off Chittaranhan Avenue, lies one of Calcutta's most extraordinary sights: the **Marble Palace**. This Palladian mansion and its ornamental garden was built in 1835 by a wealthy Bengali merchant, Raja Rajendra Mullick, who was orphaned at three and given an English guardian, Sir James Hogg, by the Supreme Court. He started building it at the age of 16, amassing an eclectic mix of 126 varieties of marble to line the floors, wall panels, and tables. Pelicans and peacocks strut through the colonnaded inner courtyard, and tiny stairwells lead to rooms and apartments crammed with

Respecting the wishes of Mullick senior, they allow beggar children to play in their fairy-tale garden, and provide free meals for lines of the destitute every day at noon. It's closed on Monday and Thursdays.

Nearby, off Rabindra Sarani, is the **Rabindra-Bharati Museum**, the stately ancestral home of the gifted and influential Tagore family. This is where India's famous poet, philosopher and fervent nationalist Rabindranath Tagore was born and later died. His talents as poet won him the Nobel Prize in 1913, and he also composed the song "Jana Gana Mana Adhinayaka," which was adopted as the national anthem after Independence. It's a fascinating treasure-trove filled with family heirlooms, manuscripts, and paintings. It's open from Monday to Friday from 10 AM to 7 PM, Saturdays 10 AM to 1 PM, and Sundays, 11 AM to 2 PM.

It's a 15-minute drive northeast to the **Jain Temple**, built by the fabulously rich Birla family in 1867. It's actually a collection of four pagoda-like shrines set in geometrical gardens and ponds. They have exquisite interiors encrusted with mirror-glass mosaics, Venetian glass, gilt dome ceilings and precious stones, inlaid by a jeweler — all dedicated to Sitalnathji, tenth of the 24 Jain *tirthankaras* (prophets).

Returning to the city center, make a short detour to the junction of Rabindra Sarani and Zakaria Street, to see the magnificent **Nakhoda Mosque**, whose giant two 46-m (150-ft)-high minarets and copper-green domes are visible from afar. It's the center of Calcutta's Muslim community, modeled on Akbar's tomb at Sikandra near Agra and able to accommodate up to 10,000 people during major festivals. The most spectacular of these is Muharram (held in May or June), when the surrounding streets come alive with bands, and men dancing like whirling dervishes with long curving swords.

Back in central Calcutta, round off sightseeing with a visit to the historic **South Park Cemetery**, in Park Street, a leafy enclosure congested with classical mausoleums of Calcutta's distinguished Europeans, replacing Saint John's cemetery in 1767. Among those buried here are William Hickey's wife Charlotte Barry; Colonel Charles Russell Deare, who perished in the fight against Tipu Sultan; Colonel Kyd, the founder of the Botanical Gardens; the early Indologist William Jones, founder of the Royal Asiatic Society; the novelist William Makepeace Thackeray's father; and sons of Charles Dickens and Captain Cook. Among the crumbling tombstones is that of Rose Aylmer, a young beauty who captured Thackeray's heart but died in her late teens after eating infected pineapple. The custodian is full of stories, and it's open all day.

Goddess Kali and the Sisters of Mercy

Take the underground metro to Kalighat to see the temple of Calcutta's patron goddess, Kali, the malevolent destroyer, located about 10 minutes walk from the station. The present temple was built in 1809, but this site of **Kali Khetra** — from which Calcutta derived its name — has long been associated with legend. It is said to be the home of Kali, "the black one," who rose as an incarnation of Devi, Shiva's wife.

The story goes that Shiva was so distraught when Devi died that the other gods feared he would pound the earth to dust in his grief. So Vishnu surreptitiously removed Devi's offending corpse from Shiva's sight, slicing it into 52 pieces. One of her severed toes fell here, becoming Kali.

Devi represented Shiva's feminine energy in its manifold forms. Thus she took on many incarnations, of which Kali and the more saintly

Durga (the focus of Calcutta's annual Durga Puja festival) are the most important. Rather unappetizingly, the temple is notorious for its daily animal sacrifice — usually goats or sheep — when pilgrims are whipped into a frenzy, scrabbling up the marble stairs to make *puja* of sweetmeats, flowers, or coconuts. Kali is usually depicted as a gorgon-like creature with beady red eyes, dripping with blood, and triumphantly holding up weapons, snakes, and severed heads in her ten arms. Of all the Hindu deities, her wrath is most feared, and hence propitiated most slavishly. The temple is open until 10 PM.

Nirmal Hriday, the Place of the Pure Heart, the most famous of homes founded by Mother

Theresa for the destitute and dying, stands beside the Kali temple in a former pilgrim's hostel, at 54A Lower Circular Road. Visitors are allowed during the early morning and between 4 PM and 6 PM. It's here that dying men and women with nothing and no one come to be cared for by the Sisters of Mercy in their distinctive white blue-bordered saris, before "going home to God."

Mother Theresa started alone in 1948 in a Calcutta slum, and since then the Missionary Sisters have grown to more than a 1,000-strong and a separate Brotherhood has also been formed. Mother Theresa died in 1997, but her work continues without her all the same.

OPPOSITE: The Marble Palace is truly the "Miss Haversham" of grand Calcutta mansions, full of cobwebbed charm. ABOVE: Imposing façade of the Writer's Building in BBD Bagh.

Bengali Biblomania

Calcuttans pride themselves on being a literary people. The British began the trend, founding the prestigious Royal Asiatic Society and the National Library here, but the Bengalis were behind Calcutta's nineteenth century literary renaissance that gave zeal to the early independence movement. There are more than 800 newspapers in the state, more than 1,600 poetry magazines, and the bulk of India's creative theater emerges from here. Even the subway system reflects Calcutta's mania for poetical message — Kalighat station is almost entirely covered in Tagore's poems and artistic doodles. Provocative graffiti crams the city's walls, usually a compelling mixture of the poetic and the political.

Nowhere is the Bengali obsession with words so amply illustrated than the city's Portabello Road of books, **College Street**, near the university, where the air is thick with dust particles from countless books stacked high on the pavement.

You'll find almost anything in almost every language — Victorian lithographs to Russian textbooks — along this kilometer-long strip. Nearby is the **National Library**, the grand former residence of the British Lieutenant Governor, with its eight million books, including rare manuscripts. For brand-new books go to the **Oxford Book Company** on Park Street.

Arrive well primed for Calcutta by reading Geoffrey Moorehouse's classic 1971 book *Calcutta*, published by Penguin — easily the most fascinating in-depth study around. Dominique Lapierre's *City of Joy* is less critically acclaimed, but also makes compulsive reading.

Terracotta Pompeii

The unsung heroes of Calcutta's spectacular Durga Puja parade are the idol-makers who fashion clay gods by the thousands. Squatting in cotton *lungis*, deftly molding wet mud over straw cones, these pavement artisans work in the community known as **Kumar Tulli**, or Potter's Lane, located near the river in north Calcutta, just off Chitpur Road. Unpainted yet extraordinarily lifelike terracotta images of Durga, Kali, Ganesha, and Lakshmi and many other gods clutter the streets to bake in the sun, looking eerily like a kind of terracotta Pompeii. Later they will be painted up in gaudy colors, draped with tinsel, and dressed in glittering costumes as part of the Durga Puja's mammoth float parade.

Culture and Crafts Round-Up

Of all Indian cities, Calcutta has the most fascinating array of museums, art galleries, and cultural "happenings."

Keep an eye out for what's on by consulting the daily newspapers, the *Amrita Bazaar Patrika*

and the *Sunday Telegraph*, or consult the tourist office's *Calcutta This Fortnight* leaflet.

Opposite the Calcutta Club on Acharaya Bose Road is an excellent information center that is also a box office for the arts. The most active hall is the **Rabindra Sadan (** (033) 247 2413 on Cathedral Road, Calcutta's cultural hub, where Indian dancers, writers, and musicians perform. You're bound to find something happening here most nights. Other main halls include the **Academy of Fine Arts**, the **Birla Academy**, and the **Sisir Mancha**.

It's worth catching a performance of Indian classical dance, particularly the eastern dance styles of *Manipuri*, *Odissi*, and *Chahau*, usually recounting stories from the *Mahabharata* or the *Ramayana*.

Of Calcutta's 30 or so museums, make time for the country's largest, and most extensive, the **Indian Museum**, located at the junction of Chowringhee and Sudder Street. Founded in 1814 to house the burgeoning collection of the prestigious Asiatic Society, it's a huge Classical-style building with a Corinthian portico and a cavernous proscenium-style arch auditorium.

Its vast collection is spread across six departments: archaeology, anthropology, zoology, geology, botany and art. Look especially for its fine coin collection, textiles, *bidri* ware, Indian miniature paintings, and the Sunga and Gandhara sculpture. Intriguing oddities abound, including giant prehistoric coconuts, an eight-legged, four-eared preserved goat, bangles from the belly of a captured crocodile.

At the entrance, get a map to help you find your way around its giant corridors, some barely disturbed, with priceless treasures sharing dust-filled rooms with nesting pigeons. It's open daily except Mondays from 10 AM to 4:30 PM.

Equally impressive is the **Ashutosh Museum of Modern Art**, housed in Calcutta University on College Street, a fabulous showcase of the rich artistic legacy of eastern India, with sculpture, folk art, textiles and fine collection of Kalighat paintings and terracottas. It's open from Monday to Friday from 10:30 AM to 5 PM and only to noon on Saturdays.

Of other museums to explore, the following are closed on Mondays unless otherwise specified. The **Academy of Fine Arts**, Cathedral Road, is open 3 PM to 8 PM. The **Birla Academy of Art and Culture**, at 108-9 Southern Avenue, is open 4 PM to 8 PM. The **Birla Planetarium** at 96 Jawaharlal Nehru Road, the largest and best organized in India, is well patronized by city workers for its air-conditioned environment during the hot summers — most seem to doze off during the soothing drone of its lectures! There are at least two English sessions daily between 2:30 PM and 6:30 PM.

You can visit the preserved home of **Netaji Subhas Chandra Bose**, the errant Indian nationalist leader who joined forces with the Japanese during World War II, at 38/2 Lala Lajpat Rai Sarani, open Monday to Friday from 6 PM to 8 PM and on Sundays 9 AM to 12 PM.

The **Nehru Children's Museum**, 94 Jawaharlal Nehru Road, is open noon to 8 PM. The **Royal Asiatic Society**, 1 Park Street, is open for studying only from Monday to Friday, noon to 7 PM. The **State Archaeological Museum**, 33 Chittaranhan Avenue, is open Monday to Friday 11 AM to 5:30 PM, Saturdays from 11 AM to 2 PM.

SHOPPING

Calcutta is the perfect place to shop for Bengali handicrafts and textiles. Try browsing first at the **Bengal Home Industries Association**, at 57 Jawaharlal Nehru Road and the **West Bengal Government Sales Emporium** on Lindsay Street.

Best buys include village terracotta figurines, rice-measuring bowls made from wood inlaid with brass, brass oil lamps crafted to resemble people or animals, conch-shell bangles, carved ivory, delicate silver jewelry, and dolls made from papier-mâché or cotton.

The queen of Bengali textiles is the Baluchari brocade sari, noted for its complex floral and storytelling motifs, developed by eighteenth-century Gujarati immigrants. Delicate cotton and lace embroidery is another specialty, best bought at **All Bengal Women's Home**, 89 Elliot Street.

Round off any shopping with a visit to the historic **Hogg's Market**, now known as **New Market**, tucked behind the Oberoi Grand. Its Victorian red-brickwork and awnings were built almost a century ago, and it remains Calcutta's chief bartering place, particularly for its brimming animal and bird mart. Squads of eager porters clamor for the job of lugging your purchases around in pannier-like baskets before you've even bought them.

WHERE TO STAY

Luxury
Oberoi Grand ((033) 2492323 FAX (033) 2491217, 15 Chowringhee Road, is one of India's most stylish and efficient hotels, rated by frequent business travelers as their personal favorite, and even compared favorably by some with London's Savoy Hotel. Tucked behind Chowringhee's bustling arcades, it is a haven of luxury, with its sweeping Georgian façade, brass-buttoned bellhops, immaculate 1930s-style marble interior, and staff in period uniforms. Renovations to further modernize the hotel were in process at the time of writing, and should be complete by the time you have this book in your hands.

The Oberoi's fortunes are a mini-chronicle of Calcutta: originally built as a fantasy home by one Colonel Grand in the late nineteenth century then sold to an entrepreneurial Armenian, during World War II it became a glorified doss-house for British troops, known locally as Mrs. Monks Guesthouse. It's now the Oberoi chain's flagship hotel. It has a beautiful swimming pool and terrace garden, excellent health club facilities including saunas, Turkish baths, gymnasiums, and massage-cum-beauty parlors. It offers Calcutta's best restaurants, cultural Dances of India performances, a stylish cocktail lounge, and an airy 24-hour coffee shop. Other facilities include a well-equipped business center, shopping arcade, travel desk, and in-house

astrologer. Stylish comfort extends to all rooms, with their pastel pink, marble, and mahogany decor. Rates are from US$260.

The Oberoi's main competitor in town is the Taj Group's **Taj Bengal** ((033) 2233939 FAX (033) 2231776, Belvedere Road. It lacks the class and intimacy of the Oberoi, but there's no denying all the same that it is a first-class hotel and has seized a significant proportion of the luxury market in Calcutta. Its bar and disco are among the most elite in town.

Running a close third place, and with a great location on fashionable Park Street, the **Park Hotel** ((033) 2497336 FAX (033) 2497343 is also worth recommending. It has all the luxury amenities you would expect of a first-rate five-star hotel and is tastefully furbished throughout. Room rates at both the Taj and the Park are slightly cheaper than at the Oberoi.

Lastly, if you need quality accommodation in the vicinity of the airport, the **Hotel Airport Ashok** ((033) 5119111 FAX (033) 5119137 has a shopping arcade, swimming pool, health facilities, restaurants, and a bar. Room rates start at around US$100.

The Oberoi Grand Hotel, considered by many Calcuttans to be the epitome of elegance and the good life.

Mid-range

Although Calcutta has some modern mid-range hotels, by far the more interesting option in this category is to stay at one of its lingering Raj-era establishments.

In the south of town, and within walking distance of Tollygunge subway station, The **Tollygunge Club** ((033) 4732316 FAX (033) 4731903, 120 Deshpran Sasmal Road, is a charming anachronism. Set amid a beautiful 81-hectare (200-acre) estate, this historic clubhouse was built in 1788 and for a time became the residence of the deposed sons of Tipu "Tiger" Sultan. During the heyday of the British Raj, it became the most exclusive of all European clubs.

Today, in all honesty, the rooms, which range from around US$30, are nothing to write home about. But a stay here gives you full use of the club's extensive facilities and access to its inexpensive restaurants. Facilities include polo and horse-riding fields, squash and tennis courts, a golf course, and a swimming pool. Advance bookings are essential.

The **Fairlawn Hotel** ((033) 2451510 FAX (033) 2441835, 13A Sudder Street, is even more delightfully eccentric, dressed up like a Brighton boarding house. It is dominated by its formidable Armenian proprietress, Mrs. Smith, whose entourage includes a fleet of lap dogs and a corps of beaming retainers in faded khaki and Nehru caps. Once the entrance gate is closed, Calcutta's tumultuous street-life recedes (although rickshaw boys bed down on the pavement outside), and the guests can unwind in the small leafy courtyard strewn with cane chairs, statues and fairy-lights. Rooms come with floral drapes, lace dollies, and old fashioned baths — and you'll have a "bearer" assigned to your room to bring "bed-tea" and Britannica biscuits, collect washing for the *dhobi-wallah* and refill water.

Mealtimes are sounded with a resounding gong, with as many as four courses ritually served in a dining room crammed with extraordinary monarchist memorabilia. The daily Anglo-Indian menus read like samples from a Victorian handbook for *memsahibs* in the tropics: frequently delicious, particularly the fish course. With its homely, time-warped atmosphere, the Fairlawn often steals nostalgic British guests away from the more luxurious Oberoi, and attracts an interesting array of travelers, who are more or less thrown into each other's company. Videotaped episodes of English sit-coms *The Good Life* and *Yes Minister* can be viewed in the lounge. Rates are moderate and include three huge meals a day. It's best to avoid the cheaper rooms.

The **Old Kennilworth Hotel** ((033) 2828394 FAX (033) 2825136, 1-2 Little Russell Street, conveniently located close to the tourist office and government emporia, is an atmospheric and

comfortable place to base yourself. The old block, close by at No. 7 Little Russell Street, oozes character, but sadly little else.

Just around the corner, the **Astor Hotel** ((033) 2829957, 15 Shakespeare Sarani, is a quaint, inexpensive Tudor-style establishment in a peaceful courtyard that features evening barbecues.

Budget

Sudder Street, conveniently located close to the Indian Museum, Park Street, and the Maidan, is Calcutta's budget hotel headquarters.

Particularly good value in this part of town is the **Astoria Hotel** ((033) 2449679 FAX (033) 2448589. It's all air-conditioned, and while it has little in the way of amenities its rooms are far more spacious than many others in this price range — around US$20.

At 2 Sudder Street is the **Salvation Army Red Shield Guesthouse** ((033) 2450599, with Spartan but spotless fan-cooled singles and doubles with attached bath. Dorm beds cost US$1, but simple doubles with attached bathrooms are also available for around US$5. Budget travelers rate it highly, although its water supply is not always up to scratch. It's possible to put valuables into "safekeeping" at the front desk.

Another popular and cheap tourist lodge is the **Shilton Hotel** ((033) 2451512, a few doors away, at 5A. It's a slightly dilapidated looking place, but the rooms are acceptable.

Calcutta's YMCAs are quite grand. The most creakily Gothic of all, the **YMCA** ((033) 2492192, 25 Chowringhee Road, was originally built in 1902 and has a spooky "Turn of the Screw" feel. It still retains its mystifying plaque "No pets or private servants allowed!" It's unisex and the room rates of US$8 upwards include breakfast and dinner.

WHERE TO EAT

Calcutta has a fabulous array of restaurants, but it is still surprisingly difficult to sample Calcutta's exotic Bengali cuisine. Most Calcuttan families tend to eat in — believing, quite rightly, that home cooking is best. This may stem partly from tradition and partly because Bengali dishes rely heavily on subtle herbs, fresh fish, and mustard oil — a combination that does not keep well together for long. Traditionally, meals are served course by course on plantain leaves. And when Calcuttans go out, they like to do so in style — opting for swish European, Chinese or northern Indian food.

The **Suruchi** at 89 Elliot Road, near Sudder Street, gets the highest praise from locals for its typical Bengali dishes. It's best to concentrate on their fresh fish dishes, particularly *doi mach*, an unforgettable curry of river fish, yogurt, ginger, raisins and spices; *dabey chingri*, shellfish baked with coconut; *maccher paturi*, steamed mustard fish; delicious but bony smoked hilsa fish; and prawns sautéed in mustard oil and spiced with coriander and garlic. All are eaten with a variety of rice dishes or with *loochi*, a deep-fried bread, and spicy, syrupy mango chutney. Bengali sweets are positively devilish for sugar-addicts — usually milk and curd based, like *barfi*, *rasgulla*, *rasmalai*, and *sandhesh* — all made to tantalize the taste buds. Another favorite Bengali dessert is *misthi dohi*, a sweet curd with raw jaggery date-palm sugar.

The Oberoi Grand offers some of the best dining in Calcutta. For Mughalai cuisine, treat yourself to a splash-out meal at **Gharana**; **Baan Thai**, with its imported Thai chefs and authentic decor, is rated as one of the best Thai restaurants in the country. And don't forget the Oberoi coffee shop's wonderful lunchtime buffet, which is usually packed with local notables queuing for seconds.

Calcutta's main drag, Park Street, is festooned with faded neon, garish "cabaret" club porticoes and shop façades left over from the thirties and forties, crammed with the city's best-loved restaurants.

The **Sky Room**, 57 Park Street, was once the height of fashion, with its quirky Art Deco decor, fake "sky" ceiling, and old-fashioned waiters clad in spotless white. Nowadays it looks and tastes tired.

Other long-running Park Street restaurants have weathered the years better. **Kwality (** (033) 2485680, at No. 17, is one of the biggest and best of the India-wide chain. The **Moulin Rouge (** (033) 298950, at No. 31, fronted by a fake windmill façade, is a tacky stab at Parisian ambiance, but the meals remain reliable, if a bit slow in arriving. The **Blue Fox (** (033) 297993, at No. 55, is as popular as ever, serving drinks and novelties such as "sizzlers." **Tandoor (** (033) 298885, at No. 43, is recommended for its cuisine of the same name. And, lastly, at No. 17B, there's **Trinca's (** (033) 298947 — a massive complex with highly rated meals.

Just behind Sudder Street, **Amber (** (033) 2483018, 11 Waterloo Road, is the place to sample northern Indian Punjabi food. It's a massive place, covering three entire floors, and the tandoori here is reputed to be the city's best.

Calcutta's Chinese immigrants have endowed the city with numerous authentic regional Chinese restaurants, still mainly catering to the small colony who patronize them for their Peking duck, home-cooked treats, and continuous green tea. One of the best is **How Hwa**, Mirza Ghalib Road, which offers a staggering 32 different kinds of soups, including the house specialty, Chimney Soup, a mix of prawn wantons, fish, crab meat, and homemade bean curd all cooked with a garlic-ginger stock in a Mongolian hot-pot. Special dishes can be ordered in 24 hours in advance, notably

luscious roasted Peking duck served with plum sauce, scallions and pancakes. Another popular Chinese restaurant is the **Peiping**, 1/1 Park Street, with its partitioned sections a concession to Muslim patrons, renowned for its steamed garlic and ginger fish and giant king prawns.

Flury's ((033) 297664, 18 Park Street, is a classic Raj-era tearoom with an adjoining pastry shop. It's open early for British breakfasts of baked beans on toast and is a popular rendezvous place for all-day pastries, club sandwiches and Vienna coffees.

Kathleen's, 12 Free School Street, at the end of Sudder Street, also has a great restaurant-cum-bakery, always well patronized since Calcuttans adore their cream cakes!

In Sudder Street, backpackers gravitate to the **Blue Sky Café**, which serves good fruit *lassis*, Western-style breakfasts, and burgers. For inexpensive food in this area, however, you're much better heading over to **Khalsa**, on Madge Lane, close to the Salvation Army Hostel. It does superb Punjabi cuisine at rock-bottom prices.

If you're strolling down College Street's "book strip" don't miss one of Calcutta's most lively hangouts, the **India Coffee House**. It occupies the cavernous Albert Hall, noted as the venue for the First National Congress Conference in 1885. Climb up the "balcony seat" for a delicious iced coffee and observe this hub of political and cultural discussion echoing to the sounds of urgent Bengali, wafts of highbrow English and emphatic fists on tables. Calcutta's Bengali students may look threadbare and exist only on coffee and cigarettes, but they sure know their Marxist dialectics. Giant fans dangle like low propellers, waiters flit about dressed in bizarre plumed caps, soiled white uniforms and cummerbunds. It's a great place to strike up conversations and dine well for next to nothing.

The restaurant at the **Fairlawn Hotel** is the perfect place for a leisurely set lunch or dinner. The daily menu is posted outside and is always a bargain. Even if you don't eat here, evening drinks in the garden are a Calcutta institution — and you won't find a cheaper bottle of Kingfisher or Royal Challenge anywhere in the city.

HOW TO GET THERE

Indian Airlines run direct flights to Calcutta from Delhi, Bombay, Bangalore, Bagdogra (for Darjeeling), Bhubaneswar, Hyderabad, Madras, Varanasi, Patna, and Port Blair in the Andaman Islands. Various international carriers connect it with Rome, London, Bangkok, Tokyo, Dubai, New York, Osaka, Moscow, Katmandu, and Dhaka.

Calcutta's Dum Dum Airport complex combines both international and domestic services and functions reasonably smoothly. It's named after a small-arms factory nearby, which in 1898 produced the notoriously effective Dum Dum bullet that punched fist-sized holes into tribal Afridis and was banned after the Boer War. It's best to get a prepaid taxi for the 40-minute ride into the city center, costing about US$5 either way. There's also a US$1 airport bus, which stops at Chowringhee near the Oberoi Grand and Sudder Street, but this service becomes irregular in the evenings.

There are two rail stations, but travelers are most likely to enter the city through the teeming bedlam of Howrah Station, just over the Howrah bridge, which has overnight and day rail services out to most major destinations, including Madras (27 hours), Delhi (18 hours), Bombay (33 hours), and Varanasi (11 hours). Give yourself at least an hour to reach Howrah by taxi from the city center. The less congested Sealdah Station, 20 minutes northeast of the city, services Darjeeling (24 hours).

AROUND CALCUTTA

THE BANYAN BOULEVARD

Across the Hooghly's banks, south of Howrah, are India's most beautiful **Botanical Gardens** — a perfect bolt-hole from Calcutta proper, and a 40-minute drive (20 km or 11.4 miles) from the city center. Laid out by one Colonel Kyd in 1786 as a pleasure retreat for the East India Company, it stretches for about a kilometer along the riverfront, with palm, orchid, and cacti houses, a herbarium, lakes, and altogether some 30,000 varieties of tropical plants and trees. It was at these gardens that the tea now grown in Assam and Darjeeling was first developed. Its world-famous attraction is its 225 year-old Banyan tree, the largest on earth. It has a circumference of 417 m (1,367 ft) and some 1,600 aerial roots, resembling a small forest, not a single tree. It's most pleasant to make this a morning excursion, taking a ferry cruise across the Hooghly from Chandpal or Takta Ghats, checking first that the Botanical Gardens Ghat is open.

THE BELUR MATH

Some 10 km (just over six miles) north, still on the east bank of the Hooghly, is the **Belur Math**, the headquarters of the Ramakrishna Mission. This was established in 1898 by Swami Vivekananda, resuscitating the ideals of the sage Rama Krishna who preached the essential unity of all religions. Illustrating this belief, it looks like a church, Hindu temple, or mosque — depending on the way you look at it.

TOP: Pastoral peace as the sun slowly sets over the marshlands. BOTTOM: Waiting for a boat to ferry passengers through the mangrove swamps.

MANGROVES AND TIGERS

The **Sunderbans**, which lies 131 km (81 miles) east of Calcutta, where the Ganges spills into the Bay of Bengal, is the world's largest mangrove swamp and the home of the magnificent Royal Bengal tiger. Few tourists ever venture as far as this vast 2,500 sq km (965 sq miles) estuarine land of mud flats, mangroves, and dense forest, which sprawls across to Bangladesh and is accessible only by riverine waterways.

Among those who returned impressed was Alfred Hitchcock, who begged the then prime minister Indira Gandhi to let him make a horror film here, writing that it was the most "devilish, foreboding landscape" he had ever seen. She turned Hitchcock down, having already refused him permission to film in the Taj Mahal.

However lonely or perilous its landscape, it is certainly crammed with spectacular wildlife. Tribal villagers who eke out a living by honey collecting and fishing here wear brightly painted masks on the backs of their heads to lessen their chances of becoming tiger fodder. This is the largest natural habitat of tigers in the world, with some 250 roaming free in the central Project Tiger reserve. Nevertheless, it's not wise to get your hopes up too high for a sighting — many visitors miss out.

Among other wildlife, you have a good chance of seeing wild boar, jungle cats, spotted deer, giant crocodiles, king cobras, lizards, and monitors including the rare Salvator lizard. Part of the Sunderbans is the **Sajnakhali Bird Sanctuary**.

The main embarkation point for river cruises through the sanctuary is **Canning**, 54 km (33.5 miles) from Calcutta, reached by car, train, or bus. It's possible to hire private launches, but safest and easiest to go on the conducted trips run by the West Bengal Tourist Bureau ((033) 2488271, 3/2 BBD Bagh, Calcutta, who operate a luxury launch that provides sleeping quarters and armed guards for Project Tiger areas. Accommodation is also available at the **Sajnakhali Tourist Lodge** at Sajnakhali.

The reserve is best visited from mid-September to mid-March. Foreign visitors have to contact the Secretary, Department of Forest and Tourism, Government of West Bengal, Writer's Building, in Calcutta.

BIHAR: THE BUDDHIST TRAIL

Buddha lived and preached most of his life in the northeastern state of rural Bihar. Of special interest to Buddhists, Bihar is off the beaten track for most tourists.

In the sixth century BC, Pataliputra, the site of Bihar's modern capital Patna, became first the capital of the Magadhas, and then later of the

Mauryas and other successive empires that promoted Buddhist culture and philosophy.

Within the state, Bodhgaya is a hallowed place for Buddhists, as the place where Buddha achieved enlightenment beneath the Bodhi Tree. Close by are Nalanda, with the ruins of the world's oldest university, and Rajgir, capital of the Magadha empire, and the place where Buddha and Mahavira (founder of the Jain faith) lived in retreat and delivered sermons.

PATNA

Few travelers stop in Patna, most preferring to make straight for Gaya (see below), which is on

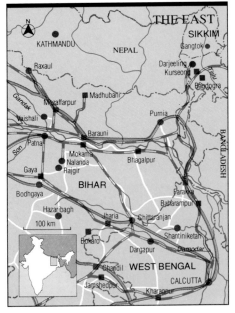

the main Delhi-Calcutta rail line and has easy access to Bihar's main tourist destination, Bodhgaya.

Nevertheless, you might care to call in and take a look at the jumbled display of exhibits at the **Patna Museum**. Labeling is minimal, but the first-floor display of terracotta images is interesting.

In the south of Patna, at the **Kumrahar** excavation site, you can see ruins that date back to around 500 BC: the remains of the ancient city of Pataliputra. You have to be something of an archeology buff, however, to make much of them.

The Government of India Tourist Office ((0612) 226721 can organize local tours.

Patna has some surprisingly good hotels for such an off-the-beaten-track destination. The best in town is the **Maurya Patna** ((0612) 222061 FAX (0612) 222069, South Gandhi Maidan, which comes with a shopping arcade, a swimming

pool, and a travel counter. Room rates start at around US$50.

A more budget option in Patna is the **Hotel President** ((0612) 220600 FAX (0612) 224455, Fraser Road, which has a mixture of economical air-conditioned rooms and even cheaper air-cooled rooms. It's a good value place with a decent south Indian restaurant.

Indian Airlines has flights daily to Patna from Delhi and Calcutta. By train, you can expect to take six hours to reach Calcutta or around 12 hours to Delhi. By bus, it is just seven hours to the Nepalese border (Raxaul) from Patna.

BODHGAYA

Bodhgaya, where Sakyamuni achieved enlightenment, is the world's most important Buddhist pilgrimage destination and Bihar's premiere tourist attraction.

In the center of the small town, next to the Deer Park, is the **Mahabodhi Temple**, a nineteenth-century reconstruction of the seventh-century original that was destroyed by Ashoka before his conversion to Buddhism. The nearby bodhi tree traces its ancestry back to the very tree under which the Buddha sat and meditated.

Almost every country in the world that has been touched by Buddhism has a representative temple here in this holiest of places. Thus, you can find a Japanese Temple, a Burmese Temple, a Thai Temple, a Chinese Temple, a Vietnamese Temple, and three temples representing the major schools of Tibetan Buddhism.

Meditation courses and courses in Buddhism are popular with many visiting foreigners. The best place to apply at short notice is the Root Institute for Wisdom Culture ((0631) 400714, which also has budget — and very basic — accommodation.

If you value your comforts, you are best off basing yourself in Gaya rather than Bodhgaya. The **Hotel Siddhartha International** ((0631) 436243 FAX (0631) 436368, has a somewhat shabby air about it, but there's no denying that it's the best hotel in the area. Air-conditioned doubles start at US$60, and there's an excellent multi-cuisine restaurant.

In Bodhgaya itself, where most of the accommodation is of a budget nature, stay at the **Bodhgaya Ashok** ((0631) 400725, a pleasant bungalow outfit with a good restaurant. Air-conditioned rooms start at around US$30.

It's easily accessible by bus or auto-rickshaw from Gaya, which is 14 km (nine miles) and on the main Delhi-Calcutta railway line. Buses from Patna to Gaya take around four hours. Due to increasing incidences of robbery, local tourist officials recommend that travelers avoid the road between Gaya and Bodhgaya after dark.

DARJEELING

Darjeeling was the unsurpassed "Queen of the Hill Stations" during the British Raj, the goal of jaded Europeans seeking to revive their tempers amid its refreshing cool charm and lovely scenery, far away from muggy Calcutta. It is an exotic patch of Anglo–Himalaya, perched on the Ghoom–Senchal Ridge at an altitude of 2,134 m (7,000 ft), with magnificent views across the mountains Kanchenjunga and Everest.

Its surrounding landscape has range upon range of snowy mountain peaks, with steeply sloping conifer forests and terraced tea plantations.

lost their domain to invading tribes of Gurkhas from Nepal in 1780. Two British officers stumbled on this remote Shangri-La in 1828, realizing its potential as a strategic link with the Nepal and Tibet, as well as a hill-station sanitarium. At that time, locals called their home "Dorje Ling" or "Place of the Thunderbolt." According to legend, Darjeeling was struck by a mystic thunderbolt of the Lamaist religion, said to be the scepter of Indra, Lord of the Gods, which supposedly fell on the site known as Observatory Hill.

Darjeeling is steeped in British legacies that are today preserved best in its architecture (Anglican, Scottish and Roman Catholic churches, Tudor-style cottages, village squares), its polo

The lively town is a labyrinth of stairways, chalet-style huts, and colorful bazaars selling handicrafts, the famous Darjeeling tea, and an object of much practical value in Darjeeling — the umbrella. Its cobbled streets bustle with all the races of the Himalayas, often in colorful tribal costume: the martially formidable Gurkhas; the famous mountaineering Sherpas; Nepalese women swaddled in red flannel, their chests hung with huge silver and turquoise necklaces; Mongol-featured urchins; elfin Lepchas and fair-skinned Sikkimese; Tibetan Lamas in saffron robes; Gurung farmers from western Nepal; and serene-faced Bhutanese. Stunted ponies lumber up and down the steps, taking market goods down to town, and giggling apple-cheeked schoolchildren on the way up, bundled in large baskets.

Until the beginning of the eighteenth century, Darjeeling was ruled by the Rajahs of Sikkim, who

ground, and above all its tea plantations, which were first established by the British, using seeds smuggled from China.

Darjeeling is a major base for trekking expeditions in the eastern Himalayas, the center of the Himalayan Mountaineering Institute. It's also a botanist's paradise, with over 4,000 species of flowers. Nearby destinations include Tiger Hill, which offers incomparable views of the Himalayas, and the Ghoom Monastery, dedicated to Maitreya, said by the Tibetans to be the "Buddha to Come."

Darjeeling is of course renowned throughout the world for its tea. However, what is so good for the tea plantations is not always so good for

Impoverished villagers swaddled against steam fumes as they are sped on a ticketless journey through the arid hinterland of Bihar.

the visitor. The torrential monsoon, which erupts from mid-June to mid-September, can blot out the views, wash out the roads, and seriously dampen the pleasure of a visit to Darjeeling. The hill station is most idyllic from March to mid-June, when rhododendron, magnolia, and hollyhocks bloom. Views across to the divine mass of the Himalayas are at their most crisply spectacular during the wintry months from mid-September to December, when Darjeeling is carpeted with snow.

GENERAL INFORMATION

Only the most dedicated sightseer could rise bright and early for an energetic expedition on the first day in Darjeeling. Its high altitude leaves most people feeling slightly enervated for at least a day or so. Bearing this is mind, allow yourself at least three days to see Darjeeling's main attractions, which can be covered on foot if you've a penchant for healthy, rugged walking. Alternately, you can inquire at the **Tourist Bureau** ((0354) 54050, 1 Laden-La Road, about hiring private taxis, jeeps, and Land-rovers for getting about. They also have a useful local map. Ponies might look spindly, but their sturdy legs are bred for lugging heavy loads around — including visiting tourists.

GETTING AROUND

On the first day, develop your Himalayan sea legs by winding your way around Darjeeling town's two main thoroughfares: Laden-La, officially known as Nehru Road, leading up to Chowrasta Square. The latter is a bustling strip where you'll find most of the hotels, restaurants, shops, banks, cinemas, and the Tourist Bureau; and Cart Road at the bottom of the steep ridge, which is crammed with winding bazaars overflowing with odd-shaped vegetables, putrid-smelling Tibetan potions, and colorful Himalayan handicrafts — a mixture of Nepali, Tibetan, Sikkimese and Bhutanese folk art, wooden carvings, woven fabric, knits, carpets, local jewelry, and bric-a-brac.

Look especially for the interesting, well-organized **Tibetan Self Help Center**, established in 1959 to assist Darjeeling's large Tibetan refugee community (who fled China-occupied Tibet to India along with the thirteenth Dalai Lama). It's crammed with curios, carpets, leatherwork, jewelry, and wood carvings. Also visit **Hayden Hall**, where Tibetan women in striped tunics sell their brilliantly-hued, knitted creations.

Darjeeling's main markets pack away their baskets and stalls all day Thursday, while shops are shuttered on Sundays and half-day Saturdays. Cart Road is where you'll find the rail and bus stations, as well as the taxi stand.

WHAT TO SEE AND DO

Witnessing dawn is the ultimate experience in Darjeeling. The curtain is raised and there they are: Mount Kanchenjunga and, on a clear morning Mount Everest in the background, surrounded by Markala, Lhotse, and other Eastern Himalayan peaks, their snows flushed rosy-pink with first light, fringed by glittering pyramids of ice, snow, and rock.

The best vantage point is **Tiger Hill**, at an altitude of 2,590 m (8,482 ft), situated 11 km (just under seven miles) away. On a clear day, you'll become part of a noisy, exhaust-spluttering convoy along the mountain roads all sharing the same objective. Sightseeing buses and jeeps make the hour-long trip there each morning, leaving at 4:30 AM to await dawn on the hilltop.

It's worth making the rugged 40-minute trek from the Tiger Hill viewing platform to **Ghoom Buddhist Monastery**, the largest and most famous religious center of its kind in Darjeeling, with an entrance of fluttering prayer flags.

It was established in 1850 by a Mongolian astrologer-monk and contains a giant seated image of Maitreya (the "Buddha to Come") surrounded by sticks of incense, bells, drums, and ornate *thanka* scrolls. You can ask to view a collection of precious Buddhist manuscripts and will be asked for a small donation in return. The fun part of this excursion is returning to Darjeeling by another miniature "toy train," which leaves from Ghoom's small station, a half-hour scenic trip.

Flora and Fauna

In town there are plenty of attractions worth a look. Start with the institutions founded by scholarly British lepidopterists and botanists.

The Bengal Natural History Museum, set up in 1903, is quite simply a taxidermist's heaven. Expertly presented, it's eccentric enough to warrant a visit purely for the sensation of being "watched" by 4,300 beady-eyed stuffed animals and pinned insects, all captured along the Eastern Himalayan belt. It's open from 10 AM to 4 PM, closed Thursdays.

Lloyd's Botanical Gardens, laid out in 1865, has beautiful orchid hothouses containing over 2,000 species and a representative collection of the flora of the Sikkim Himalayas. It's open from 6 AM to 5 PM, and admission is free.

Take directions from the gardens to Victoria Road, then proceed along the pretty half-hour walk to the **Victoria Falls** — one of the most beautiful, secluded strolls in the area, although the waterfall itself is hardly impressive.

Darjeeling's **Zoo** is notorious for shutting its inmates — mostly Siberian tigers, Himalayan black bears, deer, pandas, and black jaguars — up in squalid little cages.

Also worth visiting is the **Himalayan Mountaineering Institute**, famous for its training courses. It also has a museum with fascinating photos, equipment, and exhibits relating to famous mountaineering expeditions. It's open daily 9 AM to 5 PM (summer), 9 AM to 4 AM (winter).

Close by, there's an interesting, well-manicured cemetery of former Raj residents, also containing the tomb of nineteenth century Alexander Krs, a Hungarian orientalist who traveled to Darjeeling set on establishing that Tibetan and Hungarian peoples shared a common ancestry. He became a national hero to the Tibetan people after publishing his dictionary and grammar of the Tibetan language.

Kalimpong, 51 km (32 miles) from Darjeeling, makes a pleasant day's excursion. This scenic mountain bazaar town, perched at an altitude of 1,250 m (4,100 ft) has spectacular views, picturesque hill-folk, and flower nurseries.

Tea Plantations

Darjeeling is one of the world's most famous tea-growing centers, producing India's most celebrated tea, its refined taste apparently due to its uniquely favorable climate. Altogether, the hill station is dotted with more than 70 tea plantations, which employ around 50,000 people, many of them Nepalese, and produce some 10.5 million kilos (23 million pounds) of tea annually, all of which is packed in giant tea crates and sent off to Calcutta's tea auctions.

Pure Darjeeling tea is so expensive — more than US$300 dollars per kilo in one exceptional, world-record-breaking example — that it's usually blended with leaves from other areas. India is still the largest consumer of its own tea, but the Soviet Union is a major importer of pure Darjeeling tea, which they mix with their own leaves and then sell off as "pure" Russian tea!

The traditional way of judging tea is to take a pinch in the palm of your hand, then breathe on it to moisten the leaves and judge the quality from the aroma. Darjeeling's leaves end up at the world's longest tea tasting table at Calcutta's Nilhat House, where highly trained tannin testers fastidiously sip, sniff, and swill in the practiced manner of wine-tasters.

You're welcome to visit the **Happy Valley Tea Gardens**, three kilometers (nearly two miles) from the center of town, to see how tea is produced in the so called "orthodox" method: fresh leaves are placed in "withering" troughs, dried out by high-speed fan, then successively rolled, pressed, and painstakingly fermented on a conveyer belt. Finally the tea is sorted out into grades of Golden Flowery Orange Pekoe (unbroken leaves), then Golden Broken Orange Pekoe, Orange Fanning, and Dust (broken leaves). It's open daily, except Mondays, from 8 AM to noon and 1 PM to 4:30 PM; open only from 1 PM to 4:30 PM on Sundays.

Recreation

Just combing this hillside town's vertiginous slopes should be enough to ensure that most visitors sink into their beds at night with their muscles aching all over. If all this pony-riding and strolling doesn't satisfy athletic urges for the great outdoors, try **golfing** at the Senchal Golf Club, one of the world's highest, or **fishing** on the Rangeet River at Singla (eight kilometers or five miles away) or at the Teesta River at Riyand (41 km or 25 miles away), first obtaining permits from the District Magistrate, Deputy Commissioner's Office, Hillcart Road.

Darjeeling's **treks** are another popular option, since they are short — two to three days to a week — easily managed, and cover spectacular scenery. If you decide to embark on an organized trek, with Sherpa guides, ponies and tents, contact either Summit or Himal Ventures, both located at Indreni Lodge. These agencies will arrange everything for the equivalent of US$10 a day, but you can organize your own guide at any of the hotels or lodges around town for half that price. If you'd prefer to go it alone, trails are well marked with plenty of good lodges for overnight stays along the routes.

The most popular trails go to **Sandakphu**, **Tonglu** and **Phalut**, all offering marvelous views of the whole Kanchenjunga range and Mount Everest. For detailed information on various trekking possibilities, contact the Tourist Bureau in Darjeeling.

WHERE TO STAY

Darjeeling offers a wide-range of hotels, many with breathtaking mountain and valley views. Prices vary a good deal according to season and most hotels include meals in their rates. Whatever your accommodation, you'll require heating facilities (Darjeeling gets bone-pinchingly chilly) and a window across the surrounding landscape.

The **Windamere Hotel** ((0354) 54041, FAX (0354) 54043, The Mall, has a delightfully eccentric Raj-era ambiance — rather like Calcutta's Fairlawn — with homely log fires in the bedrooms and a hot-water-bottle magically slipped beneath the floral bedspread at night. There's a fusty library, a bar, a sweet garden, a miniature golf course, and a badminton court. Good quality Indian, Chinese, and continental dishes are guaranteed to restore the body and soul after a long day's traipsing. It's perhaps not quite the lap of luxury, but the Windamere more than compensates with its time-travel ambiance. Doubles start at US$110.

A similar old-world atmosphere can be found at the **New Elgin Hotel** ((0354) 54114 FAX (0354) 54267, 18 HD Lama Road. This old bungalow comes complete with musty anglophile memorabilia, fireplaces in the rooms, and splendid views. The restaurant is recommended. Rates start at around US$60.

The **Hotel Sinclairs** ((0354) 56431 FAX (0354) 54355, Gandhi Road, is a more modern setup with a sun deck, a children's playing room, and a library among its facilities. The centrally heated rooms range from around US$20 to US$60.

Out of town, on Ghoom Monastery Road, **Sterling Holiday Resorts** ((0354) 51215 is a centrally heated hotel complex that pitches itself at the family market. Room rates start from around US$40.

In the budget to mid-range category, the **Bellevue Hotel** ((0354) 54075, Chowrasta, offers some of the best views in town and retains an old-world charm. It has another, less impressive branch on The Mall.

Opposite the Bellevue, and somewhat cheaper, is the **Pineridge Hotel** ((0354) 53909. Although this faded hotel has some very inexpensive rooms, you are best off securing one of the suites (around US$25), which have views from their bay windows.

For real budget accommodation, the **Hotel Shamrock**, Beechwood Lane, is a popular choice. It has some extremely pleasant rooms with attached washing facilities, but you will have to forego luxuries such as running water.

The **Youth Hostel**, Dr. Zakir Hussain Road, is cheap and sports great views, but other than that has little to recommend it. Not only has it seen better days but, being situated high up on the ridge, it requires a mandatory 15-minute puffing ascent from the bus or rail stations.

WHERE TO EAT

Darjeeling is not renowned for its appetizing cuisine. Addicts of traditional Tibetan *momos*, steamed mincemeat balls flavored with onion and ginger, will have a field day — otherwise expect your taste-buds to remain untantalized.

The best food is found at the **Windamere**, which also has an atmospheric small bar. Reservations are required at the Windamere if you are not a guest, and the loosen-the-belt meals are enlivened by a time-warped pianist. The **Silver Restaurant** at the New Elgin is similarly recommended.

Glenary's, The Mall, has long been celebrated as one of Darjeeling's best, and it's still going strong. Ask one of the quaintly cummerbunded waiters for an Irish coffee, or alternatively try the tandoori in the upstairs restaurant.

To try Tibet's simple cuisine in an environment that also offers Chinese dishes, the **Penang Restaurant**, on Laden-La Road, is popular with locals and foreigners alike. It's opposite the General Post Office.

HOW TO GET THERE

Indian Airlines and Jet Airways operate flights to Bagdogra airport from Delhi, Calcutta, and Guwahati. Bagdogra airport is 90 km (56 miles) from Darjeeling and reached either by a three-hour drive by airport bus, taxi, or jeep; or by taking the famous miniature two-foot narrow gauge "toy train," completed in 1881, from nearby Siliguri/ New Jalpaiguri.

The "express" *Darjeeling Mail* (12 hours) leaves Calcutta's Sealdah Station daily at 7 PM, bound for New Jalpaiguri. Reservations can be made at the Eastern Railways Booking Office, Fairlee Place, Calcutta. The last leg of the journey takes place on a miniature railway (about three departures daily), which huffs and puffs through deep jungles, tea gardens and pine forests, culminating in the famous "Agony Loop" just outside Darjeeling.

Train addicts have called it India's greatest train journey, but mere mortals often find that the spectacular scenery begins to pall at the crawling pace of 10 kph (6 mph). It frequently takes much longer than its advertised time of seven to eight hours, and some travelers reported arriving in Darjeeling in the small hours after an epic 12-hour run, finding all hotels closed. Check with the tourist office in Calcutta whether the Toy Train is running, as there have occasionally been times when the service has been disrupted.

You will reach Darjeeling much more quickly (and still get the same views) by taking the express bus, although you'll also anticipate a hundred deaths along the journey! Quirky roadside signs, with warnings such as "Lovers, Don't Leap!" or perhaps "Beware of Falling Trucks" will quickly convince you that it's not just you being neurotic.

SIKKIM

Buttonholed between Bhutan and Nepal, Sikkim was a remote independent Himalayan kingdom until it was annexed by India in 1975. It still has a hermitic flavor, with its Buddhist monasteries, prayer flags fluttering from pagoda-style houses, and red-robed lamas chanting mantras to the sound of drums and man-size horns, all against the breathtaking backdrop of the mighty Kanchenjunga range.

The Sikkimese are a friendly mix of Lepcha, Bhutanese, and Nepalese communities, and their land offers beautiful mountain scenery, good trekking, exotic varieties of fauna and flora. It boasts 600 species of orchid.

Bathed in bright Himalayan sunshine, the ornate Yiga Chhoiling monastery is worthy of a detour in Ghoom.

The best season to visit is from February to May and October to December.

To visit Sikkim you will need a permit. You can apply for one when you apply for your Indian visa, or alternatively you can apply later in India. In India, permits can be obtained at any of the Foreigners' Registration Offices in Delhi (1F Hans Bhavan, Tilak Bridge, New Delhi), Bombay (Office of the Commissioner of Police, Dadabhoy Naoroji Road), Calcutta (237 Acharya JC Bose Road), or Darjeeling (Laden-La Road).

Permits are valid for 15 days, but can be extended for a further 15 days. The permit allows you to visit Gangtok, Phodong, Rumtek, and Pemayangtse. For trips further afield, you will

need to apply for yet another permit for at the Gangtok Home Office, Government of Sikkim, Tashiling Secretariat.

WHAT TO SEE AND DO

In Gangtok, the **Tsuklakhang** is Sikkim's royal palace. You can admire the palace from the outside, but the only time visitors are generally allowed inside is during the Tibetan New Year celebrations, known as *losar* — late February or early March.

The **Institute of Tibetology** is dedicated to the study of Tibetan religion, but it also has an impressive collection of manuscripts and art works.

The **Orchid Sanctuary** is reputedly home to some 200 varieties of this much loved bloom, though you will need to be in Gangtok in April or May to see them at their best.

Other local Gangtok attractions include the **Cottage Industries Institute** and the **Enchey Monastery**, and **Deer Park**.

The main attraction out of town is the Karmapa ("black hat") monastery of **Rumtek**. It is an active monastery and there are usually monkish activities of some kind or another on a daily basis.

The Kagyupa ("red hat") monastery of **Phodong** is less impressive but still worth a visit.

The Tourist Information Center ((03592) 23425 in Gangtok bazaar can assist with tours, car rental, and guide hire. Good trekking firms in Gangtok are Sikkim Himalaya Adventure ((03592) 23638, 1 Supermarket Complex; Yak and Yeti Travels ((03592) 22714, Hotel Superview Himalchuli; and Mahayana Tours and Travels ((03592) 23885, 23 Supermarket Complex.

WHERE TO STAY

The best of Gangtok's hotels is the **Nor-Khill Hotel** ((03592) 25637 FAX (03592) 23187, Paljor Stadium Road. Formerly the royal guesthouse, it now features a gift shop, a multi-cuisine restaurant, a bar, direct-dial phones, and well-appointed rooms from around US$80.

The **Hotel Tashi Delek** ((03592) 22991 FAX (04592) 22362, Mahatma Gandhi Marg, with its tasteful Tibetan theme decor, has slightly cheaper rooms, but also take a look at the hotel's mountain-view suites before making budget your first priority.

For something cheaper and less ostentatious, the **Hotel Tibet** ((03592) 23468 FAX (03592) 26233, Paljor Stadium Road, is a superb choice. It has a bewildering pricing system, which seems to vary room by room, but essentially you can choose from small budget rooms (around US$12) or spacious, tasteful suites (US$30).

The **Denzong Inn** ((03592) 22692 FAX (03592) 22362 is recommended for budget travelers. The roof terrace here is particularly pleasant, and the rooms come equipped with bathrooms.

HOW TO GET THERE

The nearest airport to Sikkim is Bagdogra, which has regular connections with Indian Airlines and Jet Airways to New Delhi and Calcutta. It's a four-and-a-half-hour bus journey from Bagdogra to Gangtok, the Sikkim capital.

Bus connections from Gangtok to Darjeeling take around seven hours. The better way to do this trip is in a share jeep taxi, which covers the distance in a mere four or five hours.

THE NORTHEAST

The northeast is India's last frontier and regrettably is mostly forbidden to travelers hoping to explore this vast fertile region of rice paddies, mountains, and jungle wedged between Nepal and China to the north, Bangladesh to the west, and Burma to the east. Connected to the rest of Hindu-dominated India by a sliver of territory above Bangladesh, its inhabitants have cultural affinities more toward Southeast Asia than the subcontinent.

Nagaland and Tripura states and the territory of Mizoram are sensitive border zones and are off limits. But visitors who do not mind the lack of comforts and can tolerate some restrictions on their movements can, with prior planning, visit the states of Assam, Meghalaya, and Manipur. Traveling here yields magnificent scenery and exotic wildlife, and the experience of one of the

least known areas of the globe. The northeast is home to many tribal peoples, with many different cultures and languages, and an infectious love of festivals, music, and dance. Part of the Indian government's policy of banning outsiders stems from the government's fear that wholesale exposure to newcomers could spell doom for these unique cultures.

ENTRY FORMALITIES

Foreign tourists need a separate permit for each state. The permit may specify that only part of the state can be visited, and it may only be valid for seven days. If you are planning to visit this area, try to obtain all the necessary papers from your Indian mission before leaving home, as some states can require up to four months' notice. If booking the trip in India, apply for

permits at any Foreigners Registration Office. For the most up-to-date information, contact the Deputy Secretary, Ministry of Home Affairs, Government of New Delhi, (F-10), North Block, New Delhi 110001.

ASSAM

Assam may be synonymous with fine tea, but exotic wildlife reserves are its principal attraction, and it is home to India's rare one-horned rhinoceros that Marco Polo called the "hideous unicorn."

The state capital, **Guwahati,** lies on the banks of the great Brahmaputra, classified in Hindu cosmology as India's only male river. The city has

some grand Hindu temples but is primarily an airport gateway to the northeast and a jump-off spot for visiting the wildlife reserves.

The **Tourist Information Center (** (0361) 544475 is on Station Road. The best season to visit is January to March and November to December, and the Assamese mark the harvesting season with *bihus*, festivals celebrated by bathing in the Brahmaputra.

In town, visit the **Kamakshya Temple**, which honors the Hindu goddess Shakti, the essence of female energy, and the **Assam State Zoo and Museum**.

OPPOSITE: The magical spectacle of dawn unfolding over the lofty peaks of Mount Kanchenjunga above Darjeeling. ABOVE: The brass-studded interior of the Ghoom Monastery famous for its enshrined image of the Maitreya Buddha.

Chug 20 km (12 miles) up the Brahmaputra by steamer to visit the silk-weaving community at **Sualkashi**, where the rich Endi, Muga, and Pat silks are made.

In Guwahati, one of the best places to stay is the **Hotel Brahmaputra Ashok** ((0361) 541064, Mahatma Gandhi Road. Rates are mid-range.

The **Dynasty Hotel** ((0361) 510496 FAX (0361) 522112, on Lakhotia SS Road, has similar rates and is in a prime central location. It has two good restaurants, serving an interesting mixture of southern Indian, Mughalai, European, and Chinese, cuisine.

The **Raj Mahal Hotel** ((0361) 522478 FAX (0361) 521559, Assam Trunk Road, Paltan Bazaar, is a

fairly cheerless place, but it has good value air-conditioned rooms from US$15.

For true budget accommodation, try the **Hotel Kuber International** ((0361) 514353 FAX (0361) 541465, Hem Barua Road, Fancy Bazaar, which has basic air-conditioned rooms for under US$10 and air-cooled rooms with attached bathrooms for around US$5.

You can either fly there directly from Calcutta, or make the 24-hour journey by train. New Delhi is 40 hours away, even on the express *Assam Mail*.

ABOVE: Layered tea gardens at the Happy Valley Plantation are typical of the landscape of Darjeeling. OPPOSITE: Tibetan-style façade of Rumtek Monastery, 24 km from Gangtok in Sikkim.

WILDLIFE PARKS

Kaziranga Wildlife Sanctuary is located northeast of Guwahati on the banks of the Brahmaputra. Assam's premier nature park has some 430 sq km (158 sq miles) of steamy primeval forest, which can be explored by elephant, car, and boat. It is home to as many as 1,300 wild rhinos and large numbers of wild elephants and buffalo, along with swamp deer, hog deer, tigers, and Himalayan bears. The rhinos are watched closely by park guards, but poaching is rife, with astronomical amounts being fetched for powdered rhinocerous horn, which is prized as an aphrodisiac by the Chinese.

Kaziranga can be reached by air from Calcutta to **Jorhat**, 84 km (52 miles) from the park, or the 235-km (146-mile) trip from Guwahati can be made by bus or taxi through verdant rice paddies and thatched hut villages.

Accommodation can be arranged at numerous forest lodges by making reservations in advance through the Divisional Forest Officer, Sibasagar Division, PO Box Kaziranga.

Manas Wildlife Sanctuary is nestled in the Himalayan foothills bordering Bhutan, 175 km (108 miles) northwest of Guwahati. It has 270 sq km (104 sq miles) of riverine forest, which attracts many varieties of bird and animal life, and was where Project Tiger was launched.

Stay at the **Forestry Department Bungalow** or the **Manas Tourist Lodge**, which can be booked through the Division Forest Officer, Wildlife Division, Sarania, Guwahati.

MEGHALAYA

Only 100 km (62 miles) from Guwahati, Meghalaya's capital of **Shillong** is 1,495 m (4,900 ft) high, a pretty Raj-era hill station with landscape and climate that British colonialists called the "Scotland of the East." It is noted for its quaint cottages, waterfalls, pine groves, and flowers, as well as for the dances of the local Khasi, Jantia, and Garo tribes.

It has a year-round temperate climate, though it is wise to avoid the monsoon months — **Cherrapunji**, just 60 km (37 miles) away, was for a long time reported to be the wettest place on the planet, with an annual average rainfall of nearly 11.5 m (40 ft) and a record of 23 m (75 ft) in a single year! Nearby Mawsynram, it seems, is now the wettest place in the world.

Shillong is a regional melting pot, and **Bara** bazaar bustles with colorful costumed Nagas, Mizos, and Manipurs from the neighboring states. There are Naga-style woven rugs, silver jewelry, bamboo handicrafts, and rare butterflies compressed in glass to buy.

Arrive via Guwahati and stay at the modest and inexpensive **Hotel Pinewood Ashok** ((0364) 223116. In town, play golf at an 18-hole course, and go fishing on Umiam Lake, 16 km (10 miles) away.

MANIPUR

Bordering Nagaland, Mizoram, and Burma, **Manipur** is rich in tribal culture, wooded hills and lakes. The capital, **Imphal** is known for its spectacular Rash Lila festival every October/ November, which features Manipuri dance. Other highlights include the golden **Shri Govindaji** temple museum and the tribal village of **Moriang**, 37 km (23 miles) away. Woven goods and other local handicrafts can be bought in the large **Khwairamband** bazaar.

Stay at the inexpensive **Hotel Ranjit** ((0385) 220382 on Thangal Bazaar.

Most people approach Imphal from Calcutta, which has daily flights with Indian Airlines.

ORISSA

Tucked alongside the northeastern coastline off the Bay of Bengal, this green, semitropical state is one of India's undiscovered gems — it is said that if one knows Orissa, one knows India. To a visitor's eyes, this quiet, rural state seems barely industrialized at all. Its capital, Bhubaneswar is surrounded by intricate beehive-sculpted temples and tiny villages of ocher-red mud huts whose exteriors are traced with pretty rice-flour patterns. Its unspoiled pastoral landscape is a patchwork of palm and cashew plantations and pools covered with mauve water-hyacinths. It is a state empty of tourists, yet busy with ebony-skinned villagers dressed in loincloths, bullock-carts, and plumaged parakeets flickering through the trees.

Orissa has a rich culture, colorful festivals, and distinctive folk art. What's more, it has white-sanded beaches, a tantalizing local cuisine, and a growing network of luxury hotels — in other words, a perfect place just to switch off and relax. For generations, Bengalis have come here to escape the madness of Calcutta. It's only a matter of time before foreign tourists start flocking to Orissa too.

Above all else, Orissa is famous for its astonishing number of magnificent Hindu and Jain temples. The state is best visited with a view to exploring its compact "temple triangle."

Begin with the state capital, **Bhubaneswar**, a city of more than 500 temples, built during the heyday of Orissan Hindu culture between the seventh and fifteenth centuries, and including some of the most superb religious architecture the world has ever produced. It also has Jain and Buddhist caves, fine museums, and beautiful botanical and zoological gardens.

The seaside resort of **Puri** lies 61 km (38 miles) away, and is a vital pilgrimage center where life revolves around the famous temple of Lord Jagannath, where one of India's most extraordinary and spectacular festivals, the Rath Yatra, is held every summer.

Just 31 km (19 miles) along the coastal road from Puri, past paddy fields and villages, is **Konarak** with its magnificent, densely-carved Sun Temple, built in the shape of a huge chariot.

Recorded history documents Orissa's earliest ruler as Kalinga, a powerful warlord who lost his domain to Ashoka, the powerful Mauryan emperor, in 260 BC at a battlefield near modern-day Bhubaneswar. According to lore, Ashoka was so repulsed by the bloody carnage he witnessed here that he pledged to renounce warfare, taking up the Buddhist faith of nonviolence and compassion. To commemorate his epoch-making conversion, he left a famous set of rock edicts at Dhauli, eight kilometers (five miles) south of Bhubaneswar.

Buddhism rapidly declined however, and Jainism took root, reaching its zenith during the second century BC under the Chedi king, Khavravela, who encouraged monks to create the excavated cave temples of Udaigiri and Khandagiri, eight kilometers (five miles) west of Bhubaneswar. By the seventh century, Orissa had adopted Hinduism, like much of south India, and entered its golden age of temple architecture.

Under successive Hindu Kesari and Ganga kings, the temple for Lord Jagannath was built at Puri; the cult of Shiva, or Shaivism, inspired the creation of many temples in Bhubaneswar, and the worship of Surya, the Sun God, flourished,

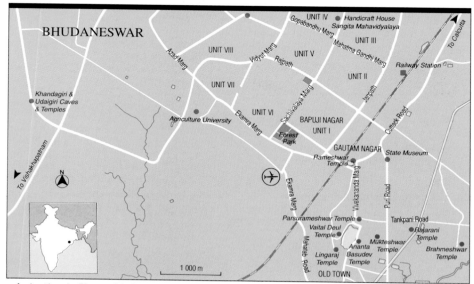

BHUDANESWAR

culminating in Konarak's famous Sun Temple, built during the thirteenth century.

Yet Muslim invasions from both the north and the southern kingdom of Golconda resulted in the overthrow of the Hindu rulers, not to mention the decimation of countless temples. Thereafter, Orissa was claimed successively by the Afghans, the Marathas, and the British in 1803.

Orissa is at its most steamy, lush, and beautiful just after the monsoon in October, and is comfortable to visit until February, when the mercury starts to climb. Puri is pleasant and popular as a bolt-hole from Calcutta all year round. Otherwise, it's well worth braving heat and human waves to witness the Rath Yatra festival held every June/July. Pre-monsoon breakers (May to June) produce the best coasters if you like body-surfing. Puri and Bhubaneswar make the best bases for day-long excursions — there are few hotels of any repute at Konarak.

BHUBANESWAR

In ancient times, Bhubaneswar was known as Ekamrakshetra, one of five religious cities in the ancient Kalingan state that now comprises modern-day Orissa. Locals will tell you that Lord Shiva makes his "holidays" here, ranking it second only to Varanasi as his favorite "resort." Here in Bhubaneswar, Shiva is known as Tribuhuvaneswara or "Lord of the Three Worlds," from which the city derives its name.

In its heyday, between the seventh and the fifteenth centuries, Bhubaneswar was a magnetic and powerful pilgrimage center. More than 7000 sandstone temples once fringed its sacred Bindusagar "Ocean Drop," tank, said to contain

water from every holy stream, river, and pool in India, and hence a great place for washing away sins. All but 500 or so were destroyed during the Mughal conquest of the sixteenth century. Among the survivors are many perfectly preserved examples of the profusely carved Orissan style of temple architecture.

Modern Bhubaneswar is delightfully rural for a state capital that administers the affairs of 25 million Orissans—largely free of pollution, traffic and highrise buildings. Its hallowed temples are concentrated in the old town, very exotic with its cobbled alleys, palm groves, and frangipani trees dotted around the khaki-colored Bindusagar Tank, where local lads go spear-fishing for sacred fish.

General Information

In town, use taxis, auto-rickshaws, or buses. Go temple-hopping by cycle-rickshaw; these are often wired up with black sun-umbrellas. Bicycles can be hired easily through any hotel, perfect for a day's excursion.

The Orissa Tourism Development Corporation (OTDC) **Tourist Information Center ℂ** (0674) 50099, Jayadev Marg, near Pantha Niwas Tourist Bungalow runs useful sightseeing tours. The city tour (8:45 AM to 6 PM daily, except Monday) costs US$2, and covers Bhubaneswar's major temples, the Udaigiri and Khandagiri caves, Nandankanan Park, and Dhauli. There's also a regular Puri/Konarak tour (9 AM to 6 PM). Both have good guides and leave from the Pantha Niwas Tourist Bungalow. You can also hire trained guides and private cars for sightseeing here. Expect to pay about US$25 for a round trip from Bhubaneswar to Puri and Konarak, or US$15 one way.

Otherwise, frequent local buses make the one-and-a-half-hour journey to Puri, leaving from the main bus station. Buses to Konarak can be irregular, and it's wise to check departures with the tourist office before planning your day. From Puri to Konarak, regular minibuses take passengers on a "fill-her-up" basis for the 35-minute, 30-km (18.8-mile) ride. If you take an early morning bus from Puri and an afternoon bus back (or on to Bhubaneswar), you'll have ample time to see the Sun Temple.

What to See and Do

Bhubaneswar's famous temples are best covered at your own leisurely pace, preferably in the quiet

cool of early morning. By concentrating on a cluster of impeccably preserved temples, you will be taken on a curator's walk though five centuries of temple architecture, able to see style and form developing, expanding and refining before your eyes.

Orissan temple design was governed by mathematical formulae, even down to the most seemingly innocuous detail. All followed an essential structure consisting of an entrance porch (*jagamohan*) and an inner sanctum for the image of the deity (*deul*), above which a ribbed conical tower (*shikara*) rises. Endless additions could be incorporated — sub-shrines, halls where offerings could be made, and dancing halls for the ritualized dance that later blossomed into the lithe, exotic *Odissi* style. The exterior was always lavishly carved with geometrical designs, flowers, animals, human and mythological figures, and gods. In the earlier, squat shrines,

these carvings are simple storytelling devices, but in the later extravagant, tapering temples, the stone comes alive with sharp precision, and provocative female figures appear, at their most poutingly playful at the Rajarani and Brahmeshwar temples and at the Sun Temple at Konarak, where scrutiny of close-up detail reveals some highly athletic dalliances.

Bhubaneswar's eleventh-century **Lingaraj Temple**, dedicated to Shiva as Lord Lingaraj, or "Lord of the Universe," is considered the pinnacle of Orissan architecture, but it's so sacred to Hindus that "heathens" aren't allowed inside and instead are restricted to peering at it from a platform (erected for Lord Curzon) outside the compound

wall. Binoculars are useful; you'll see the temple's ornately carved 46-m (150-ft)-high spire, covered with sculpted lions crushing elephants, said to symbolize the reemergence of Hinduism over Buddhism. There's little else for foreigners to look at except elderly temple priests napping under a giant Banyan tree.

The temple is dedicated to Lord Shiva, and the granite *lingam* which represents him is dutifully lathered each day with water, milk, and *bhang* (hashish). Amazingly, the entire walled compound contains some 50 small shrines, each of importance to the gift-bearing devotees. Thousands of pilgrims gather here for the major Shivrati festival in February / March, holding candles on the night of the full moon, as the Lingaraj deity is ritually bathed in the nearby Bindusagar tank to mark the anniversary of his birth.

Skirting the eastern side of Bindusagar is a cluster of about 20 smaller temples. Look especially for the small, decorative **Sisneswar Temple** and the two-story **Vaital Deul Temple**, both dating from the eighth century, the latter thought to be a tantric shrine where humans were once sacrificed for the presiding eight-armed deity, Kapalini, depicted here wearing garlands of skulls and reclining on a corpse. It's one of the few non-Shiva temples in Bhubaneswar, being dedicated to the Goddess Durga.

At the top of Tankpani Road, you'll find the **Parsurameshwar Temple** (seventh century), said to be the home of Ganesha's brother, Parsurameshwar (Muruga). It's the best preserved of all Bhubaneswar's most ancient temples, and has finely detailed bas-reliefs of elephant and horse processions.

Close by is the **Mukteshwar Temple** (ninth century), with its exquisite carved lotus entrance canopy, each petal bearing an image of a deity. Within its enclosure are many mango and jackfruit trees, plus a pint-sized sacred tank, where childless women bathe on the full moon of March / April to become fertile.

Continuing along Tankpani Road, look out for the **Rajarani Temple** (twelfth century), set in pretty gardens. It is a "love temple," covered with coyly erotic carvings of women and couples, built by a Rajah for his wife, the Rani — hence the name. Once the Rajah was interred within, the temple became a mausoleum and was no longer used for worship.

Lastly, the **Brahmeshwar Temple** (eleventh century) lies on the outskirts of the old city. It's actually a complex of shrines, notable for its elaborate exterior carvings, particularly its dancing girls, and higher up, the Orissan lion, which was hunted to extinction during the British Raj.

If you care to take a look, just across the field from the Brahmeshwar Temple are the part-excavated ruins of **Sisupalgarh**, thought to be the remains of the city founded by Ashoka, occupied from the third century BC to the fourth century AD.

In town, also visit the **Orissa State Museum**, opposite the Kalinga Ashok for its rich collection relating to Orissa's history, culture, architecture and many tribal people, open 10 AM to 5 PM every day except Monday.

The Tribal Research Bureau here is filled with sheaves of yellowing theses on Orissa's 62 distinct tribal groups of aboriginal people, whose ancestors existed before the Aryan invasion of India. These "hunter-gatherers" live according to their own customs in the mountain ridges of central Orissa. Among the better known are the Kondhs, the bugbear of British missionaries for their reluctance to give up their habit of human sacrifice — today slaughter is mostly confined to roosters, goats, and bullocks. Then there are the Bondas, famous in India for their licentious attitude to premarital sex, and the fact that their young women choose their husbands on the basis of their sexual skills. Other major tribes are the Juangs, the Santals, the Parajas, the Koyas, and the Godabas.

Shopping

Orissa was traditionally known as "Utkal," or "Land of Art" for its talented communities of sculptors, painters, potters, weavers, and embroiderers whose skills created her exquisite temple complexes and kept her rulers beautifully garbed — today these arts are kept alive in Orissa's timeless villages.

By far the most popular tourist purchase is Orissa's famous colorful patchwork appliqué, fashioned into sun umbrellas, hanging lanterns, canopies, and cushions, and her silk and cotton handloomed *ikat* design textiles. Other good buys include the animal motif papier-mâché masks originally used for epic play; *patachitra* paintings on muslin cloth; etched palm-leaf manuscripts, silver filigree jewelry, soapstone and wood carvings, brass and bell metal work, and shellcraft. At Puri you can buy little carved replicas of Lord Jagannath and his brother and sister.

In Bhubaneswar the best places to shop are the **Utkalika Handicrafts Emporium** and the **Handloom Cooperative Society**, both in the Market Building halfway up Rajpath. These give an overview of contemporary Orissan crafts, with everything sold at fixed prices. They can also arrange visits to see skilled craftsmen at work.

Throughout the state, you'll find lanes, neighborhoods and sometimes, entire villages devoted to one particular craft. Wander into any of these areas, and you'll be welcome to watch the work in progress, meet the family and, if you like, make a purchase.

OPPOSITE: Youthful Buddhist monks in Sikkim.
ABOVE: Gangtok's bustling marketplace.

All of this commercial activity comes to a head in **Pipli**, 20 km (12.5 miles) en route from Bhubaneswar to Puri, where the main street consists entirely of stalls aimed at passing tourists. The specialty here is colorful appliqué work, often utilizing decorative motifs of animals, birds, and flowers. Much of it has become rather mass-produced, although there are still elderly artists who remember how to make the delicate and elaborate work of the 1800s.

Other places to visit include the bell-metal village of **Belakati**, only nine kilometers (five and a half miles) from Bhubaneswar; the palm-etcher's village of **Ragurajpur**, which is just outside Puri; and the beautiful fresco-covered

houses of **Pathuria Sahi** or "Stone Carver's Lane" in Puri itself.

In the major bazaar areas, such as that around the Jagannath Temple in Puri, bargaining is expected, and whittling down prices is part of the fun, carried out with bantering good humor. By contrast, the individual artists working from their homes tend to quote fair prices for their work — exceedingly low in relation to the painstaking time, skill, and talent that has gone into its making.

Out of Town

Either take the OTDC tour or hire a taxi for the afternoon to round off Bhubaneswar's sights.

Some eight kilometers (five miles) into the surrounding countryside lie the twin hills of **Udaigiri** and **Khandagiri**, honeycombed with ancient Jain and Buddhist caves. Scattered at various levels, they were hollowed out by monks

during the reign of Khavravela, the Kalinga emperor during the second century BC. Udaigiri has 44 caves, many extensively carved. The most historically interesting is the Hathi Gumpha or Elephant Cave, which contains one of India's most important extant Pali scripts — a detailed record of Khavravela's religious, military and civil accomplishments. Khandagiri has 19 caves, and is crowned by a series of Jain temples.

Ashoka's famous **Dhauli Edicts** are about eight kilometers (five miles) south of Bhubaneswar, carved on a giant rock overlooking the plain below where the climactic Kalinga battle took place. The 13 inscriptions are still remarkably legible after 2000 years. The elephant carved out of the rock above symbolizes Buddha and is the earliest known sculpture in Orissa. The hill is topped by the modern white Shanti Stupa, or Peace Pagoda, built by Japanese Buddhists and visible for miles and notable for its marked resemblance to a UFO, with its five antennae-like "umbrella" representing the Buddhist virtues of faith, hope, compassion, forgiveness, and nonviolence.

The extensive **Nandankanan Park**, 20 km (12.5 miles) away, is a scenic wildlife and botanical garden, unique as the only place where the rare white tiger has ever been bred in captivity. It's India's largest Lion Safari Park, measuring over 20 hectares (50 acres) and is also home to rhinos, monkeys, gharials (a species of fish-eating crocodile), pelicans, pythons, brown bear, and India's rare white crocodile.

Buses run visitors out on regular "wildlife patrols." There are pleasant facilities at the Tourist Cottages or Forest Rest House. It's open 7 AM to 6 PM during April to September, and 7:30 AM to 5 PM, September to March. Local buses ply there every hour from Bhubaneswar.

Where to Stay

The **Hotel Oberoi Bhubaneswar** ((0674) 440890 FAX (0674) 440898, Nayapalli, offers luxury accommodation at remarkably reasonable rates. One of India's most beautiful hotels, its distinctive, temple-inspired design features polished sandstone, Orissan decor and brass lamps throughout, with a lovely swimming pool and tennis courts set in palm-dotted landscaped gardens. A choice of restaurants offers excellent food, ranging from local specialties to Mughalai, Western, and Chinese cuisine. Facilities include a health club, a shopping arcade, a travel desk, and a beauty salon with car rental for temple-hopping. It's located seven kilometers (just over four miles) from the capital. There's a courtesy shuttle service between the airport and the hotel.

Within the city center, choose from several moderately priced hotels, all close to the temples. The best is the **New Kennilworth Hotel** ((0674) 433600 FAX (0674) 433351, at Gautam Nagar, which has comfortably furnished rooms, efficient staff, good restaurants, and a travel desk. Breakfast at their coffee shop — delicious yogurt, fresh fruit, toast, eggs, and coffee — is astoundingly good at only US$1.50.

Around the corner, the ITDC-run **Kalinga Ashok** ((0674) 431055 FAX (0674) 507524, is quite stylish, and its useful facilities include a bank, several restaurants, a travel agency, a swimming pool, and a doctor. The **Hotel Swosti** ((0674) 504178 FAX (0674) 507524, 103 Janpath, is more expensive and has similar facilities and standards.

Hotel Prachi ((0674) 402366 FAX (0674) 403287, farther along Janpath, is functional and clean, with good food, a swimming pool, and tennis courts.

the local caramel custard, *chena purd patha* (cheese-burnt-sweet) or *khiri*, rice cooked with milk, sugar, cardamom, and cashew nuts.

Other delicious specialties to look out for are *dahi maccha*, fish cooked with curd and coriander; *saag bhaja*, fried spinach; and *khajun khata*, an unusual combination of tomato cooked with dates. Local curd is devastatingly rich and creamy — perfect with fresh fruit for breakfast.

A pleasant ride north of town, the **Hotel Oberoi** offers the most stylish dining experience — its **Pushpaneri** restaurant has exceptional Orissan and Indian fare (both vegetarian and non-vegetarian) for around US$10 per head. You'll also dine well at slightly cheaper prices at the **Hotel**

Rates start at around US$30. The state-run **Pantha Niwas Tourist Bungalow** ((0674) 432515 is a good budget choice located close to the temples on Lewis Road. Each room comes with fans, mosquito net, and shower. It's right next door to the tourist office and is the departure point for sightseeing tours. Cheaper again, the big, well-kept **Bhubaneswar Hotel** ((0674) 416977, directly behind the railway station, is popular with backpackers.

Where to Eat

Orissa's cuisine is similar to that of Bengal — liberal quantities of fresh seafood (lobster, prawns, crab, and fish), traditionally cooked with coconut milk or curd and given zing with pinches of *fenugreek* and mustard seeds. Order an Orissan *thali* for starters — fluffy white rice, *bekti* or *rui* fish, vegetable dishes including the staple green, *kara saag* (spinach), delicate *puris*, rounded off with

Swosti and the **Hotel Kalinga Ashok**, both of which offer incredibly good value lunchtime Orissan *thalis*, as well as a diverse range of Indian, continental, and Chinese food.

Few restaurants are worth visiting outside the hotels. Try **East and West**, which is opposite the New Kennilworth, for palatable Chinese fare.

How to Get There

You can fly to Bhubaneswar from Calcutta and Delhi, and there are direct flights from Madras, Hyderabad, and Varanasi.

It can be more fun to make the journey by overnight train — at least one way. Bhubaneswar

OPPOSITE: Detail of an exquisitely ornate frieze adorning the Rajarani Temple in Bhubaneswar. ABOVE: Post-monsoon ablutions at the Mukteshwar Temple in Bhubaneswar.

is on the main Calcutta to Madras railway line so there are plenty of trains to Bhubaneswar, as well as trains terminating at Puri. From Calcutta, take the "superfast" overnight *Coromandel Express* to Bhubaneswar (7 hours) or the slower pilgrim-packed *Howrah-Puri Express* (12 hours). Bhubaneswar also has direct rail links with Hyderabad, Delhi, and Bombay.

PURI

Fringed by sand dunes and casuarina trees, Puri is one of India's four holiest places, a goal for countless pilgrims, from ash-smeared fakirs to Bombay film-stars. It's also a popular seaside resort with a rambling country-club style hotel, dilapidated Bengali villas, and conical-capped lifeguards.

Puri is home to the "Formless One," Lord century Jagannath Temple, the focus of this atmospheric, worship-obsessed town. He is an incarnation of Lord Krishna, and one of the reasons for his popularity is that all castes are equal before him.

Millions have dropped to their knees before his image — a white-faced, legless, brightly-painted wooden idol with glaring eyes. Stumpy arms emerge from his forehead, which glitters with a large diamond. He shares the temple with his black-faced brother Balaram, and his yellow-faced sister Subhadra. He commands more than six thousand "servants" who dedicate their lives to him, either as priests, temple wardens, or pilgrim guides, altogether forming a complex hierarchy of 37 orders and 97 classes. Like an infant emperor, Lord Jagannath has his teeth brushed, his face anointed, his fine clothes changed, his body given a fragrant sandalwood-scented bath and laid out for siesta. Meals are placed before him and later removed — untouched but sanctified. None of these age-old ceremonies may be witnessed by a non-Hindu, for the temple is a forbidden citadel to outsiders.

Puri's religious fervor reaches a spectacular pitch during the **Rath Yatra**, the "Cart Festival," held during June and July. To celebrate Krishna's journey from Gokul to Mathura, the images of Lord Jagannath and his siblings are hauled through Puri on vast *rathas* (chariots) to the nearby Gundicha Mandir (garden house) for their annual week's vacation, before being dragged back home.

Puri becomes massed with hundreds of thousands of delirious, swaying humans, riveted by the spectacle of three huge wooden chariots as large as houses and surmounted by decorated pavilions in which the three gods sit on brocade cushions for their mile-long journey. The largest is Jagannath: some 14 m (45 ft) high, 11 m (35 ft) square and supported by 16 wheels, each 2.1 m (seven feet) tall — adding the word Juggernaut to the English language.

Ritual decrees that each wagon is pulled by 4,200 men girdled with thick rope and accompanied by musicians bashing cymbals, drums, and horns in wild abandon. People press forward, throwing rice, marigolds, and coconut shards for blessings, and cases of frenzied self-sacrifice beneath the wheels are not unknown. After delivering the gods back home, the chariots are broken up and the discarded timbers are sold as sacred relics.

What to See and Do

Puri's endless white sand beach is good for long strolls, fresh air, swims, and watching sunrises, sunsets and local fishermen dressed in loincloths and conical hats repairing nets and putting out to sea in their catamarans. Local urchins tag along, selling shells, cloth, and semiprecious gems. Pilgrims take a holy dip, staggering and giggling in the surf getting their clothes drenched, believing that its extremely salty waters will, in the words of a local guide, "bring broadness of mind and do away with all meanness."

Tourists preparing to don skimpy swimsuits will soon discover that sunbathing is considered highly eccentric in Orissa — what goes in Goa does not "go" here. The sight of partially exposed flesh causes local fishermen to stampede across the sands, rapt at having cornered a rare Westerner on their shores. You'll be peppered with friendly invitations to explore their village, become a star guest at a seafood sizzle-up on the sands, or spend a day going fishing with them. It's certainly fascinating to watch their catamarans being constructed on the sands, made from solid tree trunks, split longitudinally and bound together. When they're not being used, they're untied and the planks laid out on the beach to dry out, like giant matchsticks.

Strong currents fringe the shoreline, resulting in Puri's eccentric corps of elderly "lifeguards," actually retired fishermen, easily recognized by their wickerwork hats. They'll lead you down to surf with heroic displays of chivalry, then "guard" your clothes for a few rupees. One Dutch traveler related that he was snatched by a current out to sea and started shouting for help, only to see the "lifeguard" wave encouragingly from the shore, while his traveling companions had to swim out to rescue him!

Unfortunately, locals seem to use much of their otherwise glorious beach as a public latrine — a good reason for escaping to the more pristine (and hygienic) sands at Gopalpur-on-Sea, further south.

All sandy tracks in Puri lead to its broad central **Baradand**, or **Grand Road**, which runs from the Jagannath Temple to the Gundicha Mandir. It's best to visit at sunset, when gas lamps and candles form a flickering, action-packed strip of jostling pilgrims, prospecting beggars, bullock carts, cycle-rickshaws, and street stalls selling trinkets, vegetarian snacks, and religious paraphernalia.

The magnificent **Jagannath Temple** stands at the center, built during the twelfth century by the Kalingan king Chodaganga. It is Orissa's tallest temple, and its 65 m high (212 ft) spire is a landmark for miles around. Each of its four gates has an animal theme: horse (south), elephant (north), tiger (west), and lion (east). Pilgrims enter by the Lion Gate to pay respects to Lord Jagannath, laden with gifts of coconuts and flowers. Devout women emerge bald-headed, having offered their shining tresses as a symbol of sacrifice. In front of the main entrance is a beautiful pillar, uprooted from the Sun Temple at Konarak.

Non-Hindus aren't allowed inside, but can peer over the walls on a nearby viewing platform on the roof of the Raghunandan Library. A sign inside warns "Be Aware of Monkeys" and you are given a big stick, just in case. From here you'll get a clear view all the way down to the Gundicha Mandir, Lord Jagannath's summer temple. On the way down, ask to see the library's good collection of antique Pali manuscripts — you'll be asked for a donation in any case, so you might as well.

Where to Stay

One of the best places to stay in Puri is the **Mayfair Beach Resort** ((06752) 24041 FAX (06752) 24242, Chakratirtha Road, a tasteful beachside place with restaurants and a swimming pool. Room rates are very reasonable, in the US$40 to US$60 range.

The **Toshali Sands Resort** ((06752) 23571 FAX (06752) 23899, Konark, Marine Drive, is a better class of resort, but has a remote location and is far from the beach. It has a restaurant, bar, swimming pool, health facilities, tennis and badminton, and more.

The **South Eastern Railway Hotel** ((06752) 22063 is caught in a pre-World War I timewarp and is a must for Raj-fiends. Set in a manicured garden on the sand's edge, it was originally built as the grand residence of one Lady Ashworth, but was taken over by the Bengal Nagpur Railway and opened as a hotel in 1925. It's now run by the South Eastern Railway, but still referred to as the "BNR."

Rooms are kept spotless, with sand whisked out twice a day, and have quaint four-posters, mosquito nets, porcelain baths, sea-facing shuttered windows and adjoining verandahs. Some are grander than others and priced accordingly. Convalescent bath-chairs are set for taking "bed tea" and "after tea," delivered by hotel "boys" wearing cummerbunds and BNR hats with big brass buttons. Huge quantities of Raj-era food are served downstairs in the dining room; included in the room rates but open to nonresidents. Signs

in the hallway request silence during siesta hours. Facilities include billiards, table tennis, a bar, and a library. The manager is friendly and helpful, particularly for travel arrangements. As you open your shutters in the morning, lifeguards wave hopefully from the gate, cooing, "*Sahib*, Madam, beach is ready and waiting!"

If all that Raj-era to-do is not your thing, and you'd prefer an economical and modern resort by the sea, the **Hans Coco Palms** ((06752) 22638 FAX (06752) 23165 is recommended. It has simple but comfortable rooms with balconies overlooking the sea, a swimming pool, a restaurant, and a bar. The **Pantha Niwas Tourist Bungalow**, ((06752) 22562 has clean comfortable rooms, with an

attached restaurant for good mealtime *thalis*. Rates get a little over US$10 for best rooms.

Puri's budget guesthouse enclave lies east of the South Eastern Railway Hotel. The best idea is to take a stroll around and check out the rooms personally, but you may want to take a special look at the recommended **Z Hotel** ((06752) 22554 and the **Hotel Shankar International** ((06752) 23637, both of which have a range of rooms that cost from next to nothing to around US$10 (usually with a bathroom, balcony, and sea views).

How to Get There

The nearest transport hub is Bhubaneswar, which is just an hour away by minibus.

A white-clad widow clasps her hands and gazes with fretful adoration at a garish painted idol before the commencement of the Rath Yatra or Car festival in Puri.

ALONG THE COAST

If you're looking for a good place to get away from it all, you should head for **Gopalpur-on-Sea**, around three hours drive south of Puri. Be warned, however, unless you are staying at the Oberoi Palm Beach Hotel, the beach is not all that great. It is nevertheless a relatively good base for an excursion to the lovely **Chilka Lake**, which is on the coast en-route to Puri. Chilka is a beautiful island-dotted bird sanctuary best seen at sunrise by taking a boat out from Balligan or Rambha.

The **Oberoi Palm Beach Hotel** ((0680) 282021 FAX (0680) 282300, is a charming British country house-style resort just 100 m (109 yards) from a delightfully secluded stretch of private beach. The Oberoi has excellent facilities, including several good restaurants, reasonably priced car rental, and badminton and tennis courts. Arrangements can also be made for horseback riding, sailing, or even fishing.

Gopalpur-on-Sea is 172 km (107 miles) from Bhubaneswar and 16 km (10 miles) from the Berhampur railway station, which links with Bhubaneswar and Calcutta.

Four faces of devotion at Puri's Rath Yatra. Clockwise from ABOVE LEFT: Fierce gaze from a shaven-headed woman, one of thousands, has dedicated her locks to Lord Jagganath; A "servant" of Lord Jagganath bears a totemic staff in the image of his master; Ash-smeared *sadhu* or holy man; A Shaivite or follower of Lord Shiva, his forehead smeared with the phallic symbol of the lingam.

KONARAK

The thirteenth-century **Sun Temple** stands on a desolate stretch of wind-flung sand, an awesome relic of Konarak's ancient legacy as a busy center of Orissan culture and commerce. This unique ruin was conceived as a chariot to pull the Sun God, Surya, across the heavens. Steps ascend to the main entrance, flanked by seven gigantic straining horses, representing the seven colors of the prism. Around

its base are 24 huge wheels, each signifying the changing cycle of the sun. The entire structure is covered with carvings, sculptures, figures, and bas-reliefs. It was designed so that the sun's first rays strike the dancing hall first, then the hall of audience, and finally the head of the Sun God in the main temple, harnessing its energy and life-force.

According to popular lore, it was here that the cult of sun-worship began some 5,000 years ago. The legend relates that Krishna, irritated by a disrespectful son-in-law, Samba, cursed him with leprosy, and advised him to do penance for the sun-god Surya for 12 years. Once cured of his disease, Samba erected a small temple to Surya — said to be buried beneath the present temple.

The Sun Temple was commissioned by King Narasimha of the Ganga dynasty to commemorate his victorious expansion into Bengal, and as a symbol of Hindu might against the encroaching Muslims. It took 1,200 masons and sculptors, and 12,000 laborers, 12 years to complete it, between 1243 and 1255. The main temple has fallen into ruins, yet a remaining audience hall is proof of the colossal scale on which the temple was executed. Every aspect of contemporary life was recorded in its painstaking carvings, from courtly procedures like law, administration, civic life, and war to erotic imagery of human love as marvelous and detailed as those seen at Khajuraho.

Originally the temple had a huge spire, soaring to 70 m (277 ft), and was nicknamed the "Black Pagoda" by early mariners navigating their passage to Calcutta, apparently due to the superstition that the temple's iron filings magnetically pulled unwary ships to the shore.

Outside the temple grounds, there's a small but interesting **museum** which houses excavated sculptures — whole and fragmented. It's open 10 AM to 5 PM, closed on Fridays.

Konarak's deserted, beautiful beach may tempt some travelers to stay on. The **Tourist Bungalow** ((06758) 35831 is next to the temple, has clean rooms — some with air-conditioning — all with attached baths.

It's a short bus journey of just one hour from Puri to Konarak.

ANDAMAN AND NICOBAR ISLANDS

This chain of 321 virgin tropical islands stretches across the eastern Bay of Bengal, midway between India and the tip of Sumatra. Only 38 of the islands are inhabited. The archipelago possesses a smoldering primitive beauty, with dense forests woven with canopies of vines and deserted white sand beaches lapped by clear turquoise waters. This exotic, unspoiled landscape hardly feels part of India at all.

Port Blair, the Andaman' capital, is tranquil and rustic, with wooden houses smothered in bougainvillea, scenic views across to nearby islands, and an unpolluted wharf with old ships and cackling seagulls.

There is still much that is pristine on the archipelago, which is home to six aboriginal tribal groups, each with unique customs, languages, and beliefs, some little changed since the Paleolithic age. Many of these indigenous tribes are hostile toward intruders, be they government officials carrying presents of plastic buckets, watches, or chocolates, or gaping tourists fumbling for their cameras.

Islands inhabited by these tribes are now off limits to casual visitors. Nevertheless, only the xenophobic and handsome Sentinelese, who live on North Sentinel Island, have remained completely isolated from the world, repulsing all intruders with their expertly hurled two-meter (six-and-a-half-foot) poisoned arrows.

The Greater Andamese from the north, the Jarawas from the Middle Andamans, and the Nicobarese and Shompens from the Nicobar Islands would simply prefer to be left alone. Then there are others, like the naked, body-painted Onges from South Andaman, a tribe of hunters and gatherers, have become quite blasé about visits from anthropologists and curious onlookers, and will often eagerly swap their tasseled G-strings for polyester nighties or T-shirts, and their freshly caught fish for tins of baked beans.

The powerful Marathas from central India first annexed the Andaman and Nicobar islands in the late seventeenth century as a convenient base for plundering British, Dutch, and Portuguese merchant ships. After several attempts, the British finally ousted the Marathas in the nineteenth century and established a penal colony at Port Blair in the aftermath of the 1857 Indian Mutiny, earning the archipelago the notorious sobriquet "kala pani", or "water of death". During World War II, the Andamans were the only part of India to be occupied by the Japanese, who between 1942 and 1945 massacred large numbers of prisoners and local tribespeople.

Port Blair's main industry is the export of timber, and vast areas of its teak, mahogany, and rosewood forests have been razed. The capital has a mixed community of mainland Indians and Burmese, and makes a perfect base for exploring the nearby coral reefs.

Entry Formalities

Foreigners can visit only the Andaman Islands, and a permit is required. If you are flying, this is granted as a matter of course on arrival at Port Blair. It is valid for 30 days. Travelers arriving by sea are required to obtain a permit before purchasing their ticket. This can be arranged at the Foreigners' Registration Offices in either Calcutta, 237 Acharya JC Bose Road; or in Madras, Shastri Bhavan Annex, 26 Haddows Road; or at your Indian embassy when you apply for an Indian visa. After arriving by ship, you are required to report to the superintendent of police in Port Blair.

A permit for the Andaman islands allows you to visit South Andaman, Middle Andaman, Little Andaman, North Passage, Neil, Havelock, Bharatang, and Long islands.

When to Go

The Andamans are at their most idyllic between mid-November and mid-May, when the weather is generally warm with cooling sea breezes. Port Blair's "off" season coincides with the monsoon period (late May to early October), when it has a steamy, primeval beauty, but snorkeling and scuba diving become impossible.

What to See and Do

What most people have in mind when they visit the Andamans Islands is a week or two of idyllic leisure, hopping from one secluded oyster-shell bay to another, basking in clear waters, and exploring the underwater enchantment of colorful coral reefs. But Port Blair has its own charm, and it's worth spending a day or two making a relaxed bicycle tour of its sights.

Start with the **Cellular Jail**, the eerie edifice constructed by the British in 1906 and used to incarcerate many hundreds of "dangerous" Indian political prisoners until 1938. Set on the sea coast of Atlanta Point, it resembles a vast wheel, with the central watchtower joined by seven triple-storied wings, all pocketed with hundreds of tiny crypt-like cells where prisoners were kept in solitary confinement. For the British, it was a highly effective way of paralyzing the Independence movement: elite and literate freedom fighters shared their plight of isolation, hard labor, and brutal torture with common criminals, and many were driven to insanity and suicide.

But by far the worst atrocities took place during the Japanese occupation of Port Blair, from

1942 to 1945, when there were mass executions of prisoners as well as villagers suspected of being spies for the Allied forces.

The prison grounds are open from 9 AM to noon and 2 PM to 5 PM every day. A sound-and-light show runs daily except Sunday at 7 PM. There are several informative booklets for sale at the entrance booth.

Winding down the road to Aberdeen Jetty you'll find the **Marine Museum**, a dusty chamber which has over 350 pickled exhibits of different species, charts of tropical fish, shells, coral, and an exotic collection of turtle eggs. Come here before you start scuba diving so you'll recognize what lurks beneath the Andamans' ocean waves. The museum is open from 8:30 AM to 12:30 PM and from 1:30 PM to 4 PM, but is closed on Sundays and public holidays.

It's a hilly climb through Aberdeen Bazaar up to the **Anthropological Museum**, which has a fascinating collection of photographs and descriptions of the Andaman and Nicobar tribal

OPPOSITE: Seething crowds and enough medieval pageantry to rival a Cecil B. de Mille epic at the Rath Yatra. ABOVE: Frenzied devotees hurl themselves on a fragment of a painted wooden *rath* or chariot.

groups, and displays of ceremonial costumes and objects, such as crab claw pipes, flax tassel G-strings, leaf-palm umbrellas, human mandible necklaces, and nautilus shell cups. But there is frustratingly little solid information, and if you wish to know more about the region's tribal people, try to strike up a conversation with the head researcher in residence, Mr. Baha. The museum is open from 9 AM to noon and again from 1 PM to 4 PM; it is closed Saturdays and public holidays.

From here, ask for directions to the nearby **Cottage Industries Emporium**, which sells delicate shell jewelry, shell-lamps, and a wide range of local handicrafts. It's open 8:15 AM to

studded Bristol boats that meander around the harbor, stopping at places of interest, and return just as sunset casts a molten light over the landscape.

First stop is at the **Bamboo Jetty Market**, where excited islanders in folded-up *dhotis* and large lapels haggle passionately for fish, jackfruit, and Tupperware. The most interesting stop on this trip is at **Viper Island**. The first prison for chain-gang convicts in British India was built here in 1867; later it was used for female prisoners. Ironically, the view from the gallows — all that remains of the prison — is one of incomparable loveliness. The boat leaves from the end of the Phoenix Bay dockyard at 3 PM.

12:30 PM, and from 1 PM to 4:45 PM, except during the weekend.

Halfway down the road leading to Chatham Wharf is Port Blair's well-kept **Mini Zoo** which houses an array of indigenous plumed birds, monitor lizards, wild boars, macaque monkeys, bears, and deer. There's also a crocodile breeding farm and a captivating Painted Stork, as poised and eccentric as an old count in a multicolored tuxedo. It's open from 7 AM to noon and from 1 PM to 5 PM, and is closed on Mondays. The two last stops are eccentric Port Blair tourist attractions: the gigantic Victorian-era **Chatham Saw Mill** and the **Wimco Match Factory**, where most of India's matchsticks are made.

HARBOR CRUISES

The tourist office employs old khaki-clad sailors to run afternoon cruises on quaint, brass-

There's also an early morning cruise from the same jetty across to **Ross Island**, which was once a well-fortified cantonment from which the British could survey their penal settlement in style, well protected from convicts and naked "heathen" tribespeople.

Established in 1858, Ross Island had a splendid Georgian-style Residency, a combined officers' mess and club, colonial bungalows, a church and graveyard, numerous administrative offices, and even a printing press and swimming pool. Its residents dressed formally for dinner, as though they were dining in a Pall Mall club. Lady Duff Cooper once spent a night here while fleeing Singapore for England, and thought it very "select."

Banyan trees now have the crumbling settlement in a macabre embrace that resembles flesh grafted onto stone. Spotted deer and peacocks run wild and take shelter in the deserted buildings.

Ferries leave for the island from Phoenix Bay Jetty approximately every two hours from 8:30 AM until 2 PM.

On the west coast, and accessible from Port Blair by bus, lies **Wandoor Beach** with secluded clear waters and rich coral reefs. It's a convenient base for exploring nearby **Jolly Buoy** and **Red Skin** islands.

BEACH PARADISE AND CORAL REEFS

The easiest way to arrange a visit to the outer islands is to contact either Island Travels ((03192) 21358, Aberdeen Bazaar, their branch at the Bay Island Hotel, or the TCI travel desk at the Andaman Beach Resort. They'll give you an update on which islands are open to visitors and save you the hassle of hiring a boat or organizing helicopter transport to **Havelock** and **Neil** islands (where it's possible to stay overnight at PWD bungalows). They'll also arrange snorkeling and scubadiving equipment.

To organize your own trip, contact the Marine Department or the Oceanic Company, on Mahatma Gandhi Road, Middle Point. Boat trips include visits to the paradisiacal, uninhabited islands of **Red Skin**, **Jolly Buoy**, and **Cinque** (actually a handful of small islands connected by sandbars), all fringed by beaches and sheer blue waters with visibility down to six meters (20 ft). The calm lagoons enclosed by coral reefs around these islands are particularly good for snorkeling and diving — just like floating through a huge aquarium with shifting kaleidoscopic hues and Technicolor tropical fish. As you cruise between the islands, you'll quite often see gamboling dolphins, flying fish, and large sea crocodiles.

If you plan a diving trip to the Andamans, be sure to avoid the monsoon period between June and September when the sea is turbulent, khaki-colored, and massed with venomous jellyfish. During this period of sudden squalls, boat-owners usually refuse to take tourists to the outer islands.

Where to Stay and Eat

The **Welcomgroup Bay Island** ((03192) 20881 FAX (03192) 21389 is a spacious, well-designed resort hotel atop Marine Hill, fitted out with local and natural wood furniture. The rooms all have balconies, which provide breathtaking views across Phoenix Bay. Both the bar and restaurant overlook the sea, and hotel fare includes Indian, Burmese, and local seafood dishes. Rates are moderate. Facilities include a seawater pool (there is no attached beach), health club, indoor games, and video screenings of several interesting films on the tribal people of the islands. Mrs. Vasan operates the hotel's travel desk, and her efficiency and prodigious knowledge of the islands make this service far superior to that provided by the sleepy tourist office. She'll take rapid care of any ticketing and can arrange transport facilities (taxi, boat hire, helicopter rides) as well as snorkeling and scuba equipment.

The **Peerless Resort** ((03192) 21462 FAX (03192) 21463 is modern and functional with a beachfront location at Corbyn's Cove, Port Blair's most swimmable beach. The hotel supplies equipment for windsurfing, waterskiing, sailing, scuba diving, snorkeling, and fishing. Other facilities include a restaurant, bar, travel desk, and tennis courts. Rates are moderate.

The **Shompen Hotel** ((03192) 20360, at Middle Point, has friendly service, a restaurant, and rooms with attached bathrooms. It's a less expensive option, with rooms ranging from around US$12. The popular **Megapode Nest** ((03192) 20207, Haddo, overlooking Phoenix Bay, is excellent value, featuring spacious doubles at bargain prices.

The two resort hotels have the town's only established restaurants — otherwise go to Aberdeen Bazaar to stock up on provisions and delicious local fruits, or sample fish patties and samosas from cheap *chai* cafés.

If you're in the vicinity of Corbyn's Cove, try **The Waves**, a popular alfresco restaurant and a great place to unwind with a cold beer.

How to Get There

Indian Airlines operates three flights weekly to Port Blair and back from Calcutta and Madras. The flight takes about two hours. Book well in advance — preferably before you arrive in India — if you want to be sure of getting a flight.

The other alternative is to make the three-day sea crossing to Port Blair from either Calcutta or Madras. Schedules are erratic and infrequent however, particularly during the monsoon months, and the lurching journey can easily induce seasickness. Fares for foreigners start at around US$50. Shipboard meals cost extra and tend to be monotonous *thali* affairs, although the Western-style breakfasts are good. To book berths or to inquire about the next sailing, contact the Shipping Corporation of India ((033) 2842854, 13 Strand Road in Calcutta, or ((044) 5226873 Jawahar Building, Rajahi Salai, Madras.

OPPOSITE LEFT: An elderly *dhoti*-clad couple admire friezes worn to a spidery frailty after seven enturies of exposure to the elements at the Sun Temple in Konarak. RIGHT: One of the 24 gigantic wheels adorning the base of the sun temple.

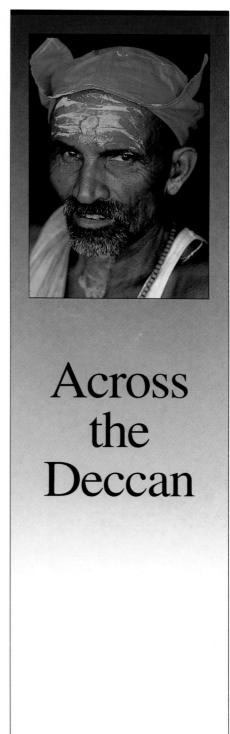

Across the Deccan

HYDERABAD

Capital of Andhra Pradesh, Hyderabad is India's sixth largest city. The beautiful architectural relics of its legendary Muslim grandeur are rapidly being swallowed up by an ugly industrial hinterland that sprawls across to Secunderabad, the modern twin capital. Yet locked within Hyderabad's heart are countless layers of its medieval Islamic heritage. Magnificent mosques and peeling nineteenth-century courtly mansions stand cheek by jowl with a shanty town of modern buildings and factory shacks.

With a skyline distinguished by slender minarets, Hyderabad represents a curious Muslim foothold in the south's Hindu heartland. It was founded in 1591 by the Qutb Shahi dynasty, a line of Muslim rulers who had ruled the mainly Hindu subjects of the surrounding southern Deccan since the fourteenth century. Muhammad Quli, the fourth of the Qutb Shahis, built his new capital near the Musi River as an alternative to his cramped, disease-ridden fortress city at Golconda, 11 km (seven miles) away, which today lends its name to locally produced wine.

Hyderabad's first major monument remains its most magnificent emblem: the Charminar arch, which straddles the city's original grid of broad intersecting boulevards. As a thriving trading center, Hyderabad — and the lure of its local diamond industry — proved irresistible to the Mughal emperor Aurangzeb who captured the region in 1650. In the wake of Aurangzeb's death in 1707, Hyderabad was snatched up in 1713 by one of the dead emperor's most trusted generals, Mir Kamruddin Khan, of the Asaf Jahn dynasty. He retained his Mughal title, Nizam-ul-Mulk and became the independent ruler of Hyderabad.

Successive Nizams amassed legendary fortunes, despite having their Deccan domain chipped down to the size of Italy by the French, the Marathas, and the British. When the tenth and last Nizam, Mir Osman Ali Khan, came to power in 1911, he was arguably the richest man in the world. His giant palace teemed with some 11,000 servants (38 were required to dust the chandeliers, while others did nothing except grind spices), entire wings were used to house mammoth quantities of precious jewels and gold bullion, and he used egg-sized diamonds as paperweights. Yet the Nizam's parsimony was equally fabled: he wore the same oil-streaked fez and soiled jacket for 30 years, was said to knit his own socks, and haggled over the price of local Charminar cigarettes. When India gained its independence in 1947, the Nizam flatly refused to relinquish his control of the state, grimly hanging on for two years before Indian troops massed at his borders forced him to capitulate.

Hyderabad's landscape is fringed by its boulder-strewn Banjara Hills, once the rugged home of a gypsy tribe from distant Rajasthan and now an elite enclave. The Banjara tribes-people still add their colorful presence to the city's bazaars, their women costumed in rustic Rajput finery with heavy, jingling jewelry and embroidered camel slippers.

It's most pleasant to visit the city between October and February, when it is fanned by cool breezes from its numerous reservoirs. But from March onwards, Hyderabad becomes unbearably stifling, with the waves of dry, sauna-hot air reducing even determined sightseers to a dehydrated frazzle.

GENERAL INFORMATION

The **Andhra Pradesh Tourist Information Bureau** ((040) 501519, first and fifth floors, Gargan Vihar, Mukkaram Jahi Road, provides local information, city maps, and tickets for their conducted city tours (open 8 AM to 6 PM every day except Friday).

WHAT TO SEE AND DO

Hyderabad is very spread out, so it's worth having a definite strategy before setting off for a day's sightseeing. Golconda Fort (see page 296) is best enjoyed in the cool early morning, leaving you free to explore the city's museums, mosques, and markets in the afternoon. Conducted city tours are convenient time-savers, but offer only a fleeting glimpse of Hyderabad's real charm, which is concentrated in its vibrantly colorful bazaars. Personal guides and transportation can be hired at the Tourist Information Bureau and if you're set on cycling the 11 km (seven miles) out to Golconda Fort — a pleasant, relatively straight-forward route if you've got a map on hand — hotels should be able to advise on bicycle rental.

Mosques, Markets, and Museums

At the heart of the old walled city stands Hyderabad's emblematic **Charminar**, a magnificent archway framed by four tapering minarets, each 56 m (184 ft) high. It was built in 1591 by Muhammad Quli Qutb Shahi as a sort of architectural talisman against a plague that was

minarets. Pigeons and hornets swoop around it like dark clouds and build nests in its inaccessible upper regions.

In contrast to its severe granite walls, the interior glitters with dangling Belgian chandeliers and decorative marbled inscriptions from the Koran. This is Hyderabad's principal place of Muslim worship, and on Fridays and Muslim festivals it can accommodate more than 10,000 kneeling devotees. During the Muslim holy month of Ramadan, many thousands more spill across the streets outside.

To the left of the courtyard is a marbled row of the Nizam's decorative tombstones — their womenfolk lie beneath flat tablets. Old men with

devastating the newly-founded city. Today the image of the Charminar follows you all across India on the country's No. 1 brand of beedi cigarettes.

You can make the spiraling ascent up to a tiny second-floor mosque for views across the city. It's open from 9 AM to 4:30 PM, and expect to find its cavernous interior teeming with swaddled alms-seekers.

Just beyond the Charminar, you'll see the colossal **Mecca Masjid**, the largest mosque in southern India.

Construction began under Muhammad Quli Qutb Shahi in 1614, but it was finished as an act of Islamic faith by the next conqueror of the Deccan, the Mughal emperor Aurangzeb, in 1687. Modeled on the famous mosque at Mecca, it's built on an awe-inspiring scale, with lofty monolithic pillars, vast calligraphy-emblazoned archways, and towering gold-tipped 30-m (100-ft)-high

hennaed beards commiserate with each other in the shadows, and ragged urchins sprawl across the tombstones. The mosque's workers scatter grain across the courtyard for bedraggled flocks of goats, pigeons, chickens, and in the courtyard's far right-hand corner is a solid black marble seat brought from Iran 200 years ago. Locals say that those who sit on it are destined to return to Hyderabad — you'll have to find out for yourself!

From here, any number of cobbled lanes will plunge you into the bustling medieval pantomime of Hyderabad's **Old Bazaar**. Wind your way through crowded alleys strewn with sandalwood screw-curls and dung, sidestep loitering buffaloes and knots of conversing merchants, and charge bravely through the riotous traffic.

A view of Hyderabad, a Muslim island in the Hindu south.

Crocheted-capped merchants gossip on upturned flowerpots; burqa-clad women with heavily kohl-rimmed downcast eyes flit by; and craftsmen stoop over spun silver or run plump fingers through rows of pearls. The lanes glitter with glass bangles and open sacks dot the pavement with the color and scent of every imaginable spice.

Hyderabad is a major processing center for pearls from the Middle East, Japan, and China, and loose pearls can be bought at about 20% of London prices, provided you bargain hard. Himroo brocades, delicate silver jewelry, rare Urdu books or decadently gilded Korans, lacquered sandalwood toys, and traditional bidri work with its distinctive silver on black designs are other popular products.

Several old and decaying city palaces lie within walking distance of the bazaar area. They include the **Panch Mahal**, **Chow Mahal**, **King Kothi**, and **Baradari** palaces, the latter notable for the battalions of Amazonian female sepoys who once patrolled the palace's zenana, or women's quarters, during the reign of Nizam Ali in the eighteenth century. Court documents as well as local lore record that this Nizam made his Italian mistress the colonel in charge of these female soldiers. But having gained military clout, she lost her original appeal for the Nizam, and he resolved to remove her. Acting on a tip-off, she escaped to Poona (now Pune, in Maharashtra state) accompanied by her loyal female sepoys, where she lived until her death. The next resident of the Baradari was a prime minister renowned for his elegant eccentricities, who trained his soldiers to ride ostriches in the gardens.

By far the most extravagant of the palaces is the **Faluknuma Palace**, five kilometers (three miles) south, a neoclassical mansion fronted by a vast marble stairway and vestibule fountains. It was built in 1897 and was used as the Nizam's guesthouse, accommodating touring viceroys and graced by British royalty. Its grand gilt-edged reception room is left just as it was, cluttered with period furniture, chandeliers, and figurines.

On the south bank of the Musi River, the **Salar Jung Museum** is one of Hyderabad's highlights. It houses the eclectic private collection of Nawab Salar Jung III, who served as prime minister to the Nizam of Hyderabad in the early 1900s until he resigned in 1914 to devote himself to the serious pursuit of collecting.

Armed with immense reserves of gold, the nawab traveled incessantly in pursuit of collectibles, making him the toast of Europe's leading auction houses. He died in 1949, aged 60 and a bachelor, and his priceless collection of over 35,000 exhibits from all over the world spans 35 galleries, each devoted to a certain theme. There's a vast range of Indian antiques — family heirlooms, sculptures, paintings, manuscripts, textiles, ivory and jade carvings, arms and armor — as well as galleries devoted to Middle Eastern, Far Eastern, and European art, with novelty collections of toys and antique clocks. The top floor contains an India researcher's gold mine — the nawab's library of over 60,000 books, many original historical documents, and rare state annals. In one corner, an army of plaster busts, a veritable Who's Who of British Empire builders, gathers dust. On the ground floor a cafeteria offers tea and snacks. The museum is open daily except Fridays from 10 AM to 5 PM, and bags and cameras must be deposited at the entrance.

On the other side of the Musi River lies the former **British Residency**, a fine Greco-colonial building built in 1803, fronted by two crouching sphinxes, and now used as a college. Other nearby architectural relics include the remarkable ocher-red **High Court** and the **Osmania Hospital**, both built in the Indo–Saracenic style in the late nineteenth century.

The **Government Archaeological Museum**, adjacent to the imposing colonial-era Indo–Saracenic Secretariat near the Public Gardens, has a fine collection of antique Indian sculpture, prehistoric utensils, coins, manuscripts, old arms, eighteenth-century bidri-ware, textiles, and china. Close by is the **Ajanta Pavilion**, which displays full-size copies of the Ajanta frescoes. The gardens are good for a peaceful stroll away from the city's chaotic muddle. Rather incongruously, just outside the Secretariat, a row of medicine men seem to have claimed their turf, selling a lurid array of peacock feathers, musty pills, tiger teeth, flayed buffalo skin, and cats' and rats' tails.

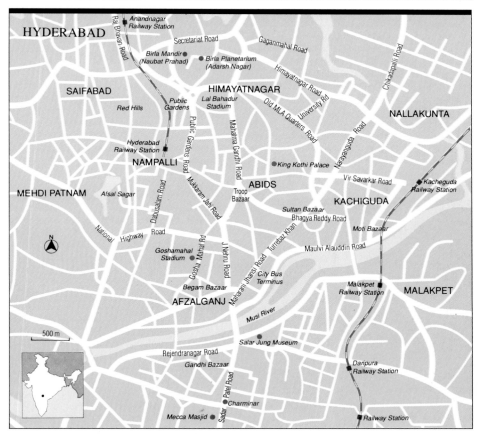

If you're going to visit any zoo in India, then make it the **Nehru Zoological Park**, located just outside the old city walls on Bangalore Road, quite near the Charminar. Wandering around its lush, well-landscaped, miniature lake-studded 121-hectare (300-acre) enclosure makes an enjoyable afternoon's excursion. Some 1,600 animals and 240 species of birds live in the near-natural surroundings. The highlight is undoubtedly the **Lion Safari Park**, with its free-roaming herds of lions. It's about a 20-minute walk from the zoo's main entrance, and every 15 minutes between 9:30 AM and 12:15 PM and 2 PM and 4:30 PM crowded minibuses leave for a "safari" circuit. There are several cafeterias and leafy grounds for picnics. Avoid Sundays; during the hot season, avoid visiting in the afternoon, when the animals are slumped in deep siesta.

The **National History Museum**, the **Aquarium**, and the **Ancient Life Museum** are worth visiting, located just near the entrance. The complex is open between 9 AM and 6 PM daily, except Monday.

If you're still in need of stimulation, visit the **Birla Mandir** (Naubat Prahad), the modern white marble temple atop a rocky hill opposite the Public Gardens. During the reign of the Qutb Shahis, royal proclamations were announced from here, with drum rolls for effect. Built by the mega-wealthy Birla family and decorated with ornate bas-reliefs depicting scenes from the Hindu epics, the temple is open to all castes and creeds. It's liveliest at sunset, when crowds clamor to offer scented garlands and coconuts — a symbol of a fulfilling life — to the temple deity, Lord Venkateshwara. So many coconuts are offered, in fact, that a sign says: "Please Leave Your Coconuts Here" at a locker used to baby-sit coconuts at the rate of 10 paise an hour! Hawkers sell medicinal bottles of "Guaranteed Pure Ganga Water," plastic trinkets, and cotton-candy at the temple's entrance.

On the adjacent hill stands the **Birla Planetarium** (Adarsh Nagar), which offers "Japanese Technology Sky Theatre" with English sessions at 11:30 AM, 4 PM, and 6 PM daily (Sundays at 11:30 AM, 3:45 PM, and 6 PM).

The archways and minarets of Hyderabad make it one of the most picturesque cities in the south.

Golconda Fort

The majestic ruins of this rambling fortress capital have an almost biblical quality, looming high above dusty, sepia scrubland, 11 km (seven miles) west of Hyderabad. Golconda was the virtually impregnable medieval citadel of the Qutb Shahi kings, a city fabled for its exotic bazaars selling diamonds, silver jewelry, and precious gems. Its mines produced the legendary Orloff, Regent, and Koh-i-noor diamonds.

Eyewitness accounts by Marco Polo and the seventeenth-century French traveler Jean-Baptiste Tavernier spread the legend of Golconda's decadence and wealth. Founded in the thirteenth century by the Hindu Kakatiya kings of Warangal,

it was originally just a simple hilltop mud settlement called "Golla (shepherd) Konda (hill).". Golconda was ceded to the powerful fourteenth-century Muslim Bahmani rulers and later passed into the hands of the Persian Qutb Shahi dynasty, who ruled the surrounding region between 1518 and 1687.

Under the Qutb Shahis, Golconda emerged as a formidable stronghold; built entirely of solid granite boulders, it seemed almost part of the mountain itself. The city within its walls had a complex civil and military administration, gem-studded royal palaces, mosques, harem quarters with interior fountains, Turkish baths, assembly halls, pavilioned gardens, and even a mortuary. Water was raised by an ingenious system through laminated clay pipes and Persian water wheels gushed water through the fountains and irrigated the flower-strewn roof gardens at the citadel's heights.

One of Golconda's most intriguing features is its acoustic system, which enables a handclap sounded at the gates to be heard clearly right up in the citadel. Golconda was virtually impregnable: it was encircled by some seven kilometers (four and a half miles) of triple-tiered ramparts dotted with eight formidable iron-spiked gates, 87 semicircular watch-posts, and a wide moat. It

withstood over eight months under siege by Aurangzeb's armies, falling only when a turncoat general betrayed the Qutb Shahis and allowed the enemy's forces to stream through the grand entrance gate. Aurangzeb annexed Golconda as part of his empire in 1687 and the fortress citadel soon crumbled into decline.

Golconda's fragmented ruins and winding medieval passages come to life with the help of a knowledgeable guide — but it's also the sort of place that is enjoyable to ramble about in at will, making discoveries of your own. Experienced guides can be hired from the tourist bureau, or you can buy the very informative Guide of Golconda Fort, which has a clearly marked map.

Northwest of Golconda lie the **Qutb Shahi Tombs**, a necropolis of more than a dozen magnificent domed tombs built for the Qutb Shahi rulers and their families set amid peaceful gardens. The tombs are reminiscent of the famous Lodi tombs of Delhi, and the finest is that of Muhammad Quli Qutb Shahi, the founder of Hyderabad, which rises to a height of 55 m (180 ft).

WHERE TO STAY

Hyderabad's luxury hotels are in the northwest of town on Road No. 1. The **Krishna Oberoi** ((040) 3392323 FAX (040) 3393079, Road No. 1, Banjara Hills, is Hyderabad's most elegant luxury hotel, with plush pastel decor, indoor fountains, and impeccably efficient staff. It's situated 10 minutes from the airport amid landscaped gardens that overlook the city. (From the top floors you can see Golconda Fort, 13 km or eight miles, away). Comfortable, tastefully furnished double rooms come with all modern conveniences — push-button telephones, vast televisions linked to cable, and mini-bars.

Its two stylish restaurants, which offer excellent Hyderabadi and Chinese cuisine, are heavily patronized by the city's elite, and there's also a good bar and 24-hour coffee shop. Facilities include a very modern health club with grounds for squash, tennis, and golf, a beauty parlor, a swimming pool, a travel desk, and the adjacent Krishna Plaza, a slick shopping arcade. Room rates start at US$120 for doubles.

The **Taj Residency** ((040) 3399999 FAX (040) 3392218, Road No. 1, Banjara Hills, is a close runner-up. It has a swimming pool, a business center, three restaurants, a fitness center, and even a private lake. Doubles start at US$115, and it's highly recommended.

Not quite as luxurious and with room rates that start at around US$75, the **Holiday Inn Krishna** ((040) 3393939 FAX (040) 3392684, Road No. 1, Banjara Hills, is a modern hotel with a swimming pool, tennis and squash courts, a health club, and an Italian restaurant.

In the mid-range category, **The Residency** ((040) 204060 FAX (040) 204040, Public Gardens Road, is a reliable air-conditioned hotel with a good central location. It has a shopping arcade and a dependable multi-cuisine restaurant. Doubles start at around US$30.

The **Hotel Bhaskar Palace** ((040) 3301523, Road No. 1, Banjara Hills, is a cheaper option, though it is looking a little tired these days. It has a swimming pool, a bar, and even a revolving restaurant.

The **Ritz Hotel** ((040) 233571, Hillfort Palace, has far more character. Built in a Scottish baronial style, this former palace is now a charming — if slightly dilapidated — hotel smothered with

whitewash, dusty chandeliers, and bright bougainvillea creepers. The dining room serves Indian, continental, and Chinese food, but has dreary 1950s decor. There are tennis courts and a small pool, which is used by locals for swimming lessons. Spacious, air-conditioned ground floor rooms with quaint furniture are best. Doubles start at about US$30.

For inexpensive accommodation, try the **Rock Castle Hotel** ((040) 222541, Road No. 6, Banjara Hills, a colonial-era lodging house now slightly rundown but still quaint, with friendly staff and good food.

Within the city center, the budget **Hotel Sarovar** ((0842) 3227638, on Secretariat Road, has clean and comfortable air-conditioned rooms for less than US$10, and incorporates an excellent all-day south Indian restaurant with generous *thalis*. Also recommended in the budget category

is the **Hotel Suhail** ((040) 510142, in Abids, the city's bustling shopping area, which is very popular with budget travelers. The Suhail has some extremely good value air-conditioned rooms for around US$7.

WHERE TO EAT

For sophisticated dining and good service: the Krishna Oberoi hotel has two plush restaurants, both overlooking cascading fountains: **Firdaus** for faultless Persian-influenced Hyderabadi Mughalai dishes — with delicious baronial *raan*, tandoor leg of lamb — and the **Szechwan Garden** for regional Chinese food.

Hotel Banjara's evening **Kebab-e-Bahar** outdoor terrace restaurant is deservedly popular for its Mughalai dishes, aromatic kebabs, and handkerchief-thin *romali rotis*.

No visit to Hyderabad is complete without an authentic experience of the city's Islamic culture in one of the Irani cafés: always cheap, filthy, full of capped Muslims, *burqa*-clad matrons, marble-topped tables, and glittering mosaic walls. The best (cleanest) to try are the **Hotel Madina**, near the Charminar, and **Rainbow Restaurant** on Abid Road (also known as Mahatma Gandhi Road). Specialties to order include *haleem*, a spiced mutton curry cooked with delicately pounded

OPPOSITE: At a dobhi laundry clothes are pounded clean on rocks. ABOVE LEFT: The Qutub Shahi Tombs of Golconda. RIGHT: A more common sight in the south of India: a Hindu temple.

wheat; *paya*, chicken soup served with flat bread; and *pauna*, sweet spiced tea. Local sweetmeats include *ashrafi*, an edible "coin" stamped with a Mughal seal, and *badam ki jali*, almond-studded *halwa*.

Good south Indian food is found at the **Kamath Hotel** in Abids, near the Indian Airlines office. Prices are inexpensive.

Well-heeled locals favor a handful of "classy" restaurants, all heavily air-conditioned with fake rococo, mirror-lined decor and a pulsating disco beat, serving good Mughalai, Chinese, and continental dishes. The **Golden Deer** restaurant, just opposite the Santhosh cinema in Abids, is a good example of this style. Others include the rooftop **Palace Heights** nearby (just look up, you can't miss its towering neon sign), **Fifth Avenue** and **Blue Fox**, both next to each other on Lakdiakapol.

The **Indian Coffee House**, in the Secretariat grounds, has delicious hot or cold coffee and south Indian snacks — good for a break after visiting the nearby Government Archaeological Museum in the Public Gardens. It's open 9:30 AM to 5 PM.

HOW TO GET THERE

Indian Airlines operates daily direct flights to Hyderabad from Delhi, Bangalore, Bombay, Madras, and Calcutta, and regular flights from Bhubaneswar and Nagpur. Jet Airways and NEPC also fly to some major destinations.

Hyderabad is connected by train to all major Indian cities, and popular rail journeys to south Indian destinations include the 16-hour trip to Bangalore and the 15-hour overnight express to Madras. Both these trains can be taken from the central Kachiguda station, saving the drive to the main station in Secunderabad, eight kilometers (five miles) away. As elsewhere in India, the express overnight trains are frequently booked out, so try to reserve your sleeper as soon as possible.

Regular buses run between Hyderabad and Bangalore, Madras, and Bombay, among other destinations.

THE DECCAN TRAIL TO BANGALORE

From Hyderabad, many travelers head straight for Karnataka's capital, Bangalore, picking up the popular route through Mysore to Ooty. Few venture southwest across the Deccan Plateau's arid, boulder-strewn terrain to explore its deserted medieval cities, forts, and temples — the legacy of the powerful Mughal Chalukya, Telegu and the Hoysala kingdoms who made this region their battleground. Those who make the effort — involving long, hot hours of bus and train travel — will be richly rewarded. The region is full of decaying architectural treasures and rustic towns where life seems barely to have changed for centuries. A good network of state-run hotels offer overnight facilities at all main destinations.

Ideally you could spend a week or so on the Deccan trail, starting in north Karnataka with **Bidar**, 130 km (81 miles) from Hyderabad, the former capital of the Muslim Bahmanis, with its well-preserved fifteenth-century city fort, palaces, pavilions, and fine tombs; and the fabulous medieval walled city of **Bijapur**, described by historian James Grant Duff as "exceeding anything of its kind in Europe."

Bijapur was the sixteenth-century stronghold of the Adil Shahi dynasty, whose legacy of majestic monuments includes the Gol Gumbaz, with a massive dome said to be second in size only to that of St. Peter's in Rome, and a "whispering gallery," where the slightest whisper echoes inside the dome 12 times over.

To the south lie a clustered trio of sculptured caves and stone temple sites: **Badami**, **Pattadakal**, and **Aihole**. All date back to the sixth century, when the early Chalukya kings ruled the region.

The culmination of the Deccan trail is found in the splendid isolation of **Hampi**, the fourteenth-century kingdom of the mighty Vijayanagars, whose Hindu empire was the largest in India's history.

Hampi is also known as Vijayanagar, or "City of Victory." Its impressive medieval ruins — full of fortified battlements, palaces, temples, pavilions, shrines, baths, and bazaars — spread across 26 sq km (10 sq miles). They sit in a surreal setting of brown granite boulders.

Close to the ruins is the equally impressive **Vittala Temple**. It was built in the sixteenth century and is dedicated to Vishnu. UNESCO has declared it a world heritage monument. The Hampi tourist office is on the Hampi Main Bazaar and has maps of the site.

Hampi itself has limited accommodation, but in Kamalapuram, about four kilometers (two miles) to the south, you can find the **Hotel Mayura Bhuvaneshwari** ((08394) 51574, which has simple but comfortable rooms, both air-cooled and air-conditioned, and a restaurant.

Most people arrive in Hampi via nearby Hospet which has express bus and limited rail connections with Bangalore, 358 km (222 miles) away.

BANGALORE

Karnataka's state capital is an attractive, efficient city with a well-planned grid of tree-lined boulevards, stately old public buildings, and beautiful gardens. Dubbed India's "Silicon Valley"

ABOVE: Southern India's largest mosque, the Mecca Masjid. BELOW: A betel nut seller with his wares.

Across the Deccan

for its burgeoning computer industry, Bangalore is the country's main center for scientific and technological research, eclipsing the city's traditional industries of coffee-trading, horse breeding, and indefatigable moviemaking.

There's a cosmopolitan, almost campus-like air to Bangalore, which has a constant stream of foreign business travelers and draws people from all over India for higher education, business opportunities, and research. It's an ideal base for planning trips through south India, with several interesting sights of its own, plenty of good hotels, and a thriving nightlife, with an array of restaurants, bars, and 1930s-era art deco cinemas.

Legend has it that Kempe Gowda, a feudal chief from the Vijayanagar kingdom, founded Bangalore (which means "city of boiled beans") in 1537 in memory of the spot where he was offered a meal of beans by a kindly hermit when lost in the forest. His medieval mud fort was later enlarged and rebuilt in stone by the Muslim leader Hyder Ali and his son, Tipu Sultan, in the late eighteenth century.

After defeating Tipu "Tiger" Sultan at Srirangapatna, the British arrived in 1809 to build a cantonment, and present-day Bangalore is dotted with Raj-era bougainvillea-shrouded bungalows, churches, clubs, pavilioned gardens, quaint shopping malls, as well as racing grounds and breweries. Ironically, it was the Maharaja of Mysore who produced the most extravagant parody of Victorian England in his Bangalore Palace: a vast, ivy-swathed turreted model of Windsor Palace, now eerily silent amidst its large gardens on the outskirts of the old cantonment town.

Set high above the stifling plains, Bangalore is a popular summer bolt-hole, though its climate is pleasant all year round. The city's extensive parks — notably Cubbon Park and Lalbagh — are at their best during January and August, and it can be fun to participate in the horse-racing mania that grips Bangaloreans between November and March and from mid-April to July.

GENERAL INFORMATION

The Karnataka Tourist Office ((080) 578901, at 10/4 Kasturba Road in Queen's Circle, is the most efficient of a handful of offices that are dotted around the city. It's worth investigating a number of the well-planned and reasonably priced sightseeing tours they have on offer. Aside from useful city tours, there's an excellent 16-hour tour out to Mysore, Srirangapatna, and Brindhaven Gardens, with various overnight tours to the Hoysala temple towns of Belur and Halebid, the Vijayanagar ruins of Hampi, Ootacamund, and the wildlife sanctuaries of Bandipur and Nagarhole.

Indian Airlines ((080) 79413, is in the Cauvery Bhavan complex in District Office Road.

WHAT TO SEE AND DO

Bangalore's few places of interest are concentrated around its large sprawling gardens. In the city center, it's worth making a promenade down Vidhana Vidhi (Bangalore's Champs-Elysées) to see an extraordinary Raj-era palisade of Greco-colonial public buildings bordering Cubbon Park. Here you'll see India's most impressive **Post Office**, the sienna-colored **High Court**, and the ash-red public library. The most magnificent building of all stands on the north side of the park — the palatial **Vidhana Soudha**, which houses the Secretariat and Legislature. Built in 1954, this four-story Neo-Dravidian-style citadel is worth a closer look. Permission to visit after 5:30 PM can be obtained from the Under Secretary (Protocol) ((080) 79401, Department of Social and Administrative Reforms, Vidhana Soudha.

The **Government Museum** is located on Kasturba Road. Established in 1886, it has 18 wings displaying an extensive collection of sculptures, coins, artifacts, inscriptions, and paintings excavated from both the Neolithic-period Chandraval site and the great Harappan site at Mohenjo-Daro in Sind Province, as well as a portrait gallery with rare miniatures and paintings of the bejeweled, sybaritic Tanjore and Mysore rulers. The **Venkatappa Art Gallery** is a spacious modern extension, and houses many paintings by Venkatappa, who was court painter to the Mysore maharaja in the early 1900s. Works by India's top contemporary artists are also on display. It's open every day except Wednesday from 9 AM to 5 PM. Neither the **Technological Museum** nor the **Aquarium** close by are really worth visiting. This could be a useful time to visit the Tourist Office, almost directly across the road, for information on sightseeing tours.

At the entrance to **Cubbon Park**, opposite, it's impossible to miss one of the few imposing statues of Queen Victoria allowed to remain standing in India. Laid out in 1864, the park's wide sweeping green has original wrought-iron benches and is relaxing for sunset strolls.

About four kilometers (two and a half miles) south of the city's bustling market area stands Bangalore's historic **Kempegowda Fort**, Hyder Ali's eighteenth-century stone reconstruction of the original mud fort. Inside the fort walls is Tipu Sultan's wooden palace, with just enough elaborate paint-work surviving on the walls, niches, and twirling columns to give an idea of its former glory. Don't miss the tiny museum here; the antique etchings, documents, and family portraits provide a pocket history of legendary Muslim leader Tipu Sultan (British India's arch rival)

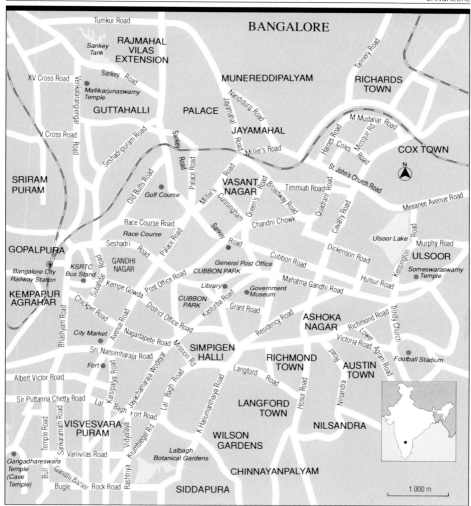

BANGALORE

Tumkur Road

RAJMAHAL
VILAS
EXTENSION
Sankey Tank

MUNEREDDIPALYAM

RICHARDS
TOWN

XV Cross Road

Sankey Road

Mallikarjunaswamy
Temple

GUTTAHALLI   PALACE

JAYAMAHAL

V Cross Road

COX TOWN

Seshadripuram Road

Miller's Road

St John's Church Road

SRIRAM
PURAM

Golf Course

VASANT
NAGAR

Timmiah Road

Meeanee Avenue Road

Old Bulls Road

Palace Road

Cunningham

Chandni Chowk

Ulsoor Lake   Murphy Road

GOPALPURA

Race Course Road
Race Course

Seshadri

Cubbon Road

Dickenson Road

ULSOOR

Someswaraswamy
Temple

Bangalore City
Railway Station

KSRTC
Bus Stand

GANDHI
NAGAR

General Post Office
CUBBON PARK

Mahatma Gandhi Road

Hulsur Road

Kempe Gowda

Post Office Road

KEMPAPUR
AGRAHAR

Chickpet Road

District Office Road

CUBBON
PARK

Library

Government
Museum

Grant Road

ASHOKA
NAGAR

Richmond Road

Trinity Church

City Market

Nagartapete Road

Mission Rd

SIMPIGEN
HALLI

Residency Road

Victoria Road

Football Stadium

Sri Narsimharaja Road

RICHMOND
TOWN

AUSTIN
TOWN

Fort

Langford Road

Hosur Road

Albert Victor Road

Sir Puttanna Chetty Road

Lal Bagh Fort Road

LANGFORD
TOWN

NILSANDRA

VISVESVARA
PURAM

Vidyalaya

WILSON
GARDENS

Vanivilas Road

Lalbagh
Botanical Gardens

CHINNAYANPALYAM

Gangadhareswara
Temple
(Cave
Temple)

Rock Road

Bugle

SIDDAPURA

1 000 m

and his life and times. It's open from 6 AM to 6 PM daily and is particularly worth seeing if you plan to visit Tipu Sultan's fortress capital, Srirangapatna, 125 km (77.5 miles) away. The finely wrought marble temple almost directly adjacent to Tipu's palace will undoubtedly catch your eye: the **Venkataramanaswamy Temple**, built by the Wodeyars in the seventeenth century.

Bangalore's beautiful **Lalbagh Botanical Gardens**, situated a two kilometers (just over a mile) southeast of the city center, were laid out over 100 hectares (240 acres) by Hyder Ali in 1760 with exotic plants supplied by ambassadors from Persia, Kabul, Mauritius, and France. With much zeal, the British added nineteenth-century pavilions, pebble paths lined with elegant lamps, fountains, flowerbeds, and a beautiful cast-iron glasshouse modeled on Crystal Palace. Every afternoon, a band comprised of aged pensioners

in epauletted costumes sends warbling, reedy notes from a bygone era wafting across the park. Magnificent flower shows are held twice a year — on August 15 to mark Independence Day and on January 26, Republic Day.

From the gardens, you can make a detour up the nearby Bugle Hill to see the **Bull Temple** with its 6.2-m (20-ft)-high stone monolith Nandi bull, which locals claim grows larger every year. Close by is the **Ganesha Temple**, with a devotional idol of the elephant-headed god carved in 110 kilos (243 lb) of solid butter! Amazingly, it never seems to melt, and when it is ritually cut up every four years and meted out to pilgrims, another replica is created from the proceeds donated by wealthy patrons.

Cultural entertainment in Bangalore is best from March to April, being the peak season for performances of traditional Karnataka dance and music. Performances are always listed alongside the cinema guide in the city's daily *Deccan Herald*. Otherwise inquire at the Chowdiah Memorial Hall Sankey Road, or Bharatiya Bhavan on Race Course Road, where the shows are usually held.

WHERE TO STAY

Luxury

The Oberoi ((080) 5585858 FAX (080) 5585960, 39 Mahatma Gandhi Road, is Bangalore's best hotel. Luxuriously appointed rooms look out onto perfectly manicured gardens, and guests can choose from a number of international class restaurants.

barbecue. Rooms are plush, pastel-colored, and fitted with cable television. Doubles start at around US$150.

Facilities include a swimming pool, health club, beauty salon, bookshop, travel counter, and business desk. A classic English bar serves pints of chilled draft beer.

Mid-range

The **Gateway Hotel** ((080) 5584545 FAX (080) 5584030, 66 Residency Road, is a good value upper middle-range hotel, with tasteful, all air-conditioned rooms from US$80. Facilities include restaurants, a bar, a swimming pool, a business center, and more.

The renowned **Taj West End Hotel** ((080) 2255055 FAX (080) 2200010, Race Course Road, is Bangalore's oldest hotel, though you might not guess it by the stylish interior. Set amid eight hectares (twenty acres) of landscaped gardens, it radiates Raj-era charm, despite a characterless modern annex.

Ask for a Victorian room in the original whitewashed hotel, where rooms come with balconies, wicker furniture, and huge British bathtubs. Doubles start at around US$215. There's a good pool, several restaurants, and the lawns are perfect for candlelit cocktails.

The **Windsor Manor Sheraton** ((080) 2269898 FAX (080) 2264941, 25 Sankey Road, is very stylish with meticulous Regency-style decor throughout — from the lobby's balustraded marble staircase to the staff uniforms, prompt service, excellent restaurants, and a poolside

For something a little less expensive, try the **Ramanashree Comforts** ((080) 2225152 FAX (080) 2221214, 16 Raja Ram Mohan Roy Road, an all air-conditioned hotel with a good restaurant and very friendly service.

Cheaper again is the **New Victoria Hotel** ((080) 5584076 FAX (080) 5584985, 47–48 Residency Road. Set in leafy gardens, everybody who stays here is charmed by the hotel's Raj-era atmosphere. There's a good restaurant and bar. The New Victoria has some budget-priced rooms for less than US$10, but the US$30 suites are particularly charming and good value for money. Book in advance.

Budget

One of Bangalore's most popular budget hotels is the **Ajantha** ((080) 5584321 FAX (080) 5584780, 22A Mahatma Gandhi Road. It has a good location, friendly staff, an excellent south Indian restaurant, and spacious air-cooled rooms cost as little as US$5. The Ajantha also has some reasonably priced air-conditioned rooms. Bookings are essential.

Also recommended is the **Airline's Hotel** ((080) 2271602, 4 Madras Bank Road. Set in pleasant grounds, it has an alfresco restaurant and large rooms ranging from US$5 to US$10. Again, bookings are essential.

WHERE TO EAT AND NIGHTLIFE

Bangalore is the only south Indian city with a thriving nightlife, and most travelers find it a welcome oasis of good restaurants, bars, English-style pubs, and even discos. It's also the only place in India which makes decent draft beer, best sampled at the curiously eclectic **Pub World**, Mahatma Gandhi Road, which is something like an exhibition of pub styles from around the world all crammed into one drinking space. **Nasa**, on Church Street, is the upmarket option.

If you plan to make the most of Bangalore's pub culture, you may as well make the most of the city's international cuisine too. On the pizza front, **Casa Piccolo**, Devata Plaza, 131 Residency Road, and **US Pizza**, Church Street, are commonly agreed to be the best. Of course, you may simply want to take the easy option and dine in the familiar surroundings of the **Pizza Hut** (India's first though nowadays not the only) on Cunningham Road.

There are other fast food options in Bangalore. The British chain **Wimpy**, Mahatma Gandhi Road, is virtually indistinguishable from those "at home," while **K.F.C.** can be found on Brigade Road. **Mac's Fast Food**, a casual eatery with (buffalo meat) hamburgers, french fries, pizzas, and shakes, can be found on Church Street.

Of the leading hotels, the **Windsor Manor** has several elegant restaurants serving particularly good Indian, Northwest Frontier, Chinese, and continental food. Discriminating locals flock to the lobby-level Royal Derby, a classic London tavern that serves excellent pub lunches with a pint of draft beer.

The garden restaurant at the **New Victoria Hotel** on Residency Road has a good lunch buffet that pulls in the crowds.

In town, try **Princes**, 9 Brigade Road, the last word in Bangalore chic, with its plush Regency decor, potted palms, and tailored waiters. A blowout three-course meal of Waldorf Salad, Prawns Crème Gratin, and Chateaubriand Steak, plus coffee comes to around US$10. Farther up Brigade Road, at No. 44, the **Kwality Restaurant** has excellent Indian cuisine at affordable prices.

Other local favorites, with very good and reasonably priced Mughalai, Chinese, and continental dishes, are the **Blue Fox**, at 80 Mahatma Gandhi Road, with its old-time band and two-step

dance-floor; and the **Jewel Box** and **Koshy's Parade Café**, both with vintage waiters and excellent food, located within the quaint Raj-era Koshy's Corner, opposite St. Mark's Cathedral on Church Street.

If you are in town for any time, you will hear about **Coconut Grove**, also on Church Street, the most popular seafood restaurant in town. Vegetarian and meat dishes also appear on the menu of this leafy terrace restaurant, most of prepared in delicious coconut sauces.

Excellent Andhra-style food, served on a banana leaf platter, can be found at both **Amaravathi**, off Mahatma Gandhi Road, and **RR Plantation Leaf** restaurants, opposite The Pub in Church Street.

The **Woodlands Hotel**, 5 Sampangi Tank Road, offers delicious south Indian vegetarian food, with as-much-as-you-can-eat bargain mealtime *thalis*, and delicious freshly squeezed grape juice.

At Bangalore's clean, proletarian Udipi cafés — located mainly around the Gandhi Nagar–Chickpet area near the rail and bus stations — it's possible to dine well on delicious south Indian fare for less than US$0.50! One of the best to try, the **Dai Vihar**, is a few doors down from the Badami House Tourist Office on NR Square. It has cheap *thalis*, fresh fruit juices, and great *lassis* mixed in a machine that looks just like a 1920s dentist's drill.

There's a quaint **Indian Coffee House** at 78 Mahatma Gandhi Road which is good for early breakfasts with excellant strong coffee. It's full of amusement value — with its aged waiters in Nehru caps, worn convict-like cotton uniforms, and walls plastered with faded posters of Mahatma Gandhi.

OPPOSITE: The Lalbagh Botanical Gardens in Bangalore. ABOVE: Exuberantly-colored powders coaxed into finger-swirled pyramids, terra-cotta pots and dangling necklaces make up some of the *puja* items sold at this stall in Mysore's Devaraja Market.

How to Get There

Bangalore has excellent air connections to the rest of India, with daily direct flights to Bombay, Delhi, Hyderabad, Calcutta, and Madras, as well as regular services to Ahmedabad, Calcutta, Cochin, Coimbature, Goa, Trivandrum, and other centers.

Daily express trains run to Bangalore from all major Indian cities, and popular journeys include the six-hour *Brindhavan Express* or *Shatabdi Express* (all air-conditioned) from Madras, the twice-weekly 40-hour *Karnataka Express* from Delhi, and the 24-hour *Kurla Express* from Bombay.

Bangalore is also well-serviced by state coaches from all the main Indian cities, with an efficient daily network of buses plying throughout southern and central India. When planning a long bus journey, try to avoid the notorious "video coaches," which feature Hindi movies in "glorious technicolor" as a ploy to lure customers. Insomniac Indians seem to adore these spoof extravaganzas full of wet saris, paunchy villains, and dance sequences on wildly elaborate sets. Most video coaches carry the sign "If the Video Fails We Are Not Responsible," but alas, it rarely does.

MYSORE

Mysore once held sway as Karnataka's princely capital, and an aura of faded grandeur still lingers in this leisurely city of angel-cake palaces, manicured gardens, and tree-lined avenues. Eclipsed by bustling, industrial Bangalore as the modern capital, Mysore is a quaintly rustic town with thirties-era architecture. This is India's "Sandalwood City," where much of the country's incense is produced, filling the air with dusky whiffs of jasmine, sandalwood, musk, and rose.

Mysore's name stems from Mahishasura, a ruthless demon king who, according to Hindu lore, tyrannized the people of this region until he was slaughtered by the goddess Chamundi. The city has been the seat of a succession of powerful ruling dynasties of the south since ancient times. The first to leave a significant legacy were the Hoysalas, who governed the area from the twelfth to the fourteenth century and were renowned for their patronage of art and architecture. Their magnificent temples and buildings can be seen at nearby Somnathpur, Belur, and Halebid. The Wadiyar maharajas then made Mysore their capital, ruling until 1759 when their kingdom was snatched away by the monarch's own commander-in-chief, the renegade Hyder Ali. In 1799, the British defeated Tipu Sultan, Hyder Ali's powerful son, annexed half his state, and restored an infant Wadiyar heir to the Mysore throne. The British set about expanding their empire in the south, and the Wadiyar maharajas ruled more or

less under the protective thumb of the Raj until Independence in 1947.

The British referred to prosperous, semi-democratic Mysore as a "model princely state," and adored attending the domain's lavish royal extravaganzas. The most famous of these was the annual *khedda*, a ritual roundup of wild elephants with specially constructed spectators' huts complete with electricity and running water, as well as evening entertainment in the form of banquets and a full-piece orchestra — all in the middle of dense jungle.

Today, Mysore boasts India's most spectacular Dassera festival (called Dussehra in northern India). Held during September/October, it celebrates the goddess Chamundi's victory over Mahishasura. This 10-day carnival of dance and musical festivities climaxes with a stunning procession of richly caparisoned elephants,

liveried cavalry, and regal silver and gold carriages, accompanied by parading bands, flower-strewn floats, and fireworks.

WHAT TO SEE AND DO

Mysore is pleasantly small, so most of its sights can easily be covered on foot or in short hops by taxi or auto-rickshaw. The Tourist Office runs excellent all-day city sightseeing tours that include visits to Brindhavan Gardens and excursions to Somnathpur and Srirangapatna.

The city tour starts with **Saint. Philomena's Church**, three kilometers (two miles) north of town. Built in 1931, this neo-Gothic cathedral with its two tapering spires and dazzling medieval-style stained-glass interior appears to have been uprooted from rural France and set down again on the other side of the world.

In town is the **Sri Chamarajendra Art Gallery**, housed in the eighteenth-century Jaganmohan Palace near Gandhi Square, with many fine oil portraits of Mysore's royal family, miniature paintings, and all sorts of antique treasures including fine pieces of sculpture, Hoysala carvings, and rare musical instruments. It's open daily from 8 AM to 5 PM.

There's a brief stop at the **Zoological Gardens**, on Lalitha Palace Road, open daily 8 AM to 5 PM, where over 1,500 species of animals and birds reside in leafy captivity.

The city's main attraction is **Amber Villas**, the late maharaja's palace. A lavish Arabian Nights fantasy of domes, turrets, archways, and fluted

A scalloped archway frames Amber Villas, the fantasy palace built for the Maharaja of Mysore, a passionate Anglophile who also created a replica of Windsor Palace on the outskirts of Bangalore.

Across the Deccan

colonnades, which stands amid garden pavilions in the town center, it was designed by the English architect Henry Irwin in the Indo–Saracenic style, and built over a period of 15 years (1897–1912) to replace the former palace which had been partially destroyed by fire. Only the public quarters of this rambling fairytale palace are open to view, it is still a royal residence.

It's filled with eccentric enchantments: a vast Durbar Hall dotted with candy-striped gilt pillars, lined with giant murals depicting the life of the maharaja, and topped by a beautiful stained-glass roof. One extravagant room is followed by another, each a confused marvel of styles, with Italianate furniture, Byzantine mosaics, the local Hoysala-

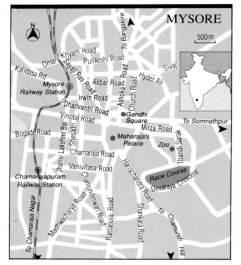

style carvings, solid silver doors, art deco statues, sweeping marble staircases, and plumed ostrich-feather chairs with *punkah-wallah* attachments. A fascinating portrait gallery is incorporated within the palace, with another museum of paintings and royal relics in the courtyard near several ornate temples. The palace is open daily from 10:30 AM to 5:30 PM. Cameras and shoes must be left at the entrance. Avoid the nightmarish crowds during weekends and public holidays, and return on Sunday evenings when the palace, lit up by thousands of flame-colored bulbs, looks like an illuminated mirage.

The tour goes to **Chamundi Hill** (13 km, eight miles, by road, or four kilometers, two and a half miles, by climbing the seventeenth-century pilgrims' steps), a picnic spot 1,065 m (3,500 ft) above the city. It was named for the goddess Chamundi, the family deity of the Mysore rulers. Atop the hill is the 2,000-year-old **Chamundeshwari Temple**, with its sculpted multitiered pyramidal tower added only three centuries ago. Nearby is the lurid statue of the ferocious demon

Mahishasura — complete with a caddish, cheesy leer — who, according to legend, met his death at the hands of the vengeful goddess Chamundi, thus bringing peace to the local people. Halfway down the hill you'll see the 4.9-m (16-ft)-high **Nandi**, Shiva's holy bull, hewn in 1859 from a single black boulder with wreaths of carved bells and garlands.

The tour ends with a visit to the beautifully terraced **Brindhavan Gardens**, 19 km (12 miles) from Mysore, laid out against the Krishnarajasagar Dam on the Cauvery River. Evenings have a gala atmosphere, with the whole park illuminated like a fluorescent fishbowl with sparkling lights and cascading computer-controlled fountains synchronized with music!

It's possible to stay overnight at the ex-palace **Hotel Krishnarajasagar (** (0821) 57322 FAX (0821) 420854, where air-conditioned rooms with garden views range from around US$30.

Back in Mysore, one of the city's highlights is the **Devaraja Fruit and Spice Market**, located behind Gandhi Square. It's an intoxicating mazelike strip of heaped flowers, incense stalls, and exotic fruit.

Even if you're not shopping for Mysore's famous incense, sandalwood handicrafts, or silks, it's fun to stroll through the city's excellent emporia. Among the best are **Cauvery Arts and Crafts Emporium** on Sayaji Rao Road, **Karnataka Silk Industries Corporation** on Mananthody Road, and the **Government Sandalwood Oil Factory**, located in the city's southern outskirts, where you can watch the distilling process and see how incense is made and then browse in the shop (open Monday to Saturday 9 AM to 11 AM and from 2 PM to 4 PM).

Train buffs should visit the **Rail Museum**, in KRS Road near the railway station, with its rows of vintage engines, decadent royal coaches, signals, and Raj-era memorabilia. It's open daily from 10 AM to 1 PM and from 3 PM to 5 PM.

It's well worth making an excursion to the island fortress at **Srirangapatna**, 16 km (10 miles) from Mysore, standing between two tributaries of the Cauvery River. It was once the stronghold of the powerful eighteenth-century Muslim ruler Hyder Ali and his legendary son, Tipu Sultan. Tipu Sultan was British India's most mercilessly powerful foe. He led two successful battles against the East India Company forces before finally dying while defending his fortress capital against Lord Wellesley's army in 1799.

Tipu's larger-than-life persona, virulent hatred of Englishmen, and obsession with surrounding himself with tigers (both live and symbolic) make him one of India's most flamboyant historical figures. One of his most famous artifacts now lies in the Victoria and Albert Museum — the so-called Tiger Man Organ, an ingenious mechanical toy that represents a gleeful tiger swallowing a petrified English *sahib*.

Only sprawling battle-scarred ruins remain of Tipu Sultan's splendid fortress, although the dungeon where many British soldiers were imprisoned has been preserved. To the right of the entrance, look for a small plaque commemorating the exact spot where the fatally wounded leader died. Also see Tipu's mosque with its twin minarets and the ancient multi-columned **Sri Ranganathawamy Temple**, built in 894, with its large reclining image of Vishnu — in his *avatar* as a sea serpent — and central brass pillar.

Tipu Sultan's magnificent summer palace, **Daria Daulat Bagh**, and the family mausoleum, the white-domed **Gumbaz** — with its interior

most conveniently located is **Lalitha Mahal Palace Hotel ((0821) 571265 FAX (0821) 571770, on T. Narasipur Road overlooking the city, an immense former guest palace painted with a confectioner's palette of white marble, lemon yellow, pale blue, and peppermint green. Its dome was designed after Saint Paul's Cathedral in London. The suites are crammed with rickety period furniture and they open onto balustraded terraces. Room prices range from US$70 to US$230 and up.

In the city center, **Quality Inn Southern Star ((0821) 43814 FAX (0821) 421689, 13 Vinoba Road, is a comfortable mid-range hotel with a swimming pool and other amenities.

lacquered with Tipu's tiger stripe emblem — stand unscathed amid ornamental gardens outside the fort. The Indo–Islamic palace, built in 1784 almost entirely of wood, has an extravagant multicolored interior of gilded walls and ornate arches. Stylized eighteenth-century frescoes depict the lifestyles of the Muslim nawabs and famous battle scenes, each full of symbolic intrigue. Upstairs is a fascinating museum displaying an array of Tipu's tiger-studded possessions, documents, and lithographs, as well as fine ink drawings of him and his family. The palace is open from 9 AM to 5 PM daily.

WHERE TO STAY

There are two luxury palace-hotels, both moderately priced, quirkily grand, and built by the Maharaja of Mysore during the thirties. The

In the mid-range category too, the **King's Kourt Hotel ((0821) 421142 FAX (0821) 438384, JLB Road, is also recommended — a modern hotel, where air-conditioned rooms range from around US$30 to US$120.

Heartily recommended for its comfortable colonial charm is the **Hotel Metropole ((0821) 420681 FAX (0821) 420854, 5 Jhansi Lakshmi Bai Road, in the city's heart. It has affable khaki-clad staff, rattan-lined verandas, and leafy gardens for sipping cold beer at twilight. Spacious Raj-era rooms have mosquito-netted bedsteads and old tiled bathrooms. Rates are around US$30 and upwards, and excellent Indian, Chinese, and Western dishes are served at the restaurant.

Victorian-era steam-train and an old Austin colorfully adapted into a bogie are two of the exhibits at Mysore's Rail Museum.

The Karnataka Tourist Development Corporation (KSTDC) **Hotel Mayura Hoysala** ((0821) 425349, JLB Road, is an excellent budget hotel. A courtyard restaurant serves good travelers' fare, and the Tourist Office is just next door. Another good option is **Hotel Dasaprakash** ((0821) 24444, Gandhi Square, with a vegetarian restaurant and an ice cream parlor. Cheaper budget lodges are crammed around the central Gandhi Square area.

WHERE TO EAT

Even if you're not staying there, treat yourself to a meal at the **Lalitha Mahal Palace Hotel**, where you can try the best in Mysore cuisine while enjoying entertaining performances of classical Indian music.

Adventurous eaters will favor Mysore's unexpectedly good, street-side south Indian cafés in and around Dhanvantri Road, over the predictable fare provided by the main hotels. Try **RRR Restaurant** on Gandhi Square, or **RR Plantation Leaf Restaurant** on Chandragupta Road, for delicious Andhra Pradesh-style *thalis* served on a banana leaf.

The **Hotel Dasaprakash's** cafeteria serves freshly prepared south Indian snacks throughout the day and great mealtime "tiffins" with 15 or so assorted dishes. Freshly squeezed grape juice is their specialty, though it's much nicer if you ask them to leave out the sugar.

The **Hotel Shilpashi**, in the CPC Building, Gandhi Square, is a travelers' favorite for relaxed evening dining. There's a good bar and the pretty rooftop restaurant serves excellent Mughalai food, as well as Chinese and Western-style dishes.

Another popular establishment is the **Punjabi Restaurant and Bombay Juice Center**, 397 Dhanvantri Road, for good north Indian dishes and fluffy cappuccinos. It's run by an eccentric and always entertaining proprietor.

The **New Bombay Tiffinys**, near the Thesus Complex on Sayaji Rao Road, is renowned for its overwhelming array of Indian confectionery, with an upstairs café for sampling them with a glass of chilled *lassi*. The vintage **Cold Drinks House** (founded in 1934 as the Brahman Soda Factory), Sardar Patel Road near Gandhi Square, has excellent chilled sweetened milk and fresh fruit juices served in clean glasses with straws.

HOW TO GET THERE

Bangalore (140 km or 87 miles away) is the nearest destination for flight connections with the rest of India. From Bangalore, buses depart throughout the day for the three-hour journey to Mysore. Trains are much less frequent, but the daily *Shatabdi Express* does the trip to Bangalore in just two hours, before going on to Madras (seven hours).

THE HOYSALA TEMPLES

No visit to Karnataka is quite complete without appreciating the artistic grandeur of the Hoysala dynasty in the magnificent temple architecture found at **Somnathpur**, **Belur**, and **Halebid**. The Hoysala dynasty ruled the surrounding region from about 950 to 1310, when they were crushed by the iconoclastic Muslim rulers of Delhi. The finesse and artistry of these Hoysala temples is remarkable, with the black stone so finely chiseled that it attains the lace-like delicacy of carved sandalwood or ivory. Hoysala temples typically have origami-pleated walls and ascending friezes. They rise from a star-shaped platform, and unlike other south Indian temples have no towering *goporams*.

BELUR

Belur, 39 km (14 miles) from Hassan, which flourished as the Hoysala capital 800 years ago, contains the ornately carved **Chennakeshava Temple**, built in 1116. According to local lore, the Muslim conquerors came to Belur intent on razing this temple, but left awed by its magnificence. Every deity in the Hindu pantheon is said to be represented here, and some many times over.

HALEBID

Halebid, 16 km (10 miles) away, offers the equally splendid double-shrined **Hoysalesvara Temple**, built in 1126, and considered one of the most skilled architectural feats in the world. As you walk around the temple, the carved walls begin to seem like a voluminous scroll unfurled before your eyes, laden with an infinite variety of ornamental decoration. Nearby, an open-air museum displays an excellent collection of Hoysala-period sculpture salvaged from other temples. The Hassan Tourist Office runs day tours to Belur and Halebid every Wednesday, Friday, and Sunday.

SOMNATHPUR

Somnathpur, built in the thirteenth century, was the last of the Hoysala temples and is the culmination of their artistic achievement.

The triple-shrined temple, dedicated to Keshava, stands on a star-shaped base within a cloistered enclosure and is covered with panels of exquisite sculpted friezes depicting narratives from the great Hindu epics, the *Ramayana*, *Mahabharata*, and *Bhagavad-Gita*. It ranks alongside the temples of Khajuraho and Bhubaneswar for the skilled execution and delicacy of its exterior carvings, and is especially noted for the six horizontal bands of decorative friezes ascending with lathe-turn precision from the temple base. The temple is open from 9 AM to 5 PM daily. For a more informed account of the temple's history, ask the curator for a copy of P.K. Mishra's book *The Hoysalas*.

WHERE TO STAY

The best accommodation in the vicinity of Belur and Halebid is at Hassan, 187 km (116 miles) northwest of Bangalore, or 120 km (74 miles) northwest of Mysore. Though, with the accommodation situation at Belur improving in recent years, some budget travelers now opt to stay there instead.

The **Hassan Ashok Hotel** ((08712) 68731 FAX (08712) 67154, is the best place to stay, or there's a choice of several budget hostels.

HOW TO GET THERE

Somnathpur is an hour or so from Mysore by bus, with a change at either Narsipu or at Bannur.

For Belur and Halebid, you will probably need to overnight in Hassan, which can be reached from either Mysore or Bangalore in around four hours by bus. Hassan also has a train station that connects it with Mysore, though services are sparse.

En route to Hassan, if you have the time, make a detour to **Sravanabelagola**, 93 km (58 miles) from Mysore, to see its astonishing 1,000 year-old, 17-m (56 ft)-high monolithic statue of the naked Jain saint Lord Gomateswara. Every 12 years, there's a near riot here as Jain pilgrims clamber up scaffolding to pour thousands of pots of water, milk, curds, ghee, flowers, vermilion, and saffron across the saint's implacable face in a sacred anointing ritual.

KARNATAKA'S WILDLIFE SANCTUARIES

From Mysore, two of Karnataka's loveliest wildlife sanctuaries are only a couple of hours' driving distance away. **Bandipur Wildlife Sanctuary** in the Nilgiri foothills, lies 80 km (50 miles) south on the Mysore–Ooty Road. Amidst Bandipur's lush 400 sq km (154 sq miles) of bamboo, teak, and rosewood jungle live many elephants, leopards, Indian bison, spotted deer, macaques, and a great variety of birdlife. It's possible to observe the animals at close range, particularly elephant herds, from the road, from atop an elephant, or from a boat on the Moyer River. The best season is from September to April.

Accommodation (which must be pre-booked) as well as all transport within the forest is arranged through Bandipur's **Forest Lodge and Guesthouse**. Contact the Field Director ((0821) 20901 or (0821) 24980, Project Tiger, Government House Complex, Mysore.

Nagarhole National Park, 94 km (58 miles) southwest of Mysore in the beautiful Kodagu district, spans 294 sq km (114 sq miles) of tropical forest, undulating streams, and swampland. It's inhabited by tigers, elephants, leopards, sloth bears, wild boar, several species of crocodile, and a rich variety of birdlife. Nagarhole, which translates as "snaking water," is crisscrossed with meandering streams thick with plump mahseer for fishing. Arrangements for hiring jeeps, elephants, and boats, for visiting Heballa elephant training camp, are made either through your hotel or Nagarhole's Forest Department.

Delightful accommodation is also offered by the **Kabini River Lodge**, where room rates are generally around US$100, depending on the season. The Kabini is located just outside Nagarhole Park, and it is a converted royal hunting lodge. Excellent food is served, and the lodge has a well-stocked and comfortable bar. The same proprietors also run the safari-style **Karapur Tented Camp**, six kilometers (four miles) into the forest, and both are open to coincide with the park's season from mid-September to mid-June. Either can be booked through **Jungle Lodges and Resorts** ((080) 362820, 348/9 Brooklands, 13th Main, Rajmahal Villas Extension, Bangalore.

Everything from silver and pearls to daily fruit and vegetables are on sale at Hyderabad's bustling and colorful bazaars.

OOTACAMUND (OOTY)

Set 2,285 m (7,500 ft) high in the lush Nilgiri Hills at the apex of Tamil Nadu, Kerala, and Karnataka, "Ooty" was the former summer headquarters of the British Government of Madras. Ooty was their mock-Sussex retreat: a bracing, eucalyptus-scented region of softly undulating hills grazed by plump Jersey cows, rhododendron-lined country roads, Victorian gingerbread cottages, milky streams thrashing with trout, and a cobbled town bazaar called Charing Cross. Today, India's elite spend their summers in a "Snooty Ooty" slightly gone to seed, playing snooker in the Ooty Club (a young subaltern called Neville Chamberlain first invented snooker here in 1875), and attending the annual fox-hunting, garden, and dog galas.

Ooty derives its name from the local Toda word *udhagamandalam*, or "village of huts." The area's original settlers were the Todas, a cattle-worshipping tribe whose women often have as many as four husbands apiece, and who still live in small beehive huts on Ooty's outskirts. John Sullivan, the Collector of Coimbature and avid botanist who founded the first European settlement here, stumbled across Ooty's idyllic scenery in 1819 during one of his nomadic searches for rare flowers. By 1869, Ooty was the southern summer capital and an icon of Victorian India with its full social season and pastoral round of "at home" calls, horse riding, and punting on the lake. Indian royalty soon followed, each vying to build a more extravagant palace than the last.

Raj relics survive everywhere in the pavilioned Botanical Gardens, the Anglican church spires, the nineteenth-century shops, and the dwindling community of British pensioners who preferred to stay on after Independence.

Ooty's main industry is oil extraction, particularly from the eucalyptus trees introduced during the nineteenth century, but also from lemongrass, geranium, clove, and camphor. Tea plantations in the neighboring hills produce distinctive blends of masala, chocolate, and cardamom tea.

Ooty's popular "season" is from September to October and from April to May, and it is best avoided at these busy times of the year. The place is far more peaceful and less expensive during February and March. In winter and during the nippy (sometimes downright freezing) monsoon months, bring warm clothing and waterproof shoes to guard against sudden flash floods.

GENERAL INFORMATION

The **Tourist Office (** (0423) 43977, on Commercial Road, runs daily sightseeing tours around Ooty, as well as to Coonoor and the Mudumalai Wildlife Sanctuary.

WHAT TO SEE AND DO

Ooty's charming landscape provides a soothing break from the scorched lowlands, with plenty of opportunities for long strolls in the Nilgiri Hills, horseback riding, boating on the lake, or simply relaxing in rickety Raj-era splendor. Ooty town is very small, and its sights are easily covered on foot in a day; longer distances can be covered by bus, taxi, or auto-rickshaw.

Start with the terraced **Botanical Gardens**, a sprawling 21-hectare (50-acre) manicured paradise created by the Marquis of Tweedale in 1847 and brimming with some 650 varieties of plants. Visitors can buy seedlings and fresh-cut flowers from the curator's office. Ooty's "season" reaches its peak during May, with the annual Flower Show and Dog Show.

A half-hour climb up the main winding path past ornamental floral beds and exotic thickets is the grand Raj-era Government House, still used by the Tamil Nadu Governor as a summer retreat. At the top of the ridge is a Toda community, whose lifestyle has been "modernized" with concrete shacks and Western-style clothing. (To see a Toda settlement where the tribespeople live traditionally in tiny domed huts and wear decorative tattoos, vivid handwoven shawls, and corkscrew curls, go to **Kandal Mund**, a village nine kilometers, or five and a half miles, from Ooty.)

From the Gardens' high cast-iron entrance gates, it's a 20-minute stroll back along Garden Road (turning left at Higgins Road) to **Saint Stephen's**, a parish church set in an English cemetery. It was built during the early nineteenth century with immense teak beams pillaged from Tipu Sultan's palace at Srirangapatna.

Nearby is **Spencer's Store**, an old British emporium with 1940s merchandise and excellent local Cheddar and Wensleydale cheeses, and the red-brick Scottish **Nilgiri Library**, opened in 1868, where old men wearing pince-nez and mufflers study dated copies of *Punch* magazine and glance disapprovingly at intruders.

Just down the road, near the Savoy Hotel, is the Ooty Club (more properly called the Ootacamund Planter's Club). From here, either jump aboard a bus or take a two-kilometer (one-and-a-quarter-mile) stroll to Ooty's scenic **lake**, the main focus of activity for coy honeymooners and large, raucous family groups. The **Boat House** (open from 8 AM to 6 PM) rents out row-, paddle-, and motorboats, and also has facilities for fishing. A hand-painted sign proclaims: "Rowers are available for rowing capacity including the rower's rowing cooly charges extra!"

Nearby is a children's toy railway that circles the lake, and a small snack bar. At the open-air market by the lakeside, you can rent ponies, with or without a hired escort, to trot along Ooty's mountain trails. You can also arrange to have ponies delivered to your hotel for a day excursion.

Ooty's **bazaar**, which stretches from Hospital Road and Commercial Road down to Charing Cross, is good for a leisurely stroll. There are all sorts of musty oddities: Chinese tailors who still use 1930s pattern books, shops specializing only in rosewood pipes and walking sticks, and photographers' shops displaying "Box Brownies" and yellowing photographs of pale-skinned debutantes. For the best collection of antique silver Toda jewelry go to **Suraaj**, about midway down the main bazaar (with a twin shop at the Savoy Hotel), and buy embroidered Toda shawls from a

views across the Nilgiri Hills to **Dodabatta Heights**, 10 km (just over six miles), which looms behind the Botanical Gardens and is the highest peak in Tamil Nadu, at nearly 3,000 m (9,845 ft). Take a bus there from the main bus stand and enjoy spectacular views all the way down to the Coimbature lowlands from the topmost observation point. From there, it's a glorious 45-minute walk back to town, descending past tea gardens, forest thickets, and rolling meadows. (If you start to wilt, there are plenty of buses plying the route back to town.)

Nearby picnic spots include **Catherine Falls** and **Elk Hill** (both eight kilometers or five miles). **Kodanad View Point** (16 km or 10 miles) has

cluster of shops near Charing Cross. The bazaar is crammed with tiny shops selling oils, tea, and delicious Nilgiri honey. The Tourist Office at Charing Cross seems consistently to lack useful Ooty maps and pamphlets; you'll have better luck at Higginbothams Bookshop nearby.

OOTY EXCURSIONS

Aside from walking, pony riding, boating, and a scenic golf course open to paying nonmembers, anglers will find excellent trout and carp fishing in streams at Avalanche Emerald and Parson's valleys, as well as in Ooty Lake. A license and tackle are available from the Assistant Director of Fisheries, ((0423) 2232, Fishdale, near the bus-stand.

There are plenty of invigorating walks across the hills, particularly to **Wenlock Downs**, eight kilometers (five miles) away, with impressive

superb views across the hazel-colored mountains, and at the hill station of **Coonoor** (13 km or eight miles), you can stay overnight at the delightful Raj-era Taj Garden Retreat ((04264) 30021 FAX (04264) on Church Road, which offers period suites. Visits to **Glen Morgan** (24 km or 15 miles), one of the most beautiful tea estates in the region, can be arranged through Mr. Gordon of the Savoy Hotel. Given advance notice, the owners will guide visitors and explain the tea production process; they can also arrange an afternoon tea.

To visit **Mudumalai Wildlife Sanctuary**, 64 km (40 miles) away, take the two-hour express bus to **Theppukady**, where the sanctuary's reception center is located. Mudumalai covers some 320 sq km (about 125 sq miles); a dense, deciduous hill forest wedged between Bandipur and

The Raj-era parish church of Saint Stephen's in Ooty.

Wynad sanctuaries. Its remoter regions are exceptionally rich in wildlife and can be explored by jeep or atop elephants on a four-seat howdah. You're likely to see tigers, panthers, wild bears, spotted deer, gaur (Indian bison), sambar, reptiles (including the scaly anteater), and a great variety of birdlife. The park also contains an Elephant Camp, where the harnessed heavyweights are tutored in the logging trade. The best season to visit is February to May, and you can conveniently arrange accommodation and in-park transportation while in Ooty through the District Forest Officer (North) ((0423) 2235. There are lots of options ranging from basic dormitory beds in forest lodges to the most comfortable deluxe rooms for US$5 to US$10 at **Bamboo Banks Farm House** in Musingudi Village.

WHERE TO STAY

Savoy Hotel ((0423) 2572 or (0423) 44142 FAX (0423) 43318, 77 Sylks Road, which first opened in 1841, offers deluxe rooms in the original old hotel or in whitewashed cottages, both with comfortable 1930s-era furniture and wooden floors, from US$90. On nippy winter nights, aged retainers shuffle in with hot-water bottles and light the wood fires. Good Anglo–Indian cuisine is served in the rosewood-paneled dining room, with afternoon cream teas served on the lawn. Mr. Gordon at the front desk can arrange pony riding, trout fishing, golf, and visits to nearby tea plantations.

The **Fernhill Palace** ((0423) 43910, a vast Swiss Alpine-style former summer palace of the Maharaja of Mysore, had been acquired by the Taj group and was undergoing renovations at the time of writing. It offers views across the blue Nilgiri mountains, romantically overgrown gardens, pavilions, and tennis courts, and should be Ooty's best accommodation.

For mid-range and budget accommodation with some atmosphere, the **Regency Villa** ((0423) 42555 is recommended. It comes complete with lawns and wicker furniture. Less grand, but also very good value is the **Willow Hill** ((0423) 42686, Havelock Road, a small, family-run hotel with a good Indian and Chinese restaurant.

The **YWCA** ((0423) 42218, Anandagri, which takes both men and women, is particularly good value. It has carpeted single rooms with log-fires and a good restaurant. The **Youth Hostel** ((0423) 43665 has cheap dormitory beds for just over US$1 and simple doubles for under US$10.

For lakeside vistas — most pleasant during the peaceful off-season — stay at **Hotel Lakeview** ((0423) 43904, located outside town on West Lake Road overlooking Ooty Lake.

During the off-season, hotels and lodges reduce their rates substantially.

WHERE TO EAT

Ooty's main bazaar area is crammed with eating places catering for the seasonal droves of Indian tourists, but the **Hotel Hills Palace**, at 66 Commercial Road, has particularly good Gujarati mealtime *thalis* and a never-ending menu with something to please everyone from fussy Brahmans to brain-eating Zoroastrians. Your status as a "meat-eater or not, *sahib*?" is demanded at the door, as a kind of food apartheid is in force: partition walls separate the carnivorous types from the herds of herbivores.

Up the road is **Tandoori Mahal**, good for Mughalai and tandoor dishes, and the ice cream parlor next door serves creamy concoctions made with real strawberries, figs, and mango.

Both **Chungwah**, on Commercial Road, and **Shinkows**, on Commissioner's Road, are run by Chinese families and offer appetizing curry-laced Sino–Indian dishes. For Indian fast food, the **Kurinji Snack Bar** on Commercial Road is popular with locals and foreign travelers alike.

Prohibition is in force, but both the Savoy and Fernhill Palace hotel bars serve liquor without demanding permits.

HOW TO GET THERE

Ooty's nearest airport is at **Coimbature**, 88 km (55 miles) away, with direct flights to Madras, Bombay, and Bangalore. Coimbature is also a major rail junction, with an efficient network of trains to all the main cities.

From Mysore, the 159-km (100-mile) bus journey takes about four hours. The route corkscrews up thickly forested slopes dotted with precarious alpine villages, past the sun-drenched glades of Karnataka's Bandipur and Tamil Nadu's Mudumalai wildlife sanctuaries where elephants and monkeys loiter by the roadside. Mysore–Ooty buses leave the depot throughout the day, but the 6:15 AM bus is best for quieter roads.

If you're heading for Coimbature from Ooty, the quickest option is the three-hour bus trip. But be warned: this is a white-knuckle affair, as the bus tends to hurtle down the switchback roads. Between 20 and 30 buses leave Ooty station each day.

The best option is India's most enchanting rail journey. Ooty's vintage Swiss miniature train steams slowly down the steep slopes via the Coonoor Hills with their soaring rainforests and waterfalls to the lowland railhead of Mettapalayam. There are daily services to and from Ooty timed to connect with the *Nilgiri Express* (which also stops in Coimbature an hour later en route to Madras).

A village woman carries firewood across a rustic meadow in Ooty.

Across the Deccan

Madras
and the
Temple
Towns

TAMIL NADU

Tamil Nadu, India's most southern state—dubbed India's Bible Belt — brims with magnificent architecture, exotic pageantry, and age-old traditions — the legacy of the South's ancient Dravidian culture. Following the route from Madras through Kanchipuram, Mahabalipuram, and Madurai — the main trio of temple towns — you'll see some of India's most impressive temple architecture and experience the warmth and color of rustic Tamil Nadu.

TEMPLE ARCHITECTURE OF THE SOUTH

Dravidian architecture and sculpture achieved its zenith with the construction of vast, imposing temple complexes. These were not the single buildings of further north, but sprawling edifices in which the main shrine was lost amidst a warren of passages, sweeping pillared halls, courtyards, bazaars, and sacred bathing pools. Encased by concentric outer walls and dominated by gigantic, multitiered *goporam* gateway towers, they are stunning in their rich decorative detail. These places of worship were also public forums, where villagers would come to gossip, listen to devotional readings from ancient palm leaf manuscripts, and debate administrative and court matters.

Dravidian temple architecture follows a basic pattern, regardless of a temple's size, with a rectangular ground plan dominated by the distinctive *goporam*, believed to exert talismanic protection over the temple complex. Often rising to a height of more than 50 m (164 ft), these archways swarm with cavorting deities and mythological creatures — some human and some fantastic hybrids — which act out scenes from the great Hindu epics. Up until iIndependence, caste Hindus barred *harijans*, or so-called "untouchables," from entering the temples, so these poor pariahs could only worship the deities on the *goporams*, getting cricked necks in the bargain. Nowadays, temple authorities bow to modern public taste and have them painted up in an outrageous technicolor gloss, disfiguring their great antiquity.

Inside the temple complex stands the pyramid-shaped *vimana*, the wall and tower over the main shrine. This is entered through *mandapas*, cool cloistered passages. In the later Dravidian temple complexes, the designs of these passages became more elaborate, culminating in the so-called "thousand-pillared halls," although rarely do these halls contain this exact number. For instance, Madurai's famous Meenakshi Temple's Hall of Thousand Pillars actually has only 997. Each temple also has its own sacred tank, several smaller shrines, often a score of ceremonial elephants, and its own ornate *ratha*, or wooden temple chariot. On the

annual chariot festival day, the *ratha* is mounted with ornate bronze idols and paraded through the town in a ritual climax of religious fanfare. Most temples you'll encounter in Tamil Nadu's temple towns bar non-Hindus from entering the inner shrine, the sacred *sanctum sanctorum*, but there's still much to admire, with each detail crafted as though that particular panel, door, or fresco was in itself an individual work of art.

SOUTH INDIAN CUISINE

While south Indian dishes are often very spicy, they are tempered with plenty of cooling fresh yogurt, grated coconut, and rice, and are generally much lighter on the palate than the rich, ghee-laden cuisine of the north. Fish is always plentiful along the coastal stretches of the south, and you can usually take your pick of pomfret, lobster, mussels, prawns, and crabs, traditionally cooked with spice-laced coconut milk.

The easiest way to order is to request a "tiffin" *thali*, which will either be served the traditional way on a banana leaf or on a large round metal tray. Even in modest cafés — known variously as *udipi vihars*, tiffin houses, and military hotels (the latter denoting non-vegetarian) — you'll be given six or so assorted vegetarian dishes that are constantly refurbished, a dollop of steaming rice, *papads*, puffed wheat *puri*, fresh *dahi* (yogurt), chutneys, and mango pickles. You'll soon catch on to the south Indian way of using fingers as expert all-purpose eating utensils — and marvel how Madras girls manage to make this look almost graceful — but remember to observe the Indian etiquette of using only your right hand, as using the left will earn you horrified glances from neighboring tables. You'll notice how the locals scrub their hands scrupulously clean before settling down to their finger-scrum meal. Don't touch the water that is slapped down as soon as you sit down; stick to bottled drinks, or well-boiled tea and coffee.

Typical south Indian staples include a dozen varieties of *dosa*, a crispy-thin rice pancake filled with spiced vegetables; *idli*, steamed fermented rice cakes; *vadai*, peppercorn-studded doughnut-shaped balls of deep-fried lentils and rice; and *utthapam*, a thick rice pancake that always comes with a topping — akin to a pizza — of tomatoes, onions, and green chilies. All are accomspicy lentil dish, and make a nourishing protein-packed meal in themselves.

Soothe away the chilies with a *lassi*, freshly squeezed fruit juice, or refreshing fresh coconut milk sipped straight from the husk with a straw. The finale to any meal is always a cup or two of

Weathered stone bulls guard the seventh century Shore Temple at Mahabalipuram.

the local filtered coffee, which is hard to beat anywhere in the world. Don't be alarmed at the waiter's antics if he starts sloshing the boiling brew from one beaker to another at rapid speed — he's performing "coffee by the yard," a south Indian courtesy that froths and cools it down to drinking temperature.

MADRAS (CHENNAI): THE SOUTHERN GATEWAY

As a gateway to Tamil Nadu, Madras, nowadays officially called Chennai, offers relative comfort, good cuisine, and a refined charm to travelers embarking on a tour through the state's temple heartland. Tamil Nadu's tropical seaside capital is full of commercial bustle, yet despite its sprawling skyline, it lacks the brash poverty of India's three larger cities — Bombay, New Delhi, and Calcutta — and has a languid, almost rustic, atmosphere that reflects the essence of south India. This is partly due to its breezy, surf-sprayed locale on the eastern Coromandel Coast, but also to the city's irrepressibly affable, Dravidian-featured, dark-skinned Tamils, whose easygoing ways, lilting language, vivacious culture, and devastatingly spicy cuisine give even the seasoned India traveler the odd sensation of encountering another nation altogether.

BACKGROUND

Four centuries ago, Madras was still Madraspatnam, a small fishing village within a region that was ruled over by the greatest dynasties of the south, the Cholas and the Pallavas. Yet Madras has a long, colorful history of association with seafaring traders and missionaries: Saint Thomas the Apostle was thought to have been martyred here in AD 72, and Arab, Chinese, and Phoenician merchants first began trading along the Coromandel Coast some 1,500 years ago. A Portuguese cathedral bears witness to a transient occupation by traders from Lisbon during the fourteenth century.

In the early seventeenth century, Madras played a strategic role in the history of the British in India, long before India Britannica was a gleam in Queen Victoria's eye. The founder of the city, Sir Francis Day, arrived with the East India Company in 1639, and leased 10 km (six miles) of coastal territory from a descendant of the Raja of Vijayanagar to build Fort Saint George. The garrison camp within the fort's walls became known as "White Town;" outside sprang up Madraspatnam or "Black Town," where the Indian community lived, many of whom were employed as weavers for the cloth trade.

This was the husk of modern Madras, which rapidly eclipsed the East India Company's original settlement at Surat on India's northwest coast. In

1688, James II granted Fort Saint George the first municipal charter in India, and by 1740, Company trade represented over 10% of the entire British public revenue. At this time, however, the Company faced a formidable rival in the French who were just as intent as the British on reaping profits from India. They finally came to blows after war broke out in Europe — first the War of the Austrian Succession (1740–1748) then, with reversed alliances, the Seven Years War (1756–1763).

The French attacked and took Fort Saint George in 1746, although in the pause between the two European wars, Madras was restored to the British in exchange for Cape Breton Island in North America. Madras was barely back in British hands before another battle for supremacy in the south followed — but this time the British defeated the French in a dramatic, unexpected assault on nearby Arcot in 1751, taking it against a force twice its size and saved only by timely reinforcements. From this battle emerged one of British India's lasting heroes — the young Robert Clive, who had persuaded his commander to let him seize Arcot and who later became the governor of Madras.

By 1772, Calcutta had become the most important British city, and Madras, despite its busy commerce, grand Victorian buildings, spacious mansions, and glorious coastline, was destined to be the most provincial of British India's quartet of major capitals.

Nowadays, Madras combines its old legacy with a sprawling manufacturing belt for its main industries — textiles, tannery, cycles, and automobiles. It's also a major producer of films, and gaudy cinema billboards are the city's trademark.

Madras offers the perfect introduction for a first-time India traveler, as it lacks the push-and-shove crowds of Bombay, New Delhi, and Calcutta, and is both unusually spacious and easy to negotiate. Madrassis are often ingenuously friendly, forever flashing mirthful grins at passing tourists. Somehow, long after you've left Madras, you'll be charmed by its simplicity — the men perfectly at ease in a knotted, sarong-style *lungi*, and the women with fragrant blossoms wound into their hair with the same artless grace.

GENERAL INFORMATION

The **Tamil Nadu Government Tourist Office** ((044) 830 3390, 143 Anna Salai (Mount Road), is essentially just a place to book a highly rewarding many of the top-range hotels and restaurants.

Further south lies the Guindy/Adyar area, bordered by Elliot's Beach, with the nearby attractions of the Guindy reserves and temples. Along the Adyar River, one of the city's major waterways, stands a leafy pocket of grand old mansions, including the Madras Club, the Raja's Chettinad Palace, and the Theosophical Society.

Getting around can seem intimidating to the first-time visitor, with streets and lanes arranged in haphazard fashion, and many of the old British place-names still in currency, despite an official emphasis on new, tongue-twisting, post-Independence names. To save problems, it's often worth asking someone to write in Tamil the names of places you want to visit before setting out.

It's most enjoyable to explore Madras by taxi, stopping off at the city's three main sightseeing areas and then simply strolling at whim. You'll find cabs at any of the major hotels and at the main railway station, and can also hail them in the street. Fares are very reasonable and you can always bargain for a day rate, giving a list of the places you wish to see. Auto-rickshaws can do the same job for much less, taking you as far as the airport if desired, and cycle-rickshaws are perfect for negotiating the frenetic back-alleys of the city center, but remember to agree on the fare before climbing aboard. Madras has an easy-to-use city bus system — almost orderly compared to India's other main cities — and if you plan to cover much distance this way, buy the useful *Hallo Madras* booklet for a list of all the city bus routes.

Otherwise, the tourist office runs excellent conducted tours, staffed by knowledgeable guides, which whisk you to all the main places of interest in an afternoon. You'll get a good overview of Madras this way and can always return to Fort Saint George and the Government Museum — where the tour stops are tantalizingly brief — for a less-harried inspection. The tours leave daily at 2 PM from outside the Government of India Tourist Office at 154 Anna Salai.

Bicycles are perfect for gliding along Madras's flat Italianate Marina Parade for panoramic views across the steel-gray Bay of Bengal and lungfuls of salty, incense-scented air, dodging balloon-sellers, donkeys, fakirs, and family scrums. If you follow your nose southward, you'll eventually arrive at Elliot's Beach, 11 km (seven miles) away.

WHAT TO SEE AND DO

The highlights of Madras are the historic Raj-era architecture within the city's environs, and the many surrounding attractions in the southern Guindy/Adyar area.

If you're taking the guided tour, you'll first stop at **Fort Saint George**, established by the East India Company in 1641. The husk of the fort's original "White Town" still stands, much of it rebuilt after the French surrendered the fort in 1749. The ghosts of the Company's East Indiamen still seem to linger in these Georgian gesso-surfaced buildings.

The imposing eleventh-century **Governor's House**, with its grand black Charnockite Corinthian columns, now serves as the city's Legislative Assembly and Council, as well as the

offices of the State Secretariat. Its marble-like surface is actually *chunam*, a hard plaster made from ground shells, which gleams with high polish.

Party men come to chat in the cool of the nearby **Cornwallis Cupola**, above which soars India's tallest flagpole.

Other fine historic buildings include **Clive House** (next to the Archaeological Survey Office), **Wellesley House**, and the original Officers' Mess (1780–1790), now converted into the **Fort Saint George Museum**.

The latter has an extraordinarily rich collection of East India Company memorabilia, including original historical documents, a superb portrait gallery, armory, coins, medals, uniforms, antique clocks, and furniture. The museum houses many fine eighteenth-century lithographs and paintings by the Daniell brothers, and a George Chinnery painting of the East India Company's plump adventurer Major Stringer Lawrence walking with the Nawab of Carnatic. There is also a tiny wooden cage into which one Captain Phillip Anstruther of the Madras Artillery, a huge, bearded officer, was squashed from September 1839 to February 1840, after he had been captured in China while on a forgotten imperial mission. He spent his time sketching on old scraps of bark, the result of which so impressed his captors that they built him a slightly larger cage for more arm movement! Admission is free and the museum is open daily except Fridays from 9 AM to 5 PM.

The oldest of the Anglican churches in the East, **Saint Mary's Church** stands in a leafy, shaded corner of the garrison and still attracts a large congregation of Madras Christians. Designed by William Dixon and built from solid stone between 1678 and 1680 this exquisite chapel is suffused with the spirit of early Empire. Its courtyard is paved with some of the oldest British tombstones in Asia. The church's interior is cluttered with ornate marble sarcophagi decorated with mourning angels. Job Charnock, the founder of Calcutta, who rescued his Indian mistress from her suttee pyre, baptized their three daughters at the church font; Lord Robert Clive married at an altarpiece captured from the French at Pondicherry; and eight former governors lie buried within its environs. Permission can be granted to look at the register of baptisms, marriages, and burials dating from 1680. Saint Mary's Church is open daily from 8:30 AM to 5:30 PM.

Just north of the fort, near Parry's Corner, stands the bulbously domed, ash-red **High Court**, one of India's most remarkable Indo-Saracenic structures and the second-largest judicial building in the world, after London. Designed by Henry Irwin (who also designed the Mysore Palace) and J.H. Stephens in 1892, it towers surrealistically over the bustling chaos of modern Madras.

If you're on a tour bus, you will probably make a mental note to return for a more lingering inspection. You're free to wander through to its grand central cupola, where impromptu affidavits can be typed out by spectacled, cross-legged peons, and through its vaulted arcades where black-cloaked lawyers, wigs askew, converse in the shade of giant sparrow-infested matted *tatties*. Other spectacularly pompous Victorian buildings clustered nearby to include in your own tour of Madras are the Southern Headquarters of the State Bank of India and the General Post Office further north. Westward from here stands the Indo-Saracenic Central Railway Station with its classic clock-tower, Moore Market, and the Government Museum and National Art Gallery, all of which were designed by Irwin, one of the most prolific architects of the Raj period.

The tour stops at the **Government Museum** in Pantheon Road, Egmore. First opened in 1857, it is one of the country's best museums, with entire wings devoted to natural history and archaeological relics. Its highlight is India's most extensive collection of Dravidian bronze sculpture, mainly from the Pallava (700–900), Chola (850–1350) and Vijayanagar (1350–1600) periods.

Pallava bronzes are easily identified by their elongated grace and distinctive oval faces. The Cholas achieved an artistic peak with their robustly sensuous and ornately-clad bronzes, their archetypal females dressed in bejeweled harem pants, exposing boyish waists, perfect navels, and protruding breasts. Perhaps the best-known of Chola bronzes is the *Nataraj*, or Shiva, in a cosmic dance pose framed by a decorative ring.

Also on display are many rare second-century Buddhist sculptures and the immense Amaravathi stupa, said to have been erected over Gautama Buddha's relics.

A pebble path leads to the turreted and domed **National Art Gallery**, which has a fine collection of old and modern paintings, including rare Rajput-, Mughal-, and south Indian-style paintings. Both complexes are open from 10 AM to 5 PM daily except Friday, and there's a small cafeteria for cool drinks and snacks.

Heading southward, the next stop is **Valluvar Kottam**, in Nungambakkum, a giant concrete memorial to the ancient poet-saint Thiruvalluvar, impressive only for its ornate "temple chariot" shrine, a replica of the famed temple chariot at Tiruvarur. Opened in 1976, its vast auditorium looks like an aircraft hanger, and contains 1,330 of the poet's verses inscribed on granite tablets.

A further six kilometers (just under four miles) south lies the **Guindy Snake Park**, the brainchild of American conservationist Romulus Whitiker. It houses a fascinating, well-documented reptilium, with over 200 species of snakes, lizards, crocodiles, tortoises, and spiders, all living in pits.

Look especially for the massive 11-m (33-ft)-long Regal Python and the very poisonous Russell's Viper, whose fangs inspired the invention of the hypodermic needle, and the swarming "Snake-Worship Termite-Hill," decked with flowers and lamps every Friday. There's an impressive hourly bout of un-fanged snake handling, and you can witness venom extraction on Saturdays and Sundays between 4 PM and 5 PM. The fully-fledged research center here manufactures anti-venom for snakebite cures. The park is open every day from 8:30 AM to 5:30 PM.

You can return later to visit the nearby **Raj Bhavan**, a former governor's Banqueting Hall built in the style of a Greek temple, with grand Corinthian and Ionic columns and marble terraces. It was commissioned by Edward Clive, son of Lord Robert Clive, in 1802. Renamed Rajaji Hall, and used for important public functions, it is open to visitors from 10 AM to 6 PM daily. It lies on the periphery of the **Guindy National Park**, a 121-hectare (300-acre) reserve only eight kilometers (five miles) from central Madras. This was once part of the governor's gigantic domain, and rare black buck, spotted deer, cheetah, civet cats, jackals, mongoose, and monkeys roam wild. You can return for an enjoyable day's excursion, either taking the urban train or the No. 45 bus from Anna Square.

Crossing the Cooum River into the historic Mylapore district, the tour continues to the **Kapaleeswarar Temple**, off Ramakrishna Mutt Road down an alley lined with hawkers selling flowers, sacred ash, and tulsi-wood beads. It's a magnificent example of Dravidian temple architecture, dominated by a towering *goporam* gateway writhing with colorful, ornately-carved mythological figures.

The present Shiva temple was built by the Vijayanagar kings in the sixteenth century on the site of an earlier temple destroyed during the Portuguese occupation of Mylapore in 1566. Its spacious flagstone-paved courtyard has a bustling, forum-like atmosphere. It is best visited at sunset, when the temple priest conducts the evening *puja*, or worshiping ceremony, to a backdrop of cymbals, flutes, gongs, smoldering incense, and muttered prayers. Pilgrims stream in, clutching blossoms, shredded coconuts, and rice-strands and stopping to have their temples smeared with a blood-red *tikka* mark.

The colorful 11-day Arupathumoovar festival staged here every March to April is most spectacular on the eighth day, when bronze images of the 63 *nayanmars*, or devotees of Lord Shiva, are paraded around the courtyard. You can also unearth treasures — silks, jewelry, and traditional brass vessels — from the tiny shops surrounding the temples.

Another ancient temple is the **Krishna Parthasarathy Temple** on Triplicane High Road.

The tour makes a paddle-stop at **Elliot's Beach**, the Long Beach of Madras, which is more peaceful than Marina Beach but not recommended for swimming. You'll notice a small memorial facing the sea, erected in the memory of a sixteenth-century Danish sailor called Schimdt who fell in love with a beautiful Tamil girl. So disconsolate was Schimdt when his mistress drowned at sea that he set sail, vowing to comb the waves in search of her body, and was never seen again.

The tour finishes at the **San Thome Cathedral Basilica** on the Main Beach Road, said to contain the mortal remains of Saint Thomas the Apostle, who was martyred by stone-throwing assailants in AD 72 at the nearby hillock (you'll see it on your

way in from the airport) now called **Saint Thomas Mount**. The present Gothic cathedral, with sepia-colored towers and lovely stained-glass windows, was built in 1896 on a site occupied by several churches since the original fourteenth-century Portuguese church. If you venture to Saint Thomas Mount, you'll find a little chapel and a cell, said to have been his dwelling, with holes in the ground worn away by his knees in constant prayer.

It is worth making a special visit to the stately nineteenth-century mansion that houses the **Theosophical Society**, located amid an oasis of 100 hectares (247 acres) of forested parkland on the southern banks of the Adyar River. The Society, whose advocates essentially explored the spiritual nature of man, was cofounded in 1875 by the Russian Madame Blavatsky and her American financial mentor, Colonel Henry Olcott, who established their world headquarters in Madras

two years later. A tireless traveler, Madame Blavatsky survived a disastrous marriage at the age of 14, and despite being described as "fat, unprepossessing and irascible," went on to build an impressive international organization, astounding skeptics by such feats as causing a shower of roses to materialize from nowhere

In her later years, she taught that evolution would soon dispense with the human sexual organs and that there would be two spinal cords in the body. Among those profoundly influenced by her doctrines were the poet W.B. Yeats, the artists Kandinsky and Mondrian, India-reformer Annie Besant, and Oscar Wilde's wife, Constance.

There's an enormous library—open from 9 AM to 10 AM and from 2 PM to 4 PM — stacked with some 17,000 books and many ancient manuscripts encompassing all religions and philosophies. You can picnic undisturbed in the leafy gardens, which are massed with ancient Banyan trees, and house a spiritual supermarket of a church, Buddhist and Hindu temples, a Zoroastrian shrine, and a mosque. The Society is open daily from 8 AM to 11 AM and from 2 PM to 5 PM except Sundays, and the gardens from sunrise to sunset.

Nearby is the **Kalashetra Center**, where students come from all over India (and overseas) to study *Bharatanatayam*, possibly India's most ancient classical dance form, traditionally performed by *devadasis*, young girls dedicated to south Indian temples.

Beaches and Bazaars

Marina Beach stands between Madras and the deep-blue Bay of Bengal. This 13-km (eight-mile)-long mustard-yellow sandy strip fringed by palms and casuarina trees is not exactly the French Riviera, but its balmy seafront throbs with activity. By twilight it throngs with milling families, resembling a sort of shantytown Hades of lamp-lit stalls, pavement entertainers, and wandering hawkers. Along its Italianate Raj-era esplanade lie several imposing public buildings facing the ocean — the Nabob's Palace, the university, Presidency College, and the new lighthouse.

Along Marina Beach are parks dotted with statues of famous Tamil writers and sages, flanked at either end by memorials to two former chief ministers, the late C.N. Annadurai and M.G. Ramachandran, a former matinee idol known for his Superman roles before he turned to politics.

Fishing fleets bob into shore on their catamarans (from the Tamil, meaning "tied-logs") just before dusk, providing an interesting spectacle as they pile their seething catch on the sands and haggle with waiting marketers. Walking southward, at the junction of Pycroft Road and South Beach Corner, you'll reach the **Aquarium** and the historic eighteenth-century **Ice House**, which used to store immense chunks of ice brought by ships from American lakes before the days of refrigerators and air-conditioners.

If you're serious about swimming, head out for **Golden Beach**, about 21 km (13 miles) south of Madras, where the sea is clean and calm, or simply head for the more established beach resorts of Mahabalipuram, 61 km (38 miles) away.

Back in the city, much of Madras's maritime history is crammed into the spice-laden cobbled bazaars of central **Georgetown**, west of the dock area and north of Fort Saint George. When King George V visited Madras in 1911, he raised his eyebrows at Blacktown, the original East India Company's indelicate sobriquet for the native quarter, and suggested it be renamed.

life you can go to the modern **Burma Bazaar**, located directly opposite the Customs House on First Line Beach Road near Parry's Corner. It's full of cheap electronics smuggled from the Gulf, fake Rolex watches, murky bottles of Johnny Walker, reflective sunglasses by the case-load, and shifty salesmen. Moving southwest toward Anna Salai, the **Evening Bazaar** is riddled with tiny alleys each specializing in different household items. Its musty antique shops are open until about 9:30 PM.

SHOPPING

Madras is one of India's largest cottage industry centers for textiles, glazed Thanjuver pottery,

During Madras's late seventeenth-century trading heyday, Blacktown had an added oriental swagger in its shifting population of merchants from Portugal, China, Europe, and Arabia who all added their personality to this historic grid of interlocking streets filled with crumbling façades and decaying godowns.

A good walk starts at **Armenian Street**, just off Parry's Corner or Netaji Subhas Chandra Bose Road. Don't miss the **Armenian Church**, built in 1724, with its whitewashed interior hung with icons and paintings, and a leafy inner courtyard and cemetery containing a Christian gravestone dated 1630, the oldest in Madras. The church is beautifully maintained, with a fascinating array of documents relating to the history of Armenians in India, yet has no priest or congregation.

Clustered nearby, you'll find the **China Bazaar** and **Portuguese Church Street**. For livelier street-

leather ware, and numerous types of handicrafts. Treasure-hunters will also find Madras full of musty curio shops and excellent well-stocked state emporia, and may find themselves making improbable "impulse" buys of giant brass-studded temple doors, elaborate south Indian temple lamps, or irresistible brightly painted terracotta horses known as *ayyanars*, traditionally made throughout Tamil Nadu as symbolic protection of home and hearth.

The best, and most convenient, items to buy are inexpensive, good quality silks, cottons, and handloom fabrics. **Co-Optrex**, Kuralagam, on Netaji Subhas Chandra Bose Road, has the most extensive range, with a ground floor devoted just

OPPOSITE: An army *jawan* bicycles past a historic building within Fort Saint George. ABOVE: The bulbously-domed Indo-Saracenic High Court is the second largest judicial building in the world.

to silks and handloom fabrics, sold at fixed prices. **India Silk House**, at 846 Anna Salai, also has an excellent range.

If you're beginning to feel rather travel-worn, Madras is the perfect place to stock up on fresh cheap cotton garments, many of them "export seconds" in the latest designs. Try **Hanif Bros**, 15-A Nungambakkum High Road, for quality "Madras plaid" shirts, or simply comb an almost endless line of hawkers' wares along Anna Salai. Here you'll also find the state emporia, of which Tamil Nadu's **Poompahur** (at No. 818), Kerala's **Kairali** (at No. 138), Karnataka's **Kaveri** in the LIC Building, and the **Victoria Technical Institute** (at No. 765) are the best. Poompahur has an especially good range of bronze figures, all reproductions of original tenth- to twelfth-century Chola sculptures.

Interesting curio shops to poke through for sculpture, Raj-era relics, brass, and paintings include **N. Balakrishnan and Company**, 62 Montieth Lane; the **Heritage**, 135 Anna Salai; **Kalimuthi**, Krishnamuthi Mudali Street, next to Triplicane High Road, and **Aparna Art Gallery**, 781 Anna Salai. However, bear in mind that faking antiques is a welldeveloped business throughout India, and that it's illegal to take anything more than a hundred years old out of the country. Reproductions are often excellent, provided they are presented and priced as such and not as the genuine article.

Excellent quality leather goods — stylish luggage, wallets, jackets, belts, and shoes — is best at **Sarala Art Center**, at the Hotel Connemara. The **Reptile House**, 161 Anna Salai, is also worth a try, while its neighbor, **Higginbothams Bookshop**, established in 1844, is the city's largest.

WHERE TO STAY

Luxury

The **Taj Coromandel** ((044) 8272827 FAX (044) 8257104, 17 Mahatma Gandhi Road, is the best Madras has to offer, and on a par with the best of the Taj hotels elsewhere around India. Rates range from US$195 to US$750. Of several restaurants, the Taj's Mysore restaurant is particularly worthwhile for Mughalai and regional Indian specialties, with evening *Bharatanatayam* dance performances and musicians.

Not quite as luxurious as the Taj is the **Welcomgroup Chola Sheraton** ((044) 8280101 FAX (044) 8278779, 10 Cathedral Road. It has executive business facilities, a good swimming pool, and a variety of restaurants, including the city's best Northwest Frontier cuisine at its replica of the Maurya Sheraton's famous Bukhara restaurant in New Delhi. The best rooms for panoramic city views are those on the top floor.

Welcomgroup Park Sheraton ((044) 4994104 FAX (044) 4997201, 132 TTK Road, lies about

15 minutes' drive from the city center and is popular with business travelers for its comfort and efficiency. Facilities include excellent Indian and Chinese restaurants, a health club, and a large swimming pool that at night sets the scene for an evening barbecue. Rates range from US$150.

The stately **Hotel Connemara** ((044) 8520123 FAX (044) 8523361, Binny Road, has served as both a palace and a British residency and is an elegant oasis within the city's business district. Its ornately carved wooden lobby is filled with centerpieces from a dismantled antique Dravidian temple, and service is splendidly efficient. Ask to be put in the delightful old wing overlooking the pool, with spacious, luxurious Raj-era rooms. Facilities include possibly the best bookshop in Madras, a choice of bars, a good shopping arcade, travel desk, beauty salon, several excellent restaurants, a coffee shop, and a pastry shop. Rates are from US$140.

Mid-range

At the top of the middle range, the **Ambassador Pallava Hotel** ((044) 8554476 FAX (044) 855 4492, 53 Montieth Road, offers air-conditioned comforts, a swimming pool, health club, and other four-star amenities at rates from US$50.

Slightly cheaper, and less of a class act, is the **Hotel President** ((044) 8542211 FAX (044) 8542299, Dr. Radhakrishnan Road, which has similar, if slightly shabbier, amenities from around US$30.

Other good, centrally located mid-range hotels with rates around US$30 include the **Hotel New Victoria** ((044) 8253638, 3 Kennet Lane, Egmore; and **The Residency** ((044) 8253434 FAX (044) 8250085, 45 GN Chetty Road — a good family choice, though it does have an "alcohol permit room" too.

Budget

Great value at around US$12 for a simple air-conditioned double with attached bathroom is the **Hotel Maris** ((044) 8270541, right next door to the Chola Sheraton on Cathedral Road.

In more secluded, downtown Mylapore, at 72 Dr. Radhakrishnan Road, the **New Woodland's Hotel** ((044) 8273111 FAX (044) 8260460 has two restaurants, including an excellent, cheap south Indian vegetarian restaurant, and even a swimming pool, at rates of around US$12 with air-conditioning.

But by far the best hotel in the very cheap range is **Broadlands Lodge** ((044) 8545573, 16 Vallabha Agraham Street, opposite Star Talkies in Triplicane. It's an immaculate old Moorish merchant's house with pastel-blue shutters — a traveler's oasis with simple rooms, a sunroof, a peaceful garden courtyard strewn with deck chairs and swing-seats,

Kapaleeswarar Temple in Madras, dominated by a giant multi-tiered pyramid goporum (gateway) that is believed to exert a protective influence over the temple complex.

room-service meals, and boiled and filtered water. Rooms range from as little as US$4 (if you don't mind using the communal bathing facilities) to US$9 for the "suites." The rooftop terrace, popular for sunbathing, overlooks a large modern mosque.

WHERE TO EAT

For stylish dining, try the Hotel Connemara's outdoor mock-rustic **Raintree** restaurant ((044) 8520123, which serves the delicious Tamil Nadu Chettinad cuisine. Specialties include *chettinadu meen kozambu*, an aromatic fish curry; *kozhi varutha*, a subtly spiced chicken curry; and *paayasam*, a moist rice pudding with almonds, raisins, and cardamom.

Each of the four main hotels has a potpourri of good restaurants and bars, but some are outstanding: the Chola Sheraton's **Peshawri** ((044) 8280101 for superb Northwest Frontier food, the Taj Coromandel's **Mysore** ((044) 8272827 for a variety of Indian regional dishes and evening dance performances, and the **Golden Dragon** (same phone number) for Chinese food. The Hotel Connemara also offers outstanding buffet lunches — with a pick-and-choose mixture of Indian, Chinese, and Western dishes — complete with dessert and coffee for around US$7 per head.

For those with a newly acquired enthusiasm for the almost exclusively vegetarian south Indian cuisine, Madras is a goldmine for good, extraordinarily cheap restaurants — it's fun to try south Indian cuisine in authentic surroundings.

Amaravathi ((044) 8276416, 1 Cathedral Road, is nothing less than an eating experience, and consistently wins praise and awards for its superb Andhra-style food. Try their crab *masala* and *sora puttu*, grilled fish with spices, or opt for their spectacular set meal served on a banana leaf. This includes a variety of vegetarian dishes, fish, prawns, or chicken, and, if desired, curd and fluffy rice, which the waiter liberally sprinkles with a fine lentil powder and hot ghee, leaving the traditional tamarind paste up to your discretion. Your fingers are supposed to do the rest (you're given finger bowls and hot towels before and after the meal), but if you find the idea off-putting just ask for a fork and spoon.

Other excellent south Indian restaurants are **Woodlands Drive-In** ((044) 8271981 near the top of Cathedral Road, open daily for early morning breakfasts of fresh *idlis*, *dosas*, and *vadas*, with generous *thali* platters served for lunch and dinner; the **Hotel Dasaprakash's** pleasant rooftop restaurant on Poonamallee Road; and the **Mathura** restaurant ((044) 8521777, on the second floor, Tarapore Towers, Anna Salai, specializing in regional vegetarian fare, with a bewildering array of *thali* choices. You can dine on the pretty terrace lit with fairy lights, or in air-conditioned comfort.

For "multi-cuisine" — in this case a mixture of southern-style vegetarianism and northern-style barbecued meats — the **Carnival Multi-Cuisine Restaurant** ((044) 4993142, 68 CP Ramaswamy Road, Abhiramapuram, is an air-conditioned treat that delivers the goods.

For Malabar cuisine, coconut curry food of Kerala, the **Coconut Grove** ((044) 8268800, 95 Harrington Road, Chetpet, is a smart but not overly expensive place for a delicious meal.

Outside the hotels, the best Chinese restaurant is **Chinatown** ((044) 8276221, 4 Cathedral Road, Gopalapuram, opposite the Chola Sheraton, where the Madras chic converge for excellent Sichuan and Chinese regional dishes amidst an attractive bold red and green decor, dangling Chinese lanterns, and monkey-box screens.

The **Chungking** ((044) 8570134, 67 Anna Salai, is another local old-time favorite for Sino-Indian fare. Set in a quiet leafy cul-de-sac above a musty music shop, it serves good garlic prawns, sweet and sour pomfret, and spring rolls.

Lastly, if you feel like splashing out on that most unexpected of things in Madras — Japanese cuisine — head over to **Dahlia** ((044) 8265240, Kaveri Complex, 96 104 Nungambakkum High Road. The chefs are from Japan, the ambience is right, and prices are around US$20 per head for dinner.

NIGHTLIFE

Enthusiasts of Indian classical dance and music should time their visit to Madras to coincide with the annual cultural bonanza held in December and January, when performances are staged each evening.

A dozen cultural halls regulary stage performances, notably the **Kalashetra Center**, the **Music Academy Raja Anamalai Hall**, and the **Fairlands Tourist Exhibition Center** on Marina Beach.

The week's upcoming events are listed in Friday's *The Daily Hindu*. Otherwise, this is your once-in-a-lifetime chance to experience the outrageous fortunes and lachrymose antics of south Indian cinema. The best centrally located air-conditioned cinemas are Sathyam, Devi, and Safire, and if that only whets your appetite, approach the Tourist Office about arranging a visit to one of Madras's film studios.

HOW TO GET THERE

International travelers can fly direct to Madras from Colombo, Kuala Lumpur, Singapore, Jakarta, Shahjah, and Abu Dhabi, and British Airways operate direct flights from London.

Madras is the most convenient base from which to explore south India, with direct Indian Airlines flights to Ahmedabad, Bangalore, Bombay, Calcutta, Cochin, Delhi, Hyderabad, Madurai, Port Blair, Trivandrum, and several other centers.

Both the smart domestic terminal and the international airport are quite close together, about 15 km (nine miles) from the city. If arriving by air, there's a PTC bus service (from 5 AM to 10 PM) running between both airports and the city, which drops passengers at Egmore railway station and most major hotels on request. Madras port has passenger shipping links with Penang, Singapore, and Port Blair.

Madras has two railway stations: Egmore, which serves most of south India, and Central for the rest of India. Both are located quite close together in the city center near Poomallee High Road.

Popular train journeys include the overnight *Alleppey Express* to Cochin, the *Bangalore Mail*

THE TEMPLE TOWNS

Tamil Nadu's main trio of temple towns — Kanchipuram, Mahabalipuram, and Madurai — offer the perfect introduction to the cultural fabric of south India, with its Hindu faith, rustic simplicity, and deep respect for tradition.

At least two days are recommended for both Kanchipuram and Mahabalipuram, with excellent accommodation at the latter. Buses travel from these temple towns to Madurai, but it's more interesting and comfortable to return to Madras along the scenic coastal road and take the daily flight, eight-hour train trip, or deluxe bus to Madurai.

(seven hours) and the *Shatabdi Express* (five hours) to Bangalore, and the *Charminar Express* (14 hours) to Hyderabad.

From either station, it is a short city hop north to Fort Saint George, and only eight kilometers (five miles) south to the Guindy National Park.

Avoid bottleneck lines for rail tickets and head for the Indrail office on the second floor of the Central station, open from 10 AM to 6 PM.

Trains are generally slower, but safer, than the battered sardine-tin state buses, which make traveling long distances a grueling endurance test. Both the Tamil Nadu State Transport and the privately run Thiruvalluvar Transport Corporation have their terminals off Esplanade Road. If you intend to do much traveling by bus, buy the monthly *Jaico Time table* from any newsstand, which lists all destinations, revised schedules, and fares in south India.

KANCHIPURAM

Kanchipuram, or "Golden City," 76 km (47 miles) southwest of Madras, is one of the most spectacular of Tamil Nadu's pilgrimage centers. The skyline of this rustic town is massed with towering *goporams*, for within its environs stand no less than a thousand ancient temples, many of them well-preserved masterpieces of Dravidian architecture.

Kanchipuram is one of India's Seven Sacred Cities, but differs from the others — Varanasi, Mathura, Ujjian, Haridwar, Dwarka, and Ayodhya — in that it offers worship to both Shiva and Vishnu, rather than one or the other. Few of Tamil Nadu's temple towns are as interesting and beguiling as Kanchipuram, with its almost constant festival

Windbreaking palm trees along lonely coastal stretch in Tamil Nadu.

pageantry, exquisite temples, swarms of kohl-eyed children, and tiny hut porticos decorated with rice-powder *kolam*. Outside the entrance to the main temples, wizened hawkers sell assorted piles of blossoms, coconuts, powdered ash, camphor, sugar lumps (a symbol of wealth), incense sticks, conch shells, and sacred threads for Brahmans (with a point-of-sale mantra hummed over them!).

Kanchipuram is also renowned for its brightly colored, fine-quality silk, and silver and gold brocaded fabrics. In the surrounding countryside, skeins of brilliant silk and cotton hang to dry beneath the trees, and the town itself is a hive of weaving activity: back alleys are matted with silk threads and hum with the click-clacking of looms.

just a major religious pilgrimage center, but also a seat of learning, attracting scholars, artists, and musicians. Sixth-century sage Shankaracharya, who has been called the "Brahman Aquinas," set up an episcopal seat here that exists to this day. But by the ninth century, the Pallavas were on the wane, and Kanchipuram fell to a succession of rulers (the Cholas, Badami Chalukyas, and Vijayanagar rajas) who all stamped their own artistic style on the elaborate temples that can be seen today.

To see Kanchipuram at its exuberant best, try to time your visit to coincide with one of the major temple festivals. The most spectacular is the "cart festival" held at the Kamakshiamman Temple on the lunar cusp of February and March,

Kanchipuram first flourished as the capital of the Pallava dynasty, great patrons of art who ruled much of the far south between the sixth and eighth centuries. The Pallavas were prolific builders who also turned their talents to establishing the traditions of silk-weaving and the choreography of *Bharatanatayam* dance, performed within pillared halls by barefoot *devadasis*, half-hidden by silken veils, who lived within the temple enclosures.

Of all the Pallava kings, Mahendravarman I (600–630), a dramatist and poet, encouraged the most inspired developments in Dravidian (the Pallava term for Tamil Nadu) temple architecture. His reign witnessed not only some of the mono-lithic carved *rathas*, or "chariot temples," at Mahabalipuram, but also the beginnings of the towering *goporam* gate-towers clustered with writhing deities that became a Dravidian temple trademark. In its heyday, Kanchipuram was not

when temple deities are paraded in elaborately decorated wooden chariots against an extravagant backdrop of firecrackers, fairs, street acrobats, and folk theater. Similar festivals are held on a smaller scale by every temple to celebrate the south Indian New Year during April, including the equally carnival-like *Brahmothsavam* festival.

Bicycles are perfect for cruising Kanchipuram's flat, spacious streets, and there are plenty of bike-rental places. There is no tourist office, but the Archaeological Survey Office opposite the Kailasanatha Temple can usually supplies maps.

What to See and Do
Scattered in and around Kanchipuram are some 1,000 temples, about 200 of which are within the city itself. Only a handful are especially outstanding, and these are mainly clustered toward the northern end of the town, near the bus station.

There are a few basic guidelines to bear in mind before setting off on your temple tour. First, all "living" temples (where pilgrims still come to make *puja* worship) take a siesta break between 1 PM and 4 PM, so that early mornings and late afternoon are best for sightseeing. Secondly, be prepared for a barrage of dirty beggars and frantic, credential-waving "guides," and remember that one stern-faced "No!" is more effective than a dozen apologetic smiles. But have plenty of spare change at hand anyway in case you get talking with temple priests or custodians, whose knowledge is genuine and their tales often fascinating. They will sometimes let you clamber to the top of temple *goporam* for stunning views,

but they'll expect a token of thanks, something in the realm of Rs 20.

The **Kailasanatha Temple**, located east of the town center down Nellukkara and Putteri Streets, is one of Kanchipuram's earliest and most exquisite temples. It's a masterpiece of early Dravidian architecture, with a small prototypical *goporam* and *mandapa*, and its sculptures, carved reliefs, and overall design poses a vitality and austere elegance closer in style to the monolithic rock-cut temples at Mahabalipuram. It was built entirely in sandstone by the Pallava king Rayasimha in the late seventh century, with the more elaborate frontispiece added later by his son, Mahendravarman III.

Within the temple pavilion stand the three telltale signs of a "living" temple in which pilgrims gather to worship Lord Shiva: the Nandi bull (Shiva's trusty steed), the tall *durajasthamba* flagstaff, and the *balipitha*, shaped like an inverted lotus leaf, where offerings are made. The temple's inner courtyard wall contains many miniature shrines, and if you peer closely, some of these have the fragments of beautifully painted stucco-work frescoes, just enough to give an impression of the temple's original splendor.

To the left of the nearby Nellukkara and Putteri Streets junction lies the **Ekambareshwara Temple**, with its soaring 57-m (187-ft)-high *rajagoporam* and massive fortress-like outer walls built by the Vijayanagar king Krishna Devaraja in 1500.

Dedicated to Shiva, this is Kanchipuram's largest, most magnificent "living" temple, spread across nine hectares (22 acres). It was originally built by the Pallavas and became a fusion of successive Chola and Vijayanagar craftsmanship. Within the dim coolness of its airy sandalwood-scented enclosures, the barefoot pilgrims seem dwarfed. Long pillared hallways lead to a monkey puzzle of ornately-carved enclosures, small shrines, and the inner *sanctum sanctorum*. Within a tiny courtyard stands a gnarled mango tree, said to be some. The temple was built around this tree, and owes its name to a corruption of *Eka Amra Nathar*, Lord of the Mango Tree. Novice priests seem to materialize like ghosts from the shadows — some are barely eight years old, already self-assured, with sacred threads twined across their thin chests, heads shaved but for a tuft of hair.

A five-minute stroll further left, you'll find the **Kamakshiamman Temple**, with its large watchtower *goporams*. Built by the Cholas during the fourteenth century, it is one of India's three holy places dedicated to Sakthi (the goddess Parvati when she married Lord Shiva), considered particularly auspicious for marriage-blessings. Close by is the large Vishnu temple, the **Vaikuntha Perumal**, built by Pallava emperor, Nadivarman II, in the seventh century. It has beautiful lion-pillared cloisters and sculpted bas-reliefs around the main shrine, portraying the history of the Pallavas and the wars fought by them.

Another impressive Vishnu temple is the Vijayanagar **Varasdaraja Temple**, with its 30-m (98-ft)-high *goporam*, thousand-pillared hall, and many ornate sculptures, among which is a huge chain carved out of a single piece of stone.

But these are only the most famous of the town's temples, and you're bound to stumble across countless discoveries of your own, not to mention fascinating weaving workshops.

If you're serious about shopping, drop in at the **Weaver's Service Center**, at 20 Station Road, or **Srinivas Silk House**, at 17A TK Nambi Street,

OPPOSITE and ABOVE: South India is well known for its traditional dance and drama. Special performances are held in Madras in December and January.

for reasonably priced fine silks and brocades. Kanchipuram's **India Coffee House,** just down Gandhi Road, serves excellent cold coffee.

Where to Stay and Eat
It's best to explore at your own leisurely pace, staying overnight at the **Hotel Tamil Nadu** ((04112) 22552, Station Road, near the railway station, which is cheaply priced and serves good south Indian fare. It is managed by the Tamil Nadu Tourism Development Corporation (TTDC).

How to Get There
Kanchipuram is easily reached from Madras, either by regular bus services or daily trains from Madras, connecting at Chengalpattu. If you're taking the TTDC tour, which leaves Madras at 6:45 AM and returns at 6 PM, you'll make only a brief morning stop at the main temples.

THIRUKALIKUNDRAM

The TTDC tour makes a brief stop at this small pilgrimage town, 50 km (31 miles) out from Kanchipuram and 15 km (nine miles) from Mahabalipuram. It's notable for its medieval Shiva temple atop the 160-m (525-ft)-high Vedagiri hill, where two eagles are said to come to be fed by temple priests every day at noon.

Legend has it that these two eagles are actually saints who stop to rest at this temple on their daily flight between the holy cities of Varanasi and Rameswaram. But somehow, the birds have either "just been" or are "delayed," when visitors clamber up to witness this daily ritual!

The vertiginous climb up the hill's 500 granite-hewn steps is the equivalent of a Jane Fonda workout and earns spectacular views. The less-fit get themselves slung into baskets for an alarmingly swaying ascent at the hands of the *dandi-wallahs*: one false step could send their human baggage plummeting all the way down!

Another much larger Shiva temple stands within the village center and houses Tamil Nadu's Lourdes — a tank believed to have healing powers. Locals swear that every 12 years a conch mysteriously rises from its waters, a phenomenon that attracts streams of pilgrims. These conchs are displayed in the Shiva temple.

MAHABALIPURAM (MAMALLAPURAM)

This popular seaside resort lies on the gloriously empty white-sanded Coromandel Coast, 65 km (40 miles) east of Kanchipuram, or 58 km (36 miles) south of Madras, and is easily reached by bus. It began as a seaport almost 2,000 years ago and was known to Phoenician, Arab, and Greek traders. Between the seventh and tenth centuries, the port thrived as a busy trade center

established by Narasimhavarman I, nicknamed "*mamalla*" or "great wrestler," hence the village's original name of Mamallapuram. The Pallavas left an astonishing legacy of unique monolithic rock-cut temples, caves, massive bas-reliefs, and one remaining shore temple — and these are the oriental marvels that visitors flock to see today.

Collectively, these open-air structures are the earliest known examples of Dravidian architecture in existence, built by the Pallava kings during a creative frenzy of temple-building in the seventh century. Mysteriously, the Pallavas deserted the site, and these ancient architectural treasures lay undiscovered until the late eighteenth century.

You could start your tour close to the village center, with the most famous of the bas-reliefs: the immense **Arjuna's Penance,** a huge 27-m (88-ft)-long and nine-meter (30-ft)-high frieze crammed with a Noah's Ark of beasts, birds, and mytho-logical figures — including life-sized elephants — sculpted across a whaleback-shaped rock.

Built during the reign of Narasimhavarman Pallava (circa 630-670), archaeologists have long debated whether it portrays the Mahabharata fable in which the mortal Arjuna undergoes penance to Lord Shiva for his guilt in killing his fellow humans alongside Krishna; or the mythical tale of the descent of the holy river Ganges to the earth —

OPPOSITE: Courtyard view of the Ekambareshwara Temple in Kanchipuram. ABOVE: Temple wall buttressed by stone guardians in the pilgrimage town of Kanchipuram.

depicted by a natural fissure in the rock face. To the right, you'll see Lord Shiva letting the floodwaters flow through his hair, preventing the world from being destroyed by the impact of its descent. Either way, the panel is nothing less than a brilliant piece of artistry, filled with realistic, humorous touches: cavorting mice at the elephants' feet, a deer scratching its face with its hoof, and an emaciated hermit doing penance by standing on one foot, whose ascetic posturing is mocked by a cat striking the same pose.

The nearby hillside is dotted with eight *mandapas*, shallow rock-cut cave temples, each sculpted with fine bas-reliefs depicting scenes from Hindu mythology, although two were left

Back on Beach Road, take the road to your left for a 15-minute walk down to the casuarina tree-sheltered sandy clearing containing the monolithic seventh-century **Five Rathas**. Each of these miniature "temple chariots" is a stupendous work of art, sculpted into architecture from gigantic boulders, and covered with ornate porches, pillars, and statuary. Although these temples have stylistic links to early Buddhist chapels and monasteries, they contain the embryonic forms of later Dravidian architecture — the *goporams*, *vimanas*, and multi-pillared halls. They are named after the Pancha Pandava, the five hero brothers of the epic *Mahabharata*, and guarded by three stone guardians: a lion, an elephant, and a Nandi-bull.

unfinished. The finest and largest of these is the **Krishna Mandapa**, which shows Krishna using Mount Govardhann as a sort of protective umbrella to save his flocks of shepherds and animals from Indra, a vengeful rain-god.

Take the path just left of the "Penance" for an easy climb up the hill — site of several scattered temple *mandapas*, and **Krishna's Butterball**, a massive boulder precariously balanced on the hill's slope. For stunning views across Mahabalipuram, climb the tall lighthouse at the rear of the hill, open to visitors until noon.

The **Mahishasuramardhini Cave,** just below the lighthouse, fronted by a lion-pillared portico, has especially exquisite reliefs, particularly those of Lord Vishnu sleeping on the coils of the serpent Adisesha and of the Goddess Durga, better known as Kali, seated on a lion about to kill the buffalo-headed demon, Mahishasura.

Of Mahabalipuram's ancient Seven Pagodas, only a single desolate **Shore Temple** stands on the coastline, at the end of the main Beach Road.

Built by the Pallava king Rayasimha during the late seventh century, this simple, pagoda-roofed structure is one of south India's oldest temples. Assaulted by the elements, many of the temple's exquisite reliefs have been worn to obscurity, but its original splendor is still visible. This two-spired temple is unique in that it houses shrines to both Shiva and Vishnu, the latter containing a splendid 2.5-m (eight-foot)-long bas-relief of Vishnu reclining on his serpent couch. A rear chamber contains remnants of a 16-sided granite phallic *lingam*, which originally touched the ceiling, and a bas-relief depicting a sacred cow forever in the throes of sacrificial slaughter. Rows of stone bulls guard the temple courtyard. The temple's modern neighbor is a bulbously ugly nuclear power plant, visible 10 km (six miles) further up the coastline.

Back in town, there's a good open-air museum, dozens of tiny souvenir shops, and a government-funded **School of Sculpture**, where sculptors create excellent replicas of ancient Indian carvings in marble, soapstone, and granite, all sold at reasonable prices. It's diagonally opposite the bus-stop and is open from 9 AM to 1 PM, and 2 PM to 6 PM, closed Tuesdays.

Local information is provided by the Tourist Office ((04113) 232, on East Raja Street, and the useful *Guide to Mahabalipuram* booklet.

The **Mahabalipuram-Madras Road** is worth several stops. This 58-km (36-mile)-long coastal ribbon of road takes you first to the **Crocodile Farm**, which lies 16 km (10 miles) from Mahabalipuram. Like Madras' Snake Farm, it was established by Romulus Whitaker to breed rare species of crocodiles in captivity. Visitors peer down into large swampy enclosures housing some 516 reptiles. "Jaws 3," the largest captive crocodile in India, is the star attraction, and crowds form to watch him chew his way through a lunch of bandicoots and buffalo steaks.

Just 18 km (11 miles) short of Madras is the **Cholamandalam Artists Village**, a seaside commune started during the 1960s where a community of artists, sculptors, and potters live and work. There's a continual exhibition of works for sale, and visitors are often invited in to meet the artists. Those with a creative bent can stay at a clean, simple guesthouse and attend workshops in batik-dyeing, sculpture, painting, or fabric-printing.

Where to Stay and Eat

The ITDC-run **Ashok Temple Bay Resort** ((04114) 42251 FAX (04114) 42255 has secluded cottages, a swimming pool, restaurant, and bar. Rates for the cottages start at around US$70 in season, but drop to as low as US$30 out of season (May to June).

For a winning combination of comfortable lodgings, excellent food, and a perfect, quiet stretch of surf for swimming, go to **Silversands Beach Resort** ((04114) 42228, about two kilometers (a little over a mile) along the coast. It has sea-facing air-conditioned deluxe rooms or deluxe beach villas, all with tasteful south Indian decor. Good Indian, continental, and Chinese food is served, but fresh seafood dishes here are simply outstanding. Rates range from around US$15.

Cheaper again, and peacefully situated, is the **TTDC Hotel Tamil Nadu Beach Resort** ((04114) 42235 where you can enjoy a swimming pool and other smart amenities for as little as US$8, if you forsake the air conditioning.

Shoestring budget lodges in town include the recommended **Vinayak Cottages** ((04114) 42445, which has cottages for less than US$5.

Some visitors swear by the "authentic" experience of lodging with village families, paying about US$4 per week for the local version of "bed and breakfast" — *charpoy* (a rope bed) and *chai*.

On the food front, among the friendly, ramshackle budget beach-cafés, try the **Village Restaurant**, the **Sunset**, and the **Rose Garden** for excellent fresh seafood and travelers' fare.

MADURAI

Lying 472 km (293 miles) south of Madras, Madurai is one of India's oldest and most illustrious cities, an oasis of traditional Tamil culture that is dominated by magnificent

towering temple complexes. Founded over 2,500 years ago on the lushly fertile banks of the Vaigai River, Madurai today still retains much of its distinctive heritage, along with a leisurely old-world charm.

The most famous of all of Tamil Nadu's pilgrimage centers, Madurai's overwhelming attraction for visitors is the giant fortress-like medieval **Meenakshi Temple**, with its nine soaring stucco-work *goporams*. Acknowledged as the finest, and one of the largest, examples of Dravidian architecture, it embraces much of the city with ever-rippling rings of stone battlements, tanks, and corridors. The elaborate ebb and flow of its temple life has changed little for centuries, and its exotic bazaars hum with a carnival atmosphere and are full of temple-offerings, barefoot devotees, sacred ash-smeared mystics, and wailing music. Tiny shops are full of unexpected treasures — traditional brass temple lamps, jewelry, handwoven silks, tie-dye fabrics, and stone carvings.

OPPOSITE: Ancient stone-hewn temples within the group of the Five Rathas at Mabalipuram. ABOVE: Gypsy waifs are eerily dwarfed beside Krishna's gravity-defying "Butterball" on the mountain slopes of Mahabalipuram.

Legend tells how Madurai, "the city of nectar," was formed by a single drop of water shaken from Lord Shiva's locks, in answer to a prayer of the Pandya king Kulasekera for a new capital during the sixth century BC. The Pandyas ruled much of south India from Madurai until the thirteenth century, initiating a renaissance of Tamil literature, art, and architecture as the seat of the *Sangam*, or Tamil Academy. The city fell to the Cholas during the eleventh and twelfth centuries, and was to change hands several times — first to the Delhi Sultans, then the Vijayanagars, followed by the cultivated Nayak rulers who built Madurai as we see it today, laid out in the pattern of a lotus flower with the immense Meenakshi Temple at its core.

The Nayaks ruled from 1599 to 1781, when they were ousted by British troops who destroyed the temple's defenses, filled in its moat fort, and built four broad streets known as the *veli*, or "outer streets," which now mark the limits of the old city. You'll find most of Madurai's sights concentrated here, as well as the budget lodges, restaurants, the main **Tourist Office** ((0452) 34757, West Veli Street, the General Post Office, bus stations, and railway station.

Madurai's modern cantonment area lies on the northern banks of the Vaigai River — there's little to see here, but this is where the better hotels are located. Allow yourself at least two days for leisurely sightseeing, either on foot or by handy cycle-rickshaw, nicest in the cool of early evening.

When to Go

The best time to visit is the cool season from October to March, but it's worth coming a little later for the most spectacular month-long **Chithirai Festival** in April and May, when Madurai explodes with bizarre and wonderful pageantry for the "marriage" of Goddess Meenakshi and Lord Sundareswarar. As many as 10,000 pilgrims stream into the city each day. The **Teppam**, or **Float Festival**, which is just as interesting, is held during January and February at the Mariamman tank's island temple.

What to See and Do

In the center of the old town, the magnificent **Meenakshi Temple** is the classic monument to Madurai's Dravidian heritage and seethes with an astonishing profusion of sculpted figures, ornamental pillars, and cloistered courtyards. Much of this massive complex — which covers six hectares (15 acres) — was built during the seventeenth century by the Nayak kings, although the Vijayanagar rulers renovated it extensively.

It comprises two main sanctums, one dedicated to the goddess Meenakshi — a "fish-eyed" Pandya princess born with three breasts, one of which miraculously disappeared when she met her true love, Shiva, in the form of Lord up on Mount Kailas;

the other sanctum is dedicated to her famous consort, Shiva himself. Of four leviathan tapering *goporams* surrounding the temple complex, the southern gateway eclipses them all with a height of nearly 50 m (164 ft).

Within are five smaller *goporams*, enclosing two slender, gilt-smothered *vimanas*, or central shrines. Highlights include its famous **Musical Pillars** — 22 tapering rods, each carved out of a single block of granite, which sound an arpeggio of musical notes when tapped; and the ornate **Hall of a Thousand Pillars**, actually 985, with two small shrines standing in the space reserved for the remaining 15 pillars. Part of the hall has been turned into a museum with a fascinating, though poorly-lit, display of antique art treasures, sculpture, religious icons, and photographs charting the development of Dravidian architecture. There's plenty to see — one enthusiastic visitor said he spent two entire days wandering through its imposing enclosure — and only the inner sanctum is barred to non-Hindus.

Evenings can be spent very pleasantly listening to temple music performed outside the Meenakshi Amman shrine between 6 PM to 7:30 PM and 9 PM to 10 PM. The main temple complex is open daily from 5 AM to 12:30 PM and from 4 PM to 10 PM, and there's a peculiar rule that photos can only be taken between 1 PM and 4 PM on payment of Rs 5.

A short 10-minute cycle-rickshaw ride brings you to the seventeenth-century **Tirumali Nayak Palace**, a vast Indo-Saracenic abode notable for its elegant domes, colonnades, and pavilions. As a sort of south Indian Versailles, it so captivated Lord Napier, the Governor of Madras during the 1860s, that he restored it, although today it is only a quarter of its original size. Its imposing Main Hall, as big as a football field, was originally Tirumali Nayak's boudoir, where he was royally entertained by dancers, musicians, and court fakirs. The courtyard outside was used for religious pageants and gladiatorial fights. It is open from 8 AM to 4 PM daily, there's a museum and a good sound-and-light show here daily at 6:30 PM relating the history of the Nayak dynasty.

There are several other places of interest. The **Mariamman Teppakkulam Tank**, built in 1646, with its picturesque island temple reached by boat, lies five kilometers (three miles) east of the city center. There's a good **Gandhi Museum**, five kilometers (three miles) north of the city center, which houses many of the Mahatma's personal relics, including the bloodstained *dhoti* he was assassinated in and his glasses. Within the same complex is the **Government Museum** and various south Indian crafts and textile displays, all open daily between 10 AM and 1 PM and 2 PM and 6 PM, except Wednesdays.

From the central bus-stand, you can take a No.5 bus out to the impressive rock-cut temple of

Tirupparankundrum, just eight kilometers (five miles) away. Carved into the side of a mountain, it is one of the six holy shrines of Subrahmanya, the second son of Shiva, and throbs with colorful activity as pilgrims, holy-men, and vacationing Indians come armed with lamp-lit bowls, coconuts, garlands, and incense for Shiva's blessings.

Where to Stay

Madurai's best hotel is the **Taj Garden Retreat** ((0452) 601020 FAX (0452) 604004 in which rooms are mostly housed in a delightfully restored colonial villa. The most expensive deluxe rooms are in new but tastefully appointed cottages.

air-conditioned doubles, even cheaper fan-cooled rooms and classic south Indian meals. You'll see dozens of very cheap hotels and cafes clustered along Town Hall Road within the old town, but there's little to distinguish one from another.

Outside the hotels, good, simple south Indian breakfasts and *thali* meals can be had at **Amutham** and the **Indo-Ceylon Restaurant**, both on Town Hall Road.

HOW TO GET THERE

Madurai is easily accessible from Madras, with a choice of a near-daily flight, an eight-hour train journey, and frequent buses.

Of Madurai's two other top-class hotels, the better is the three-star **Pandyan** ((0452) 537090 FAX (0452) 533424, Race Course Road, set in a pretty garden with pleasant, well-furnished rooms. Rates start at less than US$50. It has Madurai's best restaurant, and has car rental, a travel agency, a bank, beauty parlor, and a shopping arcade.

The similarly priced **Hotel Madurai Ashok** ((0452) 537531 FAX 537530, Algarkoil Road, is also recommended. Unlike the Pandyan, it has a swimming pool.

Going down in price again, the **Hotel Supreme** ((0452) 742151 FAX (0452) 742637 is a well-managed lower-mid-range hotel with a rooftop southern Indian-style restaurant and doubles from around US$10 (fan-cooled) and US$15 (air conditioning).

Budget travelers should take a look at the central, cheaply priced TTDC-run **Hotel Tamil Nadu** ((0452) 537471, West Veli Street, with good

From either Kanchipuram or Mahabalipuram, buses take about 10 wearisome hours. Madurai is also connected by air to Cochin and Bangalore, and well-connected by rail directly with Bangalore, Quilon, and — for temple-addicts — the other major Tamil temple cities of Rameswaram, Tiruchirapalli (Trichy), Thanjavur (Tanjore), and Tirupati. Buses ply to all major south Indian centers, and from here, Kanya Kumari, the "Land's End" of India, is only 150 km (94 miles), a six-hour bus journey. From Kanya Kumari you can conveniently continue traveling through Kerala state by taking the early morning express bus to Kovalam beach, a pleasant three-and-a-half-hour trip.

A wandering showman orchestrates a beachfront battle between a mongoose and a cobra near the Shore Temple.

The Deep
South

KERALA INSTANTLY DISARMS TRAVEL-WEARY VISITORS with its beautiful, shimmering beaches, sun-filtered glades of palm trees, and green lowlands.

Villagers claim their land was created by the warmongering god Parashurama who was persuaded to change his bloodthirsty ways and throw away his axe. When the axe fell from heaven, the legend says, it landed in southern India and formed the fertile Malabar Coast on the Arabian Sea.

This narrow, verdant strip of land is one of India's wealthiest states, crisscrossed with mossed backwaters and bursting with paddy fields and coconut, rubber, and cashew plantations. Cut off from the rest of India by the towering Sahyadri mountain range to the east, Kerala evolved a distinctive culture of dance, drama, and temple arts under the royal Chera dynasty and defied even the Mughal's efforts to incorporate it into their empire.

Although isolated by land, Kerala claims an unusually cosmopolitan history. Missionaries were among its earliest visitors: St. Thomas the Apostle is believed to have established the earliest Christian colony in Kerala in AD 52, followed by Syrian Christian settlers from Alexandria, whose cathedrals and churches still attract large congregations throughout the state. Kerala's lush Malabar coast lured legions of ancient Phoenician, Chinese, Arab, and Jewish traders in search of ivory, pepper, spices, incense, and myrrh. In the period spanning the fifteenth to the seventeenth century, Kerala became the battleground for numerous colonizing struggles between the Portuguese, the French, the Dutch, and, finally, the British, who gained control in 1795.

Modern Kerala — "land of *kera*" (coconuts) — was created in 1956 by the joining together of lands that comprised the ancient kingdoms of Travancore, Cochin, and Malabar. A year later, the people of Kerala were the first in the world to voluntarily elect a Communist regime. Today, religious piety and Marxist-Leninism are the reigning passions. Novelist Arthur Koestler described the state as "a kind of tropical Marxist Ruritania, where Cabinet Ministers were known to consult their horoscopes to deduce the Party-line from the stars and Catholic missions, deriving from Saint Francis Xavier, were still the most important cultural influence."

Kerala does not suffer from the extreme poverty that is found in the larger northern cities of Bombay, Delhi, and Calcutta. The state boasts a literacy rate of over 70%, along with one of the lowest birthrates in India. The balmy climate is softened by strong sea breezes, and is most pleasant from December to January, although it's still comfortable to travel between October and March.

TRIVANDRUM

Trivandrum, nowadays also known as Kerala's languid seaside capital, sprawls over seven hills covered with colonial-era government buildings and traditional wooden houses hidden among lush parks and gardens.

Trivandrum was originally called Thiru Ananthapuram, or "abode of the snake," after an ancient myth that it was the home of Anantha, the sacred serpent often depicted curling around Lord Vishnu's body. Raja Marthanda Varma of Travancore made this his capital in 1750 and dedicated his entire kingdom to Lord Vishnu, the god of creation. He decreed that he and his successors would be the *dasis*, or servants of Vishnu. The present ex-raja still makes a daily morning pilgrimage from his palace to the Padmanabhaswamy Temple to prostrate himself before the reclining image of the family deity.

Most travelers prefer the sunny indolence of Kovalam's beaches, which are only 13 km (eight miles) away, and visit Trivandrum for a full-day tour of its museums, art galleries, temples, and zoo.

GENERAL INFORMATION

The **Tourist Information Center** ((0471) 61132, on Park View Road, Trivandrum, is functional and conveniently located just opposite the gateway entrance to the zoo, gardens, and museum. You can ask here about *kathakali* dance performances run by the Trivandrum Kathakali Club.

The **Kerala Tourism Development Corporation (KTDC) office** ((0471) 330031, Station Road, Thampanoor, runs good sightseeing tours around the city, to Padmanabhapuram palace and Kanya Kumari, and to the Periyar Wildlife Sanctuary in Thekkady.

WHAT TO SEE AND DO

Padmanabhaswamy Temple has a seven-story *goporam*, or pyramid-shaped archway, writhing with carved mythological figures. In 1733 Raja Marthanda Varma poured much of his personal wealth into glorifying this temple as his tribute to Lord Vishnu.

Non-Hindus are not allowed inside, and can only admire its ornate exterior — the interior has fine murals and reliefs — and observe male devotees self-consciously disrobing on the temple stairs, partly concealed behind their wives. Clad in rented *dhotis*, they disappear into the cool, sandalwood scented interior, from which is heard occasional humming and the clang of a temple bell.

Bustling street scene in the Connemara Market, Trivandrum.

Two major temple festivals take place here in March to April and October to November, each lasting 10 days and climaxing in processions of caparisoned elephants, devotees carrying golden deities on palanquins, and marching musicians, all led by the *dhoti*-clad maharaja down to the sea.

It's worth timing your visit around noon to catch the daily procession of temple priests. Then stroll through the back streets branching off Mahatma Gandhi Road for a poke through the government emporium, and the book and antique shops dotted throughout the area. Look out for **Kairali**, the excellent government handicrafts emporium, opposite the Secretariat.

The **Connemara Market**, which is easily found by its entrance archway near the Secretariat along Mahatma Gandhi Road, is an interesting place to wander through: a joss-scented strip lined with merchants squatting under black umbrellas like wizened monkeys, wiry boys splashing water on heaped blossoms, and chickens running among piles of mangoes, jackfruit and coconuts. This is the city's colorful market forum, where everything from wedding finery to pet parrots can be found.

WHERE TO STAY

Probably the best hotel in Trivandrum is the **South Park** ((0471) 333333 FAX (0471) 331861, Mahatma

From here it's a short rickshaw ride north to Trivandrum's magnificent hilltop **Zoo and Botanical Gardens** (64 acres or 26 hectares), which are open daily and have several museums within the grounds. The **Napier Museum** is a brightly turreted pagoda designed in 1880 by an English architect to honor the Governor of Madras, Lord Napier. It houses a superb collection of rare eighth-century, Chola-period sculpture, stone carvings, delicate antique jewelry, intriguing musical instruments, and memorabilia from the royal Travancore household. An excellent guidebook with anecdotes about the various items on display is sold at the front desk. The museum is open from 10 AM to 5 PM except Mondays and Wednesdays.

Other museums include the **Sri Chitra Art Gallery**, with its fine collection of contemporary Indian paintings, and the **Aquarium**, with natural history displays of ghoulish stuffed specimens.

Gandhi Road. The centrally air-conditioned rooms come with satellite television, direct-dial phones and other modern conveniences. Rates range from around US$50.

The three-star **Hotel Lucia** ((0471) 463443 FAX (0471) 463347, East Fort, is another reasonably luxurious hotel. The novelty suites in Arabic, Chinese, and Keralan styles, are an interesting feature, but for most visitors it is the swimming pool that makes the difference. Rates are similar to those at the South Park.

The KTDC-run **Hotel Mascot** ((0471) 438990 FAX (0471) 434406 is a quaint colonial bungalow set in a quiet and leafy part of town. The best rooms are on the top floor. It's very conveniently located, with the Indian Airlines office just opposite, and the museum, zoo, and tourist office within a 10-minute walk. Rates are from around US$30.

A good mid-range option is **Hotel Chaithram** ((0471) 330977, near the railway station on Thampanoor Road, which has a cafeteria-style coffee shop that serves reliably good south Indian *thalis* and refreshing fruit *lassis*.

Also recommended in the mid-range category is the **Jas Hotel** ((0471) 324881 FAX (0471) 324443, in Thycaud — a small but well-maintained establishment with rates for air-conditioned rooms from US$20.

For comfortable budget accommodation, a popular choice is the **Hotel Regency**, ((0471) 330377, Manjalikuam Cross Road, where well appointed air-conditioned rooms can be had for as little as US$10; less if you forego the air-conditioning and opt for a fan.

Find rock-bottom accommodation at the **YMCA Guesthouse** ((0471) 330059, in Palatam.

WHERE TO EAT

Trivandrum has plenty of small eating houses that serve very good south Indian vegetarian food for next to nothing.

One of the best is **Arul Jyothi**, just across the road from the Secretariat, where plentiful *thalis* with fresh red grape juice cost next to nothing. They serve "rocket roasts;" immense paper-thin *dosas* curved up like Stetsons and served with *sambhar* and coconut chutney, and have a large selection of delicious *lassis* and sweets.

For a good sit-down meal, the restaurants at the **South Park** and **Lucia** hotels are particularly recommended, and not very expensive.

The **Indian Coffee House** has two branches: one on Mahatma Gandhi Road and one north of Statue Road between the museum and the Secretariat. Both are recommended for coffee and snacks.

The **Khyber Restaurant**, near Station Road, has Chinese and Western food. The railway station's cafeteria must be India's cleanest, with delicious and cheap *thalis* and south Indian snacks served with a mug of steaming cardamom tea.

HOW TO GET THERE

Trivandrum's airport is a useful jumping-off point for Air India or Air Lanka flights to Sri Lanka. Indian Airlines and Air Maldives fly to the Maldives. Indian Airlines flies direct from Madras, Cochin, Bombay, Goa, Bangalore, and Delhi.

Kerala offers some of India's most enjoyable train journeys — gentle swaying rides past spectacular palm-fringed coastal backwaters and vast fields busy with *lungi*-clad rice-planters. Many travelers make the 18-hour, 920-km (570-mile) journey from Madras by the *Trivandrum Mail*, and then continue up Kerala's coastline to Cochin, 219 km (136 miles) away, by a combination of train, backwater trails, and buses.

From Trivandrum, KSRTC runs frequent buses to all the main cities in Kerala as well as long-distance services to Madras, Madurai, Mysore, and Bangalore; all leave from the bus depot opposite the railway station. If you're planning to take the backwater trip from Quilon (71 km or 44 miles), buses start at 7:30 AM for Ernakulam/Cochin and pass through Quilon about two hours later. There's also a daily bus to the Periyar Wildlife Sanctuary at Thekkady (272 km, or 170 miles), which takes eight hours.

Locating the right bus at Trivandrum's bus depot can be quite infuriating, as destinations are written in Malayam script and there are no bus bays, so that you have to join the mêlée each time a bus arrives to find out if it is the one you want. It's usually possible to find a seat on these buses but near impossible to book.

EXCURSIONS FROM TRIVANDRUM

Trivandrum makes a good base for visiting **Kanya Kumari**, also known as Cape Comorin, 87 km (54 miles) to the southeast in neighboring Tamil Nadu state. This is India's "Land's End," where the waters of the Arabian Sea, Indian Ocean, and the Bay of Bengal merge. Hindu pilgrims throng to its beachfront *ghats*, or steps, in the belief that bathing in these waters washes away their sins. It's a spectacular, windblown location, with nothing but endless sky and sea on the horizon, and its sunsets and sunrises are unique. On full moon nights, sunset and moonrise occur simultaneously, hovering together like a tangerine and a golf ball. It's worth staying overnight to see at least one sunset and one sunrise.

It's highly recommended that you also visit **Padmanabhapuram Palace**, which is just under 32 km (20 miles) from Kanya Kumari and 55 km (34 miles) from Trivandrum.

Padmanbhapuram Palace is one of Kerala's most impressive buildings, built in 1550 for the Travancore rulers of this former capital city. It's a marvel of design and delicate craftsmanship, built of teak wood, with Chinese-influenced low gabled roofs and elaborate carved interiors opening out onto private courtyards and some 40 panels of murals throughout. As you wander through, look for the carved open hall where the king held court, and the ornate council chambers, dance hall, temple, women's quarters, and the palace tower, whose topmost room was reserved for the god Vishnu, complete with murals and a bed — the maharaja occupied the room just beneath it. The complex is open daily, except Mondays, from 7 AM to 9 PM.

OPPOSITE: The multi-storied Padmanabhaswamy Temple in Trivandrum makes an easy landmark in the low-lying capital. OVERLEAF: An idyllic scene at Trivandrum beach.

At Kanya Kumari the TTDC-run **Hotel Tamil Nadu** ((04652) 71257 has an attractive beach-front location, rooms overlooking the sea, and mealtime *thalis*. Rates range from as little as US$3 to around US$15.

The **Hotel Samudra** ((04652) 71162, has some very smart air-conditioned rooms, if you are looking for a little more comfort.

To get to Kanya Kumari, you can either take a local bus from Trivandrum (or Kovalam Beach), or go on the US$3 day-tour organized by the Kerala Tourist Development Corporation (KTDC), which leaves at 7:30 AM and returns at 9 PM. The tour offers the advantage of stopping off at Padmanbhapuram Palace.

own secluded bay. The other main beach, just to the south, resembles a seaside commune crammed with budget hotels, well-tanned tourists, and cheap restaurants serving delicious fresh seafood and Western-style dishes.

It's not a place for peaceful solitude. Garrulous fisherwomen try to barter their haul of wriggling crabs or sackfuls of pawpaw for your wristwatch, and semi-nude body-surfers attract regular busloads of daytripping Indians.

Swimmers should keep close to the shore as Kovalam's waters are renowned for dangerous undertows that frequently carry the unwitting out to sea. After a record 11 deaths in 1986, a long-term Kovalam resident, clothes-designer Tim

KOVALAM

Kerala's dramatic Malabar coast is a continuous stretch of unspoiled, white-sanded bays, but the only beach resort is at Kovalam, just 13 km (eight miles) from Trivandrum. Here you'll find a series of small, sheltered coves with powder-soft sand, fringed by palm groves and paddy fields. Kovalam is perfect for unwinding after a bout of travel, with its good range of hotels, beach cafés, and plenty of sun and surf.

WHAT TO SEE AND DO

Compared to Goa's sprawling sands, Kovalam's two main beaches are quite contained and both within easy strolling distance of each other. At one end is Kovalam's five-star Beach Resort, landscaped across a palm-lined hillside with its

Heineman, an American citizen born in Tamil Nadu who has adopted Indian nationality, formed India's first professional team of lifeguards, who rescue an average of two swimmers a day.

Apart from these two beaches, there's an almost endless unspoiled coastline to explore. Further south, strung between Kovalam's candy-striped lighthouse and a mini Taj Mahal-style mosque perched on the headland's tip, is a sheltered, slightly more private, beach. In the opposite direction, the almost deserted bay just beyond the Hotel Samudra (past Kovalam's Beach Resort) makes a pleasant afternoon's excursion and is safe for swimming. From here, the beaches get more bewitching the further you stroll.

It's worth rising early one morning to witness Kovalam's fishing community hauling ashore their catamarans and proudly inspecting the morning's catch of tuna, squid, crabs, lobster, sharks and, occasionally, an illicit turtle. From the lighthouse, it's a 10-minute walk across the headland to the fishing village, with a small path leading down to the beach. En route, stop by at the Marine Research Laboratory, which has displays of local marine life and the methods used to catch them. There is also an extensive library, though you must first request permission from the custodian to browse.

WHERE TO STAY

Kerala's luxury five-star resort, the **Kovalam Ashok Beach Resort** ((0471) 480101 FAX (0471) 481522 is stunningly located atop a palm-scattered cliff face. Of a Mediterranean-style design that has won awards from the Royal Institute of British Architects, it sprawls across several tiers that drop down to the beach.

Facilities include an extensive yoga and massage center, watersports (including water skiing, motorboats, and paddleboats), a large pool, and a tennis court. Kovalam's only bank is located within the main lobby. Either stay in the main hotel building, or at the Kovalam Grove, a cluster of self-contained cottages, each with a terrace, along the seafront sands. For quaint vintage splendor, stay at a suite in the 100-year-old Halcyon Castle, the Maharaja of Travancore's former summer palace which has beautiful views across the Lakshadweep Sea. High season rates are from US$135 to US$450.

The KTDC-run **Hotel Samudra** ((0471) 480089 FAX (0471) 480242, overlooking the adjacent secluded bay, is pleasant and inexpensively priced.

Along the main tourist beach, **Rockholm** ((0471) 480306 FAX (0471) 480607, just above the lighthouse, has a winning combination of spacious, clean rooms (complete with vases of fresh flowers), a friendly management, the beach's most attractive balcony restaurant, and a well-thumbed library. Try to snare one of the coveted rooftop rooms for privacy and a spectacular view. Rates are from around US$20.and you will find any number of "resorts" offering simple but functional rooms from around US$10 in season, less out of season.

WHERE TO EAT

The ex-fishermen chefs who staff Kovalam's many beach cafés are culinary dynamos, serving up delectable seafood as well as popular Italian, Chinese, English, and French dishes. So many restaurants line the beach nowadays that recommendations are almost pointless. Most serve excellent seafood meals and have their wares on display — take a stroll and see what takes your fancy.

The Rockholm Hotel's **Balcony Restaurant** has an enchanting view, and serves chilled beer, excellent seafood dishes, and strong, fragrant coffee. Portions are gargantuan by Kovalam standards.

The **Lucky Coral** rooftop restaurant above Hotel Seaweed is almost as pleasant, and plays Talking Heads and David Bowie for its music-conscious patrons. Try Fish Welewska, served with a velouté sauce with shrimps or Lobster Thermidor.

On the beach, **Hotel Searock's Café** has a talented Goan chef, whose classic Goan dishes are as good as his grilled or baked seafood served with the house lemon-butter garlic sauce. This is also the place for an excellent "executive breakfast," with your toes in the sand and a crumpled copy of yesterday's *Indian Express*.

But for almost unbelievably good value and haphazard charm, both **Velvet Dawn**, and **Leo's Restaurant**, inexpensive beachside restaurants, do excellent tiger prawns and grilled fish, and are heartily recommended.

HOW TO GET THERE

Kovalam is only 13 km (eight miles) from Trivandrum and can be reached either by taxi, which costs about US$4 to US$5 one way, or a bus service every half-hour from platform 19 at Trivandrum's city bus depot opposite the Padmanabhaswamy Temple.

Kovalam's lush scenery and palm-fringed beaches are a perfect location for tropical indolence. OPPOSITE: Poolside vista from the Kovalam Ashok Beach Hotel. ABOVE: A seemingly endless stretch of unspoiled coastline.

Kovalam's optimum season is from September to April, after which the summer's heat and the monsoon send most tourists fleeing to Kashmir and the Himalayas.

BACKWATERS

The palm-fringed, balmy backwaters, or *kayals*, stretch along the coastal strip from Quilon (also known as Kollam) to Cochin. Local ferries chug gently through this unexpected version of rural India, providing one of south India's most profound pleasures: a cruise in the heart of a tropical Venice. Go armed with a large floppy hat, binoculars, a zoom-lens camera, and a bagful of oranges and delicious fresh cashews for optimum enjoyment.

Local ferries from **Quilon**, **Alleppey**, or **Kottayam** — the main backwater towns — cost less than the cashew nuts and offer an *African Queen* fantasy, plowing through winding waterways that are peopled by slender riverbank dwellers, and heady with the scent of frangipani and ripe jackfruit trees.

Tour cruises have become increasingly popular in recent years, and an eight-hour journey costs around US$6 per head, a small and very worthwhile investment.

It's worth traveling to Alleppey and Kottayam for the late August/early September 10-day *Onam* harvest festival, when the backwaters churn with colorful water carnivals and snake boat races. The most spectacular is the Nehru Trophy Boat Race, held in Alleppey on the second Saturday of August, when boats carrying up to 100 paddlers each compete in a colorful regatta.

The backwaters are best visited from December to February, because by early March the heat becomes oppressive and the swarms of mosquitoes can be deflected only by applying continual lathers of repellent.

QUILON (KOLLAM)

On the edge of Ashtamudi Lake, 73 km (45 miles) from Trivandrum, Quilon is the most picturesque of the *kayal* towns. It's full of pastel-painted wooden villas and labyrinthine alleys, and policemen wearing quaint Raj-style topees. It's also one of Kerala's most historic ports: the Phoenicians, Persians, Greeks, Romans, and Arabs all used Quilon as a stopover for plying the backwaters.

From the seventh to the tenth century, the Chinese established a busy trading base here, leaving a visible legacy of low-slung, pagoda-style architecture and Chinese fishing nets. This strategic, fertile district later became a source of rivalry between the Portuguese, Dutch, and British. It's still possible to see the dilapidated ruins of an old Portuguese fort near Thangasseri Beach, three kilometers (almost two miles) away.

Travelers come to Quilon to embark on the longest and most varied of the backwater routes. It takes eight and a half hours to meander along the 85-km (53-mile) stretch to Alleppey. There are two ferries daily, but you'll see more if you take the earlier one that departs at 10 AM and glides into Alleppey just after dusk. (This trip can also be made in the opposite direction.)

It's worth staying overnight in Quilon for one of Kerala's best accommodation surprises, the charming lakeside **Yatri Niwas ℂ** (0474) 78638 a former British Residency set in leafy gardens on the outskirts of town. Pristine rooms are furnished in local wooden furniture, all with shower, tub, and hot water and all rooms under US$10, even with air-conditioning.

The more central **Hotel Sudarsan ℂ** (0474) 744322 FAX (0474) 740480, on Parameswar Nagar, is only 10 minutes' walk from the ferry jetty, and has very cheap, fan-cooled rooms or slightly more expensive air-conditioned ones. You can dine well at either of its two restaurants on a choice of Indian, Chinese, and European specialties, or opt for cheap, delicious vegetarian *thalis* at Hotel Guru Prasad on Main Street.

ALLEPPEY (ALAPPUZHA)

Alleppey, 83 km (52 miles) from Quilon, is a small, picturesque, oriental Amsterdam, with inter-locking canals and bridges, and a center for backwater cruises.

From here you can take the two-and-a-half-hour scenic cruise to Kottayam, which for many is quite long enough to enjoy the *kayals*. Gliding along the canals, which cross the extensive Vembanad Lake stretching north to Cochin, you'll see flotillas of dugouts laden with coconuts, and lovely inland lagoons snaking into narrow, water lily-covered stretches.

The two-star **Alleppey Prince Hotel ℂ** (0477) 243752 FAX (0477) 243758, AS Road, provides very comfortable rooms from around US$15 in a pleasant setting a short distance out of town, and has a good restaurant and swimming pool.

Just opposite the boat jetty is **Hotel Komala ℂ** (0411) 243631, with a choice of air-conditioned doubles at US$10 or non-air-conditioned at US$4.

Other hotels in the vicinity are best avoided.

KOTTAYAM

Less than 30 km (18 miles) from Alleppey, and situated slightly inland from the Malabar coast, Kottayam is a busy commercial city, famous for its rubber, tea, coffee, pepper, and cardamom

---

The picturesque town of Allepey is a favorite setting out point for barge cruises through Kerala's winding coils of backwaters.

plantations, and primarily visited by tourists as a stopping-off point on the way to the Periyar Wildlife Sanctuary, 117 km (73 miles) away. A stronghold of the Syrian Christian sect, which has existed in Kerala since AD 190, Kottayam has many beautiful churches, including the Valiapalli Church, five kilometers (three miles) northwest of the railway station, which contains a cross believed to have come from the original church founded by St. Thomas the Apostle in Cranganore.

Stay at the **Vembanad Lake Resort** ((0481) 564866, Kodimatha, five kilometers (three miles) out of town, with peaceful, cheap rooms. And regardless of whether you choose to stay at the

THE DEEP SOUTH

resort or not, you should take the mid-morning Alleppey-Kottayam ferry and arrive at the Vembanad at lunchtime to order Keralan specialties such as *karimeen*, a local freshwater fish prepared in a fiery sauce of onions, green chilies, and spices, for an alfresco meal by the lakeside at Kottayam's best restaurant.

In town, the **Anjali Hotel** ((0481) 563661 FAX (0481) 563889, on KK Road, well appointed air-conditioned rooms for around US$20. It also has a good coffee shop and a bar.

For something a little cheaper but still comfortable, the **Hotel Aida** ((0481) 568391 FAX (0481) 568399 is recommended. Like the Anjali it has a bar and restaurant.

Kottayam is part of the rail network and has two bus stations: a local depot and an interstate stand that is roughly a kilometer (just over half a mile) from the boat jetty.

PERIYAR (THEKKADY)

The **Periyar Wildlife Sanctuary** is one of the most beautiful forest stretches of the south. Set in the Cardamom Hills near the border with Tamil Nadu, it is a 777 sq km (300 sq mile) jungle refuge for tigers, elephants, bison, antelopes, sloth bears, otters, monkeys, and the occasional panther or leopard. Among the sanctuary's creepers, spice vines, and blossoming trees, bird-watchers may spot darters, flycatchers, hornbills, blue-winged parakeets, bulbuls, herons, and egrets.

This is the finest Indian sanctuary for watching and photographing wild elephants, and as a member of Project Tiger, it has 40 of India's 3,000 or so remaining tigers. The enormous Periyar Lake, 24 sq km (just over nine square miles) in area, was created in 1895 by the British government in Madras for use in irrigation, but it became part of the newly formed sanctuary in 1934. While cruising along the shore in a motorboat, you can watch herds of elephants, bison, deer, and the occasional tiger, grazing at the water's edge.

What to See and Do

Tickets for one-hour motorboat cruises on Lake Periyar are available from the Wildlife Office, near the boat jetty. You're likely to see more if you take the earliest boat at 7 AM, when the misty waters resemble England's Lake District, and the herds come down for their morning drink.

The Wildlife Office also organizes three-hour group treks through the forest, which are most informative about the sanctuary's flora and fauna, but frustrating as the noise of so many people frightens most animals away. A far more satisfying alternative is to hire a private Wildlife Office guide to take you to the best vantage points and *machans*, or tree houses, so that you see far more wildlife at close range. The Wildlife Office can also arrange elephant rides and private boat rides.

Where to Stay

The **Lake Palace Hotel** ((04869) 22023 (booked at the Aranya Niwas Hotel below) has the most romantic location for overnight stays. This large old bungalow sits on a small island on Thekkady Lake, has a good bar and restaurant, and guests have been known to spot tigers from the windows of their rooms. Rooms have an antiquated Raj-era charm, and cost from around US$100.

On the lake's edge, the **Aranya Niwas Hotel** ((04869) 22023 has comfortable rooms ranging from around US$25 to US$50. The restaurant is recommended, and there's a bar too.

For something more stylish and upmarket, try the **Spice Village** ((04869) 22315, a resort-style operation with rustic cottages arranged around a swimming pool. Rates are from US$100.

The KTDC-run **Periyar House** ((04869) 22026, about a kilometer (just over half a mile) away, in the forest, has pleasant airy rooms, hot water, and food that is worth the hike.

At Kumily town, five kilometers (three miles) away, the inexpensive **Lake Queen Tourist Home** ((04869) 22084, opposite the post office is another pleasant option. Rates start at less than US$5.

It's best to book in advance for hotels in Periyar, which can be done through any KTDC office; otherwise, you can ask the staff at the tourist office in Kumily to check which hotels have rooms available. They'll also give you useful boat-trip tickets, maps, and walking/ trekking permits.

charm and is perfect to explore on foot or by boat.

Phoenician, Israelite, Greek, Roman, Arab, and Chinese traders all visited or settled in this tropical port, leaving behind Muslim, Christian, and Jewish communities that still exist today. It was Cochin's Jews who founded the first large community, over 1,000 years ago. These were the "black Jews," who arrived as early as AD 52 from Yemen and Babylon to trade olive oil and dates for peacocks and spices, and intermarried with the local population. Another wave of Jewish refugees came from Spain in the fifteenth century and were given protection by the Raja of Cochin. These "white Jews" were more insular and frowned on mixed marriages; they still exist, though in ever-dwindling numbers, today.

How to Get There

There are buses to Periyar from all main cities in Kerala, but the most popular scenic route is from Kottayam, 117 km (73 miles) away. The four-to five-hour journey winds up to a 305 m (1000 ft) plateau of leafy cardamom, pepper, and coffee plantations.

COCHIN (KOCHI)

Cochin is Kerala's largest and most beautiful city, with its lush islands, backwaters, faded colonial architecture, and an unusual history. It comprises the Fort Cochin/Mattancherry peninsula, the modern business district on Ernakulam mainland, and Willingdon, Bolgatty, Gundu, and Vypeen islands. It is one of India's biggest naval bases and busiest ports, exporting vast amounts of coir, rubber, seafood, and spices to foreign countries. Despite its bustling harbor, Cochin is full of languid

Vasco da Gama took Cochin for Lisbon in 1502, but the Dutch, who coveted its spices, incense, myrrh, and ivory, usurped the Portuguese in 1663. In 1795 the city passed to the British. Fort Cochin and Mattancherry Island are littered with architectural relics — Dutch palaces, Portuguese churches, and British bungalows — of these conquerors.

GENERAL INFORMATION

The **Government of India Tourist Office** ((0484) 666045, Willingdon Island (next to the Malabar Hotel), is open 9 AM to 2 PM except Sunday. Contact the KTDC **Tourist Reception Center** ((0484) 330031, Shanmugham Road, Ernakulam, to reserve a conducted boat tour around Cochin.

Rice-beds create lush headlands all the way along the backwater trail.

WHAT TO SEE AND DO

If you take a ferry to the historic Fort Cochin/ Mattancherry district, you'll alight at the old docks, now a sprawling neighborhood of shuttered merchants' houses and warehouses. Almost directly opposite is the elegant **Mattancherry Palace**, set in a cluster of mango trees. Built by the Portuguese in 1557, it was presented to the Cochin raja, Veera Kerala Varma (1537–1567), in exchange for trading privileges. It was later repaired by the occupying Dutch, gaining the misnomer "Dutch Palace." An annex of the Mattancherry is now a museum. One room contains portraits of former Cochin rajas, a line of imperious mandarin-like faces with fixed, inscrutable gazes; another displays a collection of their elaborate costumes, including ornate robes, brilliant turbans, silk parasols, and an ivory palanquin. The upstairs bedchambers are adorned with seventeenth-century frescoes depicting lively scenes from the Indian epics, the *Ramayana* and the *Mahabharata*, painted with colors created from charcoal, lime, leaves, and flowers. Open from 10 AM to 5 PM, except Friday and public holidays.

Near Mattancherry Palace, up a winding street filled with interesting antique shops and heady with the scent of pepper, cardamom, and cloves, is **Jewtown**. The Jews of Cochin once numbered as many as 4,000, but today only eight families remain, with many families having emigrated to Israel, Australia, and Canada. Almost hidden at the end of a cul-de-sac is the **Jewish Synagogue**, built in 1568. It was destroyed by the Portuguese in 1662, and rebuilt by the Dutch in 1664. Its interior glitters with nineteenth-century Belgian chandeliers, hand-painted eighteenth-century Chinese willow-pattern tiles, and in one corner, a brass pulpit and gold raja's crown.

Jackie Cohen, the synagogue's custodian, has an expert knowledge of Jewish settlements in Asia and displays the synagogue's prized possessions on request: a papyrus whorl that is an ancient copy of the Great Scrolls of the Old Testament and the Cochin rajas' copperplate grants of privilege to the Jewish merchant Joseph Rabin. The synagogue is open from 10 AM to noon, and from 3 PM to 5 PM every day except Saturday and Jewish holidays.

By cycle or rickshaw, it's two kilometers (one and a quarter miles) to the northern isthmus of **Fort Cochin**, a neighborhood of pastel villas and cobbled streets. Along the way, stop to watch Cochin's fishermen working their Chinese fishing nets, first introduced by visitors from the court of Kublai Khan, whose influence also remains throughout Kerala in pagoda-style temples, conical fishermen's hats, and Chinese methods of making porcelain and paper. The filmy blue nets, suspended from poles lashed together and

cantilevered out over the water, are counter-balanced with a primitive system of rock-weights. To see them in action, return an hour before dusk, when the nets look like giant birds dipping in and out of the water with their silvery cargo.

It's a 10-minute stroll through the winding streets to **St. Francis Church**, established by Portuguese Franciscan friars in 1504. This unadorned structure, originally made from wood and later rebuilt in stone, is the oldest European church in India. As invaders conquered Cochin, it passed from the Catholic Portuguese to the Protestant Dutch and the British Anglican, and today functions as a Church of Southern India. The Portuguese explorer Vasco da Gama, who landed in Cochin in 1498 and was known to have terror-ized the natives by slicing off the noses, ears, and hands of his captives, was buried here in 1524, although his remains were shipped back to Lisbon 14 years later. The tombstones of da Gama and

other settlers, engraved in Portuguese on one side, and Dutch on the other, can be seen in Saint Francis Church.

A short stroll south, down Prince Street, is the Roman Catholic **Santa Cruz Church**, built in 1557, with a mock-marble interior painted in lurid colors.

Across the water, on **Gundu Island**, is an old Raj-era coir factory where weavers use the area's abundant supply of coconut husks to fashion practical doormats, ropes, and matting.

The easiest way to become acquainted with Cochin is to take the KTDC's boat tour. It leaves twice a day (9:30 AM and 1:30 PM) from Ernakulam's boat jetty opposite the Sealord Hotel and includes a stop at Bolgatty Palace. Tickets must be purchased at the tourist office, not on board the boat.

If you have a free afternoon, Cochin's scenic backwaters between Ernakulam and Varpaoja make a pleasant trip. The ferry leaves from Ernakulam's main jetty every hour, and takes two hours each way.

In Ernakulam, see the **Cochin Archaeological Museum** in Durbar Hall Road, with its assortment of exhibits plucked from the Cochin royal family's collection. Otherwise buy teas, spices, and fresh cashew nuts in Ernakulam market, and meander along Mahatma Gandhi Road where various emporia sell *lungis* the colorful cloth worn tied at the waist, rosewood carvings, jewelry, and *kathakali* masks. At the government emporium, look out for a curious collection of Hindu deities with bobbing heads in contemporary garb, with Hanuman, the Monkey god, dressed up like a Japanese *yakuza*!

WHERE TO STAY

The **Taj Malabar Hotel** ((0484) 666811 FAX (0484) 668297, Willingdon Island, is by far the best hotel in Cochin, with air-conditioned rooms tastefully

A timeless moment on the waters of Cochin, Kerala.

decorated with woven rugs and wicker furniture. Set on the edge of the island with its own lawns and jetty, it has a glorious view across the busy harbor to Mattancherry Island. The hotel has a swimming pool, a restaurant, an unexceptional coffee shop, and a bar and, as part of the Taj-Group, it is being expanded to a total of 100 sea-facing rooms. Located right next to the tourist office, the hotel is convenient to the airport and a short ferry or taxi ride from either Fort Cochin or Ernakulam. Rates are from US$110 to US$300.

Also on Willingdon Island is the **Casino Hotel** ((0484) 668221 FAX (0484) 668001. Built in the 1950s, it lacks a harbor view, but is very efficient, with a pleasant old wing. There's a swimming pool and

an excellent seafood restaurant. Both hotels have boat services to neighboring islands.

Back on mainland Ernakulam, the **Taj Residency** ((0484) 371471 FAX (0484) 371481 is a slightly drab but reliable luxury hotel with rates from US$80, with all the usual amenities bar the swimming pool.

For travelers in search of faded elegance, the 250-year-old **Bolgatty Palace Hotel** ((0484) 355003 has antique furniture, ceiling fans, mosquito nets draped on four-poster beds and a languid terrace for sipping afternoon beers. Located on the narrow, palm-fringed Bolgatty Island, this was once a Dutch Palace and later the British Residency. Run by the state government, it is deluged with Indian vacationers during peak season, and becomes a haven of peace only during off-season. Rates are from around US$20.

In Ernakulam, the three-star **Sealord Hotel** ((0484) 382472 FAX (0484) 370135, Shanmugham Road, has air-conditioned rooms from US$20.

Slightly more expensive is **Hotel International** ((0484) 382091 FAX (0484) 373929, Mahatma Gandhi Road, a smart mid-range hotel with a central location.

The **Woodlands Hotel** ((0484) 382051 FAX (0484) 382080, Mahatma Gandhi Road, has comfortable, air-conditioned and fan-cooled rooms from US$7 to US$30, and an excellent vegetarian restaurant.

Biju's Tourist Home ((0484) 369881 is the best of the budget hotels. It's friendly and has a convenient location opposite the ferry jetty.

On Fort Cochin, the **Hotel Seagull** ((0484) 228128, Calvety Road, overlooks the harbor and the Chinese fishing nets in a sleepy, cul-de-sac of pastel-hued villas, just five-minutes' walk from the jetty. It has pleasant rooms from just US$10 with bath, and a popular balcony restaurant.

For even cheaper accommodation in Fort Cochin, try **Tharavadu Lodge** ((0484) 226897. Rooms with shared baths cost as little as US$3.

WHERE TO EAT

Kerala cuisine is distinctive for its variety of spicy, coconut-flavored dishes and fresh seafood specialties. The **Riceboat Restaurant** at the Malabar Hotel is decorated to resemble Kerala's cargo boats. The walls are adorned with paddles and coolie hats, and their seafood specialties are very good, especially the prawn shashlik Oriental. Also recommended at the same hotel is the **Waterfront Café**.

In Ernakulam, the **Sealord Restaurant**, at the Sealord Hotel, serves a special fish Veronique (stuffed with grapes), and offers a range of delicious seafood dishes.

Swagath, the bustling upstairs eatery at Dwarka Hotel on Mahatma Gandhi Road, is a favorite of Cochin's locals for its air-conditioned annex and generous *thalis*. It offers a staggering array of dishes including the massive mini-*thali*, or the "executive power lunch" *thalis*, as well as good *lassis* and south Indian specialties.

Also on Mahatma Gandhi Road is the **Pandhal Restaurant**, an air-conditioned place that serves good north Indian cuisine.

The Woodlands Hotel, just down the road, has a couple of recommended restaurants, notably the **Lotus** for excellent cheap vegetarian *thalis*.

Nearby, on Warriom Road, behind the Dwarka Hotel, is Cochin's best Chinese restaurant, the **Chinese Garden**, serving excellent seafood dishes.

The **Indian Coffee House**, opposite the ferry jetty, serves strong, freshly ground coffee, Western-style omelets, and "butter jam" toast from 6 AM.

Jancy Café, on Shanmugham Road, has delicious south Indian snacks, with particularly good fluffy *idlis* and crisp, doughnut-shaped *vadas*.

NIGHTLIFE

A performance of the traditional *kathakali* dance is one of Cochin's highlights. This form of dance theater, dating back 500 years, can be seen nightly, with explanation and narration, all over the city. By tradition, all dancers are male and wear elaborate costumes and mask-like makeup to mime stories from the great Hindu epics, the

Ramayana and the *Mahabharata*. Arrive early for the performance and peer backstage to see the lean, athletic performers transform themselves into oversized deities attired in bulky tutu-like burlap underskirts, layers of bright garments, heavy jewelry, and headdress. The makeup is highly symbolic: green denotes the hero king or god and black and red denote demons. The actor slips a seed from the *cunlappuvu*, or eggplant vine, under his eyelids to make his eyes red.

As much an act of worship as a highly dramatic folk theater, *kathakali* is traditionally performed by the flickering light of temple-lamps, accompanied by musicians and a chanting Brahman priest. Artists use a vast repertoire of acrobatic eye

movements, dramatic facial expressions, and perfect muscle control that require years of training. In Ernakulam, there are three equally good daily performances: at the **Cochin Cultural Centre** ((0484) 367866, at the Durbar Hall Ground next to the Cochin Museum, from 6:30 PM to 8 PM; **Art Kerala**, Menon and Krishna Annex, from 7 PM to 8:30 PM and **See India Foundation** ((0484) 369471, Kathathi-Parambil Lane, from 7 PM to 8:30 PM.

HOW TO GET THERE

Cochin can be reached by daily direct flights from Madras, Trivandrum, Bangalore, Goa, Bombay, and Delhi. There are also direct train routes linking the city with all major cities. Daily trains service nearby destinations from Cochin: an Ernakulam-Kottayam train at 7 AM and 5:30 PM, and the Ernakulam-Quilon service at 11:30 AM.

Buses depart from the Central Bus Station on Stadium Road in Ernakulam, with shuttles several times daily to Trichur, Alleppey, Quilon, Thekkady, and Trivandrum, and links to major cities in neighboring Karnataka and Tamil Nadu states.

OUT OF COCHIN: TRICHUR (THRISSUR)

Trichur, a picturesque pilgrimage town just south of the Nilgiri Hills, set amongst paddy fields and coconut and pineapple plantations, makes an enjoyable overnight excursion from Cochin, 80 km (50 miles) away. If you're visiting Kerala during late April to early May, it's worth planning your itinerary around Trichur's exuberant Pooram procession, the most spectacular of Kerala's temple festivals. Trichur's streets explode into rich pageantry, with a day-long parade of 30 gaily caparisoned "tusker" elephants, each carrying a Brahman priest seated under silk parasols and giant feathers. After dusk, there's a massive fireworks display that lasts until dawn.

Trichur's most remarkable feature is its magnificent **Vadakkunath Temple** complex in the low-slung, wooden pagoda style unique to Kerala's traditional temple architecture. The main temple shrine contains a curious three-meter (10-ft) mound of hardened cows' ghee, or clarified butter, under which a devotional *lingam* dedicated to Lord Shiva is completely embedded. The shrine also contains a panel of exquisite murals narrating the epic *Mahabharata*.

A museum and a zoo with a renowned collection of snakes are the other attractions.

Accommodation is for the most part basic. The best choice is the **Hotel Elite International** ((0487) 21033, Chembottil Lane, which, despite the name, is a lower mid-range hotel with functional air-conditioned doubles from around US$20.

If you've discovered a fascination for *kathakali* dance, it's well worth making the 27-km (17-mile) trip to Cheruthuruthy where the **Kerala Kala Mandalam**, the state's renowned *kathakali* dance school, is located. The instructors are usually delighted to let you watch their rigorous early morning training sessions, and there are evening dance performances.

Trichur is easily reached from Cochin by train (one and a half hours), though note that the Cochin train station is known as Ernakulam.

OPPOSITE: A vestige of the Portuguese legacy in the old European enclave of Fort Cochin. ABOVE: A Kathakali dance artiste displays their traditional elaborate make-up and stylized dress.

Travelers'
Tips

GETTING THERE

Getting to India is easy. The nation's main gateways of New Delhi and Bombay are serviced by most major international airlines. Some international airlines also fly to Madras and Calcutta. Each airport is linked to the rest of India by its internal air network. It is best to book tickets well in advance, so that you have a firm reservation with the airline of your choice and a date around which to begin planning travel arrangements within India. When booking your international flight, seats on internal Indian Airlines flights can also be booked through your travel agent.

AIR INDIA

Flagship Air India offers flights from Asian capitals, Australia, Europe, the Middle East, Africa, the Soviet Union, and North America.

FROM THE UNITED STATES

American visitors, for whom India is virtually the opposite side of the world, are provided with limited direct air connections and are advised to explore discount fares offered in New York, Los Angeles, and San Francisco, mostly by Asian carriers. Only a few airlines, notably Air India, Delta, and United, service India directly. New York has the greatest frequency of direct flights to New Delhi, Bombay, and Madras, and has at least one weekly flight to Calcutta. The cheapest round-trip fares to India from the east coast are around US$1,400; from the west coast expect to pay around US$1000.

For good deals on either around-the-world or circle-Pacific airfares try **High Adventure Travel** US TOLL-FREE (800) 350 0612 E-MAIL airtreks @highadv.com WEB SITE www.highadv.com, 4th Floor, 442 Post Street, San Francisco, CA 94102 — overland segments can be incorporated.

Check the Sunday travel sections of papers like the *New York Times*, the *Los Angeles Times*, or the *San Francisco Examiner/Chronicle*. American travelers may wish to forsake the direct-flight option and travel to India via London or from an Asian gateway city. From Hong Kong, Bangkok, and Singapore you can find one-way flights for around US$250 to US$400.

FROM EUROPE

The London *Independent's* travel section is good for checking out tours and package deals. Many cut-price flights are offered by Arab or Asian airlines, which often make long stopovers and can be delayed in obscure or bizarre locations. It is much better to pay the extra amount and take a direct flight on an established international carrier that at least gives a certain guarantee of arriving on time. Air India, Alitalia, Air France, British Airways, Air Canada, Japan Airlines, Lufthansa, Delta, SAS, Swissair, Singapore Airlines, Thai Airways, and Qantas all have good, regular and reliable services to India.

Reliable London travel agencies for low-cost tickets are **Trailfinders Travel Centre** ((0171) 9383939 FAX (0171) 9383305, at 194 Kensington High Street, W8 7RG, and at ((0171) 9383366, 42-50 Earls Court Road, London W8 6FT; and **STA Travel** ((0171) 937 9962 (United Kingdom telephone information and bookings), 74 Old Brompton Road, London SW7. Typical fares (London to Delhi) are around £300 one way or £350 to £450 round trip. Prices depend very much on the carrier and tour operator.

From the United Kingdom and Europe, bargain-hunting can be rewarded by some remarkably cheap deals. ("Bucket shops" advertise in the newspapers and in magazines like *Time Out*, *LAM*, and the *Australasian Express*.)

FROM AUSTRALASIA

Travelers from Australasia often stop off in India for very little extra cost on the grand overland route to Europe. It's possible to get cheap or Apex fares to Singapore, Bangkok or Hong Kong, and then fly on to India from there. Advance-purchase round-trip fares from Australia to London or other European cities with India as a stopover cost around A$2,000 to A$2,500. The price varies according to the season and destination in India, and Sydney and Perth offer the cheapest deals. **Travel Specialists**, 7 Piccadilly Arcade, 222 Pitt Street, Sydney 2000, has a good reputation.

VISAS

A tourist visa is required for all visitors to India. Depending on the embassy, visas can take anywhere from a day to a week to issue, and as long as four weeks for mailed applications. Immigration officials steadfastly refuse to allow entry to anyone without proper documentation, and most airlines check the passports of all India-bound passengers as in the past they have borne the cost of deporting numerous travelers.

Visas are delivered for 15 days, one month, three months and six months, though the latter starts counting down from the moment it's issued.

Indian embassies abroad include:

Australia ((06) 273 3999, 3-5 Moonah Place, Yarralumla, Canberra, ACT, 2600.
Austria ((01) 5058666, Karntnerring 2, A 1010 Vienna.
Belgium ((02) 640 9140, 217 chausée de Vleurgat, 1050 Brussels.

Canada ((613) 744 3751, 10 Springfield Road, Ottawa, Ontario, KIM 1C9.
France ((01) 40.50.70.70, 15, rue Alfred Dehodencq, 75016 Paris.
Germany ((228) 54050, Adenauerallee 262 264, 53113 Bonn.
Ireland ((01) 497 0843, 6 Leeson Park, Dublin 6.
Italy ((06) 488 4642, Via XX Septembre 5, 00187, Rome.
Japan ((03) 3262 2391, 2-2-11 Kudan Minami, Chiyoda-ku, Tokyo 102.
The Netherlands ((070) 346 9771, Buitenrustweg 2, 2517 KD, The Hague.
New Zealand ((04) 473 6390, 180 Molesworth Street, Wellington.
Spain ((01) 345 0406, Avenida Pio XII 30-32, 28016, Madrid.
Sweden ((08) 248505, Adolf Fredriks, Kyrkogata, 11183 Stockholm.
Switzerland ((031) 382 3111, Effingerstrasse 45, CH 3008 Berne.
United Kingdom ((0171) 836 8484, India House, Aldwych, London WC2 4NA.
United States ((202) 939 7000, 2107 Massachusetts Avenue NW, Washington DC, 20008.

Visa extensions are only possible for those traveling on six-month visas. Applications should be submitted to a Superintendent of Police in any district headquarters, or the **Foreigner's Regional Registration Offices** in Bombay, Office of the Commissioner of Police, Dadabhoy Naoroji Road; in Calcutta, 237 Acharya JC Bose Road; and in Madras, Shastri Bhavan Annex, 26 Haddows Road. In Delhi the **Foreigner's Registration Office** ((011) 3319781, is at First Floor, Hans Bhavan, Tilak Bridge, New Delhi 110 002.

Special permits for entry into "restricted areas" are requested from the **Under Secretary**, **Foreigner's Division**, at the Ministry of Home Affairs, Lok Nayak Bhavan, Khan Market, Delhi. After the six-month period, officials prefer you to leave, and Indian missions will be reluctant to grant you another entry visa for at least a year.

CUSTOMS

Visitors are allowed to carry in one duty-free bottle of spirits and 200 cigarettes. Customs officials are less scrupulous these days about visitors declaring luxury items that might be resold in India, but video cameras are still required to be declared.

India has extremely heavy penalties for smuggling, and unless you really desire a jail term in the country, don't even think about bringing in any illicit goods, or smuggling in expensive items. Ongoing political extremism has led to greatly enhanced security, so don't be surprised if after you have been cleared through Customs, your bags are run through an X-ray machine.

All four of India's main international airports have red and green channels, and customs officials will be available at the red channel for any foreigners wishing to register dutiable goods. There is no restriction on how much money you may bring in to the country, but when you leave you may be asked to show exchange receipts from a state-owned bank to prove that any hard currency you had was not swapped on the black-market.

CURRENCY

Strictly speaking, the Indian currency, known as the rupee, is divided into 100 paise, however

paise are of so little value as to be virtually worthless nowadays. Paper bills come in denominations of 10, 20, 50, 100 and 500, while coins are issued for denominations of one, two and five rupees.

The exchange rate at press time was 43 rupees to US$1. Exchanging cash and travelers' checks can be a hassle, involving the filling in of endless forms and being referred to at least four different officers before you get the money in your pocket. For this reason, it is often best to change a sizable sum of money at a time so as to minimize the time spent on such procedures. Your passport is essential identification for changing money, and travelers' checks generally have a better rate of exchange than cash.

Swaying palms dwarf a canal-side village along the backwaters of Cochin.

It can be difficult to change a Rs 100 or Rs 500 note on the street, so it is wise to get some small change at the bank for rickshaws, tips, and fending off persistent street urchins.

There is also commonly a reluctance to accept any bills that are ripped or worn, so be careful that your change does not include notes that will prove difficult to get rid of. Banks and five-star hotels will graciously accept this exhausted currency.

Credit cards have found widespread acceptance at shops and restaurants across India, and you will find the American Express and Visa logos in some of the most distant and obscure locations. While plastic is a convenient way of reserving

travel funds, most private shopkeepers will try to charge you the percentage that they are meant to pay the card company. It is rare that wily traders can be persuaded out of this uncharitable state of mind, so be prepared to pay three percent for American Express, and six percent for credit cards such as Visa and Diners Club.

However, plastic is an advantage when paying in five-star hotels, which will add a seven-percent "luxury tax" for food and accommodation if you are paying with foreign currency.

Foreigners are generally required to use foreign currencies to settle accounts at hotels, but can use rupees if they present a certificate proving the source of their local currency was an official bank. This system is chaotic, and you can repeatedly use the same certificate, which may not have any correlation to the rupees you are spending.

WHEN TO GO

It is possible to go to India at any time of the year and avoid extreme heat and monsoons, provided you select the right area. When it is blisteringly hot in the south, it can be crisply pleasant in Delhi and the Himalayas.

In general, the optimum season to travel to northern India — to Delhi, Agra, and Rajasthan — is between September and March, although it can get very cold during the winter months of December and January. It is best to avoid the plains during the hot months between April and June. Southern India is hot all the time, but is best between November and February. To the east, a combination of heat, humidity, and monsoon again makes November to February the most comfortable time to visit. The Himalayas are best appreciated between May and July, so unless you have been bitten by the ski-bug, avoid the winter snows. The extreme pre-monsoon heat, the torrential rain, and the post-monsoon humidity apply everywhere, at varying times, between May and September.

WHAT TO TAKE

Naturally, it is best to travel as lightly as possible if you want to avoid your trip becoming an endurance test, and unless you have a safe base to leave luggage, confine yourself to one main bag. You'll find it near impossible not to accumulate purchases as you travel, so that you'll leave with considerably more than when you arrived. A sound lock, preferably a combination lock, is constantly useful to guard against having your luggage pilfered. Always keep all your important documents in your hand luggage: passports, air tickets, credit cards, insurance policies, and immunization certificates, etcetera.

The type of clothing you take naturally depends on your destination. Many travelers, believing that India is a land of perpetual heat and dust, have landed in New Delhi in midwinter with a bag full of breezy Hawaiian shirts. Although for most of the year, the most practical clothing for India will be loose cotton clothes and sensible walking shoes, check a temperature guide before deciding your wardrobe. Sunglasses provide essential protection against the relentless sun.

There are other items worth taking to India, to cope more easily with the unforeseen. Bring spare passport photographs, as these are often required for permits to restricted areas. A basic first aid kit should include Lomotil tablets (nonantibiotic pills for diarrhea), sunscreen, water purification pills, multivitamins, aspirin, insect repellent, and antiseptic cream. As far as toiletries go, bring whatever you feel you couldn't live without for more than a week. Indian chemists usually have a baffling array of pharmaceuticals, but are short on good quality shampoo, cosmetics, suntan lotion, razors, dental floss, contraceptives, and tampons.

Photographic film should be purchased outside India, as items sold in India have often been spoiled from not being refrigerated. A small flashlight will provide illumination during power cuts and while exploring caves and gloomy ruins. Electrical appliances such as hair dryers, travel irons, and shavers must run on 220 volts. A small pair of binoculars can be useful for spotting wildlife.

India has a great range of bookshops that stock most leading titles, so it is not necessary to bring with you all the books you think you might need.

hospital, but may impair your health permanently. Have your shots at least two weeks before you go, so that they have time to take effect and you can recover from any lingering reaction. Cholera vaccines remain active for six months. The vaccine against hepatitis A, gamma globulin, is effective for two months, so those intending a longer stay should ask for a double dose.

Also make sure that your teeth are in good order, as Indian dentistry can look fearsomely antiquated to Western eyes! If you have capped teeth, you may want to take spare caps and a glue kit. India's swirling dust spells pure hell for travelers who wear contact lenses, so it's more comfortable to wear glasses.

It can be a good idea to carry a supply of music cassettes, film, cigarettes, alcohol, toiletries, lighters, and pens to be given away as gifts in return for favors or hospitality.

HEALTH

Prevention
Prevention is always the best cure. A course of immunization vaccinations and a supply of malaria tablets are essential to safeguard you against most of the dreaded maladies India has to offer. These are not essential requirements for entering the country unless you have arrived from Africa, South America, or any area infested with smallpox, yellow-fever, or cholera.

Vaccinations are recommended for cholera, typhoid, tetanus, and hepatitis A, which can all be contracted easily and will not only put you in

Malaria is a widespread problem, particularly during the monsoon and in tropical areas where mosquitoes are rampant, and there are numerous theories as to the pros and cons of anti-malaria preparations. There is evidence that long-term use can be damaging to the retina and the liver, and many travelers prefer to smother themselves with mosquito repellents and string up nets around their beds at night. Also, pills do not offer complete protection. However, many people who have contracted a severe case of malaria have survived only because they were on a course of pills.

Doctors usually prescribe Chloroquine tablets, taken either daily or weekly. Pregnant women should avoid Chloroquine, and instead take

OPPOSITE: A detail from a Hindu shrine in Goa.
ABOVE: Platform hawkers sell their spicy wares as a train comes to a halt at a rural station.

Proguanil, while an antimalarial syrup is available for children. Other alternatives, known by the brand names Fansidar, Faladar, Antemal, and Methidox, can trigger adverse reactions. It's best to start taking the tablets 10 days before departure, which will give you a chance to change them if they don't agree with you. For full protection, you are supposed to continue taking them for six weeks after you leave the country, as malaria germs are incredibly resilient.

Antimalarial tablets are overpriced in the United States when compared with prices in Europe or Australia. In most parts of Asia, antimalarials are sold without a prescription and are very inexpensive.

Rabies vaccinations are now readily available, but as a general rule, you should avoid stray dogs and monkeys. Macaque monkeys may look cuddlesome as they gambol across ancient forts and temples, but they can become vicious if they decide to take food from you. If bitten by any animal, clean the wound thoroughly and then admit yourself into the nearest hospital for the 14-day-long series of injections to thwart the potentially fatal disease.

On the Road

It's quite normal to experience a few minor bodily hiccups in adjusting to the Indian diet and climate, especially during the first few days after arrival, when your system is particularly sensitive. There are plenty of tales about India's vacation-ruining ailments, but if you observe some basic rules you should return home in good shape.

Food and drink tend to be the biggest worries for most visitors. Since most diseases in the subcontinent are waterborne, you will need to be particularly careful about your liquid consumption, especially as several liters of fluid a day is necessary to stave off dehydration from India's notoriously hot and dusty summer months.

No matter what old India-hands tell you, avoid any water that has not been boiled for at least 10 minutes and filtered or sterilized with water purification tablets. Always inquire whether water served in hotels and restaurants has been processed, as water that has only been filtered may still harbor a few resilient bugs. Indian Airlines serves unfiltered, un-boiled water on its flights, and it is best to carry a few bottles of mineral water onto planes, buses, and trains. When ordering bottled water, make sure that the seal is removed before your eyes, since crafty vendors and waiters have been known to top bottles up with tap water so that they can make a little money on the sly. Also avoid ice cubes, which are, after all, just frozen water.

You'll need to take twice as much water on train or bus journeys as you think you will consume, and if your supply runs out, stick to hot tea, soft drinks, or juicy oranges. It's a good idea to bring an all-purpose plastic cup with you, so that you avoid using dirty *chai* glasses which can carry hepatitis. Get into the habit of brushing your teeth with boiled, bottled, or even soda water, and try to remember not to swallow water while you practice arias in the shower!

Adjust to the highly-spiced Indian diet slowly, sticking for the first couple of days to fairly bland dishes like rice, yogurt, breads, and boiled eggs. In general, it is risky to eat street food prepared by pavement vendors, raw vegetables, unpeeled or unsterilized fruits, and food with a high water content, such as lettuce, tomatoes, and watermelon. India has a fantastic array of vegetarian dishes and many travelers avoid red meats and pork, as these can contain nasty parasites. Poultry is usually safe but can contain salmonella, particularly if it is under-cooked, and it is advisable to choose chicken *tikka* over chicken tandoori, as the former dish is equally as tasty but cooked more thoroughly, being served off the bone. Seafood is best eaten in the coastal regions and avoided inland, as refrigerated trucks have been known to break down.

However, you must not be overly fastidious or you will miss sampling the remarkable fare that India offers. Food freshly cooked and sold straight from the brazier at roadside *dhabas*, or cafés, is delicious and usually safe. Ice cream can be a breeding ground for typhoid when thawed and refrozen, but is also a most delicious treat, particularly in the dairy state of Gujarat.

The best rule is to eat at places with a high turnover so that the food served is usually fresh.

Ironically, five-star hotels often produce tummy troubles as they serve food with sauces and dressings such as mayonnaise that are best left alone. Be sensible, and if something looks or smells borderline, do not eat it. Smaller restaurants often do not provide utensils, in keeping with the Indian custom of eating with one's right hand, and so it is best to wash your hands before chowing down.

If you are smitten by diarrhea or an upset tummy, treat all spiced and oily foods as taboo. Eat sparing amounts of bland boiled rice, yogurt, and bananas, and drink plenty of black tea and water. It is best to try and work the bugs out of your system, but if your travel itinerary demands an immediate calmed stomach, take some Lomotil tablets to halt diarrhea. Avoid taking antibiotics immediately, as these will kill the bugs but also any other bacterial resistance you have accumulated, making you susceptible for a second bout. If problems persist for more than two days, particularly if accompanied by fever, consult a doctor as you may be suffering from dysentery, an illness that will require treatment.

ACCOMMODATION

India has a vast array of accommodation, from opulent palaces to seedy dives, and as tourism becomes a major industry, service standards have generally improved.

In this guide, accommodation has been divided into categories which fall into set price ranges, as follows:

Luxury: more than US$80.
Mid-range: US$30 to US$80.
Budget: less than US$30.

Five-star hotels are the scene of much socializing in the major cities and are usually up to international standards, having an array of restaurants, health clubs, business centers, and all essential services.

Rajasthan has many former palaces converted into hotels, and it is worth staying in one of these for an unforgettable experience of comfort, cuisine and service amid architectural magnificence — a pleasant change from the modern hotels of the West.

Former lodges of British colonial rulers provide solid and often sumptuous accommodation in the hill stations, and wildlife parks often have comfortable bungalows run by state authorities.

Quite frequently, you will arrive at your hotel and the staff will deny all knowledge of your booking, usually because your room has been given to a guest willing to pay a higher price. In such a situation, have ready all the paperwork necessary to prove your booking, and usually a room will suddenly become vacant.

Cheap accommodation is typically clustered around bus or rail stations, and despite being Spartan, is usually available for under US$5 a night.

If you are traveling through malaria-infested areas and see slogans declaring "get blood test for all fever cases," this is a cue to use a mosquito net. Cotton nets are better than nylon as cotton breathes and allows your sweat to evaporate from the net, cooling you underneath. If you have no net, turn on a ceiling fan — mosquitoes hate direct air currents so this will hopefully ward them off.

Always lock up your luggage when you leave your room if your accommodation is in any way disreputable. The real thieves, sad to say, are usually other foreign tourists who have fallen on hard times or are into hard drugs. French and Italian junkies have the worst reputation for ripping off everything you own, so if you see

anyone acting suspiciously, change hotels or take protective measures by either carrying your cash and passport with you or leaving it with the hotel manager for safekeeping.

TOURIST INFORMATION

The main **Government of India Tourist Office** is in Delhi ((011) 332 0008, 88 Janpath, and is open from 9 AM to 6 PM daily except Sundays. It offers answers to queries about all Indian destinations.

State Tourist Offices in Delhi are useful for gathering specialized material:
The joint **Andaman and Nicobar** office ((011) 6871443, is at 12 Chanakyapuri.

OPPOSITE: A wedding-cake haveli tower in the Rajasthan fortress city of Jaisalmer. ABOVE: Luckily for these hardy travelers, India is a land of endless horizons and few life-endangering tunnels.

Andhra Pradesh ((011) 3382031, Ashoka Road.
Assam ((011) 3343961, B1 Bhagat Kharak Singh Marg.
Bihar ((011) 3361087, Bihar State Emporium, Bhagat Kharak Singh Marg.
Goa ((011) 4629967, 18 Amrita Shergil Marg.
Gujarat ((011) 3340305, A6 Bhagat Kharak Singh Marg.
Haryana ((011) 3324911, Chandralok Building, 36 Janpath.
Himachal Pradesh ((011) 3325320, Chandralok Building, 36 Janpath.
Jammu and Kashmir ((011) 3345373, Chandralok Building, 36 Janpath.
Karnataka ((011) 3363862, State Emporia Building Bhagat Kharak Singh Marg.
Kerala ((011) 3368541, Kanishka Hotel Shopping Complex, Ashoka Road.
Madhya Pradesh ((011) 3341187, State Emporia Building Bhagat Kharak Singh Marg.
Maharashtra ((011) 3363773, A8 Bhagat Kharak Singh Marg.
Meghalaya ((011) 3014417, 9 Aurangzeb Road.
Orissa ((011) 3364580, B4 Bhagat Kharak Singh Marg.
Rajasthan ((011) 3383837, Bikaner House, India Gate.
Sikkim ((011) 6883026, New Sikkim House, 14 Panchsheel Marg, Chanakyapuri.
Uttar Pradesh ((011) 3322251, Chandralok Building, 36 Janpath.
West Bengal ((011) 3732695, A2 Bhagat Kharak Singh Marg.

Tourist information can also be obtained from the following overseas offices of the Government of India Tourist Office:
Australia ((02) 9264 4855, Level 2, Picadilly, 210 Pitt Street, Sydney, NSW 2000.
Canada ((416) 962 3787/88, 60 Bloor Street, West Suite No. 1003, Toronto, Ontario M4W 3B8.
France ((01) 42.65.83.86, 8, boulevard de la Madeleine, 75009 Paris.
Germany ((069) 235423, Kaiserstrasse 777-III, D-6000 Frankfurt-am-Main 1.
Switzerland ((022) 7321813, 1-3 rue de Chante-poulet, 1202 Geneva.
United Kingdom ((0171) 494 1048, 7 Cork Street, London W1X 2AB.
United States of America ((213) 380 8855, 3550 Wilshire Boulevard, Suite 204, Los Angeles, CA 90010; or ((212) 586 4901/2, 30 Rockefeller Plaza, Room 15, North Mezzanine, New York, NY 10020.

GETTING AROUND

India is different for everyone. Some people swear that a rough-and-tumble style of traveling is the only way to get close to its soul. Others enjoy adventurous sightseeing, but not at the expense of comfort.

Perhaps the best strategy is the middle ground of traveling independently with an emphasis on comfort. Try to strike a balance between insulation from India's grand panorama that comes from the cloistered atmosphere of organized tours and five-star hotels, and being snared by the day-to-day hassles of tight budget traveling.

Most people underestimate India's size, and many itineraries have been thrown out of kilter by failing to appreciate the considerable time it takes to cover distances. The country has a remarkable transport infrastructure that somehow always gets you where you want to go, and mostly it is a trade-off between time by train and money by plane.

DOMESTIC AIRLINES

Until quite recently there was little alternative to flying Indian Airlines, India's main domestic carrier. It is still the main carrier, however both Jet Airways and Demania Airways cover major tourist routes with daily flights. There are several other private airlines with less extensive routes including Modiluft, Jagson, Archana and East West.

The general information/reservation numbers in India for the above airlines are:
Indian Airlines (main offices): Bombay ((022) 2876161; Calcutta ((033) 2472356, Delhi ((011) 331 0517; Madras ((044) 8251677.
Jet Airways: Bangalore ((080) 2276620; Bombay ((022) 2855086; Delhi ((011) 6853700; Goa ((0832) 221472; Hyderabad ((0842) 231263; Madras ((044) 8555353.
East West Airlines: Bombay ((022) 6436678; Calcutta ((033) 552 8782; Delhi ((011) 372 1510; Goa ((0832) 224108; Madras ((044) 827 7007.

Flights on these airlines generally cost about double that of a first-class rail ticket, but the investment is usually worthwhile for covering long hauls that would take days by train.

Try to buy tickets well in advance and ensure that seats are confirmed, as flights are typically overbooked. If you purchase your ticket with rupees, you will be asked to produce a bank receipt to prove your foreign currency was changed at a bank. Foreigners pay 50% more than residents, but are given a higher priority on flights and greater flexibility in changing tickets.

Political extremism has made tight security a facet of Indian air travel, so ensure that any pocketknives are stashed inside your checked luggage, and expect batteries to be confiscated as they are seen as capable of powering a bomb.

Indian civil aviation is overstretched. It is best to give yourself plenty of time between connections as planes are frequently delayed.

Indian Airlines offer several discount travel schemes. The "Youth Fare," restricted to 12- to 30-year-olds, gives a 25% discount on the United States dollar fare for any internal flight for up to

90 days. The "Discover India" scheme offers 21 days' unlimited travel for a flat US$500. The "Wonder Fare" ticket (US$300 for seven days) is similar. With all these schemes, you are allowed to visit no airport more than once, except for the purpose of a connecting flight or when in transit.

RIDING THE RAILS

The Indian rail system was established by the British, largely as a means of transporting troops and extracting raw materials, and it remains one of the more beneficial colonial legacies, carrying more than three billion passengers each year on its services that ply across the country. In contrast to the brisk, buckled-up anxiety of a plane journey, Indian train trips are made vivid by one's fellow passengers, and a ticket buys a front-row seat for the greatest drama on earth: the human condition.

The network services the most far-flung areas of the country, and no visit to India would be complete without experiencing a train journey, which remains the most practical and reliable form of travel. There are several scenic routes worth taking during the day, but it is generally best to cover longer distances by overnight sleeper, which will save you money and time.

From first-class air-conditioned sleeper to third-class bench, there will be a mode of rail travel to suit your budget. A quota of berths are reserved for tourists, but these are rapidly allocated so it is best to book well in advance. The system works surprisingly well, and many an astonished traveler has arrived at a remote station to see a clerk open an immense ledger in which their name is listed for a reserved seat. Ticketing is computerized along the main trunk routes, where there are also international travel bureaus that save you the inconvenience of queuing for hours in the main ticket hall.

Not all trains have first-class compartments, and the second-class compartments are usually overcrowded. Even if you have reserved a berth, it can be difficult to avoid unlikely bed partners. An old man may respectfully request that he be allowed to perch on the edge of your seat, and when you consent, he may be joined by many relatives. In a totally crammed train, it would look very selfish for you to want to take so much room when such people have so little. For this reason, request the top bench that unfolds from the wall. These cannot be shared and usually provide a cozy location for a good night's sleep.

Thieves do prey upon snoozing travelers, so be sure to use your luggage as a pillow. Dining cars are rare on Indian trains, as snacks and refreshments are sold by hawkers at each station. For a more comfortable journey it is best to take along some food and bottles of mineral water.

Indrail Passes are only good value if you are going to be doing a lot of traveling by train. Passes are issued for periods of 7, 21, 30, 60, and 90 days. They must be purchased in foreign currency by foreign nationals or by Indians living abroad, and can be obtained from all main railway stations in India or through your travel agent. There are three prices: air-conditioned, first class, and second class. The prices for travel for seven days in these categories is US$300/$150/$80 and for 90 days, US$1060/$530/$235.

Railway schedules are available from most large stations; the most useful ones are the *All India Railway Timetable* and the concise but comprehensive *Trains at a Glance*.

Travelers who enjoy luxury may want to experience the Palace on Wheels (see RIDE THE PALACE ON WHEELS, page 15 in TOP SPOTS), a remarkable eight-day rail tour through Rajasthan aboard sumptuous carriages belonging to erstwhile maharajas. Scarlet-turbaned waiters serve Indian and continental cuisine as you chug through the desert state aboard the vintage train, which has private cabins with showers. The tour rolls out from Delhi and stops at Jaipur, Chittaurgarh, Udaipur, Jaisalmer, Jodhpur, and Bharatpur/Fatehpur Sikri/Agra. The tour runs between October and May.

BUSES

Buses are less comfortable than trains, but are cheaper and go to more obscure locations not reached by rail. Buses are another quintessential Indian experience, and no one ever quite forgets the near-collisions above mountain ravines or the constant blaring of horns. The latest addition are "video buses," complete with televisions showing the latest Hindi-language films. While these productions yield remarkable insights into the dynamics of India, their soundtracks ensure insomnia.

Cruising to school by Vespa, Jaipur.

At the height of summer, it is worth paying extra to travel aboard an air-conditioned vehicle.

URBAN TRANSPORTATION

Indian towns and cities usually have bus and sometimes rail systems, but most travelers find it best to get around by taxi and auto-rickshaw, for which there are certain ground rules.

Drivers will often insist their meter is not working so that they can charge more; and if you accept this principle, always agree on a price before setting off. It can be helpful to ask a local what a fair price should be. If there is a line of auto-rickshaws, the lead driver may turn you down if he feels the fare is too low to justify losing his place at the front of the line. If this is the case, just go to the last driver, who will have little to lose by taking you to your destination, even if it is nearby.

Auto-rickshaws are the cheapest and most convenient way of negotiating short distances, but are best avoided for longer trips, as it is invariably a rough ride and the vehicles are prone to accidents and breakdowns.

Taxis are about double the price, but it is worth paying for the added comfort and speed. The vehicle will either be the ubiquitous Ambassador, a clanking 1957 Morris Oxford still produced in India, or the Padmini, a zippier 1950s-model Fiat.

Drivers will also wait quite happily if you want to retain them while you go off for an hour of so of sightseeing or shopping, but you must agree to pay a waiting charge of about Rs 40 per hour. Drivers are also entitled to charge on top of the meter a 25% "night charge" between 10 PM and 6 AM. Different rules apply in different cities, and it is best to check with hotel personnel as to the correct local rate.

COMMUNICATIONS

TIME

Indian Standard Time is five and a half hours ahead of Greenwich Mean Time and nine and a half hours ahead of United States Eastern Standard Time. However time is a very elastic concept in India. Indeed in Hindi, the same word is used to describe both "yesterday" and "tomorrow."

POSTAL SERVICES

Mail services in India are generally good, although it's best to make sure that staff frank letters to ensure that the stamp is not immediately peeled off and resold — a common practice. Sending a parcel abroad can be a complicated, time-consuming business. Either bear with excess luggage or get government emporia to ship your shopping home.

TELEPHONES

Until not that long ago India had one of the world's oldest telephone systems, an archaic network established by the British during Queen Victoria's reign. Blessedly, the government has updated its mechanical exchanges with digital systems, and most numbers are obtainable by direct dialing. Use the area code (indicated in parentheses in this book) if dialing from outside the area, and the local number only if in the area. To reach a subscriber in India from overseas, dial your overseas access number, then "91" for India, the area code (dropping the initial "0") and the number.

If you are staying in a good city hotel, it is quite easy to make calls internationally or long-distance within India by direct-dialing. Otherwise, calls must be made from crowded booths at the local post office.

Hotels usually whack a stiff service charge on telephone calls, so it is worth checking their terms before you begin a calling binge.

E-MAIL AND FACSIMILE

Domestic and international telex and telegram services in India are fairly reliable and reasonably priced. Again, you have a choice of either lining up at the General Post Office or using the facilities of a large hotel. Telex is rarely used nowadays, having been superceded by fax and e-mail.

Fax and e-mail are increasingly popular in India, though it is hard to log on outside the major cities. Most five star hotels have business centers with fax services, but rates tend to be pricey, with an additional 10% service charge for an international destination.

In India's major cities, cybercafés are popular with the young middle class, and provide an inexpensive opportunity to do your e-mail.

MEDIA

India has a large number of English-language dailies and hundreds of vernacular newspapers, for one of its beauties is an unshackled press. The dailies, written in a dense Edwardian prose packed with remarkable colloquialisms, become an addictive beginning to the day if you wish to understand the complexities of Indian politics.

The *Times of India* has the largest circulation and, along with the *Statesman of Calcutta*, plots a centrist path. The *Indian Express* is anti-government and prone to printing glaring exposés on its front page. The *Hindu of Madras* has a strong science section and solid coverage of southern India, while the *Hindustan Times* is pro-government and good for getting the views of the status quo. The *Telegraph* and the *India Post* are more upbeat, with solid features and good photographs.

Newspapers also advertise ongoing cultural events, but the coverage is haphazard, with events often being advertised after they have occurred. Major cities usually have a weekly journal dedicated to local events, such as the *Delhi Diary*, *Bombay Calling*, and *Hallo Madras*, brimming with practical information and directory listings.

Sunday newspapers contain matrimonial columns that amply illustrate how Indian marriages are frequently transactions based on pragmatic assessment. For women, a "wheatish complexion" is an asset, and both sexes are rated by their caste, profession, income, and prospects.

More in-depth coverage is found in news magazines, such as The *Illustrated Weekly* or *Sunday*.

But the best read is *India Today*, a fortnightly publication crammed with well-written and well-researched articles covering all aspects of Indian life.

The government controls the electronic media, and All India Radio and the two-channel Doordarshan television network are notoriously dull, essentially reporting on news of process (politicians planting trees) or cricket matches. Television does have its high points, notably the screening of soap operas based on the Hindu epics. The programs enjoy a massive following, with entire villages turning out to watch a television set that has been garlanded and blessed for the weekly showing.

India has the world's largest film industry, annually churning out more than 1,000 films compared with Hollywood's paltry 400. The industry is centered in Bombay, and to the Western eye the finished products usually resemble 1940s-style pantomimes of heroes, villains, and damsels in distress bursting into song between gun battles.

Cinema has been seriously undermined throughout the country by the rise of the video. Cassettes of new Western films are pirated and appear in India within weeks of their release in the United States or Europe.

INDIA'S NIGHTLIFE

Nightlife is virtually nonexistent in small towns and villages, but New Delhi, Bombay, and Calcutta have discos and an array of cultural events that will keep you out until the wee hours.

Wealthy, well-educated, and socially elite Indians tend to lead incredibly hectic social lives, and simply adore formal dress functions, which is what the winter wedding season is all about. Visitors drawn into well-connected party circles will encounter a high-powered series of social engagements in private homes, five-star hotels, and exclusive clubs. Here, dress, manners, and informed conversation count for everything. Time-honored tradition ensures that while guests are plied with drinks, food often doesn't arrive until past midnight. By the time it does, your surroundings may have become an amiable blur of perfume, silk brocade saris, handlebar mustaches, and tinkling laughs. Most guests tend to eat very quickly, then melt away into the night. Whiskey on an empty stomach followed by rich, spicy food taxes the body, and the best counter-measure is to have a snack before going out and then to drink and eat lightly.

Discos are found in most five-star hotels in the big cities, but cover charges and bar prices tend to be outrageously high. Hotel guests are charged only a nominal amount, but otherwise high membership fees deter all but the wealthy sons and daughters of the shakers and movers.

BENEATH THE WHIRLING FAN

Every visitor to India encounters its bureaucracy, the leviathan that runs the affairs of the nation's multitudes.

Many formalities in India require bouts of form-filling, but anything slightly more complex — like getting a refund on a railway ticket or permission to go to a restricted area — can escalate into a Kafkaesque adventure. India's bureaucratic warrens usually house rows of bespectacled, shrunken clerks, cowering peons in faded khaki shuffling about delivering *sahib*'s tea, whirring fans, and great sheaves of yellowing files held down by paperweights or quite literally bound by "red tape." The expression was born in India

An Indian policeman wearing a *kepi* in Pondicherry, Tamil Nadu, once a French enclave.

during the early days of the British Civil Service, when red ribbons were first used to hold together official documents. To the untutored eye, these office dens may appear totally haphazard — bustling with people and transactions, while replies to your queries may appear confusing, or even cryptic. You may find yourself wondering what originally launched you on your bureaucratic odyssey in the first place.

But take heart. Be assured that behind every formality lies a reason. By following some general ground rules, keeping reasonably patient, and always maintaining a sense of humor, you'll find things can get done. As a foreigner, it is sometimes difficult to understand all the labyrinthine ins-and-outs of the system. Since transactions can often be frustrating and time-consuming, use an age-old management technique: delegate responsibility. Most hotels can produce a number of willing young men who for a small tip will wait in long lines to purchase tickets at airline offices, rail, or bus stations. In local parlance, they will "do the needful" while you follow your own schedule. Always check that the person you are about to trust with your money has been vetted by hotel staff. Travel agencies in India tend to charge only nominal rates for their services, and often secure bookings magically through their own quotas, even on services you've been assured are completely "full up."

More important procedures, such as extending one's visa or seeking a permit to visit a restricted area, require making a personal appearance. Often all that is required is a stamp and an indecipherable scrawl in the right place on the right piece of paper by the right official, but without this your vacation may be ruined. Officials tend to take a very dim view of foreigners who arrive in India without a visa, overstay, or wind up in areas deemed strategically "sensitive."

The trials and eventual triumphs of dealing with officialdom in India are just part of adjusting to the pace of life on the subcontinent. Never underestimate the power of the person wielding the needed rubber stamp, and always conduct your business in a very polite, but reasonably firm manner.

Officials usually sit in a cramped room and deal with hundreds of people daily, all of whom think their case is more important than yours, so it is easy to see why any display of rudeness or arrogance can go against the grain. Heat and inexplicable delays can drive even paragons of patience to tantrums, but try to remember that India is run according to different rules.

Jovial small talk and a zestful handshake with the appropriate official will go a long way toward getting your case cleared. Some travelers swear that a tip oils the cogs, and this may work in distant regions. But most Indian officials staunchly oppose the suggestion of a bribe, and unless a demand is clearly made, do not risk being arrested for trying to corrupt an officer of the government of India.

BAKSHEESH, BEGGING, AND BARGAINING

One of the first words a traveler learns in India is *baksheesh*. Loosely translated, it is something you pay to get things done — a little gift or a bribe, a payment for services rendered. It is usually a small amount, generally less than Rs 10. Beggars moan "*baksheesh, sahib,*" on street corners. Taxi drivers keep their palms out and demand "*baksheesh*" after you've just given them the correct fare.

Begging is a part of Indian life, despite being officially illegal. India forces the traveler to make choices, and the *baksheesh* decision is one for which there can be no guidance. Coping with beggars is all part of traveling in India.

The most deserving of your sympathy are the lepers, multiple amputees, and other unfortunates whose permanent life-crippling diseases prohibit them from doing much else. Elderly women begging on the streets are invariably widows, who have a lowly place in society once their husband has died. Half-naked children with large eyes can be very endearing, but are often employed by local rackets who make begging a profession. Mothers with screaming babies whom they deliberately pinch should come much lower on the compassion scale.

Bargaining is one of India's great institutions. Once you have experienced the satisfaction of whittling down the price of a carpet, silver necklace, or carved statue, no shopping expedition in India will ever be the same again. Traders expect their customers to haggle and are inwardly astonished if items are purchased without even a hint of dissent.

Bargaining requires a little acting ability. Traders do their showmanship routine, offering sweetened tea and pulling out stock so that their shop takes on the appearance of a pigpen. For your part, you are advised to keep poker-faced about the items that you covet. Remember that your trump card is a nonchalant walkout, a tactic that invariably brings prices crashing down. Bear in mind though that no merchant worth his salt

widely spoken that you can use it almost throughout the country.

The fact is — and this is one of the reasons that English is such a popular compromise — of India's 18 major tongues, Hindi is spoken only by around 20% of the population as their native language. The 200 million speakers of Bengali are more likely to want to converse with you in English than in a rival Indian language such as Hindi.

Be that as it may, these are not excuses to toss out the phrasebook. Those who make an effort to learn a little Hindi will usually be rewarded with smiles, and every now and again they may even find their language skills to come in useful.

is going to sell at anything less than his cost price — and they'll often try to sell goods at up to 70% higher than that.

The main thing to remember is that bargaining is only the means to an end. When you see something that you really want, or that you know will make a perfect gift for someone, don't feel that if you can't whittle the price down then it's not worth having. In India as anywhere, quality and fine workmanship will always come with a price-tag attached.

TRAVELERS' HINDI

In all honesty, unless you get very far off the beaten track indeed (and then in a Hindi-speaking area), you are unlikely to ever need to speak a word of India's official national tongue. After all, English is the unofficial national language, and it's so

Note that an *e* at the end of a word is generally pronounced like the English "ay," as in "say," whereas the combination *ai* is pronounced more like the "y" in "sky."

Basic Vocabulary

Hello/Good-bye   *Namaste*
Good-bye/See you again   *Phir milenge*
How are you?   *Aap kaise hain?*
Very good   *Bahut Acha*
Bad   *Kharab*
Please   *Kripaya*
Thank you   *Dhanyavad, Shukriya*
Yes   *Han, Anchi*
No   *Nahi*
Excuse me   *Maaf Karna*
What is your name?   *Aap ka naam kya hai?*

Fisherman at work, Cochin, Kerala.

My name is Kate   *Meera naam Kate hai*
What is the time?   *Kya bara hai?*
Where is the…?   *Kahan hai…?*
How much is this?   *Kitne ka hai?*
Too much   *Bahut zyada hai*
Lower your price   *Kum karo*
Left   *Bai*
Right   *Dai*
Stop   *Roko/Bas*
Go straight   *Seedha jaaiye*
Hurry up   *Jaldi kare*
Slow down   *Aahista*
Go away   *Chale jao or Chelo*
Big   *Bada*
Small   *Chhota*

Beautiful   *Sundar*
Toilet   *Bakhana*
Train   *Gadi*
Prayer   *Puja, pratha*
Sleep   *Sana*
Friend   *Dosta*
Smile   *Muskarana*
Bill please   *Bill lao*
Water   *Panni*
Rice   *Chawal*
Fruit   *Phal*
Vegetables   *Sabzi*
Bread   *Chapati*
Tea   *Chai*
Coffee   *Kafi*
Milk   *Dudh*
Sugar   *Chini*
Laundry   *Dhobi*
O.K.   *Achha*

Numbers

1   *ek*
2   *do*
3   *teen*
4   *char*
5   *panch*
6   *chhe*
7   *saat*
8   *aarth*
9   *nau*
10   *das*
20   *bis*
30   *tish*
40   *chalish*
50   *pachash*
60   *sahath*
70   *setur*
80   *aashi*
90   *numba*
100   *sau*
1000   *hazar*

GLOSSARY OF COMMON FOODS, CUISINES, AND DISHES

COMMON DISHES

baingan mumtaz   stuffed eggplant.
biryani   chicken or lamb in orange-flavored rice, sprinkled with rose water, almonds, and dried fruits.
dal makhni   a dish of rich spiced lentils with coriander.
dosa   south Indian crisp rice pancake often with a mashed potato filling served with *sambhar*.
gushtaba   spicy meat pounded to pâté consistency, formed into balls and simmered in spiced yogurt.
idlis   steamed rice-cake eaten with fresh coconut chutney.
khatte alloo   spiced potato.
firni   a kind of exotic rice pudding served in earthenware bowl.
kheer   a rich thickened milk sweetened with raisins and nuts.
khulfi   Indian ice cream accompanied by transparent sweet vermicelli called *falooda*.
rogon josh   curried lamb.
roomali   a snack or meal of handkerchief-thin *rotis* or *parathas*, layered and stuffed with minced meat or *paneer* cheese.
sambhar   a chili-laced lentil soup.
shahi paneer   cheese in cream and tomatoes.
subze   spiced vegetable dishes.

Cooking Terms

masala   a pungent blend of spices that can include any or all of turmeric, saffron, chili, cinnamon, coriander (both leaf and seed), ginger, garlic, cardamom, mustard (seeds), pepper and cumin — among others.
tandoori   a clay oven in which is baked chicken, meat, or fish that has been marinated in spices, yoghurt, and saffron.
thali   a large round metal tray filled with little bowls that are constantly refilled.
tikka   the same principle as *tandoori*, but applied to boned cuts of meat.

UNLEAVENED BREADS

These are generally baked clinging to the inside of a tandoor clay oven:

chapati   crispy bread.

dosa   a form of crepe made from lightly fermented rice flour and stuffed with spiced potato, eaten with fresh coconut chutney and *sambhar*.

khulcha bhatura   a soft doughy bread eaten with spicy chick-peas.

naan   fluffy, yogurt-leavened bread.

paratha   millet-based, sprinkled with cumin, or caraway seeds, stuffed with peas, onions, or potato.

romali roti   handkerchief-thin bread.

SNACKS

masala dosa   a potato-based curry wrapped in a crispy pancake.

pakoras — a combination of fresh vegetables cooked together in a blend of sweet spices, rolled in a ball, then dipped in chick-pea flour before being crispily deep-frie.

samosas   deep-fried triangles of thin dough encasing vegetables cooked in a pungent mixture of spices.

DESERTS AND CONFECTIONS

barfi   a creamy, fudge-like confection made from sweetened milk that has been slowly boiled down until it almost caramelizes.

gulab jamun   spongy ground almond balls, served dripping with honeyed syrup.

jalebi   cartwheel-shaped sweets, served dripping with honeyed syrup.

kulfi   ice cream, flavored with cardamom, pistachio nuts, and saffron.

paan   a mixture of betel nut and spices wrapped in a betel leaf.

rasgulla   cream cheese balls in rose-water syrup.

burfi   halwa sweets covered in wafer-thin silver paper.

BEVERAGES

chai   tea that has been boiled together with milk and sugar.

lassi   yogurt-based drink, sweet or salty.

nimbu   lime soda, served sweet, salted, or plain.

WEB SITES

Probably the best overall introduction to what's out there — and there's definitely a lot out there — would be the **Infohub India Travel Guide** www.infohub.com/TRAVEL/TRAVELLER/ASIA/india.html, packed with links to far more sites than you will possibly have time to explore.

For overall India information it's hard to beat **INDOlink** www.indolink.com/, a huge site brimming with everything from cricket trivia to Bollywood gossip. Another good overall introduction to the country, its culture and people is **Almost Everything About India and Indians Abroad** www.indiaxs.com/travel/index.htm, which has travel information on over 100 Indian destinations.

For a photographic tour through the best of Rajasthan with some practical information included on the state's major attractions, take a look at **Rajasthan** www.ent.ohiou.edu/~kartik/raj.html. Slightly less exciting, but still worth a look if you are heading their is the Rajasthan site called by the **Rajasthan Tourism Development Corporation** www.inetindia.com/travel/state/rajasthan/.

The ultimate resource on India's festivals, complete with clickable lists, is the **Festivals of India** www.indiagov.org/culture/festival/festival.htm. It is part of the massive **Discover India** site maintained by India's Ministry of External Affairs: www.indiagov.org/1page.htm. It's broad range of cultural pages and links can be viewed at http://www.indiagov.org/culture/overview.htm#links.

The scholarly with an interest in Indian arts should take a look at N.S. Sundar's excellent **Indian Classical Arts Home Page**, an informed labor of love if ever there was one: www.cis.ohio-state.edu/~sundar/. It has a special focus on the Carnatic (Karnatic) classical music of southern India.

For an analysis of Hinduism, its art, its philosophy, and its religious significance, **Hinduism** www. geocities.com/RodeoDrive/1415/indexd.html is a site that can keep you busy for days, not just with its own content but with its extensive links. You can continue your quest at the **Hindu Universe — Dharma and Philosophy** www.geocities.com/RodeoDrive/1415/indexd.html, which as the name suggests is a fairly serious rundown of the seminal Hindu concepts.

For something lighter, but still cultural, check out the **Cuisine of India** www.incore.com/india/cuisine.html, a fabulous site that not only takes you by the hand and guides you through complexities of regional culinary variations but also includes links to recipes that enable you try them out yourself.

Lastly, all of India's major destinations have web sites promoting their attractions, hotels and restaurants — do a search to find them — but few of them do it as well as **Mumbai on the Net** www.mumbainet.com/mainmenu.htm, which is useful for its up-to-date listings.

Chefs display tantalizing Mughali fare at the famous Rambagh Palace Hotel in Jaipur.

Recommended Reading

History and Religion

BASHAM, A.L. *The Wonder That Was India*. New York: Taplinger Publishing Co., 1967.

GANDHI, M.K. *An Autobiography or The Story of My Experiments With Truth*. 1948; translated by Mahadev Desai; New York: Dover, 1983.

HIBBERT, C. *The History of the Indian Mutiny*. London, 1980.

KEAY, JOHN. *Into India*. London: J. Murray, 1973.

KEAY, JOHN. *India Rediscovered*. London: Collins, 1988.

MEHTA, VED. *Mahatma Gandhi and His Apostles*. London: Deutsch, 1977.

MOOREHOUSE, GEOFFREY. *Calcutta*. London: Penguin Books, 1983

MOOREHOUSE, GEOFFREY. *India Britannica*. London: Harvill Press, 1983

THAPAR, ROMILA. *A History of India*. London: Pelican, 1980.

WATSON, FRANCIS. *A Concise History of India*. London: Thames and Hudson, 1974.

Novels, Travel Writing, and Commentaries

ACKERLEY, JOE RANDOLPH. *Hindoo Holiday: An Indian Journal*. 1931; New York: Poseiden Press, 1980.

CAMERON, JAMES. *An Indian Summer*. London: Macmillan, 1974.

COLLINS, LARRY and DOMINIQUE LAPIERRE. *Freedom at Midnight*. New York: Simon and Schuster, 1975.

FISHLOCK, TREVOR. *India File*. London: J. Murray, 1983.

FORSTER, E.M. *A Passage To India*. 1924; London: Everyman's, 1992.

JHABVALA, RUTH PRAWER. *The Heat and the Dust*. New York: Simon and Schuster, 1987.

LAPIERRE, DOMINIQUE. *The City of Joy*. Translated from the French by Kathlyn Spink; Boston, Massachusetts: G.K. Hall, 1986.

NAIPAUL, V.S. *An Area Of Darkness*. London/New York: Penguin, 1968.

NAIPAUL, V.S. *India: A Wounded Civilization*. London: Deutsch, 1977.

RUSHDIE, SALMAN. *Midnight's Children*. 1981; New York: Knopf, 1995.

THEROUX, PAUL. *The Great Railway Bazaar*. 1975; New York: Penguin Books, 1995.

WOOD, HEATHER. *Third Class Ticket*. London/Boston: Routledge and Kegan Paul, 1980.

Photo Credits

Photographs by **Robert Holmes** except those listed below:

Mohamed Amin and Duncan Willetts: *pages* 23, 27

Derek Davies: Pages 4, 12, 39, 69, 76, 77, 81, 85, 94, 99, 182, 192, 200, 201, 208, 250, 311, 313, 330, 338, 340, 344, 345, 349.

Alain Evrard: Pages 210, 211, 215, 218, 220, 221, 222, 224, 228, 233, 236-237, 332, 333, 335.

Greg Girard: Pages 43, 79, 213.

Dieter Ludwig: Pages 5, 7, 8 *left*, 21, 29, 45, 54, 61, 66, 72, 86, 87 *top*, 89, 90, 91, 93 *left*, 95 *bottom*, 96, 97, 121, 150, 151, 164-165, 176, 177, 181, 184, 191, 230, 251, 255, 258, 259, 261, 267, 271, 280, 281, 283, 284, 285, 286, 287, 288, 291, 329, 354, 355, 359, 361.

Nik Wheeler: Pages 13, 14, 15, 16, 17, 19, 24, 25, 31, 32, 33, 35, 36, 37, 38, 40, 41, 43, 47, 48, 50, 51, 52, 53, 56, 57, 95 *top*, 107, 118, 125, 129, 152, 157, 162, 163 *bottom*, 169, 170, 171, 174, 185, 216, 225, 229, 231, 232, 256, 257, 292-293, 294, 296, 297, 299, 342-343, 351, 358, 360, 363, 367.

Quick Reference A–Z Guide
to Places and Topics of Interest with Listed Accommodation, Restaurants and Useful Telephone Numbers